D0138398

Evolutionary Psychology

Evolutionary Psychology

The New Science of the Mind

David M. Buss
University of Texas at Austin

Allyn and Bacon

Boston • London • Toronto • Sydney • Tokyo • Singapore

Vice President, Social Sciences: *Sean W. Wakely*
Series Editorial Assistant: *Jessica Barnard*
Marketing Manager: *Joyce Nilsen*
Sr. Editorial Production Administrator: *Susan McIntyre*
Editorial Production Service: *Ruttle, Shaw & Wetherill, Inc.*
Composition Buyer: *Linda Cox*
Manufacturing Buyer: *Megan Cochran*
Cover Administrator: *Jenny Hart*
Electronic Composition: *Omegatype Typography, Inc.*

Copyright © 1999 by Allyn & Bacon
A Viacom Company
160 Gould Street
Needham Heights, MA 02494

Internet: www. abacon.com

Photo credits appear on page 441, which constitutes an extension of the copyright page.

Library of Congress Cataloging-in-Publication Data

Buss, David M.
    Evolutionary psychology: the new science of the mind / David M.
  Buss.
      p.   cm.
    Includes bibliographical references and index.
    ISBN 0-205-19358-7
    1. Genetic psychology.   2. Human evolution.   I. Title.
  BF701.B84   1999
  155.7—dc21   98-28483
                                                          CIP

Printed in the United States of America

10 9 8 7 6 5 4   04 03 02 01 00 99

This book is dedicated to:

Charles Darwin
Francis Galton
Gregor Mendel
R. A. Fisher
W. D. Hamilton
George C. Williams
John Maynard-Smith
Robert Trivers
Richard Dawkins
Donald Symons
Martin Daly
Margo Wilson
Leda Cosmides
John Tooby

And to all students of evolutionary psychology,
past, present, and future

BRIEF CONTENTS

C O N T E N T S

6 Short-Term Sexual Strategies   161

PART FOUR   Challenges of Parenting and Kinship   187

7 Problems of Parenting   189

PREFACE

It is especially exciting to be an evolutionary psychologist during this time in the history of science. Most scientists operate within long-established paradigms. Evolutionary psychology, in contrast, is a revolutionary new science, a true synthesis of modern principles of psychology and evolutionary biology. By taking stock of the field at this time, I hope this book contributes in some modest measure to the fulfillment of a scientific revolution that will provide the foundation for psychology in the new millennium.

Charles Darwin must be considered the first evolutionary psychologist for this prophesy at the end of his classic treatise, *On the Origin of Species* (1859): "In the distant future I see open fields for far more important researches. Psychology will be based on a new foundation." More than 140 years later, after many false starts and halting steps, the science of evolutionary psychology is finally emerging. The purpose of this book is to showcase the foundations of this new science and the fascinating discoveries of its practitioners.

When I first started to conduct research in evolutionary psychology as a young assistant professor at Harvard University in 1981, evolutionary speculations about humans abounded, but practically no empirical research had been conducted to back them up. Part of the problem was that scientists interested in evolutionary questions could not bridge the gap between the grand evolutionary theories and the actual scientific study of human behavior. Today that gap has closed considerably, because of both conceptual breakthroughs and an avalanche of hard-won empirical achievements. Many exciting questions still cry out for empirical scrutiny, of course, but the existing base of findings is currently so large that the problem I faced was how to keep this book to a reasonable length while still doing justice to the dazzling array of theoretical and empirical insights.

Despite the emergence of evolutionary psychology over the past decade, until now no text on the discipline existed. This book is meant to fill that gap. Although it is written with undergraduates in mind, it is also designed to appeal to a wider audience of laypersons, graduate students, and professionals who seek an up-to-date overview of evolutionary psychology.

I wrote this book with another purpose as well—frankly, a revolutionary one. I wrote it so that the hundreds of professors at universities throughout the world who have been thinking and writing about evolution and human behavior will be motivated to teach formal courses in evolutionary psychology and get those courses established as part of required psychology curricula. Already evolutionary psychology is attracting the best and the brightest young minds. I hope that this book helps to accelerate the trend and in some small way contribute to the fulfillment of Darwin's prophesy.

ACKNOWLEDGMENTS

The acknowledgments for this book must include not just colleagues who have directly commented on its contents, but those who have influenced my personal evolutionary odyssey, which has spanned more than twenty years. My interest in evolution began in an undergraduate geology class in the mid-1970s, when I first realized that there were theories designed specifically to explain the origins of things. My first evolutionary groping was a term paper for a course in 1975 in which I speculated, drawing on now-laughable primate comparisons, that the main reason men have evolved a status-striving motive is because higher status produced increased sexual opportunities.

My interest in evolution and human behavior grew when I was in graduate school at the University of California at Berkeley, but I found the most fertile evolutionary soil at Harvard University, which offered me a position as assistant professor of Psychology in 1981. There I began teaching a course on human motivation using evolutionary principles, although the text scarcely mentioned evolution. My lectures were based on the works of Charles Darwin, W. D. Hamilton, Robert Trivers, and Don Symons. I started corresponding with Don Symons, whose 1979 book is considered by many the first modern treatise on human evolutionary psychology. I owe Don a special thanks; his friendship and insightful commentary have informed practically everything that I've written on the subject of evolutionary psychology. Influenced by Don's ideas, in 1982 I designed my first evolutionary research project on human mating, which eventually mushroomed into a cross-cultural study of 10,047 participants from thirty-seven cultures around the world.

After word got around about my evolutionary interests, a brilliant young Harvard graduate student named Leda Cosmides rapped on my office door and introduced herself. We had the first of many discussions (actually arguments) about evolution and human behavior. Leda introduced me to her equally brilliant husband and collaborator John Tooby, and together they tried to correct some of the more egregious errors in my thinking—something they continue to do to this day. Through Leda and John I met Irv DeVore, a prominent Harvard anthropologist who conducted "simian seminars" at his Cambridge home, and Martin Daly and Margo Wilson, who came to Harvard on sabbatical. At that point, the early to mid-1980s, Leda and John had not yet published anything on evolutionary psychology, and no one was called an evolutionary psychologist.

The next pivotal event in my evolutionary quest occurred when I was elected to be a fellow at the Center for Advanced Study in the Behavioral Sciences in Palo Alto. Thanks to the encouragement of Director Gardner Lindzey, I proposed a special center project entitled "Foundations of Evolutionary Psychology." The acceptance of this proposal led Leda Cosmides, John Tooby, Martin Daly, Margo Wilson, and me to spend 1989 and 1990 at the center working on the foundations of evolutionary psychology, even through the earthquake that rocked the Bay Area. In the writing of this book I owe the greatest intellectual debt to Leda Cosmides, John Tooby, Don Symons,

Martin Daly, and Margo Wilson, pioneers and founders of the emerging field of evolutionary psychology.

Harvard on one coast and the Center for Advanced Study on the other provided a bounty for budding evolutionary scholars, but I must also thank two other institutions and their inhabitants. First, the University of Michigan supported the Evolution and Human Behavior group between 1986 and 1994. I owe special thanks to Al Cain, Richard Nisbett, Richard Alexander, Robert Axelrod, Barb Smuts, Randolph Nesse, Richard Wrangham, Bobbi Low, Kim Hill, Warren Holmes, Laura Betzig, Paul Turke, Eugene Burnstein, and John Mitani for playing key roles at Michigan. Second, I thank the Department of Psychology at the University of Texas at Austin, which had the prescience to form one of the first graduate programs in evolutionary psychology in the world under the heading of Individual Differences and Evolutionary Psychology. Special thanks go to Joe Horn, Dev Singh, Del Thiessen, Lee Willerman, Peter Mac-Neilage, David Cohen, and the department chair, Randy Diehl, for their roles at UT.

I owe tremendous thanks to friends and colleagues who have contributed to the ideas in this book in one form or another: Dick Alexander, Bob Axelrod, Robin Baker, Jerry Barkow, Jay Belsky, Laura Betzig, George Bittner, Don Brown, Eugene Burnstein, Arnold Buss, Bram Buunk, Liz Cashden, Nap Chagnon, Jim Chisholm, Helena Cronin, Michael Cunningham, Richard Dawkins, Irv DeVore, Frans de Waal, Mike Domjan, Paul Ekman, Steve Emlen, Mark Flinn, Robin Fox, Robert Frank, Steve Gangestad, Karl Grammer, W. D. Hamilton, Kim Hill, Warren Holmes, Sarah Hrdy, Bill Jankowiak, Doug Jones, Doug Kenrick, Lee Kirkpatrick, Judy Langlois, Bobbi Low, Kevin MacDonald, Neil Malamuth, Janet Mann, Linda Mealey, Geoffrey Miller, Randolph Nesse, Dick Nisbett, Steve Pinker, David Rowe, Paul Rozin, Joanna Scheib, Paul Sherman, Irwin Silverman, Jeff Simpson, Dev Singh, Barb Smuts, Michael Studd, Frank Sulloway, Del Thiessen, Nancy Thornhill, Randy Thornhill, Lionel Tiger, Bill Tooke, John Townsend, Robert Trivers, Jerry Wakefield, Lee Willerman, George Williams, D. S. Wilson, E. O. Wilson, and Richard Wrangham.

I would like to thank the following reviewers for their feedback on the manuscript: Clifford R. Mynatt, Bowling Green State University; Richard C. Keefe, Scottsdale College; Paul M. Bronstein, University of Michigan-Flint; Margo Wilson, McMaster University; W. Jake Jacobs, University of Arizona; and A. J. Figueredo, University of Arizona.

Thanks go to my students past and present who are making major contributions to the field of evolutionary psychology: April Bleske, Mike Botwin, Todd DeKay, Josh Duntley, Bruce Ellis, Barry Friedman, Heidi Greiling, Arlette Greer, Martie Haselton, Liisa Kyl-Heku, Anne McGuire, David Schmitt, and Todd Shackelford. Special thanks also to Kevin Daly, Todd DeKay, Josh Duntley, A. J. Figueredo, Barry Friedman, Martie Haselton, Rebecca Sage, Todd Shackelford, and W. Jake Jacobs for generously providing detailed comments on the entire book.

And to Cindy.

PART ONE

Foundations of Evolutionary Psychology

Two chapters introduce the foundations of evolutionary psychology. Chapter 1 traces the scientific movements leading to evolutionary psychology. First the landmarks in the history of evolutionary theory are described, starting with theories of evolution developed before Charles Darwin and ending with modern formulations of evolutionary theory widely accepted in the biological sciences today. Next five common misunderstandings about evolutionary theory are examined. Finally we trace landmarks in the field of psychology, starting with the influence Darwin had on the psychoanalytic theories of Sigmund Freud and ending with modern formulations of cognitive psychology.

Chapter 2 provides the conceptual foundations of modern evolutionary psychology and introduces the scientific tools used to test evolutionary psychological hypotheses. The first section examines theories about the origins of human nature. Then we turn to a definition of the core concept of an evolved psychological mechanism and outline the properties of these mechanisms. The middle portion of Chapter 2 describes the major methods used to test evolutionary psychological hypotheses and the sources of evidence on which these tests are based. Because the remainder of the book is organized around human adaptive problems, the end of Chapter 2 focuses on the tools evolutionary psychologists use to identify adaptive problems, starting with survival and ending with the problems of group living.

1 The Scientific Movements Leading to Evolutionary Psychology

Psychology will be based on a new foundation.
—Charles Darwin, 1859

As the archeologist dusted off the dirt and debris from the skeleton, she noticed something strange: the left side of the skull had a large dent, apparently from a ferocious blow, and the rib cage—also on the left side—had the head of spear lodged in it. Back in the laboratory scientists determined that the skeleton was that of a Neanderthal man who had died roughly 50,000 years ago, the earliest known homicide victim. His killer, judging from the damage to the skull and rib cage, bore the lethal weapon in his right hand.

The fossil record of injuries to bones reveals two strikingly common patterns (Trinkaus & Zimmerman, 1982; Walker, 1995). First, the skeletons of men contain far more fractures and dents than do the skeletons of women. Second, the injuries are located mainly on the left frontal sides of the skulls and skeletons, suggesting right-handed attackers. The bone record alone cannot tell us with certainty that combat among men was a central feature of human ancestral social life. Nor can it tell us with certainty that men evolved to be the more physically aggressive sex. But skeletal remains provide clues that yield a fascinating piece of the puzzle of where we came from, the forces that shaped who we are, and the very nature of our minds.

The huge human brain, approximately 1,400 cubic centimeters, is the most complex organic structure in the known world. Understanding the human mind/brain mechanisms in evolutionary perspective is the goal of the new scientific discipline called evolutionary psychology. *Evolutionary psychology* focuses on four key questions: (1) *Why* is the mind designed the way it is—that is, what causal processes created, fashioned, or shaped the human mind into its current form? (2) *How* is the human mind designed—what are its mechanisms or component parts, and how are they organized? (3) *What are the functions* of the component parts and their organized structure—that is, what is the mind designed to do? (4) *How* does input from the current environment, especially the social environment, interact with the design of the human mind to produce observable behavior?

Contemplating the mysteries of the human mind is not new. Ancient Greeks such as Aristotle and Plato wrote manifestos on the subject. More recently, theories of the human mind such as the Freudian theory of psychoanalysis, the Skinnerian theory of reinforcement, and connectionism have vied for the attention of psychologists.

Only within the past few decades have we acquired the conceptual tools to synthesize our understanding of the human mind under one unifying theoretical framework—that of evolutionary psychology. This discipline pulls together findings from all disciplines of the mind, including those of brain imaging; learning and memory; attention, emotion, and passion; attraction, jealousy, and sex; self-esteem, status, and self-sacrifice; parenting, persuasion, and perception; kinship, warfare, and aggression; cooperation, altruism, and helping; ethics, morality, and medicine; commitment, culture, and consciousness. This book offers an introduction to evolutionary psychology and provides a road map to this new science of the mind.

This chapter starts by tracing the major landmarks in the history of evolutionary biology that were critical in the emergence of evolutionary psychology. Then we turn to the history of the field of psychology and show the progression of accomplishments that led to the need for integrating evolutionary theory with modern psychology.

Landmarks in the History of Evolutionary Thinking

We begin our examination of the history of evolutionary thinking well before the contributions of Charles Darwin and then consider the various milestones in its development through the end of the twentieth century.

Evolution before Darwin

Evolution refers to change over time in organic (living) structure. Change in life forms was postulated by scientists to have occurred long before Darwin published his classic 1859 book, *On the Origin of Species* (see Glass, Temkin, & Straus, 1959; and Harris, 1992, for historical treatments).

Jean Pierre Antoine de Monet de Lamarck (1744–1829) was one of the first scientists to use the word *biologie*, thus recognizing the study of life as a distinct science. Lamarck believed in two major causes of species change: first, a natural tendency for each species to progress toward a higher form and, second, the inheritance of acquired characteristics. Lamarck said that animals must struggle to survive and that this struggle causes their nerves to secrete a fluid that enlarges the organs involved in the struggle. Giraffes evolved long necks, he thought, through their attempts to eat from higher and higher leaves (recent evidence suggests that long necks may also play a role in mate competition). Lamarck believed that the neck changes that came about from these strivings were passed down to succeeding generations of giraffes, hence the phrase "the inheritance of acquired characteristics." Another theory of change in life forms was developed by Baron Georges

Léopold Chrétien Frédérick Dagobert Cuvier (1769–1832). Cuvier proposed a theory called *catastrophism*, according to which, species are extinguished periodically by sudden catastrophes, such as meteorites, and then replaced by different species.

Biologists before Darwin also noticed the bewildering variety of species, some of which seemed to contain astonishing structural similarities. Humans, chimpanzees, and orangutans, for example, all have exactly five digits on each hand and foot. The wings of birds are similar to the flippers of seals, perhaps suggesting that one was modified from the other (Daly & Wilson, 1983). Comparisons among these species suggested that life was not static, as some scientists and theologians had argued. Further evidence suggesting change over time also came from the fossil record. Bones from older geological strata were not the same as bones from more recent geological strata. These bones would not be different, scientists reasoned, unless there had been a change in organic structure over time.

Another source of evidence came from comparing the embryological development of different species (Mayr, 1982). Biologists noticed that such development was strikingly similar in species that otherwise seemed very different from one another. An unusual loop-like pattern of arteries close to the bronchial slits characterize the embryos of mammals, birds, and frogs. This evidence suggested, perhaps, that these species might have come from the same ancestors many years ago. All these pieces of evidence, present before 1859, suggested that life was not fixed or unchanging. The biologists who believed that organic structure changed over time called themselves evolutionists.

Another key observation had been made by various evolutionists before Darwin: Many species possess characteristics that seem to have a purpose. The porcupine's quills help it fend off predators. The turtle's shell helps to protect its tender organs from the hostile forces of nature. The beaks of many birds are designed to aid in cracking nuts. This apparent functionality, so seemingly abundant in nature, also required an explanation.

Missing from the evolutionists' accounts before Darwin, however, was a theory to explain how change might take place over time and how such seemingly purposeful structures like the giraffe's long neck and the porcupine's sharp quills could have come about. A causal mechanism or process to explain these biological phenomena was needed. Charles Darwin provided the theory of just such a mechanism.

Darwin's Theory of Natural Selection

Darwin's task was more difficult than it might at first appear. He wanted not only to explain why change takes place over time in life forms, but also to account for the particular ways in which it changes. He wanted to determine how new species emerge (hence the title of his book, *On the Origin of Species*), as well as how others vanish. Darwin wanted to explain why the component parts of animals—the long necks of giraffes, the wings of birds, the trunks of elephants—existed in those particular forms. And he wanted to explain the apparent purposive quality of those forms, or why they seem to function to help organisms accomplish specific tasks.

Charles Darwin created a scientific revolution in biology with his theory of natural selection. His book, On the Origin of Species *(1859), is packed with theoretical arguments and detailed empirical data that he amassed over the twenty-five years prior to the book's publication.*

   The answers to these puzzles can be traced to a voyage Darwin took after graduating from Cambridge University. He traveled the world as a naturalist on a ship, the *Beagle*, for a five-year period, from 1831 to 1836. During this voyage he collected dozens of samples of birds and other animals from the Galápagos Islands in the Pacific Ocean. On returning from his voyage he discovered that the Galápagos finches, which he had presumed were all of the same species, actually varied so much that they constituted different species. Indeed, each island in the Galápagos had a distinct species of finch. Darwin determined that these different finches had a common ancestor but had diverged from each other because of the local ecological conditions on each island. This geographic variation was likely pivotal to Darwin's conclusion that species are not immutable but can change over time.

   What could account for why species change? This was the next challenge. Darwin struggled with several different theories of the origins of change, but rejected all of them because they failed to consider a critical fact: the existence of adaptations. Darwin wanted to account for change, of course, but perhaps even more important he wanted to account for why organisms appeared so well designed for their local environments.

   It was . . . evident that [these others theories] could [not] account for the innumerable cases in which organisms of every kind are beautifully adapted to their habits of life—for instance, a woodpecker or tree-frog to climb trees, or a seed for dispersal by hooks and plumes. I had always been much struck by such adaptations, and until these could be explained it seemed to me almost useless to endeavour to prove by indirect evidence that species have been modified. (Darwin, from his autobiography; cited in Ridley, 1996, p. 9)

Darwin unearthed a key to the puzzle of adaptations in Thomas Malthus's *An Essay on the Principle of Population* (published in 1798), which introduced Darwin to the notion that organisms exist in numbers far greater than can survive and reproduce. The result must be a "struggle for existence," in which favorable variations tend to be preserved and unfavorable ones tend to die out. When this process is repeated generation after generation, the end result is the formation of a new species.

More formally, Darwin's answer to all these puzzles of life was the theory of *natural selection* and its three essential ingredients: *variation, inheritance,* and *selection*.[1] First, organisms vary in all sorts of ways, such as in wing length, trunk strength, bone mass, cell structure, fighting ability, defensive ability, and social cunning. Variation is essential for the process of evolution to operate—it provides the "raw materials" for evolution.

Second, only some of these variations are inherited—that is, passed down reliably from parents to their offspring, which then pass them on to their offspring down through the generations. Other variations, such as a wing deformity caused by an environmental accident, are not inherited by offspring. Only those variations that are inherited play a role in the evolutionary process.

The third critical ingredient of Darwin's theory is selection. Organisms with some heritable variants leave more offspring *because* those attributes help with the tasks of *survival* and/or *reproduction*. In an environment in which the primary food source might be nut-bearing trees or bushes, some finches with a particular shape of beak, for example, might be better able to crack nuts and get at their meat than would finches with other shapes of beaks. More finches who have beaks better shaped for nut cracking survive than those with beaks poorly shaped for nut cracking and thereby can contribute to the next generation.

An organism can survive for many years, however, and still not pass on its inherited qualities to future generations. To pass its inherited qualities to future generations it must reproduce. Thus, *differential reproductive success*, brought about by the possession of heritable variants that increase or decrease an individual's chances of surviving and reproducing, is the "bottom line" of evolution by natural selection. Differential reproductive success or failure is defined by reproductive success relative to others. The characteristics of organisms who reproduce more than others, therefore, get passed down to future generations at a relatively greater frequency. Because survival is usually necessary for reproduction, it took on a critical role in Darwin's theory of natural selection.

Darwin envisioned two classes of evolved variations—one playing a role in survival and another playing a role in reproduction. Among human beings, for example, sweat glands help maintain a constant body temperature, and thus help us to survive. Our tastes for sugar and fat help guide us to eat certain foods, and thus help us to survive. Likewise,

---

[1] The theory of natural selection was discovered independently by Alfred Russel Wallace (Wallace, 1858) and Darwin and Wallace co-presented the theory at a meeting of the Linnaen Society.

other inherited attributes aid in reproduction. The elaborate songs of some bird species, for example, help them to attract mates and hence to reproduce but do nothing to enhance an individual bird's survival. In summary, differential reproductive success of inherited variants is the crux of Darwin's theory of natural selection. It is useful to think of two classes of characteristics that evolve through this process—those that help organisms survive and those that help them reproduce.

Evolution by natural selection is not forward-looking and is not "intentional." The giraffe does not spy the juicy leaves stirring high in the tree and "evolve" a longer neck. Rather, those giraffes that due to an inherited variant happen to have longer necks have an advantage over other giraffes in getting to those leaves. Hence they have a greater chance of surviving and thus of passing on their slightly longer necks to their offspring (recent work suggests that the long neck of giraffes may serve other functions, such as success in same-sex combat). Natural selection merely acts on those variants that happen to exist. Evolution is not intentional and cannot look into the future and foresee distant needs.

Another critical feature of natural selection is that it is *gradual*, at least when evaluated relative to the human life span. The short-necked ancestors of giraffes did not evolve long necks overnight, or even over the course of a few generations. It has taken dozens, hundreds, thousands, and in some cases millions of generations for the process of natural selection to gradually shape the organic mechanisms we see today. Of course, some changes occur extremely slowly, others more rapidly. And there can be long periods of no change, followed by a relatively sudden change, a phenomenon known as "punctuated equilibrium" (Gould & Eldredge, 1977). But even these "rapid" changes occur in tiny increments each generation and take hundreds or thousands of generations to occur.

Darwin's theory of natural selection offered a powerful explanation for many of the baffling aspects of life and one that proved pivotal for the origin of new species (although Darwin failed to recognize the full importance of geographic isolation as a precursor to natural selection in the formation of new species; see Cronin, 1991). It accounted for the modification of organic structures over time. It also accounted for the apparent purposive quality of the component parts of those structures—that is, that they seem "designed" to serve particular functions linked with survival and reproduction.

Perhaps most astonishing to some (but appalling to others), in 1859 natural selection united all species into one grand tree of descent in one bold stroke. For the first time in recorded history, each species was viewed as being connected with all other species through a common ancestry. Human beings and chimpanzees, for example, share more than 98 percent of each other's DNA, and shared a common ancestor perhaps 15 to 20 million years ago (Wrangham & Peterson, 1996). Even more startling is the recent finding that many human genes turn out to have counterpart genes in a transparent worm called *Caenorhabditis elegans*. They are highly similar in chemical structure, suggesting that humans and this worm evolved from a distant common ancestor (Wade, 1997). In short, Darwin's theory made it possible to locate humans in the grand tree of life, showing their place in nature and their links with all other living creatures.

Darwin's theory of natural selection created a storm of controversy. Lady Ashley, a contemporary of Darwin, remarked on hearing his theory that human beings descended from apes: "Let's hope it's not true; but if it is true, let's hope that it does not become widely known." In a famous debate at Oxford University, Bishop Wilberforce bitingly asked his rival debater Thomas Huxley whether the "ape" from which Huxley descended was on his grandmother's or his grandfather's side.

Even biologists at the time were highly skeptical of Darwin's theory of natural selection. One objection was that Darwinian evolution lacked a coherent theory of inheritance. Darwin himself preferred a "blending" theory of inheritance, in which off-spring are mixtures of their parents, much like pink paint is a mixture of red and white paint. This theory of inheritance is now known to be wrong, as we will see later in the discussion of the work of Gregor Mendel, so early critics were correct in the objection that evolution by natural selection lacked a solid theory of heredity.

Another objection was that some biologists could not imagine how the early stages of the evolution of an adaptation could be useful to an organism. How could a partial wing help a bird, if a partial wing is insufficient for flight? How could a partial eye help a reptile, if a partial eye is insufficient for sight? Darwin's theory of natural selection requires that each and every step in the gradual evolution of an adaptation be advantageous in the currency of reproduction. Thus, partial wings and eyes must yield an adaptive advantage, even before they evolve into fully developed wings and eyes. For now it is sufficient to note that partial forms can indeed offer adaptive advantages; this objection to Darwin's theory is therefore surmountable (Dawkins, 1986). Further, it is important to stress that just because biologists or other scientists have difficulty imagining certain forms of evolution, such as how a partial wing might be useful, that is not a good argument against such forms having evolved. This "argument from ignorance," or as Dawkins (1982) calls it "the argument from personal incredulity," is not good science, however intuitively compelling it might sound.

A third objection came from religious creationists, many of whom viewed species as immutable (unchanging) and created by a deity rather than by the gradual process of evolution by selection. Furthermore, Darwin's theory implied that the emergence of humans and other species was "blind," resulting from the slow, un-planned, cumulative process of selection. This contrasted with the view that creation-ists held of humans (and other species) as part of God's grand plan or intentional design. Darwin had anticipated this reaction, and apparently delayed the publication of his theory in part because he was worried about upsetting his wife, Emma, who was deeply religious.

The controversy continues to this day. Although Darwin's theory of evolution, with some important modifications, is the unifying and nearly universally accepted theory within the biological sciences, its application to humans, which Darwin clearly envisioned, still meets with vigorous resistance. But humans are not exempt from the evolutionary process, despite our profound resistance to being analyzed through the same lens used to analyze other species. As we head into the twenty-first century we finally have the conceptual tools to complete Darwin's revolution and forge an evolu-tionary psychology of the human species.

Evolutionary psychology is able to take advantage of key theoretical insights and scientific discoveries that were not known in Darwin's day. The first among these is the physical basis of inheritance—the gene.

The Modern Synthesis: Genes and Particulate Inheritance

When Darwin published *On the Origin of Species* he did not know the nature of the mechanism by which "inheritance" occurred. Indeed, as mentioned previously, the dominant thinking at the time was that inheritance constituted a sort of "blending" of the two parents, whereby offspring would be an intermediate between them. A short and a tall parent, for example, would produce a child of intermediate height, according to the blending theory. This theory is now known to be wrong.

An Austrian monk named Gregor Mendel showed why it did not work. Inheritance was "particulate," he argued, and not blended. That is, the qualities of the parents are not blended with each other, but rather are passed on intact to their offspring in distinct packets called *genes*. Furthermore, parents must be born with the genes they pass on; they cannot be acquired by experience.

Unfortunately for the advancement of science, Mendel's discovery that inheritance is particulate, which he demonstrated by cross-breeding different strains of pea plants, remained unknown to most of the scientific community for some thirty years. Mendel had sent Darwin copies of his papers, but either they remained unread or their significance was not recognized.

A *gene* is defined as the smallest discrete unit that is inherited by offspring intact, without being broken up or blended—this was Mendel's critical insight. *Genotypes*, in contrast, refer to the entire collection of genes within an individual. Genotypes, unlike genes, are not passed down to offspring intact. Rather, in sexually reproducing species such as our own genotypes are broken up with each generation. Thus, each of us inherits a random half of genes from our mother's genotype and a random half from our father's genotype. The specific half of the genes we inherit from each parent, however, is identical to half of those possessed by that parent because they get transmitted as a discrete bundle, without modification.

The unification of Darwin's theory of evolution by natural selection with the discovery of particulate gene inheritance culminated in a movement in the 1930s and 1940s called the "Modern Synthesis" (Dobzhansky, 1937; Huxley, 1942; Mayr, 1942; Simpson, 1944). The Modern Synthesis discarded a number of misconceptions in biology, including Lamarck's theory of the inheritance of acquired characteristics and the blending theory of inheritance. It emphatically confirmed the importance of Darwin's theory of natural selection, but put it on a firmer footing with a well-articulated understanding of the nature of inheritance.

The Ethology Movement

To some people, evolution is most clearly envisioned when it applies to physical structures. We can easily see how a turtle's shell is an adaptation for protection and a bird's wings an adaptation for flight. We recognize similarities between ourselves and chimpanzees, and so most people find it relatively easy to believe that human beings and chimps have a common ancestry. The paleontological record of skulls, although incomplete, shows enough evidence of physical evolution that most concede that change has taken place over time. The evolution of behavior, however, has historically been more difficult for scientists and laypeople to imagine. Behavior, after all, leaves no fossils.

Darwin clearly envisioned his theory of natural selection as being just as applicable to behavior, including social behavior, as to physical structures. Several lines of evidence support this view. First, all behavior requires underlying physical structures. Bipedal locomotion is a behavior, for example, and requires the physical structures of two legs and a multitude of muscles to support those legs while the body is in an upright position. Second, species can be bred for certain behavioral characteristics using the principle of selection. Dogs, for example, can be bred (artificial selection) for aggressiveness or passivity. These lines of evidence all point to the conclusion that behavior is not exempt from the sculpting hand of evolution. The first major discipline to form around the study of behavior from an evolutionary perspective was the field of ethology, and one of the first phenomena the ethologists documented was imprinting.

Ducklings *imprint* on the first moving object they observe in life—forming an association during a critical period of development. Usually this object is the duck's mother. After imprinting, the baby ducks follow the object of their imprinting wherever it goes. Imprinting is clearly a form of learning—an association is formed between the duckling and the mother that was not there before the exposure to her motion. This form of learning, however, is "preprogrammed" and clearly part of the evolved structures of the duckling's biology. Although many have seen pictures of a line of baby ducks following their mother, if the first object a duck sees is a human leg, it will follow that person instead. Konrad Lorenz was the first to demonstrate this imprinting phenomenon by showing that baby birds would follow him for days rather than their own mother if exposed to his leg during the critical period shortly after birth. Lorenz (1965) started a new branch of evolutionary biology called *ethology*, and imprinting in birds was a vivid phenomenon used to launch this new field. Ethology is defined as "the study of the proximate mechanisms and adaptive value of animal behavior" (Alcock, 1989, p. 548).

The ethology movement was in part a reaction to the extreme environmentalism in American psychology. Ethologists were interested in four key issues, which have become known as the four "whys" of behavior advanced by one of the founders of ethology, Niko Tinbergen (1951): (1) the *immediate causes* of behavior (e.g., the movement of the mother); (2) the *developmental causes* of behavior (e.g., the events during the duck's lifetime that cause changes); (3) the *function* of behavior, or the "adaptive purpose" it seems to fulfill (e.g., keeping the baby duck close to the mother, which helps it to survive), and (4) the *evolutionary* or *phylogenetic origins* of behavior (e.g., what sequence of evolutionary events led to the origins of an imprinting mechanism in the duck).

Ethologists developed an array of concepts to describe what they believed to be the innate properties of animals. *Fixed action patterns* are the stereotypic behavioral sequences in which an animal engages, triggered by a well-defined stimulus (Tinbergen, 1951). Once a fixed action pattern is triggered, the animal performs it to completion. Showing certain male ducks a wooden facsimile of a female duck, for example, will trigger a rigid sequence of courting behavior. Concepts such as fixed action patterns were useful in allowing ethologists to partition the ongoing stream of behavior into discrete units for analysis.

The ethology movement went a long way toward orienting biologists to focus on the importance of adaptation. Indeed, the glimmerings of evolutionary psychology itself may be seen in the early writings of Lorenz, who wrote, "our cognitive and perceptual categories, given to us prior to individual experience, are adapted to the environment for the same reasons that the horse's hoof is suited for the plains before the horse is born, and the fin of a fish is adapted for water before the fish hatches from its egg" (Lorenz, 1941, p. 99; translated from the original German by I. Eibl-Eibesfeldt, 1989, p. 8).

Ethology ran into three problems, however. First, many descriptions acted more as "labels" for behavior patterns and did not really go very far in explaining them. Second, ethologists tended to focus on observable behavior—much like their American behaviorist counterparts—and so did not look "inside the heads" of animals to the underlying mechanisms responsible for generating that behavior. And third, although ethology was concerned with adaptation (one of the four critical issues listed by Tinbergen), it did not develop rigorous criteria for discovering adaptations. Ethologists did, however, turn up many useful findings, documenting, for example, the imprinting that occurs in a variety of bird species and stereotypic fixed action patterns that are released by particular stimuli. Ethology also forced psychologists to reconsider the role of biology in the study of human behavior. This set the stage for an important scientific revolution, which was brought about by a fundamental reformulation of Darwin's theory of natural selection—a reformulation known as inclusive fitness theory.

The Inclusive Fitness Revolution

In the early 1960's a young graduate student named William D. Hamilton was working on his doctoral dissertation at Oxford University. Hamilton proposed a radical new revision of evolutionary theory, which he termed "inclusive fitness theory." Legend has it that his professors failed to understand the dissertation or its significance (perhaps because it was highly mathematical), and so his work was initially rejected. When it was finally accepted by the Oxford dons and published in 1964 in the *Journal of Theoretical Biology*, however, Hamilton's theory sparked a revolution that transformed the entire field of biology.

Hamilton reasoned that *classical fitness*—the measure of an individual's direct reproductive success in passing on genes through the production of offspring—was too narrow to describe the process of evolution by selection. He theorized that natural selection favors characteristics that cause an organism's genes to be passed on, regardless of whether the organism produces offspring directly. Parental care—investing in your own children—was reinterpreted as merely a special case of caring for kin who carry copies of your genes in their bodies. An organism can also increase the reproduction of its genes by helping brothers, sisters, nieces, or nephews to survive and reproduce. All these relatives have some probability of carrying copies of the organism's

William D. Hamilton revolutionized evolutionary biology with his theory of inclusive fitness, published in 1964. He has continued to make profound theoretical contributions on topics as diverse as the evolution of spite and the origins of sexual reproduction. Hamilton is now on the faculty of Oxford University.

genes. Hamilton's genius was in the recognition that the definition of classical fitness was too narrow and should be broadened to *inclusive fitness*.

Technically, inclusive fitness is not a property of an individual or an organism but rather a property of its *actions* or *effects*. Thus, inclusive fitness can be viewed as the sum of an individual's own reproductive success (classical fitness) *plus the effects* the individual's actions have on the reproductive success of his or her genetic relatives. For this second component the effects on relatives must be weighted by the appropriate degree of genetic relatedness to the target organism—for example, 0.50 for brothers and sisters (because they are genetically related by 50 percent with the target organism), 0.25 for grandparents and grandchildren (25 percent genetic relatedness), 0.125 for first cousins (12.5 percent genetic relatedness), and so on (see Figure 1.1 on page 14).

The inclusive fitness revolution marshaled a new era that may be called "gene's eye thinking." If you were a gene, what would facilitate your survival and reproduction? First, you might try to ensure the well-being of the "vehicle" or body in which you reside (survival). Second, you might try directly to make many copies of yourself (direct reproduction). Third, you might want to help the survival and reproduction of vehicles that contain copies of you (inclusive fitness). Genes, of course, do not have thoughts, and none of this occurs with consciousness or intentionality. The key point is

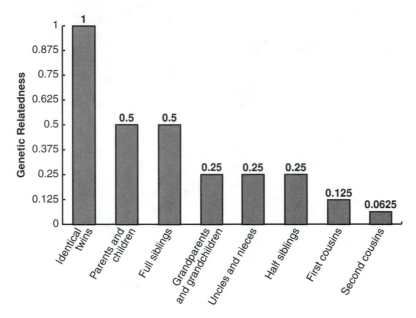

FIGURE 1.1   Genetic Relatedness among Different Types of Relatives. One implication of inclusive fitness theory is that acts of altruism will be directed more toward closely related individuals than more distantly related individuals. Extrapolated from Hamilton (1964).

that the gene is the fundamental unit of inheritance, the unit that is passed on intact in the process of reproduction. Adaptations arise by the process of inclusive fitness. Genes that have effects that increase their replicative success will replace other genes, producing evolution over time.

Thinking about selection from the perspective of the gene offered a wealth of insights to evolutionary biologists. The theory of inclusive fitness has profound consequences for how we think about the psychology of the family, altruism, helping, the formation of groups, and even aggression—topics we explore in later chapters. The scientific citations to Hamilton's theory went from three or four per year in the 1960s to thousands in the 1970s and beyond; it is appropriately considered the unifying theory in evolutionary biology. As for W. D. Hamilton himself—after a stint at the University of Michigan, Oxford University made him an offer he couldn't refuse, and so he returned to the department that had belatedly recognized his genius.

Clarifying Adaptation and Natural Selection

The rapid inclusive fitness revolution in evolutionary biology owes part of its debt to George C. Williams, who in 1966 published a now-classic work, *Adaptation and Natural Selection*. This seminal book contributed to at least three key shifts in thinking in the field.

First, Williams (1966) challenged the prevailing endorsement of *group selection*, the notion that adaptations evolved for the benefit of the group through the differential survival and reproduction of groups (Wynne-Edwards, 1962), as opposed to benefit for the gene arising through the differential reproduction of genes. According to the theory of group selection, for example, an animal might limit its personal reproduction to keep the population low, thus avoiding the destruction of the food base on which the population relied. According to group selection theory, only species that possessed characteristics that were beneficial to their group survived. Those that acted more selfishly perished because of the overexploitation of the critical food resources on which the species relied. Williams argued persuasively that group selection, although theoretically possible, was likely to be an extraordinarily weak force in evolution, for the following reason. Imagine a bird species with two types of individuals—one that sacrifices itself by committing suicide so as not to deplete its food resources and another that selfishly continues to eat the food, even when supplies are low. In the next generation, which type is likely to have descendants? The answer is that the suicidal birds will have died out and failed to reproduce, while those who refused to sacrifice themselves for the group will have survived and left descendants. Selection operating on individual differences *within* a species, in other words, undermines the power of selection operating at the level of the group. Within five years of the book's publication most biologists had relinquished their subscription to group selection, although recently there has been a resurgence of interest in the potential potency of group selection (Wilson & Sober, 1994; Sober & Wilson, 1998).

Williams's second contribution was in translating Hamilton's highly quantitative theory of inclusive fitness into clear prose that could be comprehended by everyone. Once biologists understood inclusive fitness, they began vigorously researching its implications. To mention one prominent example, inclusive fitness theory partially solved the "problem of altruism": How could altruism evolve—incurring reproductive costs to oneself to benefit the reproduction of others—if evolution favors genes that have the effect of self-replication? Inclusive fitness theory solved this problem (at least in part) because altruism could evolve if the recipients of one's help were one's genetic kin. Parents, for example, might sacrifice their own lives to save the lives of their children, who carry copies of the parents' genes within them. The same logic applies to making sacrifices for other genetic relatives, such as sisters or cousins. The benefit to one's relatives in fitness currencies must be greater than the costs to the self. If this condition is satisfied, then kin altruism can evolve. In later chapters we review evidence showing that genetic relatedness is indeed a powerful predictor of helping among humans.

The third contribution of *Adaptation and Natural Selection* was Williams's careful analysis of adaptation, which he referred to as "an onerous concept." *Adaptations* may be defined as evolved solutions to specific problems that contribute either directly or indirectly to successful reproduction. Sweat glands, for example, may be adaptations that help solve the survival problem of thermal regulation. Taste preferences may be adaptations that guide the successful consumption of nutritious food. Mate preferences may be adaptations that guide the successful selection of mates. The problem is how to determine which attributes of organisms are adaptations. Williams established several standards for invoking adaptation and believed that it should be invoked only when necessary to explain the phenomenon at hand. When a flying fish leaps out of a wave and falls back into the water, for example, we do not need to invoke an adaptation for "getting back to water." This behavior is explained more simply by the physical law of gravity, which explains why what goes up must come down.

In addition to providing conditions in which we should not invoke the concept of adaptation, Williams provided criteria for determining when we should invoke the concept: *reliability*, *efficiency*, and *economy*. Does the mechanism regularly develop in all members of the species across all "normal" environments (reliability)? Does the mechanism solve a particular adaptive problem well (efficiency)? Does the mechanism solve the adaptive problem without extorting huge costs from the organism (economy)? In other words, adaptation is invoked not merely to explain the usefulness of a biological mechanism, but to explain *improbable usefulness* (Pinker, 1997). Hypotheses about adaptations are, in essence, probability statements about why a reliable, efficient, and economic set of design features could not have arisen by chance alone (Williams, 1966; Tooby & Cosmides, 1992).

In the next chapter we explore the key concept of adaptation in greater depth. For now, it is sufficient to note that Williams's book brought the scientific community one step closer to the Darwinian revolution by creating the downfall of group selection as a preferred and dominant explanation, by illuminating Hamilton's theory of inclusive fitness, and by putting the concept of adaptation on a more rigorous and scientific footing.

Trivers's Seminal Theories

In the late 1960s and early 1970s a graduate student at Harvard University, Robert Trivers, studied William's 1966 book on adaptation. He was struck by the revolutionary consequences that gene-level thinking had for conceptualizing entire domains. A sentence or brief paragraph in Williams's book might contain the seed of an idea that could blossom into a full theory if nurtured properly.

Trivers contributed three seminal papers, all published in the early 1970s. The first was the theory of reciprocal altruism among nonkin—the conditions under which mutually beneficial exchange relationships or transactions could evolve (Trivers, 1971). The second was parental investment theory, which provided a powerful statement of the conditions under which sexual selection would occur for each sex (1972). The third was the theory of parent-offspring conflict—the notion that even parents and their progeny will get into predictable sorts of conflicts because they share only 50 percent of their genes (1974). Parents may try to wean children before the children want to be weaned, for example, in order to free up resources to invest in other children. More generally, what might be optimal for a child (e.g., securing a larger share of parental resources) might not be optimal for the parents (e.g., distributing resources more equally across children). We explore these theories in greater depth in later chapters because they have influenced literally thousands of empirical research projects, including many on humans.

The Sociobiology Controversy

Eleven years after Hamilton's pivotal paper on inclusive fitness was published, a Harvard biologist named Edward O. Wilson caused a scientific and public uproar that rivaled the outrage caused by Charles Darwin in 1859. Wilson's 1975 book, *Sociobiology: The New Synthesis*, was monumental in both size and scope, at nearly 700 double-column pages. It offered a synthesis of cellular biology, integrative neurophysiology, ethology, comparative psychology, population biology, and behavioral ecology. Further, it examined species from ants to humans, proclaiming that the same fundamental explanatory principles could be applied to both.

Sociobiology is not generally regarded as containing fundamentally new theoretical contributions to evolutionary theory. The bulk of its theoretical tools—most prominently inclusive fitness theory and the theories of parental investment and sexual selection—had already been developed by others (Hamilton, 1964; Trivers, 1972, respectively). What it did do is synthesize under one umbrella a tremendous diversity of scientific endeavors and give the emerging field a visible name.

The chapter on humans, the last in the book and running a mere twenty-nine pages, created the most controversy. At public talks audience members shouted him down, and once a pitcher of water was dumped on his head. His work sparked attacks from Marxists, radicals, creationists, other scientists, and even members of his own department at Harvard. Part of the controversy stemmed from the nature of Wilson's claims. He asserted that sociobiology would "cannibalize psychology," which of course was not greeted with warmth by most psychologists. Further, he speculated that many cherished human phenomena, such as culture, religion, ethics, and even aesthetics, would ultimately be explained by the new synthesis. These assertions strongly contradicted the dominant theories in the social sciences, that branch of science for which our species is nearly the sole focus. Culture, learning, socialization, rationality, and consciousness, not evolutionary biology, were presumed by most social scientists to explain the uniqueness of humans.

Despite Wilson's grand claims for a new synthesis that would explain human nature, he had little empirical evidence on humans to support his views. The bulk of the scientific evidence came from nonhuman animals, many far removed phylogenetically from humans. Most social scientists could not see what ants and fruit flies had to do with people. Although scientific revolutions always meet resistance, often from within the ranks of established scientists (Sulloway, 1996), Wilson's lack of relevant scientific data on humans did not help.

Furthermore, the tremendous resistance to Wilson's inclusion of humans within the purview of evolutionary theory was based on several common misunderstandings about evolutionary theory and its application to humans. It is worth highlighting a few of these before turning to parallel movements within psychology that laid the groundwork for evolutionary psychology.

Common Misunderstandings about Evolutionary Theory

The theory of evolution by selection, although elegant in its simplicity, generates a number of common misunderstandings. Perhaps its very simplicity leads people to think that they can understand it completely after only brief exposure to it—after reading an article or two in the popular press, for example. Even professors and researchers in the field get mired in these misunderstandings.

Misunderstanding 1: Human Behavior Is Genetically Determined

Genetic determinism is the doctrine that argues that behavior is controlled exclusively by genes, with little or no role for environmental influence. Much of the resistance to applying evolutionary theory to the understanding of human behavior stems from the misconception that evolutionary theory implies genetic determinism. Contrary to this misunderstanding, evolutionary theory in fact represents a truly interactionist framework. Human behavior cannot occur without two ingredients: (1) evolved adaptations and (2) environmental input that triggers the development and activation of these adaptations. Consider calluses as an illustration. Calluses cannot occur without an evolved callus-producing adaptation, combined with the environmental influence of repeated friction to the skin. Therefore, to invoke evolutionary theory as an explanation for calluses we would never say "calluses are genetically determined and occur regardless of input from the environment." Instead, calluses are the result of a specific form of interaction between an environmental input (repeated friction to the skin) and an adaptation that is sensitive to repeated friction and contains instructions to grow extra new skin cells when it experiences repeated friction. Indeed, the reason that adaptations evolve is that they afford organisms tools to grapple with the problems posed by the environment.

So notions of genetic determinism—behaviors caused by genes without input or influence from the environment—are simply false. They are in no way implied by evolutionary theory. A related misunderstanding, stemming from the mistaken doctrine of genetic determinism, is that evolutionary theory implies an inability to change behavior.

Misunderstanding 2: If It's Evolutionary We Can't Change It

A second misunderstanding is that evolutionary theory implies that human behavior is impervious to change. Consider the simple example of calluses again. Humans can and do create physical environments that are relatively free of friction. These friction-free environments mean that we have designed change—a change that prevents the activation of the underlying callus-producing mechanisms. Knowledge of these mechanisms and the environmental input that triggers their activation gives us the power to alter our "behavior," in this case the number and thickness of calluses we develop.

In a similar manner, knowledge of our evolved social psychological adaptations along with the social inputs that activate them gives us tremendous power to alter social behavior, if that is the desired goal. Consider one example. There is evidence that men have lower thresholds than women for inferring sexual intent. When a woman smiles at a man, male observers are more likely than female observers to infer that the woman is sexually interested in the man (Abbey, 1982). This is most likely part of an evolved psychological mechanism in men that motivates them to seek casual sexual opportunities (Buss, 1994).

Knowledge of this mechanism, however, allows for the possibility of change. Men, for example, can be educated with the information that they have lower thresholds for inferring sexual intent when a woman smiles at them. This knowledge can then be used by men, in principle, to reduce the number of times they act on their faulty inferences of sexual interest and decrease the amount of unwanted sexual advances they make toward women.

Knowledge about our evolved psychological adaptations along with the social inputs that they were designed to be responsive to, far from dooming us to an unchangeable fate, can have the liberating effect of changing behavior in areas in which change is desired. This does *not* mean that changing behavior is simple or easy. More knowledge about our evolved psychology gives us more power to change when change is desired.

Misunderstanding 3: Evolutionary Theory Requires Improbable Computational Abilities of Organisms

This misunderstanding is best exemplified by a passage from a critic of evolution as applied to humans:

> Hunters and gatherers do not have counting systems beyond *one*, *two*, and *three*. I refrain from comment on the even greater problem of how animals are supposed to figure that *r* [genetic relationship between the animal and its first cousin] = 1/8. The failure of [evolutionists] to address this problem introduces considerable mysticism in their theory. (Sahlins, 1977, pp. 444–445)

In essence, for adaptations to be created by the process of selection via inclusive fitness, such as the propensity to help a brother more than a cousin, humans must have evolved mathematical abilities that are highly improbable. To understand why this represents a misunderstanding, consider the spider's web (Dawkins, 1979, p. 188). To describe the marvelous complexities of the spider's web—including the angles of the threads, the progressively larger concentric circles, and so on—we need a pretty complex mathematical description. No one would argue, however, that spiders are mathematicians or use mathematics to create their webs. And yet everyone would agree that the spider's web is an adaptation. The spider spins its web through various "rules of thumb." Although these rules are probably complex, the spider does not need complex mathematical computations to execute them.

Similar reasoning occurs for humans and their adaptations to kin. Let's say hypothetically that humans have evolved the following rule of thumb: "The more someone looks like me, the more help I'll give her or him." Because a person and his or her siblings look more alike, on average, than a person and his or her cousins, this rule of thumb will have the effect of helping close genetic relatives more than distant ones. This adaptation can evolve in humans and can be carried out by each individual without performing any mathematics at all.

The actual psychological adaptations involved in helping kin are probably more complex. But the key point is this: As scientists, we may need complex mathematics as an aid to *describe* adaptations such as the spider's web or human helping. This does not mean that the spider or the human has to be a sophisticated mathematician to execute the adaptations.

Misunderstanding 4: Current Mechanisms Are Optimally Designed for the Environment & Costs

The concept of adaptation, the notion that mechanisms have evolved functions, has led to many outstanding discoveries over the past century (Dawkins, 1982). This does not mean, however, that the current collection of adaptive mechanisms that make up humans is in any way "optimally designed." An engineer might cringe at some of the ways in which our mechanisms are structured, which sometimes appear to be assembled with a piece here and bit there. In fact, many factors cause the existing design of our adaptations to be far from optimal. Let's consider two of them (see Dawkins, 1982, Chapter 3).

One constraint on optimal design is *evolutionary time lags*. Recall that evolution refers to change over time. Each change in the environment brings new selection pressures. Because evolutionary change occurs slowly, requiring thousands of generations of recurrent selection pressure, existing humans are necessarily designed for the previous environments of which they are a product. Stated differently, we carry around a stone-aged brain in a modern environment. A strong desire for fat, adaptive in a past environment of scarce food resources, now leads to clogged arteries and heart attacks. The lag in time between the environment that fashioned our mechanisms (the hunter-gatherer past that created much of our selective environment) and today's environment means that our existing evolved mechanisms are not optimally designed for the current environment.

A second constraint on optimal design pertains to the *costs of adaptations*. Consider as an analogy the risk of being killed driving a car. In principle, we could reduce this risk to near zero if we imposed a ten mile-per-hour speed limit and forced everyone to drive in armored trucks with ten feet of padding on the inside (Symons, 1993). But we consider the costs of this solution to be ridiculously high. Similarly, we might consider a hypothetical example in which natural selection built into humans such a severe terror of snakes that people never ventured outdoors. Such a fear would surely reduce the incidence of snake bites, but it would carry a prohibitively high cost. Further, it would prevent people from solving other adaptive problems, such as gathering fruits, plants, and other food resources necessary for survival. In short, the existing fear of snakes that characterizes humans is not optimally designed—after all, thousands of people do get bitten by snakes every year, and some die as a result. But it works reasonably well, on average, given the costs that would otherwise follow.

All adaptations carry costs. Selection favors a mechanism when the benefits outweigh the costs relative to other designs. Thus we have a collection of evolved mechanisms that are reasonably good at solving adaptive problems efficiently but are not designed as optimally as they might be if costs were not a constraint. Evolutionary time lags and the costs of adaptations are just two of the many reasons why adaptations are not optimally designed (Williams, 1992).

Misunderstanding 5: Evolutionary Theory Implies a Motivation to Maximize Gene Reproduction

Psychologist Brian Little (1989) studies what he calls "personal projects." He asks people to write down all the things they are working on at the moment. People mention small things such as training their cat to use a litter box or trying to grow long fingernails. They also mention larger projects such as getting a college degree, working on their relationships, and even "changing Western civilization." But *never* in roughly twenty years of research has someone responded, "I'm trying to maximize the replication of my genes."

Differential gene replication caused by differences in design is the causal process responsible for creating fundamental human motivations. But the motives and goals we have as products of this evolutionary process do not embody the process itself. As we will discuss later, some evidence indicates that humans have goals such as the desire to get ahead on a social or dominance hierarchy. On average, presumably, those who had these goals outreproduced those who lacked them, perhaps by securing access to better food, covering greater territory, or finding more desirable mates. As descendants of those ancestors, we carry with us the goals and motives that led to their success. Nowhere, however, is the goal of "fitness maximization" present in humans or any other species, either consciously or unconsciously.

Consider a hypothesis developed by Donald Symons: "The best female 'strategy' is to obtain the best possible husband, to be fertilized by the fittest male . . . and to maximize returns on sexual favors bestowed" (Symons, 1979, p. 180). The word *strategy* is in quotation marks precisely because Symons does not mean to imply that a woman is consciously calculating the reproductive returns from bestowing sexual favors. This shorthand, however, provides an efficient means for conveying the essence of Symons's evolutionary hypothesis, without using each time the more cumbersome but more technically correct phrasing: "A long history of evolution by selection fashioned in women complex and specific psychological mechanisms, not necessarily consciously articulated ones, that inclined them to make behavioral decisions that had the effect in ancestral environments of maximizing their returns on sexual favors bestowed."

It can be shown that the goal of fitness maximization cannot possibly have evolved. One reason is that fitness is not something that can be tracked directly in one's lifetime, and we can't have goals for things we cannot track. A second reason is that the factors that affect fitness are different for men and women, different for children and adolescents, and different even for you in one situation compared with other situations. Humans cannot have a general goal of fitness maximization for the simple reason that there is no general course of action that maximizes fitness for both sexes, for all ages, and for all situations (Symons, 1992; Tooby and Cosmides, 1992).

Humans are collections of mechanisms, each one of which was forged over evolutionary time by the process of selection. The products of this process tend to be problem specific—keep warm, avoid predators, get food, find a mate, have sex, socialize children, help kin in need, and so on. The product of the evolutionary process is not, and cannot be, the goal of maximal gene propagation.

In summary, part of the resistance to the application of evolutionary theory to humans is based on several common misconceptions. Contrary to these misconceptions, evolutionary theory does not imply genetic determinism. It does not imply that we are powerless to change things. It does not imply that organisms can compute complex mathematical formulas. It does not mean that our existing adaptations are optimally designed. And it does not mean that organisms have as a goal, either consciously or unconsciously, the desire to maximize the replication of their genes. With these common misunderstandings about evolutionary theory clarified, let's turn now to the field of psychology and examine the landmarks that led to the emergence of evolutionary psychology.

Landmarks in the Field of Psychology

While changes have been taking place in evolutionary biology since Darwin's 1859 book, psychology proceeded along a different path. Sigmund Freud, whose contributions came a few decades after Darwin, was significantly influenced by Darwin's theory of evolution by natural selection. So was William James. In the 1920s, however, psychology took a sharp turn away from evolutionary theory and embraced a radical behaviorism that reigned over the field for half a century. Then important empirical discoveries made radical behaviorism untenable, forcing a turn back to evolutionary theory. In this section we briefly trace the historical influence—and lack of influence— of evolutionary theory on the field of psychology.

Freud's Psychoanalytic Theory

In the late 1800s Sigmund Freud rocked the scientific community by proposing a theory of psychology that had a foundation in sexuality. To the Victorian culture Freud's theory was shocking. Not only was sexuality a motivating force for adults, Freud proposed that it was *the* driving force of human behavior regardless of age, from the smallest newborn infant to the oldest senior citizen. All of our psychological structures, according to Freud, are merely ways of channeling our sexuality.

At the core of Freud's theory of psychoanalysis was his proposal of the *instinctual system*, which included two fundamental classes of instincts. The first were the *life-preservative instincts*. These included the needs for air, food, water, and shelter and the fears of snakes, heights, and dangerous humans. These instincts served the function of survival.

Freud's second major class of motivators consisted of the *sexual instincts*. Freud conceptualized sex in an extraordinarily broad fashion. Sex was not merely adult intercourse. It included among others the sucking of the mother's breast during infancy (the oral stage) as well as sneezing, spitting, and defecating (the anal stage). "Mature sexuality" for Freud culminated in the final stage of adult development—the genital stage, which led directly to reproduction, the essential feature of Freud's mature sexuality.

Astute readers might sense an eerie familiarity. Freud's two major classes of instincts correspond almost precisely to Darwin's two major theories of evolution. Freud's life-preservative instincts correspond to Darwin's theory of natural selection, which many refer to as "survival selection." And his theory of the sexual instincts correspond closely to Darwin's theory of sexual selection.

Despite these rough parallels, Freud's theory of psychoanalysis lacks a clear understanding of adaptation and natural selection. Indeed, because Freud wanted to create psychoanalysis as an autonomous discipline, he moved farther away from a Darwinian anchoring. A contemporary of Sigmund Freud, William James, however, took Darwinism more seriously.

William James and the Psychology of Instincts

William James published his classic treatise, *Principles of Psychology*, in 1890, right around the time Freud was publishing a flurry of papers on psychoanalysis. At the core of James's theory was also a system of "instincts," in many ways far more sophisticated than Freud's theory.

James defined *instincts* as "the faculty of acting in such a way as to produce certain ends, without foresight of the ends, and without previous education in the performance" (James, 1890/1962, p. 392). Instincts were not always blind, nor were they inevitably expressed. They could be modified by experience or overridden by other instincts. In fact, said James, we possess many instincts that contradict each other and so cannot always be expressed. For example, we have sexual desire but also can be coy, are curious but also timid, aggressive but also cooperative.

Undoubtedly the most controversial part of James's theory was his list of instincts. Most psychologists of the day believed, like Freud, that instincts were few in number. One contemporary of James, for example, argued that "instinctive acts are in man few in number, and, apart from those connected with the sexual passion, difficult to recognize after early youth is past" (cited in James, 1890/1962, p. 405). James argued, to the contrary, that human instincts are many.

James's list of instincts begins at birth: "crying on contact with the air, sneezing, snuffling, snoring, coughing, sighing, sobbing, gagging, vomiting, hiccuping, staring, moving the limbs when touched, and sucking . . . later on come biting, clasping objects, and carrying them to the mouth, sitting up, standing, creeping, and walking" (p. 406). By age two the child has displayed a veritable avalanche of instincts.

And it continues. As each child grows, the instincts of *imitation, vocalization, emulation, pugnacity, fear of definite objects, shyness, sociability, play, curiosity*, and *acquisitiveness* blossom. Still later, adults display the instincts for *hunting, modesty, love*, and *parenting*. Subsumed by each of these instincts is more *specificity* of our innate psychological nature. The fear instinct, for example, includes specific fears of strange men, strange animals, noises, spiders, snakes, solitude, dark places such as holes and caverns, and high places such as cliffs. The key point about all these instincts is that they evolved through natural selection and were adaptations to solve specific adaptive problems.

Contrary to the common view, James believed that humans had many *more* instincts than other animals: "no other mammal, not even the monkey, shows so large a list" (p. 406). And it was in part the length of the list that was its downfall. Many psychologists found it preposterous that humans would have such a large set of innate propensities. By 1920 these skeptics believed that they had a theory to explain why instincts in humans are few in number and highly general: the behaviorist theory of learning.

The Rise of Behaviorism

If William James believed that much of human behavior was driven by a variety of instincts, James B. Watson believed just the opposite. Watson emphasized a single all-purpose learning mechanism called *classical conditioning*—a type of learning in which two previously unconnected events come to be associated (Pavlov, 1927; Watson, 1924). An initially neutral stimulus such as the ring of a bell, for example, can be paired with another stimulus such as food. After many such pairings, because it has been paired repeatedly with food, the sound of the bell can elicit salivation from dogs and other animals (Pavlov, 1927). Classical conditioning offered the promise of accounting for the staggeringly complex diversity of human behavior with a simple theory of learning that could be applied to all behavioral domains.

Behavior, Watson argued, is determined primarily by forces in the environment of each individual. As much as James stressed nature, Watson stressed nurture. Watson not only argued against the existence of instincts, he also argued against all proposals that stressed internal mechanisms, including psychological concepts such as fear, desire, and consciousness. The only proper province for psychological inquiry was overt, observable behavior. The postulation of internal entities was judged unscientific.

A decade after Watson's major work, a young Harvard graduate student named B. F. Skinner pioneered a new brand of environmentalism called *radical behaviorism* and a principle of operant conditioning. According to this principle the reinforcing consequences of behavior were the critical causes of subsequent behavior. Behavior followed by reinforcement would be repeated in the future. Behavior not followed by reinforcement (or followed by punishment) would not be repeated in the future. All behavior, except random behavior, could be explained by the "contingencies" of reinforcement.

Interestingly, the elements in the structure of Skinner's operant conditioning paralleled those of Darwin's theory of natural selection, but on a different time scale. Darwin's theory considered variation (heritable individual differences) and selective retention (the propagation of the selected variants). Likewise, Skinner's theory included variation (random behaviors emitted) and selective retention (the proliferation of behavior that had been reinforced by its previous consequences). Indeed, Skinner even called his theory one of "selection by consequences" and drew parallels between behaviorism and natural selection (Skinner, 1981).

Perhaps more important than the details of Skinner's behaviorism are the fundamental assumptions about human nature on which the formulation rests. First, in sharp contrast to instinctivists like William James, behaviorists assumed that the innate properties of humans were few in number. What was innate, the behaviorists believed, was merely a *general ability to learn* by reinforcing consequences. Second, the behaviorists made what is called the *equipotentiality assumption*, that the mechanisms of learning are the same regardless of the stimuli, responses, or reinforcers (Domjan, 1997). That is, any reinforcer could be paired with any behavior and learning would occur equally in all cases. Thus any behavior could be shaped as easily as any other behavior merely by manipulating the contingencies of reinforcement.

Although not all behaviorists endorsed all of these principles, the fundamental assumptions—few innate qualities, the equipotentiality of learning, and the power of environmental contingencies of reinforcement—dominated the field of psychology for more than half a century (Herrnstein, 1977). The nature of human nature, it was asserted, is that humans have no nature. Humans could be shaped and molded into anything as long as one had control of the reinforcement contingencies. In light of these basic assumptions, it is not surprising that the findings of astonishing cross-cultural variability were enthusiastically embraced by social scientists.

The Astonishing Discoveries of Cultural Variability

If humans are general learning machines, built without innate propensities or proclivities, then all of the "content" of human behavior—the emotions, passions, yearnings, desires, beliefs, attitudes, and investments—must be added during each person's life. If learning theory offered the promise of identifying the *process* by which adults were formed, cultural anthropologists offered the promise of providing the *contents* (specific thoughts, behaviors, and rituals) on which those processes could operate (Tooby & Cosmides, 1992).

Most people are interested in stories of other cultures, and the stranger and more discrepant from our own, the more interesting such stories are. Americans wear earrings and finger rings, but certain African cultures insert bones through their noses and tattoo their lips. The mainland Chinese prize virginity, whereas the Swedes think virgins are a bit odd (Buss, 1989a). Many Iranian women wear veils over their hair and faces; many American women (especially in southern California) wear "dental floss" bikinis and cover practically nothing.

Likewise, anthropologists coming back from their field work have long celebrated the cultural diversity they found. Perhaps most influential was Margaret Mead, who purported to discover cultures in which the "sex roles" were totally reversed and sexual jealousy entirely absent. Mead depicted island paradises inhabited by peaceful peoples who celebrated shared sexuality and free love and did not compete, rape, fight, or murder.

The more discrepant the findings from other cultures were from North American culture, the more they were celebrated, repeated in textbooks, and splashed over the news media. If tropical paradises existed in other cultures, then perhaps our own problems of jealousy, conflict, and competition were due to American culture, Western values, or capitalism.

The reports of exotically variable cultures meshed perfectly with the dominance of the equipotentiality assumption in psychology. The psychologists' and the anthropologists' theories complemented each other in a harmonious symbiosis that lasted most of the twentieth century. Anthropologists proclaimed that "cultural phenomena . . . are in no respect hereditary but are characteristically and without exception acquired" (Murdock, 1932, p. 200). Forty years later, the prominent anthropologist Clifford Geertz echoed Murdock: "Undirected by cultural patterns—organized systems of significant symbols—man's behavior would be virtually ungovernable, a mere chaos of pointless acts and exploding emotions, his experience virtually shapeless" (Geertz, 1973, p. 46). The human mind had the "capacity for culture," but it was the specific culture that was the causal agent responsible for filling in the blanks.

But closer scrutiny revealed snakes in the tropical cultural paradises. Subsequent researchers found that many of the original reports of these tropical cultures were simply false. Derek Freeman (1983), for example, found that the Samoan islanders whom Mead had depicted in such utopian terms were intensely competitive and had murder and rape rates higher than those in the United States! Furthermore, the men were intensely sexually jealous, which contrasted sharply with Mead's depiction of "free love" among the Samoans.

Freeman's debunking of Margaret Mead's findings created a storm of controversy, and he was widely criticized by a social science community that had embraced what now appeared to be the myths perpetrated by cultural anthropologists such as Mead. But subsequent research has confirmed the findings of Freeman and, more important, the existence of numerous human universals (Brown, 1991). Male sexual jealousy, for example, turned out to be a human universal and the leading cause of spousal homicide in the many cultures that have been surveyed so far (Daly & Wilson, 1988). Emotional expressions such as fear, rage, and joy were recognized by people in cultures that had no access to television or movies (Ekman, 1973). Even feelings of love, thought to be a recent invention by white Europeans a few hundred years ago, show universality (Jankowiak, 1995).

Some still cling to the myths of infinite cultural variability. As noted by Melvin Konner: "We have never quite outgrown the idea that, somewhere, there are people living in perfect harmony with nature and one another, and that we might do the same were it not for the corrupting influences of Western culture" (1990).

The weight of the evidence started to make the portrait painted by social scientists increasingly difficult to cling to. In addition, new movements were rumbling in other branches of science, suggesting even deeper problems with the view of humans as merely having "the capacity for culture," all of its matter inserted by the social environment.

The Garcia Effect, Prepared Fears, and the Decline of Radical Behaviorism

One rumbling of discontent came from Harry Harlow (1971), who raised a group of monkeys in isolation from other monkeys in a laboratory that housed two artificial "mothers." One mother was made of wire mesh, the other of the same wire mesh covered with a soft terry-cloth cover. Food was dispensed to the monkeys through the wire-mesh mother, not through the terry cloth mother.

According to the principles of operant conditioning, because the monkeys were receiving their primary reinforcement of food from the wire mothers, in behavioral terms such as clinging to a mother when frightened they should have become more attached to the wire mother rather than to the terry cloth mother. Yet precisely the opposite occurred. The baby monkeys would climb onto the wire mothers for food, but chose to spend the rest of their time with the terry cloth mothers. When frightened the monkeys ran not to the food-reinforcing mother but to the one that gave them "contact comfort." Clearly, something was going on inside the monkeys other than a response to the primary reinforcement of food.

Another rumbling of discontent came from John Garcia at the University of California at Berkeley. Garcia was interested in examining two of the fundamental assumptions of behaviorism—equipotentiality and the contiguity principle (Garcia & Koelling, 1966). Recall that the equipotentiality assumption is that the rules of learning do not depend on the stimuli used. The contiguity principle is that reinforcement will be more powerful if it is followed closely in time and space (hence contiguous with) the behavior that is being reinforced.

Garcia showed that even in rats neither of these fundamental assumptions held. In a series of studies he gave rats some food, and then several hours later he gave them a dose of radiation that made them sick (Garcia, Ervin, & Koelling, 1966). Although the nausea occurred several hours after they ate, the rats generally learned in a single trial never to eat that type of food—seemingly responsible for their illness—again. When Garcia paired the nausea with buzzers or light flashes, however, he could not train the rats to avoid them. In other words, rats seem to come into the world "preprogrammed" to learn some things easily, such as to avoid foods linked with nausea, but find it extraordinarily difficult to learn other things, such as to avoid buzzers and lights that are linked with nausea.

Although these sorts of findings may seem obvious in retrospect, at the time they were hotly disputed. In fact, editors of the major psychology journals consistently rejected Garcia's papers because they went against the dominant assumptions of behaviorism, which were widely believed to be "laws." Only after Garcia replicated his findings many times and similar findings began to emerge from other laboratories did the journals grudgingly accept his papers for publication.

In short, Garcia and others after him documented violations of two principles widely believed to be fundamental. The contiguity principle was violated because the reinforcement did not have to be linked closely in time or space to the behavior being reinforced. The equipotentiality assumption was violated because some pairings proved extremely easy to learn (e.g., nausea and avoiding food), whereas others proved extremely difficult to learn. This suggested that rats were somehow "prepared" to learn some things easily and rapidly and not at all prepared to learn other things. Findings such as these caused some behaviorists to attend to evolutionary considerations.

The proposition that organisms might come into this world "prepared" by evolution to learn some things and not others was picked up by Martin Seligman. Seligman and his colleagues proposed that it was indeed quite easy to "condition" people to develop certain types of fears—a fear of snakes, for example—but extremely difficult to condition people to develop other, less natural fears such as of electrical outlets or cars (Seligman & Hager, 1972).

These hypothesized violations of the equipotentiality assumption showed up even in observational learning studies with monkeys. In one series of studies Susan Mineka (1992) showed monkeys one of two videotapes. In one tape a monkey was shown displaying tremendous fear of a snake. Mineka then altered the videotape by splicing in a flower instead of the snake. Monkeys witnessing another member of their species showing a fear of snakes subsequently avoided snakes themselves, exhibiting observational learning (Bandura, 1977). But the monkeys witnessing one of their own species showing exactly the same fear response to a flower did not subsequently avoid flowers and showed no observational learning. Even explaining observational learning—learning derived from watching others—requires positing prepared propensities inside the organism.

In summary, some fundamental assumptions were being violated, which suggested two important conclusions. First, rats, monkeys, and even humans seemed "wired" to learn some things very easily and to not learn other things at all. This conclusion suggests that learning does not constitute an alternative explanation to evolutionary theory. Instead, the particular types of learning that organisms come equipped with must themselves be explained, and evolutionary theory provides a valuable tool for doing so.

Second, the external environment is not the sole determinant of behavior. Something goes on inside the minds and brains of organisms that must be taken into account when considering behaviors. These conclusions, in conjunction with other forces in science, led to the decline of radical behaviorism and the beginnings of a new model of the human mind.

Peering into the Black Box: The Cognitive Revolution

A number of forces converged in psychology to bring back the legitimacy of looking inside the "black box" to explore the psychology underlying behavior. One force came from the mushrooming violations of the fundamental "laws" of learning. A second came from the study of language, in Noam Chomsky's powerful arguments for a universal "language organ" with an underlying structure that turned out to be invariable across languages (Chomsky, 1957; Pinker, 1994). A third force came with the rise of computers and the "information-processing metaphor." All three forces coalesced into what became known as the *cognitive revolution.*

The cognitive revolution returned to psychology the respectability of looking "inside the heads" of people rather than at just the external contingencies of reinforcement. The revolution was required, in part, simply because external contingencies alone could not successfully account for the behavior being observed. Furthermore, with the rise of the computer psychologists began to be more explicit about the exact causal processes they were proposing.

> The cognitive revolution is more or less now equated with *information processing:* A cognitive description specifies what kinds of information the mechanism takes as input, what procedures it uses to transform that information, what kinds of data structures (representations) those procedures operate on, and what kinds of representations or behaviors it generates as output. (Tooby & Cosmides, 1992, p. 64)

For an organism to accomplish certain tasks it must solve a number of information-processing problems. To successfully accomplish the tasks of seeing, hearing, walking bipedally, and categorizing, for example, requires a tremendous amount of information-processing machinery. Although seeing with our eyes seems to come effortlessly and naturally for most of us—we just open our eyes and look—in fact it takes thousands of specialized mechanisms to accomplish, including a lens, a retina, a cornea, a pupil, specific edge detectors, rods, cones, specific motion detectors, a specialized optic nerve, and so on. Psychologists came to realize that they needed to understand the information-processing machinery in our brains to understand the causal underpinnings of human performance.

Information-processing mechanisms—the cognitive machinery—require the "hardware" in which they are housed, the neurobiology of the brain. But the information-processing description of a mechanism such as the eye is not the same as the description of the underlying neurobiology. Consider as an analogy the word-processing software on a computer, which contains a program that deletes sentences, moves paragraphs, and italicizes characters. But the program can run on an IBM computer, a Macintosh, or any number of clone computers. Even though the underlying "hardware" of the machines differs, the information-processing description of the program is the same. By analogy, in principle, one could build a robot to "see" in a manner similar to a human, but the hardware would be different from the neurobiology of the human. Thus the cognitive level of description (i.e., input, representations, decision-rules, output) is useful, and perhaps even necessary, whether or not all the underlying hardware is understood.

With the downfall of certain assumptions of behaviorism and the emergence of the cognitive revolution it became respectable to look "inside the head" of the human. No longer was it viewed as "unscientific" to posit internal mental states and processes. On the contrary, it was considered absolutely necessary.

But most cognitive psychologists carried over one unfortunate assumption from the behaviorist paradigm: the equipotentiality assumption of domain-generality (Tooby & Cosmides, 1992). The domain-general learning processes proposed by behaviorists were simply replaced by domain-general cognitive mechanisms. Missing was the idea that there might be privileged classes of information that the cognitive mechanisms were specifically designed to process.

The image of human cognitive machinery was that of a large computer designed to process any information it was fed. Computers could be programmed to play chess, do calculus, predict the weather, manipulate symbols, or guide missiles. In this sense the computer is a domain-general information processor. But to solve any particular problem, it must be "programmed" in very specific ways. Programming a computer to play chess, for example, takes millions of lines of "if . . . then" statements of programming.

One of the main problems with a domain-general (equipotential) assumption about the information-processing mind is the problem of *combinatorial explosion*. With a domain-general program lacking specialized processing rules, the number of alternative options open to it in any given situation is infinite. The evolutionary psychologists John Tooby and Leda Cosmides (1992) present the following example. Suppose that within the next minute you could perform any one of one hundred possible actions—read the next paragraph in this book, eat an apple, blink your eyes, dream about tomorrow, and so on. And within the second minute you could also perform any one of one hundred actions. After only two minutes there would be ten thousand possible combinations of behavioral options (100 × 100). After three minutes there would be one million behavioral sequences you could perform (100 × 100 × 100), and so on. This is combinatorial explosion—the rapid proliferation of response options caused by combining two or more sequential possibilities.

To get a computer or a person to accomplish a specific task, special programming must narrow sharply the infinite possibilities. So combinatorial explosion renders a computer or a person incapable of solving even the simplest tasks without special programming. The computer, of course, can be programmed to perform a staggering variety of tasks, limited mainly by the imagination and wizardry of the programmer. But what about humans? How are we programmed? What special information-processing problems are we "designed" to solve with our large, 1,400 cubic centimeter brain?

The idea that there might be some information-processing problems that the human mind was specially designed to process was missing from the cognitive revolution in psychology. Humans went from being blank slates on which contingencies of reinforcement do the writing (learning theory) to general-purpose computers on which cultures write the software (cognitive theory). It was this gap, along with accumulated empirical findings and convergence from a variety of empirical sciences, that finally set the stage for the emergence of evolutionary psychology. Evolutionary psychology furnished the missing piece of the puzzle by providing a broad specification of the kinds of information-processing problems the human mind was designed to solve—problems of survival and reproduction.

Summary

Evolutionary biology has undergone many historical developments. Evolution—change over time in organisms—was suspected to occur long before Charles Darwin came on the scene. Missing, before him, however, was a theory about a causal process that could explain how organic change could occur. This theory, the theory of natural selection, was Darwin's crowning contribution to evolutionary biology. The theory of natural selection has three essential ingredients—variation, inheritance, and selection. Natural selection occurs when some inherited variations lead to greater reproductive success than other inherited variations. In short, natural selection is defined as changes over time due to the differential reproductive success of inherited variations.

Natural selection provided a unifying theory for the biological sciences and solved several important mysteries. First, it provided a causal process by which change, the modification of organic structures, takes place over time. Second, it proposed a theory to account for the origin of new species. And third, it united all living forms into one grand tree of descent and simultaneously revealed the place of humans in the grand scheme of life.

A major stumbling block for many biologists was that Darwin lacked a workable theory of inheritance. This theory was provided when the work of Gregor Mendel was recognized and synthesized with Darwin's theory of natural selection in a movement called the Modern Synthesis. According to this theory, inheritance does not involve "blending" of the two parents but rather is particulate. That is, genes, the fundamental unit of inheritance, come in discrete packets that are not blended but rather are passed on intact from parent to child. The particulate theory of inheritance provided the missing ingredient to Darwin's theory of natural selection.

Following the Modern Synthesis, two European biologists, Konrad Lorenz and Niko Tinbergen, started a new movement called ethology, which sought to place animal behavior within an evolutionary context by focusing on both the origins and functions of behavior. The imprinting of ducklings on their mother, for example, served a survival function by keeping the ducklings close to the mother for protection. The ethology movement forced psychologists to reconsider the role of biology in human behavior.

In 1964 the theory of natural selection itself was reformulated in a revolutionary pair of articles published by William D. Hamilton. The process by which selection operates, according to Hamilton, involves not just classical fitness (the direct production of offspring), but inclusive fitness, which includes the effects of an individual's actions on the reproductive success of genetic relatives, weighted by the appropriate degree of genetic relatedness. The inclusive fitness reformulation provided a more precise theory of the process of natural selection by promoting a "gene's eye" view of evolutionary selection pressures. It also solved, in part, the problem of altruism in its explanation of why organisms would incur personal costs to help other individuals, if those other individuals carried copies of their genes.

In 1966 George Williams published the now classic *Adaptation and Natural Selection*, which had three effects. First, it led to the downfall of group selection, the theory that adaptations evolve through differential group reproduction for the benefit of the group. Second, it promoted the Hamiltonian revolution by translating the highly mathematical inclusive fitness theory into a language more readily comprehensible to most biologists. And third, it provided rigorous criteria for identifying adaptations, such as efficiency, reliability, and precision. In 1972 Robert Trivers built on the work of Hamilton and Williams, offering three seminal theories that remain important today: reciprocal altruism, parental investment, and parent-offspring conflict.

In 1975 Edward O. Wilson published *Sociobiology: A New Synthesis*, which attempted to synthesize the key developments in evolutionary biology and then give the synthesis a recognizable name. Wilson's book created a storm of controversy, mostly because of its final chapter, on humans, which offered a series of hypotheses but little empirical data.

Much of the resistance to Wilson's book, as well as to using evolutionary theory to explain human behavior, may be traced to several core misunderstandings. Contrary to these misunderstandings, however, evolutionary theory does not imply that human behavior is genetically determined, nor that human behavior is unchangeable. It does not imply improbable feats of computation, such as calculating fractions of genetic relatedness. It does not imply optimal design. And it does not imply that humans have as a motive the drive to maximize gene reproduction.

While all these changes were taking place within evolutionary biology, the field of psychology was following a different course, one that was essential to its eventual integration with evolutionary theory. Following Darwin, two key psychological theories were developed that were profoundly influenced by evolutionary ideas. Sigmund Freud drew attention to the importance of survival and sexuality by proposing a theory of life-preserving and sexual instincts, paralleling Darwin's distinction between natural selection and sexual selection. In 1890, William James published *Principles of Psychology*, which proposed that humans have a number of specific instincts.

In the 1920s, however, American psychology turned away from evolutionary ideas and embraced a version of radical behaviorism—the idea that a few highly general principles of learning could account for the complexity of human behavior. At the same time the apparent discoveries of astonishing cultural variability seemed to support radical behaviorism, because they purported to show the extreme plasticity and malleability of human behavior.

In the 1960s, however, empirical findings that suggested important violations of the general laws of learning began to accumulate. Harry Harlow demonstrated that monkeys do not prefer wire-mesh "mothers," even when they receive their primary food reinforcement from those mothers. John Garcia showed that organisms could learn some things readily and rapidly, such as an aversion to food when its consumption was followed several hours later by illness but failed to learn other things even after thousands of trials. Something was going on inside the brains of organisms that could not be accounted for solely by the external contingencies of reinforcement.

The accumulation of these findings led to the cognitive revolution, reinstating the importance and respectability of looking "inside the heads" of people. The cognitive revolution was based on the information-processing metaphor—descriptions of mechanisms inside the head that take in specific forms of information as input, transform that information through decision rules, and generate behavior as output.

The idea that humans might come predisposed or specially equipped to process some kinds of information and not others set the stage for the emergence of evolutionary psychology, which represents a true synthesis of modern psychology and modern evolutionary biology. With this historical background in place we turn now to the foundations of evolutionary psychology.

The New Science of Evolutionary Psychology

Darwin took [a] radical step toward uniting the mental and physical worlds, by showing how the mental world—whatever it might be composed of—arguably owed its complex organization to the same process of natural selection that explained the physical organization of living things. Psychology became united with the biological and hence evolutionary sciences.

—Tooby & Cosmides, 1992, p. 20

Robin Baker and Mark Bellis, British biologists, stared with disbelief into the microscope at the astonishing shape of a human sperm. Conventional wisdom in the field told them that humans have one primary shape or *morph* of sperm—that of a cone-shaped head and a wavy tail. Conventional wisdom also told them that deviations from this standard sperm shape were malformations, perhaps due to the toxins in our modern environment or to the common habit among men of wearing tight underwear and pants—the so-called "tight trousers" hypothesis.

Baker and Bellis's finding, that sperm came in several different predictable shapes, would challenge this view (1995). It is true that the most common sperm morph, in roughly 50 percent of all human sperm, is the standard cone-shaped head with a long, wavy tail. These sperm seem well designed to swim fast. The shapes of the head and tail enable them to race quickly up the female reproductive tract, at a rate of two inches per hour. But other sperm came in different shapes. One of the sperm morphs, for example, has a coiled tail. In one study, Baker and Bellis mixed sperm from two different men in the laboratory and watched them interact. In one dramatic sequence, a sperm of one male attacked and killed a sperm of the other male. This led Baker and Bellis to formulate the kamikaze sperm hypothesis, which suggests that "sperm warfare" is a general phenomenon among mammals. According to this hypothesis, males have different types of sperm, each designed to carry out different functions. The cone-shaped standard sperm are the "egg getters," designed to race as quickly as possible to fertilize the egg. The coil-tailed sperm have a "kamikaze" function, and instead of racing to the egg, these "seek and destroy" sperm prevent the sperm of other males from reaching the egg. This is not science fiction. It is fact, and it highlights the exciting process of scientific discovery.

This finding, along with other discoveries, provides a powerful clue to an adaptive problem faced by our male ancestors—that of sperm competition. The existence of these sperm morphs suggests a long evolutionary history in which women regularly mated with more than one man within the span of a week (the length of time human sperm can remain viable in the female reproductive tract). This discovery, in turn, led to other hypotheses about humans, including hypotheses about the potential benefits to women of mating with more than one man. Ancestral women who mated with more than one man are likely to have benefited in some way. There is indeed evidence for this suggestion, as we will see later (Greiling and Buss, under review).

This example highlights several features of the exciting science of evolutionary psychology. One feature is that hypotheses about human evolution—in this case hypotheses about women's mating psychology—can come from the strangest of places, in this case a study of sperm. Second, the science of evolutionary psychology is not a sterile enterprise, but a vibrant and cutting-edge field in which fascinating new discoveries are made almost daily. And third, knowledge of evolutionary theory is what led Baker and Bellis to make their discovery. Thinking about function—seeing the component parts of organisms as designed for specific purposes—provided a powerful guide to new insights.

This chapter focuses on the logic and methods of the science of evolutionary psychology, a new scientific synthesis of modern evolutionary biology and modern psychology. It utilizes the most recent theoretical advances in evolutionary biology such as inclusive fitness theory, the theory of parental investment and sexual selection, and the development of more rigorous standards for evaluating the presence or absence of adaptation. Evolutionary psychology also incorporates the most recent conceptual and empirical advances in psychology, including information-processing models; knowledge from artificial intelligence; and discoveries such as universal emotional expression (Ekman, 1973), universals in the ways people categorize plants and animals (Atran, 1990; Berlin, Breedlove, & Raven, 1973), and universals in the dimensions that people use to categorize other people (White, 1980). The goal of this chapter is to introduce the conceptual foundations of this new synthesis. Later chapters will build on this foundation. Let's start by asking why psychology needs to be integrated with evolutionary biology.

The Origins of Human Nature

Three Theories of the Origins of Complex Adaptive Mechanisms

If you walk around with bare feet for a few weeks you will develop calluses on your soles. The callus-producing mechanisms—manufacturing numerous new skin cells when repeated friction is encountered—function to protect the anatomical and physiological structures of your feet from damage. If you ride around in your car for a few weeks, however, your car tires will not get thicker. Why not?

Your feet and your car tires are both subject to the laws of physics. Friction tends to wear down physical objects, not build them up. But your feet, unlike your tires, are subject to another set of laws—the laws of organic natural selection. Your feet have callus-producing mechanisms because of natural selection. Evolution by selection is a creative process; the callus-producing mechanisms are the adaptive products of that creative process. They exist now because in the past those who tended, however slightly, to have genes that predisposed them to develop extra skin thickness as a result of friction had this extra element to aid in their survival, and hence lived to reproduce more than those without the beneficial predisposition. As descendants of these successful ancestors, we carry with us the adaptive mechanisms that led to their success.

In the past century three major theories have been proposed to account for the origins of adaptations such as callus-producing mechanisms (Daly & Wilson, 1988). One theory is *creationism*, the idea that a supreme deity created all of the plants and animals, from the largest whales to the smallest plankton in the ocean, from the simple single-celled amoebas to the complex human brain. Creationism is not viewed as a "scientific theory" for three reasons. First, it cannot be tested because specific empirical predictions do not follow from its major premise. Whatever exists does so simply because the supreme being has created it. Second, creationism has not guided researchers to any new scientific discoveries. No new knowledge has been uncovered as a result of the theory that a supreme deity created all forms of life on earth. Third, creationism has not proved useful as a scientific explanation for already discovered organic mechanisms. Creationism, therefore, is a matter of religion and belief, not a matter of science. It cannot be proved false, but it has not proven useful as a predictive or an explanatory theory.

A second theory is *seeding theory* (Buss, 1995a). According to seeding theorists, life did not originate on earth. In one version of this theory the seeds of life arrived on earth via a meteorite, a version that gained some credibility with the recent discovery of possible signs of life on Mars. In a second version of seeding theory extraterrestrial intelligent beings came down from other planets or galaxies and planted the seeds of life on earth. Regardless of the origins of the seeds, however, evolution by natural selection presumably took over, and the seeds eventually evolved into humans and the other extant life forms observed today.

Seeding theory, unlike creationism, is in principle testable. We can study meteorites for signs of life, which would lend plausibility to the theory that life originated elsewhere. We can scour the earth for signs of extraterrestrial landings. We can look for evidence of life forms that could not have originated on earth. We can scan the universe for intelligent life coming from beyond our solar system. Seeding theory, however, runs into three problems. First, there is currently no solid scientific evidence on earth that such "seedings" have taken place. Second, seeding theory has not led to any new scientific discoveries, nor has it explained any existing scientific puzzles. Most important, however, seeding theory runs into a fundamental problem—it simply pushes the causal explanation for origins of life back in time. If the earth was really seeded by extraterrestrial beings, what causal processes led to the origins of these intelligent beings? And what causal process is responsible for developing the existing seeds into the life forms we see on earth today?

We are left with the third option—*evolution by natural selection.* Although evolution by natural selection is called a theory, its fundamental principles have been confirmed so many times—and never disconfirmed—that it is viewed by most biologists as a fact (Alcock, 1993; Mayr, 1982). The components of its operation—differential reproduction due to inherited design differences—have been shown to work in both the laboratory and the wild. The differing sizes of the beaks of finches on different islands in the Galápagos, for example, have been shown to have evolved to correspond to the size of the seeds prevalent on each island (Grant, 1991). Larger beaks are needed when the seeds are large, whereas smaller beaks are better when the seeds are small. The theory of natural selection has many virtues that scientists seek in a profound scientific theory: (1) it organizes known facts about organic life; (2) it leads to new predictions; and (3) it provides guidance to important domains of scientific inquiry.

So among the three theories—creationism, seeding theory, and natural selection—there is really no real contest. Evolution by natural selection is the only known *scientific* theory that can account for the astonishing diversity of life we see around us today. Although it is always possible that in the future a better theory might come along, at present natural selection is the only one that unites all living things—plants, animals, insects, and birds, from the smallest single-celled organisms in the sea to the most complex mammals on land—into one grand tree of descent. And it is the only known scientific theory that has the power to account for the origins and structure of complex adaptive mechanisms—from callus-producing mechanisms to oversized brains—that comprise human nature.

The Three Products of Evolution

There are three products of the evolutionary process—*adaptations, byproducts* (or concomitants) of adaptation, and *random effects* (or noise), as shown in Table 2.1 (Buss, Haselton, Shackelford, Bleske & Wakefield, 1998; Tooby & Cosmides, 1990). Let's start by examining adaptations, the most important and fundamental product of the evolutionary process.

An adaptation may be defined as an inherited and reliably developing characteristic that came into existence through natural selection because it helped to solve a problem of survival or reproduction during the period of its evolution (after Tooby & Cosmides, 1992, pp. 61–62; see also Thornhill, 1997).

Let's break down this definition into its core elements. An adaptation must have genes "for" that adaptation. Those genes are required for the passage of the adaptation from parents to children; hence the adaptation can be inherited.

An adaptation must develop reliably among species members in all "normal" environments. That is, to qualify as an adaptation it must emerge at the appropriate time during an organism's life in reasonably intact form, and hence be characteristic of most or all of the members of a given species (but see Wilson, 1994, for an alternative view). There are important exceptions to this, such as mechanisms that exist in only one sex or in a specific subset of the population, which will be covered later, but for now it is important to stress that most adaptations are species-typical.

TABLE 2.1   Three Products of the Evolutionary Process

Product	Brief Definition
Adaptations	Inherited and reliably developing characteristics that came into existence through natural selection because they helped to solve problems of survival or reproduction during the period of their evolution; example: umbilical cord
By-products	Characteristics that do not solve adaptive problems and do not have functional design; they are "carried along" with characteristics that do have functional design because they happen to be coupled with those adaptations; example: belly button
Noise	Random effects produced by forces such as chance mutations, sudden and unprecedented changes in the environment, or chance effects during development; example: particular shape of a person's belly button

The reliably developing feature of adaptations does *not* mean that the adaptation must appear at birth. Indeed, many adaptations develop long after birth. Walking is a reliably developing characteristic of humans, but most humans do not begin to walk until a full year after birth. Breasts are reliably developing features in women, but do not develop until puberty. Characteristics that are transient, temporary, easily perturbed by the environment, or appear in only a few members of a species are not reliably developing, and hence do not meet the definitional standards for adaptations.

Adaptations are fashioned by the process of selection. Selection acts as a sieve in each generation, filtering out the many features that do not contribute to propagation and letting through those that do (Dawkins, 1996). This sieving process recurs generation after generation, so that each new generation is a bit different from its parent generation. This process of natural selection is necessary for the creation of adaptations.

Those characteristics that make it through the filtering process in each generation do so because they contribute to the solution of an adaptive problem of either survival or reproduction. The contributions to these adaptive problems can be *direct*, such as a fear of dangerous snakes, which solves a problem of survival or a desire to mate with particular members of one's species, which helps to solve a reproductive problem; or *indirect*, as in the desire to ascend a social hierarchy, which many years later might provide better access to mates. Or they can be even more indirect, such as when a person helps his or her brother or sister, which eventually helps that sibling to reproduce (recall the concept of inclusive fitness). Unless a feature contributes to the successful solution of an adaptive problem, it cannot be selected for and hence cannot become an adaptation.

Each adaptation has its own period of evolution. Initially a *mutation*, a spontaneous change in the structure of a piece of DNA, occurs in a single individual. Mutations are thought to arise from mistakes in the replication of DNA. Although most mutations hinder survival or reproduction, some, by chance alone, end up helping the organism survive and reproduce. If the mutation is helpful it will be passed down to the next generation in greater numbers. In the next generation, therefore, more individuals possess the characteristic that was initially a mutation in a single person. Over many generations, if it continues to be successful, the mutation will spread to the entire population so that every member of the species will have it. The *environment of evolutionary adaptedness*, or *EEA*, refers to the statistical composite of selection pressures that occurred during an adaptation's period of evolution responsible for producing the adaptation (Tooby & Cosmides, 1992). Most adaptations, of course, are not caused by single genes, but rather are the products of many genes. The human eye, for example, is constructed by thousands of genes. The adaptation's *period of evolution* refers to the time span during which it was constructed, piece by piece, until it came to characterize a universal design of the species.

Although adaptations are the primary products of evolution, they are certainly not the only products. The evolutionary process also produces *byproducts* of adaptations. Byproducts are characteristics that do not solve adaptive problems and do not have functional design. They are "carried along" with characteristics that do have functional design because they happen to be coupled with those adaptations, just as the heat from a light bulb is a by-product of design for light.

Consider the human belly button. There is no evidence that the belly button, per se, helps humans survive or reproduce. A belly button is not good for catching food, detecting predators, avoiding snakes, finding good habitats, or choosing mates. It does not seem to be directly or indirectly involved in the solution to an adaptive problem. Rather, the belly button is a byproduct of something that is an adaptation—namely, the umbilical cord that provided food to the growing fetus. The hypothesis that something is a byproduct of an adaptation, therefore, requires identifying the adaptation of which it is a byproduct and the reason why its existence is associated with that adaptation (Tooby & Cosmides, 1992). The hypothesis that something is a byproduct, just like the hypothesis that something is an adaptation, must be subjected to rigorous standards of scientific confirmation.

The third and final product of the evolutionary process is *noise* or *random effects*. Random effects can be produced by forces such as mutations (most of which are random), sudden and unprecedented changes in the environment, or accidents during development. These random effects sometimes harm the smooth functioning of an organism, much as throwing a monkey wrench into a machine or spilling scalding coffee onto the hard drive of your computer will ruin its functional operation. Some random effects are neutral—they neither contribute to nor detract from adaptive functioning—and some are beneficial to an organism. The glass encasement of a lightbulb, for example, often contains perturbations from smoothness due to imperfection in the materials and the process of manufacturing that do not affect the functioning of the bulb; a bulb can function equally well with or without such perturbations. In self-reproducing systems, these random effects can be carried along and passed down to succeeding generations, as long as they do not impair the functioning of the mechanisms that are adaptations. Noise is distinguished from incidental by-products in that it is not linked to the adaptive aspects of design features but rather is independent of such features.

In summary, the evolutionary process produces three products—adaptations, byproducts of adaptations, and random effects. In principle, we can analyze the component parts of a species and conduct studies to determine which are adaptations, which are by-products, and which are due merely to random effects. Evolutionary scientists differ in their estimates of the relative sizes of these three categories of products. Some believe that even uniquely human qualities, such as language, are merely incidental by-products of our large brains (Gould, 1991). Others see overwhelming evidence that human language is an adaptation *par excellence* and shows all of the features of adaptations described above (Pinker, 1994). Fortunately, we do not have to rely solely on the inventions of scientists because we can test their ideas ourselves. We now have stringent tests, reviewed later in this chapter, for determining whether a characteristic is an adaptation, a by-product, or merely a random effect.

Despite scientific quibbles about the relative size of the three categories of evolutionary products, all evolutionary scientists agree on one fundamental point: adaptations are the primary product of evolution by selection (Dawkins, 1982; Dennett, 1995; Gould, 1997; Trivers, 1985; Williams, 1992). Those characteristics that pass through the selective sieve generation after generation for hundreds, thousands, and even millions of years, are those that helped to solve the problems of survival and reproduction.

And so the core of all animal natures, including humans, consists of a large collection of adaptations. Some of these adaptations are sense organs—eyes, ears, nose, taste buds—that provide windows to adaptively relevant information in our environment. Some of these adaptations help us to move through our environment, such as an upright skeletal posture, leg bones, and our big toes. Evolutionary psychologists tend to focus on one special subclass of the adaptations that comprise human nature—psychological adaptations. Before we look at those, however, let us consider a critical concept for evolutionary theorizing about humans: levels of analysis in evolutionary psychology.

Levels of Evolutionary Analysis in Evolutionary Psychology

One of the essential features of any science is the formulation of hypotheses. In the case of evolutionary psychology the nature of hypotheses centers on the adaptive problems and their solutions. More specifically, it centers on the adaptive problems faced by our ancestors and on the adaptive psychological solutions to those problems. In order to see precisely how evolutionary psychologists formulate these hypotheses, we must describe a hierarchy of levels of analysis within evolutionary psychology, as shown in Figure 2.1 on page 40.

General Evolutionary Theory.   The first level of analysis is general evolutionary theory. In its modern form, general evolutionary theory, as described in Chapter 1, is understood as inclusive fitness theory. Inclusive fitness theory describes the process of evolution by changes that increase the likelihood of producing viable offspring (classical fitness) and the likelihood that one's genetic kin will produce offspring (inclusive fitness). Recall that inclusive fitness is defined as the sum of an individual's direct fitness in producing offspring and the effects on the fitness of kin who carry copies of the individual's genes.

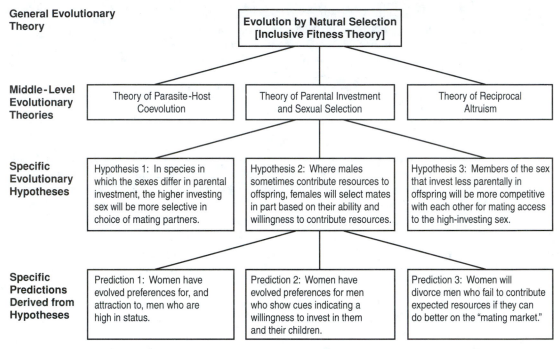

General Evolutionary
Theory

Evolution by Natural Selection
[Inclusive Fitness Theory]

Middle-Level
Evolutionary
Theories

Theory of Parasite-Host
Coevolution

Theory of Parental Investment
and Sexual Selection

Theory of Reciprocal
Altruism

Specific
Evolutionary
Hypotheses

Hypothesis 1: In species in
which the sexes differ in parental
investment, the higher investing
sex will be more selective in
choice of mating partners.

Hypothesis 2: Where males
sometimes contribute resources to
offspring, females will select mates
in part based on their ability and
willingness to contribute resources.

Hypothesis 3: Members of the sex
that invest less parentally in
offspring will be more competitive
with each other for mating access
to the high-investing sex.

Specific
Predictions
Derived from
Hypotheses

Prediction 1: Women have
evolved preferences for, and
attraction to, men who are
high in status.

Prediction 2: Women have
evolved preferences for men
who show cues indicating a
willingness to invest in them
and their children.

Prediction 3: Women will
divorce men who fail to contribute
expected resources if they can
do better on the "mating market."

FIGURE 2.1   Three Levels of Evolutionary Analysis. The figure shows one version of
the hierarchy of levels of analysis in evolutionary psychology. General evolutionary theory,
understood in the context of modern inclusive fitness theory, occupies the highest level in
the hierarchy. Each middle-level theory must be consistent with general evolutionary theory,
but cannot be derived from it. Specific evolutionary hypotheses about evolved psychological
mechanisms or behavior patterns are derived from each middle-level theory. Each specific
evolutionary hypothesis can generate a variety of specific testable predictions. Support for
each hypothesis and theory is evaluated by the cumulative weight of empirical evidence.

At this general level, even though we talk about evolutionary "theory," it is widely
accepted by biological scientists as fact. Most of the research in evolutionary psychology proceeds from the assumption that evolutionary theory is correct, but the research
does not test that assumption directly. The fundamental processes underlying evolution by selection have been observed many times in the laboratory and in the field, and
have never been falsified by a single study or finding.

The principles of evolution by selection have been used successfully, for example, to
breed aggressive or passive dogs and maze-bright or maze-dull rats (Plomin, DeFries, &
McClearn, 1997). Predominantly white-colored moths were replaced by predominantly
dark-colored moths in England when the soot from Industrial Revolution-era factories
darkened the tree trunks (Ridley, 1996). The darker tree trunks made the lighter-colored
moths easier for predators to spot, and hence they died at a more rapid rate than the darker
moths. New reproductively distinct species, including dog and plant species, have been
produced experimentally through the principles of selection (Ridley, 1996).

There are observations that could, in principle, falsify general evolutionary theory. If scientists observed complex life forms that were created in time periods too short for natural selection to have operated (e.g., in seven days), then the theory would be proved false. If scientists discovered adaptations that functioned for the benefit of other species, then the theory would be proved false. If scientists discovered adaptations that functioned for the benefit of same-sex competitors, then the theory would be proved false (Darwin, 1859; Mayr, 1982; Williams, 1966). But no such phenomena have ever been documented.

General evolutionary theory is the guiding paradigm for the entire field of biology as well as for evolutionary psychology. So when an evolutionary psychologist tests an evolutionary hypothesis, he or she is not testing "general evolutionary theory," which is assumed to be true in its general outlines. Because no compelling alternatives have been proposed over the past century, and because there is overwhelming evidence supporting general evolutionary theory, these assumptions are reasonable.

Middle-Level Evolutionary Theories.   Moving one level down (see Figure 2.1), we find middle-level theories such as Trivers's theory of parental investment and sexual selection. These middle-level theories are still fairly broad, covering entire domains of functioning. They are also fair game for scientific testing and possibly being proved false. Let's examine just one theory to illustrate this point—Trivers's theory of parental investment as the driving force behind sexual selection. This theory, which is itself an elaboration of Darwin's own theory of sexual selection (1871), provided one of the key theoretical ingredients for predicting the operation of mate choice and the operation of intrasexual competition (competition between members of the same sex). Leaving aside the details for now (see Chapter 4), Trivers argued that the sex that invests greater resources in its offspring (often, but not always, the female) will evolve to be more choosy or discriminating in selecting a mate. The sex that invests less in offspring, in contrast, will evolve to be less choosy and hence more competitive with members of its own sex for sexual access to the valuable, high-investing opposite sex. The more an organism invests in reproduction, in other words, the more it has to lose by making a bad mate choice.

In the case of humans, women's absolute minimum parental investment is internal fertilization followed by a nine-month period of gestation. Women bear the heavy burdens of pregnancy. Men do not. Women, therefore, are predicted to have evolved mechanisms that lead to greater choosiness when it comes to picking a mate. Men, whose minimum parental investment is the contribution of sperm, are predicted to be less choosy.

The differences between women and men in terms of the fitness costs of making a poor mate choice are profound. An ancestral man who made a poor choice when selecting a mate could have walked away without incurring much loss. An ancestral woman who made a poor choice when choosing a mate might risk becoming pregnant and perhaps having to raise the child alone, without help.

Now let's consider the flip side. The benefits to a woman of making a wise mate choice would have been significant. A woman could have chosen a man on the basis of his intelligence and reliability and whether he showed signs that he would be likely to stick around to help raise a child. A man, too, would have benefited from choosing a mate carefully; for example, by selecting a woman who was likely to be fertile and who would be a good parent to their children. However, if the man were seeking a casual sex partner, then the benefits to him of being highly choosy would be fewer. In fact, being extremely choosy under these conditions might lower his chances of succeeding in getting a short-term mate. These differences between the sexes in the costs and benefits of being choosy created selection pressure for sex differences in mate preferences.

It turns out that the fundamental tenets of Trivers's theory have been strongly supported by empirical evidence from a variety of species (Trivers, 1985). In the many species in which females invest more heavily in offspring than males, including our own, females are in fact more likely to be choosy and discriminating (Buss, 1994; Kenrick, Sadallan, Groth, & Trost, 1990; Symons, 1979). There are a few species, however, in which males invest more than females. In some species, for example, the female implants her eggs in the male, and he is the one who carries the offspring until they are born. In species such as the Mormon cricket, poison-arrow frog, and pipefish seahorse, for example, males invest more than females in this way (Trivers, 1985).

The male pipefish seahorse receives the eggs from the female and then carries them around in his kangaroo-like pouch (Trivers, 1985). These females compete aggressively with each other for the "best" males, and males in turn are choosy about who they mate with. This so-called "sex-role reversed" species supports Trivers's theory, showing that it is not "maleness" or "femaleness" itself that causes the sex difference in choosiness. Rather, it is the relative parental investment of the two sexes. So the cumulative weight of the evidence, coming from species in which females invest more than males (the most common pattern) and from species in which males invest more than females, provides substantial support for Trivers's middle-level theory of parental investment as a determinant of relative choosiness and competitiveness for mates.

Look again at Figure 2.1 (page 40). You can see that Trivers's middle-level theory is compatible with general evolutionary theory; he is not proposing something that could not come about by the evolutionary process. At the same time, however, parental investment theory is not logically derivable from general evolutionary theory. There is nothing in inclusive fitness theory itself that says anything about parental investment theory. Thus, middle-level theories must be compatible with general evolutionary theory, but they must also stand or fall on their own merits.

Specific Evolutionary Hypotheses. Let's move one level down on Figure 2.1 to examine the specific evolutionary hypotheses. One hypothesis that has been advanced for humans, for example, is that women have evolved specific preferences for men who have a lot of resources to offer (Buss, 1989a; Symons, 1979). The logic is as follows. First, because women invest heavily in children, they have evolved to be choosy when they pick mates (standard prediction from parental investment theory). Second, the *content* of women's choices should reflect whatever has historically increased the survival and reproduction of their children. Therefore, women are hypothesized to have evolved mate preferences for men who are both able and willing to contribute resources to them and their children. This is an evolutionary psychological hypothesis because it proposes the existence of a specific psychological mechanism—a desire—that is designed to solve a specific human adaptive problem—that of securing a man who appears highly capable of investing in children.

This specific evolutionary psychological hypothesis can be tested empirically. Scientists can study women across a wide variety of cultures and see whether they in fact prefer men who are both able and willing to contribute resources to them and their children. To provide strong tests of the hypothesis, however, we must see what specific predictions it generates—moving to the lowest level of the hierarchy in Figure 2.1. Based on the hypothesis that women prefer men who have a lot of resources to offer, we could make the following predictions: (1) women will value in men specific qualities known to be linked with the acquisition of resources such as social status, intelligence, and somewhat older age; (2) in a singles bar, women's attention, as measured by eye gaze, will be drawn more to men who appear to have resources than to men who do not; and (3) women whose husbands fail to provide economic resources will be more likely to divorce them than women whose husbands do contribute economic resources.

All of these predictions follow from the evolutionary psychological hypothesis that women have a specific evolved preference for men with resources. The value of the hypothesis rests with the scientific tests of predictions derived from it. If the predictions fail—if women are shown not to desire personality characteristics known to be linked with resource acquisition, do not gaze more at men with resources in singles bars, and are not more likely to divorce husbands who fail to provide resources—then the hypothesis will be proved false. If the predictions succeed, then the hypothesis is supported, at least for the moment.

This is highly oversimplified, of course, and several additional levels of analysis are often involved. We could perform an even more detailed analysis of the sorts of information-processing mechanisms needed to solve the adaptive problem of securing a man's investment and use as a guide an analysis of the relevant ancestral cues that would have been available to our human ancestors in those environments. Because we know that humans spent 99 percent of their evolutionary history as hunter-gatherers (Tooby & DeVore, 1987), for example, we could predict that part of women's evolved preference will include the specific qualities needed for successful hunting such as athletic prowess, good hand-eye coordination, and the physical endurance needed for long hunts.

All the conditions of standard science hold in testing these predictions. If the predictions do not pan out empirically, then the hypotheses on which they were based are called into question. If key hypotheses are called into question by several predictive failures, then the truth or value of the middle-level theory that generated the hypotheses is doubtable. Theories that are consistently supported—as, for example, Trivers's theory of parental investment and sexual selection has been in hundreds of empirical studies— are hailed as major middle-level theories, especially if they generate interesting and fruitful avenues of research. Theories that fail to generate such avenues or that produce a series of predictive failures are abandoned or replaced by better theories.

This hierarchy of levels of analysis is useful in answering questions such as what evidence could falsify evolutionary formulations? A particular hypothesis about a psychological mechanism could be wrong, even if the theory one level up that led to the hypothesis is entirely correct. Trivers's middle-level theory of parental investment could be correct, for example, even if it turned out that women have not evolved specific mate preferences for men with resources. Perhaps the relevant mutations for women's preferences did not arise, or perhaps women in ancestral conditions were constrained from making their own mating choices.

Similarly, even if the specific evolutionary psychology hypothesis is correct—in this case, that women have evolved specific mate preferences for men with resources—there is no guarantee that each and every prediction derived from it will be correct. It might be the case, for example, that women do desire qualities in men linked with resources and do gaze at resource-laden men more in singles bars, but do not divorce men who fail to provide for them. Perhaps women whose husbands fail to provide are stuck with them because of laws that prohibit divorce. Or perhaps the woman perceives that she won't be able to do much better, and so decides to stick it out. Maybe she thinks her children will be better off with their father around, even if he does not bring in economic resources. Any of these factors could render our specific prediction false. The key point is that the evaluation of evolutionary formulations rests with the cumulative weight of the evidence, and not necessarily with any single prediction.

Two Strategies for Generating and Testing Evolutionary Hypotheses.   The hierarchy of levels in Figure 2.1 shows one scientific strategy for generating evolutionary hypotheses and predictions. This strategy is called the top-down or theory-driven approach to hypothesis generation. One can start at the top with general evolutionary theory and derive hypotheses. For example, we could predict solely based on the inclusive fitness formulation of evolutionary theory that humans will help close genetic relatives more than they will distant genetic relatives. Or we could generate a hypothesis based on Trivers's middle-level theory of parental investment. Either way, the derivations flow downward in the diagram, going from the general to the specific.

The top-down strategy illustrates one of the ways in which theories can be extraordinarily useful. Theories provide both a set of working premises from which specific hypotheses can be generated, and a framework for guiding researchers to important domains of inquiry such as investing in kin or children.

There is a second strategy for generating evolutionary psychological hypotheses (see Table 2.2). Instead of starting with a theory, we can start with an observation. Once the observation is made about the existence of a phenomenon, we can then proceed in a bottom-up fashion and generate a hypothesis about its function. Because humans are keen perceivers of other people, they generally notice things even without a formal theory to direct attention to them. For example, most people don't need a theory to tell them that humans communicate through spoken language, walk upright on two legs, and sometimes wage war on other groups. There is nothing in general evolutionary theory that would have generated the hypothesis that language, bipedal locomotion, or group-on-group warfare would have evolved.

The fact that we observe many things about both ourselves and other species that were not predicted in advance by evolutionary theory does not undermine the theory. But it does raise a problem: How can we explain these phenomena? Can evolutionary thinking help us understand them? Can these unpredicted phenomena be located within the grand edifice of evolutionary psychology, or do they somehow fall outside it?

TABLE 2.2   Two Strategies of Generating and Testing Evolutionary Hypotheses

Strategy 1: Theory-Driven or "Top-Down" Strategy	Strategy 2: Observation-Driven or "Bottom-Up" Strategy
Step 1: Derive Hypothesis from Existing Theory Example: From parental investment theory we can derive the hypothesis that because women have a greater obligatory investment in offspring than men, women will tend to be more choosy or discriminating in their selection of a mate.	*Step 1: Develop Hypothesis about Adaptive Function Based on a Known Observation* Example: A. Observation: Men seem to give higher priority than women to physical appearance in the selection of a mate. B. Hypothesis: Women's physical appearance provided ancestral men with cues to fertility.
Step 2: Test Predictions Based on the Hypothesis Example: Conduct an experiment to test the prediction that a woman will impose a longer delay and more stringent standards before consenting to sex to evaluate a man's quality and commitment.	*Step 2: Test Predictions Based on Hypothesis* Example: Conduct experiments to determine whether men's standards of attractiveness are closely based on cues to a woman's fertility.
Step 3: Evaluate Whether Empirical Results Confirm Predictions Example: Women impose longer delays and impose more stringent standards than men before consenting to sex (Buss & Schmitt, 1993; Kenrick et al., 1990).	*Step 3: Evaluate Whether Empirical Results Confirm Predictions* Example: Men find a low WHR a known fertility correlate, attractive (Singh, 1993).

Consider a common observation that has been documented by scientific research: A woman's physical appearance is a significant part of her desirability to men. This is something many people observe without the guidance of any scientific theory. Even your grandmother could probably have told you that most men prefer attractive women. But an evolutionary perspective probes deeper. It asks why.

The most widely advocated evolutionary hypothesis is that a woman's appearance provides a wealth of cues to her fertility. What men find attractive, according to this hypothesis, should be specific physical features that are linked with fertility. Over evolutionary time, men who were drawn to women showing these fertility cues would have outreproduced men who were drawn to women lacking fertility cues, or who were indifferent to a woman's physical appearance altogether.

Psychologist Devendra Singh has proposed one such feature—the ratio of the waist to the hips, or WHR (Singh, 1993). A low WHR, indicating that the waist is smaller in circumference than the hips, is linked with fertility for two reasons. First, women in fertility clinics with low WHRs get pregnant sooner than women with higher WHRs. Second, women with higher WHRs show a higher incidence of heart disease and endocrinological problems, both of which are linked with lower fertility. So

Singh proposed that men will prefer women with low WHRs, and that a desire evolved in men to home in on this powerful physical cue to women's fertility.

In a series of studies across several different cultures Singh presented men with line drawings of women with various WHRs. Some showed a WHR of .70 (waist seven-tenths the size of the hips), others a WHR of .80, and still others a WHR of .90. Men were instructed to circle the figure they found most attractive. In each culture, in samples ranging from Africa to Brazil to the United States, men of varied ages found the .70 WHR woman to be the most attractive. So although the notion that men value physical appearance in women is a common observation, specific evolutionary hypotheses can be generated and tested about *why* this phenomenon occurs.

Two general conclusions about this "bottom-up" strategy of generating and testing hypotheses can be drawn. First, it is perfectly legitimate for scientists to observe phenomena and subsequently formulate hypotheses about their origins and functions. In astronomy, for example, the finding of the expanding universe was observed first, followed by theories that attempted to explain it. Within biology, the phenomenon of sexual reproduction, as contrasted with clonal or asexual reproduction, remains a known phenomenon for which several theories have been advanced (e.g., Hamilton, 1980; Tooby, 1982; Williams, 1975). Thus, the bottom-up strategy of discovering phenomena and then generating hypotheses about function provides a nice complement to the "top-down" theory-driven hypotheses about phenomena that might occur, but have yet to be documented.

Second, the value of an evolutionary hypothesis depends in part on its precision. The more precise the hypothesis, the easier it is to generate specific predictions that follow from it. These predictions are most often based on an analysis of the "design features" the hypothesized adaptation should have if the hypothesis is correct. Step by step, prediction by prediction, hypotheses that fail to yield empirically verified predictions are scrapped; those that consistently yield empirically verified predictions are retained. So the entire enterprise shows a cumulative quality as the science moves closer and closer to discovering the existence, complexity, and functionality of evolved psychological mechanisms.

The Core of Human Nature: Fundamentals of Evolved Psychological Mechanisms

In this section we will address the core of human nature from an evolutionary psychological perspective. First we argue that all species, including humans, have a nature that can be described and explained. Second we provide a definition of evolved psychological mechanisms—the core units that comprise human nature. Finally, we explore two illustrations of evolved psychological mechanisms.

All Species Have a Nature

It is part of the male lion's nature to walk on four legs, grow a large furry mane, and hunt other animals for food. It is part of the butterfly's nature to enter a flightless pupa state, wrap itself in a cocoon, and emerge to soar, fluttering gracefully in search of food and mates. It is part of the porcupine's nature to defend itself with quills, the skunk's to defend itself with a spray of acrid liquid smell, the stag's to defend itself with antlers, and the turtle's to defend itself with a shell. All species have a nature; that nature is different for each species. Each species has faced unique selection pressures during its evolutionary history and therefore has confronted a unique set of adaptive problems.

Humans also have a nature—qualities that define us as a unique species—and all psychological theories imply its existence. For Sigmund Freud human nature consisted of raging sexual and aggressive impulses. For William James human nature consisted of dozens or hundreds of instincts. Even the most ardently environmentalist theories, such as B. F. Skinner's theory of radical behaviorism, assume that humans have a nature—in this case consisting of a few highly general learning mechanisms. All psychological theories require as their core a specification of, or fundamental premises about, human nature.

Because evolution by selection is the only known causal process that is capable of producing the fundamental components of that human nature, all psychological theories are implicitly or explicitly evolutionary. Although many psychologists fail to specify their assumptions about the evolution of human nature (hence keeping those assumptions implicit), not one has ever proposed a psychological theory that has presumed some other causal process to be responsible for creating human nature.

If humans have a nature and evolution by selection is the causal process that produced that nature, then the next question is what great insights into human nature can be provided by examining our evolutionary origins. Can examining the *process* of evolution tell us anything about the *products* of that process in the human case? Answers to these key questions form the core of the rest of this book.

Whereas the broader field of evolutionary biology is concerned with the evolutionary analysis of grandly integrated parts of an organism, evolutionary psychology focuses more narrowly on those parts that are psychological—the analysis of the human mind as a collection of evolved mechanisms, the contexts that activate those mechanisms, and the behavior generated by those mechanisms. And so we turn now directly to the subclass of adaptations that make up the human mind—evolved psychological mechanisms.

Definition of an Evolved Psychological Mechanism

An *evolved psychological mechanism* is a set of processes inside an organism with the following properties:

1. *An evolved psychological mechanism exists in the form that it does because it solved a specific problem of survival or reproduction recurrently over evolutionary history.* This means that the form of the mechanism, its set of *design features,* is like a key made to fit a particular lock (Tooby & Cosmides, 1992). Just as the shape of the key must be coordinated to fit the internal features of the lock, the shape of the design features of a psychological mechanism must be coordinated with the features required to solve an adaptive problem of survival or reproduction. Failure to mesh with the adaptive problem meant failure to pass through the selective sieve of evolution.

2. *An evolved psychological mechanism is designed to take in only a narrow slice of information.* Consider the human eye. Although it seems as though we open our eyes and see nearly everything, the eye is actually sensitive only to a narrow range of input from the broad spectrum of electromagnetic waves. Our eyes are designed to process input from only a very narrow wedge of waves—those within the visual spectrum. We do not see X rays, which are shorter radiations than those in the visual spectrum. Nor do we see radio waves, which are longer than those in the visual spectrum.

Even within the visual spectrum, however, our eyes are designed to process a narrower subset of information (Marr, 1982). Human eyes have specific edge detectors that pick up contrasting reflections from objects and motion detectors that pick up movement. They also have specific cones designed to pick up certain information about the colors of objects. So the eye is not an all-purpose seeing device. It is designed to process only narrow slices of information—waves within a particular range of frequency, edges, motion, and so on—from among the much larger domain of potential information.

Similarly, the psychological mechanism of a predisposition to learn to fear snakes is designed to take in only a narrow slice of information—slithery movements from self-propelled elongated objects. Our evolved preferences for food, landscapes, and mates are all designed to take in only a limited subset of information from among the infinite array that could potentially constitute input. The limited cues that activate each mechanism are those that recurred during the EEA (environment of evolutionary adaptedness) or those in the modern environment that closely mimic these ancestral cues.

3. *The input of an evolved psychological mechanism tells an organism the particular adaptive problem it is facing.* The input of seeing a slithering snake tells you that you are confronting a particular survival problem, namely physical damage and perhaps death if bitten. The different smells of potentially edible objects—rancid and rotting versus sweet and fragrant—tell you that you are facing an adaptive survival problem of food selection. The input, in short, lets the organism know which adaptive problem it is dealing with. This occurs almost invariably out of consciousness. Humans do not smell a pizza baking and think "Aha! I am facing an adaptive problem of food selection!" Instead, the smell unconsciously triggers food selection mechanisms, and no consciousness or awareness of the adaptive problem is necessary.

4. *The input of an evolved psychological mechanism is transformed through decision rules into output.* Upon seeing a snake you can decide to attack it, run away from it, or freeze. Upon smelling a pizza just out of the oven you can choose to devour it or walk away from it (perhaps if you are on a diet). The decision rules are a set of procedures—"if, then" statements—for channeling an organism down one path or another.

5. *The output of an evolved psychological mechanism can be physiological activity, information to other psychological mechanisms, or manifest behavior.* Upon seeing a snake you may get autonomically aroused or frightened (physiological output); you may use this information to evaluate your behavioral options such as freezing or fleeing (information to other psychological mechanisms) and the consequence of this evaluation is an action, such as running away (behavioral output).

Consider another example, sexual jealousy. Let's say you go to a party with your romantic partner and then leave the room to get a drink. When you return, you spot your partner talking animatedly with another person. They are standing very close to each other and looking deeply into each other's eyes, and you notice that they are lightly touching each other. These cues might trigger a reaction we can call sexual jealousy. The cues act as input to the mechanism, signaling to you an adaptive problem—the threat of losing your partner. This input is then evaluated according to a set of decision rules. One option is to ignore the two of them and feign indifference. Another option is to threaten the rival. A third option is to become enraged and hit your partner. Still another option would be to reevaluate your relationship. Thus, the output of a psychological mechanism can be physiological (arousal), behavioral (confronting, threatening, hitting), or input into other psychological mechanisms (reevaluating the status of your relationship).

6. *The output of an evolved psychological mechanism is directed toward the solution to a specific adaptive problem.* Just as the cues to a partner's potential infidelity signal the presence of an adaptive problem, the output of the sexual jealousy mechanism is geared toward solving that problem. The threatened rival may leave the scene, your romantic partner may be deterred from flirting with others, or your reevaluation of the relationship may cause you to cut your losses and move on. Any of these might help with the solution to your adaptive problem.

Stating that the output of a psychological mechanism leads to solutions to specific adaptive problems does not imply that the solutions will always be optimal or successful. The rival may not be deterred by your threats. Your partner may have a fling with your rival despite your display of jealousy. The main point is *not* that the output of a psychological mechanism *always* leads to a successful solution, but rather that the output of the mechanism *on average* tended to solve the adaptive problem in the environment in which it evolved.

An important point to keep in mind is that a mechanism that led to a successful solution in the evolutionary past may or may not lead to a successful solution now. Our strong taste preferences for fat, for example, were clearly adaptive in our evolutionary past because fat was a valuable and scarce source of calories. Now, however, with hamburger and pizza joints on every street corner, fat is no longer a scarce resource. Thus, our strong taste for fatty substances now causes us to overconsume fat, which can lead to clogged arteries and heart attacks and thereby hinder our survival. The central point is that evolved mechanisms exist in the forms that they do because they led to success on average during the period in which they evolved. Whether they are currently adaptive— that is, whether they currently lead to increased survival and reproduction—is an empirical matter that must be determined on a case-by-case basis.

In summary, an evolved psychological mechanism is a set of procedures within the organism that is designed to take in a particular slice of information and transform that information via decision rules into output that historically has helped with the solution to an adaptive problem. The psychological mechanism exists in current organisms because it led, on average, to the successful solution of a specific adaptive problem for that organism's ancestors. (See Box 2.1 on page 50 for two examples.)

B O X **2.1**

Two Illustrations of Evolved Psychological Mechanisms: Fear of Spiders and Landscape Preferences

At this early stage in the development of the field of evolutionary psychology no psychological mechanism has been completely described. We do not know all of the decision rules, the precise range of events that trigger their activation, or the complete range of outputs of any mechanism. Nonetheless, two illustrations of *possible* psychological mechanisms will help to convey the scientific goals of this enterprise.

Let's consider the fear of spiders and preferences for certain landscapes. An evolved fear of spiders exists in the form that it does because it solved a specific problem of survival in human ancestral environments (Marks, 1987). The fear is triggered only by a narrow range of inputs, such as the specific shapes and movements associated with spiders. Once a spider is perceived as dangerous and within striking range this information is transformed via decision rules that might activate physiological arousal and perhaps the implementation of a host of behavioral options. The options—such as stomping on the spider, fleeing, or yelling for help—would presumably have lowered the odds of receiving a deadly spider bite in ancestral environments. Thus, the output of the fear-of-spiders mechanism solves an ancestral adaptive problem. It is not by chance that human fears and phobias tend to be concentrated heavily around environmental events that threatened human survival. Fears of snakes, spiders, heights, darkness, and strangers provide a window for viewing the survival hazards that our human ancestors faced (Marks, 1987).

Preferences are evolved psychological mechanisms of a different sort than fears. Preferences motivate an organism to seek things rich in the "resource providing potential" needed for survival or reproduction (Orians & Heerwagen, 1992). Landscape preferences provide an illustration. Studies of landscape preferences show that savanna-like environments are consistently preferred to other environments. In particular, people like landscapes that provide food, water, and

safety and places that offer protection from hazards such as bad weather or landslides. They also like places that offer freedom from predators, parasites, toxic foods, and unfriendly humans (Orians & Heerwagen, 1992). Furthermore, people prefer places where they can see without being seen, places allowing multiple views for surveillance, and places offering multiple ways of moving through space for escape.

As a human walks through a variety of places searching for a place to stay for a while, some particular landscapes fail to fulfill these evolved preferences. Those that do trigger a set of cognitive procedures or decision rules, depending in part on other contextual input such as one's state of hunger or thirst, the size of one's group, and one's knowledge about the presence of hostile humans in the vicinity. Eventually these procedures produce output in the form of a behavioral decision to remain in the habitat or continue the search for a better habitat. These behavioral decisions presumably led those who had them to survive and reproduce better than either those who did not or those who possessed alternative preferences that were less effective at securing resources and reducing risk.

Although psychological mechanisms such as landscape preferences clearly differ in important ways from mechanisms such as spider fears, they share critical ingredients that qualify them as evolved psychological mechanisms: They exist thanks to a history of natural selection; they are triggered only by a narrow range of information; they are characterized by a particular set of decision rules; and they produce behavioral output that solved an adaptive problem in ancestral times.

Given the infinite courses of action a human could pursue in principle, evolved psychological mechanisms are necessary for channeling action into the narrow pockets of adaptive choices. Psychological mechanisms are necessary for seeking and extracting particular forms of information. Decision rules are necessary for producing action based on that information.

Important Properties of Evolved Psychological Mechanisms

This section examines several important properties of evolved psychological mechanisms. They provide nonarbitrary criteria for "carving the mind at its natural joints" and tend to be problem specific, numerous, and complex. These features combine to yield the tremendous flexibility of behavior that characterizes modern humans.

Evolved Psychological Mechanisms Provide Nonarbitrary Criteria for "Carving the Mind at Its Joints."   A central premise of evolutionary psychology is that the primary nonarbitrary way to identify, describe, and understand psychological mechanisms is to articulate their functions—the specific adaptive problems they were designed by selection to solve.

Consider the human body. In principle the mechanisms of the body could be described in an infinite number of ways. Why do anatomists identify as separate mechanisms the liver, the heart, the hand, the nose, and the eyes? What makes these divisions nonarbitrary compared with alternative ways of dividing the human body? The answer is function. The liver is recognized as a mechanism that performs functions different from those performed by the heart or the hand. The eyes and the nose, although located close together, perform different functions and operate according to different inputs (electromagnetic waves in the visual spectrum versus odors). If an anatomist tried to lump the eyes and the nose into one category it would seem ludicrous. Understanding the component parts of the body requires the identification of function. Function provides a sensible nonarbitrary way to understand these component parts.

Evolutionary psychologists believe that similar principles should be used for understanding the mechanisms of the mind. Although the mind could be divided in an infinite number of ways, most of them would simply be arbitrary. A powerful nonarbitrary analysis of the human mind is one that rests on function. If two components of the mind perform different functions, they can be regarded as separate mechanisms (although they may interact with each other in interesting ways).

Evolved Psychological Mechanisms Tend to Be Problem Specific.   Imagine giving directions to someone to get from New York City to a specific street address in San Francisco, California. If you gave general directions such as "head west," the person might end up as far south as Texas or as far north as Alaska. The general direction would not reliably get the person to the right state.

Now let's suppose that the person did get to the right state. The "go west" direction would be virtually useless because west of California is ocean. The general direction would not provide any guidance to get to the right city within California, let alone the right street address. To get the person to the right state, city, street, and location on that street you would need to give more specific instructions. Furthermore, although there are many ways to get to a particular street address, some paths will be far more efficient and time saving than others.

The search for a specific street address on the other side of the country is a good analogy for what is needed to reach a specific adaptive solution. Adaptive problems, like street addresses, are specific—don't get bitten by that snake, select a habitat with running water and places to hide, avoid eating food that is poisonous, select a mate who is fertile, and so on. There is no such thing as a "general adaptive problem" (Symons, 1992). All problems are content specific.

Because adaptive problems are specific, their solutions tend to be specific as well. Just as general instructions fail to get you to the correct location, general solutions fail to get you to the right adaptive solution. Consider two adaptive problems: selecting the right foods to eat (a survival problem) and selecting the right mate with whom to have children (a reproductive problem). What counts as a "successful solution" is quite different for the two problems. Successful food selection involves identifying objects that have calories and particular vitamins and minerals and do not contain poisonous substances. Successful mate selection involves, among other things, identifying a partner who is fertile and will be a good parent.

What might be a general solution to these two selection problems, and how effective would it be at solving them? One general solution would be "select the first thing that comes along." This would be disastrous because it might lead to eating poisonous plants or marrying an infertile person. If anyone ever had developed such a general solution to these adaptive problems in human evolutionary history, he or she failed to become one of our ancestors.

To solve these selection problems in a reasonable way one would need more specific guidance about the important qualities of foods and mates. Fruit that looks fresh and ripe, for example, will signal better nutrients than fruit that looks rotten. People who look young and healthy will be more fertile, on average, than people who look old and ill. We need *specific selection criteria*—qualities that are part of our selection mechanisms—to solve these selection problems successfully.

The specificity of mechanisms is further illustrated by errors in selection. If you make an error in food selection, there is an array of mechanisms tailored to correcting that error. When you bite a piece of bad food, it may taste terrible, in which case you would spit it out. You may gag on it if it makes its way past your taste buds. And if it makes its way all the way down to your stomach, you may vomit—a specific mechanism designed to get rid of toxic or harmful ingested substances. But if you make an error in mate selection you do not spit, gag, or throw up (at least not usually). You correct your error in other ways—by leaving him or her, selecting someone else, or simply telling the person that you don't want to see him or her anymore.

In summary, problem specificity of adaptive mechanisms is favored over generality because (1) general solutions fail to guide the organism to the correct adaptive solutions; (2) even if they do work, general solutions lead to too many errors and thus are costly to the organism; and (3) what constitutes a "successful solution" differs from problem to problem (the criteria for successful food selection differ from the criteria for successful mate selection). The adaptive solutions, in short, must have dedicated procedures and content-sensitive elements to solve adaptive problems successfully.

Humans Possess Many Evolved Psychological Mechanisms.   Humans, like most organisms, face a large number of adaptive problems. The problems of survival alone number in the dozens or hundreds—problems of thermal regulation (being too cold or too hot), avoiding predators and parasites, ingesting life-sustaining foods, and so on. Then there are problems of mating such as selecting, attracting, and keeping a good mate and getting rid of a bad mate. There are also problems of parenting such as breastfeeding, weaning, socializing, attending to the varying needs of different children, and so on. Then there are the problems of investing in kin, such as brothers, sisters, nephews, and nieces; dealing with social conflicts; defending against aggressive groups; grappling with the social hierarchy; and so on.

Because specific problems require specific solutions, numerous specific problems will require numerous specific solutions. Just as our bodies contain thousands of specific mechanisms—a heart to pump blood, lungs for oxygen uptake, a liver to filter out toxins—the mind, according to this analysis, must also contain hundreds or thousands of specific mechanisms. Because a large number of different adaptive problems cannot be solved with just a few mechanisms, the human mind must be made up of a large number of evolved psychological mechanisms.

The Specificity, Complexity, and Numerousness of Evolved Psychological Mechanisms Give Humans Behavioral Flexibility.

The definition of a psychological mechanism, including the key components of input, decision rules, and output, highlights why adaptations are not rigid "instincts" that invariably show up in behavior. Recall the example of callus-producing mechanisms that have evolved to protect the structures beneath the skin. You can design your environment so that you don't experience repeated friction. In this case your callus-producing mechanisms will not be activated. The activation of the mechanisms depends on contextual input from the environment. In the same way, all psychological mechanisms require input for their activation.

Psychological mechanisms are not like rigid instincts for another important reason—the decision rules. Decision rules are "if, then" procedures such as "if the snake hisses, then run for your life" or "if the person I'm attracted to shows interest, then smile and decrease distance." For most mechanisms these decision rules permit at least several possible response options. Even in the simple case of encountering a snake, you have the options of attacking it with a stick, freezing and hoping it will go away, or running away. In general, the more complex the mechanism, the greater the number of response options there will be.

Consider a carpenter's tool box. The carpenter gains flexibility not by having one "highly general tool" that can be used to cut, poke, saw, screw, twist, wrench, plane, balance, and hammer. Instead, the carpenter gains flexibility by having a large number of highly specific tools in the tool box. These highly specific tools can then be used in many combinations that would not be possible with one highly "flexible" tool. Indeed, it is difficult to imagine what a "general" tool would even look like, since there is no such thing as a "general carpenter's problem." In a similar fashion, humans gain their flexibility from having a large number of complex, specific, functional psychological mechanisms.

With each new mechanism that is added to the mind, an organism can perform a new task. A bird has feet that enable it to walk; adding wings enables it to fly. Adding a beak to a bird enables it to break the shells of seeds and nuts and get at their edible core.

With each new specific mechanism that is added, the bird can complete a new task that it could not have done before. Having feet as well as wings gives the bird the flexibility to both walk and fly.

This leads to a conclusion contrary to human intuitions, which for most of us holds that having a lot of innate mechanisms causes behavior to be inflexible. In fact just the opposite is the case. The more mechanisms we have, the greater the range of behaviors we can perform, and hence the greater the flexibility of our behavior.

Methods for Testing Evolutionary Hypotheses

Once clearly formulated hypotheses about evolved psychological mechanisms and associated predictions are specified, the next step is to test them empirically. Evolutionary psychologists have a wide array of scientific methods at their disposal. The scientific foundation of evolutionary psychology, as we will see, rests not on a single method, but rather on convergent evidence from a variety of methods and sources of data (see Table 2.3).

Comparing Different Species

Comparing species that differ along particular dimensions provides one source of evidence for testing functional hypotheses. The comparative method involves "testing predictions about the occurrence of the trait among species other than the animals whose behavior the researcher is trying to understand" (Alcock, 1993, p. 221). As an example, consider the following sperm competition hypothesis: The function of producing large sperm volume is to displace competing males' sperm, and hence increase the odds of fertilizing a female's egg.

One strategy for testing this hypothesis is to compare species that differ in the prevalence of sperm competition. In highly monogamous species sperm competition is

TABLE 2.3   Methods and Data Sources for Testing Evolutionary Hypotheses

Methods for Testing Evolutionary Hypotheses	Sources of Data for Testing Evolutionary Hypotheses
1. Compare different species	1. Archeological records
2. Compare males and females	2. Data from hunter-gatherer societies
3. Compare individuals within a species	3. Observations
4. Compare the same individuals in different contexts	4. Self-reports
5. Experimental methods	5. Life-history data and public records
	6. Human products

rare or absent. In certain species of birds (e.g., ring doves) and mammals (e.g., gibbons), males and females pair off to produce offspring and rarely have sex outside the pair-bond. In other species, such as bonobo chimpanzees, females will copulate with a number of males (Small, 1992). In this species there is a great deal of sperm competition. Thus we know that sperm competition is high in promiscuous species and low in monogamous species.

Now comes the test. We can line up species by the degree to which sperm competition is likely to be prevalent. Among primates, for example, gorillas tend to be the least promiscuous, followed by orangutans, humans, and chimpanzees, who are the most promiscuous. Next we can obtain comparative data on the sperm volume in each of these species as indicated by testicular weight, corrected for body size. The prediction from the sperm competition hypothesis is that males in species that show a lot of sperm competition should have higher testicular weight (indicating a high volume of sperm) compared with species that show lower levels of sperm competition.

The comparative evidence yields the following findings. The testes of male gorillas account for 0.02 percent of body weight; of male orangutans, 0.05 percent of body weight; of human males, 0.08 percent of body weight; and of the highly promiscuous chimpanzees, 0.27 percent of body weight (Short, 1979; Smith, 1984). In sum, males in the species showing intense sperm competition display larger testicular volume; males in the species with the least sperm competition display the lowest testicular volume. The comparative method thus supports the sperm competition hypothesis.

The method of comparing different species, of course, is not limited to sperm competition and testicular volume. We can also compare species that are known to face a particular adaptive problem with those known not to face that problem. We can compare cliff-dwelling goats and non–cliff-dwelling goats to test the hypothesis that goats that graze on cliffs will have specialized adaptations to avoid falling such as better spatial orientation abilities. We can compare species with known predators with those lacking those predators to test the hypothesis that there are specific adaptations to combat those predators (e.g., specific alarm calls sounded when encountering an image of the predator). Comparing different species, in short, is a powerful method for testing hypotheses about adaptive function.

Comparing Males and Females

Sexually reproducing species usually come in two forms—male and female. Comparing the sexes provides another method for testing hypotheses about adaptation. One comparative strategy involves analyzing the different natures of the adaptive problems faced by males and females. In species with internal female fertilization, for example, males face the adaptive problem of "paternity uncertainty." They never can "know" with complete certainty whether they are the genetic father of their mate's offspring. The females, however, do not confront this adaptive problem. They "know" that their own eggs, not a rival's eggs, are fertilized because they can only come from within them.

Based on this analysis we can compare males and females to see whether males have evolved specific adaptations that have the function of increasing their chances of paternity. We will examine these adaptations in detail in Chapter 5, but one example will suffice to make the point here: male sexual jealousy. Although both sexes are equally jealous overall, recent studies have shown that men's jealousy, far more than women's, is activated specifically by signals of *sexual* infidelity, suggesting one solution to the problem of paternity uncertainty (Buss, Larsen, Westen, & Semmelroth, 1992). Once activated, men's jealousy motivates behavior designed to repel a rival or to dissuade a mate from an infidelity. The fact that men's jealousy is especially triggered by cues to sexual infidelity (rather than by cues to emotional infidelity) points to a facet of men's psychology that corresponds to a sex-linked adaptive problem—that of uncertainty of parenthood. Adaptations such as these are predicted to be lacking in women, who have not faced the adaptive problem of "knowing" whether the offspring are their own. In sum, comparing the sexes within one species can be a powerful method of testing evolutionary hypotheses.

Comparing Individuals within a Species

A third method involves comparing some individuals with other individuals within one species. Consider young and older women. Teenage girls have many years of potential reproduction ahead of them; women in their late thirties have fewer fertile years left. We can use these differences to formulate and test hypotheses about adaptation.

For example, suppose you hypothesized that younger women would be more likely to abort a developing fetus than older women if there weren't an investing man around to help. The evolutionary rationale is this: because they have many reproductive years left, younger women can "afford" to lose the chance to have a child to wait for a more opportune time to reproduce. The older woman may not get another chance to have a child. Comparing the rates of abortion, miscarriage, and infanticide in the two groups of women provides one method for testing this hypothesis.

Comparing individuals within a species is not restricted, of course, to age. We can compare individuals who are poor to those who are rich to test the hypothesis that the poor will engage in "riskier" strategies of acquiring resources: the rich might be more "conservative" to protect their wealth. We can compare women who have many strong brothers around to protect them with women who are only children to see whether women in the second group are more vulnerable to abuse at the hands of men. We can compare individuals who differ in their desirability as mates or individuals who differ in the sizes of their extended families. In short, within-species comparison also constitutes a powerful method for testing evolutionary hypotheses about adaptation.

Comparing the Same Individuals in Different Contexts

Another approach is to compare the same individuals in different situations. Among the Siriono of eastern Bolivia, for example, one man who was a particularly unsuccessful hunter had lost several wives to men who were better hunters. He suffered a loss of status within the group, due to both his poor hunting and his loss of wives to other men. Anthropologist A. R. Holmberg took up hunting with this man, gave him game that others were later told the man had killed, and taught him the art of killing game with a shotgun. Eventually, as a result of the man's increased hunting success, he enjoyed an increase in social status, attracted several women as sex partners, and started insulting others rather than being the victim of insults (Holmberg, 1950).

Comparing the same individuals in different situations is a powerful method for revealing evolved psychological mechanisms. Hypotheses can be formulated about the adaptive problems confronted in two different situations, and hence about which psychological mechanisms will be activated in each. In the case of the Siriono man who went from low to high status thanks to a change in his hunting ability, the higher status apparently caused him to be more self-confident. It also seems to have affected the psychological mechanisms of other Siriono men, who shifted from insulting the man to being more respectful.

Unfortunately, it is sometimes difficult for researchers to wait until a person moves from one context to another. People often find a niche and stay there. Furthermore, even when people do shift situations, many things tend to change at once, making it difficult for researchers to isolate the specific causal factor responsible for a change. In the case of the Siriono man, for example, did the change in other men's behavior toward him occur because he was bringing in meat, because he was attracting women, or even perhaps because he was carrying a shotgun? Because of the problems of separating the specific causal factors responsible, scientists sometimes try to "control" the situation in psychological experiments.

Experimental Methods

In experiments, one group of subjects is typically exposed to a "manipulation" and a second group serves as a "control." Let's say that we develop a hypothesis about the effect of threat on the tightness of "in-group cohesion." The hypothesis states that humans have evolved a specific psychological mechanism whose function is to react adaptively to threats from the outside, such as an invasion by a hostile group of humans. Under threat conditions group cohesion should increase, as manifested by such tendencies as showing favoritism toward in-group members and showing an increase in prejudice toward out-group members.

In the laboratory experimenters choose one group of subjects at random and tell them they may have to go to a smaller room because another group has first priority on the room they are in. Before they leave the experimenter gives them $100 as payment for participating in the study, with instructions to divide the money between the two groups however they want. The control group is also charged with dividing the money between their group and another group, but is not told that the other group is taking over their room. We can then compare how the control group and the experimental group decide to split up the money. If there is no difference between the experimental and control groups we would conclude that our prediction had failed. On the other hand, if the threatened group allocated more money to itself and shortchanged the other group, but the control group allocated equally, then our prediction would be confirmed—external threat increases in-group favoritism.

In sum, the experimental method—subjecting different groups to different conditions (sometimes called manipulations)—can be used to test hypotheses about adaptations.

Sources of Data for Testing Evolutionary Hypotheses

Evolutionary psychologists have a wealth of sources from which they can obtain data for testing hypotheses. This section briefly presents some of these sources.

Archeological Records

Bone fragments secured from around the world reveal a paleontological record filled with interesting artifacts. Through carbon-dating methods we can obtain rough estimates of the ages of skulls and skeletons and trace the evolution of brain size through the millennia. Bones from large game animals found at ancestral campsites can reveal how our ancestors solved the adaptive problem of securing food. Fossilized feces can provide information about other features of the ancestral diet. Analyses of bone fragments can also reveal sources of injury, disease, and death. The archeological record provides one set of clues about how we lived and evolved, and the nature of the adaptive problems our ancestors confronted.

Data from Hunter-Gatherer Societies

Current studies of traditional peoples, especially those relatively isolated from Western civilization, also provide a rich source of data for testing evolutionary hypotheses. Studies by anthropologists Kim Hill and Hillard Kaplan (1988), for example, show that successful hunters do not benefit directly from their efforts because meat is shared by the group, but they do benefit in other reproductively relevant ways. The children of successful hunters receive more care and attention from the group, resulting in superior health. Successful hunters also are sexually attractive to women, and tend to have more mistresses and more desirable wives.

Findings from contemporary hunter-gatherers, of course, are not definitive. There are many differences among the various groups of tribal societies. But these findings do provide suggestive evidence that, in conjunction with other sources of data, allow us to formulate and test hypotheses about human evolutionary psychology.

Observations

Systematic observations provide a third method for testing evolutionary hypotheses. Anthropologist Mark Flinn devised a behavioral scanning technique for systematically gathering observations in Trinidad (Flinn, 1988a). Every day he walked through the targeted village, visiting every household and recording each observation he made on a record sheet. He was able to confirm, for example, the hypothesis that men with fertile wives engaged in more intense "mate guarding" than men with less fertile wives (i.e., those who were pregnant or old). He determined this through behavioral scans that showed that men tended to get into more fights with other men when their wives were fertile and fewer fights when their wives were not fertile. Observational data can be collected from a variety of sources—trained observers such as Flinn, husbands or wives of the target subjects, friends and relatives, even casual acquaintances. Data from observations, like all sources of data, contain potential flaws and biases. An observer may have preconceptions about what he or she expects to observe, which could color the recordings. Observers also may not be privy to important domains of behavior, such as sexual behavior, because people prefer to guard their privacy. Researchers must be sensitive to these sources of bias and be sure to supplement their observations with other sources of data.

Self-Reports

Reports by the actual subjects provide an invaluable source of data. Self-report data can be secured through interviews or questionnaires. There are some psychological phenomena that can only be examined through self-report. Consider sexual fantasies. These are private experiences that leave no fossils and cannot be observed by outsiders. In one study evolutionary psychologists Bruce Ellis and Donald Symons were able to test hypotheses about sex differences in sexual fantasy (Ellis & Symons, 1990). They found that men's sexual fantasies tended to involve more sexual partners and more partner switching, and were more visually oriented. Women's sexual fantasies tended to have more mystery, romance, emotional expressions, and context. Without self-report, this sort of study could not be conducted.

Self-report has been used to test a variety of evolutionary psychological hypotheses about mate preferences (Buss, 1989a), violence against spouses (Daly & Wilson, 1988), tactics of deception (Tooke & Camire, 1991), tactics of getting ahead in social hierarchies (Kyl-Heku & Buss, 1996), and patterns of cooperation and helping (McGuire, 1994).

Like all data sources, self-report carries with it biases and limitations. People may be reluctant to divulge behavior or thoughts they fear will be judged undesirable, such as extramarital affairs or unusual sexual fantasies. People may lie outright or, if they don't lie, they may be unaware of what information is relevant. Subjects may say things just to please the experimenter or to sabotage the study. For these reasons evolutionary psychologists try not to rely exclusively on self-report. Conclusions derived from multiple sources of data are always more convincing.

Life-History Data and Public Records

People leave traces of their lives on public documents. Marriages and divorces, births and deaths, crimes and misdemeanors, are all part of the public record. In one series of studies the evolutionary biologist Bobbi Low was able to unearth data on marriages, divorces, and remarriages from different parishes in Sweden recorded many centuries ago. The priests of these parishes kept scrupulously accurate and detailed records of these public events. By looking at marriage and divorce rates from four hundred years ago we can see whether the patterns that occur today are longstanding and recurrent over human history, or merely products of our modern times. Low was able to test a number of evolutionary hypotheses using these public records. She confirmed, for example, that wealthier men tended to marry younger (and hence more fertile) women compared with poorer men (Low, 1991). Furthermore, the older the man, the larger the age gap between him and his bride—a finding that we also see today across cultures (Kenrick & Keefe, 1992).

Public records, in short, provide an invaluable source of data for testing evolutionary hypotheses. They are limited, of course, in many ways. For instance, the statistics they draw on can be inaccurate or biased, and rarely do the public records contain all the information researchers seek to rule out potential alternative explanations. Yet public records, especially if used in conjunction with other sources of data, can be treasure troves for creative scientists.

Human Products

The things humans make are products of their evolved minds. Modern fast-food restaurants, for example, are products of evolved taste preferences. Hamburgers, French fries, milk shakes, and pizza are filled with fat, sugar, salt, and protein. They sell well precisely because they correspond to, and exploit, evolved desires for these substances. Thus, food creations reveal evolved taste preferences.

Other sorts of human products reveal the design of our evolved minds. The pornography and romance novel industries, for example, can be viewed as creations of common fantasies. The fact that "skin magazines" are consumed mainly by men and romance novels mainly by women reveals something about the evolved sexual natures of men and women (Ellis & Symons, 1990; Symons, 1979). The themes common in plays, paintings, movies, music, operas, novels, soap operas, and popular songs all reveal something about our evolved psychology. Human creations thus can serve as an additional data source for testing evolutionary hypotheses.

Transcending the Limitations of Single Data Sources

All data sources have limitations. The fossil record is fragmentary and has large gaps. With contemporary hunter-gatherers we do not know the degree to which current practices are contaminated by modern influences such as television. In self-report people may lie or fail to know the truth. With observational reports many important domains of behavior are hidden from prying eyes; those that are not may be distorted due to observer bias. Laboratory experiments are often contrived and artificial, rendering their generalizability to real-world contexts questionable. Life data from public records, although seemingly objective, can also be subject to systematic biases. Even human products must be interpreted through a chain of inferences that may or may not be valid.

The solution to these problems is to use multiple data sources in testing evolutionary hypotheses. Findings that emerge consistently across data sources that do not share methodological limitations are especially powerful. By using multiple data sources researchers can transcend the limitations of any single data source and arrive at a firmer empirical foundation for evolutionary psychology.

Identifying Adaptive Problems

It is clear that humans, like many species, have faced an extraordinary number of adaptive problems over human evolutionary history, giving rise to many complex adaptive mechanisms. The next critical question is: How do we know what these adaptive problems are?

To approach this question, a crucial qualification is needed. No amount of conceptual work can definitively yield a complete list of all the adaptive problems humans have faced. This indeterminacy is caused by several factors. First, we cannot rewind the evolutionary clock and see all the things our ancestors confronted in the past. Second, each new adaptation creates new adaptive problems of its own, such as becoming coordinated with other adaptive mechanisms. Identifying the full set of human adaptive problems is an enormous task that will occupy scientists for decades to come. Nonetheless, several guidelines will give us a start.

Guidance from Modern Evolutionary Theory

One guideline is the structure of modern evolutionary theory itself, which tells us that the differential reproduction of genes coding for design differences, either through producing descendants or helping genetic relatives produce descendants, is the engine of the evolutionary process. Therefore, all adaptive problems must by definition be things that are required for reproduction or that aid reproduction, however indirectly.

So to start, we can think of the following broad classes of adaptive problems.

1. *Problems of survival and growth:* getting the organism to the point at which it is capable of reproduction.
2. *Problems of mating:* selecting, attracting, and retaining a mate and performing the needed sexual behavior required for successful reproduction.
3. *Problems of parenting:* helping offspring survive and grow to the point at which they are capable of reproduction.
4. *Problems of aiding genetic relatives:* the tasks entailed in aiding the reproduction of those nondescendant kin who carry copies of one's genes.

These four classes of problems provide a reasonable starting point and a set of guidelines to the search. Taken alone, however, these classes of adaptive problems are highly general and do not tell us what adaptive problems humans, as opposed to other sexually reproducing organisms, have faced.

Guidance from Knowledge of Universal Human Structures

A second source of guidance to identifying adaptive problems comes from the accumulated knowledge of universal human structures. All humans, aside from an occasional hermit, live in groups. Knowledge of that fact suggests a host of potential adaptive problems to which humans might have evolved solutions. One obvious problem, for example, is how to make sure that you are included in the group and are not ostracized or cast out (Baumeister & Leary, 1995). Another problem is that group living means that conspecifics live closer, and hence are in more direct competition with one another for access to the resources needed to survive and reproduce.

All known human groups have social hierarchies—another structural feature of our species. The fact that hierarchies are universal suggests another class of adaptive problems (see Chapter 12). These include the problem of getting ahead (because resources increase as one rises in the hierarchy); the problem of preventing slips in status; the problem of upcoming competitors vying for your position; and the problem of incurring costs due to the wrath of someone higher up who is threatened by your rise. In sum, identifying universal features of human social interaction—such as group living and social hierarchies—provides a guide to identifying human adaptive problems.

Guidance from Traditional Societies

A third source of guidance comes from traditional societies, such as hunter-gatherers. There is evidence that these societies more closely resemble the conditions under which we evolved than do modern societies. There is strong evidence, for example, that humans have been hunters and gatherers for 99 percent of human history— roughly the past several million years before the advent of agriculture ten thousand years ago (Tooby & DeVore, 1987). Furthermore, large game animals were frequent targets of hunting activities. Examining hunter-gatherer societies, therefore, provides clues about the sorts of adaptive problems our ancestors faced.

It is virtually impossible to hunt large game alone, at least with the tools that were available prior to the invention of guns and other weapons. In hunter-gatherer societies large game hunting almost invariably occurs in groups or coalitions. To be successful these coalitions must solve an array of adaptive problems, such as how to divide the work and how to coordinate the efforts of the group, both of which require clear communication.

Guidance from the Paleoarcheology

A fourth source of guidance comes from the archeological record. Analyses of the teeth of our human ancestors, for example, reveal information about the nature of the ancestral diet. Analyses of skeletal fractures reveal information about how our ancestors died. Bones can even give clues as to what sorts of diseases plagued ancestral human populations, and thereby reveal another set of adaptive problems.

Guidance from Current Mechanisms

A fifth and highly informative source of information comes from the current psychological mechanisms characteristic of humans. The fact that the most common human phobias across cultures are snakes, spiders, heights, darkness, and strange men and not, for example, cars or electrical outlets reveals a wealth of information about ancestral survival problems. It tells us that we have evolved propensities to fear likely ancestral dangers, but not modern dangers. The universality of sexual jealousy tells us that an-cestral women and men were not necessarily sexually faithful to their mates. If they had always been faithful, there would be no need for men to have such a powerful psycho-logical mechanism of sexual jealousy—a mechanism known to be the leading cause of spouse battering and spouse homicide (Daly & Wilson, 1988). In short, our current psy-chological mechanisms provide windows for viewing the nature of the adaptive prob-lems that plagued our ancestors.

Guidance from Task Analysis

A more formal procedure for identifying adaptive problems (and subproblems) is known as task analysis (Marr, 1982). Task analysis starts with an observation about a human structure (e.g., humans live in groups with status hierarchies) or a well-documented phenomenon (e.g., humans favor their genetic relatives). A task analysis poses this ques-tion: For this structure or phenomenon to occur, what cognitive and behavioral tasks must be solved?

Let's consider the observation that people tend to aid genetic relatives over non-relatives. If you are a college student, the odds are high that your parents are helping you out in some way, with tuition, room, board, clothes, or a method of transportation. The odds are also high that your parents are not helping your neighbor's children, even if they like them a lot. Parental aid, of course, is just one limited example of the wide-spread tendency of people to help those who carry copies of their genes. People also tend to help close genetic relatives more than distant genetic relatives, especially in life-or-death situations (Burnstein, Crandall, & Kitayama, 1994).

A task analysis involves analyzing this phenomenon by identifying the cognitive tasks that must be solved for it to occur using only information that would have been available in ancestral environments. For example, people need a way to identify those who carry copies of their genes—the problem of kin recognition. They must have solved this problem using only information that was available at the time, such as features of physical appearance. Furthermore, people need to solve the problem of gauging how closely related their genetic relatives are—the problem of closeness of kinship. People don't think about these things consciously most of the time; they happen automatically. A task analysis, in short, enables us to identify the adaptive problems that *must* be solved for the phenomenon we observe to occur.

Organization of Adaptive Problems

The bulk of this book is organized around human adaptive problems and the psycho-logical solutions that have evolved to solve them. We begin with survival problems be-cause without survival there can be no reproduction. We then move directly to the problem of mating, including the issues of selecting, attracting, and retaining a desir-able mate. Then we shift to the products of mating—children. Human children cannot survive and thrive without parental help, so this section covers the ways in which par-ents invest in their children. All of this occurs within a larger kin group, the strands of DNA that humans share with genetic relatives.

The book then shifts to the larger social sphere within which we live. Chapters on cooperation, aggression, conflict between the sexes, and social status form the core of this section.

The final chapter pans back to take a broader focus, covering two topics. The first focuses on the most unique aspect of human nature—culture. This chapter discusses the implications of having a stone-age mind in the modern world, and makes some speculations about the future of *Homo sapiens*. Next it focuses on reformulating the major branches of psychology using an evolutionary perspective, considering topics such as reasoning (cognitive psychology), dominance (personality psychology), psychopathology (clinical psychology), and social relationships (social psychology).

Summary

This chapter covered four topics: (1) the logic of generating hypotheses about our evolved psychological mechanisms, (2) the products of the evolutionary process, (3) the nature of evolved psychological mechanisms, and (4) the scientific procedures by which we test these hypotheses.

The logic of evolutionary hypotheses starts with an examination of the four levels of analysis, going from most general to most specific—general evolutionary theory, middle-level evolutionary theories, specific evolutionary hypotheses, and specific predictions about empirical phenomena derived from these hypotheses. One method of hypothesis generation is to start at the higher levels and move down. A middle-level theory can produce several hypotheses, each of which in turn yields several testable predictions. This can be described as the "top-down" strategy of hypothesis and prediction formation.

A second method is to start with a phenomenon known or observed to exist, such as the importance men attach to a woman's appearance. From this phenomenon one can generate hypotheses about the possible function for which it was designed. This bottom-up method is called reverse engineering, and is a useful supplement to the top-down method, especially because we know about the existence of many human phenomena long before we have solid scientific explanations for them.

The evolutionary process produces three products: adaptations, byproducts of adaptations, and random noise. Although all three products are important and evolutionary scientists differ in their estimates of the prevalence of these products, evolutionary psychologists tend to focus on adaptations. More specifically, they focus on one special subclass of adaptations that comprises human nature: psychological mechanisms.

Psychological mechanisms are information processing devices that exist in the form they do because they have solved specific problems of survival or reproduction recurrently over the long course of human evolutionary history. They are designed to take in only a narrow slice of information, transform that information through decision rules, and produce output in the form of physiological activity, information to other psychological mechanisms, or manifest behavior. The output of an evolved psychological mechanism is directed toward the solution to a specific adaptive problem. Evolved psychological mechanisms provide nonarbitrary criteria for "carving the mind at its joints," tend to be problem specific, and are large in number and functional in nature.

Once a hypothesis about an evolved psychological mechanism is formulated, the next step in the scientific endeavor is testing it. Testing evolutionary hypotheses relies on comparisons, finding out whether groups that are predicted to differ in a particular way actually do. This method can be used to test hypotheses by comparing different species, comparing males and females within a species, comparing individuals of each sex, and comparing the same individuals in different contexts.

After deciding on a particular comparative research design, the next step is to decide which source of data to use. Evolutionary psychology has a wealth of potential sources to draw on including the archeological record, contemporary hunter-gatherer societies, self-report, observer-report, data evoked from subjects in laboratory experiments, life-history data from public records, and products made by people.

Every source of data has strengths, but each also has limitations. Each provides information that typically cannot be obtained in the same form through other data sources. And each has flaws and weaknesses not shared by others. As a rule of thumb, therefore, studies that test evolutionary hypotheses using two or more data sources are better than studies that rely on a single source, thus establishing a firm empirical foundation.

The final section of this chapter outlined major classes of adaptive problems, some that form the core of the remainder of the book. Four classes of adaptive problems follow from modern evolutionary theory: problems of survival and growth, problems of mating, problems of parenting, and problems of genetic relatives. Additional insights into identifying adaptive problems come from knowledge of universal human structures, traditional tribal societies, paleoarcheology, task analysis, and current psychological mechanisms. Current mechanisms such as a fear of heights, a taste for fatty foods, and a preference for savannalike landscapes provide windows for viewing the nature of past adaptive problems.

PART TWO

Problems of Survival

This part consists of a single chapter devoted to what is known about human adaptations to the problems of survival. Darwin coined the phrase "the hostile forces of nature" to describe the forces that impede survival. Modern humans are descendants of ancestors who succeeded in combating these hostile forces. The beginning of Chapter 3 covers the problem of food acquisition and selection and examines hypotheses about how ancestral humans acquired food—the hunting hypothesis, the gathering hypothesis, and the scavenging hypothesis. Next human adaptations of habitat selection, the preferences that guide our decisions about places to live, are examined. Next we explore fears, phobias, anxieties, and other adaptations designed to combat various environmental dangers ranging from snakes to diseases. Then the intriguing question of whether humans are programmed to die is addressed, and Chapter 3 ends with a provocative analysis of a genuine evolutionary mystery—why some people commit suicide.

3 Combating the Hostile Forces of Nature

Human Survival Problems

There is nothing in the body that never goes wrong.
—Randolph Nesse and George Williams, 1994, p. 19

Differential reproduction is the "bottom line" of the evolutionary process, the engine that drives natural selection. To reproduce, organisms must survive—at least for a while. Charles Darwin summed it up best: "As more individuals are produced than can possibly survive, there must in every case be a struggle for existence, either one individual with another of the same species, or with the individuals of distinct species, or with the physical conditions of life" (1859, p. 53). So an examination of the adaptive problems of survival is a logical starting point for human evolutionary psychology.

Living poses a problem, or rather a number of problems. Although our current style of living protects us a great deal, everyone has at some point encountered forces that endanger survival. Darwin called these the "hostile forces of nature," and they include climate, weather, food shortages, toxins, diseases, parasites, predators, and hostile conspecifics (members of the same species).

Each of these hostile forces has created adaptive problems for humans—problems that have recurred in each generation over the long expanse of evolutionary history. The adaptive problems were important in the determination of successful survival solutions. They imposed a filter through which those who succumbed to disease, parasites, predators, harsh winters, and long dry summers, for example, failed to pass. As Darwin noted, "in the great battle of life . . . the structure of every organic being is related, in the most essential yet often hidden manner, to that of all the other organic beings, with which it comes into competition for food and residence, or from which it has to escape, or on which it preys" (1859, p. 61).

Let us look, then, at the fascinating collection of adaptations that make up the human survival machine—the mechanisms of the body and mind that have evolved to combat the hostile forces of nature. The first problem to be faced is finding fuel for the machine.

Food Acquisition and Selection

Without food and water we would all die: "Diet is the primary factor allowing or constraining the rest of a species' system of adaptations" (Tooby & DeVore, 1987, p. 234). Indeed, most animals spend more waking hours engaged in the search, capture, and intake of food than in any other activity (Rozin, 1996). Finding food is as necessary for survival as finding a mate is for reproduction. In the modern world humans simply go to the grocery store or a restaurant. Our ancestors, roaming the grassy savanna plains, did not have it so easy. Many obstacles lay between waking up hungry and dozing off at night with a full belly.

The most pressing general problem in food selection is how to obtain adequate amounts of calories and specific nutrients such as sodium, calcium, and zinc without at the same time consuming dangerous levels of toxins that could rapidly lead to death (Rozin & Schull, 1988). This requires searching for food; recognizing, capturing, handling, and consuming it; and digesting it to absorb its nutrients. And these activities must be coordinated with an assessment of one's internal metabolic state, including whether one is suffering from a negative energy balance—burning up more calories than are being taken in—or a specific nutritional deficiency (Rozin & Schull, 1988).

The problems of food selection become especially crucial for omnivores—species that regularly eat both plants and animals—for example, rats and humans. Eating a wide range of foods—plants, nuts, seeds, fruits, meats—increases one's odds of being poisoned because toxins are widespread throughout the plant world. A profound evolutionary insight is that plant toxins themselves are adaptations that reduce the odds of the plants' being eaten. Toxins thus help plants defend themselves from predators, as it were, but they hurt humans and other animals that rely on the plants for survival. In a very real sense, our ancestors were in conflict with plants.

Food Selection in Rats

Rats, one of the most commonly studied species of omnivores, provide an instructive example for illuminating the adaptive problems of food and fluid selection. Rats solve the problem of food seeking and consumption in infancy by getting all the needed calories from mother's milk. This prevents the baby rat from consuming lethal toxins until it can start foraging for food on its own.

Rats have evolved taste preferences for sweet foods, which provide rich sources of calories, and avoid bitter foods, which tend to contain toxins. Rats adaptively adjust their eating behavior in response to at least three internal states: deficits in water, calories, and salt (Rozin & Schull, 1988). Experiments show that rats display an immediate liking for salt the first time they experience a salt deficiency. They likewise increase their intake of sweets and water when their energy and fluids become depleted. These appear to be specific evolved mechanisms, designed to deal with the adaptive problem of food selection, and coordinate the rat's consumption patterns with its physical needs (Rozin, 1976).

That is not all, however. Rats show an astonishing *neophobia*, or a strong aversion to new foods. Rats typically sample new and unfamiliar food only in very small doses, and when they do so, they eat the new foods separately—never together. By keeping samples small and new foods separate, the rats have the opportunity to learn what makes them sick, thus avoiding a potentially deadly overconsumption of poisons. Interestingly, when a rat eats both a familiar food and a new food at the same meal and subsequently gets sick, it thereafter avoids only the new food. It seems to "assume" that the familiar food is safe and the new food is the source of the sickness.

So even the rat has an elaborate set of evolved mechanisms to solve the adaptive problems of food selection. The adaptive solutions of another omnivore—humans—are no less elaborate.

Food Selection in Humans

All over the world, people spend more money on food than practically anything else. People in Western countries such as Germany and the United States spend 21 percent of their income on food, which is second only to income spent on leisure activities (Rozin, 1996). In less wealthy countries such as India and China fully 50 percent of all income is spent on food. World wide, however, food takes center stage in parent-infant interactions. There may be nothing more important for survival early in life than determining what should be ingested or avoided (Rozin, 1996).

The sharing of food is a major social activity for humans. Among some societies such as the Kwakiutl of the northwest coast of North America, rich men throw "pot-latches" for the group, in which they feast on food and drink for hours and evaluate a man's status by the lavishness of the spread (Piddocke, 1965; Vayda, 1961). Other cultures such as the !Kung San of Botswana have specific words for special kinds of hunger, such as being "meat hungry" (Shostak, 1981). Sharing food is also a strategy of courtship, a sign of the closeness of relationships, and a means for reconciling after a conflict (Buss, 1994). In America, family holidays such as Thanksgiving typically involve lavish feasts at which turkey, stuffing, cranberries, and pumpkin pie are shared by all.

Fishermen tell tales about the fish they catch, farmers about the size of their vegetables, hunters about their prowess in taking down a large animal. Failure to provide food can lead a man to lose status in the group (Hill & Hurtado, 1996; Holmberg, 1950). Further, it is not uncommon among cultures such as the Ganda and Thonga tribes in Central Africa and the Ashanti in the coastal region of Nigeria for women to seek to divorce husbands who fail to provide food (Betzig, 1989). Even the myths and religions of cultures abound with stories of food and drink—Eve and Adam eating the apple, Jesus turning water into wine, the three small fish and two barley loaves multiplying to feed the masses and, the prohibitions against eating pork.

Food and its consumption have become frequently used metaphors. We find tall tales "hard to swallow," thick prose "difficult to digest," a stroke of good fortune "sweet," a good book "juicy," and a social disappointment "bitter" (Lakoff & Johnson, 1980). Food, in short, permeates our psychological preoccupations, verbal discourse, social interaction, and religious beliefs on a daily basis.

Humans have evolved mechanisms to combat natural toxins. The things that we find terrible smelling and bitter tasting, for example, are not random. Gagging, spitting, and vomiting are responses designed to prevent us from eating harmful things or getting rid of those that happen to make it past our taste and smell defenses. The fact

Food shortages are one of the most important "hostile forces of nature" for many species. In humans, food sharing serves functions beyond securing fuel for the body, including courtship attraction and solidifying social bonds.

that many children dislike vegetables such as broccoli and brussels sprouts is not by chance. These vegetables contain the chemical allylisothiocynate, which can be toxic, especially to children (Nesse & Williams, 1994).

One cross-cultural study asked Americans and Japanese to list the things they found most disgusting. Feces and other body wastes were the most frequently mentioned items, at 25 percent of the written responses (Rozin, 1996). Feces in particular are known to harbor harmful elements, including parasites and toxins, and are particularly dangerous to humans. After all, feces are what the body is getting rid of. Other responses to the survey included poor hygiene (possible conduit for disease transmission), body boundary violations such as a gaping wound, inappropriate sex, and death. Rozin (1996) interprets these cross-cultural data as a universal human abhorrence for any reminder that humans have commonalities with animals. It seems plausible, however, that humans have evolved a predisposition to be disgusted by specific classes of objects—such as feces and other disease conduits—that jeopardized their survival. The disgust reaction, according to this adaptationist account, would function to protect the body from ingesting or coming into contact with substances that might be detrimental to human health and survival.

At this point we cannot judge whether either Rozin's (1996) explanation or the adaptationist explanation (or some other explanation) is adequate to clarify the nature and patterning of disgust reactions, in part because so little research has been devoted to exploring disgust. Rozin (1996) notes that among the eight leading textbooks in introductory psychology, with an average length of 668 pages, the median number of pages devoted to the entire topic of what humans eat and why is less than half a page. We can look forward to future research to clarify the nature of human adaptations to the survival problems of food selection and avoidance.

Sickness in Pregnant Women

During the first three months of pregnancy some women develop pregnancy sickness—a heightened sensitivity and a nauseous reaction to particular foods commonly known as morning sickness. The percentage of women who report experiencing such reactions range from 75 (Brandes, 1967) to 89 percent (Tierson, Olsen, & Hook, 1986). Actual vomiting percentages are lower, with roughly 55 percent of the women reporting that symptom. Profet (1992) argues that all these figures probably underestimate the prevalence of pregnancy sickness for two reasons. First, the interviews with the women were conducted *after* the peak period of pregnancy sickness, and therefore index only the instances remembered from earlier weeks or months. Second, the studies all define pregnancy sickness as the presence of nausea or vomiting and fail to include food aversions. If food aversions are added to the definition, as Profet believes they should be, then it is likely that close to 100 percent of all pregnant women would report pregnancy sickness during the first trimester.

Women who experience pregnancy sickness often seek remedies to alleviate it, from folk advice to physician's prescriptions. Although the term "sickness" implies that something is malfunctioning, recent evidence suggests precisely the opposite. Profet has marshaled a powerful case for viewing pregnancy sickness as an adaptation that prevents mothers from consuming and absorbing *teratogens*—toxins that might be harmful to the developing baby.

As noted above, many plants produce toxins as a defense against predators. These toxins occur in a wide variety of plants, including many we consume regularly such as apples, bananas, potatoes, oranges, and celery. The black pepper that we use to spice our food contains sarole, which is both carcinogenic (causes cancer) and mutagenic (causes mutations). The special problem that humans face, which becomes more pronounced during pregnancy, is how to get the valuable nutrients from plants without at the same time incurring the costs of their toxins.

Plants and the predators that consume them seem to have coevolved (Profet, 1992). Plants signal their toxicity with chemicals. Vegetables such as cabbage, cauliflower, broccoli, and brussels sprouts, for example, get their strong tastes from allylisothiocyanate. Rhubarb leaves contain oxalate (Nesse & Williams, 1994). Humans find these chemicals bitter and unpleasant—an adaptation that helps them avoid consuming toxins. At the same time, the chemicals help the plant by deterring animals from eating it.

The specific foods pregnant women report finding distasteful include coffee (129 women out of the sample of 400), meat (124), alcohol (79), and vegetables (44). In sharp contrast, only three women reported aversions to bread and not a single woman reported an aversion to cereals (Tierson et al., 1985). Another study of one hundred women experiencing their first pregnancies found similar results (Dickens & Threthowan, 1971). Of the one hundred women, thirty-two described aversions to coffee, tea, and cocoa;

eighteen cited aversions to vegetables; and sixteen cited aversions to meat and eggs. Many became nauseated when smelling fried or barbecued food, which contains carcinogens, and some nearly fainted when smelling spoiled meat, which is teeming with toxin-producing bacteria. If pregnant women do consume these foods, they are more likely to vomit. Vomiting prevents the toxins from entering the mother's bloodstream and passing through the placenta to the developing fetus, thus is a seemingly important and healthful reaction (Profet, 1992).

A variety of sources of evidence support Profet's hypothesis that pregnancy sickness is an adaptation to prevent the ingestion of teratogens. First, the foods pregnant women find repugnant appear to correspond to those carrying the highest doses of toxins. Meats, for example, often contain toxins due to fungal and bacterial decomposition (Nesse & Williams, 1994). Likewise, certain vegetables such as cabbage, cauliflower, and brussels sprouts contain the carcinogen allylisothiocyanate (Buttery, Guadagni, Ling, Seifert, & Lipton, 1976). Second, pregnancy sickness occurs precisely at the time when the fetus is most vulnerable to toxins, roughly two to four weeks after conception, which is when many of the fetus's major organs are being formed. Third, pregnancy sickness decreases around the eighth week and generally disappears entirely by the fourteenth week, coinciding with the end of the sensitive period for organ development.

Perhaps the clinching piece of evidence comes from the success of the pregnancy itself. Women who do *not* have pregnancy sickness during the first trimester are roughly three times more likely to experience a spontaneous abortion than women who do experience such sickness (Profet, 1992). In one study of 3,853 pregnant women, only 3.8 percent of the women who experienced pregnancy sickness had spontaneous abortions, whereas 10.4 percent of the women who had not experienced pregnancy sickness had spontaneous abortions (Yerushalmy & Milkovich, 1965). Women who experience pregnancy sickness seem more likely to have successful pregnancies and carry to term. In short, it appears to be an adaptation that prevents women from eating foods that would harm developing fetuses.

Adaptations are expected to be universal, so cross-cultural evidence is critical. Although pregnancy sickness has not been explored much in other cultures, the ethnographic record contains evidence of its existence among the !Kung of Botswana, the Efe Pygmies of Zaire, and the Australian Aborigines. The mother of a !Kung woman, Nisa, reported why she suspected that Nisa was pregnant: "If you are throwing up like this, it means you have a little thing inside your stomach" (Shostak, 1981, p. 187).

Profet's analysis of pregnancy sickness highlights one of the benefits of adaptationist thinking. A phenomenon previously regarded as an illness, and hence perhaps something dysfunctional and to be avoided, appears to be an exquisitely tailored mechanism designed to combat a hostile force of nature—one that would impair the survival of a child even before it is born.

The Hunting Hypothesis

Aside from illuminating modern human taste preferences, another reason food acquisition is important from an evolutionary perspective is that ancestral methods of secur-

Large game hunting typically requires cooperation and communication among several hunters. According to the hunting hypothesis, large game hunting provided a major driving force for human evolution, with ramifications for tool making, tool use, language, and the enlargement of the brain.

ing food have been linked to the rapid emergence of modern humans. The importance of hunting in human evolution, for example, has been a major source of controversy in anthropology and evolutionary psychology. One widely held view is the model of "man the hunter" (Tooby & DeVore, 1987). According to this view, the transition from mere foraging to large-game hunting provided a major impetus for human evolution, with a cascading set of consequences including a rapid expansion of tool making and tool use, the development of a large human brain, and the evolution of complex language skills necessary for communication on cooperative hunts.

All known human groups consume far more meat than any other primate species. Among chimpanzees, for example, meat constitutes a small 4 percent of the diet. Among humans, estimates of the proportion of meat in the diet range from 20 to 40 percent, and go as high as 90 percent during cold and hunting seasons. Even the lowest estimates of the percentage of meat in the human diet are far higher than the highest estimates for any one of the other 222 primate species. Furthermore, it is extremely difficult for humans to get all essential nutrients, such as cyanocobolamine, from an exclusively vegetarian diet (Tooby & DeVore, 1987). This suggests that meat has been a central feature of the human diet for thousands of generations.

Modern tribal societies often hunt as a major method for food acquisition. For example, the Aka Pygmies, who dwell in the tropical rain forests of the Central African Republic, spend roughly 56 percent of their subsistence time hunting, 27 percent of their subsistence time gathering, and 17 percent of their subsistence time processing food (see Hewlett, 1991). The !Kung of Botswana, another example, are excellent hunters and devote a lot of time to hunting and talking about hunting. On average, hunting provides 40 percent of the calories in the !Kung diet, but this can dip below 20 percent in a lean season and can reach more than 90 percent during a successful hunting season (Lee, 1979).

!Kung men differ greatly in their hunting prowess, but there are strong sanctions against boasting. The !Kung have an interesting strategy of promoting sharing and cooperation—they say that "the owner of the arrow is the owner of the meat" (Lee,

1979, p. 247), even if the owner of the arrow is not the one who shot it. In fact, there is widespread sharing of arrows, which reinforces cooperation and helps distribute responsibility for the kill. The owner of the arrow is in charge of distributing the meat, which is shared communally, often with the man's kin, mate, and friends. Stinginess with meat causes a rapid decline in prestige and status.

Our bodies are walking archives that show a long history of meat eating (Allman, 1994). Contrast the gut of an ape with that of a human. The ape's gut consists mainly of a colon, a large winding tube well designed for processing a vegetarian diet permeated with tough fiber. The human gut, in contrast, is dominated by the small intestines, distinguishing us from all other primates. The small intestines provide the place where proteins are rapidly broken down and nutrients absorbed, suggesting that humans have a long evolutionary history of eating protein-rich food such as meat.

The fossil record of the teeth of human ancestors provides another clue to diet. The thin enamel coating on human tooth fossils does not show the heavy wear and tear known to occur from a diet mainly of fibrous plants.

Vitamin evidence provides a third clue. The human body cannot produce vitamins A and B12, even though these are vital for human survival. Precisely these two vitamins are found in meat.

A fourth clue comes from a bounty of bones found in Olduvai Gorge in Tanzania, Africa, discovered in the summer of 1979 by three independent researchers, Richard Potts, Pat Shipman, and Henry Bunn (Leakey & Lewin, 1992). These bones were ancient, estimated to be nearly two million years old, and many bore cut marks, tangible evidence of ancestral butchers. All of these clues suggest a long evolutionary history in which meat was an essential part of the diet of human ancestors.

The Provisioning Hypothesis.   Proponents of the hunting hypothesis argue that it can explain a large number of unusual features of human evolution (Tooby & DeVore, 1987). Perhaps most important, it can explain the fact that human males are unique among primates in their heavy parental investment in children. This has been called the *provisioning hypothesis*. Because meat is an economical and concentrated food resource it can be transported effectively back to the home base to feed the young. In contrast, it is far less efficient to transport low-calorie food over long distances. Hunting thus provides a plausible explanation for the emergence of the heavy investment and provisioning that men channel toward their children. In fact, high male investment among mammals tends to be extremely rare in the absence of carnivorousness (Tooby & DeVore, 1987).

Although provisioning is often regarded as the most important adaptive explanation for the evolution of hunting, the hunting hypothesis can also explain several other aspects that characterize humans. One is the emergence of *strong male coalitions*, which appear to be characteristic of humans worldwide (Tooby & DeVore, 1987). The fact that human males tend to form coalitions, characterized by cooperation over long periods of time, must be explained, and hunting provides one such plausible explanation (chimpanzees form male-male coalitions as well, but these tend to be transient and opportunistic rather than enduring; see de Waal, 1982). Large game hunting requires the coordinated action of cooperators. Single individuals can rarely succeed in taking down a large animal. The primary plausible alternatives to hunting as a hypothesis for the emergence of male coalitions are group-on-group aggression and defense and in-group political alliances, activities that also could have selected for strong male coalitions (Tooby & DeVore, 1987).

Hunting can also account for the emergence in humans of *strong reciprocal altruism* and *social exchange.* Humans seem to be unique among primates in showing extensive reciprocal relationships that can last years, decades, or a lifetime (Tooby & DeVore, 1987). Meat from a large game animal comes in quantities that far exceed what a single hunter could possibly consume. Furthermore, hunting success is highly variable; a hunter who is successful one week might fail the next (Hill & Hurtado, 1996). These conditions favor food sharing from hunting. The costs to a hunter of giving away meat he cannot eat immediately are low because he cannot consume all the meat himself anyway and leftovers will soon spoil. The benefits can be large, however, when the recipients of his food return the favor at a later time. Thus, hunting can help explain the emergence in humans of the prolonged social exchanges characteristic to our species.

Hunting also provides a plausible explanation for the *sexual division of labor.* Men's larger size, upper body strength, and ability to throw projectiles accurately over long distances makes them well suited for hunting. Ancestral women, often preoccupied by pregnancy and children, were less well suited for hunting. Among modern hunter-gatherers the division of labor is strong—men hunt and women gather, often carrying their young with them. The sexes can exchange food—meat provided by men from the hunt and plant foods provided by women from gathering. In sum, hunting provides a plausible explanation for the strong division of labor that characterizes modern humans (Tooby & DeVore, 1987).

Finally, hunting also provides a powerful explanation for the emergence of stone tool use. Stone tools are regularly found at the same sites as bones from large animals—sites dating back two million years. Their main function seems to have been for killing and then separating the valuable meat from the bones and cartilage. In short, hunting provides an explanation for the emergence and refinement of stone tools that clearly characterized our ancestors.

In summary, while the provisioning of women and children is often hypothesized to be the primary adaptive explanation for the origins of hunting, the hunting hypothesis can explain a host of other human phenomena as well. In addition to the heavily male parental investment in children, it can at least partially explain the emergence of strong coalitions among men, reciprocal alliance and social exchange among friends, the sexual division of labor, and the development of stone tools.

The Showoff Hypothesis.   Hunting produces resources that are unique among the food groups in two respects. First, meat comes in large packages, sometimes larger than the hunter and his immediate family can consume. Second, the packages are unpredictable. A successful streak of taking down two large animals in a week can be followed by a long period of less successful hunting. These qualities establish the conditions for the sharing of meat beyond the confines of one's immediate family, and these periodic "bonanzas" would become known to everyone in the community (Hawkes, 1991).

These considerations led anthropologist Kristen Hawkes to propose the *showoff hypothesis* (Hawkes, 1991). Hawkes suggests that women would prefer to have neighbors who are showoffs—men who go for the rare but valuable bonanzas of meat—because they benefit by gaining a portion of it. If women benefit from these gifts, especially in times of shortage, then it would be to their advantage to reward men who pursue the showoff strategy. They could give such hunters favorable treatment, such as siding with them in times of dispute, providing health care to their children, and, perhaps most important, offering sexual favors.

Men pursuing the risky hunting strategy would therefore benefit in several ways. By gaining increased sexual access to women they increase their odds of fathering more children. The favored treatment of their children from neighbors increases the survival and possible reproductive success of those children. Finally, the costs to men of pursuing this showoff strategy might not be large—although large game hunting certainly entails risks that cannot be discounted, the large meat bounties are far more than the hunter or his family can consume, and so they do not suffer by sharing the meat widely.

Some evidence supports the showoff hypothesis, mostly coming from in-depth study of the Ache, a native population of eastern Paraguay (Hill & Hurtado, 1996; Hill & Kaplan, 1988). Historically the Ache have been a nomadic group and have used both hunting and gathering to secure food. Anthropologists Kim Hill and Hillard Kaplan lived with the Ache for several years, using data from foraging trips in the forest directly observed between 1980 and 1985. On the foraging trips the Ache move in small bands, shifting to a new camp almost daily. On a typical day the Ache band sets out from the camp in the early morning, starting in a single file but then fanning out systematically. The men hunt for game or search for honey. When hunting, the men space themselves out so that they do not overlap in their search efforts, but remain close enough so that they can call to one another if they need help taking down game.

Among the Ache, although gathered food is consumed primarily by the gatherer and his immediate family, meat from the hunt is distributed widely within the group. In fact, the hunter himself sometimes gets less meat than others outside his nuclear family (Kaplan, Hill, & Hurtado, 1984). Hawkes (1991) found that fully 84 percent of the resources acquired by men were shared outside the immediate family—that is, to people other than himself, his wife, and his children. In contrast, only 58 percent of the foods gathered by women were shared outside of the immediate family. This is true even of the foods they collect. Ache men are more likely than Ache women to go after foods such as honey that come in larger packets and can be widely shared, rather than foods such as palm starch or virella (Hawkes, 1991).

The showoff hypothesis can be considered a rival of the provisioning hypothesis, at least in its pure form. Men hunted, Hawkes argues, not to provide for their own families, but rather to gain the benefits of sharing their bounty with neighbors. The fact that successful Ache hunters do benefit in the currencies of increased sexual access and better survival of their children supports the showoff hypothesis. As Kristen Hawkes concluded:

"men may choose risky endeavors, not in spite of, but partly because the gamble gives them the chance to claim favors they can win by showing off" (1991, p. 51). Nonetheless, the two hypotheses are not incompatible. Men may have hunted to provide for their families *and* to gain the status, sexual, and survival benefits outside of their families.

In summary, the hunting hypothesis provides a powerful explanation for a wide variety of phenomena that characterize humans but not other primates. It provides a plausible account of heavy male parental investment, the formation of male coalitions, the extended levels of reciprocity and social exchange, the sexual division of labor, and the use of stone tools. Despite these features, the hunting hypothesis has been attacked on various grounds. It turns out, for example, that the majority of calories even in hunter-gatherer societies are obtained through gathering. In these societies hunting provides no more than 20 to 40 percent of calories in the diet (Lee, 1979; Tooby & DeVore, 1987). This leads to an alternative proposal that gathering was primary and hunting trivial in human evolution.

The Gathering Hypothesis

In contrast to the view that men provided the critical evolutionary impetus for the emergence of modern humans through hunting, an opposing view suggests that women provided the critical impetus, through gathering (Tanner, 1983; Tanner & Zihlman, 1976; Zihlman, 1981). According to this hypothesis, stone tools were invented and used not for hunting, but rather for digging and gathering various plants. The gathering hypothesis would explain the transition from forests to savanna woodlands and grasslands because the use of tools made the securing of gathered food possible and more economical (Tanner, 1983). After the invention of stone tools for gathering was the invention of containers to hold the food and the elaboration of tools for hunting, skinning, and butchering animals. According to the gathering hypothesis, securing plant food through the use of stone tools provided the primary evolutionary impetus for the emergence of modern humans. According to this view, hunting only came much later and did not play a role in the emergence of modern humans.

The gathering hypothesis provides a useful corrective to the exclusive focus on male hunting in the development of humans and helps account for the fact that the diet of our primate relatives, and hence likely our prehominid ancestors, consisted mainly of plant food. It also helps account for the fact that roughly 50 to 80 percent of the diets of modern hunter-gatherers consist of gathered plant foods. Finally, it highlights the fact that all members of the population—females and males—are important in evolutionary terms—women have often been overlooked as central agents in the evolution of modern humans (Hrdy, 1981).

Women worldwide spend considerable time and energy acquiring food and caring for children (e.g., Hurtado, Hill, Kaplan, & Hurtado, 1992; Shostak, 1981). These two activities sometimes conflict with each other. Gathering in subtropical forests, for example, poses substantial risks to infants and children. Ache children risk bites from ants, bees, wasps, snakes, spiders, poisonous caterpillars, mosquitoes, gnats, and ticks (Hurtado et al., 1992). Thorns and stinging nettles threaten to jab the young as the mother

In nearly every traditional society, food secured through gathering accounts for the majority of calories consumed by all members of the group. According to the gathering hypothesis, gathering gave rise to the making and use of stone tools, providing a driving force for the evolution of modern humans.

forages through the brush. It should come as no surprise that women with younger and more numerous children spend less time gathering than women with older children or women who are postreproductive (Hurtado et al., 1992; Lee, 1979). By gathering less, women with young children sacrifice some calories to better care for their children.

Furthermore, a key predictor of the amount of time a woman spends foraging is how much food her husband brings back. Women with husbands who provide well spend less time foraging than women with husbands who provide little (Hurtado et al., 1992). Women seem to adjust their behavior to changing adaptive demands, increasing gathering to compensate for a poor provider and decreasing it to avoid exposing young children to environmental hazards.

Comparing the Hunting and Gathering Hypotheses

Despite the importance of women's gathering, the gathering hypothesis has been criticized by those who don't think it can successfully explain the divergence of humans in the primate lineage (see Tooby & DeVore, 1987). Men worldwide do, in fact, hunt. If gathering were the sole or even the most productive human method of food getting, then why wouldn't men just gather, and stop wasting their time hunting? The gathering hypothesis, in other words, does not account for the division of labor between the sexes observed across a wide variety of cultures, with men hunting and women gathering.

The hunting hypothesis, in contrast, can explain this division of labor. It explains why women do not hunt regularly—they are occupied with pregnancy and dependent children, which makes hunting a more onerous, more risky, and less profitable enterprise. In short, hunting is more cost effective for men than for women. In addition, the division of labor allows both types of resources—animals and plants—to be exploited.

Another problem with the gathering hypothesis is that plant collecting is something that is also done by the great apes. Stone tools, of course, would make gathering more efficient, but the increment does not seem powerful enough to explain the massive changes that occurred in the transition to modern humans. The gathering hypothesis, for example, does not explain the high parental investment by human males. It does not account for the emergence of a powerful male coalitional psychology. And it does not account for why humans penetrated many environments that lack plant resources—the Eskimos, for example, live almost entirely on animal meat and fat.

The gathering hypothesis has trouble explaining why humans form strong extended reciprocal alliances that can last for decades. It also has trouble explaining why women should share their food with men, who would be essentially parasites sponging off women's labor unless they gave them something in return, such as meat. An exchange of gathered food for meat, however, could explain why women would have been willing to share with men the food they collected and processed.

In summary, it is clear that over millions of years primate and human ancestral females have gathered plant foods. Stone tools undoubtedly made plant gathering more efficient, and gathering likely played a key role in reciprocal exchanges between the sexes. But the gathering hypothesis falls short in accounting for several known facts about humans—the division of labor between the sexes, the emergence of high male parental investment, and the sharp differences between humans and apes.

Meat has clearly been central to human evolution. But perhaps we did not always hunt. Perhaps we exploited the killings of other predators. This is the basis of a third hypothesis for human food acquisition: the scavenging hypothesis.

The Scavenging Hypothesis

The scavenging hypothesis argues that at least some of the meat our ancestors did eat might have been secured through *scavenging*, the retrieval of dead carcasses killed by other animals (Isaac, 1978; Shipman, 1985). Perhaps the stone tools found along with the animal bones were designed for processing scavenged remains rather than fresh kill from the hunt.

Let's examine the evidence. In addition to cut marks, many bones found at the "stone cache" at Olduvai Gorge in Africa bore gnaw marks, suggesting that other animals had feasted on the bones (and the meat on them) as well. So did those bones come from animals hunted by ancestral humans? Or did ancestral humans simply scavenge the remains of prey killed by other predators?

Unfortunately the evidence is not definitive. Sometimes the gnaw marks were on top of the cut marks, suggesting that humans hunted the animals and left the remains to be scavenged by other animals. But other times the cut marks were on top of the gnaw marks, suggesting that our ancestors may have capitalized on the kills of other carnivores. Of all the bones with both types of marks, about half showed the cut mark on top of the gnaw mark; the other half showed the gnaw mark on top of the cut mark (Leakey & Lewin, 1992).

These findings suggest that humans might have been both scavengers and hunters. In fact, in nature we find very few pure predators (the cheetah is an exception) and few pure scavengers (the vulture is an exception). Most meat-eating animals do some scavenging and some hunting. Perhaps human ancestors also did a bit of both.

Nonetheless, the scavenging hypothesis leaves too many holes, at least in its suggestion that scavenging was the primary source of meat for our ancestors (Tooby & DeVore, 1987). First, within any geographical range kills by large predators are rare. Humans would have had to cover extremely large ranges to find enough meat for themselves and their families from scavenged remains. Second, scavenging depends on what is left over after the predator that killed the animal has feasted. This would have required our ancestors to travel even greater distances to get enough food to subsist.

A third problem is that humans would have had to compete with dozens of other species for the small remains—insects, vultures, microorganisms, mammalian carnivores, and perhaps even the predator or its kin returning to the site of the kill (Tooby & DeVore, 1987, p. 221). Most mammalian scavengers are themselves predators, so our ancestors would likely have had to compete with them. Heavy competition for the remains would have made scavenging quite dangerous for our ancestors.

Fourth, meat left for any length of time quickly rots, proliferating with microorganisms and maggots that render the meat dangerous for humans. Primates, in fact, rarely eat dead carcasses unless they have killed them themselves (DeVore & Hall, 1965; Strum, 1981). Furthermore, modern tribal societies rarely scavenge, despite the fact that they can neutralize many of the parasites through cooking (Tooby & DeVore, 1987).

In short, the scavenging hypothesis runs into formidable difficulties as a major account of human food acquisition. Occasional scavenging might have occurred among our ancestors, but it could not have rivaled hunting as a major means of food acquisition.

The controversy continues, with some arguing that no single food collection pattern characterized our ancestors. Rather, the tremendous diversity of food-procuring techniques—gathering, scavenging, hunting, and fishing—defies any singular ancestral portrait.

These debates are often filled with ideology, and accusations of ideological bias are directed against all competing theorists. Some argue that the view of "man the hunter" glorifies men too much, imbuing this male-dominated activity with more importance than the female-dominated gathering, thus supporting "patriarchy" or enforcing the view of male dominance and superiority. Others argue that those advocating the gathering hypothesis are driven by a reverse bias, the desire to glorify women's contribution to the food needed for human survival. One must sift through the ideology to get a reasonable sense of the importance of hunting and gathering (and occasional scavenging) in human evolutionary history.

In summary, although the controversy has not yet been settled there is clear agreement that human ancestors were omnivores and that both meat and gathered plants were important ingredients in their diet. The high prevalence of male hunters and female gatherers among tribal societies, although not definitive evidence, provides one more clue that both activities are part of the human pattern of procuring food.

Finding a Place to Live: Shelter and Landscape Preferences

Imagine you are on a camping trip (Orians & Heerwagen, 1992). You wake up in the morning with an empty stomach and need to urinate. As you go about your business, the sun beats down on your head and thirst parches your throat, and you quickly come to appreciate the nearby stream with its cold, clean water. But it's time to head off for the day. You pack your gear and look around you. In which directions are you drawn? Some seem beautiful. They promise attractive vistas, perhaps a running stream for water and fishing, lush vegetation, and a safe place to camp. But there are also dangers that you must attend to—wild animals, steep cliffs, the harsh heat of the sun.

Now imagine that this camping trip lasts not a few days or weeks, but your entire lifetime! This is what our ancestors faced, roaming the savanna of Africa, continuously looking for habitable places to land, if only momentarily. Because there are large costs to choosing a poor place to inhabit, for example one with meager food resources and vulnerability to hostile forces, and great benefits to choosing a good place to inhabit, one can readily hypothesize that selection would have forged in us adaptations designed to make our choices wisely. This hypothesis has been the subject of extensive testing by evolutionary psychologists (Kaplan, 1992; Orians & Heerwagen, 1992).

The Savanna Hypothesis

Orians (1980, 1986) has championed the *savanna hypothesis* of habitat preferences. This hypothesis states that selection has favored preferences, motivations, and cognitions to explore and settle in environments abundant with the resources needed to sustain life while simultaneously avoiding environments lacking resources and posing risks to survival. The savanna of Africa, widely believed to be the site in which humans originated, fulfills these requirements.

The savanna houses large terrestrial animals, including many primates such as baboons and chimpanzees. It offers more game for meat than do tropical forests, more vegetation for grazing, and wide-open vistas conducive to a nomadic lifestyle (Orians & Heerwagen, 1992). Trees there protect sensitive human skin from the harsh sun and provide a refuge for escaping from danger.

Studies of landscape preferences offer support for the savanna hypothesis. In one study subjects from Australia, Argentina, and the United States evaluated a series of photographs of trees taken in Kenya by the biologist Gordon Orians. Each photograph focused on a single tree, and pictures were taken under standardized conditions such as in similar daylight and weather. The trees selected for inclusion in the study varied in four qualities—canopy shape, canopy density, trunk height, and branching pattern. At the time of this writing the final data analyses had not been reported, but the authors could offer a preliminary summary of the results. Participants from all three cultures showed similar judgments. All showed a strong preference for savannalike trees—those forming a moderately dense canopy and trunks that separated in two near the ground. Participants also tended to dislike skimpy and dense canopies (Orians & Heerwagen, 1992).

A large body of evidence supports the conclusion that natural environments are consistently preferred to human-made environments (Kaplan & Kaplan, 1982). One study (Kaplan 1992) summarizes the results from thirty different studies in which participants rated color photographs or slides on a five-point scale. The studies varied widely, including scenes from Western Australia, Egypt, Korea, British Columbia, and the United States. Participants included college students and teenagers, Koreans and Australians. Based on this large body of research, it is clear that natural environments are consistently preferred over human-made environments. And when the latter contain trees and other vegetation, they are rated more positively than similar environments that lack trees or vegetation (Ulrich, 1983). Subjects placed in a stressful situation show less physiological distress when viewing slides of nature scenes (Ulrich, 1986). These results may not be surprising, but they support the notion that humans have evolved preferences that are consistent across at least some cultures and that different landscapes can have profound effects on our psychology and physiology.

In a more elaborate extension of the savanna hypothesis, Orians and Heerwagen (1992) proposed three stages of habitat selection. *Stage 1* may be called *selection*. On first encounter with a habitat or landscape, the key decision is whether to explore or to leave. These initial responses tend to be highly affective or emotional. Open environments devoid of cover are abandoned. Completely closed forest canopies, which restrict viewing and movement, also are abandoned.

If the initial reaction is positive in the selection stage, people enter *stage 2*, which may be called *information gathering*. In this stage the environment is explored for its resources and potential dangers. One study determined that people have a great fondness for mystery at this stage (Kaplan, 1992). People tend to like paths that wind around a bend until they are out of sight and hills that promise something lying beyond them. Mapping also includes an assessment of risk. The same promise of resources around the bend may contain a snake or a lion. So mapping at this stage also entails scrutiny for places for hiding, refuges to conceal oneself and one's family. Multiple places for concealment also afford evaluation from multiple perspectives and multiple routes for escape, should that prove necessary.

Stage 3 of habitat selection may be called *exploitation*, and involves another decision about whether to stay in the habitat long enough to reap the benefits of the resources it offers. This decision involves tradeoffs—the same site that provides good foraging may leave one vulnerable to predators (Orians & Heerwagen, 1992). A craggy cliff that provides good opportunities for surveillance may leave one at risk of making a precipitous fall. Thus, the final decision in this stage, to stay long enough to reap the benefits of the habitat, requires complex cognitive calculations.

There are further complexities. Another set of calculations pertains to the time frame of decisions (Orians & Heerwagen, 1992). This temporal dimension can range from the need to assess immediate transitory states to predictions of events over the course of years. Weather patterns are crucial to immediate time frames. Thunder and lighting may signal the need for immediate cover. Humans have poor vision at night, and so have to take cover as darkness falls. The lengthening of shadows and reddening of the sun as it approaches the horizon may trigger the selection of a temporary campsite.

On a longer time frame are seasonal changes, a shift from winter to spring or fall to winter. Seasonal changes bring new information that must be freshly evaluated. Spring brings the budding of lush vegetation and the promise of ripe fruit. Fall turns vegetation brown and signals an impending winter. The savanna hypothesis predicts that people will show strong preferences for signals of harvest—the greenness of grass, the budding of trees, the appearance of fruit on bushes. Bare tree limbs and brown grass should therefore be less agreeable. As noted by Orians and Heerwagen: "It may be difficult for many of us, with the year-round supplies of a wide array of fruits and vegetables in our supermarkets, to understand the importance of the first salad greens of the season to people throughout most of human history" (1992, p. 569).

Flowers, although not commonly eaten by humans, are universally loved. They signal the onset of greens and fruits long absent during the winter months. Bringing flowers to hospital patients may have a real purpose: Studies show the mere presence of flowers in a hospital room improves the rate of recovery of hospital patients and puts them in a more positive psychological state (Watson & Burlingame, 1960).

Although tests of the savanna hypothesis have just begun, and many of its tenets and predictions remain to be evaluated empirically, the results so far are promising. Given the supreme importance for survival of selecting a place to live, from transient habitats to permanent homes, it would be astonishing if evolution left our environmental preferences untouched.

Selection has grooved and scored our environmental preferences as much as our food and mate preferences. Although we live in a modern world far from the savanna plain, we modify our environments to correspond to that ancient habitat. Humans create architecture that mimics the comfortable sensation of living under a forest canopy. We love views, and hate living in basements. We recover more quickly from hospital stays if we can view trees outside the hospital window (Ulrich, 1984). And we paint pictures and shoot photographs that recreate the vistas and mysteries of an ancient savanna habitat (Appleton, 1975).

Combating Predators and Other Environmental Dangers: Fears, Phobias, Anxieties, and "Evolutionary Memories"

All humans experience anxiety and fear that signal danger on certain occasions. The adaptive rationale for human fears seems obvious—they cause us to deal with the source of danger, serving a survival function. This is widely recognized, as reflected in a recent book, *The Gift of Fear: Survival Signals that Protect Us from Violence*, which was on the *New York Times* bestseller list for weeks (De Becker, 1997). The main message of the book is an exhortation for readers to listen to the intuitive nature of fear because it provides the most important guide we have for avoiding danger.

Psychologist Isaac Marks (1987) phrased the evolutionary function of fear crisply:

Fear is a vital evolutionary legacy that leads an organism to avoid threat, and has obvious survival value. It is an emotion produced by the perception of present or impending

danger and is normal in appropriate situations. Without fear few would survive long
under natural conditions. Fear girds our loins for rapid action in the face of danger and
alerts us to perform well under stress. It helps us fight the enemy, drive carefully, para-
chute safely, take exams, speak well to a critical audience, keep a foothold in climbing a
mountain. (p. 3)

Fear may be defined as "the usually unpleasant feeling that arises as a normal response to
realistic danger" (Marks, 1987, p. 5). Fears are distinguished from *phobias*, which are fears
that are wildly out of proportion to the realistic danger, are typically beyond voluntary
control, and lead to the avoidance of the feared situation. Recently evolutionary psychologists have begun to develop detailed theories of the evolution of fears and phobias.

Marks (1987) outlines four ways in which fear and anxiety can afford protection.

1. *Freezing or becoming immobile:* This response aids the vigilant assessment of the situation, helps conceal one from the predator, and sometimes inhibits an aggressive
   attack. If you are not sure that you've been spotted or cannot readily determine the
   location of the predator, freezing may be better than lashing out or fleeing.
2. *Escape or avoidance:* These responses distance the organism from specific threats.
   When you encounter a snake, for example, running away may be the easiest and
   safest way to avoid receiving a poisonous bite.
3. *Aggressive defense:* Attacking, bashing, or hitting a threatening predator may neutralize the threat by destroying it or causing it to flee. This mode of protection
   undoubtedly entails an assessment of whether the predator can be successfully
   vanquished or repelled. A spider can be squashed more easily than can a hungry
   two thousand-pound bear.
4. *Submission or appeasement:* This response typically works mainly when the threat
   is a member of one's own species. Among chimpanzees, performing submissive
   greetings to the alpha male effectively prevents a physical attack. The same might
   be true for humans.

In addition to these behavioral responses, fear also brings about a predictable set
of *evolved physiological reactions* (Marks & Nesse, 1994). Epinephrine, for example, is
produced by fear, and this acts on certain blood receptors to aid blood clotting, should
one sustain a wound. Epinephrine also acts on the liver to release glucose, making
energy available to the muscles for fight or flight. Heart rate speeds up, increasing the
blood flow and hence circulation. The pattern of blood flow gets diverted from the
stomach to the muscles. If you are faced with a threatening lion, digestion can wait!
People also start to breathe more rapidly, even to hyperventilate, increasing the oxygen
supply to the muscles and speeding the exhalation of carbon dioxide.

Most Common Human Fears

Table 3.1 shows a catalogue of the common subtypes of fears, along with the hypothesized adaptive problems for which they might have evolved (Nesse, 1990, p. 271).
Charles Darwin succinctly forecast a major movement in psychology that would occur a

TABLE 3.1   Subtypes of Fear and Corresponding Adaptive Problem

Subtype of Fear	Adaptive Problem
Fear of snakes	Receiving poisonous bite
Fear of spiders	Receiving poisonous bite
Fear of heights	Damage from falls from cliffs or trees
Panic	Imminent attack by predator or human
Agoraphobia	Crowded places from which one cannot escape
Small animal phobias	Dangerous small animals
Hypochondriasis	Disease
Separation anxiety	Separation from protection of parent
Stranger anxiety	Harm from strange humans, especially males
Fear of blood from injury	Dangerous predators or humans

Source: Reprinted with permission from: R. M. Nesse, Evolutionary explanations of emotions in *Human Nature* 1:3 (1990), (New York: Aldine de Gruyter) Copyright © 1990, Walter de Gruyter, Inc.

century later when he declared: "May we not suspect that the . . . fears of children, which are quite independent of experience, are the inherited effects of real dangers . . . during ancient savage time?" (Darwin, 1877, pp. 285–294). A large body of evidence suggests that humans are far more likely to develop fears of dangers that were present in the ancestral environment, but far less to dangers in the current environment. Snakes, for example, are hardly a problem in large urban cities, but automobiles are. Fears of cars, guns, electrical outlets, and cigarettes are virtually unheard of, since these are evolutionarily novel hazards—too recent for selection to have fashioned specific fears. The fact that more city dwellers go to psychiatrists with fears of snakes and strangers than fears of cars and electrical outlets provides a window into the hazards of our ancestral environment.

The specific fears of humans seem to emerge in development at precisely the time when the danger would have been encountered (Marks, 1987). Fears of heights and strangers, for example, emerge in infants around six months of age, which coincides with the time when they start to crawl away from their mothers (Scarr & Salapatek, 1970). In one study, 80 percent of infants who had been crawling for forty-one or more days avoided crossing over a "visual cliff" (an apparent vertical drop that was in fact covered with sturdy glass) to get to their mothers (Bertenthal, Campos, & Caplovitz, 1983). Crawling increases the risk of dangerous falls and encounters with strangers without the protective mother in close proximity, and so the emergence of the fear of heights and strangers at this time seems to coincide with the onset of the adaptive problems. Human infants' fear of strangers has been documented in a variety of different cultures, including Guatemalans, Zambians, !Kung bushmen, and Hopi Indians (Smith, 1979). In fact, the risk of infants' being killed by strangers appears to be a common "hostile force of nature" in nonhuman primates (Hrdy, 1977; Wrangham & Peterson, 1996), as well as in humans (Daly & Wilson, 1988).

BOX 3.1
The Adaptive Conservatism Hypothesis of Fears

A common characteristic of anxiety disorders in humans is the tendency to overgeneralize—to show fear of a wider range of objects or situations than actually pose the threat (Marks, 1987; Mineka, 1992). This overgeneralization is especially likely to occur with the passage of time. A person with agoraphobia, for example, might initially be fearful of large crowds. Over time, however, the phobia tends to worsen, so that he or she might fear being in a grocery store. The fear might eventually constrain the agoraphobic to his or her backyard, and, in extreme cases, the fear might leave him or her housebound.

The *adaptive conservatism hypothesis* has been proposed to explain this overgeneralization phenomenon (Hendersen, 1985; Tomarken, Mineka, & Cook, 1989). To understand this hypothesis, consider two scenarios. In scenario 1 a person assumes that something is not dangerous, but then it bites him and he dies. In scenario 2 the person assumes that something is dangerous, when it is in fact not dangerous. According to the adaptive conservatism hypothesis, the cost of mistakenly assuming that an object was safe when it was in fact dangerous would have been much higher in the currency of survival than the cost of erring on the safe side and assuming that some objects were dangerous, even if they were not. Thus some overgeneralization can be adaptive, even if it sometimes results in mistakenly avoiding objects that are in fact harmless.

Several studies support the adaptive conservatism hypothesis. In one, women were shown slides of a feared image (such as a snake or a spider), and slides of a neutral image such as a flower or a mushroom (Tomarken, Mineka, & Cook, 1989). After each slide, subjects received either an electric shock, which caused pain, a tone, or noth-

ing. These events occurred randomly, a third of the time each, so that the odds of receiving a shock after seeing a snake was one-third, a tone one-third, and nothing one-third.

When the women were asked afterward how often a shock followed seeing the snake, they consistently overestimated this conditional probability. That is, they estimated that shocks followed the appearance of a snake anywhere from 42 to 52 percent of the time, when in fact they only followed the appearance of the snake 33 percent of the time. This bias was especially strong in women diagnosed as having a high fear of snakes to begin with.

When the same experiment was conducted using an evolutionarily novel danger—damaged electrical outlets—the overestimate effect did not occur. Participants perceived that shock followed the image of a damaged electrical outlet 34 percent of the time, which is astonishingly close to the 33 percent of the time in which the shocks actually followed. These findings suggest that fear is linked to systematic biases in perception that cause people to overestimate the extent to which the feared object results in a negative consequence.

Although more research needs to be done, the findings so far support the adaptive conservatism hypothesis. People seem "wired" to overgeneralize negative consequences coming from historically dangerous objects, but not from evolutionarily novel dangerous objects. Fears tend to bias the processing of information in a way that confirms the danger of the feared object, which may function to maintain or enhance the fear. This overgeneralization would cause people to be adaptively conservative—to err on the side of avoiding the ancestrally dangerous objects, even at the cost of making some mistakes.

Separation anxiety is another kind of fear for which there is widespread cross-cultural documentation, peaking between nine and thirteen months of age (Kagan, Kearsley, & Zelazo, 1978). In one cross-cultural study experimenters recorded the percentage of infants who cried after their mothers left the room. At the peak age of separation anxiety, 62 percent of Guatemalan Indians, 60 percent of Israelis, 82 percent of Antigua Guatemalans, and 100 percent of African bush infants exhibited this overt display of separation anxiety.

Animal fears emerge around age two, as the child begins a more expansive exploration of its environment. *Agoraphobia*, the fear of being in public places or spaces from which escape might be difficult, can emerge later, as the young leave the home base (Marks & Nesse, 1994). The developmental timing of the emergence of fears, in short, seems to correspond precisely to the onset of the adaptive problem, in this case a threat to survival. This illustrates the point that psychological mechanisms do not have to show up "at birth" to qualify as evolved adaptations. The onset of specific fears, like the onset of puberty, is a developmentally timed psychological emergence.

Although there is much evidence that the patterning of fears appears to correspond fairly precisely to specific adaptive problems of ancestral environments and displays some evidence of cross-cultural generality, there remains controversy in the psychological literature about the precise status of fears and phobias as evolved adaptations (e.g., McNally, 1987). The standard evolutionary account implies that fears of evolutionary significance should be extinguished only with great difficulty. Behavioral research, however, demonstrates that phobias about heights and animals in adults are among the easiest phobias to treat (Mathews, 1978). As noted before, however, phobias are defined as irrational fears that are disproportionate to the realistic hazard. So it is not clear that evidence for the treatability of phobias of heights and animals in adulthood necessarily contradicts the concept of an evolved predisposition to fear heights and specific animals that emerges reliably in childhood. (See Box 3.1 for additional information on fears.)

Avoiding Toxins: The Functions of Allergies

The world is filled with toxins—substances poisonous to humans and other animals. Pollen grains contain acids and alkaloids. Hay dust contains toxic fungal spores. Nickel is one of many toxic metals found in the natural environment. Some nuts contain heavy concentrations of metals that would be harmful if eaten in large amounts. Even bananas, potatoes, and broccoli contain toxins. Plants produce toxins to defend themselves against herbivores (plant-eating animals), who feed on them for survival.

In addition, many insect and animal species produce venom as a defense against predators or as a means to capture prey. The snake's venom and the bee's sting sometimes result in death. In Burma, for example, more than one thousand people are killed each year by a single species of snake, the Russell's viper (Than-Than et al., 1988). These toxic substances in animals, insects, and plants can hurt humans by interfering with cell functioning, blocking brain receptor sites, and even blocking our natural defenses against other types of toxins (Profet, 1991). If the substances make their way past our other defenses—such as our food selection preferences—they can cause substantial damage. Toxins can cause cell mutations and even cancer from cumulative exposure—in short, they are ever present in our environment and represent a serious "hostile force of nature."

According to Margie Profet, allergies have evolved to combat these hostile forces of nature (Profet, 1991). She proposes the *toxin hypothesis* of allergies to explain the particular substances to which humans are allergic, those bodily mechanisms that are triggered when we encounter these substances, and the specific functional properties that allergies seem to exhibit.

Let's first consider the bodily mechanisms that allergic responses trigger. Mild forms of allergic response include sneezing, which extrudes the toxin from the nasal passages; coughing, which expels the toxin from the lungs; eye watering, which gets it out of the eyes; and scratching, which gets it off the skin. More extreme allergic responses include vomiting, which ejects the toxin out of the stomach, and diarrhea, which extrudes the toxin from the intestines. All these responses seem well designed to defend the body against toxins by preventing their entry into the bloodstream and hence their circulation to vulnerable body organs.

Extreme allergies also cause a drop in blood pressure. This drop is common after venomous snake bites, insect bites, or jellyfish stings. A drop in blood pressure slows the rate at which the toxin circulates through the bloodstream, decreasing the rate of exposure of the body organs to the toxins. Interestingly, individuals who are especially susceptible to insect venom are *not* the same individuals who are susceptible to pollen or food allergies (Evan & Summers, 1986). This suggests that selection may have fashioned immune systems in a domain-specific manner to recognize different classes of toxins (Profet, 1991).

Allergies are more common in industrial societies than they would have been among our forebears (Profet, 1991). Estimates of the number of people in modern industrial societies who suffer from respiratory allergies alone average around 16 percent but range as high as 27 percent. Three factors may be responsible for the prevalence of allergies in modern society. First, among hunter-gatherer societies the substances that produced an allergic response could usually be identified and then avoided. An ancestral human who ate a fruit, vegetable, or fish and subsequently developed allergic symptoms could thereafter avoid simply the source of the symptoms. In modern life, however, we are exposed to many hidden ingredients in the foods we eat—preservatives are found in manufactured foods and fish oil is sometimes added to ice cream. These hidden ingredients are not as easily identifiable, and hence not as easily avoided.

Second, modern humans are exposed to detergents, soaps, and shampoos, all containing mixtures of substances not found in hunter-gatherer societies. Even coffee beans can produce allergies because they contain up to 5 percent chlorogenic acid.

A third possible cause of the increase in allergies among modern humans is the dramatic reduction in breastfeeding. Several studies have documented that infants who are breastfed (usually for at least six months) develop far fewer allergies in adulthood than those who are not (Profet, 1991). Although we don't know precisely why this occurs, one possibility is that the mother's milk contains antibodies that combat toxins to which an infant might be exposed. The mother's supply of antibodies could prevent the infant from producing an excessive amount of its own antibodies, and hence prevent allergic sensitivities later in life.

So, although more research must be conducted, the toxin hypothesis can explain a host of known phenomena. It can account for the known manifestations of allergy, such as tearing, sneezing, coughing, scratching, vomiting, and diarrhea. It can account for the drop in blood pressure that accompanies a strong allergic response. It can explain why allergies occur to specific classes of food, pollens, venom, metals, and drugs—because these substances contain toxins. And it can account for why individuals differ in the nature and strength of their reactions to allergies—different individuals are exposed to different amounts and classes of toxins, and hence develop different degrees of allergies to different classes of substances. In short, by taking a functional approach to the human body and the hostile forces it encounters, the toxin hypothesis makes sense of a variety of otherwise puzzling facts about the nature of human allergies.

Combating Disease

Diseases infect humans many times during the course of life. Humans have evolved adaptations to combat diseases, but not all of these are intuitively obvious. The emerging science of Darwinian medicine is overturning conventional wisdom in how we react to common things like the fever that makes us sweat and reduces iron levels in our blood—both of which occur as a result of infectious disease (Williams & Nesse, 1991).

Fever. When you go to a physician with a fever, the timeworn recommendation to take two aspirin and call in the morning might be offered. Millions of Americans each year take aspirin and other drugs to reduce fever. Recent research suggests, however, that fever-reducing drugs may prolong disease. Fever, it turns out, may be a natural and useful defense against disease.

When cold-blooded lizards are infected with a disease, they commonly find a hot rock on which to bask. This raises their body temperature, which combats the disease. Lizards that cannot find a warm place on which to perch are more likely to die. A similar relationship between body temperature and disease has been observed in rabbits. When given a drug to block fever, diseased rabbits are more likely to die (Kluger, 1990).

Early in the twentieth century, a physician named Julian Wagner-Jauregg observed that syphilis was rarely seen in places where malaria was common (Nesse & Williams, 1994). At the time, syphilis killed 99 percent of those who were infected. Wagner-Jauregg intentionally infected syphilis patients with malaria, which produces a fever, and found that 30 percent of those patients survived—a huge increase in survival over patients not intentionally infected with malaria. The fever from malaria apparently helped to cure the fatal effects of syphilis.

A more recent study found that children with chicken pox whose fevers were reduced by acetaminophen took nearly a day longer to recover than children whose fevers were not reduced (Doran et al., 1989). Another researcher intentionally infected subjects with a cold virus and gave half the subjects a fever-reducing drug and half a placebo (a pill containing no active substances). Those given the fever-reducing drug had more nasal stuffiness, a worse antibody response, and a slightly longer-lasting cold (Graham et al., 1990).

Iron-Poor Blood. It turns out that iron is food for bacteria. They thrive on it. Humans have apparently evolved a means of starving these bacteria. When a person gets an infection, the body produces a chemical (leukocyte endogenous mediator) that reduces blood levels of iron. At the same time, people spontaneously reduce their consumption of iron-rich food such as ham and eggs, and the human body reduces the absorption of whatever iron is consumed (Nesse & Williams, 1994). These natural bodily reactions essentially starve the bacteria, paving the way to combat the infection for a quick recovery.

Although this information has been available since the 1970s, apparently few physicians and pharmacists know about it (Kluger, 1991). They continue to recommend iron supplements, which interfere with our evolved means for combating the hostile force of infections.

Among the Masai tribe, fewer than 10 percent suffered infections caused by an amoeba. When a subgroup was given iron supplements, 88 percent of them developed infections (Weinberg, 1984). Somali nomads have naturally low levels of iron in their diets. When investigators sought to correct this with iron supplements, there was a 30 percent jump in infections within a month (Weinberg, 1984). Old people and women in America are routinely given iron supplements to combat "iron-poor blood," which might paradoxically increase their rate of infections.

In sum, humans have evolved natural defense mechanisms such as fever and blood iron depletion that help combat disease. Interfering with these adaptations by artificially reducing fever or increasing blood iron seems to cause more harm than healing.

Are Humans Programmed to Die?

Because survival is so important for reproduction, and we have so many adaptations designed to keep us alive, why do we die at all? Why couldn't selection have fashioned mechanisms that allow us to live forever, or at least for a few hundred years? And why do some people commit suicide, an act that seems so contrary to anything that evolution would favor? This final section, on survival problems, explores these puzzling questions.

The Theory of Senescence

The answer to these mysteries has been partially solved by senescence theory (Williams, 1957). *Senescence* is not a specific disease, but rather *the deterioration of all bodily mechanisms as organisms grow older.* Senescence theory starts with an interesting observation: The power of natural selection decreases dramatically with increasing age. To understand why this occurs, consider a twenty-year-old woman and a fifty-year-old woman. Selection operates far more intensely on the younger woman, since anything that happens to her could affect most of her future reproductive years. A gene activated at age twenty that weakened a woman's immune system, for example, could damage her entire reproductive capacity. If the same damaging gene became activated in the fifty-year-old instead, it would have almost no impact on the woman's reproductive capacity. Selection operates only weakly on the older woman, since most or all of her reproduction has already occurred (Nesse & Williams, 1994).

Williams (1957) took this observation as a starting point and developed a pleiotropic theory of senescence. *Pleiotropy* is the phenomenon whereby a gene can have two or more different effects. Let's say that there is a gene that boosts testosterone in men, causing them to be more successful in competing with other men for status early in life, such as in their twenties and thirties. But the elevated testosterone also has a negative effect later in life—increasing the risk of prostate cancer. This pleiotropic gene can be favored by selection—that is, it increases in frequency in subsequent generations—because the early advantage in status gains for men outweighs the later cost in lowered survival due to prostate cancer. Through this pleiotropic process, we have evolved a number of genes that help us early in life but cause damaging pleiotropic effects later in life, when selection is weak or absent.

The pleiotropic theory of senescence helps to explain not only why our organs all wear out at roughly the same time late in life, but also why men die younger than women —roughly seven years earlier on average (Williams & Nesse, 1991). The effects of selection operate more strongly on men than on women because the reproductive variance of men is higher than that of women. Stated differently, most fertile women reproduce, and the maximum number of children they can have is sharply restricted—roughly twelve, for all practical purposes. Men, in contrast, can produce hundreds or thousands of children *or* be shut out of reproduction entirely. Because men have greater variability in reproduction, selection can operate more intensely on them than on women. In particular, selection will favor genes that enable a man to compete successfully for mates early in life to be one of the few who reproduces a lot or to avoid being excluded entirely.

Selection for men's success in mate competition will be favored, even if it means that these genes have detrimental effects on survival later in life. Even though men can and sometimes do reproduce for a longer period of time than women, senescence theory explains why these later reproductive events will have a much smaller impact than events occurring earlier in life for men. Genes will be selected for early success in mate competition more strongly in men than in women, at the expense of genes that promote survival later. This strong selection for early advantage produces a higher proportion of pleiotropic genes that cause early death. As one researcher noted, "it seems likely that males suffer higher mortality than do females because in the past they have enjoyed higher *potential* reproductive success, and this has selected for traits that are positively associated with high reproductive success but at a cost of decreased survival" (Trivers, 1985, p. 314). Men, in short, are programmed to die sooner than women, and the theory of senescence helps to solve the mystery of why.

In summary, selection is most potent early in life because any events that happen early can affect the entire span of a person's reproductive years. As people get older, however, the power of selection weakens. In the extreme case something that happened to you in old age right before you died would likely have no effect on your reproductive capacity. This means that selection will favor genes that have pleiotropic effects— adaptations that give beneficial effects early in life, even if they come with heavy costs later on. These heavy costs cumulate in old age, resulting in the deterioration of all body parts at roughly the same time. In this sense organisms can be said to be programmed to die.

The Puzzle of Suicide

The senescence of organisms, eventually resulting in death, may be inevitable, but there is an even deeper puzzle for evolutionary psychology: Why would anyone intentionally take his or her own life? Evolutionary theory tells us that reproduction is the engine of the evolutionary process and survival is surely necessary for reproduction. So what could account for suicide?

Evolutionary psychologist Denys de Catanzaro (1991, 1995) has addressed this issue, developing an evolutionary theory of suicide and testing his theory on many samples of subjects, ranging from the general public to many "high-risk" samples such as the elderly and those in a psychiatric ward. Let's first examine the logic of his theory. De Catanzaro's central argument is that suicide will be most likely to occur when an individual has a dramatically reduced ability to contribute to his or her own inclusive fitness, defined as the welfare and reproduction of self and kin. Indicators of this dramatically reduced capacity to contribute to fitness include expectations of poor future health, chronic infirmity, disgrace or failure, poor prospects for successful heterosexual mating, and perceptions of being a burden on one's genetic kin. Under these conditions it is at least plausible that the replication of an individual's genes would have a better chance without him or her around. If a person is a burden to his or her family, for example, then the kin's reproduction, and hence the person's own fitness might suffer as a result of his or her survival.

To test this evolutionary theory of suicide de Catanzaro looked at *suicidal ideation:* whether a person had ever considered suicide, had recently considered suicide, intended to kill him- or herself within one year, intended to kill him- or herself ever, or had previously engaged in suicidal behavior. The dependent measure was a sum of responses to these items. Suicidal ideation is not actual suicide, of course. Many people have thoughts of suicide without actually killing themselves. Nonetheless, because suicide is usually a premeditated event, a lot of suicidal ideation will almost invariably precede an actual suicide. So suicidal ideation is a reasonable index to examine as a proxy for actual suicide.

In another part of the questionnaire de Catanzaro asked participants a series of questions about their perceived burdensomeness to family, perceived significance of contributions to family and society, frequency of sexual activity, success with members of the opposite sex, homosexuality, number of friends, treatment by others, financial welfare, and physical health. Participants responded to each item using a seven-point scale ranging from –3 to +3. The participants varied—a large public sample, a sample of the elderly, a sample from a mental hospital, a sample of inmates at a maximum security center housing those who had committed antisocial crimes, and two samples of homosexuals.

The results provided support for de Catanzaro's evolutionary theory of suicide. When the measure of suicidal ideation was correlated with the other items on the questionnaire, he found the following results.[1] Across all samples, the strongest correlate of suicidal ideation was burdensomeness to family and, for males, lack of success in heterosexual activity. For men in the public sample, ages eighteen to thirty years, the following correlations were found with suicidal ideation: burden to family (+.56), sex in last month (–.67), success in heterosexual relations (–.49), sex ever (–.45), stability of heterosexual relations (–.45), sex last year (–.40), and number of children (–.36). For

---

[1]Correlations describe the relationships between variables, and range from +1.00 to –1.00. A positive correlation means that as one variable increases, the other variable also increases. A negative correlation means that as one variable increases, the other decreases.

young women in the public sample, ages eighteen to thirty years, similar results were found, although they were not quite as strong: burden to family (+.44), sex ever (–.37), and contribution to family (–.36).

For older samples health burdens took on increased importance and showed a strong correlation with suicidal ideation. For the public sample of men over the age of fifty, for example, the following significant correlations were found with suicidal ideation: health (–.48), future financial problems (+.46), burden to family (+.38), homosexuality (+.38), and number of friends (–.36). Women over the age of fifty in the public sample showed similar results: loneliness (+.62), burden to family (+.47), future financial problems (+.45), and health (–.42). Similar results were found with all the samples.

Findings such as these have now been reported by independent researchers. In a study of 175 American university students, Michael Brown and his colleagues tested de Catanzaro's theory of suicide using a 164-item questionnaire (Brown, Dahlen, Mills, Rick, & Biblarz, in press). They found that individuals with low reproductive potential (e.g., who perceive they are not attractive to members of the opposite sex) and high burdensomeness to kin reported more suicidal ideation, as well as more depression and hopelessness.

In summary, results from independent investigators provide reasonable preliminary support for de Catanzaro's evolutionary psychological theory of suicide. More precise tests need to be done and the next step might be a prospective study of people who actually commit suicide. In the meantime, however, we can conclude, theoretically, that there are conditions that could select for psychological mechanisms that would prompt a person to commit suicide. These conditions center around failing in the heterosexual world and being a burden on close kin. Thoughts of suicide are most likely to occur when people are confronted with these fitness-threatening social contexts.

Summary

Food shortages, toxins, predators, parasites, diseases, and extremes of climate are hostile forces of nature that recurrently plagued our ancestors. Humans have evolved many adaptive mechanisms to combat these impediments to survival. One of the most important survival problems is obtaining food. Food acquisition and consumption are difficult and complex problems. In addition to the problem of food shortages, organisms face the problem of selecting which foods to consume (e.g., those that are rich in calories and nutrients), selecting which foods to avoid (e.g., those that are filled with toxins), and actually procuring those foods. Humans evolved as omnivores, consuming a wide variety of plants and animals. Among the apparent human adaptations are specific food preferences for calorically rich food; specific mechanisms for avoiding the consumption of toxic food, such as the emotion of disgust in response to feces; and mechanisms for getting rid of toxins such as gagging, spitting, vomiting, coughing, sneezing, diarrhea, and pregnancy sickness.

One of the most controversial topics in human evolution is how human ancestors procured their food. Three basic hypotheses have been advanced: the hunting hypothesis, the gathering hypothesis, and the scavenging hypothesis. All available evidence points to an ancestral pattern characterized by male hunting, female gathering, and perhaps occasional opportunistic scavenging.

Another adaptive problem of survival involves finding a place to live. Humans appear to have evolved preferences for landscapes rich in resources and places where one can see without being seen, mimicking the savanna habitats of our ancestors.

All habitats, even those rich in resources and offering places of refuge, contain hostile forces that impede survival. Humans have evolved a variety of specific fears to avoid these dangers. The human fears of snakes, spiders, heights, and strangers, for example, appear to be present across a variety of cultures and emerge at specific times in development, suggesting adaptive patterning. The fears of heights and strangers, for example, emerge when infants begin to crawl and are increasingly exposed to the hazards of heights and strangers.

Diseases and parasites are ubiquitous hostile forces of nature, especially for long-lived organisms. Humans appear to have evolved a variety of adaptive mechanisms to combat diseases and parasites. Contrary to conventional medical wisdom, the human mechanism that elevates body temperature and creates a fever is a natural bodily function to combat infectious diseases. Taking aspirin or similar drugs to combat fever has the paradoxical effect of prolonging disease.

Given the importance of survival in the evolutionary scheme of things, why people die (or do not live longer) poses an interesting puzzle. The theory of senescence explains why. Basically, selection is most potent early in life because any events that happen early can affect the entire span of a person's reproductive years. As people get older, however, the power of selection weakens—in the extreme, a bad event that happened to you right before you died would have little or no consequences on your reproduction. This means that selection will favor genes that have pleiotropic effects—adaptations that give beneficial effects early in life, even if they come with heavy costs later on. Testosterone production in men, for example, appears to provide benefits in young adulthood in the form of mating success, but has detrimental consequences later on in the form of prostate cancer.

Perhaps even more puzzling than the fact that people appear programmed to die is the phenomenon of suicide—when a person intentionally ends his or her own life. Could psychological mechanisms for suicide, which seems to fly in the face of evolution, possibly have evolved? According to one evolutionary psychologist the answer is yes. Suicidal ideation occurs most commonly among those with poor reproductive prospects, who experience failure at heterosexual mating, are in poor health, have poor financial prospects for the future, and who perceive themselves to be a large burden on their kin. Although more research is needed on this important topic, current evidence points to the possibility that humans have evolved context-sensitive psychological mechanisms to evaluate future reproductive potential and net cost to genetic kin.

All these evolved mechanisms help humans to survive long enough to reach adulthood. Once there, however, humans still encounter hostile forces that impede survival. But they also face a new set of adaptive challenges—those of mating, a topic to which we now turn.

PART THREE

Challenges of Sex and Mating

Because differential reproduction is the engine that drives the evolutionary process, the psychological mechanisms surrounding reproduction should be especially strong targets of selection. If selection has not sculpted psychological mechanisms designed to solve adaptive problems posed by sex and mating, then evolutionary psychology would be "out of business" before it even got off the ground. In this part we consider the problems of mating and examine the large empirical foundation that evolutionary psychology has established in this domain.

Part three is divided into three chapters. Chapter 4 examines how women select mates. It presents evidence from large-scale cross-cultural studies designed to test evolutionary psychological hypotheses. Women's mate preferences are complex and sophisticated because of the large number of complex adaptive problems that women have had to solve over the expanse of evolutionary history. The chapter concludes with an examination of how women's desires affect actual mating behavior.

Chapter 5 deals with men's mate preferences and how they are designed to solve a somewhat different set of adaptive problems. According to the metatheory of evolutionary psychology, men and women are predicted to differ only in domains in which they have recurrently faced different adaptive problems over human evolutionary history. In all other domains the sexes are predicted to be similar. This chapter highlights the domains in which the adaptive problems that men have confronted are distinct—problems such as selecting a fertile partner and ensuring certainty in paternity when investing in a long-term mate.

Chapter 6 focuses on a relatively hidden side of human mating—short-term sexual strategies. This chapter reviews recent scientific findings on sperm competition and female orgasm—physiological clues that suggest a long ancestral history of nonmonogamous mating. Because humans experience both short-term and long-term mating, they show a degree of flexibility rarely observed in other species. Which strategy an individual pursues often depends on context. The chapter ends with a review of the major contextual variables, such as individual mate value and ratio of men to women in the mating pool, that affect whether a short-term or a long-term mating strategy is pursued.

4 Women's Long-Term Mating Strategies

. . . to an extraordinary degree, the predilections of the investing sex—females
—potentially determine the direction in which the species will evolve. For it is
the female who is the ultimate arbiter of when she mates and how often and
with whom.

—Sarah Blaffer Hrdy, 1981

Nowhere do people have an equal desire for all members of the opposite sex. Everywhere some potential mates are preferred, others shunned. Imagine living as our ancestors did long ago—struggling to keep warm by the fire; hunting meat for our kin; gathering nuts, berries, and herbs; and avoiding dangerous animals and hostile humans. If we were to select a mate who failed to deliver the resources promised, who had affairs, who was lazy, who lacked hunting skills, or who heaped physical abuse on us, our survival would be tenuous, our reproduction at risk. In contrast, a mate who provided abundant resources, who protected us and our children, and who devoted time, energy, and effort to our family would be a great asset. As a result of the powerful survival and reproductive advantages that were reaped by those of our ancestors who chose mates wisely, many specific desires evolved. As descendants of those winners in the evolutionary lottery, modern humans have inherited a specific set of mate preferences.

Scientists have also documented evolved mate preferences in many nonhuman species. The African village weaverbird provides a vivid illustration (Collias & Collias, 1970). When a female weaverbird arrives in the vicinity of a male, he displays his recently built nest by suspending himself upside down from the bottom and vigorously flapping his wings. If the male impresses the female she approaches the nest, enters it, and examines the nest materials, poking and pulling them for as long as ten minutes. During this inspection the male sings to her from nearby. At any point in this sequence she may decide that the nest does not meet her standards and depart to inspect another male's nest. A male whose nest is rejected by several females will often break it down and rebuild another from scratch. By exerting a preference for males capable of building superior nests the female weaverbird addresses the problems of protecting and provisioning her chicks. Her preferences have evolved because they bestowed a reproductive advantage over other weaverbirds who had no preferences and who mated with any male who happened to come along.

Women, like weaverbirds, also prefer males with "nests" of various kinds. Consider one of the problems that women in evolutionary history had to face: selecting a man who would be willing to commit to a long-term relationship. A woman in our evolutionary past who chose to mate with a man who was flighty, impulsive, philandering, or unable to sustain relationships found herself raising her children alone and without benefit of the resources, aid, and protection that a more dependable mate might have offered. A woman who preferred to mate with a reliable man who was willing to commit to her presumably would have had children who survived, and thrived, and multiplied. Over thousands of generations, a preference for men who showed signs of being willing and able to commit evolved in women, just as preferences for mates with adequate nests evolved in weaverbirds. This preference solved key reproductive problems, just as food preferences solved key survival problems.

Theoretical Background for the Evolution of Mate Preferences

This section reviews three important theoretical issues that are key to understanding the evolution of mate preferences. The first concerns one of the greatest mysteries in evolutionary biology: Why has sexual reproduction evolved? The second topic deals with the definition of the two distinct types that exist in sexually reproducing species—males and females—and the related issue of the influence of parental investment on the nature of mating. The third topic pertains to mate preferences as evolved psychological mechanisms.

Asexual versus Sexual Reproduction

Perhaps because sexual reproduction is the method humans use, we are not always aware that this is only one possible mode of reproduction. Many species, in fact, reproduce asexually, such as certain species of mites, isopods, and monogonont rotifers. In these species there is only one sex. The offspring are identical copies of the parents, with the exception of whatever mutations occur. Asexual reproduction has many advantages (Williams, 1975). First, such organisms avoid entirely the problem of searching for and selecting a mate. Second, all the genes are typically passed on to the offspring with no loss. The advantages of asexual reproduction are precisely the disadvantages of sexual reproduction. Sexually reproducing species face the problems of mate selection and courting, which can be costly in time and resources. In sexually reproducing species, only half of one's genes are passed down to one's offspring—a full 50 percent loss compared to asexual reproduction.

Given these tremendous costs, why has sexual reproduction evolved at all? This has been one of the most persistent puzzles in evolutionary biology, and many theories have been advanced to solve it. Simply stated, the puzzle is what reproductive benefit could sexual reproduction provide that would be so large that it would outweigh all the costs?

One of the most important and well-known consequences of sexual reproduction is the generation of *genetically diverse offspring*. Compared to asexual species, in which the offspring are identical their parent (unless there is mutation), the offspring of sexually reproducing parents are genetically different from their parents. The offspring are also genetically different from each other. Siblings are genetically related by only 50 percent on average.

Most theories of the origin of sex revolve around the potential benefit of having genetically variable offspring. One theory is that having genetically variable offspring increases the number of niches that can be simultaneously occupied. The key insight here is that genetically identical individuals have the same requirements for food, habitat, and so on. Genetically different individuals have different survival requirements, and so can inhabit a somewhat broader array of niches (Trivers, 1985; Williams, 1975). Doing so also means that siblings are less likely to suffer the costs of direct competition with each other in their search for niches. Although intuitively appealing, the theory of niche variability cannot explain why sexual reproduction has not entirely replaced asexual reproduction. Indeed, asexual reproduction remains quite common today. Another theory, one that fits more precisely with the facts of sexual and asexual species, is needed.

The leading theory—the parasite theory of the origins of sex—is not an intuitively obvious one (Hamilton, 1980; Tooby, 1982). Most people think that sex can lead to parasites in the form of sexually transmitted diseases. It turns out that parasites may be responsible for sex! Parasites pose a big adaptive problem for long-lived organisms. They can evolve hundreds, thousands, or even millions of generations in the span of the single life of a long-lived organism and proliferate by spreading to other hosts, especially if the hosts to which they spread provide much the same "environment" as the original host. Since groups of asexual organisms are all alike parasites can thrive because they can move easily from host to host. This is not good for the host, however, because parasites can evolve to the point of overcoming the host's defense mechanisms and eventually kill it off.

This is where sexual reproduction comes in, according to the parasite theory. By creating genetically different offspring, sexual reproduction provides a radically different host environment for parasites compared with the original host. Thus, parasites are thwarted. They must now adapt to this new environment. But then the very next host is also genetically different, and so the process has to start again.

In the continuing evolutionary battle between parasites and hosts, an arms race has developed—a sequence of mutual counteradaptations that continues over time (Dawkins, 1982). Sexual reproduction may be one pivotal adaptation by hosts, helping host organisms and their offspring combat parasites. By doing so, sexual reproduction could have provided a benefit so large that it outweighed all of the costs.

Each new adaptation brings new adaptive challenges. One of the most serious adaptive challenges posed by sexual reproduction is finding a mate.

Parental Investment and Sexual Selection

It is a remarkable fact that what defines biological sex is simply the size of the sex cells. Mature reproductive cells are called *gametes*. Each gamete has the potential to fuse with another gamete of the opposite sex to form a *zygote*, which is defined as a fertilized gamete.

Males are defined as the sex with the small gametes, females as those with the large gametes. The female gametes remain reasonably stationary and come loaded with nutrients; the male gametes are endowed with greater mobility. Along with differences in size and mobility come a difference in quantity. Men produce millions of sperm, which are replenished at a rate of roughly twelve million per hour. Women, on the other hand, produce a fixed and unreplenishable lifetime supply of approximately four hundred ova.

Women's greater initial investment per gamete does not end with the egg. Fertilization and gestation, key components of human parental investment, occur internally in women. One act of sexual intercourse, which requires minimal male investment, can produce an obligatory and energy-consuming nine-month investment by the woman that forecloses other mating opportunities. In addition, women alone engage in the activity of lactation (breastfeeding), which lasts as long as four years in some societies (Shostak, 1981).

No biological law of the animal world dictates that females must invest more than males. Indeed, among some species such as the Mormon cricket, pipefish seahorse, and Panamanian poison arrow frog males in fact invest more (Trivers, 1985). The male Mormon cricket produces a large spermatophore that is loaded with nutrients. In areas where food is scarce, large spermatophores become extremely valuable to the female, but simultaneously become difficult for the male to produce, because they require extensive food consumption. Females compete with each other for access to the high-investing males holding the largest spermatophores. Among these so-called "sex-role reversed" species, males are more discriminating than females about mating. In particular, the females that are chosen by the males for depositing their spermatophore contain 60 percent more eggs than females who are rejected (Trivers, 1985). Among all four thousand species of mammals and the more than two hundred species of primates, however, the females—not the males—undergo internal fertilization and gestation.

The great initial parental investment of females makes them a valuable reproductive resource (Trivers, 1972). Gestating, bearing, lactating, nurturing, protecting, and feeding a child are exceptionally valuable reproductive resources that are not allocated indiscriminately. Economics 101 tells us that those who hold valuable resources do not give them away haphazardly. Because women in our evolutionary past risked investing enormously as a consequence of having sex, evolution favored women who were highly selective about their mates. Ancestral women suffered severe costs if they were indiscriminating—they experienced lower reproductive success, and fewer of their children survived to reproductive age. A man in human evolutionary history could walk away from a casual coupling having lost only a few hours or even a few minutes. His reproductive success was not seriously compromised. A woman in evolutionary history risked getting pregnant as a result, and therefore could have incurred the costs of that decision for years.

Modern birth control technology has altered this. In today's industrial nations women can have short-term sexual encounters with less fear of pregnancy. But human sexual psychology evolved over millions of years to cope with ancestral adaptive problems, before the advent of modern contraceptive technology. Humans still possess this underlying sexual psychology, even though the current environment has changed.

In summary, Trivers's (1972) theory of parental investment and sexual selection makes two profound predictions: (1) the sex that invests more in offspring (typically, but not always, the female) will be more discriminating or selective about mating; and (2) the sex that invests less in offspring will be more competitive for sexual access to the high investing sex. In the human case, it is clear that women have greater *obligatory* parental investment. To produce a single child, women must endure a nine-month pregnancy, whereas men can produce that same child with as little as a few minutes of investment. When it comes to long-term mating or marriage, however, it is equally clear that both men and women invest heavily in children, and so the theory of parental investment predicts that both sexes should be very choosy and discriminating.

Mate Preferences as Evolved Psychological Mechanisms

Consider the case of an ancestral woman trying to decide between two men, one of whom shows great generosity to her with his resources and the other of whom is stingy. All else being equal, the generous man is more valuable to her than the stingy man. The generous man may share his meat from the hunt, aiding her survival. He may sacrifice his time, energy, and resources for the benefit of the children, aiding the woman's reproductive success. In these respects the generous man has higher value than the stingy man as a mate. If, over evolutionary time, generosity in men provided these benefits repeatedly and the cues to a man's generosity were observable and reliable, selection would have favored the evolution of a preference for generosity in a mate.

This would put selection pressure on men to evolve the trait of generosity, of course, but at least two factors might contribute to the maintenance of individual differences along the generous-stingy dimension. First, generosity might be correlated with amount of resources. It's easier for a millionaire to pay the check for the group dinner than it is for the pauper. Since men differ in their resource holdings, differences in generosity might follow from this monetary disparity. Second, men can be extremely choosy about the women to whom they allocate their resources. A man might withhold resources from one woman while channeling those resources to another. All men might be stingy under some circumstances and generous under others. Women, therefore, might be especially sensitive to men who are generous toward them personally.

Now consider a more complicated and realistic scenario in which men vary not just in their generosity but also in a bewildering variety of ways that are significant in the choice of a mate. Men differ in their physical prowess, athletic skill, ambition, industriousness, kindness, empathy, emotional stability, intelligence, social skills, sense of humor, kin network, and position in the status hierarchy. Men also differ in the costs they carry into a mating relationship: some come with children, bad debts, a bad temper, a selfish disposition, and promiscuous proclivities. In addition, men differ in hundreds of ways that may be irrelevant to women. From among the thousands of ways in which men differ, selection over hundreds of thousands of years focused women's preferences, laserlike, on the most adaptively valuable characteristics. Women lacking specific adaptively relevant preferences are not our ancestors; they were out-reproduced by choosier women.

The qualities people prefer, however, are not static. Because they change over time, mate seekers must gauge the future potential of a prospective partner. A man might lack resources now but, as a medical student, might have excellent future promise. Or a man might be highly ambitious but have already reached his peak. Or he might have had children with another woman, but because they are about to leave the home, the children will not drain his resources. Gauging a man's mating value requires looking beyond his current position and evaluating his future potential.

In short, evolution has favored women who prefer men possessing those attributes that confer benefits and who dislike men possessing those attributes that impose costs. Each separate attribute constitutes one component of a man's value to a woman as a mate. Each of her preferences tracks one critical component.

Preferences that give priority to particular components, however, do not completely solve the problem of choosing a mate. In selecting a mate a woman must deal with the problem of identifying and correctly evaluating the cues that signal whether a man indeed possesses a particular resource. The assessment problem becomes especially acute in areas in which men are apt to deceive women, such as pretending greater status than they actually possess or feigning greater commitment than they are truly willing to give.

Finally, women face the problem of integrating their knowledge about a prospective mate. Suppose that one man is generous but emotionally unstable. Another man is emotionally stable but stingy. Which man should a woman choose? Selecting a mate requires psychological mechanisms that make it possible to add up the relevant attributes and give each its appropriate weight in the whole. Some attributes weigh more heavily than others in arriving at the bottom line or the final decision about whether to choose or reject a particular man. One of these heavily weighted components is the acquisition of resources.

The Content of Women's Mate Preferences

With this theoretical background in mind, we turn now to the actual content of women's mate preferences (summarized in Table 4.1). As the previous discussion implies, choosing a mate is a complex task, and so we do not expect to find simple answers to what women want. Perhaps no other topic has received as much research attention in evolutionary psychology, however, and so we have some reasonably firm answers to this long-standing question.

Preference for Economic Resources

The evolution of the female preference for males offering resources may be the most ancient and pervasive basis for female choice in the animal kingdom. Consider the gray shrike, a bird living in the Negev Desert of Israel (Yosef, 1991). Just before the start of the breeding season, male shrikes begin amassing caches of edible prey such as snails and useful objects such as feathers and pieces of cloth in numbers ranging from 90 to 120. They impale these items on thorns and other pointed projections within their ter-

TABLE 4.1   **Adaptive Problems in Long-Term Mating and Hypothesized Solutions**

Adaptive Problem	Evolved Mate Preference
Selecting a mate who is able to invest	Good financial prospects Social status Older age Ambition/industriousness Size, strength, athletic ability
Selecting a mate who is willing to invest	Dependability and stability Love and commitment cues Positive interactions with children
Selecting a mate who is able to physically protect self and children	Size (height) Strength Bravery Athletic ability
Selecting a mate who will show good parenting skills	Dependability Emotional stability Kindness Positive interactions with children
Selecting a mate who is compatible	Similar values Similar ages Similar personalities

ritories. Females scan the available males and choose to mate with those with the largest caches. When Yosef arbitrarily removed portions of some males' stock and added edible objects to the supplies of others, females still preferred to mate with the males with the larger bounties. Females avoided entirely males without resources, consigning them to bachelorhood. Wherever females show a mating preference, the male's resources are often the key criterion.

Among humans, the evolution of women's preference for a permanent mate with resources would have required three preconditions. First, resources would have to be accruable, defensible, and controllable by men during human evolutionary history. Second, men would have to differ from each other in their holdings and their willingness to invest those holdings in a woman and her children, because if all men possessed the same resources and showed an equal willingness to allocate them, there would be no need for women to develop such a preference for them. Third, the advantages of being with one man would have to outweigh the advantages of being with several men.

These conditions are easily met in humans. Territory and tools, to name just two resources, are acquired, defended, monopolized, and controlled by men worldwide. Men vary tremendously in the quantity of resources they command—from the homeless to the jet setters. Men also differ widely in how willing they are to invest their time and resources in long-term mateships. Some men prefer to mate with many women, investing little in each. Other men channel all their resources to one woman and her children (Belsky, Steinberg, & Draper, 1991).

Over the course of human evolutionary history women could often garner far more resources for their children through a single spouse than through several temporary sex partners. Men invest in their wives and children with provisions to an extent unprecedented among primates. In all other primates, females must rely solely on their own efforts to acquire food because males never share those resources with their mates (Smuts, 1995). Men, in contrast, provide food, find shelter, defend territory, and protect children. They tutor children in sports, hunting, fighting, hierarchy negotiation, friendship, and social influence. They transfer status, aiding offspring in forming reciprocal alliances later in life. These benefits are unlikely to be secured by a woman from a temporary sex partner. Not all potential husbands can confer all of these benefits, but over thousands of generations, when some men were able to provide some of these benefits, women benefited by choosing them as mates.

So the stage was set for the evolution of women's preferences for men with resources. But women needed cues to signal a man's possession of those resources. These cues might be indirect, such as personality characteristics that signal a man's upward mobility. They might be physical, such as a man's athletic ability or health. They might include reputation, such as the esteem in which a man is held by his peers. The possession of economic resources, however, provides the most obvious cue.

Preference for Good Financial Prospects

Currently held mate preferences provide a window for viewing our mating past, just as our fears of snakes and heights provide a window for viewing ancestral hazards. Evidence from dozens of studies documents that modern American women indeed value economic resources in mates substantially more than men do. In a study conducted in 1939, for example, American men and women rated eighteen characteristics for their relative desirability in a marriage partner, ranging from irrelevant to indispensable. Women did not view good financial prospects as absolutely indispensable, but they did rate them as important, whereas men rated them as merely desirable but not very important. Women in 1939 valued good financial prospects in a mate about twice as highly as men, a finding that was replicated in 1956 and again in 1967 (Hill, 1945; Hudson & Henze, 1969; McGinnis, 1958).

The sexual revolution of the late 1960s and early 1970s failed to change this sex difference. In an attempt to replicate the studies from earlier decades, in the mid-1980s 1,491 Americans were surveyed using the same questionnaire (Buss, 1989a). Women and men from Massachusetts, Michigan, Texas, and California rated eighteen personal characteristics for their value in a marriage partner. As in the previous decades, women still valued good financial prospects in a mate roughly twice as much as did men. In 1939, for example, women judged "good financial prospect" to be 1.80 in importance on a scale ranging from 0 (irrelevant) to 3 (indispensable); men in 1939 judged "good financial prospect" to be only 0.90 in importance. By 1985 women judged this quality to be 1.90 in importance, whereas men judged it to be 1.02 in importance—still roughly a twofold difference between the sexes (Buss, Shackelford, Kirkpatrick, & Larsen, under review).

The premium that women place on economic resources has been revealed in a diversity of contexts. Douglas Kenrick and his colleagues devised a useful method for revealing how much people value different attributes in a marriage partner by having men and women indicate the "minimum percentiles" of each characteristic they would find acceptable (Kenrick, Sadalla, Groth, & Trost, 1990). The percentile concept was explained with such examples as the following: "A person at the 50th percentile would be above 50% of the other people on earning capacity, and below 49% of the people on this dimension" (p. 103). American college women indicate that their minimum acceptable percentile for a husband on earning capacity is the seventieth percentile, or above 70 percent of all other men, whereas men's minimum acceptable percentile for a wife's earning capacity is only the fortieth. Women also show higher standards for economic capacity in a dating partner, in a sexual relationship, and in a steady dating context, as shown in Figure 4.1.

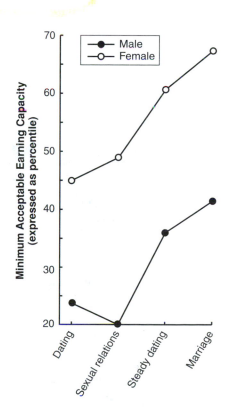

FIGURE 4.1   Minimum Acceptable Earning Capacity at Each Level of Involvement.
Women maintain considerably higher minimum standards for financial capacity in mates, reaching peak standards in the long-term mating context (marriage).

Source: Evolution, traits, and the stages of human courtship: Qualifying the parental investment model by D. T. Kenrick, E. K. Sadalla, G. Groth, & M. R. Trost, *Journal of Personality, 58,* 1990, 97–116. Reprinted with permission.

Personal ads in newspapers and magazines confirm that women actually on the marriage market desire strong financial resources. A study of 1,111 personal ads found that female advertisers seek financial resources roughly eleven times as often as male advertisers do (Wiederman, 1993). In short, sex differences in preference for resources are not limited to college students and are not bound by the method of inquiry.

Nor are these female preferences restricted to America, or to Western societies, or to capitalist countries. A large cross-cultural study was conducted of thirty-seven cultures on six continents and five islands using populations ranging from coast-dwelling Australians to urban Brazilians to shantytown South African Zulus (Buss, Abbott, Angleitner, et al., 1990). Some participants came from nations that practice *polygyny* (the mating or marriage of a single man with several women), such as Nigeria and Zambia. Other participants came from nations that are more *monogamous* (the mating of one man with one women), such as Spain and Canada. The countries included those in which living together is as common as marriage, such as Sweden and Finland, as well as countries in which living together without marriage is frowned on, such as Bulgaria and Greece. The study sampled a total of 10,047 individuals in thirty-seven cultures, as shown in Figure 4.2 (Buss, 1989a).

Male and female participants in the study rated the importance of eighteen characteristics in a potential mate or marriage partner, on a scale from unimportant to indispensable. Women across all continents, all political systems (including socialism and

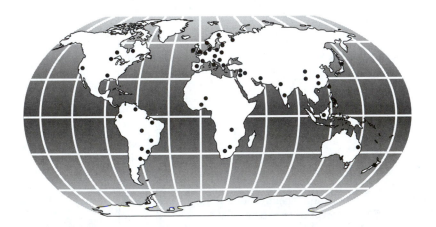

FIGURE 4.2   Locations of Thirty-Seven Cultures Studied in an International Mate Selection Project. Thirty-seven cultures, distributed as shown above, were examined by the author in his international study of male and female mating preferences. The author and his colleagues surveyed the mating desires of 10,047 people on six continents and five islands. The results provide the largest database of human mating preferences ever accumulated.

Source: Buss, D. M. (1994a). The strategies of human mating. *American Scientist, 82,* 238–249. Reprinted with permission.

communism), all racial groups, all religious groups, and all systems of mating (from intense polygyny to presumptive monogamy) placed more value than men on good financial prospects. Overall, women valued financial resources about 100 percent more than men, or roughly twice as much (see Figure 4.3). There are some cultural variations. Women from Nigeria, Zambia, India, Indonesia, Iran, Japan, Taiwan, Colombia, and Venezuela valued good financial prospects a bit higher than women from South Africa (Zulus), the Netherlands, and Finland. In Japan, for example, women valued good financial prospect roughly 150 percent more than men, whereas women from the Netherlands deem it only 36 percent more important than their male counterparts, less than women from any other country. Nonetheless, the sex difference remained invariant—women worldwide desired financial resources in a marriage partner more than men.

These findings provided the first extensive cross-cultural evidence supporting the evolutionary basis for the psychology of human mating. Because ancestral women faced the tremendous burdens of internal fertilization, a nine-month gestation, and lactation, they would have benefited tremendously by selecting mates who possessed resources. These cross-cultural data support the hypothesis that current women are the

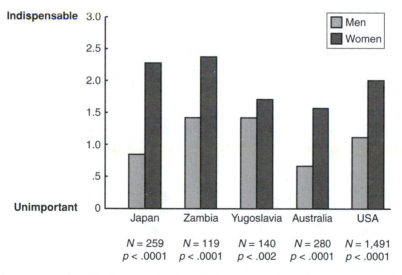

FIGURE 4.3   Preference for Good Financial Prospect in a Marriage Partner.
Participants in cultures rated this variable, in the context of eighteen other variables, on how desirable it would be in a potential long-term mate or marriage partner using a four-point rating scale, ranging from zero (irrelevant or unimportant) to three (indispensable).

N = sample size.

p values less than .05 indicate that sex difference is significant.

Source: Buss, D. M., & Schmidt, D. P. (1993). Sexual strategies theory: An evolutionary perspective on human mating. *Psychological Review, 100,* 204–232. Copyright © 1993 by the American Psychological Association. Adapted with permission.

descendants of a long line of women who had these mate preferences—preferences that helped their ancestors solve the adaptive problems of survival and reproduction.

Preference for High Social Status

Traditional hunter-gatherer societies, which are our closest guide to what ancestral conditions were probably like, suggest that ancestral men had clearly defined status hierarchies, with resources flowing freely to those at the top and trickling slowly down to those at the bottom (Betzig, 1986; Brown & Chia-yun, n.d.). Cross-culturally, groups such as the Melanesians, the early Egyptians, the Sumerians, the Japanese, and the Indonesians include people described as "head men" and "big men" who wield great power and enjoy the resource privileges of prestige. Among various South Asian languages, for example, the term "big man" is found in Sanskrit, Hindi, and several Dravidian languages. In Hindi, for example, *bara asami* means "great man, person of high position or rank" (Platts, 1960, pp. 151–152). In North America, north of Mexico, "big man" and similar terms are found among groups such as the Wappo, Dakota, Miwok, Natick, Choctaw, Kiowa, and Osage. In Mexico and South America "big man" and closely related terms are found among the Cayapa, Chatino, Mazahua, Mixe, Mixteco, Quiche, Terraba, Tzeltal, Totonaco, Tarahumara, Quechua, and Hahuatl. Linguistically, therefore, it seems that many cultures have found it important to invent words or phrases to describe men who are high in status.

Linguistic analysis suggests that these terms indicate men who are important, influential, and powerful (Brown & Chia-yun, n.d.). They refer to men at or near the top of social hierarchies, the elite in status and prestige within their groups. A man's social status, as indicated by these linguistic phrases, would provide a powerful cue to his possession of resources.

Women appear to desire men who command a high position in society because social status is a universal cue to the control of resources. Along with status come better food, more abundant territory, and superior health care. Greater social status bestows on children social opportunities missed by the children of lower-ranking males. For male children worldwide, access to more and better quality mates typically accompanies families of higher social status. In one study of 186 societies ranging from the Mbuti Pygmies of Africa to the Aleut Eskimos, high-status men invariably had greater wealth and more wives and provided better nourishment for their children (Betzig, 1986).

Women in the United States express a preference for mates who have high social status or a high-status profession, qualities that are viewed as only slightly less important than good financial prospects (Buss & Barnes, 1986; Hill, 1945; Hudson & Henze, 1969; Langhorne & Secord, 1955; McGinnis, 1958). Using a rating scale from irrelevant or unimportant (0) to indispensable (3), American women from Massachusetts, Michigan, Texas, and California all rated social status as between important and indispensable, whereas men rated it as merely desirable but not very important. In one study of five thousand college students women listed as desirable attributes of a mate status, prestige, rank, position, power, standing, station, and high place considerably more frequently than do men (Langhorne & Secord, 1955).

One study examined short-term and long-term mating to discover which characteristics people especially valued in potential spouses, as contrasted with potential sex partners (Buss & Schmitt, 1993). Participants were male and female students at the University of Michigan, a population for which both casual and marital mating issues are relevant concerns (Little, 1989). Several hundred individuals evaluated sixty-seven characteristics for their desirability or undesirability in the short or long term, rating them on a scale ranging from -3 (extremely undesirable) to +3 (extremely desirable). Women judged the likelihood of success in a profession and the possession of a promising career to be highly desirable in a spouse, giving average ratings of +2.60 and +2.70, respectively. Significantly, these cues to future status are seen by women as more desirable in spouses than in casual sex partners, with the latter ratings reaching only +1.10 and +0.40, respectively.

American women also place great value on education and professional degrees in mates—characteristics that are strongly linked with social status. The same study found that women rate lack of education as highly undesirable in a potential husband, giving it an average rating of –2.39 (Buss & Schmitt, 1993). The cliché that women prefer to marry doctors, lawyers, professors, and other professionals corresponds with reality. Women shun men who are easily dominated by other men or who fail to command the respect of the group.

The importance that women grant to social status in mates is not limited to America or even to capitalist countries. In the vast majority of the thirty-seven cultures considered in the international study on choosing a mate, women valued social status in a prospective mate more than men in both communist and socialist countries, among Africans and Asians, among Catholics and Jews, in the southern tropics and the northern climes (Buss, 1989a). In Taiwan, for example, women valued status 63 percent more than men, in Zambia women valued it 30 percent more, in West Germany women valued it 38 percent more, and in Brazil women valued it 40 percent more (see Figure 4.4 on page 112).

Hierarchies are universal features among human groups and resources tend to accumulate to those who rise in the hierarchy. Women historically appear to have solved the adaptive problem of acquiring resources in part by preferring men who are high in status. Modern women are descendants of these successful ancestors, and so have inherited their mate preferences.

Preference for Older Men

The age of a man also provides an important clue to his access to resources. Just as young male baboons must mature before they are able to enter the upper ranks in the baboon social hierarchy, human adolescents and young men rarely command the respect, status, or position of more mature men. This reaches extremes among the Tiwi, an aboriginal tribe located on two islands off the coast of Northern Australia (Hart & Pilling, 1960). The Tiwi are a gerontocracy in which the very old men wield most of the power and prestige and control the mating system through their complex networks of alliances. Even in American culture, status and wealth tend to accumulate with increasing age.

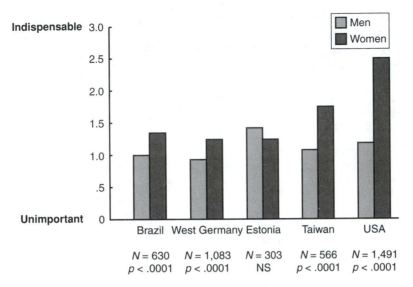

FIGURE 4.4   Preference for Social Status in a Marriage Partner. Participants in thirty-seven cultures rated this variable, in the context of eighteen other variables, on how desirable it would be in a potential long-term mate or marriage partner using a four-point rating scale, ranging from zero (irrelevant or unimportant) to three (indispensable). Data from Buss, D. M., Abbott, M., Angleitner, A., Asherian, A., Biaggio, A., and other co-authors (1990).

N = sample size.

p values less than .05 indicate that sex difference is significant.

NS indicates that sex difference is not significant.

In all thirty-seven cultures included in the international study on mate selection, women preferred older men (see Figure 4.5). Averaged over all cultures, women prefer men who are roughly three and a half years older. The preferred age difference ranges from French Canadian women, who seek husbands just a shade under two years older, to Iranian women, who seek husbands more than five years older. The worldwide average age difference between actual brides and grooms is three years, suggesting that women's marriage decisions often match their mating preferences.

To understand why women value older mates, we must consider the things that change with age. One of the most consistent changes is access to resources. In contemporary Western societies income generally increases with age (Jencks, 1979). American men who are thirty, for example, make $14,000 dollars more than men who are twenty; men who are forty make $7,000 more than men who are thirty. These status trends are not limited to the Western world. Among the Tiwi, a polygynous people, men are typically at least thirty before they have enough social status to acquire a first wife (Hart & Pilling, 1960). Rarely does a Tiwi man under the age of forty attain enough status to acquire more than one wife. Older age, resources, and status are coupled across cultures.

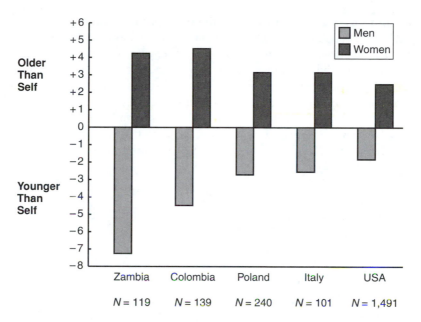

FIGURE 4.5   Age Differences Preferred between Self and Spouse. Participants recorded their preferred age difference, if any, between self and potential spouse. The scale shown is in years, with positive values signifying preference for older spouses and negative values signifying preference for younger spouses.

N = sample size.

Source: Buss, D. M., & Schmidt, D. P. (1993). Sexual strategies theory: An evolutionary perspective on human mating. *Psychological Review, 100,* 204–232. Copyright © 1993 by the American Psychological Association. Adapted with permission.

In traditional societies part of this linkage may be related to physical strength and hunting prowess. Physical strength increases in men as they get older, peaking in the late twenties and early thirties. Although there have been no systematic studies of the relationship between age and hunting ability, anthropologists believe it may peak when a man is in his mid-thirties, at which point his slight decline in physical prowess is more than compensated for by his increased knowledge, patience, skill, and wisdom (Kim Hill, personal communication, 1991) So women's preference for older men may stem from our hunter-gatherer ancestors, for whom the resources derived from hunting were critical to survival.

Twenty-year-old women in all thirty-seven cultures studied typically prefer to marry men only a few years older, not substantially older, in spite of the fact that men's financial resources generally do not peak until they are in their forties or fifties. One reason why young women are not drawn to substantially older men may be that older men have a higher risk of dying and hence are less likely to be around to continue contributing to the provisioning and protection of children. Furthermore, the potential incompatibility created by a large age discrepancy may lead to strife, thus increasing the odds of divorce. For these reasons, young women may be more drawn to men a few years older who have considerable promise, rather than to substantially older men who already have attained a high position but have a less certain future.

All these cues—economic resources, social status, and older age—add up to one thing: the ability of a man to acquire and control resources that ancestral women could use for themselves and for their children. The possession of resources, however, is not enough. Women also need men who possess traits that are likely to lead to the sustained acquisition of resources over time. A man's ambition is one of these traits.

Preference for Ambition and Industriousness

How do people get ahead in everyday life? Psychologist Liisa Kyl-Heku sought to identify the tactics that people use to elevate their position within hierarchies in the workplace and in social settings (Kyl-Heku & Buss, 1996). She asked eighty-four individuals from California and Michigan to think about people they knew well and to write down the acts they had seen these people using to get ahead in status or dominance hierarchies. Using various statistical procedures, she discovered twenty-six distinct tactics including deception, social networking, sexual favors, education, and industriousness. The industriousness tactic included actions such as putting in extra time and effort at work, managing time efficiently, prioritizing goals, and working hard to impress others. She then asked 212 individuals in their mid- to late twenties to indicate which tactics they had used. She separately asked their spouses to indicate which tactics their partners had used. Next she correlated this information to their past income and promotions and their anticipated income and promotions to see which tactics for getting ahead were most successfully linked with actual measures of getting ahead.

Among all the tactics, sheer hard work proved to be one of the best predictors of past and anticipated income and promotions. Those who said they worked hard and whose spouses agreed that they worked hard achieved higher levels of education, higher annual salaries, and anticipated greater salaries and promotions than those who failed to work hard. Industrious and ambitious men secure a higher occupational status than lazy, unmotivated men (Kyl-Heku & Buss, 1996; Jencks, 1979; Willerman, 1979).

American women seem to be aware of this connection, because they indicate a desire for men who show the characteristics linked with getting ahead. In the 1950s, for example, 5,000 undergraduates were asked to list characteristics that they sought in a potential mate. Women far more than men desired mates who enjoy their work, show career orientation, demonstrate industry, and display ambition (Langhorne & Secord, 1955). The 852 single American women and 100 married American women in the international study on mate selection unanimously rated ambition and industriousness as important or indispensable (Buss, 1989a). Women in the study of short- and long-term mating regard men who lack ambition as extremely undesirable, whereas men view lack of ambition in a wife as neither desirable nor undesirable (Buss & Schmitt, 1993). Women are likely to discontinue a long-term relationship with a man if he loses his job, lacks career goals, or shows a lazy streak (Betzig, 1989).

Women's preference for men who show ambition and industry is not limited to the United States or even to Western society. In the overwhelming majority of cultures women value ambition and industry more than men do, typically rating them as between important and indispensable. In Taiwan, for example, women rate ambition and industriousness as 26 percent more important than men do, women from Bulgaria rate it as 29 percent more important; and women from Brazil rate it as 30 percent more important.

This cross-cultural and cross-history evidence supports the key evolutionary expectation that women have evolved a preference for men possessing signs of the ability to acquire resources and a disdain for men lacking the ambition that often leads to resources. This preference helped ancestral women solve the critical adaptive problem of securing resources and it helped them gauge the likelihood of future resources when direct and easily observable signs of resources were absent. Even if directly observable resources were present, a man's ambition and industriousness provided an excellent signal of the continuation of those resources. The evidence suggests that modern women are the descendants of women who expressed this preference.

Preference for Dependability and Stability

Among the eighteen characteristics rated in the worldwide study on mate selection, the second and third most highly valued characteristics, after love, are a dependable character and emotional stability or maturity. In twenty-one of thirty-seven cultures, men and women had the same preference for dependability in a partner (Buss et al., 1990). Of the remaining sixteen cultures, women in fifteen valued dependability more than men. Averaged across all thirty-seven cultures, women rated dependable character a 2.69 where a 3 signifies indispensable; men rate it nearly as important, with an average of 2.50. In the case of emotional stability or maturity the sexes differ more. Women in twenty-three cultures value this quality significantly more than men do; in the remaining fourteen cultures men and women value emotional stability equally. Averaging across all cultures, women give this quality a 2.68, whereas men give it a 2.47. In all cultures, in effect, women place a tremendous value on these characteristics, judging them to be anywhere from important to indispensable in a potential spouse.

These characteristics may possess great value to women worldwide for two reasons. First, they are reliable signals that resources will be provided consistently over time. Second, those men lacking dependability and emotional stability provide erratically and inflict heavy emotional and other costs on their mates. In a study of newlyweds, 104 couples were selected at random from the public records of all marriages that had been licensed in a large county in Michigan during a particular six-month period (Buss, 1991). These couples completed a six-hour battery of personality tests and self-evaluations of their marital relationship and their spouse's character, and were interviewed by a male and a female interviewer. One instrument asked participants to indicate which among 147 possible costs their partner had inflicted on them over the past year.

Emotionally unstable men—as defined by themselves, their spouses, and the interviewers—are especially costly to women. They tend to be self-centered and monopolize shared resources. Furthermore, they are frequently possessive, monopolizing much of the time of their wives. They show higher than average sexual jealousy, becoming enraged when their wives merely talk with someone else, and are dependent, insisting that their mates provide for all of their needs. They tend to be abusive both verbally and physically. They display inconsiderateness, such as by failing to show up on time, and they are moodier than their more stable counterparts, often crying for no apparent reason. They have more affairs than average, suggesting further diversion of time and resources (Buss & Shackelford, 1997). All these costs indicate that such men will absorb their partners' time and resources, divert their own time and resources elsewhere, and fail to channel resources consistently over time. Dependability and stability are personal qualities that signal increased likelihood that a woman's resources will not be drained by the man.

The unpredictable aspects of emotionally unstable men inflict additional costs by preventing solutions to critical adaptive problems. The erratic supply of resources can wreak havoc with accomplishing the goals required for survival and reproduction. Meat that is suddenly not available because an unpredictable, changeable, or variable mate decided at the last minute to take a nap rather than go on the hunt is sustenance counted on but not delivered. Its absence creates problems. Resources prove most beneficial when predictable. The erratically provided resources may then go to waste when the needs they were intended to meet are met through other, more costly means. Resources that are supplied predictably can be more efficiently allocated to the many adaptive hurdles that must be overcome in everyday life.

Women place a premium on dependability and emotional stability to reap the benefits that a mate can provide to them consistently over time. In human ancestral times, women choosing stable, dependable men had a greater likelihood of ensuring the man's ability to acquire and maintain resources for use by them and their children. Women making these wise choices avoided many of the costs inflicted by undependable and unstable men.

Preference for Athletic Prowess

The importance of physical characteristics in the female choice of a mate is notable throughout the animal world. Male gladiator frogs, are responsible for creating nests and defending the eggs. In the majority of courtships, a stationary male gladiator frog is deliberately bumped by a female who is considering him. She strikes him with great force, sometimes enough to rock him back or even scare him away. If the male moves too much or bolts from the nest, the female hastily leaves to find an alternative mate. Only rarely does a female reject a male who remains firmly planted after being bumped. Bumping helps a female frog assess how successful the male will be at defending her clutch. The bump test reveals the male's physical ability to protect.

Women sometimes face physical domination by larger, stronger males, which can lead to injury and sexual domination. These conditions undoubtedly occurred with some regularity during ancestral conditions. Indeed, studies of many nonhuman primate groups reveal that male physical and sexual domination of females has been a recurrent part of our primate heritage. Primatologist Barbara Smuts lived among the baboons residing in the savanna plains of Africa and studied their mating patterns (Smuts, 1985).

She found that females frequently formed enduring "special friendships" with males who offered physical protection to themselves and their infants. In return, these females granted their "friends" preferential sexual access during times of estrus. In essence, female baboons exchange sex for protection.

Analogously, one benefit to women of long-term mating is the physical protection a man can offer. A man's size, strength, physical prowess, and athletic ability are cues that signal solutions to the problem of protection. The evidence shows that women's preferences in a mate embody these cues. In the study of temporary and permanent mating, American women rated the desirability of a series of physical traits. Women judged short men to be undesirable for either a short-term or a permanent mate (Buss & Schmitt, 1993). In contrast, women found it very desirable for a potential marriage partner to be tall, physically strong, and athletic. For example, using a rating scale ranging from –3 (extremely undesirable) to +3 (extremely desirable), women rated the quality "physically strong" to be 1.50 (in between "somewhat desirable" and "very desirable"), whereas men rated this quality only 0.87—a notable difference.

Another group of American women consistently indicated a preference for men of average or taller height, roughly 5 feet 11 inches, as the ideal marriage partner. Tall men are consistently seen as more desirable as dates and mates than are short or average men (Ellis, 1992). Furthermore, the two studies of personal ads described earlier revealed that, among women who mentioned height, 80 percent wanted a man to be 6 feet or taller (Cameron, Oskamp, & Sparks, 1978). Perhaps even more telling is the finding that ads placed by taller men received more responses from women than those placed by shorter men (Lynn & Shurgot, 1984). Tall men date more often than short men and have a larger pool of potential mates. Women solve the problem of protection from other aggressive men at least in part by preferring a mate who has the size, strength, and physical prowess to protect them.

This preference is not limited to Western cultures. Among the Mehinaku tribe of the Brazilian Amazon anthropologist Thomas Gregor (1985) noted the importance of men's wrestling skills as an arena in which these differences become acute:

> A heavily muscled, imposingly built man is likely to accumulate many girlfriends, while a small man, deprecatingly referred to as a *peristsi*, fares badly. The mere fact of height creates a measurable advantage. . . . A powerful wrestler, say the villagers, is frightening . . . he commands fear and respect. To the women, he is "beautiful" (*awitsiri*), in demand as a paramour [lover] and husband. Triumphant in politics as well as in love, the champion wrestler embodies the highest qualities of manliness. Not so fortunate the vanquished. A chronic loser, no matter what his other virtues, is regarded as a fool. As he wrestles, the men shout mock advice. . . . The women are less audible as they watch the matches from their doorways, but they too have their sarcastic jokes. None of them is proud of having a loser as a husband or lover. (pp. 35, 96)

Barbara Smuts believes that during human evolutionary history physical protection was one of the most important things a man could offer a woman. Aggressive men wishing to dominate women physically and to circumvent women's sexual choices may have exerted an important selection pressure on women in ancestral times. Given the alarming incidence of sexual coercion and rape in many cultures, a mate's protection value may well remain a selectively relevant force in modern environments. Many women do not feel safe on the streets, and a strong, tall, athletic mate acts as a deterrent for other sexually aggressive men. Evolutionary psychologist Nigal Barber summarizes the evidence for women's preferences: "traits of male body structure such as height, shoulder width, and upper-body musculature are sexually attractive to women and also intimidating to other men" (Barber, 1995, p. 406).

Preference for Good Health

Mating with someone who is unhealthy would have posed a number of adaptive risks for our ancestors. First, an unhealthy mate would have a higher risk of becoming debilitated, thus failing to deliver whatever adaptive benefits he or she might otherwise have provided such as food, protection, health care, and investment in child rearing. Second, an unhealthy mate would be at an increased risk of dying, prematurely cutting off the flow of resources and forcing a person to incur the costs of searching for a new mate. Third, an unhealthy mate might transfer communicable diseases or viruses to the chooser, impairing his or her survival and reproduction. Fourth, an unhealthy mate might infect the children of the union, imperiling their chances of surviving and reproducing. And fifth, if health is partly heritable, a person who choses an unhealthy mate would risk passing on genes for poor health to his or her children. For all these reasons, it comes as no surprise that women and men both place a premium on the health of a potential mate.

In the study of cultures, on a scale ranging from 0 (irrelevant) to +3 (indispensable), women and men both judged "good health" to be highly important. Averaged across the cultures, women gave it a +2.28 and men gave it a +2.31 (Buss et al., 1990). Using a separate instrument that requested participants to rank thirteen characteristics from most (1) to least important (13), both sexes gave "healthy" an average ranking of fourth. That quality was exceeded only by "kind and understanding" (1), "intelligent" (2), and "exciting personality" (3).

The importance people place on good health is not unique in the animal world. Some species display large, loud, and gaudy traits that are costly yet appear to signal health and vitality. Consider the bright, flamboyant, ostentatious plumage of the peacock. The mystery of the peacock's tail, which seems so contrary to survival, is on the verge of being solved. It has been proposed that the brilliant plumage of peacocks and other birds serves as a signal of a low load of parasites (Hamilton & Zuk, 1982). Peacocks with duller plumage, it turns out, carry a higher parasite load. Peahens appear to prefer the brilliant plumage because it provides a reliable signal of a healthy peacock.

Randy Thornhill, Steve Gangestad, Karl Grammer, Todd Schackelford, Randy Larsen and others have discovered an important physical marker of good health—the degree to which the face and body are symmetrical (Gangestad & Thornhill, 1997; Grammer & Thornhill, 1994; Shackelford & Larsen, 1997; Thornhill & Moeller, 1997). Their evolutionary reasoning is that various environmental events and genetic stressors produced deviations from bilateral symmetry, creating lopsided faces and bodies. Some individuals are better able to withstand such events and stresses better than others—that is, they show *developmental stability*. The presence of facial and bodily symmetry is an important health cue, reflecting an individual's ability to withstand environmental and genetic stressors. Therefore, women are hypothesized to have evolved a preference for men who show physical evidence of symmetry. Such symmetry would not only increase the odds of the mate being around to invest and less likely to pass on diseases to her children, it may have direct genetic benefits as well. By selecting a man with symmetrical features, a women may be in essence selecting a superior complement of genes to be transmitted to her children.

A considerable body of evidence supports the hypothesis that symmetry is indeed a health cue and that women especially value this quality in mates (Gangestad & Thornhill, 1997; Thornhill & Moeller, 1997). First, facially symmetric individuals score higher on tests of physiological, psychological, and emotional health (Shackelford & Larsen, 1997). Second, there is a positive relationship between facial symmetry and judgments of physical attractiveness in both sexes. Third, facially symmetrical men, compared with

Most women find men with symmetrical faces, as exemplified by the actor Denzel Washington (left) to be more attractive than men with asymmetrical faces, as illustrated by the musician and actor Lyle Lovett (right). Symmetry is hypothesized to be a health cue that signals a relative absence of parasites, genetic resistance to parasites, or a relative lack of environmental insults during development.

their more lopsided counterparts, are judged to be more sexually attractive to women, have more sexual partners during their lifetimes, have more extra-pair copulations, and begin sexual intercourse earlier in life.

Preference for Love

Women long have faced the adaptive problem of choosing men who not only have the necessary resources but also show a willingness to commit those resources to them and their children. This may be more problematic than it at first seems. Although resources can often be directly observed, commitment cannot. Instead, gauging commitment requires looking for cues that signal the likelihood of future fidelity in the channeling of resources. Love may be one of the key cues to commitment.

According to conventional wisdom in the social sciences, "love" is a relatively recent invention, introduced a few hundred years ago by romantic Europeans (Jankowiak, 1995). According to this view, love is a local product of Western culture, and will not be found across the globe in societies far removed from European influence. Recent research suggests that this conventional wisdom is radically wrong. There is evidence that loving thoughts, emotions, and actions are experienced by people in cultures worldwide —from the Zulu in the southern tip of Africa to the Eskimos in the cold northern ice caps of Alaska. In a survey of 168 diverse cultures around the world, anthropologists William Jankoviak and Edward Fisher examined four sources of evidence for the presence of love: the singing of love songs, elopement by lovers against the wishes of parents, cultural informants reporting personal anguish and longing for a loved one, and folklore depicting romantic entanglements. Using the presence of these phenomena they found evidence for the presence of romantic love in 88.5 percent of the cultures (Jankowiak, 1995; Jankowiak & Fischer, 1992). When sociologist Sue Sprecher and her colleagues interviewed 1,667 men and women in Russia, Japan, and the United States, they found that 61 percent of the Russian men and 73 percent of the Russian women were in love at that time (Sprecher, Aron, Hatfield, Cortese, Potapova, & Levitskya, 1994). Comparable figures for the Japanese were 41 percent of the men and 63 percent of the women. Among Americans, 53 percent of the men and 63 percent of the women acknowledged being in love. Clearly love is not a phenomenon limited to America or to Western culture.

To identify precisely what love is and how it is linked to commitment, one study examined acts of love (Buss, 1988a). First, fifty women and fifty men from the Universities of California and Michigan were asked to think of people they knew who were currently in love and to describe actions performed by those people that would reflect or exemplify their love. A different group of college men and women then evaluated each of the 115 acts named for how typical it was of love. Acts of commitment top women's and men's lists, being viewed as most central to love. Such acts include giving up romantic relations with others, talking of marriage, and expressing a desire to have children with this person. When performed by a man, these acts of love signal the intention to commit resources to one woman and her future children.

Commitment, however, has many facets that signal particular ways of sharing resources. One major component of commitment is fidelity, exemplified by the act of remaining faithful to a partner when not physically together. Fidelity signals the exclusive commitment of sexual resources to a single partner. Another aspect of commitment is the channeling of resources to the loved one, such as buying an expensive gift. Acts such as this signal a serious intention to commit to a long-term relationship. Emotional support is yet another facet of commitment, revealed by such behavior as being available in times of trouble and listening to the partner's problems. Commitment entails a channeling of time, energy, and effort to the partner's needs at the expense of fulfilling one's own personal goals. Acts of reproduction also represent a direct commitment to one's partner's reproduction. All these acts, which are viewed as essential to love, signal the commitment of sexual, economic, emotional, and genetic resources to one person.

Because love is a worldwide phenomenon, and because a primary function of acts of love is to signal commitment, women are predicted to place a premium on love in the process of choosing a long-term mate. To find out if this was the case, Sue Sprecher and her colleagues asked American, Russian, and Japanese students whether they would marry someone who had all the qualities they desired in a mate if they were not in love with that person (Sprecher et al., 1994). Fully 89 percent of American women and 82 percent of Japanese women say they require love for marriage, even if all other important qualities were met. Among Russians, only 59 percent of the women would *not* marry someone with whom they were not in love, no matter how many desirable qualities that person had. So, the majority of women in all three cultures see love as an indispensable ingredient in the decision to marry.

Direct studies of preferences in a mate confirm the centrality of love. In a study of 162 Texas women college students, of one hundred characteristics examined, the quality of being loving is the most strongly desired in a potential husband (Hendrick & Hendrick, 1992). The international study on choosing a mate confirmed the importance of love across cultures. Among eighteen possible characteristics, mutual attraction or love proved to be the most highly valued in a potential mate by both sexes, rated a 2.87 by women and a 2.81 by men (Buss et al., 1990). Nearly all women and men, from the tribal enclaves of South Africa to the bustling streets of Brazilian cities, gave love the top rating, indicating that it is an indispensable part of marriage.

Because women invest significantly more than men in childbearing and rearing, they have more to lose by having sexual intercourse indiscriminately. Requiring love is a way of securing a commitment of resources commensurate with the value of the resource that women give to men. Requiring love would presumably have helped ancestral women solve the critical problem of securing the commitment of resources from a man that could aid in the survival and reproduction of her offspring. We are the descendants of women who required these forms of commitment from men.

Preference for Willingness to Invest in Children

Another adaptive problem that women face when selecting a long-term mate is gauging men's willingness to invest in children. This adaptive problem is important for two reasons: (1) men sometimes seek sexual variety, and so may channel their efforts toward other women (mating effort) rather than toward children (parental effort) (see Chapter

6); and (2) men evaluate the likelihood that they are the actual genetic father of a child, and tend to withhold investment from the child when they know or suspect that the child is not their own (La Cerra, 1994). These two factors imply that men will differ widely in how willing they are to invest in a particular child; this variability is essential for the evolution of women's preferences for men who show signs of a willingness to invest in their children.

To test the hypothesis that women have an evolved preference for men who are willing to invest in children, psychologist Peggy La Cerra constructed slide images of men in several different conditions: (1) a man standing alone; (2) a man interacting with an eighteen-month-old child, including smiling, making eye contact, and reaching for the child; (3) a man ignoring the child, who was crying; (4) a man and the child simply facing forward (neutral condition); and (5) a man vacuuming a living room rug. The same models were depicted in all conditions.

After viewing these slide images, 240 undergraduate women rated each image on how attractive they found the man in each slide as a date, as a sexual partner, as a marriage partner, as a friend, and as a neighbor. The rating scale ranged from -5 (very unattractive) to +5 (very attractive). A number of fascinating results emerged from the ratings of the men as potential mates. First, women found the man interacting with the child positively to be more attractive as a marriage partner (average attractiveness rating, 2.75) than the same man either standing alone (2.0) or standing neutrally next to the child (2.0). Second, women found the man who ignored the child in distress to be low in attractiveness as a marriage partner (1.25), indeed the lowest of all. Third, the effect of interacting positively with the child proved *not* to be a result of the man showing domestic proclivities in general. Women found the man vacuuming, for example, to be less attractive (1.3) than the man simply standing alone doing nothing (2.0). From this study La Cerra concluded that "women's ratings of the attractiveness of men as potential mates are increased by cues of their affection toward a child and decreased by cues of their indifference toward a child in distress" (La Cerra, 1994, p. 67).

This study suggests that women prefer men who show a willingness to invest in children as marriage partners. Yet do humans in general have a preference for marriage partners who show a willingness to invest in children, or is this preference unique to women? To address this issue La Cerra conducted another study, this time using women as models and men as raters. Women were posed in conditions parallel to those of the male models in the first study—alone, interacting positively with a child, ignoring a child in distress, neutral, and vacuuming a rug. Also paralleling the first study, 240 undergraduate men rated how attractive each woman was as a marriage partner, a date, a sex partner, and so on.

The results for men were strikingly different from those for women. Men found the woman standing alone to be just as attractive (average attractiveness rating, 2.70) as the woman interacting positively with the child (2.70). In fact, the varying contexts made no difference to men in their judgments of how attractive the woman was as a marriage partner. Whether the woman ignored the child, stood next to the child, vacuumed a rug, or interacted positively with the child did not matter. Men's attractiveness judgments were the same across all contexts.

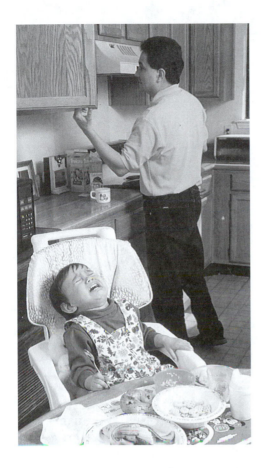

La Cerra (1994) found that women find the man interacting positively with the baby considerably more attractive, suggesting a mate preference for men who display a willingness to invest in children. Comparable photographs of women, shown either ignoring or interacting positively with a baby, produced no effect on men's judgments of women's attractiveness.

In short, women appear to have a specific preference for, and attraction to, men who show a willingness to invest in children, but the reverse is not true. On a personal note, La Cerra observed that one catalyst for her research was witnessing a poster of an attractive man holding an infant—an image that drew her attention and also proved to be a highly effective advertising technique for targeting female markets (La Cerra, 1994, p. 87). Ancestral women who failed to notice cues to a man's willingness to invest in children would have been at a disadvantage compared with women who noticed and acted on these cues.

Context Effects on Women's Mate Preferences

From an evolutionary perspective, preferences are not predicted to operate blindly, oblivious to context or condition. Just as human desires for particular foods (e.g., ripe fruit) will depend on context (e.g., whether one is hungry or full), women's preferences in a mate should also depend in part on relevant contexts. Thus far, two contexts have been explored—the magnitude of resources a woman already has prior to her search for a mate and the temporal context of mating (committed versus casual mating).

Effects of Women's Personal Resources on Mate Preferences

An alternative explanation to the evolutionary psychological theory has been offered for the preferences of women for men with resources—the structural powerlessness hypothesis (Buss & Barnes, 1986). According to this view, because women are typically excluded from power and access to resources, which are largely controlled by men, women seek mates who have power, status, and earning capacity. Women try to marry upward in socioeconomic status because this provides their primary channel for gaining access to resources. Men do not value economic resources in a mate as much as women do because they already have control over these resources and because women have fewer resources anyway.

The society of Bakweri, from Cameroon in West Africa, casts doubt on this theory by illustrating what happens when women have real power (Ardener, Ardener, & Warmington, 1960). Bakweri women hold greater personal and economic power because they have more resources and are in scarcer supply than men. Women secure resources through their own labors on plantations, but also from casual sex, which is a lucrative source of income. There are roughly 236 men for every hundred women, an imbalance that results from the continual influx of men from other areas of the country to work on the plantations. Because of the extreme imbalance in numbers of the sexes, women have considerable latitude to exercise their choice in a mate. Women thus have more money than men and more potential mates to choose from. Yet Bakweri women persist in preferring mates with resources. Wives often complain about receiving insufficient support from their husbands. Indeed, lack of sufficient economic provisioning is the reason for divorce most frequently cited by women. Bakweri women change husbands if they find a man who can offer them more money and pay a larger bride-price. When women are in a position to fulfill their evolved preference for a man with resources, they do so. Having dominant control of economic resources apparently does not negate this mate preference.

Professionally and economically successful women in America also value resources in men. A study of married couples identified women who were financially successful, as measured by their salary and income, and contrasted their preferences in a mate with those of women with lower salaries and income (Buss, 1989a). The financially successful women often made more than $50,000 a year, and a few earned more than $100,000. These women were well educated, tended to hold professional degrees, and had high self-esteem. The study showed that successful women place an even greater value than less professionally successful women on mates who have professional degrees, high social status, and greater intelligence and who are tall, independent, and self-confident. Women's personal income was positively correlated with the income they wanted in an ideal mate (+.31), the desire for a mate who is a college graduate (+.29), and the desire for a mate with a professional degree (+.35), all of which were statistically reliable. Contrary to the structural powerlessness hypothesis, these women expressed an even stronger preference for high-earning men than did women who are less financially successful.

In a separate study psychologists Michael Wiederman and Elizabeth Allgeier found that college women who expect to earn the most after college put more weight on the promising financial prospects of a potential husband than do women who expect to earn less. Professionally successful women, such as medical and law students, also place heavy importance on a mate's earning capacity (Wiederman & Allgeier, 1992). Furthermore, men low in financial resources and status do not value economic resources in a mate any more than do financially successful men (Townsend, 1989). Taken together, these results not only fail to support the structural powerlessness hypothesis, they directly contradict it.

Effects of Temporal Context on Women's Mate Preferences

A mating relationship can last for a lifetime, but often matings are of shorter duration. In Chapter 6 we will explore short-term mating in detail, but it is worthwhile to highlight now the findings that show that women's preferences shift as a function of temporal context. In one study, Buss and Schmitt (1993) asked undergraduate women to rate sixty-seven characteristics on their desirability in short-term and long-term mates. The rating scale ranged from –3 (extremely undesirable) to +3 (extremely desirable). Women found the following qualities to be more desirable in long-term marriage contexts than in short-term sexual contexts: "ambitious and career-oriented" (average rating, 2.45 in long-term versus 1.04 in short-term), "college graduate" (2.38 versus 1.05), "creative" (1.90 versus 1.29), "devoted to you" (2.80 versus 0.90), "fond of children" (2.93 versus 1.21), "kind" (2.88 versus 2.50), "understanding" (2.93 versus 2.10), "responsible" (2.75 versus 1.75), and "cooperative" (2.41 versus 1.47). These findings suggest that temporal context matters a great deal for women, causing shifts in their preferences depending on whether a marriage partner or a casual sex partner is sought (Schmitt & Buss, 1996).

In another study evolutionary psychologist Joanna Scheib (1997) constructed stimuli consisting of photographs paired with written descriptions of the personality characteristics presumed to describe the men in each photo. The written descriptions emphasized traits such as dependable, loyal, kind, mature, patient, and so on. Pairs of these photos and accompanying descriptions were shown to a sample of one hundred-sixty heterosexual women between the ages of eighteen and forty (mean age, twenty-six). Sixty of these women were or had been married or in marital-like relationships. Participants were shown five pairs of the stimulus men and asked to choose one man from each pair. Half the women were asked to choose which one they would prefer as a husband; the other half were asked to choose which one they would prefer for a brief sexual affair.

Women's choices differed profoundly as a function of temporal context. Women tended to select the men with good character traits such as dependable, kind, and mature when choosing a potential husband more than when choosing a short-term sex partner.

Specifically, of the five paired choices, most women chose roughly four with the superior character traits over those with the better looks. Furthermore, Scheib discovered an effect associated with marital status. Women who were or had been married showed a stronger preference for good character traits than women who had never been married (those never married tended more often to choose the physically attractive men). So by using an experimental manipulation in which women were forced to trade off good looks for character, context-sensitive preferences emerged. In the long-term marital context, women tended to choose character over looks.

A recent study by the social psychologist Pamela Regan (1998) explored the effects of perceived mate value and temporal context of mating on minimum standards desired in a mate. She found that women imposed higher standards than men in the short-term mating context, but not in the long-term context. Furthermore, women with high self-perceived mate value (how desirable they thought they were relative to other women) set higher minimum standards than did women lower on self-perceived mate value in both temporal contexts. In contrast, men's self-perceived mate value was unrelated to the minimum standards they imposed.

In summary, two contexts have been explored for their effects on women's preferences. The first context pertains to women's personal access to monetary resources. Contrary to the structural powerlessness hypothesis, when women have more resources, they appear to value income and education more, not less, in a potential husband. The second context pertains to the temporal duration of the relationship. Several studies show that women emphasize character traits over attractiveness when evaluating a potential husband. Qualities such as loyalty, dependability, and kindness weigh more heavily than looks in women's marital preferences. Future research could profitably explore a wider range of contextual factors, including women's "mate value," personal attractiveness, and previous mating experiences.

How Women's Mate Preferences Affect Actual Mating Behavior

For preferences to evolve, they must affect actual mating decisions because it is those decisions that have reproductive consequences. For a number of reasons, however, preferences should not show a *perfect* correspondence with actual mating behavior. People can't always get what they want for a variety of reasons. First, there are a limited number of highly desirable potential mates. Second, one's own mate value limits access to those who are highly desirable. In general only the most desirable women are in a position to attract the most desirable men, and vice versa. Third, parents and other kin sometimes influence one's mating decisions, regardless of personal preferences. Despite these factors, women's mate preferences had to have affected their actual mating decisions some of the time over the course of human evolutionary history or they would not have evolved. Following are several sources of evidence that preferences do affect mating decisions.

Women's Responses to Men's Personal Ads

One source of evidence comes from women's responses to personal ads posted by men in newspapers. If women's preferences affected their mating decisions, then they would be predicted to respond more often to men who indicate that they are financially well off. Baize and Schroeder (1995) tested this prediction using a sample of 120 personal ads placed in two different newspapers, one from the West Coast and the other from the Midwest. The authors mailed a questionnaire to those who posted the ads, asking for information about personal status, response rate, and personality characteristics. A total of ninety-two respondents returned the questionnaire, with an average age of thirty-seven. Roughly half had never been married; the other half were separated or divorced (one male respondent indicated that he was currently married).

Several variables significantly predicted the number of letters men received in response to their ads. First, *age* was a significant predictor, with women responding more often to older men than to younger men ($r = +.43$). Second, *income* and *education* were also significant predictors, with women responding more to men with ads indicating higher salaries ($r = +.30$) and more years of education ($r = +.37$). Baize and Schroeder ended their article on a humorous note by recalling the question posed by Tim Hardin in his famous folk song: "If I were a carpenter and you were a lady, would you marry me anyway, would you have my baby?" Given the cumulative research findings, the most likely answer is: No.

Women's Marriages to Men High in Occupational Status

A second source of findings pertains to women who are in a position to get what they want—women who have the qualities that men desire in a mate such as physical attractiveness (see Chapter 5). What are the mate choices of these women? In three separate sociological studies researchers discovered that physically attractive women in fact marry men who are higher in social status and financial holdings than do women who are less attractive (Elder, 1969; Taylor & Glenn, 1976; Udry & Ekland, 1984). In one study the physical attractiveness of women was correlated with the occupational prestige of their husbands (Taylor and Glenn, 1976). For different groups the correlations were all positive, ranging between +.23 and +.37.

A longitudinal study was conducted at the Institute of Human Development in Berkeley, California (Elder, 1969). Physical attractiveness ratings were made by staff members of then unmarried women when they were adolescents. Two interviewers were used, with between-judge reliabilities above +.90. This sample of women was then followed up in adulthood after they had married, and the occupational statuses of their husbands were assessed.

The results were examined separately for working-class and middle-class women. The correlations between a woman's attractiveness in adolescence and her husband's occupational status roughly a decade later was +.46 for women with working-class backgrounds and +.35 for women coming from middle-class backgrounds. These correlations were statistically significant in both cases. For the sample as a whole, a woman's physical attractiveness correlated more strongly with her husband's status (+.43) than did other women's variables such as class of origin (+.27) or IQ (+.14). In sum, attractiveness in women appears to be an important path to upward mobility; women who are most in a position to get what they want appear to select men who have the qualities that most women desire—men with status and resources.

Women's Marriages to Men Who Are Older

A third source of data on women's actual mate choices come from demographic statistics on the age differences between brides and grooms at marriage. Recall that women express a desire for men who are somewhat older. Specifically, in the international study of thirty-seven cultures, on average women preferred men who were 3.42 years older (Buss, 1989a). Demographic data on actual age differences were secured from twenty-seven of these countries. From this sample the actual age difference between brides and grooms was 2.99 years. In every country, grooms were older on average than brides, ranging from a low of 2.17 years for Ireland to a high of 4.92 years for Greece. In short, women's preferences for older husbands translates into actual marriages to older men. Of course, men's preferences are also relevant—because men prefer women younger than themselves (see Chapter 5), we would expect that men's desires might also affect the actual age differences between brides and grooms. The bottom line, however, is that the actual mating decisions of women accord well with their expressed preferences.

Summary

We now have the outlines of an answer to the enigma that is women's long-term mate preferences. Modern women have inherited from their successful ancestors wisdom and prudence about the men they consent to mate with. Ancestral women who mated indiscriminately were likely to have been less reproductively successful than those who exercised choice. Long-term mates bring with them a treasure trove of assets. Selecting a long-term mate who has the relevant assets is clearly an extraordinarily complex endeavor. It involves a number of distinctive preferences, each corresponding to a resource that helps women solve critical adaptive problems.

That women seek resources in a marriage partner may seem obvious. Because resources cannot always be directly discerned, however, women's mating preferences are keyed to other qualities that signal the likely possession, or future acquisition, of resources. Indeed, women may be less influenced by money per se than by qualities that lead to resources, such as ambition, intelligence, and older age. Women scrutinize these personal qualities carefully because they reveal a man's potential.

Potential, however, is not enough. Because many men with a rich resource potential are themselves highly discriminating and are at times content with casual sex, women are faced with the problem of commitment. Seeking love is one solution to the commitment problem. Acts of love signal that a man has in fact committed to a particular woman.

To have the love and commitment of a man who could be easily downed by other men in the physical arena, however, would have been a problematic asset for ancestral women. Women mated with small, weak men lacking physical prowess and courage would have risked damage from other men and loss of the couple's joint resources. Tall, strong, athletic men offered ancestral women protection. In this way, their personal well-being and their children's well-being could be secured against incursion. Modern women are the descendants of successful women who selected men in part for their strength and prowess.

Finally, resources, commitment, and protection do a woman little good if her husband becomes diseased or dies or if the couple is so mismatched that the partners fail to function as an effective team. The premium that women place on a man's health ensures that husbands will be capable of providing these benefits over the long haul. And the premium that women place on similarity of interests and traits with their mate helps to ensure fidelity and stability (see Box 4.1 on page 130). These multiple facets of current women's mating preferences thus correspond perfectly with those of adaptive problems that were faced by our female ancestors thousands of years ago.

Women's preferences were predicted to be sensitive to two contexts—their personal access to resources and the temporal context of short-term versus long-term mating. According to the structural powerlessness hypothesis, women who have a lot of personal access to resources are predicted not to value resources in a mate as much as women lacking resources. This hypothesis receives no support from the existing empirical data, however. Indeed, women with high incomes value a potential mate's income and education more, not less, than women with lower incomes.

Women also show sensitivity to the contexts of long-term versus short-term mating. Specifically, in long-term mating contexts women especially value qualities that signal that the man will be a good provider and a good father. These qualities are considerably less important in women's desires in a short-term mate.

For preferences to evolve they must have had a recurrent impact on actual mating behavior. For a variety of reasons, we do not expect that women's preferences will show a one-to-one correspondence with behavior. People cannot always get what they want. Nonetheless, several lines of research support the notion that women's preferences do in fact affect actual mating behavior. Women respond more to personal ads in which men indicate good financial status. Women who embody what men desire (e.g., by being physically attractive) are in the best position to get what they want, and so their mate selections are most revealing. Several studies show that physically attractive women do indeed tend to marry men with higher incomes and occupational status. Demographic statistics further show that women worldwide tend to marry older men, which directly corresponds to women's expressed preference for such men. Based on this cumulation of studies, it is reasonable to conclude that women's mate preferences have a substantial impact on their own mating behavior.

BOX **4.1**

Similarity and Compatibility

Successful long-term mating requires sustained cooperative alliances over time (Kenrick & Keefe, 1992). Similarity leads to emotional bonding, cooperation, communication, reduced risk of infidelity, and increased survival of children (Kenrick & Keefe, 1992; Keller, Thiessen, & Young, 1996; Walster, Traupmann, & Berscheid, 1979). Compatibility between mates entails a complex mesh between two different kinds of characteristics. One involves complementary traits, or a mate's possession of resources and skills that differ from one's own, in a division of labor between the sexes. The phrase "opposites attract" captures this kind of complementarity.

The other kinds of traits crucial to compatibility with a mate are those that are most likely to mesh with and are most similar to one's own. The phrase "birds of a feather flock together" captures the essence of this type of compatibility. Differences between mates in values, interests, or even personality characteristics can produce instability (Hill, Rubin, & Peplau, 1976).

One solution to the problem of compatibility is to search for a mate who is similar to oneself, a phenomenon known as assortative mating. Several sources of evidence support the hypothesis that seeking similarity is widespread in human populations (Buss, 1985). First, people actively express preferences for mates who are like them. In one study the average correlation between each participant's own personality and the personality of his or her ideal mate was approximately +.30 (Botwin, Buss, & Shackelford, 1997). Dominant people express a desire to be with dominant people, whereas extraverted people express a desire to mate with other extraverted people.

A second source of evidence comes from actual marriages. Both in the United States and worldwide, men and women who are alike on a wide spectrum of characteristics usually marry. The tendency for like people to mate shows up most obviously in the areas of age, values, intelligence, and group membership (Buss, 1985; Thiessen & Gregg, 1980). One recent study, for example, found that married couples were correlated +.86 for age, +.47 for general intelligence, and +.40 for imaginativeness (Keller, Thiessen, & Young, 1996). People seek mates with similar political and social values, such as views on abortion or capital punishment, for which couples are correlated +.50. Matches on these qualities are most likely to lead to cooperation. Even on personality characteristics, such as extraversion and conscientiousness, couples show low but significant degrees of similarity, typically around +.20 (Keller, Thiessen, & Young, 1996). People like mates who share their inclination toward parties if they are extraverted, for example, and toward quiet evenings at home if they are introverted.

A third source of evidence for the importance of similarity as a solution to the compatibility problem comes from couples who break up. Three psychologists studied 202 dating couples over the course of several years to see who stayed together (Hill, Rubin, & Peplau, 1976). They found that couples who were mismatched in values and interests tended to break up more readily than couples who were better matched. The 103 couples who broke up had more dissimilar attitudes toward sex and romance, differed more on religious beliefs and orientations, and differed more on their attitudes toward division of labor and other sex roles than did the 99 couples who stayed together.

Finding a similar mate helps to solve a host of adaptive problems. It produces emotional bonding and mutual cooperation (Kenrick & Keefe, 1992). It reduces the likelihood of sexual infidelity (Walster et al., 1978). And it lowers the odds that the couple will break up (Hill et al., 1976). Mismatched couples are more at risk for infidelity and dissolution.

5 Men's Long-Term Mating Strategies

Why does a particular maiden turn our wits so upside-down?

—William James (1890)

For selection to have produced psychological mechanisms in men that incline them to seek marriage and commit years and decades of investment to a woman, it is reasonable to assume that there were adaptive advantages to long-term mating, at least under some circumstances. This chapter examines the logic and evidence pertaining to men's long-term mating strategies. We start with the theoretical background for the evolution of men's mate preferences. Then we examine the content of men's mate preferences. The final section explores the effects of context on men's long-term mating strategies.

Theoretical Background for the Evolution of Men's Mate Preferences

This section covers the theoretical background for two topics. The first is why men would marry at all—what are the potential adaptive benefits that ancestral men could have gained from marriage? The second topic deals with complexities surrounding the content of men's desires, and how selection might have fashioned specific mate preferences in men.

Why Men Might Benefit from Commitment and Marriage

One solution to the puzzle of why men would seek marriage comes from the ground rules set by women. Because it is clear that many ancestral women required reliable signs of male commitment before consenting to sex, men who failed to commit would have suffered selectively on the mating market. For that matter, men who failed to show interest in commitment might have failed to attract any women at all. Women's requirements for consenting to sex could have made it costly for men to pursue a short-term mating strategy exclusively. In the economics of reproductive effort, the costs of not pursuing a permanent mate may have been prohibitively high for most men.

Another benefit of marriage is an increase in the quality of the woman a man would be able to attract. Men who are willing to promise long-term resources, protection, and investment in children are appealing to women, as we saw in Chapter 4, so men who are willing to commit to the long term have a wider range of women from which to choose. Such men attract desirable women because, as just noted, women typically desire lasting commitment, and highly desirable women are in the best position to get what they want. In contrast, most women can obtain a much more desirable temporary mate by offering sex without requiring commitment, since high-status men are willing to relax their standards and have sex with a variety of women if such a relationship is only short-term and carries no commitment. Men of high status typically impose more stringent standards for a spouse than most women are able to meet.

A third potential benefit would be an increase in the odds that the man is the father of the children a woman bears. Through marriage a man gains repeated sexual access—in the majority of cases, exclusive sexual access. Without this repeated or exclusive access, his certainty in paternity would be jeopardized. Thus men who marry gain the reproductive benefit of an increase in paternity certainty.

A fourth potential benefit of marriage would have been an increase in the survival of the man's children. In human ancestral environments it is likely that infants and young children more frequently died without the prolonged investment from two parents or related kin (Hill & Hurtado, 1996). Even today among the Ache Indians of Paraguay, when a man dies the other villagers sometimes make a mutual decision to kill certain of his children, even when they have a living mother. This stems from an Ache custom in which a man's living children are sometimes buried along with the dead father. The sacrificed children, known as *chape*, are usually young girls under the age of five, but they can be boys as well, and can sometimes be as old as twelve years. Often a single child is chosen, and it is not uncommon to choose one who is ill or suffers from a birth defect.

This practice was justified by the Ache on the grounds that burying the man's children would appease his angry spirit, and so the spirit would not attempt to take another living adult with him on the journey to death. Perhaps more relevant, Ache informants insist that many of the child victims would be unlikely to be cared for effectively. A child with no father, they said, would "be constantly begging for food" (Hill & Hurtado, 1996, p. 68), and thus would be a resource drain on others in the group. Overall, Ache children whose fathers died suffered a death rate more than 10 percent higher than children whose fathers remained alive. The Ache are only one group, and we must be careful not to make gross generalizations from a single group. The key point is that an increase in the survival rates of a man's children may have been one adaptive benefit that ancestral men reaped as a result of investing in a long-term marital relationship.

Over human evolutionary history, even children who did survive without their father's investment might have suffered from the absence of his teaching and political alliances, since both of these assets help to solve mating problems later in life. Fathers in many cultures past and present have had a strong hand in arranging beneficial marriages for their sons and daughters. The absence of these benefits hurts children without fathers. Such evolutionary pressures, operating over thousands of generations, would likely have given an advantage to men who married.

In summary, there are five potentially powerful adaptive benefits that would have accrued to men willing to make the commitment of marriage: (1) increased odds of succeeding in attracting a mate; (2) increased ability to attract a more desirable mate; (3) increased paternity certainty; (4) increased survival of his children; and (5) increased reproductive success of children accrued through paternal investment.

Given that there would have been powerful adaptive advantages to men willing to commit, the next question is: What qualities should they seek in women?

The Problem of Assessing a Woman's Fertility or Reproductive Value

To be reproductively successful, ancestral men had to marry women with the capacity to bear children. A woman with the capacity to bear many children would obviously have been more beneficial in reproductive currencies than a woman capable of bearing few or none. Men cannot observe a woman's reproductive value directly, and so selection could only have fashioned preferences in men for qualities that are correlated with reproductive value.

When we compare humans with their closest primate relative, the chimpanzee, we see a startling discontinuity in the female advertisement of reproductive status. When the female chimpanzee is capable of conceiving, she goes into a phase called *estrus*—the time during which she releases her eggs and shows maximal sexual receptivity. The receptivity of estrus is usually advertised by bright red swollen genitals and scents that are highly attractive to chimpanzee males. Most, although not all, of the sexual activity among the chimpanzees takes place during the estrus phase, when the female is most likely to conceive.

Humans show a markedly different form of mating. First, women's ovulation is concealed or cryptic. Unlike chimpanzee females, when women release their eggs for potential fertilization, the event is not accompanied by a pronounced genital swelling. Second, sexual activity among most humans occurs throughout the woman's ovulation cycle. Unlike the chimpanzee, sexual activity is not generally concentrated during the phase in which the female is most likely to conceive.

The transition from advertised estrus to concealed ovulation posed a poignant adaptive problem for human ancestral males. For chimpanzee males the problem of detecting a female's reproductive status is easy—all they have to do is look for the overt signals of estrus. When ovulation is not advertised, however, how could males discern a female's reproductive status? The concealment of ovulation, in short, shifted the problem from one of detecting when a woman was ovulating to one of determining which women were likely to be *capable* of conceiving children—the problem of determining a woman's reproductive value or fertility.

Reproductive value refers to the number of children a person of a given age and sex is likely to have *in the future*. A woman who is fifteen years old, for example, has a higher reproductive value than a woman who is thirty because, on average, the younger woman is likely to bear more children in the future than is the older woman. Individual women may, of course, defy these averages. The fifteen-year-old might decide never to have children, and the thirty-year-old could have six. The key is that reproductive value refers to

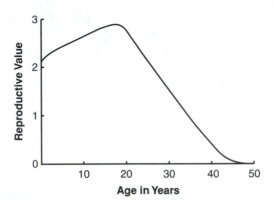

FIGURE 5.1   Typical Reproductive Value Curve for Women. The figure shows the number of children a woman of a given age is likely to have, on average, in the future. Data extrapolated from Symons (1979); Williams (1975).

the average *expected* future reproduction of a person of a given age and sex. A typical reproductive value curve for women is shown in Figure 5.1.

Reproductive value is different from *fertility*, which is defined as actual reproductive performance, measured by the number of viable offspring produced. In human populations, women in their mid-twenties tend to produce the most viable children, and so fertility among humans reaches a peak in the mid-twenties.

The differences between fertility and reproductive value can be illustrated by contrasting two females, ages fifteen and twenty-five. The younger female has a higher reproductive value because, actuarially, her *future* reproduction is expected to be higher. The twenty-five-year-old female, in contrast, would be more fertile because women in their mid-twenties produce more children, on average, than do women in their teens.

The solution to this problem of detecting fertility or reproductive value, however, is more difficult than it might at first appear. The number of children a woman is likely to bear in her lifetime is not stamped on her forehead. It is not imbued in her social reputation. Even women themselves lack direct knowledge of their reproductive value.

Ancestral men, however, could have evolved mechanisms sensitive to observable qualities of a woman that might be *correlated* with underlying reproductive value. Two potentially observable cues would have been a woman's youth and her health (Symons, 1979; Williams, 1975). Old or unhealthy women clearly could not reproduce as much as young, healthy women. But precisely which observable qualities of a woman might signal youth and health? And do men's desires in a marriage partner focus heavily on her reproductive capacity?

The Content of Men's Mate Preferences

In some ways men's mate preferences are similar to those of women. Like women, men express a desire for partners who are intelligent, kind, understanding, and healthy (Buss,

1989a). Also, like women, men look for partners who share their values and are similar to them in attitudes, personality, and religious beliefs. But because ancestral men confronted a different set of adaptive mating problems than did ancestral women, as their descendants modern men are predicted to hold a somewhat different set of mate preferences as adaptive solutions. These preferences start with one of the most powerful cues to a woman's reproductive status—her age.

Preference for Youth

Youth is a critical cue because, as noted, a woman's reproductive value declines steadily as she moves past age twenty. By the age of forty a woman's reproductive capacity is low, and by fifty it is essentially zero. The window of opportunity for reproduction is thus compressed into a fraction of women's lives.

Men's preferences capitalize on this. Within the United States men uniformly express a desire for mates who are younger than they are. Among college students surveyed from 1939 through 1988 on campuses coast to coast, the preferred age difference hovered around two and a half years (Buss, 1989a; Hill, 1945; Hudson & Henze, 1969; McGinnis, 1958). Men who are twenty-one years old prefer, on average, women who are eighteen and a half years old.

Men's preference for youthful partners is not limited to Western cultures. When anthropologist Napoleon Chagnon was asked which females are most sexually attractive to Yanomamö Indian men of the Amazon he replied without hesitation, "Females who are *moko dude*" (Symons, 1989 p. 34–35). (The word *moko*, when used with respect to fruit, means that the fruit is harvestable, and when used with respect to a woman, it means that the woman is fertile. Thus, *moko dude*, when referring to fruit means that the fruit is perfectly ripe and when referring to a woman means that she is postpubescent but has not yet borne her first child.) Comparable information on other tribal peoples suggests that the Yanomamö men are not atypical.

Nigerian, Indonesian, Iranian, and Indian men express similar preferences. Without exception, in every one of the thirty-seven societies examined in an international study on mate selection, men prefer younger wives. Nigerian men who are twenty-three years old, for example, express a preference for wives who are six and a half years younger, or just under seventeen years old (Buss, 1989a). Yugoslavian men who are twenty-one and a half years old express a desire for wives who are approximately nineteen years old. Chinese, Canadian, and Colombian men share with their Nigerian and Yugoslavian brethren a powerful desire for young women. On average, men from the thirty-seven cultures expressed a desire for wives approximately two and a half years younger than themselves (refer back to Figure 4.5, page 113).

Although men universally prefer younger women as wives, the strength of this preference varies somewhat from culture to culture. Among Scandinavian countries such as Finland, Sweden, and Norway, men prefer their brides to be only one or two years younger. Men in Nigeria and Zambia prefer their brides to be six and a half and seven and a half years younger, respectively. In Nigeria and Zambia, which practice polygyny like many cultures worldwide, men who can afford it are legally permitted to marry more than one woman. Because men in polygynous mating systems are typically older than men in monogamous systems by the time they have acquired sufficient resources to at-tract wives, the larger age difference preferred by Nigerian and Zambian men may reflect their advanced age when they acquire wives.

A comparison of the statistics offered in personal ads in newspapers reveals that a man's age has a strong effect on what he desires. As men get older they prefer as mates women who are increasingly younger. Men in their thirties prefer women who are roughly five years younger, whereas men in their fifties prefer women ten to twenty years younger (Kenrick & Keefe, 1992) (see Figure 5.2).

According to evolutionary psychologists, the evolutionary model predicts that what men desire is not youth per se, but rather features of women that are associated with reproductive value or fertility. This perspective leads to a counterintuitive predic-tion when it comes to the age preferences of adolescent males: teenage males should prefer women who are *slightly older* than they are, contrary to the typically observed pat-tern of men desiring younger partners, because slightly older women have higher fertil-ity than women their own age or women who are younger (Kenrick, Keefe, Gabrielidis, & Cornelius, 1996).

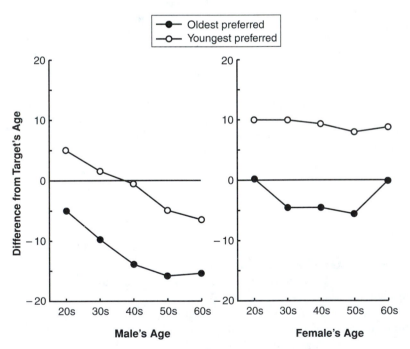

FIGURE 5.2   **Men's Age Preferences as They Get Older.** As men get older, they prefer women as mates who are increasingly younger than they are *(left)*. Women's age preferences do not show this pattern *(right)*.

Source: Kenrick, D. T., & Keefe, R. C. (1992). Age preferences in mates reflect sex differences in reproduc-tive strategies. *Behavioral and Brain Sciences, 15,* 75–133. Reprinted with permission.

To test this prediction, one study (Kenrick et al., 1996) surveyed 103 teenage males and 106 females ranging in age from twelve to nineteen. The participants received the following instructions: "I'd like you to think for a second about what type of person you would find attractive. Imagine you were going on a date with someone. Assume that the person would be interested in you, and that you were available to go on a date, and that things like parental permission and money aren't important" (Kenrick et al., 1996, p. 1505).

Each participant was then asked about his or her age limits. The experimenter began by asking, "Would you date someone who was [the subject's age]," followed by "How about someone who was [subject's age minus one]." If affirmative answers were given, the experimenter then continued until the participant stated that a particular age was too young. The experimenter then asked about the maximum acceptable age of a dating partner. Finally, participants were asked about the ideal age of a dating partner, "the most attractive person you could possibly imagine" (p. 1505). The results yielded three variables—ideal age, minimum age, and maximum age of dating partner desired. The results are shown in Figure 5.3.

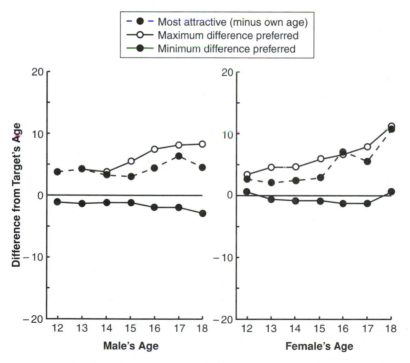

FIGURE 5.3   Age Preferences for Mates Expressed by Teenagers. Note that male teenagers, unlike older males, prefer women as mates who are somewhat older than they are *(left)*.

Source: Kenrick, D. T., Keefe, R. C., Gabrielidis, C., & Cornelius, J. S. (1996). Adolescents' age preferences for dating partners: Support for an evolutionary model of life-history strategies. *Child Development, 67,* 1499–1511. Reprinted with permission.

Although these teenage males were willing to accept dates with females who were slightly younger, they were far more willing to accept dates with older women. The "most attractive" age mirrors these findings, with adolescent males expressing a desire for dates who were several years older on average. Interestingly, this finding occurs despite the fact that these older women expressed no interest at all in dating younger men (second graph in Figure 5.3).

To get an overview of the pattern of men's preferences for the age of women as a function of their own age, the data from all age groups were combined into a single graph, shown in Figure 5.4. This graph shows clearly that at the youngest ages, teenage males prefer females a few years older then themselves. But with advancing age, men prefer women who are increasingly younger than they are.

These new data concerning teenagers are important in rendering several alternative explanations less plausible. One explanation for men's desire for young women, for exam-

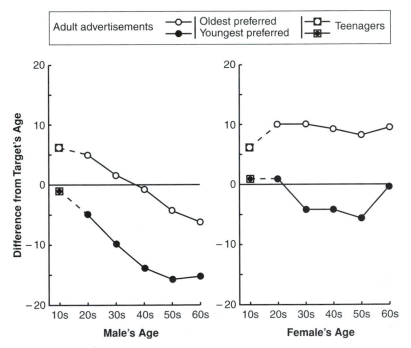

FIGURE 5.4   Comparison of Teenage Preferences with Those Expressed in Adult Advertisements. The figure shows that teenagers tend to prefer mates close to themselves in age. As they age, males increasingly prefer mates younger than themselves, whereas females prefer mates consistently a few years older.

Source: Kenrick, D. T., Keefe, R. C., Gabrielidis, C., & Cornelius, J. S. (1996). Adolescents' age preferences for dating partners: Support for an evolutionary model of life-history strategies. *Child Development, 67,* 1499–1511. Reprinted with permission.

ple, is that young women are easier to control and are less dominant than older women, and men seek to mate with women they can control (Wolf, 1992). If this were the sole reason for men's preference for young women, however, then we would expect that teenage males would also prefer younger women, but they don't. The only way the "control" explanation could work is if teenage boys think that older women are easier to dominate!

Another explanation for men's desire for young women is based on classical learning theory. Because women tend to prefer men who are somewhat older, men may have received more reward or reinforcement for seeking dates with younger women. This reinforcement explanation, however, fails to account for the preferences of the teenage males, who prefer older women despite the fact that the interest is rarely mutual.

Taken together with the cross-cultural data, these findings lend strong support to an evolutionary psychological explanation: men desire young women because over evolutionary time youth has consistently been linked with fertility. This explanation accounts for two facts that all other theories have difficulty explaining: First, that men desire women who are increasingly younger than they are as the men themselves get older; second, that teenage males prefer women a few years older than they are despite the fact that such women rarely reward them for such interest.

Evolved Standards of Physical Beauty

A preference for youth is the most obvious of men's preferences linked to a woman's reproductive capacity. Evolutionary logic leads to an even more powerful set of expectations for universal standards of beauty. Just as our standards for attractive landscapes embody cues such as water, game, and refuge, mimicking our ancestors' savanna habitats (Orians & Heerwagen, 1992), so do our standards for female beauty embody cues to women's reproductive value. Conventional wisdom dictates that beauty is in the eyes of the beholder, but those eyes and the minds behind the eyes have been shaped by millions of years of human evolution. Beauty is in the *adaptations* of the beholder (Symons, 1995).

Our ancestors had access to two types of observable evidence of a woman's reproductive value: (1) features of *physical appearance*, such as full lips, clear skin, smooth skin, clear eyes, lustrous hair, good muscle tone and body fat distribution, and (2) features of *behavior*, such as a bouncy youthful gait, an animated facial expression, and a high energy level. These physical cues to youth and health, and hence to fertility and reproductive value, have been hypothesized to be some of the key ingredients of male standards of female beauty (Symons, 1979, 1995).

Because physical and behavioral cues provide the most powerful observable evidence of a woman's reproductive value, ancestral men evolved a preference for women who displayed these cues. Men who failed to prefer qualities that signal high fertility or reproductive value—men who preferred to marry gray-haired women with somewhat less smooth skin and firm muscle tone—would have had fewer offspring, and their line would eventually have died out.

Psychologists Clelland Ford and Frank Beach discovered several universal cues that correspond precisely with the evolutionary theory of beauty (1951). Signs of youth, such as clear, smooth skin, and signs of health, such as an absence of sores and lesions, are universally regarded as attractive. Any cues to ill health or older age are seen as less attractive. Poor complexion is always considered sexually unattractive. Ringworm, facial disfigurement, and filthiness are universally undesirable. Cleanliness and freedom from disease are universally attractive.

Among the Trobriand Islanders in northwestern Melanesia, for example, anthropologist Bronislaw Malinowski reports that "sores, ulcers, and skin eruptions are naturally held to be specially repulsive from the viewpoint of erotic contact" (Malinowski, 1929, p. 244). The "essential conditions" for beauty, in contrast, are "health, strong growth of hair, sound teeth, and smooth skin." Specific features, such as bright, shining eyes, and full, well-shaped lips rather than thin or pinched lips, are especially important to the islanders.

Cues to youth are also paramount in the aesthetics of women's attractiveness. When men and women rate a series of photographs of women of different ages, judgments of facial attractiveness decline with increasing age of the woman (Henss, 1992; Jackson, 1992). The decline in ratings of beauty occurs regardless of the age or sex of the judge. As the age of the woman in the photograph increases, the value men attach to women's faces declines more rapidly than does the value other women attach, highlighting the importance to men of age as a cue to reproductive capacity.

Standards of Beauty Emerge Early in Life.   Most traditional psychological theories of attraction have assumed that standards of attractiveness are learned gradually through cultural transmission, and therefore do not emerge clearly until a child is three or four years old, or even later (Berscheid & Walster, 1974; Langlois, Roggman, Casey, Ritter, Rieser-Danner, & Jenkins, 1987). However, psychologist Judith Langlois and her colleagues have overturned this conventional wisdom by studying infants' social responses to faces (Langlois, Roggman, & Reiser-Danner, 1990).

Adults evaluated color slides of White and Black female faces for their attractiveness. Then infants two to three months and six to eight months old were shown pairs of these faces that differed in degree of attractiveness. Both younger and older infants gazed longer at the more attractive faces, suggesting that standards of beauty apparently emerge quite early in life. In a second study Langlois and her colleagues found that twelve-month-old infants showed more observable pleasure, more play involvement, less distress, and less withdrawal when interacting with strangers wearing attractive masks than when interacting with strangers wearing unattractive masks. In a third study they found that twelve-month-old infants played significantly longer with facially attractive dolls than with unattractive dolls. This evidence challenges the commonly held view that the standards of attractiveness are learned through gradual exposure to current cultural models. No training seems necessary for these standards to emerge.

Standards of Beauty Are Consistent across Cultures.   The constituents of beauty are neither arbitrary nor culture bound. When psychologist Michael Cunningham asked people of different races to judge the facial attractiveness of Asian, Hispanic, Black, and White women in photographs he found tremendous consensus about who is and is not considered good-looking (Cunningham, Roberts, Wu, Barbee, & Druen, 1995). The average correlation between racial groups in their ratings of the attractiveness of these photographs was +.93. In a second study by the same investigators, Taiwanese subjects agreed with the other groups in the average ratings of attractiveness ($r = +.91$). Degree of exposure to Western media did not affect the judgments of attractiveness in either study. In a third study, Blacks and Whites showed tremendous agreement about which women's faces were most and least attractive ($r = +.94$). Consensus has also been found among Chinese, Indian, and English subjects between South Africans and North Americans; between Black and White Americans; and between Russians, Ache Indians, and Americans (Cross & Cross, 1971; Jackson, 1992; Jones, 1996; Morse, Gruzen, & Reis, 1976; Thakerar & Iwawaki, 1979).

"Average" and Symmetrical Faces Are More Attractive.   To find out what makes an attractive face, researchers generated computer composites of the human face (Langlois & Roggman, 1990). These faces were then superimposed on each other to create new faces. The new faces differed in the number of individual faces that made them up—from four, eight, sixteen, or thirty-two faces. People were asked to rate the attractiveness of each composite face, as well as the attractiveness of each individual face that made up the composite. A startling result emerged. The composite faces were uniformly judged to be more physically attractive than any of the individual faces. The sixteen-face composite was more attractive than the four- or eight-face composites, and the thirty-two–face composite was the most attractive of all. Because superimposing individual faces tends to eliminate their irregularities and make them more symmetrical, the average or symmetrical faces may be more attractive than faces that deviate from the norm.

One line of research has shown that symmetrical faces are viewed as more attractive, and perhaps the process of computer averaging faces makes a more symmetrical composite. One study examined the relationship between facial and bodily asymmetries and judgments of attractiveness (Gangestad, Thornhill, & Yeo, 1994) and determined that a host of environmental insults produces asymmetries during development. These include not just injuries and other physical insults, which may provide a cue to poor health, but also the prevalence of parasites that inhabit the human body. Because physical asymmetries can be caused by parasites, the degree of asymmetry can be used as a cue to the health status of the individual and an index of the degree to which the individual's development has been affected by various stressors. In scorpionflies and swallows, for example, males prefer to mate with females who show almost precisely equal wing length on each side and tend to avoid those showing differences in wing length.

When Gangestad and his colleagues measured the actual asymmetry in features such as foot breadth, hand breadth, ear length, and ear breadth and independently had these people evaluated for attractiveness, they found that less symmetrical people are considered less attractive. Further, older people's faces are far more asymmetrical than younger people's faces, so symmetry also provides another cue to youth. Finally, another research project has documented that facial symmetry is positively linked with both psychological and physiological health indicators (Shackelford & Larsen, 1997). This evidence provides yet another confirmation of the theory that cues to health and youth are embodied in standards of attractiveness—standards that emerge remarkably early in life and show cross-cultural generality. Box 5.1 elaborates some findings on facial attractiveness.

Recent research has shown that symmetry may not be the sole reason that average faces are judged attractive (Langlois, Roggman, & Musselman, 1994). Rather, the effects of averageness on judgments of attractiveness occur even after the effects of symmetry have been controlled. Research found that some symmetrical faces are judged to be unattractive whereas a few asymmetrical faces received high attractiveness ratings. These findings suggest that proximity to the population average remains an important determinant of attractiveness, above and beyond the effect of symmetry.

Preference for Body Fat and the Critical Waist-to-Hip Ratio

Facial beauty, however, is only part of the picture. Features of the rest of the body may also provide cues to a woman's reproductive capacity. Standards for female bodily attractiveness vary from culture to culture, along such dimensions as a plump versus a slim body build or light versus dark skin. Emphasis on particular physical features such as eyes, ears, or genitals also varies among cultures. The most culturally variable standard of beauty seems to be in the preference for a slim versus a plump body build and is linked with the social status build conveys. In cultures where food is scarce, such as among the Bushmen of Australia, plumpness signals wealth, health, and adequate nutrition during development (Rosenblatt, 1974). In cultures where food is relatively abundant, such as the United States and many Western European countries, the relationship between plumpness and status is reversed, and the wealthy distinguish themselves by being thin (Symons, 1979).

One study revealed a disturbing aspect of American women's and men's perceptions of the desirability of plump or thin body types (Rozin & Fallon, 1988). American men and women viewed nine female figures that varied from very thin to very plump. The women were asked to indicate their ideal for themselves, as well as their perception of what men's ideal female figure was. In both cases women selected a figure slimmer than average. When men were asked to select which female figure they preferred, however, they selected the figure of exactly average body size. So American women think that men want them to be thinner than is in fact the case.

Whereas men's preferences for a particular body size vary across cultures, psychologist Devendra Singh has discovered one preference for body shape that may be universal: the preference for a particular ratio between the size of a woman's waist and the size of her hips (Singh, 1993; Singh & Young, 1995). Before puberty, boys and girls show similar fat distributions. At puberty, however, a dramatic change occurs. Men lose fat from their buttocks and thighs, whereas the release of estrogen in pubertal girls causes them to deposit fat in the lower trunk, primarily on their hips and upper thighs. Indeed, the volume of body fat in this region is 40 percent greater for women than for men.

The waist-to-hip ratio (WHR) is thus similar for the sexes before puberty, in the range of 0.85 to 0.95. After puberty, however, women's hip fat deposits cause their WHRs

BOX **5.1**

Computer-Generated Evolution of Faces

Victor Johnston and Melissa Franklin (1993) devised an ingenious method for examining standards of beauty using computer-generated graphic images. Twenty male and twenty female subjects were able to "evolve" images of women's faces on a computer screen, stopping when the faces reached the maximum of the subjects' ideal standards of beauty. The researchers then produced a computer-generated composite of these forty faces —the "beautiful composite." They then created an analogous computer-generated composite of the twenty female subjects—the "subject composite" —whose average age was twenty. When the beautiful composite (left) and the subject composite were compared, they did not differ significantly on most dimensions, with two exceptions. First, the beautiful composite had a relatively short lower face, with a short distance between the lips and the bottom of the chin. Second, the beautiful composite had a somewhat smaller mouth and fuller lips in the vertical dimension than did the subject composite. These features are all linked with youth. Fullness of the lips, for example, peaks at age fourteen in Western populations (Farkas, 1981). Similar findings have been observed by others (Perrett,

May, & Yoshikawa, 1994). Using both Japanese and English participants, they found that the most attractive composite images had larger eyes relative to face size, thinner jaws, and short distances between mouth and chin.

Evolutionary anthropologist Doug Jones (1996) documented similar findings in a cross-cultural study involving Brazilians, U.S. Americans, Russians, the Ache of Paraguay, and the Hiwi (another Indian tribe of hunter-gatherers residing in Venezuela). Jones photographed faces from each population. He then presented the photographs to separate groups of raters from each country and asked them to judge attractiveness, perceived age, and other qualities. He then measured the facial proportions and correlated them with age. Jones discovered that women who had facial proportions that suggested a younger age—such as a smaller jaw and relatively large eyes —than their actual age were perceived by male raters from all five cultures as more attractive than women whose facial proportions matched or exceeded their actual ages. These results provide further empirical evidence that cues to youth are linked with judgments of attractiveness in women.

The highest rated composite (left) *and a composite having the same features but in the proportions of the average face in the population* (right). *Courtesy of Victor Johnson.*

to become significantly lower than men's. Healthy, reproductively capable women have WHRs between 0.67 and 0.80, whereas healthy men have a ratio in the range of 0.85 to 0.95. Abundant evidence now shows that the WHR is an accurate indicator of women's reproductive status. Women with lower ratios show earlier pubertal endocrine activity. Married women with higher ratios have more difficulty becoming pregnant, and those who do get pregnant do so at a later age than women with lower ratios. The WHR is also an accurate indication of long-term health status. Diseases such as diabetes, hypertension, heart attack, stroke, and gallbladder disorders have been shown to be linked with the distribution of fat, as reflected by the ratio, rather than with the total amount of fat per se. The link between the WHR and both health and reproductive status makes it a reliable cue for ancestral men's preferences in a mate.

Singh discovered that WHR is indeed a powerful part of women's attractiveness. In a dozen studies conducted by Singh, men rated the attractiveness of female figures who varied in both WHR and total amount of fat. Again, men found the average figure to be more attractive than either a thin or a fat figure. Regardless of the total amount of fat, however, men find women with low WHRs the most attractive. Women with a WHR of 0.70 are seen as more attractive than women with a WHR of 0.80, who in turn are seen as more attractive than women with a WHR of 0.90. Studies with line drawings and with computer-generated photographic images produced the same results. Finally, Singh's analysis of *Playboy* centerfolds and winners of U.S. beauty contests over the past thirty years confirmed the invariance of this cue. Although both centerfolds and beauty contest winners got slightly thinner over that period, their WHRs remained exactly the same, at 0.70.

Is there any evidence that low WHRs are preferred across different ethnic groups? In a recent series of studies Singh and Luis (1995) presented line drawings of women differing in WHRs and body sizes to groups of young Indonesian and Black men and asked them to judge their attractiveness. The results proved almost identical to those of the original studies. Men judged female figures who were of normal weight and had low WHRs (0.70) the most attractive. Although further cross-cultural data are needed to confirm the hypothesis that WHR is a universal cue to female beauty, the existing evidence clearly points to this conclusion.

Sex Differences in the Importance of Physical Appearance

Because of the abundance of cues conveyed by a woman's physical appearance, and because male standards of beauty have evolved to correspond to these cues, men place a premium on physical appearance and attractiveness in their mate preferences. A cross-generational mating study spanning a fifty-seven–year period, from 1939 to 1996 in the United States gauged the value men and women place on different characteristics in a mate (Buss, Shackelford, Kirkpatrick, & Larsen, under review). The same eighteen characteristics were measured at roughly one-decade intervals to determine how mating preferences have changed over time in the United States. In all cases, men rated physical attractiveness and good looks as more important and desirable in a potential mate than did women. Men tend to see attractiveness as important, whereas women tend to see it as desirable but not crucial. The sex difference in the importance of attractiveness has remained constant from one generation to the next and did not vary over the entire fifty years.

This does not mean that the importance people place on attractiveness is forever fixed. On the contrary, the importance of attractiveness has increased dramatically in the United States in this century alone (Buss et al., under review). For nearly every decade since 1930, physical appearance has increased in importance for men and women about equally, corresponding with the rise in television, fashion magazines, advertising, and other media depictions of attractive models. For example, the importance attached to good looks in a marriage partner on a scale of 0 to 3 increased between 1939 and 1996 from 1.50 to 2.11 for men and from 0.94 to 1.67 for women, showing that mate preferences can change. Indeed, these changes point to the importance of cultural evolution and the impact of input from the social environment. The sex difference so far remains invariant, however. The gap between men and women is no more nor less than it was in the late 1930s.

These sex differences are not limited to the United States, or even to Western cultures. Regardless of location, habitat, marriage system, or cultural living arrangement, men in all thirty-seven cultures included in the study on choosing a mate—from Australians to Zambians—valued physical appearance in a potential mate more than women (see Figure 5.5 on page 146). China typifies the average difference in importance attached to beauty, with men a 2.06 and women a 1.59. This internationally consistent sex difference persists despite variations in race, ethnicity, religion, hemisphere, political system, or mating system. Men's preference for physically attractive mates appears to be the product of a species-wide psychological mechanism that transcends cultural variation.

Do Men Have a Preference for Ovulating Women?

Perhaps one of the most obvious predictions one could make about men's desires is that they should show a strong preference for women at the time they *ovulate*—when the egg is released into the woman's uterus to potentially be fertilized by a sperm. Ancestral men who were able to detect ovulating women would have several reproductive advantages over men who could not. First, they could channel their courtship, seduction, and sexual behavior toward women at that time, thus maximizing the odds of successful fertilization. Second, they could save a tremendous amount of effort by avoiding women who were not ovulating. Third, a married man could restrict his mate-guarding efforts to the period in which his spouse was ovulating.

Most other primate males can, in fact, detect when females of their species are ovulating. The females, in turn, make no secret of their ovulatory status. Female chimpanzees, for example, come into estrus and ovulate, giving off visual and olfactory cues that drive male chimps into a sexual frenzy. When female chimps are not ovulating they are largely ignored by the males.

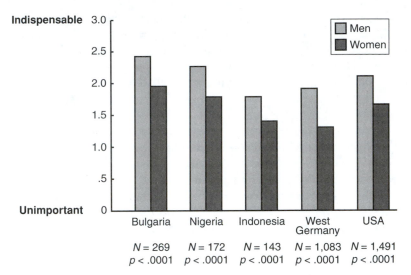

FIGURE 5.5   Desire for Physical Attractiveness in a Long-Term Mate. Participants in thirty-seven cultures rated this variable, in the context of eighteen other variables, on how desirable it would be in a potential long-term mate or marriage partner using a four-point rating scale, ranging from zero (irrelevant or unimportant) to three (indispensable).

N = sample size.

p values less than .05 indicate that sex difference is significant.

Source: Buss, D. M., & Schmitt, D. P. (1993). Sexual strategies theory: An evolutionary perspective on human mating. *Psychological Review, 100,* 204–232. Copyright © 1993 by the American Psychological Association. Adapted with permission.

In humans, however, ovulation is "concealed" or "cryptic"—conventional scientific wisdom is that there is no evidence that men can detect when women are ovulating (Symons, 1992, p. 144). Despite the tremendous reproductive advantages of detecting and desiring ovulating women, selection seems not to have given men these adaptations. Perhaps this conclusion is too hasty.

There are several lines of evidence that suggest that men might, in fact, be able to detect when women ovulate (Symons, 1995). First, during ovulation women's skin becomes "vascularized," or suffused with blood. This corresponds to the "glow" that women sometimes appear to have, a healthy reddening of the cheeks. Second, women's skin lightens slightly during ovulation as compared with other times of the menstrual cycle—a cue universally thought to be a sexual attractant (van den Berghe & Frost, 1986). A cross-cultural survey found that "of the 51 societies for which any mention of native skin preferences . . . is made, 47 state a preference for the lighter end of the locally represented spectrum, although not necessarily for the lightest possible skin color" (van den Berghe & Frost, 1986, p. 92).

Third, during ovulation women's levels of circulating estrogen increase, which produces a corresponding decrease in women's waist-to-hip ratio (Profet, personal communication, cited in Symons, 1995, p. 93). A lower WHR, as noted earlier, is known to be sexually attractive to men (Singh, 1993).

Fourth, one study watched women in singles bars to see how often they were touched by men (Grammer, 1996). One observer recorded various behaviors of each woman in the bar, including how much she was touched by men and the tightness and length of her skirt. A second member of the research team independently approached each woman as she left the bar and interviewed her about the time of her menstrual cycle. Outside the bar each woman was also photographed. Subsequently, the photographed images of the women were digitized by computer, and researchers then calculated the amount of skin each woman displayed. Researchers were careful to analyze the data for women who were taking oral contraceptives (the Pill) separately from those who were not.

Among women not taking the Pill, those who were ovulating at the time were touched by men inside the bar significantly more often than those who were at other points in their menstrual cycle. Furthermore, the ovulating women engaged in more sexual signaling, as evidenced by their showing a greater amount of skin and wearing skirts that were significantly tighter and shorter. The fact that ovulating women were touched more often by men might indicate that men can in fact detect when women ovulate. But the fact that women appear to be evoking men's interest through sexual signaling (more skin, shorter and tighter skirts) suggests an alternative explanation—that women instigate sexual overtures from men when they are ovulating. Of course, both explanations could be correct—men might be detecting ovulation and ovulating women might be initiating sexual overtures.

So we have four pieces of circumstantial evidence pointing to the possibility that men can detect when women ovulate: vascularization of the skin, lightening of the skin, reduction in WHR, and increased touching in singles bars. Because ovulating women might be sending more sexual signals to men, however, men might not be *detecting* when women ovulate so much as they are *responding* to the sexual interest the women express.

Another study lends circumstantial support to the woman-initiated contact hypothesis. Researchers looked at a sample of married women over a period of twenty-four months (Stanislaw & Rice, 1988). Ovulation was determined by measuring basal body temperature, which rises just prior to ovulation. Over the twenty-four months, women put an "X" on a chart on those days on which they experienced "sexual desire." As shown in Figure 5.6 on page 148, women's reported desire increased steadily as ovulation approached, peaked at or just after ovulation, and then decreased steadily as they approached the infertile period of menstruation. So, the fact that ovulating women are touched more at singles bars may reflect their increased sexual desire, increased exposure of skin, and perhaps other sexual signals that researchers did not examine.

In summary, definitive studies on whether men can detect when women ovulate remain to be conducted. The available evidence is sufficient to suggest that there are *potentially* observable physical changes in a woman's skin and body when she ovulates—changes known to be sexually attractive to men. Over the next few years we will be able to determine whether the conventional wisdom—that men cannot detect when women ovulate—is true or false.

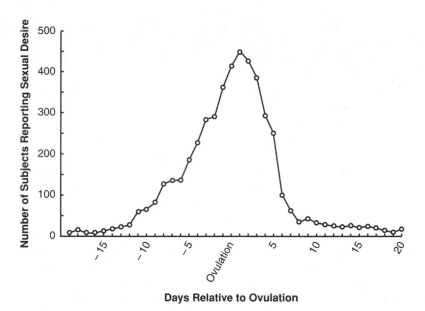

FIGURE 5.6   Women's Sexual Desire as a Function of Ovulation Cycle. Women's sexual desire tends to peak around ovulation, which was determined by shifts in basal body temperature.

Source: Stanislaw, H., & Rice, F. J. (1988). Correlation between sexual desire and menstrual cycle characteristics. *Archives of Sexual Behavior, 17*, 1988, (New York: Plenum Publishing) 499–508. Adapted with permission.

Solutions to the Problem of Paternity Uncertainty

Mammalian females typically enter estrus periodically, and thus are not sexually receptive throughout the ovulatory cycle. Vivid visual cues and strong scents often accompany estrus and powerfully attract males. Sexual intercourse occurs primarily in this narrow envelope of time. Unlike chimpanzees, women do not have genital swelling when they ovulate. Indeed, women are rare among primates in possessing the unusual adaptation of concealed or cryptic ovulation (although, as noted earlier, it may be less concealed than we think). Such relatively cryptic female ovulation obscures a woman's current reproductive status.

Concealed ovulation dramatically changed the ground rules of human mating. Women became attractive to men not just during ovulation but throughout the ovulatory cycle. Cryptic ovulation created a special adaptive problem for men by decreasing the certainty of their paternity. Consider a primate male who prevents other males from mating with a female for the brief period during which she is in estrus. In contrast to human males, he can be fairly "confident" of his paternity. The period during which he must sequester and have sex with her is sharply constrained. Before and after her estrus, he can go about his other business without running the risk that his partner will become impregnated by another male.

Ancestral men did not have this luxury. Our human ancestors probably never knew when a woman was ovulating. Because mating is not the sole activity needed for humans to survive and reproduce, women could not be "guarded" around the clock. The more time a man spent guarding, the less time he had available for grappling with critical adaptive problems. Ancestral men, therefore, were faced with a unique paternity problem not faced by other primate males—how to be certain of their paternity when ovulation was concealed.

Marriage potentially provided one solution (Alexander & Noonan, 1979; Strassman, 1981). Men who married would benefit reproductively relative to other men by substantially increasing their certainty of paternity. Repeated sexual contact throughout the ovulation cycle raised the odds that a woman would bear a given man's child. The social traditions of marriage function as public ties about the couple, by providing a clear signal about who was mated with whom, and thus potentially reducing conflict within male coalitions. Marriage also provides opportunities to learn intimately about one's mate's personality, making it difficult for her to hide signs of infidelity. These benefits of marriage would have outweighed the costs of foregoing the sexual opportunities available to ancestral bachelors, at least under some conditions.

For an ancestral man to reap the reproductive benefits of marriage he had to seek reasonable assurances that his wife would remain sexually faithful to him. Men who failed to recognize fidelity cues would have suffered in reproductive success because they lost the time and resources devoted to searching, courting, and competing. By failing to be sensitive to these cues a man risked losing the benefits of the woman's parental investment in his children, which might instead be diverted to another man's children. Perhaps even more devastating in reproductive terms, failure to ensure fidelity meant that his own efforts would be channeled to another man's offspring. Men who were indifferent to the potential sexual contact between their wives and other men are not our ancestors.

Our forebears could have solved this uniquely male adaptive problem by seeking qualities in a potential mate that might increase the odds of securing their paternity. At least two preferences in a mate could solve the problem for males: (1) the desire for *premarital chastity* and (2) the quest for *postmarital sexual fidelity*. Before the use of modern contraceptives, chastity would likely have provided a clue to the future certainty of paternity. On the assumption that a woman's proclivities toward chaste behavior would be stable over time, her premarital chastity would signal her likely future fidelity. A man who didn't select a chaste mate may have risked becoming involved with a woman who would cuckold him.

Today it seems men value virgin brides more than women value virgin grooms, at least in the United States according to a cross-generational mating study. But the value men place on virginity has declined over the past half-century, coinciding with the increasing availability of birth control (Buss et al., under review). In the 1930s men viewed chastity as close to indispensable, but in the past two decades they have rated it desirable but not crucial. Among the eighteen characteristics rated in the study, chastity went from the tenth most valued in 1939 to the seventeenth most valued in the 1990s. Furthermore, not all American men value chastity equally, generally depending on region. College students in Texas, for example, desire a chaste mate more than college students in California, rating it 1.13 as compared to 0.73 on a 3.00 scale. Despite the decline in the value of chastity in the twentieth century and despite regional variations, a significant sex difference remains—men more than women emphasize chastity as being important in a potential long-term mate.

The trend for men to value chastity more than women holds up worldwide, but it varies temendously among cultures. At one extreme, people in China, India, Indonesia, Iran, Taiwan, and the Palestinian Arab areas of Israel attach a high value to chastity in a potential mate. At the opposite extreme, people in Sweden, Norway, Finland, the Netherlands, West Germany, and France believe that virginity is largely irrelevant or unimportant in a potential mate (Buss, 1989a) (see Figure 5.7).

In contrast to the worldwide consistency in the different preferences by sex for youth and physical attractiveness, only 62 percent of the cultures in the international

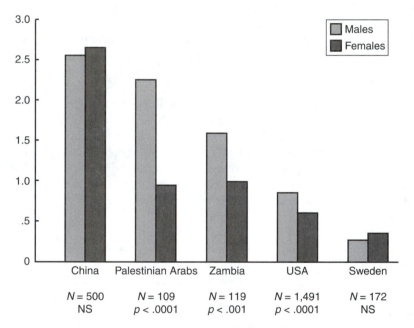

FIGURE 5.7   Desire for Chastity, or No Previous Experience with Sexual Intercourse, in a Long-Term Mate. Participants in thirty-seven cultures rated this variable, in the context of eighteen other variables, on how desirable it would be in a potential long-term mate or marriage partner using a four-point rating scale, ranging from zero (irrelevant or unimportant) to three (indispensable).

N = sample size.

p values less than .05 indicate that sex difference is significant.

NS indicates that sex difference is not significant.

Source: Buss, D. M., & Schmitt, D. P. (1993). Sexual strategies theory: An evolutionary perspective on human mating. *Psychological Review, 100,* 204–232. Copyright © 1993 by the American Psychological Association. Adapted with permission.

study on choosing a mate placed a significantly different value by gender on chastity in a committed mateship. Where sex differences in the value of virginity are found, however, men invariably placed a greater value on it than did women. In no case did women value chastity more than men.

The cultural variability in the preference of each sex for chastity may be due to several factors—the prevailing incidence of premarital sex, the degree to which chastity can be demanded in a mate, the economic independence of women, or the reliability with which it can be evaluated. Chastity differs from other attributes, such as a woman's physical attractiveness, in that it is less directly observable. Even physical tests of female virginity are unreliable, whether from variations in the structure of the hymen, its rupture due to nonsexual causes, or its deliberate alteration (Dickemann, 1981). In Japan, for example, there is currently a booming medical business of "remaking virgins" by surgically reconstructing the hymen because Japanese men continue to place a relatively high value on chaste brides, rating chastity 1.42 on a 0 to 3 scale, in comparison to American men, who rate it only 0.85, or German men, who rate it only 0.34.

Variation in the value that people place on chastity may be traceable in part to variability in the economic independence of women and in women's control of their own sexuality. In some cultures, such as Sweden, premarital sex is not discouraged and practically no one is a virgin at marriage (Posner, 1992). One reason may be that women in Sweden are far less economically reliant on men than in most other cultures. Legal scholar Richard Posner notes that marriage provides few benefits for Swedish women as compared with women in most other cultures (Posner, 1992). The Swedish social welfare system includes day care for children, long paid maternity leaves, and many other material benefits. Swedish taxpayers effectively provide what husbands formerly provided, freeing women from their economic dependence on men. That independence lowers the cost to women of a free and active sex life before marriage, or as an alternative to marriage. Thus practically no Swedish women are virgins at marriage, and hence the importance that men place on chastity has commensurably declined to a worldwide low of 0.25 on a 0 to 3 scale (Buss, 1989a).

Differences in the economic independence of women, in the benefits provided by husbands, and in the intensity of competition for husbands may be factors that drive the critical cultural variation (Tooby & Cosmides, 1989). Where women benefit from marriage and where competition for husbands is fierce, women compete with one another to signal chastity, causing the average amount of premarital sex to go down. Where women control their economic fate, do not require so much of men's investment, and hence need to compete less, they are freer to disregard men's preferences, which causes the average amount of premarital sex to go up. Men everywhere might value chastity if they could get it, but in some cultures they cannot demand it of their brides.

From a man's reproductive perspective, a more important cue than virginity to paternity certainty is a reliable signal of future fidelity. If men cannot require that their mates be virgins, they can require of them sexual loyalty. A study of short- and long-term mating found that American men view lack of sexual experience as desirable in a spouse (Buss & Schmitt, 1993). Furthermore, men see promiscuity as especially undesirable in a marriage partner, rating it –2.07 on a scale of –3 to +3. The actual amount of prior sexual activity in a potential mate, rather than virginity per se, would have provided an excellent guide for ancestral men to solve the problem of paternity uncertainty. Contemporary studies show that the best predictor of extramarital sex is premarital sexual permissiveness—people who have many sexual partners before marriage are more likely to be unfaithful than those who have few sexual partners before marriage (Thompson, 1983; Weiss & Slosnerick, 1981).

Modern men place a premium on fidelity. When American men evaluated sixty-seven possible characteristics for their desirability in a committed mateship, faithfulness and sexual loyalty emerged as the most highly valued traits (Buss & Schmitt, 1993). Nearly all men gave these traits the highest rating possible, an average of +2.85 on a scale of −3 to +3. Cross-cultural tests remain to be conducted to see whether this is a universal male desire.

Men regard unfaithfulness as the least desirable characteristic in a wife, rating it a −2.93, reflecting the high value that men place on fidelity. Unfaithfulness proves to be more upsetting to men than any other pain a spouse could inflict on her mate—a finding for which there is excellent cross-cultural evidence (Betzig, 1989; Buss, 1989b; Daly & Wilson, 1988). Women also become extremely upset over an unfaithful mate, but several other factors, such as sexual aggressiveness, exceed infidelity in the grief they cause women.

The sexual revolution of the 1960s and 1970s, with its promises of sexual freedom and lack of possessiveness, apparently has had limited impact in the sphere of men's preferences for sexual fidelity. Cues to fidelity still signal that the woman is willing to channel all of her reproductive value exclusively to her husband. A woman's future sexual conduct looms large in men's marriage decisions.

In summary, we now have the outlines of some of the qualities that men desire in a long-term mate. In addition to the personality characteristics of kindness, dependability, and compatibility, men place a premium on physical attractiveness. Standards of attractiveness correlate highly with female fertility. In essence, men's desire for physical attractiveness solves the problem of seeking women who are reproductively capable. Reproductive capability, however, is not enough. Internal female fertilization posed a second adaptive problem for men, who appear to value sexual fidelity in a long-term mate as part of a solution to the problem of paternity uncertainty.

Context Effects on Men's Mating Behavior

In this section we look at the effects of two contexts on men's mating behavior. First, we consider the fact that desires rarely show a one-to-one correspondence with actual mating behavior. As discussed in Chapter 4, where we considered women's desires, men who are high in "mate value" have better odds of getting what they want in a mate. Men who are highly desirable to women by virtue of possessing the status and resources that women prefer should be in the best position to translate that into actual mating behavior.

Second, there is a notable discrepancy between modern environments and the ancestral environments in which we evolved. Over the course of evolutionary history, humans most likely evolved in small groups containing perhaps fifty to two hundred individuals (Dunbar, 1993). In these small groups a particular man would have encountered at most perhaps a dozen to two dozen attractive women. In modern environments humans are bombarded with literally thousands of images of attractive models from billboards, magazines, television, and the movies. This section considers the possible impact of this modern environment on human mating mechanisms.

Men in Positions of Power

Although most men place a premium on youth and beauty in a mate, it is clear that not all men are successful in achieving their desires. Men lacking the status and resources that women want, for example, generally have the most difficult time attracting such women and may have to settle for less than their ideal. Evidence for this possibility comes from men who have historically been in a position to get exactly what they prefer, such as kings and other men of unusually high status. In the 1700s and 1800s, for example, wealthier men from the Krummerhörn population of Germany married younger brides than did men lacking wealth (Voland & Engel, 1990). Similarly, high-status men from the Norwegian farmers of 1700 to 1900 to the Kipsigis in contemporary Kenya consistently married younger brides than did their lower-status counterparts (Borgerhoff Mulder, 1988; Røskaft, Wara, & Viken, 1992).

Kings and despots routinely stocked their harems with young, attractive, nubile women and had sex with them frequently (Betzig, 1992). The Moroccan emperor Moulay Ismail the Bloodthirsty, for example, acknowledged siring 888 children. His harem included five hundred women. But when a woman reached the age of thirty, she was banished from the emperor's harem, sent to a lower-level leader's harem, and replaced by a younger woman. Roman, Babylonian, Egyptian, Incan, Indian, and Chinese emperors all shared the tastes of Emperor Ismail and enjoined their trustees to scour the land for as many young pretty women as could be found.

Marriage patterns in modern America confirm the fact that men with resources are most able to actualize their preferences. High-status older males, such as rock stars Rod Stewart and Mick Jagger and movie stars Warren Beatty and Jack Nicholson, frequently select women two or three decades younger. Several sociological studies have examined the impact of a man's occupational status on the physical attractiveness of the woman he marries (Elder, 1969; Taylor & Glenn, 1976; Udry & Eckland, 1984). Men high in occupational status are able to marry women who are considerably more physically attractive than can men low in occupational status. Indeed, a man's occupational status seems to be the best predictor of the attractiveness of the woman he marries. Men in a position to mate with younger, more attractive women often do.

Men who enjoy high status and income are apparently aware of their ability to attract more desirable women. In a study of a computer dating service involving 1048 German men and 1590 German women, ethologist Karl Grammer found that as men's income goes up, they seek younger partners (Grammer, 1992). Men earning more than 10,000 deutsche marks, for example, advertised for mates who were between five and fifteen years younger, whereas men earning less than 1,000 DM advertised for mates who were between zero and five years younger. Each increment in income is accompanied by a decrease in the age of the woman sought.

Not all men, however, have the status, position, or resources to attract young women, and some men end up mating with older women. Many factors determine the age of the woman at marriage, including the woman's preferences, the man's own age, his mating assets, the strength of his other mating preferences, and the woman's appearance. Mating preferences are not invariably translated into actual mating decisions for all people all of the time, just as food preferences are not invariably translated into actual eating decisions for all people all of the time. But men who are in a position to get what they want often marry young, attractive women. Ancestral men who actualized these preferences enjoyed greater reproductive success than those who did not. Modern men carry the desires of those who were reproductively successful.

Context Effects from Viewing Attractive Models

Advertisers exploit the universal appeal of beautiful, youthful women. Madison Avenue is sometimes charged with advancing a single arbitrary standard of beauty that everyone else must live up to (Wolf, 1992). This accusation is at least partially false. The standards of beauty, as we have seen, are not arbitrary but rather embody reliable cues to fertility and reproductive value. Advertisers that more closely exploit existing mate preferences are almost sure to be more successful than those that do not. Furthermore, advertisers are unlikely to have a special interest in inculcating a particular set of beauty standards. They are in the business of making money and seek to use whatever sells successfully. Advertisers perch a clear-skinned, regular-featured young woman on the hood of the latest car because the image exploits men's evolved psychological mechanisms and therefore sells cars, not because they want to promote a single standard of beauty.

The media images we are bombarded with daily, however, have a potentially pernicious consequence. In one study, after groups of men looked at photographs of either highly attractive women or women of average attractiveness, they were asked to evaluate their commitment to their current romantic partners (Kenrick, Neuberg, Zierk, & Krones, 1994). The men who had viewed pictures of attractive women thereafter judged their actual partners to be less attractive than did the men who had viewed pictures of women who were average in attractiveness. Perhaps more important, the men who had viewed attractive women thereafter rated themselves as less committed to, less satisfied with, less serious about, and less close to their actual partners. Parallel results were obtained in another study in which men viewed physically attractive nude centerfolds—they rated themselves as less attracted to their partners (Kenrick, Gutierres, & Goldberg, 1989).

The reasons for these changes are found in the unrealistic nature of the images and in the psychological mechanisms of men. The few attractive women selected for advertisements are chosen from a cast of thousands. In many cases thousands of pictures are then taken of each chosen woman. *Playboy*, for example, is reputed to shoot roughly 6,000 pictures for each monthly magazine. From these thousands of pictures, a few are selected for publication. So what men see are the most attractive women in the most attractive pose with the most attractive background in the most attractive airbrushed photograph. Contrast these photographs with what men would have witnessed 100,000 years ago, living in a band of a few dozen individuals. It is doubtful that in that environment men would have seen even a dozen women considered attractive by today's measure. The presence of a relative abundance of attractive women, however, might reasonably induce a man to consider switching mates, and hence he would decrease his commitment to his existing mate.

Consider modern times. We carry with us the same evaluative mechanisms that evolved in ancient times. Now, however, these mechanisms are artificially activated by the dozens of attractive women we witness daily in our advertisement-saturated culture, in magazines, on billboards, on TV, and in movies. These images do not represent real women in our actual social environment. Rather, these images exploit mechanisms designed for a different environment.

As a consequence of viewing such images men may become dissatisfied with, and less committed to, their mates. The potential damage inflicted by these images affects women as well because they create a spiraling and unhealthy competition with other women. Women find themselves competing with other women to embody the images they see daily—images they believe are desired by men. The unprecedented rates of anorexia nervosa and radical cosmetic surgery may stem in part from these media images. The images do not cause this unfortunate result by creating standards of beauty that were previously absent, however. Rather, they work by exploiting men's existing evolved standards of beauty and women's competitive mating mechanisms on an unprecedented and unhealthy scale.

Effect of Men's Preferences on Actual Mating Behavior

In this section we examine the impact of men's long-term mate preferences on behavior. First, we explore a study of personal ads to see whether men respond more to the ads of women who indicate qualities that embody men's desires. Second, we look at age preferences and actual mating decisions. Finally, we look at the effects of men's mate preferences on women's mating strategies, and examine whether women who are trying to attract men strive to embody the preferences that men express.

Men's Responses to Women's Personal Ads

If men act on their preferences for women who are young and physically attractive, then they should respond more to women who display these qualities. In a natural experiment two psychologists examined the responses of men to personal ads placed in two newspapers, one in the Midwest and the other on the West Coast (Baize & Schroeder, 1995; see Chapter 4). The mean age of the sample respondents was thirty-seven, with a range from twenty-six to fifty-eight.

When responses to the ads placed by men and women were compared, several striking differences emerged. First, men tended to respond to women's ads more than women responded to men's ads. Men tended to receive only 68 percent as many letters as women did. Second, and most relevant to the issue of men acting on their desires, younger women received more responses from men than did older women. Third, although mentioning *physical attractiveness* produced more responses from both sexes, it produced significantly more responses for women than for men. Interestingly, women who included self-descriptions conveying their *sexual attractiveness* received significantly more letters than women who did not mention it, but for men the result was precisely the opposite. It is reasonable to speculate that women might perceive men who mention sexual attractiveness as signaling an interest in short-term casual sexual encounters rather than long-term committed relationships.

In sum, men's responses to women's personal ads provides a natural source of evidence suggesting that men act on their preferences. Specifically, more men respond to women advertising youth and attractiveness, the qualities they desire.

Age Preferences and Marital Decisions

Actual marriage decisions confirm the preference of men for women who are increasingly younger than they are as the men age. American grooms exceed their brides in age by roughly three years at first marriage, five years at second marriage, and eight years at third marriage (Guttentag & Secord, 1983). Men's preferences for younger women also translate into actual marriage decisions worldwide. In Sweden during the 1800s, for example, church documents reveal that men who remarried following a divorce had new brides 10.6 years younger on average (Low, 1991). In all countries around the world where information is available on the ages of brides and grooms, men on average exceed their brides in age, as documented in Chapter 4 (Buss, 1989a).

The age difference between spouses as a function of the age of the man is shown dramatically in Figure 5.8. This figure shows the average age difference between brides and grooms as men get increasingly older for a sample drawn from the Island of Poro over a twenty-five-year period (Kenrick & Keefe, 1992). Men in their twenties tended to marry women just a year or two younger than themselves. Men in their thirties tended to marry women three to four years younger than themselves. Men who married in their forties, however, married women who were thirteen or fourteen years younger. These data, although limited to a single time and place, are representative of the general trend for men to marry women who are increasingly younger as they grow older (Kenrick & Keefe, 1992).

The cross-cultural data confirm the age differences between brides and grooms in actual marital decisions. The age difference ranges from about two years in Poland to roughly five years in Greece. Averaged across all countries for which we have good demographic data, grooms are three years older than their brides, or roughly the same difference that is expressly desired by men worldwide (Buss, 1989a). In polygynous cultures the age difference is even larger. Among the Tiwi of Northern Australia, for example, high-status men often have wives who are two and three decades younger (Hart & Pilling, 1960).

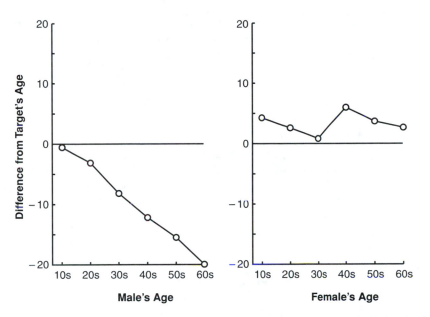

FIGURE 5.8   Actual Age Differences in 1,511 Marriages on the Island of Poro (1913–1939).

Source: Kenrick, D. T., & Keefe, R. C. (1992). Age preferences in mates reflect sex differences in reproductive strategies. *Behavioral and Brain Sciences, 15,* 75–133. Reprinted with permission.

Effect of Men's Mate Preferences on Women's Attraction Tactics

According to the theory of sexual selection, the preferences of one sex are predicted to influence the forms of competition that occur in the opposite sex (Buss, 1994). Specifically, if men's preferences have exerted an important impact on mating behavior over time, we would predict that women would compete with one another to fulfill or embody what men want. Three sources of data are relevant to examining this prediction—research on the tactics that women use to attract men, research on the tactics that women use to derogate competitors, and research on the self-descriptions that women include in their personal ads when seeking men.

In one study Buss (1988c) examined the self-reported usage and the perceived effectiveness of 101 tactics of mate attraction. Two samples of participants reported on their tactic usage—an undergraduate sample and a sample of newlywed women, the latter reporting on the tactics they had used to attract their husbands. Appearance enhancement figured prominently in both samples. Women, significantly more than men, reported using the following attraction tactics: "I wore facial makeup," "I went on a diet to improve my figure," "I learned how to apply cosmetics," "I kept myself well-groomed," "I used makeup that accentuated my looks," and "I got a new and interesting hair style." In a separate study (Buss, 1988c, study 3), an independent panel of undergraduates rated these tactics on "how effective" they would be in successfully attracting a member of the opposite sex. The ratings of perceived effectiveness matched the self-reported performance—all acts of appearance enhancement were judged to be more effective for women in attracting men than vice versa. Using a seven-point scale, acts involving enhancing facial appearance received an average effectiveness rating of 4.71 for women, but only 1.92 for men. In sum, this research supports the hypothesis that men's desires for physically attractive women have had an impact on the nature of the tactics that women use to attract men.

In a related series of studies William Tooke and Lori Camire (1991) looked at the usage and effectiveness of tactics of intersexual deception, or the ways in which men deceive women and women deceive men in the mating arena. Using a methodology similar to the study of attraction tactics (Buss, 1988c), they asked male and female undergraduates to report on their performances and rate the effectiveness of various tactics of deceiving the opposite sex. Women, more than men, used tactics of deception involving their physical appearance: "I sucked in my stomach when around members of the opposite sex," "I wore a hairpiece around members of the opposite sex," "I wore colored contact lenses to make my eyes appear to be a different color," "I dyed my hair," "I wore false fingernails," "I wore dark clothing to appear thinner than I really was," and "I wore padded clothing." As in the above study of attraction tactics, women's use of deceptive appearance enhancement was judged to be significantly more effective in attracting mates than men's use of such tactics. In sum, when it comes to attracting the opposite sex, women's behavior appears to be highly responsive to the preferences expressed by men.

Women also appear to be sensitive to the mate preferences of men in their interactions involving rivals. In one study, sixty undergraduate women rated the effectiveness of twenty-eight distinct competitor derogation tactics (Buss & Dedden, 1990, study 2). One tactic involved derogating a rival's physical appearance using acts such as "made fun of his/her appearance," "told others that the rival was fat and ugly," and "made fun of the size and shape of the rival's body." Participants used a scale of 1 (not at all effective) to 7 (extremely effective), for the goal of making the rival undesirable to members of the opposite sex. Derogating a rival's physical appearance was judged to be more effective when women used it (average rating, 3.42) than when men used it (average rating, 2.95).

An even larger sex difference pertained to derogation of the rival's sexual fidelity. Recall that men put a premium on sexual fidelity in a long-term mate, most likely as an evolved solution to the problem of paternity uncertainty. One derogation tactic, "calling competitor promiscuous," violates men's desire for a faithful wife with acts such as "called rival a tramp," "told others that the rival had slept around a lot," and "told others that the rival was loose, and would sleep with just about anybody." Calling a competitor promiscuous was judged to be 4.44 in effectiveness when used by women, but only 3.45 in effectiveness when used by men. In short, effective rival derogation tactics appear to be those that violate men's preferences in a long-term mate.

In a separate study fifty male and fifty female undergraduates reported on how often they used each of the twenty-eight derogation tactics (Buss & Dedden, 1990, study 1). Women reported a higher likelihood of derogating their rival's physical appearance than men did, with average performance reports of 4.15 and 3.69 for women and men, respectively (using a scale ranging from 1, unlikely to have ever performed tactic, to 7, highly likely to have performed tactic). Even more striking were the sex differences in the likelihood of calling a competitor promiscuous. Women (4.44) were significantly more likely than men (3.45) to derogate a rival by reputational damage on the promiscuity dimension. Based on these studies we can conclude that women's derogation tactics appear to be sensitive to men's long-term mate preferences, especially on the dimensions of physical appearance and desire for fidelity.

In summary, three sources of evidence support the notion that men's preferences affect actual behavior in the mating arena. First, men respond more to personal ads advertising qualities that fulfill men's expressed preferences, such as a desire for women who are physically attractive and young. Second, men actually marry younger women, an age difference that increases with each successive marriage. And third, women's mate attraction tactics and derogation of rival tactics map closely onto the dimensions that men prefer in a long-term mate. Specifically, women enhance their appearance as a tactic for attracting men and derogate their rivals on the dimensions of appearance and promiscuity. From all this empirical evidence we can reasonably conclude that men's preferences in a long-term mate affect not only their own mating behavior, but also the mating behavior of women in their mate competition tactics.

Summary

There were many potential benefits to ancestral men who married. They would have increased their chances of attracting a mate, specifically, a more desirable mate. By marrying, men would have increased their certainty in paternity because they gained continuous or exclusive or predominant sexual access to the woman. In the currency of fitness, men also would have benefited through the increased survival and reproductive success of their children, accrued through paternal protection and investment.

Two adaptive problems loom large in men's long-term mate selection decisions. The first is identifying women of high fertility or reproductive value—women capable of successfully bearing children. A large body of evidence suggests that men have evolved standards of attractiveness that embody clues to a woman's reproductive capacity. Signals of youth and health are central among these clues—clear skin, full lips, small lower jaw, symmetrical features, white teeth, absence of sores and lesions, and a small ratio of waist to hips.

The great importance that men place on a woman's physical appearance is not some immutable biological law of the animal world. Indeed, in many other species, such as the peacock, it is the females who place greater value on physical appearance. Nor is men's preference for youth a biological universal in the animal world. Some primate males, such as orangutans, chimpanzees, and Japanese macaques, prefer older females, who have already demonstrated their reproductive abilities by giving birth; they show low sexual interest in adolescent females because they have low fertility (Symons, 1987). Human males have faced a unique set of adaptive problems, however, and so have evolved a unique sexual psychology. They prefer youth because of the centrality of marriage in human mating. Their desires are keyed on to future reproductive potential, not just immediate reproduction. They place a premium on physical appearance because of the abundance of reliable cues it provides to the reproductive capacity of a potential mate.

The second large adaptive problem is the problem of paternity uncertainty. Over human evolutionary history men who were indifferent to this adaptive problem risked raising another man's children, which would have been tremendously costly in the currency of reproductive success. Men in many countries value virginity in potential brides, but this is not universal. A more likely candidate for a universal solution is to place a premium on cues to fidelity—the likelihood that the woman will have intercourse exclusively with him.

Men want physically attractive, young, sexually loyal wives who will remain faithful until death. These preferences cannot be attributed to Western culture, to capitalism, to white Anglo-Saxon bigotry, to the media, or to incessant brainwashing by advertisers—they appear to be universal. Not a single cultural exception to this trend has ever been documented. Men's mate preferences seem to be deeply ingrained, evolved psychological mechanisms that drive mating decisions, just as our evolved taste preferences control our decisions about food consumption.

Four sources of behavioral data confirm the hypothesis that men's mate preferences affect actual mating behavior. First, men who respond to personal ads show higher response rates to women who claim to be young and physically attractive. Second, men worldwide actually marry women who are younger by roughly three years; men who divorce and remarry tend to marry women who are even younger, with a five-year difference at second marriage and an eight-year difference at third marriage. Third, women devote much effort to enhancing their physical appearance in the context of attracting men, which suggests that women are responding to the preferences that men express. And fourth, women tend to derogate their rivals by putting down their physical appearance and calling them promiscuous—tactics that are effective in rendering rivals less attractive to men because they violate the preferences that men hold for a long-term mate.

6 Short-Term Sexual Strategies

*[Women] not rarely run away with a favoured lover. . . . We thus see that . . .
the women are not in quite so abject a state in relation to marriage as has often
been supposed. They can tempt the men they prefer, and sometimes can reject
those whom they dislike, either before or after marriage.*

—Charles Darwin, 1871

*The biological irony of the double standard is that males could not have been
selected for promiscuity if historically females had always denied them opportunity
for expression of the trait.*

—Robert Smith, 1984

Imagine an attractive person of the opposite sex walking up to you on a college campus and saying "Hi, I've been noticing you around town lately, and I find you very attractive. Would you have sex with me?" How would you respond? If you were like 100 percent of the women in one study, you would give an emphatic no. You would be offended, insulted, or just plain puzzled by the request. But if you were like the men in that study, the odds are good that you would say yes—as did 75 percent of those men (Clarke & Hatfield, 1989). As a man you would most likely be flattered by the request. Many of the 25 percent of the men who declined the sexual offer were apologetic, citing previous commitments. The idea that men and women react differently when it comes to casual sex may not be surprising. Theories in evolutionary psychology, however, provide a principled basis for predicting this difference and for explaining its magnitude.

Theories of Men's Short-Term Mating

We begin by considering theories of short-term mating. First, we will look at the adaptive logic of men's short-term mating and why it would loom larger in men's than in women's psychological repertoires. Second, we examine the potential costs that men might incur from short-term mating. And third, we explore the specific adaptive problems that men must solve if they are to successfully pursue short-term mating.

Adaptive Benefits for Men of Short-Term Mating

Trivers's (1972) theory of parental investment and sexual selection provides a powerful reproductive basis for expecting sex differences in the pursuit of short-term mating—men, more than women, are predicted to have evolved a greater desire for casual sex. The same act of sex that causes a woman to invest nine months of internal gestation obligates the man to practically no investment. Over a one-year period, an ancestral man who managed to have short-term sexual encounters with dozens of women would likely have caused many pregnancies. An ancestral woman who had sex with dozens of men in the course of the same year could only produce a single child (unless she bore twins or triplets). See Box 6.1 for a discussion of function and beneficial effects of short-term mating.

The reproductive benefits for men who successfully pursued a short-term mating strategy would have been direct: an increase in the number of offspring produced. A married man with two children, for example, could increase his reproductive success by a full 50 percent by one short-term copulation that resulted in conception and birth. This benefit assumes, of course, that the child produced by such a brief union would have survived, which would have depended in ancestral times on a woman's ability to secure resources through other means (e.g., by herself, through kin, or through other men). Historically men appear to have achieved increases in reproductive success mainly through increases in the number of sexual partners, not through increases in the number of children per partner (Betzig, 1986; Dawkins, 1986). This chapter will document the evidence for this claim, focusing on the evolved psychology of men's desire for a variety of partners.

Potential Costs of Short-Term Mating for Men

Short-term sexual strategies, however, carry potential costs for men. Over evolutionary time men risked: (1) contracting sexually transmitted diseases, risk that increases with the number of sex partners; (2) acquiring a social reputation as a "womanizer," which could impair their chances of finding a desirable long-term mate; (3) lowering the chances that their children would survive due to lack of paternal investment and protection; (4) suffering violence at the hands of jealous husbands or mates if the women with whom they pursued this strategy were married or mated; (5) suffering violence at the hands of the father or brothers of the women; and (6) risking retaliatory affairs by their wives and the potential for a costly divorce (Buss & Schmitt, 1993; Daly & Wilson, 1988; Freeman, 1983).

Given the large potential adaptive advantages of short-term mating for men, selection might have favored a short-term mating strategy despite these costs. If this were the case we would expect selection to have favored psychological mechanisms in men that were sensitive to these costs, and hence acted to reduce them where possible or preferentially pursue a short-term mating strategy only when the costs were low or could be circumvented. Pursuing a short-term mating strategy thus involves solving a number of specific adaptive problems, to which we now turn.

BOX **6.1**

Functions versus Beneficial Effects of Short-Term Mating

Short-term mating may have beneficial effects that are different from the original function. For example, "securing a part as an actor or actress in a movie" may be a beneficial effect of short-term mating, but could not have been an original function of such mating. Motion pictures are a modern invention and are not part of the selective environment in which humans evolved. Of course, this does not preclude "exchange sex for position or privilege" as a more abstract function of short-term mating.

For a benefit to qualify as a function of short-term mating means (1) that there was recurrent selection pressure over human evolutionary history such that (2) the benefit was recurrently reaped by those who engaged in short-term mating under some conditions; (3) that the costs in fitness currencies of pursuing short-term mating were less than the benefits in the contexts in which they were pursued; and (4) that selection favored the evolution of at least one psychological mechanism specifically designed to promote short-term mating in specific circumstances.

Because we cannot go back in time, we must use various standards of evidence for inferring the evolution of psychological mechanisms specifically designed to promote short-term mating. Among the criteria we can adopt are: (1) Do people in most or all cultures engage in short-term mating under particular conditions when not physically constrained from doing so? (2) Are there specific contexts that predispose men and women to engage in short-term mating that would imply the existence of psychological mechanisms sensitive to those

contexts? (3) Based on our knowledge of ancestral environments, is it reasonable to infer that those specific contexts would have provided recurrent opportunities for women to engage in short-term mating? (4) Was a potential benefit likely to be received by a woman engaging in short-term mating in those contexts? (5) Was the benefit sufficiently large so as to outweigh the potential costs of short-term mating? (6) Are the contexts in which women and men currently engage in short-term mating analogous to ancestral conditions those in which the costs were likely to be minimized and the benefits maximized?

The empirical work conducted so far cannot address all of these questions, and hence cannot unambiguously distinguish those benefits that may be actual functions of short-term mating from those that are merely side effects. Nonetheless, the available empirical evidence does provide a guide to those that are reasonably good and bad candidates for function. Given the prevalence of short-term mating across all known cultures, including tribal cultures such as the Ache (Hill & Hurtado, 1996), the Tiwi (Hart & Pilling, 1960), the !Kung (Shostak, 1981), the Hiwi (Hill & Hurtado, 1989), and the Yanomamö (Chagnon, 1983), the prevalence of infidelity in plays and novels dating back centuries, the evidence for human sperm competition (Baker & Bellis, 1995), and the prevalence of the desire for sexual variety, it is reasonable to infer that ancestral conditions would have permitted recurrent opportunities for women and men to benefit from short-term mating some of the time.

Adaptive Problems Men Must Solve When Pursuing Short-Term Mating

Ancestral men who pursued a short-term sexual strategy confronted a number of specific adaptive problems—partner number or variety, sexual accessibility, identifying which women were fertile, and avoiding commitment.

The Problem of Partner Number or Variety.   Successful pursuit of short-term mating requires an adaptation that is motivational in nature, something that would impel men toward a variety of sex partners. One first-line solution to the problem of partner number can be expected in desire. Men may have evolved over human evolutionary history a powerful desire for sexual access to a large number of women (Symons, 1979). A second specialized adaptation expected on theoretical grounds is a relaxation of standards that men might impose for an acceptable short-term partner. Elevated standards, by definition, preclude a large number of women from exceeding them. This relaxation of standards should apply to a wide range of mate characteristics, including age, intelligence, personality traits, and personal circumstances such as whether the woman is already involved with someone else. A third predicted adaptation is to impose minimum time constraints—that is, to let little time elapse before seeking sexual intercourse. The less time that is permitted to elapse, the larger the number of women a man can potentially copulate with. Like setting high standards, prolonged time delays interfere with the adaptive problem of partner number.

The Problem of Sexual Accessibility.   Men, being the less investing sex, are predicted to be less discriminating than women when seeking short-term mates. Nonetheless, reproductive advantages would accrue to men who directed their mating efforts most intensely toward women who were sexually accessible. Time, energy, and courtship resources devoted to women who are unlikely to consent to sex would interfere with the successful pursuit of short-term mating.

Specialized adaptations for solving the problem of sexual accessibility are predicted to occur in the form of men's short-term mate preferences. Specifically, women who show signs of being prudish, sexually inexperienced, conservative, or low in sex drive should be disfavored. Clothes signaling sexual openness or behavior signaling promiscuity, which would be highly undesirable in a long-term mate, might be desired by men in short-term mates because they seem to suggest sexual accessibility.

The Problem of Identifying Which Women Are Fertile.   A clear evolutionary prediction is that men seeking short-term mates would prefer women who displayed cues correlated with fertility. This is because a maximally fertile woman would have the highest probability of getting pregnant from a single act of sex. In contrast, men seeking long-term mates might be predicted to prefer younger women of higher reproductive value, because such women will be more likely to reproduce in the future (see Chapter 5 for a discussion of the distinction between fertility and reproductive value).

This distinction—fertility versus reproductive value—does not guarantee that selection will have fashioned two different standards of attraction in men, one when they are pursuing casual sex and another when they are pursuing a marriage partner. The key point is that this distinction can be used to generate a hypothesis about shifts in age preferences, which we can then test. In short-term mating a woman's fertility must be the key consideration, and men pursuing short-term mates are predicted to desire fertile women.

The Problem of Avoiding Commitment.   Men seeking short-term mates are predicted to avoid women who might demand serious commitments or investments before consenting to sex. The larger the investment in a particular woman, the fewer the number of sexual partners a given man can succeed in attracting. Women who require heavy investment effectively force men into a long-term mating strategy, which obviously conflicts with their pursuit of short-term opportunistic copulations. Men seeking short-term mates, therefore, are predicted to shun women who appear to desire long-term commitments or heavy investments before agreeing to sex.

In summary, on theoretical grounds men's pursuit of a short-term mating strategy would have carried several costs and would have required solving several adaptive problems. If over human evolutionary history men have pursued short-term mating, we should expect evolved solutions to these problems. For example, men pursuing short-term sex should especially prefer women who show signs of being immediately sexually available, high in fertility, and low in the likelihood of imposing entangling commitments. Let us now turn to the empirical evidence for the underlying psychology of short-term mating.

Evidence for an Evolved Short-Term Mating Psychology

Casual sex typically requires the consent of both sexes, no matter how eager men might be. Ancestral men could not have carried out temporary affairs alone. At least some ancestral women must have practiced the behavior some of the time, because if all women historically had mated monogamously for life with a single man and had no premarital sex, the opportunities for casual sex with consenting women would have vanished (Smith, 1984). The exception, of course, would occur in the context of coerced sex —a topic we will explore in Chapter 11.

In spite of the prevalence and evolutionary significance of casual sex, practically all research on human mating has centered on marriage. The fact that temporary mating is by definition transient and often cloaked in greater secrecy makes it difficult to study. In Kinsey's research on sexual behavior, for example, a question about extramarital sex caused many people to refuse to be interviewed altogether (Kinsey, Pomery, & Martin, 1948). Among those who did consent to an interview, many declined to answer questions about extramarital sex.

Short-term mating in the form of affairs, one-night stands, and temporary liaisons occurs in all cultures, and is not a new phenomenon. In fact, there are many clues in our existing physiology and psychology that betray a long history of casual sex stretching back to our evolutionary roots. Let's examine the physiological evidence.

Physiological Evidence for Short-Term Mating

Existing adaptations in our psychology, anatomy, physiology, and behavior reflect the scoring of prior selection pressures. Just as the modern fear of snakes reveals an ancestral hazard, so our sexual anatomy and physiology reveal an ancient story of short-term sexual strategies. That story has just recently come to light through careful studies of men's testes size, ejaculate volume, and variations in sperm production.

Testicle Size.   There are a number of physiological clues to the history of multiple matings. One clue comes from the size of men's testicles. Large testes typically evolve as a consequence of intense sperm competition—when the sperm from two or more males occupy the reproductive tract of one female at the same time because she has copulated with two or more males (Short, 1979; Smith, 1984). Sperm competition exerts a selection pressure on males to produce large ejaculates containing numerous sperm. In the race to the valuable egg, the larger, sperm-laden ejaculate has an advantage in displacing the ejaculate of other men inside the woman's reproductive tract.

Men's testes size, relative to their body weight, is far greater than that of gorillas and orangutans. Male testes account for .018 percent of body weight in gorillas and .048 percent in orangutans (Short, 1979; Smith, 1984). In contrast, human male testes account for .079 percent of men's body weight, or 60 percent more than that of orangutans and more than four times that of gorillas, corrected for body size. Men's relatively large testes provide one solid piece of evidence that women in human evolutionary history sometimes had sex with more than one man within a time span of a few days. This size of testes would have been unlikely to have evolved unless there was sperm competition. And it suggests that both sexes pursued short-term mating some of the time. But humans do not possess the largest testes of all the primates. Human testicular volume is substantially smaller than that of the highly promiscuous chimpanzee, whose testes account for .269 percent of its body weight, more than three times more than the percentage for men. These findings suggest that our human ancestors rarely reached the chimpanzee's extreme of promiscuous or relatively indiscriminate sex.

To get a concrete feel for the differences in sexuality between chimps and humans, Wrangham (1993) summarized data from a variety of studies on the estimated number of male copulation partners that females from a variety of primate species experienced per birth. The highly monogamous gorilla females averaged only one male sex partner per birth. Human females were estimated to have 1.1 male sex partners per birth, or nearly 10 percent more sex partners than gorillas. In contrast, baboon females had eight male sex partners per birth; bonobo chimp females had nine male sex partners per birth; and common chimpanzee females (*Pan troglodytes*) had thirteen male sex partners per birth. Thus, the behavior that leads to sperm competition—females having sex with a variety of males—appears to accord well with the evidence on sperm volume. Humans show higher levels of sperm competition than the monogamous gorillas but far lower levels of sperm competition than the more promiscuous chimps and bonobos.

Variations in Sperm Insemination.   Another clue to the evolutionary existence of casual mating comes from variations in sperm production and insemination (Baker & Bellis, 1995). In a study to determine the effect on sperm production of separating mates from each other, thirty-five couples agreed to provide ejaculates resulting from sexual intercourse, from either condoms or flowback, the gelatinous mass of seminal fluid that is spontaneously discharged by a woman at various points after intercourse. The partners in each couple had been separated for varying intervals of time.

Men's sperm count went up dramatically with the increasing amount of time the couple had been apart since their last sexual encounter. The more time spent apart, the more sperm the husbands inseminated in their wives when they finally did have sex.

When the couples spent 100 percent of their time together, men inseminated 389 million sperm per ejaculate, on average. But when the couples spent only 5 percent of their time together, men inseminated 712 million sperm per ejaculate, almost double the amount. The number of sperm inseminated increases when other men's sperm might be inside the wife's reproductive tract at the same time as a consequence of the opportunity provided for extramarital sex by the couple's separation. This increase in sperm insemination is precisely what is expected if humans had an ancestral history of casual sex and marital infidelity. It is important to note that this increase in sperm insemination upon being reunited did not depend on the time since the man's last ejaculation. Even when the man had masturbated to orgasm while away from his wife, he still inseminated more sperm on being reunited if he had been away from her a long time.

The increase in sperm inseminated by the husband after prolonged separation ensures that his sperm will stand a greater chance in the race to the egg by crowding out or displacing a possible interloper's sperm. Men appear to inseminate just enough sperm to replace the sperm inside the woman that have died since their last sexual episode, thereby maintaining within the woman a particular level to keep the population of his sperm inside her relatively constant. The fact that men carry a physiological mechanism that elevates sperm count when their wives may have had opportunities to be unfaithful points to an evolutionary history in which humans had extramarital affairs at least some of the time.

Different Sperm Morphs: Egg Getters and Kamikaze Sperm.   Human sperm come in more than one shape or "morph" (Baker & Bellis, 1995). The most common are those with a cone-shaped head and long wavy tail. These are the egg getters, designed to swim quickly up the female reproductive tract in the race to fertilize the egg. A second type of sperm morph is the kamikaze sperm. These typically have coiled tails and are far less efficient at swimming.

Recent evidence suggests that the coil-tailed kamikaze sperm have another function besides getting to the egg: In fact, they seem to be designed to block competing male sperm from doing so. In one study men were found to inseminate a larger fraction of these coil-tailed blockers into the female when there was an increased chance that she might have sex with another man (Baker & Bellis, 1995, p. 267). Furthermore, after the insemination of a large dose of coil-tailed blockers, women apparently retained fewer sperm from subsequent inseminations. Both pieces of evidence support the hypothesis that the coil-tailed sperm function as blockers rather than as egg getters, although clearly these provocative studies need to be replicated.

Human testicle size, variations in sperm production, and differences in sperm morphs all provide physiological clues to a human evolutionary history of short-term mating. These mechanisms suggest a long history of casual mating, but they are not the only clues. Human psychology also bears the marks of an ancestral past filled with short-term sex.

Psychological Evidence for Short-Term Mating

In this section we consider the *psychological* evidence for short-term mating—the desire for sexual variety, the amount of time that elapses before a person seeks sexual intercourse, the lowering of standards in short-term mating, the nature and frequency of sexual fantasies, and the "closing time phenomenon."

Desire for a Variety of Sex Partners.   The primary reproductive benefit of casual sex to ancestral men would have been a direct increase in the number of offspring, so that men faced a key adaptive problem of gaining sexual access to a variety of women. As a solution to this adaptive problem men have evolved a number of psychological mechanisms that have caused them to seek a variety of sexual partners (Symons, 1979).

One psychological solution to the problem of securing sexual access to a variety of partners is old-fashioned lust: men have evolved a powerful desire for sex. Men do not always act on this desire, but it is a motivating force: "Even if only one impulse in a thousand is consummated, the function of lust nonetheless is to motivate sexual intercourse" (Symons, 1979, p. 207).

To find out how many sexual partners people in fact desire, researchers asked unmarried American college students to identify how many sex partners they would ideally like to have within various time periods, ranging from the following month to their entire lives (Buss & Schmitt, 1993). The results are shown in Figure 6.1 and prove that men desire more sex partners than women at each of the different time intervals.

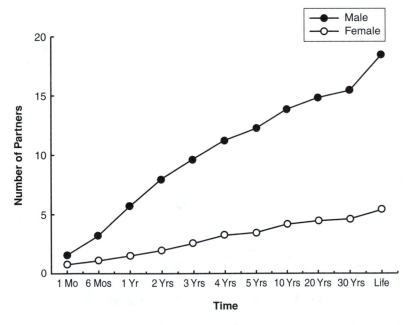

FIGURE 6.1   Number of Sexual Partners Desired. Subjects recorded in blank spaces provided how many sexual partners they would ideally like to have for each specified time interval.

Source: Buss, D. M., & Schmitt, D. P. (1993). Sexual strategies theory: An evolutionary perspective on human mating. *Psychological Review, 100,* 204–232. Copyright © 1993 by the American Psychological Association. Reprinted with permission.

Within the next year, for example, men stated on average that ideally they would like to have more than six sex partners, whereas women said that they would like to have only one. Within the next three years, men desired ten sex partners, whereas women wanted only two. The differences between men and women in ideal number desired of sex partners increase with time. On average men would like to have eighteen sex partners over their lifetime whereas women would like only four or five.

Time Elapsed before Seeking Intercourse.   Another psychological solution to the problem of gaining sexual access to a variety of partners is to let little time elapse between meeting the desired female and seeking sexual intercourse. The less time that a man permits to elapse before seeking sexual intercourse, the larger the number of women with whom he can successfully initiate sex. Large time investments absorb more of a man's mating effort and interfere with solving the problem of partner number and variety.

College men and women rated how likely they would be to consent to sex with someone they viewed as desirable if they had known the person for only an hour, a day, a week, a month, six months, a year, two years, or five years (Buss & Schmitt, 1993). Both men and women say that they would probably have sex after knowing a desirable potential mate for five years (see Figure 6.2). At every shorter interval, however, men exceeded women in the reported likelihood of having sex.

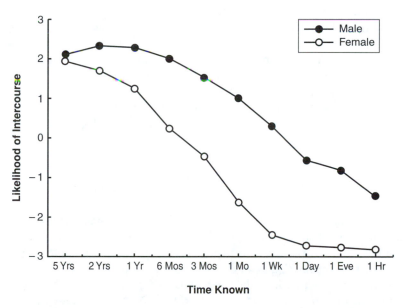

FIGURE 6.2   Probability of Consenting to Sexual Intercourse. Subjects rated the probability that they would consent to sexual intercourse after having known an attractive member of the opposite sex for each of a specified set of time intervals.

Source: Buss, D. M., & Schmitt, D. P. (1993). Sexual strategies theory: An evolutionary perspective on human mating. *Psychological Review, 100,* 204–232. Copyright © 1993 by the American Psychological Association. Reprinted with permission.

Having known a potential mate for only one week, men are still on average positive about the possibility of consenting to sex. Women, in sharp contrast, are highly unlikely to have sex after knowing someone for just a week. Upon knowing a potential mate for merely one hour, men are slightly disinclined to consider having sex, but the disinclination is not strong. For most women, sex after just one hour is a virtual impossibility. As with their desires, men's inclination to let little time elapse before seeking sexual intercourse offers a partial solution to the adaptive problem of gaining sexual access to a variety of partners.

The Lowering of Standards in Short-Term Mating.   Yet another psychological solution to securing a variety of casual sex partners is a relaxation of standards imposed by men for acceptable partners. High standards for attributes such as age, intelligence, personality, and marital status function to exclude the majority of potential mates from consideration. Relaxed standards ensure more eligible players.

College students provided information about the minimum and maximum acceptable ages of a partner for temporary and permanent sexual relationships (Buss & Schmitt, 1993). College men accept an age range roughly four years wider than do women for a temporary liaison. Men at this age are willing to mate in the short run with members of the opposite sex who are as young as sixteen and as old as twenty-eight, whereas women prefer men who are at least eighteen, but no older than twenty-six. This relaxation of age restrictions by men does not apply to committed mating, for which the minimum age is seventeen and the maximum twenty-five.

Men relax their standards for a wide variety of characteristics besides age. Men in the study expressed significantly lower standards than the women on forty-one of the sixty-seven characteristics named as potentially desirable in a casual mate. For brief encounters men require a lower level of such assets as charming, athletic, educated, generous, honest, independent, kind, intellectual, loyal, having a sense of humor, sociable, wealthy, responsible, spontaneous, cooperative, and emotionally stable. Men thus relax their standards across a range of attributes, which helps to solve the problem of gaining access to a variety of sex partners.

When the college students considered sixty-one undesirable characteristics, women rated roughly one-third of them as more undesirable than did men in the context of casual sex. Men have fewer objections in short-term relations to drawbacks such as mentally abusive, violent, bisexual, disliked by others, excessive drinker, ignorant, uneducated, possessive, promiscuous, selfish, lacking humor, and lacking sensuality. In contrast, men rate only four negative characteristics as significantly more undesirable than women, namely having a low sex drive, physically unattractive, having a need for commitment, and hairiness (the latter probably signals an endocrinological problem of too much testosterone production; women with hair on the face, chest, abdomen, and upper thighs have a higher proportion of ovulatory dysfunctions—see (Held, Nader, Rodriguez-Rigau, Smith & Steinberger, 1984; Steinberger, Rodriguez-Rigau, Smith, & Held, 1981). Men clearly relax their standards more than women for brief sexual encounters.

The relaxation of standards, however, does not mean that men have none. Indeed, the standards that men set for sexual affairs reveal a precise strategy to gain sexual access to a variety of partners. Compared with their long-term preferences, for casual sex partners men dislike women who are prudish, conservative, or have low sex drives. Also in contrast to their long-term preferences, men value sexual experience in a potential temporary sex partner, which reflects a belief that sexually experienced women are more sexually accessible to them than women who are sexually inexperienced. Men abhor promiscuity or indiscriminate sexuality in a potential wife but believe that promiscuity is either neutral or even mildly desirable in a potential sex partner. Promiscuity, high sex drive, and sexual experience in a woman probably signal an increased likelihood that a man can gain sexual access for the short run. Prudishness and low sex drive, in contrast, signal difficulty in gaining sexual access and thus interfere with men's short-term sexual strategy.

The distinguishing feature of men's relaxation of standards for a temporary sex partner involves the need for commitment. In contrast to the tremendous positive value of +2.17 that men place on commitment when seeking a marriage partner, men seeking a temporary liaison dislike women seeking a commitment, judging it to be –1.40, or undesirable in a short-term partner (Buss & Schmitt, 1993). Furthermore, men are not particularly bothered by a woman's marital status when they evaluate casual sex partners, because a woman's commitment to another man reduces the odds that she will try to extract a commitment from them. These findings confirm the prediction that men shift their desires to minimize their investment in a casual mating.

The Closing Time Phenomenon. A related psychological clue to men's strategy of casual sex comes from studies that examine shifts in judgments of attractiveness over the course of an evening at singles bars (Gladue & Delaney, 1990; Nida & Koon, 1983; Pennebaker, Dyer, Caulkins, Litowixz, Ackerman, & Anderson, 1979). In one study, 137 men and 80 women in a bar were approached at 9:00 P.M., 10:30 P.M., and 12:00 A.M. and asked to rate the attractiveness of members of the opposite sex in the bar using a ten-point scale (Gladue & Delaney, 1990). As closing time approached, men viewed women as increasingly attractive. The average judgment at 9:00 was 5.5, but by midnight it had increased to over 6.5. Women's judgments of men's attractiveness also increased over time, but women perceived the male bar patrons as less attractive overall compared with the men's perceptions of the women. Women rated the men at the bar as just below the average of 5.0 at 9:00, increasing near the midnight closing time to only 5.5 (see Figure 6.3 on page 172).

Men's shift in perceptions of attractiveness near closing time occurs regardless of how much alcohol they have consumed. Whether a man consumed a single drink or six drinks had no effect on the shift in viewing women as more attractive. The often noted "beer goggles" phenomenon whereby women are presumed to be viewed as more attractive with men's increasing intoxication, may instead be attributable to a psychological mechanism sensitive to decreasing opportunities over the course of the evening for casual sex. As the evening progresses and a man has not yet been successful in picking up a woman, he views the remaining women in the bar as increasingly attractive, a shift that will presumably increase his attempts to solicit sex from those women. The closing time phenomenon appears to represent a psychological solution to the problem of sexual accessibility—a context-specific lowering of standards as the likelihood of sexual accessibility starts to drop.

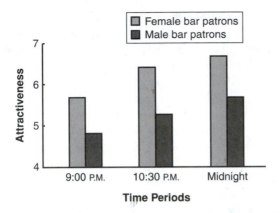

FIGURE 6.3   The Closing Time Phenomenon. As closing time approaches, both sexes, but especially men, find members of the opposite sex more attractive; the effect occurs even after controlling for the number of alcoholic drinks consumed. Female bar patrons were rated by men and male bar patrons were rated by women.

Source: Gladue, B. A., & Delaney, J. J. (1990). Gender differences in perception of attractiveness of men and women in bars. *Personality and Social Psychology Bulletin, 16*, 378–391. Copyright © 1990 by Sage Publications, Inc. Reprinted by permission of Sage Publications, Inc.

Sex Differences in Sexual Fantasies.   Sexual fantasies provide another psychological clue to an evolutionary history of men's proclivity to casual mating. Fantasies are not behaviors, of course, but they reveal something about the nature of desires that motivate men's and women's behaviors. Studies document large differences between male and female sexual fantasies. Research conducted in Japan, Great Britain, and the United States showed that men have roughly twice as many sexual fantasies as women (Ellis & Symons, 1990; Wilson, 1987). When asleep, men are more likely than women to dream about sexual events. Men's sexual fantasies more often include strangers, multiple partners, or anonymous partners. During a single fantasy episode, for example, most men report that they sometimes change sexual partners, whereas most women report that they rarely change sexual partners. Forty-three percent of women but only 12 percent of men report that they never substitute or switch sexual partners during a fantasy episode. Thirty-two percent of men but only 8 percent of women report having imagined sexual encounters with more than one thousand different partners in their lifetime. Fantasies about group sex occur among 33 percent of the men but only 18 percent of the women. A sample male fantasy is "being the mayor of a small town filled with nude girls from 20 to 24. I like to take walks, and pick out the best-looking one that day, and she engages in intercourse with me. All the women have sex with me any time I want" (Barclay, 1973, p. 209). Numbers and novelty are key ingredients of men's fantasy lives.

Men focus on body parts and sexual positions stripped of emotional context. Male sexual fantasies are heavily visual, focusing on smooth skin and moving body parts. During sexual fantasy, 81 percent of men but only 43 percent of women focus on visual images rather than feelings. Attractive women with lots of exposed skin who show signs of easy access and no commitment are the frequent contents of men's fantasies. As evolutionary psychologists Bruce Ellis and Donald Symons observed: "The most striking feature of [male fantasy] is that sex is sheer lust and physical gratification, devoid of encumbering relationships, emotional elaboration, complicated plot lines, flirtation, courtship, and extended foreplay" (Ellis & Symons, 1990, p. 544). These fantasies reveal a psychology attuned to sexual access to a variety of partners.

Women's sexual fantasies, in contrast, often contain familiar partners. Fifty-nine percent of American women but only 28 percent of American men report that their sexual fantasies typically focus on someone with whom they are already romantically and sexually involved. Emotions and personality are crucial for women. Forty-one percent of the women but only 16 percent of the men report that they focus most heavily on the personal and emotional characteristics of the fantasized partner. And 57 percent of women but only 19 percent of men report that they focus on feelings as opposed to visual images. As one woman observed: "I usually think about the guy I am with. Sometimes I realize that the feelings will overwhelm me, envelop me, sweep me away" (Barclay, 1973, p. 211). Women emphasize tenderness, romance, and personal involvement in their sexual fantasies. Women pay more attention to the way their partner responds to them than to visual images of their partner (Ellis & Symons, 1990).

Behavioral Evidence of Short-Term Mating

Physiological and psychological evidence both point strongly to a long evolutionary history in which men sought short-term mating with a variety of women. In this section we complete the picture by presenting behavioral evidence that men across cultures actually pursue short-term mating more than women.

Extramarital Affairs.   Men in most cultures pursue extramarital sex more often than do their wives. The Kinsey study, for example, estimated that 50 percent of men had extramarital affairs, whereas only 26 percent of women had them (Kinsey et al., 1948, 1953). Some studies show that the gap may be narrowing. One study of 8000 married men and women found that 40 percent of the men and 36 percent of the women reported at least one affair (Athanasiou, Shaver, & Tavris, 1970). The Hite Report on sexuality suggests figures as high as 75 percent for men and 70 percent for women, although these samples are acknowledged not to be representative (Hite, 1987). More representative samples, such as Hunt's survey of 982 men and 1044 women, yielded an incidence of 41 percent for men and 18 percent for women (Hunt, 1974). Despite these varying estimates and a possible narrowing of the gap between the sexes, all studies show sex differences in the incidence and frequency of affairs, with more men having affairs more often and with more partners than women.

Anthropologist Thomas Gregor described the sexual feelings of Amazonian Mehinaku men in this way: "Women's sexual attractiveness varies from 'flavorless' (mana) to the 'delicious' (awirintya) . . ." (1985, p. 84). Furthermore, Gregor notes that "sad to say, sex with spouses is said to be mana, in contrast with sex with lovers, which is nearly always awirintyapa" (Gregor, 1985, p. 72). Kinsey summed it up best: "There seems to be no question but that the human male would be promiscuous in his choice of sexual partners throughout the whole of his life if there were no social restrictions . . . The human female is much less interested in a variety of partners" (Kinsey, Pomeroy, & Martin, 1948, p. 589).

Prostitution.   Prostitution, the relatively indiscriminate exchange of sexual services for economic profit, is another reflection of men's greater desire for casual sex (Symons, 1979). Prostitution occurs in every society that has been thoroughly studied, from the Azande in Africa to the Zuni in North America (Burley & Symanski, 1981). Within the United States, estimates of the number of active prostitutes range from 100,000 to 500,000. Tokyo has more than 130,000 prostitutes, Poland 230,000, and Addis Ababa in Ethiopia 80,000. In Germany there are 50,000 legally registered prostitutes and triple that number working illegally. In all cultures men are overwhelmingly the consumers. Kinsey found that 69 percent of American men had solicited a prostitute and for 15 percent prostitution was a regular sexual outlet. The corresponding numbers for women were so low that they were not even reported as a percentage of the sexual outlet of women (Kinsey, et al., 1948, 1953).

The prevalence of prostitution does not imply that it is an adaptation, something that was the target of evolutionary selection. Rather, it can be understood as a consequence of two factors operating simultaneously—men's desire for casual sex and women either choosing to offer, or being forced by economic necessity to offer, sexual services for material gain.

Physiological, psychological, and behavioral evidence all point to a long evolutionary history in which short-term mating has been part of the human strategic repertoire (see Table 6.1). It is important to bear in mind that men's desire for short-term mating can have high costs in terms of psychological destructiveness and conflict between the sexes. Applying psychological knowledge to reducing social problems may require a deep understanding of basic sex differences in the desire for sexual variety.

TABLE 6.1   Clues to Ancestral Nonmonogamous Mating

Behavioral Clues
Extramarital affairs in all known cultures
Prostitution

Physiological Clues
Sperm volume
Sperm morphs—kamikaze and blocker

Psychological Clues
Male sexual jealousy
Desire for sexual variety

Women's Short-Term Mating

In this section we turn to women. First, we consider the evidence that women engage in short-term mating and likely have done so over the long course of human evolutionary history. Second, we consider hypotheses about the adaptive benefits ancestral women might have accrued from short-term mating. Third, we examine the costs of short-term mating for women. Finally, we examine the empirical evidence for the various hypotheses that have been advanced to account for women's short-term mating.

Evidence for Women's Short-Term Mating

Women bear the responsibility of a far greater minimum parental investment than men to produce a single child—nine months of gestation compared with one act of sexual intercourse. Evolutionary theories of human mating, as we have seen, therefore have emphasized the tremendous reproductive benefits to men of short-term mating (e.g., Kenrick et al., 1990; Symons, 1979; Trivers, 1972). Over human evolutionary history the reproductive benefits of short-term mating for men would have been large and direct in the form of additional children. Recall that a married man with two children could increase his reproductive success by a full 50 percent by producing one child through a casual sexual encounter. A married woman, in contrast, could not increase her direct reproductive success by sexual liaisons with dozens of men unless her husband proved to be infertile, impotent, or uninterested in sex with her.

Perhaps because of the elegance of parental investment theory and the extensive empirical support for it, many theorists have overlooked a fundamental fact about short-term mating: mathematically, the number of short-term matings must be identical, on average, for men and women. Every time a man has a casual sexual encounter with a woman he has never met, the woman is simultaneously having a casual sexual encounter with a man she has never met.

If ancestral women never engaged in short-term mating, men could not have evolved a powerful desire for sexual variety (Smith, 1984). That desire, if matings were consensual rather than forced, required the existence of some willing women some of the time. And if ancestral women willingly and recurrently engaged in short-term mating, it would defy evolutionary logic if there were no benefits to women of doing so. In fact, there are some clues that ancestral women did engage in short-term mating, starting with the physiology of the female orgasm.

Orgasm in Women.   The physiology of women's orgasm provides one clue to an evolutionary history of short-term mating. Once it was thought that a woman's orgasm functioned to make her sleepy and keep her reclined, thereby decreasing the likelihood that sperm would flow out and increasing the likelihood she would conceive. But if the function of orgasm were to keep the woman reclined so as to delay flowback, then more sperm would be retained. That is not the case. Rather, there is no link between the timing of the flowback and the number of sperm retained (Baker & Bellis, 1995).

Women discharge roughly 35 percent of sperm within thirty minutes of the time of insemination, averaged across all instances of intercourse. If the woman has an orgasm, however, she retains 70 percent of the sperm, ejecting only 30 percent. This 5 percent difference is not large, but if it occurred repeatedly, in woman after woman, generation after generation, it could add up to a large selection pressure over evolutionary time. Lack of an orgasm leads to the ejection of more sperm. This evidence is consistent with the theory that a woman's orgasm functions to draw the sperm from the vagina into the cervical canal and uterus, increasing the probability of conception.

The number of sperm a woman retains is also linked with whether she is having an affair. Women time their adulterous liaisons in a way that is reproductively detrimental to their husbands. In a nationwide sex survey of 3679 women in Britain, all women recorded their menstrual cycles as well as the timing of their copulations with their husbands and, if they were having affairs, with their lovers. It turned out that women having affairs appeared to time their copulations, most likely unconsciously, to coincide with the point in their menstrual cycle when they were most likely to be ovulating and hence were most likely to conceive (Baker & Bellis, 1995).

Behavioral Evidence of Extramarital Affairs.   The behavioral evidence also suggests that women in all but the most restrictive societies sometimes engage in extramarital sexual unions. In the United States, studies yield an affair rate ranging from 20 to 50 percent for married women (Athanasiou et al., 1970; Buss, 1994; Glass & Wright, 1992; Hunt, 1974; Kinsey et al., 1948, 1953). Affairs have also been documented, despite the shroud of secrecy that surrounds them, in dozens of tribal societies including the Ache of Paraguay (Hill & Hurtado, 1996), the Yanomamö of Venezuela (Chagnon, 1983), the Tiwi of Australia (Hart & Pilling, 1960), the !Kung of Botswana (Shostak, 1981), and the Mehinaku of Amazonia (Gregor, 1985). Modern cultural and tribal behavioral evidence, in short, does not suggest that women invariably pursue a monogamous long-term mating strategy all of the time.

In summary, a number of clues points to an ancestral past in which some women sometimes departed from monogamous mating. Physiological clues come from testes size in primates and from recent evidence on sperm insemination, sperm retention, and female orgasm. Behavioral evidence comes from the existence of extramarital affairs in all known tribal societies for which relevant data exist. And psychological clues come from the existence of the powerful male desire for sexual variety, which required willing women (in the absence of sexual coercion or force). These male mechanisms could not have evolved in a vacuum.

Hypotheses about the Adaptive Benefits to Women of Short-Term Mating

For short-term sexual psychology to evolve in women, there must have been adaptive benefits associated with casual sex in some circumstances. What might those benefits

TABLE 6.2   **Hypothesized Benefits to Women: Short-Term Mating***

Hypothesis	Author
Resource	
Investment via paternity confusion	Hrdy (1981)
Immediate economic resources	Symons (1979)
Protection through "special friendships"	Smuts (1985)
Status elevation	Smith (1984)
Genetic	
Better or "sexy son" genes	Fisher (1958)
Diverse genes	Smith (1984)
Mate Switching	
Mate expulsion	Greiling & Buss (under review)
Mate replacement	Symons (1979)
Mate insurance [backup]	Smith (1984)
Mate Skill Acquisition	
Honing skills of mate attraction	Miller (1991)
Clarifying mate preferences	Greiling & Buss (under review)
Mate Manipulation	
Increasing commitment of long-term mate	Greiling (1993)
Revenge as deterrence	Symons (1979)

*From Greiling, H. (1995).

have been? Five classes of benefits have been proposed: resources, genes, mate switching, mate skill acquisition, and mate manipulation (Greiling & Buss, under review), (Table 6.2). Let's examine these hypothesized benefits and the empirical evidence for them.

Resource Hypotheses.   One benefit of short-term mating is resource accrual (Symons, 1979). Women could engage in short-term mating in exchange for meat, goods, or services. In addition, an ancestral woman might have been able to obscure the actual paternity of her offspring through several short-term matings, and thus elicit resources from two or more men (Hrdy, 1981). According to this paternity confusion hypothesis, each man might be willing to offer some investment in the woman's children on the chance that they are genetically his own.

Another possible resource is protection (Smith, 1984; Smuts, 1985). Men typically provide protection to their mates and children, including defense against predators and aggressive men. Because a primary mate cannot always be around to defend and protect a woman, she might gain added protection by consorting with another man.

Finally, Smith (1984) proposed the status enhancement hypothesis of short-term mating. A woman might be able to elevate her social standing among her peers or gain access to a higher social circle by a temporary liaison with a high-status man. Clearly women might gain a variety of tangible and intangible resources through short-term mating.

Genetic Benefit Hypotheses.   Another class of benefits can be called genetic benefits. The first is the most obvious—*enhanced fertility.* If a woman's regular mate is infertile or impotent, a short-term mate might provide a fertility backup to aid in conception.

Second, a short-term mate might provide *superior genes* compared with a woman's regular mate, especially if she has an affair with a high-status man. These genes might give her offspring better chances for survival or reproduction. One version of this is known as the sexy son hypothesis (Fisher, 1958). By mating with an especially attractive man, a woman might be able to bear a son who is especially attractive to women in the next generation. Her son thus has increased sexual access, produces more children, and hence provides his mother with additional grandchildren.

Third, a short-term mate might provide a woman with *different genes* compared with those of her regular mate, thus enhancing the genetic diversity of her children—perhaps a hedge against environmental change (Smith, 1984). Among all the hypothesized benefits of short-term mating for women, the genetic hypotheses are the most difficult to test.

Mate Switching Hypotheses.   A third class of benefits pertains to mate switching. Sometimes a woman's husband stops bringing in resources, starts abusing her or her children, or otherwise declines in his value to her as a mate (Betzig, 1989; Fisher, 1992; Smith, 1984). Ancestral women might have benefited from short-term mating to cope with this adaptive problem.

There are several variants of this hypothesis. According to the mate expulsion hypothesis, having a short-term affair would help the woman to get rid of her long-term mate. Because men in many cultures often divorce wives who have affairs (Betzig, 1989), having an affair would be an effective means for the woman to initiate a breakup.

Another variant of this hypothesis suggests that a woman might simply find a man who is far better than her husband, and so initiate a short-term encounter as a means of switching mates. As Helen Fisher notes, ". . . infrequency of interband contact may have reduced opportunities for a female to acquire a prime mate on her first mateship, [enabling] her . . . to 'marry up' on her second try . . . [her] first mate's reproductive value might go down drastically as a result of injury; hence her second mate . . . would be of higher reproductive value than the first" (Fisher, 1992, p. 337).

Mate Skill Acquisition Hypotheses.   Another possible class of benefits for women involves acquiring mating skills (Greiling & Buss, under review). By short-term mating a woman might be able to hone her skills of attraction and seduction. She might also be able to clarify the qualities she wants in a long-term mate.

Mate Manipulation Hypotheses.   A fifth class of benefits involves manipulating her mate. By having an affair a woman might be able to gain revenge on her husband for his infidelity, thus possibly deterring him from future infidelities (Symons, 1979). Alternatively, a woman might be able to increase the commitment of her regular mate if he saw with stark evidence that other men were seriously interested in her (Greiling & Buss, under review).

Costs to Women of Short-Term Mating

Women sometimes incur more severe costs than men as a consequence of short-term mating. Women risk impairing their desirability as a long-term mate if they develop reputations for looseness or promiscuousness because men prize fidelity in potential wives. Because of men's abhorrence of promiscuity in a permanent partner, for women casual sex becomes risky to their reputations. Women known to be promiscuous suffer reputational damage even in relatively promiscuous cultures, such as among the Swedes and the Ache Indians.

Lacking a long-term mate to offer physical protection, a woman who adopts an exclusively short-term sexual strategy is at greater risk of physical and sexual abuse. Although women in marriages are also subjected to battering and even rape from their husbands, the alarming statistics on the incidence of date rape, which run as high as 15 percent in studies of college women, support the contention that women not in long-term relationships are also at considerable risk (Muehlenhard & Linton, 1987). The fact that women participating in the study of temporary and permanent partners abhor lovers who are physically abusive, violent, and mentally abusive suggests that women may be aware of the risks of abuse (Buss & Schmitt, 1993). Mate preferences, if judiciously applied to avoid potentially dangerous men, can minimize these risks.

The unmarried woman in the pursuit of casual sex risks getting pregnant and bearing children without the benefit of an investing man. In ancestral times such children would likely have been at much greater risk of disease, injury, and death. Some women commit infanticide without the presence of an investing man. In Canada, for example, single women delivered only 12 percent of the babies born between 1977 and 1983, but committed just over 50 percent of the sixty-four maternal infanticides reported to the police (Daly & Wilson, 1988). The trend of higher infanticide rates among unmarried women occurs across cultures as well, such as among the Baganda of Africa. But even infanticide does not cancel the substantial costs of nine months of gestation, reputational damage, and lost mating opportunities that women incur.

An unfaithful married woman risks the withdrawal of resources by her husband. From a reproductive standpoint she may be wasting valuable time in an extramarital liaison. Furthermore, she risks the possibility of increasing the sibling competition among her children, who may have weaker ties with each other because they were fathered by different men. Finally, women risk contracting sexually transmitted diseases from short-term mating—a risk that is greater for women than for men per act of sex (Symons, 1993).

Short-term mating thus imposes hazards for both sexes. But because there are powerful benefits as well, women and men may have evolved psychological mechanisms to select contexts in which costs are minimized and benefits maximized.

Empirical Tests of Hypothesized Benefits to Women

Despite the abundance of hypothesized benefits to women of short-term mating, they have been subjected to relatively few empirical tests. Several researchers have discovered that the woman who is engaged in short-term mating places a premium on the man's physical attractiveness, a finding consistent with the good genes and the sexy son hypotheses (Buss & Schmitt, 1993; Gangestad & Simpson, 1990; Kenrick et al., 1990). Women also seem to elevate the importance they place on immediate resources in the short-term mating context (Buss & Schmitt, 1993). Women say that they desire a short-term mate who has an extravagant lifestyle, spends a lot of money on them early on, and who gives them gifts early in the relationship. These findings support the resource accrual hypothesis.

Several studies have found that women who have affairs are significantly less happy with their current partner, emotionally and sexually, than women who do not (Glass & Wright, 1985; Kinsey et al., 1953). This provides circumstantial support for the mate switching hypothesis.

Glass and Wright (1992) examined seventeen potential "justifications" for extramarital affairs, ranging from "for fun" to "in order to advance my career." Women rated love (e.g., falling in love with the other person) and emotional intimacy (e.g., having someone who understands your problems and feelings) as the most compelling justifications for an affair. Furthermore, 77 percent of the women viewed love as a compelling justification, compared with only 43 percent of the men. These findings provide circumstantial support for the mate-switching hypothesis.

One study (Greiling & Buss, under review) examined the benefits women perceive as likely to come from affairs, how beneficial these things would be if they were received, and the contexts in which women perceive that they would be likely to have an affair. The researchers also examined women who actively pursue short-term matings, and asked them what benefits come from it. The following section summarizes the results of these studies, but several important limitations must be considered. Women's beliefs about the benefits of short-term mating do not necessarily make those benefits part of the selection pressure that led to the evolution of women's short-term mating psychology. The actual adaptive benefits that led to the evolution of women's short-term mating psychology may lie outside women's awareness and hence may not be subjectively represented. Furthermore, the benefits women actually receive in modern contexts may not mirror the adaptive benefits ancestral women received from short-term mating. With these limitations in mind, let's turn to the results.

Hypotheses Supported: Mate Switching, Mate Expulsion, and Resources. The two hypotheses receiving strong support across studies are the mate expulsion and mate switching hypotheses. Study 1 (Greiling & Buss, under review) examined women's perceptions of the likelihood of receiving twenty-eight specific benefits from extra-pair copulations. Women reported that engaging in an extra-pair mating made it easier for a woman to break up with her current partner (sixth most likely benefit to receive) and more likely that a woman would find a partner who she felt was more desirable than her current partner (fourth most likely benefit to receive). Interestingly, the benefit judged to be most likely to be received—sexual gratification—was not central to any of the hypotheses under investigation.

Another study examined the *contexts* that might prompt a woman to have an affair. Greiling and Buss (under review) found that the contexts most likely to promote an extra-pair mating were discovering that a partner was having an affair, having a partner who was unwilling to engage in sexual relations, and having a partner who was abusive to her—all contexts that might promote a breakup. Following closely on the heels of these contexts were feeling that she could find someone with whom she would be more compatible than her current partner, meeting someone who is willing to spend a lot of time with her, and meeting someone who is more successful and has better financial prospects than her current partner. These findings across studies support the hypothesis that mate switching may be a key function of short-term mating for women.

Two of the resource hypotheses received support from two or more studies. Women were judged to be highly likely to receive resources in exchange for sex, such as free dinners, money, jewelry, or clothing (tenth most likely to receive out of the list of twenty-eight). These benefits, though, were judged to be only moderately beneficial when compared with other potential benefits a woman could accrue through short-term mating. The *contexts* judged to promote an extra-pair encounter, however, included having a current partner who could not hold down a job and meeting someone with better financial prospects than her current partner. These contexts suggest that access to resources, or lack thereof, may be important in a woman's decision to have an extra-pair sexual liaison and imply a long-term interest in having a mate with resources, rather than an exchange of sex for immediate access to resources.

Hypotheses Receiving Little or No Support: Status Enhancement and Increasing a Mate's Commitment.
One hypothesis receiving no support in these studies was the status enhancement hypothesis. Study 1 (perceived likelihood of receiving benefit) found that a woman would be unlikely to raise her social status and unlikely to gain access to a higher social stratum through short-term mating. Study 2 (perceived magnitude of benefit) found that even if such a benefit were received by a woman, it would not be highly beneficial to her. These findings do not preclude the possibility that some women under some circumstances might gain tremendous social benefits from a short-term liaison with a high status man. But they do suggest that these benefits are likely to be rare, and are unlikely to have constituted a powerful enough benefit to qualify as an evolved function of short-term mating.

A second hypothesis that received little support was the notion that the commitment of a regular mate could be increased by having extra-pair sex. Although this was judged to be beneficial if it were to occur, subjects in Study 1 deemed it highly unlikely to occur. Indeed, given that sexual infidelity on the part of a woman is one of the leading causes of divorce across cultures (Betzig, 1989), it seems more likely that an affair would have the opposite effect—that is, decrease the commitment of the woman's regular mate. Although in any individual case an affair might defy the general trend and have the effect of increasing a regular mate's commitment, current evidence suggests that this effect is unlikely to have provided the evolutionary impetus for women's extra-pair matings.

It should be noted that the current studies were not able to provide tests of the various genetic hypotheses. Whether short-term extra-pair mating affords a woman adaptive advantages in currencies of better genes, more genetically diverse children, or sexy son genes must await further research. Finally, the limitations noted earlier must be kept in mind—women may not have conscious access to the adaptive benefits that gave rise to the evolution of women's short-term mating and modern benefits may not correspond to ancestral benefits.

Context Effects on Short-Term Mating

Individual Differences in Short-Term Mating

One window for viewing short-term mating is to contrast the subjective perceptions of costs and benefits of women who actively pursue short-term mating with those who do not. Greiling and Buss (under review) asked a sample of women to complete the Socio-sexuality Orientation Inventory (SOI; Gangestad & Simpson, 1990), which assesses individual differences in whether people pursue short-term or long-term mating strategies. Women's scores on the SOI were then correlated with their perceptions of the benefits they would likely receive from short-term mating and with their perceptions of the magnitude of benefits received from short-term mating. Women who pursue short-term mating have substantially different perceptions of the benefits compared to women who tend not to pursue short-term mating. This is especially true of their perceptions of the magnitude of the benefits associated with short-term mating. Women who tend to pursue short-term mating view four classes of benefits as more beneficial. One pertains to sexual resources. Women pursuing short-term mating view as highly beneficial having a sexual partner who is willing to experiment sexually ($r = +.51$), experiencing orgasms with the sexual partner ($r = +.47$), and experiencing great sexual pleasure because the partner was physically attractive ($r = +.39$).

Such women also see more benefits to improving their skills of attraction and seduction ($r = +.50$), supporting the mate skill acquisition hypothesis. They also view the resources from short-term mating as more beneficial, including expensive designer clothing ($r = +.45$), career advancement ($r = +.40$), jewelry ($r = +.37$), and the use of a partner's car ($r = +.35$).

Women who tend to pursue short-term mating also have different perceptions of the contexts likely to promote short-term mating. Having a regular partner who is fired ($r = +.29$), suffers a decrease in salary ($r = +.25$), or becomes terminally ill ($r = +.23$) is viewed as increasing the odds of short-term mating by such women. These results support the mate switching hypothesis—women who indicate that they have pursued short-term matings are more likely to cite problems with a partner as a rationale for an affair. Furthermore, meeting someone who is better looking than one's regular partner is perceived by such women as more likely to lead to an extra-pair mating ($r = +.25$).

Two clusters of costs are viewed by short-term mating women as less likely to be incurred. The first is reputational damage. Such women view reputational damage among friends, potential partners, and high-status peer groups as significantly *less* likely to occur than do women not actively oriented toward short-term mating ($r = -.47$). Perhaps such women select contexts in which these costs are less likely to be incurred, such as a large city or when the current partner is out of town. Taken together, these findings support several of the hypothesized benefits of extra-pair mating, especially resource and mate switching benefits.

Other Contexts Likely to Affect Short-Term Mating

Everyone knows some men who are womanizers and others who would never stray. Everyone knows some women who enjoy casual sex and others who could not imagine sex without commitment. Individuals differ in their proclivities for casual mating. Individuals also shift their proclivities at different times and in different contexts. These variations in sexual strategy depend on a wide variety of social, cultural, and ecological conditions.

Transitions across Life.   Casual sex is also related to people's developmental stage in life. Adolescents in many cultures are more prone to temporary mating as a means of assessing their value on the mating market, experimenting with different strategies, honing their attraction skills, and clarifying their own preferences (Frayser, 1985). After they have done so, they are more ready for marriage. The fact that premarital adolescent sexual experimentation is tolerated and even encouraged in some cultures, such as the Mehinaku of Amazonia (Gregor, 1985), provides a clue that short-term mating is related to one's stage in life.

The transition points between different committed mateships offer additional opportunities for casual sex. After a divorce, for example, it is crucial to reassess one's value on the current mating market. The existence of children from the marriage generally lowers the desirability of divorced people, compared with their hypothetical desirability if they had no children. The elevated status that comes with being more advanced in a career, on the other hand, may raise their desirability in comparison with the last time they were on the mating market. Precisely how all these changed circumstances affect a particular individual is often best evaluated by brief affairs, which allow a person to gauge more precisely how desirable he or she currently is, and hence toward whom to direct mating efforts.

Sex Ratio.   The abundance or deficit of eligible men relative to eligible women is another critical context that affects temporary mating. Many factors affect this sex ratio, including wars, which kill larger numbers of men than women; risk-taking activities such as physical fights, which more frequently affect men; intentional homicides, in which roughly seven times more men than women die; and different remarriage rates by age, whereby with increasing age women remarry less often than men. Men shift to brief encounters when many women are sexually available because the sex ratio is in their favor and they are therefore better able to satisfy their desire for variety (Pedersen, 1991). Among the Ache, for example, men appear to be highly promiscuous because there are 50 percent more women than men (Hill & Hurtado, 1996). When there is a surplus of men, in contrast, both sexes appear to shift toward a long-term mating strategy marked by stable marriages and fewer divorces (Pedersen, 1991).

Effects of Self-Perceived Mate Value and Self-Esteem on Short-Term Mating.
One final context that is likely to affect short-term mating is *mate value*, one's overall desirability to members of the opposite sex. The Self-Perceived Mating Success scale (Lalumiere, Seto, & Quinsey, 1995) assesses mate value. Sample items from this scale are: "members of the opposite sex notice me"; "I receive many compliments from members of the opposite sex"; "members of the opposite sex are attracted to me"; and "relative to my peer group, I can get dates with great ease."

Scores on the mate value scale were correlated with the reported sexual history of the participants, both male and females. The results were strikingly different for the sexes. High mate-value men, relative to their lower mate-value counterparts, tended to have sexual intercourse at an earlier age, a greater number of sex partners since puberty, a greater number of partners during the past year, a greater number of sexual invitations within the past three years, sexual intercourse a greater number of times, and did not see a need to be attached to a person before having sex. Furthermore, high mate-value men tended to score toward the high end of the Sociosexuality Inventory, suggesting that they are pursuing a short-term mating strategy.

In sharp contrast, self-perceived mate value in women was not significantly linked with their pursuit of a short-term mating strategy. Unlike for the men, there were no significant correlations for women between mate value and age of first intercourse, number of partners since puberty, number of partners in the past year, number of sexual invitations in the past three years, need to be attached before sex, or scores on the Socio-sexuality Inventory. For women, however, self-esteem proved to be a highly significant predictor of short-term mating. Women scoring low on self-esteem, relative to their high self-esteem counterparts, tended to have a greater number of sex partners since puberty, a greater number of sex partners over the past year, a greater number of one-night stands, a preference for short-term sexual relationships, and scores on the SOI indicating the pursuit of a short-term mating strategy.

In sum, individual differences in self-perceived mate value and self-esteem appear to be strongly linked with the pursuit of short-term mating, but these personal factors affect men and women differently. High mate-value men appear to pursue short-term mating, whereas mate value is not linked with short-term mating in women. In contrast, women low in self-esteem appear to pursue short-term mating, whereas self-esteem is not related to short-term mating in men. Because most men, compared to most women, indicate a desire for a variety of sex partners, one interpretation is that men who can, do; that is, men who are attractive to women express their desire for casual sex by actually having sex with a variety of partners. The picture for women is more complicated. Self-perceived mate value is unrelated to pursuit of short-term mating, but low self-esteem is related. Women with high self-esteem tend to pursue long-term committed mating, whereas women with low self-esteem tend to pursue short-term mating. Precisely why self-esteem appears to be such a powerful predictor of short-term mating for women remains an issue for future research.

Summary

The scientific study of mating over the course of the twentieth century has focused nearly exclusively on marriage. Human anatomy, physiology, and psychology, however, betray an ancestral past filled with affairs. The obvious reproductive advantages of such affairs to men may have blinded scientists to their tremendous benefits to women. Affairs require willing women. Willing women require benefits to affairs.

In this chapter we first considered men's short-term mating. According to Trivers's theory of parental investment and sexual selection, the reproductive benefits to ancestral men as a consequence of short-term mating would have been direct—an increase in the number of children produced as a function of the number of women successfully inseminated. The empirical evidence is strong that men do have a greater desire for short-term mating than do women. Compared to women, men express a greater desire for a variety of sex partners, let less time elapse before seeking sexual intercourse, lower their standards dramatically when pursuing short-term mating, have more sexual fantasies and more fantasies involving a variety of sex partners, have a larger number of extramarital affairs, and visit prostitutes more often.

Mathematically, however, short-term mating requires two. Except for forced copulation, men's desire for short-term sex could not have evolved without the presence of some willing women. We looked at the evidence that some women historically have engaged in short-term mating some of the time. The existence of physiological clues in men, such as testicle size, different sperm morphs, and variations in sperm insemination, suggest a long evolutionary history of *sperm competition*—where the sperm from two different men have inhabited a woman's reproductive tract at the same time. From an evolutionary perspective, it is unlikely that women would have recurrently engaged in short-term mating without reaping some adaptive benefits.

There are potentially five classes of adaptive benefits to women: economic or material resources, genetic benefits, mate switching benefits, mate skill acquisition benefits, and mate manipulation benefits. Based on the few studies that have been conducted, the empirical evidence supports the importance of mate switching and resource acquisition, and does not at all support status enhancement or mate manipulation benefits. Further research is needed to test hypotheses about the adaptive benefits to women of short-term mating, and to cleanly separate adaptive benefits from nonadaptive effects of short-term mating.

The final section of this chapter examined various context effects on short-term mating. Sex ratio is one context—a surplus of women tends to promote short-term mating in both sexes. Another important context is mate value, one's desirability to members of the opposite sex. Men high in self-perceived mate value are more likely to pursue short-term mating, as reflected in measures such as younger age at first intercourse and a larger number of sex partners. Women's self-perceived mate value is not related to the pursuit of short-term mating. However, women with low self-esteem appear to be more likely to pursue short-term mating than women with high self-esteem, as indexed by number of sex partners and an expressed preference for unattached, uncommitted sex.

PART FOUR

Challenges of Parenting and Kinship

This part includes two chapters, one devoted to problems of parenting and one to problems of kinship. Once an organism has successfully traversed the hurdles of survival, and then managed to solve the problem of mating and reproduction, the next challenge is to channel effort into the products of reproduction—the "vehicles" for parents' genes known as children (Chapter 7). This chapter starts with the puzzle of why mothers typically provide more parental care than fathers in nearly all species that provide any parental care at all. It goes on to explore the patterns of parental care, focusing on three key issues: the likely degree of genetic relatedness of the child to the parent, the child's ability to convert parental care into fitness, and trade-offs parents face between investing in children and using their resources for other adaptive problems. The final section provides an evolutionary explanation for a phenomenon that nearly every living human has experienced—conflict between parents and children.

Chapter 8 broadens the analysis to consider extended kin, such as grandparents, grandchildren, nieces, nephews, aunts, and uncles. The theory of inclusive fitness provides a host of implications for understanding relationships between genetic relatives, including phenomena such as helping genetic relatives in life-or-death situations, leaving resources to genetic relatives in one's will, investment by grandparents in their grandchildren, and sex differences in the importance of kin relations. The chapter concludes with a broader perspective on the evolution of extended families.

7 Problems of Parenting

My mother saith he is my father. Yet for myself I know it not. For no man knoweth who hath begotten him.

—Telemachus, son of Odysseus, from Homer's *The Odyssey*

Imagine a society in which all men and women received exactly the same income. Every able-bodied adult worked. All decisions were made communally by both sexes, and all children were raised collectively by the group. How would people react when actually faced with this social arrangement? Such an experiment was in fact conducted in Israel among those living in a kibbutz. Two anthropologists—Joseph Shepher and Lionel Tiger —studied three generations living in a kibbutz, a total of 34,040 people. In their classic 1975 book, *Women in the Kibbutz,* Shepher and Tiger tell that they found, astonishingly, that the division of labor by gender was actually greater in the kibbutz than in the rest of Israel (Tiger, 1996). Most astonishing, however, were the strong preferences exerted by women—over time they began to insist that their own children live with them rather than be raised collectively by other women. The men tried to veto this move, considering it a step backward, giving in to bourgeois values at the expense of the original utopian dream. The mothers and their mothers stood their ground and outvoted the men of the community. So the utopian experiment of communal child rearing reverted to the primacy of the mother–child bond—a pattern seen in every human culture.

From an evolutionary perspective, offspring are a sort of vehicle for their parents. They are the means by which their parents' genes may get transported to succeeding generations. Without children an individual's genes may perish forever. Given the supreme importance of offspring as genetic vehicles, then, it is reasonable to expect that natural selection would favor powerful mechanisms in parents to ensure the survival and reproductive success of their children. Aside from those of mating, perhaps no other adaptive problems are as paramount as making sure that one's offspring survive and thrive. Indeed, without the success of offspring, all the effort that an organism invested in mating would be reproductively meaningless. Evolution, in short, should produce a rich repertoire of parental mechanisms specially adapted to caring for offspring.

Given the importance of offspring, one of the astonishing facts about parental care is that many species do not engage in it at all (Alcock, 1993). Oysters, for example, simply release their sperm and eggs into the ocean, leaving their offspring adrift with not a shred of parental care. For every oyster that manages to survive under these lonely conditions, thousands die. Part of the reason for the lack of universality of parental care is that it is so costly. By investing in offspring parents lose out on resources that could be devoted to themselves. These resources could be channeled toward securing a larger territory, finding additional mates, or increasing reproductive output. Parents who protect their young risk their own survival. Some become wounded or die while fending off predators who threaten their offspring. Given the costs of parental care, then, it is reasonable to expect that whenever we do observe parental care in nature, the reproductive benefits must be large enough to outweigh the costs.

The evolution of parental care has been explored in many nonhuman animal species (Clutton-Brock, 1991). Mexican free-tailed bats provide one fascinating example of the evolution of parental care. These bats live in dark caves in large colonies containing hundreds of thousands—in some cases millions—of other bats. After a female bat gives birth she leaves the safety of the colony to forage for food. When she returns, she is faced with the problem of recognizing her own pup among the many densely packed in the cave. One square yard of the cave wall may contain several thousands pups, so the problem is not a small one. If selection operated "for the good of the species," it wouldn't matter which pup the mother bat fed, nor would there be any selection pressure to recognize and feed her own. That is not how mother bats behave, however. Eighty-three percent of the mothers actually find and feed their own pups, giving up 16 percent of their body weight in milk each day (McCracken, 1984). Mother free-tailed bats apparently have evolved sensitive mechanisms for detecting their own offspring and make tremendous sacrifices to feed them, thus ensuring their offsprings' survival. Each mother's evolved parental mechanisms were designed by selection to help her own genetic offspring, not the offspring of the bat species as a whole.

Another example of adaptations for parental care is found in nesting birds. Tinbergen (1963) explored the puzzle of why nesting birds would go to the trouble of removing the broken shells from their newly hatched chicks and laboriously take them, piece by piece, far away from the nest. He explored three hypotheses: (1) eggshell removal served a sanitary function, keeping the nest free of germs and disease that might use the broken shells as a conduit; (2) eggshell removal protected the newly hatched chicks from the sharp edges that come with broken shells; and (3) eggshell removal made the nests less salient to predators who might be inclined to prey on the young chicks. Through a series of experiments Tinbergen discovered that only the protection from predators hypothesis received support. The cost of parental care, in short, was outweighed by the benefits of increased survival of chicks through a decrease in predation.

Despite the paramount importance of parental care from an evolutionary perspective, such care has been a relatively neglected topic within the field of human psychology. When evolutionary psychologists Martin Daly and Margo Wilson prepared a chapter on the topic for the 1987 "Nebraska Symposium on Motivation," they scanned the thirty-four earlier volumes in the series in search of either psychological research or theories on parental motivation. Not a single one of those volumes contained even a paragraph on parental motivation (Daly & Wilson, 1995). Despite the widespread knowledge that mothers tend to love their children, the very phenomenon of powerful parental love appears to have baffled psychologists at a theoretical level. One prominent psychologist who has written several books on the topic of love noted, "The needs that lead many of us to feel unconditional love for our children also seem to be remarkably persistent, for reasons that are not at present altogether clear" (Sternberg, 1986, p. 133). From an evolutionary perspective, however, the reasons for deep parental love do seem clear, or at least understandable. It is reasonable to expect that selection has designed precisely such psychological mechanisms—parental mechanisms of motivation designed to ensure the survival and reproductive success of the invaluable vehicles that transport an individual's genes into the next generation. As we will see below, however, for some intriguing evolutionary reasons the love of parents is far from unconditional.

With this background in mind, let's turn to the fascinating topic of parental care and pose a question that requires us to look at humans within the broader context of species in the animal kingdom: Why do mothers in so many species, including humans, provide parental care so much more than fathers?

Although we tend to take mother-love for granted, a number of competing hypotheses have been proposed to explain why, in most species, mothers tend to invest more than fathers in their offspring.

Why Do Mothers Provide More Parental Care Than Fathers?

Evolutionary biologist John Alcock (1993) described a fascinating film, on the hunting dogs of Africa, that documented the life and hostile forces encountered by one particular dog named Solo. Solo was the only surviving offspring of a female who was subordinate in her pack. Because of the mother's status, she and her offspring were vulnerable to victimization. One by one, Solo's littermates were killed by another female in the pack, a rival with whom Solo's mother had a history of antagonism. Solo's mother fought in vain to save her pups from her murderous rival. Astonishingly, while the mother risked life and limb to save her pups, the father stood by passively and did *nothing* to protect them!

Although this story is stark, it dramatically illustrates a profound truth in the evolution of life—throughout the animal kingdom, females are far more likely than males to care for their offspring. Humans are no exception. In an amusing and telling acknowledgment, the author of a book called *The Evolution of Parental Care* said that his "greatest debt is to my wife, . . . [who] looked after our children while I wrote about parental care" (Clutton-Brock, 1991). The intriguing question is why mothers more than fathers? A variety of hypotheses have been advanced to explain the predominance of female parental care. We will consider three that are most relevant to humans: (1) the paternity uncertainty hypothesis, (2) the abandonability hypothesis, and (3) the mating opportunity costs hypothesis.

The Paternity Uncertainty Hypothesis

Mothers throughout the animal kingdom generally are 100 percent "sure" of their genetic contribution to their offspring. It is necessary to put the "sure" in quotation marks because no conscious recognition of their certainty in parenthood is necessary. When a female gives birth or lays a fertilized egg, there is no doubt that her offspring will contain 50 percent of her genes. Males can never be "sure." The problem of *paternity uncertainty* means that from a male perspective there can always be some probability that another male has fertilized the female's eggs.

Paternity uncertainty is strongest in species with internal female fertilization, including many insects, humans, all primates, and indeed all mammals. Because of internal female fertilization, when a male comes on the scene the female may already have mated with another male and so her eggs might already be fertilized. Or she might mate with another male at any time during their consortship, perhaps in secret. The problem of paternity uncertainty has tremendous consequences in human affairs, including male sexual jealousy. But for now it is important just to note that males suffer tremendous costs by channeling their resources to other men's descendants. Resources devoted to a rival's children are resources taken away from one's own. Because of the costs that males incur as a result of misdirected parental effort, any degree of paternity uncertainty means generally that it will be more advantageous for females to invest their resources in parental care. Therefore, paternity uncertainty offers one explanation for the widespread—

although by no means universal—occurrence of females investing more than males in parental care.

Alcock (1993) argues that paternity uncertainty, by itself, is not enough to preclude the evolution of male parental care. Male parental care can still evolve if the reproductive success the male gains by aiding his offspring recurrently outweighs the opportunity costs of not investing his resources elsewhere, such as in attracting additional mates. Suppose that a male's paternity probability is only 60 percent and females bear ten offspring at a time. Now let's assume that the survival rate of the offspring with no male parental care is 20 percent, with male parental care it is 50 percent. Males who do not invest in parental care can use their extra resources to gain sexual access to other females—twice as many as the males who stay around to care for their offspring. Working through the algebra of this hypothetical example yields the following outcome: Males who do *not* care for their offspring will, on average, sire twelve offspring (six offspring with each of the two females they inseminate), but only 2.4 of them will survive (on average) because of the 20 percent survival rate of offspring lacking paternal care; males who do care for their offspring will sire fewer offspring, six on average, but three of them will survive because of the 50 percent survival rate of offspring who have the advantage of investment from the father. In this hypothetical example selection will favor the evolution of male parental care because males investing in offspring end up leaving more *surviving* offspring, despite siring fewer.

Paternity uncertainty, therefore, is not enough to preclude the evolution of paternal care. But it does make it less profitable for fathers, *compared with mothers*, to invest in their offspring. Each unit of parental investment pays off more for mothers than for fathers under conditions of paternity uncertainty because some fraction of the "father's" investment will be wasted on progeny that are not his own. A full 100 percent of the mother's parental investment, in contrast, goes toward her own children. In sum, although paternity uncertainty does not preclude the evolution of male paternal care, it remains one viable cause of the widespread tendency of females to invest more in offspring than males do.

The Abandonability Hypothesis

A second hypothesis to account for widespread female parental care cites the order in which the eggs and sperm are released as the determining factor. If parental care benefits offspring, then the first one who *can* abandon the offspring does so, putting his or her mate in a cruel bind. The mate left behind can either invest in offspring and benefit as a result or can abandon the offspring. If the offspring benefit from parental care, selection will favor a parent who sticks around, even after having been abandoned by one's mate. In short, the first one who can abandon the offspring does so, and the one left behind is "forced" to care for the offspring rather than let them die (Alcock, 1993).

According to the abandonability hypothesis, internal female fertilization should be linked with heavy female parental care because the male is free to leave after contributing his sperm, and the female will be stuck with the cruel decision about whether to invest in her offspring. When fertilization occurs externally to the female, as when females deposit their eggs before the males contribute their sperm, the female would be equally free to abandon the offspring, potentially leaving the male in the bind. There-fore, according to the abandonabilty hypothesis, female parental care should be more prevalent in species with internal female fertilization, whereas male parental care should be more prevalent in species with external fertilization (Alcock, 1993).

There are some data that seem to support this hypothesis. In a study that exam-ined various fish and amphibian species, 86 percent of the species with *internal* female fertilization had females providing the bulk of the parental care (Gross & Shine, 1981). In contrast, in fish and amphibian species with *external* fertilization, only 30 percent had females providing more parental care than males. The remaining 70 percent had males providing more parental care than females.

There are two problems with this hypothesis. First, it is likely that paternity un-certainty is higher in species with internal female fertilization than in those with ex-ternal fertilization because males have fewer means of ascertaining which sperm actually fertilize the female's eggs. When fertilization occurs externally, the male has an abun-dance of cues pointing to his paternity, such as witnessing his sperm coat the eggs of the female or detecting the presence of another male's sperm on the eggs. So the real causal factor accounting for the trend of species with internal fertilization to showing a pre-dominance of female parental care could be paternity uncertainty, not ease of abandon-ment. Second, there are many species in which the sexes release their gametes *at the same time*. If the abandonability hypothesis is correct, there should be a fifty-fifty chance for either sex to evolve parental care. In a sample of forty-six species that exhibit simultane-ous gamete release, however, 78 percent (thirty-six of the forty-six species) showed male parental care (Alcock, 1993). This is substantially more than the 50 percent predicted by the abandonability hypothesis. So for two reasons—the link with paternity uncertainty and the empirical failure in species with simultaneous gamete release—the abandon-ability hypothesis by itself does not appear powerful enough to account for the wide-spread tendency of females to exhibit more parental care than males.

The Mating Opportunity Cost Hypothesis

A third hypothesis stems from sex differences in mating opportunity costs. *Mating opportunity costs* are missed additional matings as a direct result of effort devoted to off-spring. Females and males both suffer mating opportunity costs. While a mother is ges-tating or breastfeeding her child or a father is fending off predators, neither has a high probability of securing additional mates. The mating opportunity costs are higher for males than for females, however, for the reason we encountered in Chapter 6—the reproductive success of males tends to be limited primarily by the number of receptive females they can successfully inseminate. In humans, for example, males can produce more children by mating with a variety of women, but women generally cannot increase reproductive output directly by mating with a variety of men. In summary, because the mating opportunity costs of parental care will generally be higher for males than for females, males will be less likely than females to take on parental care. Instead of fo-cusing on parental care, males are more likely to channel their efforts toward securing additional mates.

According to this hypothesis, male parental care should be rare when the opportunity costs of missed matings for males are high (Alcock, 1993). When the opportunity costs males suffer from missing matings are low, however, the conditions would be more favorable for the evolution of parental care. Precisely such a condition occurs in fish species in which the males stake out and defend a specific territory (Gross & Sargent, 1985). Females then scope out the territories of various males and select one in which to lay their eggs. Males can then guard and even feed the eggs while at the same time guarding their own territory. In this case the male's mating opportunities will not suffer as a result of parental investment. Indeed, the presence of eggs laid by other females in a given male's territory appears to make males attractive to females, prompting them to lay their eggs in territories already containing eggs. Perhaps the presence of other eggs indicates to a female that the territory is safe from predators, or that another female has judged the resident male acceptable. In sum, when males do not suffer mating opportunity costs as a consequence of investing in offspring, conditions are ripe for the evolution of male parental care.

The hypothesis of mating opportunity costs may partly explain individual differences in parenting among humans. In contexts in which there is a surplus of men in the eligible mating pool, men find it difficult to pursue a short-term mating strategy. When there is a surplus of women, on the other hand, there are many more mating opportunities for men (see Chapter 6; see also Guttentag & Secord, 1983; Pedersen, 1991). Therefore, we can predict that men will be more likely to invest in children when in contexts in which there is a surplus of men but will be more negligent of children when there is a surplus of women. A great deal of empirical evidence suggests that this is the case (Pedersen, 1991).

In summary, three hypotheses have been advanced to explain the widespread prevalence of greater parental care in females than in males—paternity uncertainty, ease of abandonability, and mating opportunity costs. These hypotheses are not intrinsically incompatible, of course, and it is possible that all account in part for the sex differences in parental care. Of the three, the most viable contenders are the paternity uncertainty hypothesis and the mating opportunity cost hypothesis. We will see later in this chapter that the paternity uncertainty hypothesis can also account for variation among men in their proclivities to caring for children.

An Evolutionary Perspective on Parental Care

At the beginning of this chapter we noted that offspring are the vehicles fashioned by selection by which parental genes get transported into future generations, but not all offspring reproduce. Some are better at survival or have more promising mating prospects, and so are better bets for successfully transporting the parent's genes. Some offspring are more likely to benefit from parental care. As a general rule, selection will favor mechanisms of *parental care*—the preferential allocation of investment to one or more offspring at the expense of other forms of allocating investment—that have the effect of increasing the fitness of the parent. It follows from this definition that mechanisms of parental care will favor some offspring over others—a condition called *parental favoritism*. Stated differently, selection will favor the evolution of mechanisms in parents that favor offspring who are likely to provide a higher reproductive return on the investment (Daly & Wilson, 1995). Fathers as well as mothers should be sensitive to these conditions, as father–child bonds, although often weaker than mother–child bonds, appear to be universal across cultures (Mackey & Daly, 1995).

At the most general theoretical level, evolved mechanisms of parental care should be sensitive to three contexts (Alexander, 1979):

1. *Genetic relatedness of the offspring:* Are the children really my own?
2. *Ability of the offspring to convert parental care into fitness:* Will a given unit of my investment make a difference to the survival and reproduction of my children?
3. *Alternative uses of the resources that might be available to invest in offspring:* Will a given unit of my investment be best spent investing in children, or in other activities such as investing in my sister's children or in additional mating opportunities?

Let's now explore these three contexts in more detail and examine the empirical evidence that parental mechanisms sensitive to these contexts might have evolved in humans.

Genetic Relatedness to Offspring

Daly and Wilson (1988) describe the impact of genetic relatedness on parental motivation succinctly:

> Perhaps the most obvious prediction from a Darwinian view of parental motives is this: Substitute parents will generally tend to care less profoundly for children than natural parents, with the result that children reared by people other than their natural parents will be more often exploited and otherwise at risk. Parental investment is a precious resource, and selection must favor those parental psyches that do not squander it on nonrelatives. (p. 83)

Studies of parental feelings support this prediction. In one study of stepparents conducted in Cleveland, Ohio, only 53 percent of stepfathers and 25 percent of stepmothers claimed to have any "parental feelings" at all toward their stepchildren (Duberman, 1975). Darwinian anthropologist Mark Flinn found a similar result in a Trinidadian village—stepfathers' interactions with their stepchildren were less frequent and more aggressive than similar interactions involving genetic fathers and their children (Flinn, 1988b). Furthermore, the stepchildren apparently found these aggressive interactions unpleasant, for they left home at a younger age than genetic children.

These findings do not mean that intense feelings of parental love cannot be activated by any child other than a genetic one. Stepparents can and often do channel affection, devotion, and resources toward stepchildren. The key point is that parental love and resources are substantially *less likely* to be directed toward children by stepparents than by genetic parents. This point is recognized even in the Webster's dictionary definition of "stepmother," which includes two components: (1) the wife of one's father by a subsequent marriage, and (2) one that fails to give proper care or attention (Gova, 1986).

The conflicts of interest inherent in steprelations are frequently noted in children's tales and folklore across many cultures. One extensive cross-cultural summary of folk literature summarized these themes as follows: "Evil stepmother orders stepdaughter to be killed" and "Evil stepmother works stepdaughter to death in absence of merchant husband" (Thompson, 1955; cited in Daly & Wilson, 1988, p. 85). The theme of evil stepfathers is equally prevalent, with the two major subcategories being "lustful stepfathers" (those who are inclined to abuse a stepdaughter sexually) and "cruel stepfathers" (those who are inclined to abuse stepchildren physically or emotionally). In peoples as diverse as the Irish, Indians, Aleuts, and Indonesians, folk stories depict stepparents as villains.

Interestingly, the problems encountered in stepparent–stepchild relationships have commonly been attributed to "the myth of the cruel stepparent" or to "children's irrational fears" by the few social scientists who have observed or studied these relationships (Daly & Wilson, 1988, p. 86). But if the fears are irrational and the cruelty is indeed a myth, then it is reasonable to ask why these beliefs recur so commonly across so many diverse cultures. Even more to the point, we can ask whether these myths, beliefs, and folklore have any substance in the reality of parent–child relationships. We will examine the evidence below within the topics of child abuse and child homicide.

In species with internal female fertilization, such as our own, maternity is 100 percent certain, but paternity is sometimes in doubt. How do men assess certainty of paternity? A man has at least two sources of information to consider the likelihood that he is the genetic father of a given child: (1) information about his partner's sexual fidelity during the period in which she conceived, and (2) perceptions of the child's resemblance to him (Daly & Wilson, 1988). It is reasonable to expect that men will have evolved psychological mechanisms sensitive to both sources of information. We also expect that a mother will attempt to influence the man's perceptions around these issues, for example by trying to convince him that she has indeed been sexually faithful or that the newborn baby is the spitting image of him.

Who Are Newborn Babies Said to Resemble?   Daly and Wilson (1982) suggested that mothers should be motivated to promote a putative father's certainty of paternity by remarking on the newborn's similarity in appearance to him. Success in promoting the man's belief that he is the father should increase his willingness to invest in that child. To examine these efforts by mothers, Daly and Wilson secured videotapes of 111 American births that ranged in duration from five to forty-five minutes. The verbal utterances were recorded verbatim for subsequent scoring. Of the 111 videotapes, 68 contained explicit references to the baby's appearance (in some cases the mothers were tranquilized and in others the sound quality was too poor for the content of the utterances to be understood, so this figure probably underestimates the actual number of remarks made).

By chance alone, one would expect babies to be said to resemble the mother 50 percent of the time and the father 50 percent of the time. In fact, when the baby was said to resemble either parent, the mother's remarks about the resemblance to the father were four times as frequent (80 percent) as her remarks about the baby's resemblance to her (20 percent). Sample remarks by mothers included: "It looks like you" (one woman said this three times to her husband), "feels like you," "just like daddy," "he looks like you, got a head of hair like yours," and "he looks like you, honestly he does" (Daly & Wilson, 1982, p. 70).

In a second study in the same report, Daly and Wilson (1982) sent out 526 questionnaires to new parents whose names were gleaned from birth announcements in newspapers in Canada. Roughly 25 percent of the parents completed the questionnaires. Those who responded were asked to secure contacts with their relatives so that they also could participate in the study. Among the questions asked were "Who do you think the baby is most similar to?"

The results of this second study confirmed and elaborated on the results of the first. Of the mothers who commented on the baby's resemblance to one of the parents, 81 percent indicated that the baby was more similar to the father, whereas only 19 percent indicated greater similarity to themselves. The mother's relatives also showed this bias: Among those who commented on resemblance to either parent, 66 percent indicated that the baby was most similar to the putative father, whereas only 34 percent noted similarity to the mother.

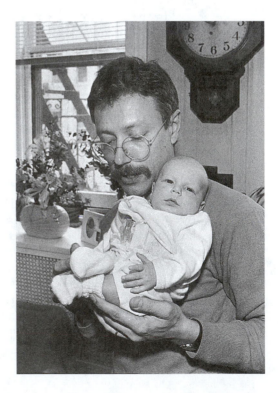

Father and infant: Is there a resemblance? Studies show that the mother, her relatives, and the father's relatives tend to declare that the infant looks more like the father than the mother. Is this a strategy to assure the man of paternity certainty and thereby ensure his investment in the child?

Contrary to Daly and Wilson's prediction, however, the mother's relatives did not show a stronger bias than the father's relatives—a prediction based on the fact that the mother's relatives, like the mother, have a vested interest in confirming paternity to activate the man's psychology of parental investment. In fact, 71 percent of the father's relatives who commented on the baby's resemblance to a parent indicated that the baby looked more similar to the putative father. The predicted effect was found, however, for first-born children. A total of 62 percent of the mother's relatives alleged paternal resemblance in first-born children, whereas only 52 percent of the father's relatives alleged paternal resemblance in first-born children.

The basic pattern of results—the greater the likelihood of the mother to insist on resemblance to the putative father—has now been replicated by a study in at least one other culture, Mexicans residing in the Yucatan (Regalski & Gaulin, 1993). In that study 198 interviews were conducted with the relatives of forty-nine Mexican infants. As in the Canadian study, relatives asserted that the infant resembled the putative father substantially more than the mother. The mother and her relatives were significantly more likely than the father and his relatives to make claims about paternal resemblance. Allegations of paternal resemblance were more common for first-born children and when the parents had only been together for a brief period of time. In summary, this cross-cultural replication is consistent with the hypothesis that mothers and their kin attempt to influence the putative father's perceptions of his paternity, presumably to encourage male parental investment in the child.

Yet many questions remain unanswered: Are mothers' attempts to manipulate fathers' confidence in paternity universal? Are mothers consciously aware that they are attempting to influence their partner's perceptions of paternity, or do these ploys operate unconsciously? Have men evolved specialized mechanisms to discount information about a baby's resemblance to them, coevolved to guard against the dangers of investing in other men's children? Answers to these questions await future research.

Who Do One-Year-Old Babies Actually Resemble?   An intriguing recent study of family photographs suggests the possibility of the evolution of a recognizable physical paternal marker in children (Christenfeld & Hill, 1995). A number of families provided photographs of one of their children at three ages—one, ten, and twenty. Half the children were girls and half were boys. A total of twenty-four family photos were studied. Photographs were also obtained of the mothers and fathers. One hundred twenty-two subjects were then asked to attempt to match each child with one of three possible mothers (one of whom was the actual mother) and with one of three possible fathers (one of whom was the actual father).

If the matchings were done randomly, a correct match would be obtained 33.3 percent of the time. The matches done between the photos of ten-year-olds and the possible parents did not deviate from this one-third figure of correct matches done by chance alone. Nor did the matches between the twenty-year-old children and their possible parents deviate from chance. There was one striking exception to these findings. Subjects correctly matched one-year-old children with their actual fathers 49.2 percent of the time. Furthermore, subjects were able to pick out the actual biological fathers for both baby boys (50 percent) and baby girls (48 percent). In contrast, subjects were not able to correctly match one-year-olds with their biological mothers at a rate greater than chance. In short, the study discovered a unique physical resemblance between one-year-olds and their biological fathers but not their biological mothers.

What do these results mean? The authors speculate that the answer lies in the sexual asymmetry in certainty of parenthood—whereas mothers are certain of their genetic contribution to their children, no matter what their children look like, fathers are not. This raises three possibilities: (1) historically, babies benefited from looking like the genetic father, which resulted in increased paternal investment; (2) historically, selection could have favored men who had physical "markers" that expressed themselves in their children so that they could channel their investment to their genetic offspring rather than to other men's offspring; (3) historically, it could have been to the mother's advantage to suppress the physical expression of her genes in the child's appearance, if doing so meant causing the actual father to recognize and invest in that child.

These theoretical possibilities await future research. But this intriguing study does raise an important question about the Daly and Wilson findings, which suggest that people comment on a newborn's resemblance to the father more often than to the mother. It suggests that such comments might be accurate—newborn babies might in fact resemble the father more than the mother. The Daly-Wilson studies were done with newborns, but the Christenfeld-Hill study was done with one-year-olds, so the two are not directly comparable. Given the importance of men's parental investment, however, we can expect future research to resolve this issue before too long.

Parents' Investment in Children's College Education. Humans live in a modern context that is in many ways different from the ancestral contexts. For one thing, modern humans have cash economies that were nonexistent in the Pleistocene era. From a research perspective, one advantage of cash economies is that they provide concrete quantitative measures of investment. Three evolutionary anthropologists exploited this opportunity to evaluate the effects of men's paternity uncertainty on their investment in children's college education (Anderson, Kaplan, & Lancaster, 1997).

The anthropologists made three predictions: (1) men will allocate more resources to their genetic children than to their step-children; (2) men who are uncertain about whether children are genetically their own will invest less than men who are certain the children are their own; and (3) men will invest more in children when the child's mother is their current mate than they will in children from former mateships. This third prediction applies to both genetic children and stepchildren. Predictions 1 and 2 follow directly from the evolutionary theory of parental care, and in particular from the premise of genetic relatedness. Prediction 3 is based on the hypothesis that men use parental care as a form of mating effort. That is, the transfer of resources to children by men is a means of attracting and retaining a mate.

The data for testing these predictions come from 615 men living in Albuquerque, New Mexico. These men parented 1,246 children, of whom 1,158 were genetic offspring and 88 were step-offspring. The researchers collected data on three dependent measures: (1) whether the child received any money at all for college from the respondent (69 percent had received some money); (2) the total amount of money each child received for college from the respondent, adjusted to 1990 dollars (on average, each offspring received $13,180 from the respondent); and (3) the percentage of the child's college expenses that were paid by the respondent (on average, 44 percent of college expenses were paid by the respondents).

The results powerfully supported all three predictions. Being genetically related to the respondent rather than being a stepchild made a large difference. Compared with stepchildren, genetic children were 5.5 times more likely to receive some money for college from the respondents; they received $15,500 more for college on average and had 65 percent more of their college expenses paid for. Prediction 1—that men would allocate more investment to genetic children than to stepchildren—was strongly supported.

The second prediction pertained to the effects of men's certainty that they were actually the fathers. In the survey the men listed every pregnancy they believed they were responsible for. Subsequently, they were asked whether they were certain that they were the fathers. A man was classified as having low confidence in paternity if he indicated that he was certain he was not the father or was unsure whether he was the father. Certainty in paternity significantly predicted two of the three dependent variables. Children of fathers with low paternity certainty were only 13 percent as likely to receive any money at all for college, all else being equal, and received a whopping $28,400 less for college than children whose fathers were confident that they were the genetic fathers. So prediction 2 appears to be supported, with a qualifier. Only six respondents in the sample indicated uncertainty about their genetic fatherhood of the children. This number is likely to underestimate true paternity uncertainty, and men may be reluctant to admit to an unknown researcher doubts about paternity. This research needs to be replicated on a larger sample, perhaps in research that either assesses the actual genetic markers to identify paternity (or lack thereof) with certainty or makes it easier for men to express whatever doubts they might have about paternity. Despite this qualification, the results support the hypothesis that men scale back their investment in children when they are uncertain of their genetic relatedness to those children.

The third prediction—that men will invest more in children of their current mates than those of their former mates, regardless of who are the genetic parents—also received strong support. A child was roughly three times as likely to receive money from the respondent if the child's mother was the respondent's mate at the time the child entered college. All else being equal, children received $14,900 more when their genetic parents were together; an additional 53 percent of the college costs of such children were paid for when the children's mothers were still mated with the respondents. The fact that men invest more in children as a function of the mating relationship with the mother, even when the children are stepchildren, supports the hypothesis that men's parental investment may function as "mating effort" rather than as strictly a "parental effort."

In summary, genetic relatedness to a child is a powerful predictor of men's monetary investment. Men invest more in genetic children than in stepchildren. They also invest more when they feel certain that they are the genetic father.

Child Abuse and Other Risks of Not Living with Both Parents.   Parental care may be viewed as a continuum. At one end is extreme self-sacrifice, in which the parent devotes all of his or her resources to a child, perhaps even risking life and limb to save the child's life. The other end of the parental care continuum is occupied by events that inflict costs on the child, such as child abuse. At the very extreme of this continuum is infanticide, the killing of an infant, which may be regarded as a reverse assay of parental care (that is, as an assessment of the extreme opposite of parental care). Inclusive fitness theory tells us that genetic relatedness to the child would be one predictor of infanticide—the less genetically related the adult was to the child, the higher the probability of infanticide. This prediction has been tested (Daly & Wilson, 1988, 1995, 1996).

In the most extensive study of its kind, Daly and Wilson surveyed 841 households that included children age seventeen or younger and ninety-nine abused children from a children's aid society in Hamilton, Ontario, Canada (Daly & Wilson, 1985). Most young children live with both genetic parents, so the rates of child abuse by stepparents and genetic parents must be corrected based on these proportions to yield a common index such as "victims per 1,000 children in population." The results are shown in Figure 7.1.

These data show that children living with one genetic parent and one stepparent are roughly *40 times* more likely to be physically abused than children living with both

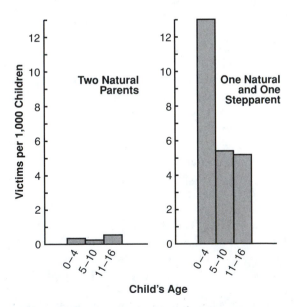

FIGURE 7.1   Per Capita Rates of Child Abuse Cases Known to Children's Aid Societies and Reported to a Provincial Registry. Hamilton, Ontario, Canada, 1983.

Source: Reprinted with permission from: Daly, Martin and Wilson, Margo. *Homicide*, 87. (New York: Aldine de Gruyter) copyright © 1988 by Aldine de Gruyter.

genetic parents. This greater risk rate occurs even when other factors such as poverty and socioeconomic status are controlled. There is indeed a higher rate of child abuse in low-income families, but it turns out that the rates in stepfamilies are roughly the same across different levels of socioeconomic status. Daly and Wilson concluded that "stepparenthood *per se* remains the single most powerful risk factor for child abuse that has yet been identified" (Daly & Wilson, 1988, pp. 87–88). Some people, of course, might claim that such findings are "obvious" or that "anyone could have predicted them." Perhaps so. But the fact remains that hundreds of previous studies of child abuse failed to identify stepparents as a risk factor for child abuse until Daly and Wilson approached the problem with an evolutionary lens.

Child Homicide as a Function of Genetic Relatedness to Offspring.

On February 20th, 1992, 2-year-old Scott M. died in a Montreal hospital of massive internal injuries caused by one or more abdominal blows. At the manslaughter trial of his mother's 24-year-old live-in boyfriend, doctors testified that Scott's body displayed "all the symptoms of a battered child," mainly because of "numerous bruises of varying ages." The accused, who portrayed himself as Scott's primary caretaker, admitted assaulting the mother and other adults, but [claimed that] "I don't hurt kids." According to an acquaintance, however, the accused had admitted striking the child with his elbow because Scott was "bothering him while he was trying to watch television." The trial outcome was conviction (Daly & Wilson, 1996, p. 77).

Events similar to this one occur every day in the United States and Canada and can be read about in every major newspaper. Unfortunately, identifying the increased risk that children suffer at the hands of stepparents has been clouded by the manner in which the U.S. Census Bureau and the Federal Bureau of Investigation (FBI) collect data—both fail to distinguish between genetic and stepparenthood (Daly & Wilson, 1996). Although existing large-scale national surveys cannot address the link between genetic relatedness and child homicide, Daly and Wilson have explored this link in a series of studies on other populations. In one study they examined 408 Canadian children who had been killed over a ten-year period by either genetic parents or stepparents. They then calculated the number of homicide victims per million coresident parent-child dyads per year. The results are shown in Figure 7.2 on page 204.

The rates of child murder are clearly far higher for stepparents than for genetic parents. The risk is highest for very young children, particularly for children age two or younger. Examining a variety of different data sets of this kind, Daly and Wilson (1988) found that the risk of a preschool-aged child being killed ranged from *40* to *100 times* higher for stepchildren than for children living with two genetic parents.

Unfortunately, cross-cultural data on child abuse and homicide as a function of stepparenthood are sparse. Daly and Wilson (1988) do cite some evidence from the ethnographic record compiled in the Human Relations Area Files (HRAF), although this evidence should be evaluated with caution because it is hardly systematic and the ethnographies were assembled without specific focus on child abuse, child homicide, or stepparents. In spite of the limitations of the ethnographic record, it is worth noting that

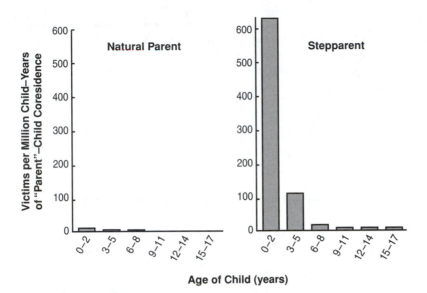

FIGURE 7.2   The Risk of Being Killed by a Stepparent Versus a Natural Parent in Relation to the Child's Age. Canada 1974–1983.

Source: Reprinted with permission from: Daly, Martin and Wilson, Margo. *Homicide,* 90. (New York: Aldine de Gruyter) copyright © 1988 by Aldine de Gruyter.

adultery, presumably resulting in some uncertainty in paternity, was mentioned as grounds for killing a child in fifteen of the thirty-nine societies in which infanticide was mentioned. In three tribal societies men reportedly insist that a child be killed if he or she displayed physical features that provoked suspicion that the child was not the man's own. Finally, among the Tikopia of Oceania and the Yanomamö of Venezuela, men who marry women who already have children by another man reportedly demand that they be killed as a condition of marriage.

Genetic relatedness is a powerful predictor of parental investment and abuse of children. Men invest more in the education of their genetic children than that of their stepchildren, and invest less in children when there is some uncertainty that they are the fathers. Children are abused and killed more often when they live with stepparents than when they live with both genetic parents. For preschool children, the risk of being physically abused and killed is at least forty times greater when they live with a stepparent than when they live with both genetic parents. Indeed, stepparenting is the single greatest risk factor that has yet been identified leading to child abuse and child homicide. Although good cross-cultural data are needed, the available evidence supports the evolutionary psychological prediction that genetic relatedness is a powerful predictor of the distribution of parental benefits or the infliction of parental costs. Parental care is costly. Humans seem to have evolved psychological mechanisms that lead them to direct their care preferentially toward their genetic progeny.

Offspring's Ability to Convert Parental Care into Reproductive Success

After considering a child's genetic relatedness (or lack thereof) to the putative parent, the next critical factor in predicting parental care is the ability of the child to utilize that care. More precisely, selection would have favored mechanisms that caused parents to invest heavily in children when it would have mattered most—that is, when the children were most able to convert the parental care into fitness by either an increase in their chances for survival or an increase in reproduction.

To understand the principle behind this prediction, consider an extreme case of a parent investing time and energy in trying to feed a child after he or she had died of some disease. Clearly we would consider such investment pathological, but from an evolutionary perspective the key point is that there would be no fitness returns on such investment. Therefore, we would expect that selection would not favor parental mechanisms to invest in children who are dead. Now consider a less extreme case—a child who is alive but terminally ill and certain to die soon. Although our moral sentiments might suggest that we should invest in these children, selection would favor the evolution of this no more than it would favor investing in dead children (unless there were reputational or other benefits to caring for a terminally ill child or a chance that such an investment would save the child's life).

This evolutionary logic does *not* imply that parents will only care for children who are robust and healthy. In fact, under some conditions parents would be predicted to invest more in an ill child than in a healthy child, simply because the same unit of investment will benefit the former more than the latter. The key theoretical point is not whether the child is ill or healthy, but rather, the child's ability to convert a given unit of parental care into fitness. Parents, of course, do not think this way, either consciously or unconsciously. No parent ever thinks "I will invest in Sally more than in Mary because Sally can convert my investment into more gene copies." Rather, selection pressures are predicted to give rise to evolved psychological mechanisms that cause shifts in investment. It is those evolved psychological mechanisms together with the current environmental events that trigger their activation and "cause" modern patterns of parental investment.

We cannot go back in time and identify with certainty which factors enabled a child to best use parental care. Nonetheless, Daly and Wilson (1988, 1995) have identified two reasonable candidates: (1) whether the child is born with an abnormality and (2) the age of the child. Children who are disabled in some way, other things being equal, are less likely to have future reproductive success than children who are healthy and intact. Younger children, all else being equal, are lower in reproductive value than are older children. Recall that reproductive value refers to the future probability of producing offspring. Let's examine the empirical data on these two candidates.

Parental Neglect and Abuse of Children with Congenital Abnormalities. Children who have a congenital disease such as spina bifida, fibrocystic disease, cleft palate, or Down syndrome are likely to be lower in reproductive value than healthy children. Is there evidence that parents treat these children differently? One index is whether they are abandoned either completely or partially. Studies show that indeed a large fraction of such seriously ill children are institutionalized. The 1976 United States census found that among those who are institutionalized, more than 16,000 children (roughly 12 percent of all institutionalized children) were never visited at all. Furthermore, roughly 30,000 (approximately 22 percent) additional patients were visited only once a year or less (U.S. Bureau of the Census, 1978). Although these findings are correlational and cannot establish causality, they are at least consistent with the hypothesis that parents invest less in children with abnormalities.

What about children with abnormalities who are neither institutionalized nor given up for adoption? The rates of child physical abuse and neglect in the U.S. population are estimated to be roughly 1.5 percent (Daly & Wilson, 1981). This provides a base rate against which the abuse of children with various characteristics can be compared. Daly and Wilson (1981) summarized a variety of studies, all of which suggest that children with abnormalities are abused at considerably higher rates. Across these studies the percentage of children born with congenital physical abnormalities who are abused ranged from 7.5 percent to 60 percent—far higher than the base rate of abuse in the general population. Although in some of these cases a child's defect may have been caused by the abuse rather than be a cause of the abuse, this is largely ruled out in children in whom the defect was present at birth, such as those with spina bifida, cystic fibrosis, talipes, cleft palate, or Down syndrome.

Maternal Care Based on the Health of the Child.   One direct test of the hypothesis that parents have proclivities to invest in children according to their reproductive value is offered by a study of twins, of whom one in each pair was healthier. Evolutionary psychologist Janet Mann conducted a study of fourteen infants, seven twin pairs, all of whom were born prematurely. When the infants were four months old Mann made detailed behavioral observations of the interactions between the mothers and their infants (Mann, 1992). The interactions were observed when the fathers were not present and when both twins were awake. Observers had more than one-hundred hours of training in behavioral observation, including extensive practice with mother–infant dyads in their homes. Among the behavioral recordings were assessments of *positive maternal behavior*, which included kissing, holding, soothing, talking to, playing with, and gazing at the infant.

Independently, the health status of each infant was assessed at birth, at discharge from the hospital, at four months of age, and at eight months of age. The health status examinations included medical, neurological, physical, cognitive, and developmental assessments.

Mann then tested the *healthy baby hypothesis:* that the health status of the child would affect the degree of positive maternal behavior. When the infants were four months old, roughly half the mothers directed more positive maternal behavior toward the healthier infants; the other half showed no preference. By the time the infants were eight months old, however, every single one of the mothers directed more positive maternal behavior toward the healthier infant, with no reversals. In sum, the results of this twin study support the healthy baby hypothesis, suggesting that mothers direct greater maternal investment toward infants who are of higher reproductive value. More extensive tests on larger samples are needed to further support this hypothesis.

Age of the Child.   Reproductive value—the expected probability of future reproduction—increases from birth to pubescence. The increase occurs primarily because some percentage of children—especially infants—die, thereby dragging down the average reproductive value of that age class. The average fourteen-year-old, for example, will have a higher reproductive value than the average infant—some infants don't survive to be fourteen years old. Surviving to puberty was a far more treacherous journey in ancestral times, when rates of infant morality were high. Based on this reasoning, Daly and Wilson made a specific prediction: The younger the child, the higher the likelihood that the parents would kill it, but this age-dependent pattern of child homicide should not occur when the killer is a nonrelative because nonrelatives do not have the same stake or interest in the child's reproductive value.

As with most other topics, the cross-cultural evidence is sparse. In the HRAF files, eleven ethnographies of diverse cultures report that a child will be killed if the birth interval is too short or the family is too large (Daly & Wilson, 1988, p. 75). In each of these eleven cases, it is the newborn that is killed; in no case does the ethnography report that the older child is put to death.

A more rigorous test of the evolutionary prediction comes from Canadian data on the risk of a child being killed by a genetic parent, depending on the child's age. These findings (Figure 7.3) show that infants are at a much higher risk of being killed by their genetic parents than any other age group of children. From that point on, the rates of child homicide decrease progressively until they reach zero at age seventeen.

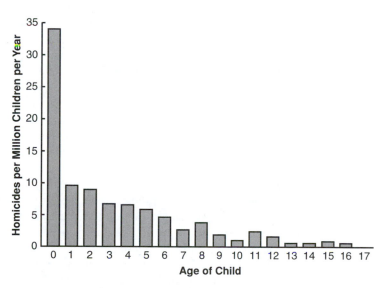

FIGURE 7.3   The Risk of Homicide by a Natural Parent in Relation to the Child's Age. Canada, 1974–1983.

Source: Reprinted with permission from: Daly, Martin and Wilson, Margo. *Homicide,* 76. (New York: Aldine de Gruyter) copyright © 1988 by Aldine de Gruyter.

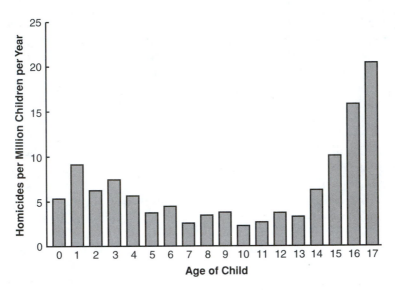

FIGURE 7.4   The Risk That a Child Will Be Killed by a Nonrelative, as a Function of Age. Canada 1974–1983.

Source: Reprinted with permission from: Daly, Martin and Wilson, Margo. *Homicide.* (New York: Aldine de Gruyter) copyright © 1988 by Aldine de Gruyter.

One possible explanation for this decrease is simply that children become increasingly capable of defending themselves physically as they get older. But this cannot account for the data, because the risk of a child being killed at the hands of a nonrelative shows a markedly different pattern, shown in Figure 7.4. Unlike genetic parents, nonrelatives are more likely to kill one-year-old children than they are to kill infants. And also unlike genetic parents, who almost never kill their teenage children, who are most physically formidable, nonrelatives kill teenagers at a higher rate than any other age category. In short, it appears to be the increasing reproductive value of children as they age that accounts for the fact that genetic parents kill older children less often, not the increased physical formidability of those children.

In summary, two negative indicators of the child's ability to promote the parent's reproductive success—birth defects and youth—predict homicides at the hands of genetic parents. Daly and Wilson (1988) take pains to point out that they are *not* proposing that "child abuse" or "child homicide" per se are adaptations; rather, they regard child homicide as an assay or test of parental feelings. They suggest that parents will feel more favorably toward children who are best able to convert parental investment into reproductive success, and less favorably toward children who are less likely to be able to do so. They capture these forms of parental feelings with the phrase *discriminative parental solicitude.* Child homicide, according to Daly and Wilson, represents an extreme and relatively uncommon manifestation of negative parental feelings, not an adaptation in and of itself. On the other hand, there is strong evidence that parents invest more care in healthy children than in unhealthy children, suggesting that selection has favored psychological mechanisms in parents sensitive to the reproductive value of their children.

Alternative Uses of Resources Available for Investment in Children

Energy and effort are finite and limited. Effort allocated to one activity must necessarily take away from that allocated to others. As applied to parenting, the principle of finite effort means that the effort expended toward caring for a child cannot be allocated toward other adaptive problems such as personal survival, attracting additional mates, or perhaps investing in other kin. At the most general level we expect that selection will have fashioned in humans decision-making rules for when to invest in children and when to devote one's energy toward other adaptive problems. From a woman's perspective, two contexts that might affect these decisions are age and marital status. From a man's perspective, one important context affecting parenting effort is his potential sexual access to women; men with high potential access to women might tilt their effort more toward mating than toward parenting. We consider each of these contexts in turn.

Women's Age and Infanticide.   Young women have many years in which to bear and invest in children, so passing up one youthful opportunity to bear and invest in a child may entail minimal cost. On the other hand, older women nearing the end of reproductive capacity who pass up an opportunity to bear and invest in children may not have another chance. As opportunities for reproduction diminish, postponing childbearing and rearing would be reproductively costly. From this perspective we expect that natural selection would favor a decision rule that causes older women to invest immediately in children rather than postponing doing so.

Daly and Wilson (1988) examined this hypothesis using infanticide as an assay of maternal investment (or lack thereof). A specific prediction follows from the above reasoning: Younger women should be more inclined than older women to commit infanticide. This hypothesis is strongly supported in data from the Ayoreo Indians (Bugos & McCarthy, 1984). The proportion of births leading to infanticide is highest among the youngest women (ages fifteen to nineteen). Infanticide is lowest among the oldest age group of women (more than thirty-nine years of age).

The Ayoreo Indians, however, appear to have an unusually high rate of infanticide —fully 38 percent of all births, so perhaps this is an atypical sample. Is there any evidence that maternal age affects infanticide in other cultures? Daly and Wilson (1988) collected data on infanticide in Canada from 1974 through 1983 (see Figure 7.5 on page 210).

As among the Ayoreo Indians, young Canadian women commit infanticide far more frequently than older Canadian women. Teenage mothers show the highest rates of infanticide, more than three times as high as any other age group. Women in their twenties show the next highest rate of infanticide, followed by women in their thirties. Figure 7.5 shows a slight increase in infanticide among the oldest group of women, which appears to contradict the hypothesis that older women will commit infanticide less often.

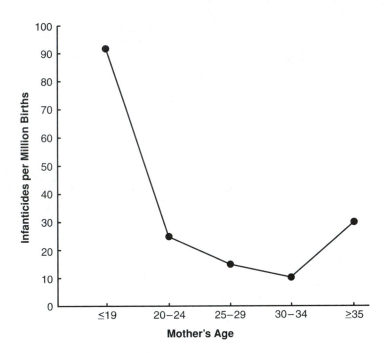

FIGURE 7.5   The Risk of Infanticide (Homicide at the Hands of the Natural Mother within the First Year of Life) as a Function of Maternal Age. Canada, 1974–1983.

Source: Reprinted with permission from: Daly, Martin and Wilson, Margo. *Homicide,* 63 (New York: Aldine de Gruyter) copyright © 1988 by Aldine de Gruyter.

Daly and Wilson note that this might not prove to be a reliable finding, however, since this group consists of only three women, one aged thirty-eight, and two age forty-one. Further research with a larger sample, including other cultures, is needed to determine whether this apparent increase among the oldest group is reliable.

So data from two cultures support the prediction that infanticide is highest among younger women, who have the most opportunities for future reproduction, and lowest among older women, who have fewer opportunities for future reproduction. Younger women presumably can use their resources for other purposes, such as stockpiling personal resources or devoting effort toward attracting investing mates. The decision rules of older women presumably tilt them toward immediate investment in children, even at the possible expense of investing in other adaptive problems. Another context that might affect the decision to invest in children is the woman's marital status.

Women's Marital Status and Infanticide.   An unmarried woman who gives birth faces three unsettling choices: she can try to raise the child without the help of an investing father; she can abandon the child or give it up for adoption; or she can kill the child and devote her efforts to trying to attract a husband, and then have children with him. Daly and Wilson (1988) propose that a woman's marital status will affect the likelihood she will commit infanticide.

They examined this prediction using two data sets. In the first they examined the HRAF files—the most extensive ethnographic database in existence. In six cultures infants were reportedly killed when no man would acknowledge that he was the father or accept an obligation to help raise the child. In an additional fourteen cultures a woman's unwed marital status was declared a compelling reason for infanticide. These data are revealing, but more quantitative data would make a more convincing case.

In sample of Canadian women studied between 1977 and 1983, two million babies were born (Daly & Wilson, 1988). Of these, unwed mothers delivered only 12 percent. Despite this relatively low percentage of unwed mothers, these women were responsible for more than half the sixty-four maternal infanticides that were reported to or discovered by the police. The astute reader might immediately think of a problem with this finding: Perhaps unwed mothers are younger, on average, than wed mothers, and so it might be youth rather than marital status that accounts for the infanticides. To address this issue Daly and Wilson (1988) examined the separate effects of age and marital status on infanticide (Figure 7.6).

The findings are clear—both age and marital status are correlated with rates of infanticide. At every age except the very oldest age bracket, unwed mothers are more likely than married mothers to commit infanticide. Daly and Wilson offer no explanation for

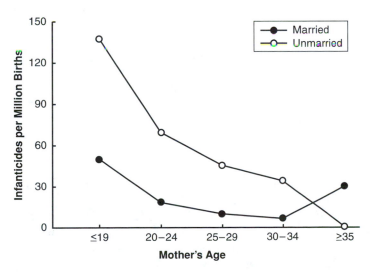

FIGURE 7.6   The Risk of Infanticide as a Function of the Mother's Age and Marital Status. Canada, 1974–1983.

Source: Reprinted with permission from: Daly, Martin and Wilson, Margo. *Homicide*, 65 (New York: Aldine de Gruyter) copyright © 1988 by Aldine de Gruyter.

the reversal of this trend among the oldest age group, where it appears that married women over the age of thirty-five are slightly more likely than unmarried women over the age of thirty-five to commit infanticide.

If we evaluate all the findings together, there appears to be substantial evidence that youth and marital status affect the likelihood that a woman will commit infanticide. Presumably these trends reflect evolved decision rules in women concerning the ways in which they allocate effort. Older married women, whose reproductive years are quickly waning, are more likely to keep and invest in a child. Younger and unwed mothers are more likely to commit infanticide, devoting their efforts more toward other adaptive problems, such as surviving or attracting investing men. It is important to bear in mind that Daly and Wilson are not arguing that infanticide per se is an adaptation. Rather, they regard infanticide as a reverse assay of parental care—the proverbial tip of the iceberg that reveals an underlying psychology of decision rules about parental investment that are sensitive to specific contexts.

Parental Effort versus Mating Effort.   Effort allocated toward parenting is effort that cannot be allocated toward securing additional mates. Recall that there are two powerful evolutionary reasons for predicting that men and women have evolved different decision rules about the tradeoffs between parenting and mating. First, men benefit more than women by gaining sexual access to additional mates. Men who succeed in mating can sire additional children through increased sexual access, whereas women cannot. Second, paternity is generally less than 100 percent certain. Therefore, the same unit of investment in a child will be less likely to increase a man's reproductive success, on average, than a woman's reproductive success. These two considerations yield a powerful prediction: Women will be more likely than men to channel energy and effort directly toward parenting rather than toward securing additional matings.

Evidence from a variety of cultures supports this prediction. Among the Ye'Kwana of the Venezuelan rain forest, for example, there is a significant gender difference in time spent holding infants. Mothers hold their infants an average of 78 percent of the time, whereas fathers hold their infants only 1.4 percent of the time (Hames, 1988). The remainder of the time the infants are held by other kin, mostly females such as sisters, aunts, and grandmothers.

The Aka pygmies of central Africa are another example (Hewlett, 1991). The Aka are known for their unusually high levels of paternal investment. Aka parents sleep in the same beds as their infants. If the child is not comforted by nursing at the mother's breast during the night, it is usually the father who cares for the infant, singing to him or her or dancing to provide comfort. The father also cleans mucus from the infant's nose and grooms the infant by cleaning off dirt, lice, or the mess from defecation. And if the mother is not around and the infant is hungry, the father will even offer the infant his own breast on which to suckle, although it obviously provides no milk.

During an average day Aka fathers hold their infants more than fathers in any other known culture—an average of fifty-seven minutes. This unusually high level of paternal investment pales in comparison to that of Aka mothers, who hold their infants 490 minutes on an average day. So even among the Aka, a culture described as a society of "mothering men," women still do the lion's share of caring for offspring.

Another cross-cultural study surveyed a variety of rural and nontechnological societies, including Mexico, Java, Quechua, Nepal, and the Philippines (reported in Barash & Lipton, 1997). The patterns of division of labor between the sexes were consistent. Fathers cared for children from 5 to 18 percent of their waking hours, with the most common amount of time being 8 percent. Mothers, in contrast, spent between 39 and 88 percent of their waking hours caring for their children, with the most common figure 85 percent. Women, in short, spent roughly ten times more time caring for children than did men. The sex difference becomes even larger if more passive forms of child care are included in the analysis, such as watching over children while they are playing. When these data are included women devote fifteen times more effort to child care than do men.

Similar differences are found in modern America, where inventions such as the baby bottle and artificial breast milk mean that men are fully able to care for children from infancy. Even there, women spend more than four times as much time as men in direct child care (Barash & Lipton, 1997). Single parenting provides another telling statistic. Roughly 90 percent of single parents are women. Despite ideologies of sexual equality, either men are reluctant to take a large role in direct parenting or women prefer to take a larger role. Most likely, the outcome may reflect the evolved decision rules of both sexes, with men tilting their investments toward mating and women tilting their investments toward parenting.

A host of other studies suggests the evolution in mothers of specific parental mechanisms that appear to be weak or absent in fathers. One series of studies examined pupillary reactions of men and women in response to various pictures (Hess, 1975). When we see something that attracts us, our pupils dilate (enlarge) more than is needed to correct for the ambient degree of illumination. Thus pupil dilation can be used as a measure of interest and attraction—a subtle measure that is reasonably immune to self-reporting biases that might affect questionnaire studies. In these studies, when women were shown slides of babies their pupils dilated more than 17 percent; men's pupils showed no dilation at all. Furthermore, when shown slides of a mother holding a baby, women's pupils dilated roughly 24 percent, whereas men's pupils dilated only 5 percent (even this small degree of dilation may be due to men's attraction to the mother rather than the infant!).

Other studies show similar sex differences in reactions to infants. Women can identify their own newborn children within six hours of birth merely by smell, whereas fathers cannot (Barash & Lipton, 1997). Women also have a greater ability to recognize the facial expression of infants when they are flashed briefly on a screen—they detect emotions such as surprise, disgust, anger, fear, and distress more quickly and accurately than do men (Barash & Lipton, 1997). Interestingly, women's accuracy was not affected in the least by the amount of previous experience with infants and children.

Women appear to have a host of parental mechanisms that are weak or absent in men. Women spend more time than do men with infants and children in all cultures for which good data exist. Women find pictures of infants more interesting and attractive than do men, as gauged by pupillary dilation. Women recognize their infants by odor hours after birth, whereas men do not. Finally, women are able to read the facial expressions of infants more quickly and accurately than can men. All these findings point to a singular conclusion: women appear to have evolved decision rules that lead them to allocate more time to parenting and have attendant evolved mechanisms of interest and emotional mind reading that render such parenting more effective.

Presumably men are using the effort not allocated toward parenting for other adaptive problems, such as mating. The direct evidence for this proposition exists, but is more tenuous. One source of evidence comes from detailed study of the Aka pygmies of central Africa. Although the Aka show heavy male parental investment compared with other cultures, there is also considerable variation among the men in how much parenting they do. When a father holds a position of high status within the tribe (*kombeti*), he devotes less than half as much effort to holding his infant as men of lower status (Hewlett, 1991). These high-status men are usually polygynous, with two or more wives. In contrast, low-status men are fortunate to have even one wife. Low-status men appear to compensate for their standing by increasing the effort they allocate to parenting, whereas high-status men appear to be channeling extra effort into attracting additional mates (Hewlett, 1991; Smuts & Gubernick, 1992).

Even when men do devote effort to parenting, it may be used as a mating tactic rather than as a means to aid the viability of the child—a hypothesis that has been developed recently by primatologists Barbara Smuts and David Gubernick (1992). Mark Flinn (1992), for example, studied male parental investment in a rural Trinidad village. He found that when a woman is single and has a child, men interact more with the woman's child before they are married than after, suggesting that men may be channeling effort to the child in an effort to attract the woman. Smuts and Gubernick argue that men's efforts toward children may reflect a strategy to secure, and perhaps to maintain, sexual access to a particular woman.

Summary.   We have examined three factors that affect the evolution of parenting: genetic relatedness to the child, ability of the child to convert parental care into survival and reproductive success, and alternative ways parents could use resources that might be channeled to children. Considerable evidence supports the notion that all three factors are important. Parents invest more in genetic children than in stepchildren; fathers, who are less certain of genetic relatedness, invest less in children than mothers, who are 100 percent certain of their genetic relatedness. Children who are healthy and high in reproductive value receive greater positive parental attention than children who are deformed, ill, or otherwise of low reproductive value. Men, who tend to have more opportunities than women to channel effort into mating, tend to provide less direct parental care of children. Among Aka men, those who are high in status appear to channel their efforts into attracting more wives, and consequently spend less time in direct parental care. Lower-status Aka men increase their investment in children, although not to levels approaching those of Aka women.

The Theory of Parent–Offspring Conflict

Evolutionary theory tells us that children are the primary vehicles for parents' reproductive success. Given the supreme importance of children to parents, you may wonder why you and your parents have ever engaged in conflict. It may come as a surprise, then, that parents and children are actually predicted by evolutionary accounts to have conflicts (Trivers, 1974).

In sexually reproducing species such as humans, parents and offspring are genetically related by 50 percent. The genetic relatedness between parent and child can exert selection pressure for intense parental care, as documented above. But it also means that parents and children *differ* genetically by 50 percent. An ideal course of action for one, therefore, will rarely coincide perfectly with an ideal course of action for the other (Trivers, 1974). Specifically, parents and children will diverge in the ideal allocation of the parent's resources, with the typical result being that children want more for themselves than parents want to give. Let's explore the logic of these parent-offspring conflicts.

Daly and Wilson (1988) offer a numerical example to illustrate this logic. Suppose you have one sibling who has the same reproductive value as you. Your mother comes home from a day of gathering with two food items to feed her children. As with many resources, there are *diminishing returns* associated with each increase in consumption—that is, the value of the first unit of food consumed is higher than the value of the second unit of food. The first unit of food, for example, may prevent starvation, whereas the second unit of food just makes you a little fuller and fatter. Let's say that the first item would raise your reproductive success by four units and the second item of food would raise it an additional three units. Your sibling's consumption of these food items would have the same result, with diminishing returns associated with each added food item.

Now comes the conflict. From your mother's perspective, the ideal allocation would be to give one unit of food to you and one to your sibling. This would net her eight units of increase, four for you and four for your sibling. If either you or your sibling monopolized all the food, however, the gain would only be seven (four for the first item plus three for the second). So from your mother's perspective an equal allocation between her children would yield the best outcome.

From your perspective, however, you are twice as valuable as your sibling—you have 100 percent of your genes, whereas your sibling only has 50 percent of your genes (on average). Therefore, your mother's ideal allocation would benefit you by the four units that you receive plus only two of the units that your sibling receives (since you benefit by only 50 percent of whatever your sibling receives), for a total of six units benefit. If you manage to get all the food, however, you benefit by seven units (four for the first item plus three for the second). Therefore, from your perspective the ideal allocation in this simplified example would be for you to get all the food and your sibling none. This conflicts with your mother's ideal allocation, which is to distribute equally, however. The general conclusion is this: The theory of parent–offspring conflict predicts that each child will generally desire a larger portion of the parents' resources than the parents want to give. Although the above example is simplified in various ways, this general conclusion applies even when siblings differ in their value to the parents and even when the parents have only a single child. If the parents were to go along with the ideal allocation of resources desired by the child, it would take away from other channels through which the parents might be reproductively successful. Interestingly, parent–child conflict over the parent's resources is predicted not merely to occur at particular times such as adolescence, but at each stage of life (Daly & Wilson, 1988).

The theory of parent–offspring conflict yields a number of specific hypotheses that can be tested: (1) parents and children will get into conflict about the time at which the child should be weaned, with the parents generally wanting to wean the child sooner and the child wanting to continue to receive resources longer; (2) parents will encourage children to value their siblings more than children are naturally inclined to value them; and (3) parents will tend to punish conflict between siblings and reward cooperation.

Mother–Offspring Conflict in Utero

Few relationships are believed to be as harmonious as that between mother and child. The mother is 100 percent certain of her genetic contribution, after all, so of all relationships the genetic interests of mother and child should coincide. In an astonishing series of recent papers, however, biologist David Haig extended the theory of parent–offspring conflict to include conflicts that occur between the mother and her offspring in utero (Haig, 1993).

The logic of mother–fetus conflict follows directly from the theory of parent–offspring conflict described above. A mother contributes 50 percent of her genes to the fetus, but the fetus also receives 50 percent of its genes from the father. Mothers will be selected to channel resources to the child who will yield the greater reproductive benefit. This child, however, has a greater stake in itself than it has in the mother's future child. Therefore, selection will create mechanisms in the fetus to manipulate the mother to provide more nutrition than will be in the mother's best interests to provide.

The conflict begins over whether the fetus is spontaneously aborted. As many as 78 percent of all fertilized eggs either fail to implant or are spontaneously aborted by the mother early in pregnancy (Nesse & Williams, 1994). Most of these occur because of chromosomal abnormalities in the fetus. Mothers appear to have evolved an adaptation that detects such abnormalities and aborts fetuses with them. This mechanism is highly functional, for it prevents the mother from investing in a baby that would be likely to die young. It's to the mother's advantage to cut her losses early so that she can preserve more investments for a future child who is more likely to thrive. Indeed, the vast majority of miscarriages occur before the twelfth week of pregnancy, and many occur before the woman misses her first period and so might not even know she was pregnant (Haig, 1993). From the fetus's perspective, however, it has only one shot at life. It will do everything it can to implant itself and prevent spontaneous abortion.

One adaptation that appears to have evolved for this function is the fetal production of human chorionic gonadotropin (hCG), a hormone the fetus secretes into the mother's bloodstream. This hormone has the effect of preventing the mother from menstruating, and thus allows the fetus to remain implanted. Producing a lot of hCG, therefore, appears to be an adaptation in the fetus to subvert the mother's attempts to spontaneously abort it. The female body appears to "interpret" high levels of hCG as a sign that a fetus is healthy and viable, and so does not spontaneously abort.

Once implantation is successful, another conflict appears to develop over the food supply, which is provided by the mother's blood. One common side effect of pregnancy is high blood pressure. When the blood pressure is so high that it causes damage to the mother's kidneys it is called preeclampsia. In the early stages of pregnancy the placental cells destroy the arteriolar muscles in the mother that are responsible for adjusting the flow of blood to the fetus. Therefore, anything that constricts the mother's other arteries will result in an elevation in her blood pressure, with the result that more blood will flow to the fetus. When the fetus "perceives" that it needs more nutrition from the mother, it releases substances into the mother's bloodstream that cause her arteries to constrict. This has the effect of raising her blood pressure and delivering more blood (and hence nutrition) to the fetus, which can damage the mother's tissues, as in preeclampsia. Clearly the mechanism has evolved to benefit the fetus, even at the risk of inflicting damage to the mother.

Two sources of evidence support the hypothesis of an evolved mechanism in fetuses that are in conflict with the mother. First, data from thousands of pregnancies show that mothers whose blood pressure increases during pregnancy tend to have lower rates of spontaneous abortions (Haig, 1993). Second, preeclampsia is more common among pregnant women whose blood supply to the fetus is more restricted, suggesting that a fetus may secrete more hCG when the blood supply is low, thus causing the mother to develop high blood pressure.

These recent theories of mother–fetus conflict may seem as bizarre as science fiction. But they follow directly from Trivers's (1974) theory of parent–offspring conflict. Conflict is predicted to occur because fetuses, like children, will be selected to take a bit more of the mother's resources than mothers will be prepared to give. Let's now turn to the implications of the theory of parent–offspring conflict after the child is born.

The Oedipal Complex Revisited

The theory of parent–offspring conflict has been examined in relation to Freud's (1900/1953) theory of the Oedipus Complex. According to Freud, the Oedipus Complex is a pivotal source of conflict between children and their same-sex parents. It has two central components. First, the son, between the ages of two and five, is hypothesized to develop a sexual attraction toward the mother. Because the father has actual sexual access to the mother, the son's sexual attraction places him in conflict with the father. This brings forth the second component of the Oedipus Complex, namely the son's unconscious desire to kill his father. The son and father, in essence, become sexual competitors for the mother. One clear prediction follows: If the theory is correct, there will be more same-sex conflict and antagonism between parent and child than opposite-sex antagonism, especially during the Oedipal stage, between the ages of two and five.

The theory of the Oedipus Complex contrasts sharply with Trivers's (1974) theory of parent–offspring conflict. According to that theory, conflicts of interest between parents and children, at least in the preschool years, have little or nothing to do with the child's gender. Instead, conflicts that occur are driven by disagreements over the allocation of the parents' investments. Sons and daughters alike are predicted to desire more parental investment than the parents are predicted to want to give, for reasons mentioned earlier in the examination of the theory of parent–offspring conflict.

Both theories predict the existence of parent–child conflict, but they differ in two key predictions. First, they differ in the resource over which parents and children conflict. In Freud's theory the conflict is sexual access to the mother, whereas in Trivers's theory the conflict is the amount of parental investment. Second, the theories differ in the importance of same-sex conflict. In Freud's theory same-sex conflict between parent and child (i.e., father and son) should be more prevalent than opposite-sex conflict (i.e., mother and son), whereas in Trivers's theory, there should not be this same-sex conflict (Daly & Wilson, 1990).

There is one important qualifier that occurs when a son becomes old enough to be a sexual competitor of his father. The standard Darwinian theory of sexual selection (see Chapter 4) would predict that members of the same sex will become rivals over sexual access to members of the opposite sex. However, there is nothing in this theory that would predict that the mother would be the target of the sexual rivalry. In fact, based on everything we know about the mate preferences that men express for younger women (see Chapter 5), we would predict that sons would rarely have any sexual interest in their mothers. The additional complication of "inbreeding depression," whereby children who are products of couplings by genetic relatives show lower intelligence scores and have more genetic diseases, suggests that selection would operate strongly against any sexual attraction that a son might have for his mother. Thus, fathers and sons might become sexual rivals, but the focus of their rivalry would be over access to other women, not their wife and mother.

In sum, according to an evolutionary account, Freud's theory of the Oedipus Complex confused two separate sources of conflict. First, there may indeed be nonsexual conflict between fathers and sons, but it would be over parental investment, not sexual access. Second, there may be sexual conflict between fathers and sons, but it would be over sexual access to other women, not to the mother. In short, Freud appears to have inappropriately combined these two distinct sources in his theory of the Oedipus Complex.

Are there any data bearing on the opposing predictions of these two theories? Daly and Wilson (1990) have collected such data, although they are indirect. They examined homicides between parents and their offspring to test the Freudian prediction that such homicides would be a special concentration of same-sex homicides during the Oedipal years (ages two to five). They used homicide as an assay of the degree of conflict or hostility in the relationship. There is some support for this assumption, as we have seen in the earlier patterning of homicides (e.g., more homicide in stepfamilies).

Using two separate samples of parent–offspring homicides, one taken from Canadian data and the other from Chicagoan data, Daly and Wilson found no evidence for a same-sex concentration of homicides during the Oedipal stages. In the Canadian sample, for example, twenty-one boys were killed by their fathers and twenty-one boys were killed by their mothers. In the same sample twenty-seven girls were killed by their fathers and twenty-seven girls were killed by their mothers. Using these homicides as an assay, there is no evidence that fathers are especially prone to killing sons or that mothers are especially prone to killing daughters, at least during the Oedipal stage.

As the children reached puberty and then adulthood, however, a clear same-sex pattern emerged. In adulthood, for example, 60 percent of familial homicides were committed by men, with other men (either the father or the son) the victims. In another 27 percent of the cases a male was the killer and a female the victim. Familial homicides in which a female was the killer are rare. Only 5 percent involved female killers with male victims, and only 9 percent involved female killers with female victims (Daly & Wilson, 1990, p. 178). In sum, in adulthood there is indeed a same-sex contingency in familial homicides, with most focused on fathers and sons. Remember that this is more than a decade after the Oedipus Complex is hypothesized to end. This pattern of data, in short, supports the Trivers theory of parent–offspring conflict more than the Freudian theory of the Oedipus Complex. (See Box 7.1 on page 220 for an example and additional studies on familial homicides.)

Summary

From an evolutionary perspective, offspring are the vehicles for parents' genes, so selection should favor parental mechanisms designed to ensure the survival and reproduction of offspring. Mechanisms of parental care have been documented in many nonhuman species. One of the most interesting puzzles is why mothers tend to provide more parental care than fathers. Three hypotheses have been advanced to explain this: (1) the paternity uncertainty hypothesis—males invest less than females because there is a lower probability that they have contributed genes to their putative offspring (maternity certainty being 100 percent and paternity certainty being less than 100 percent); (2) the abandonability hypothesis—the first one who can abandon the offspring does so, and because fertilization occurs internally in many species, males can be the first to abandon; and (3) the mating opportunity cost hypothesis—the costs to males of providing parental care are higher than for females because such investment by males precludes additional mating opportunities. Although all three factors may contribute to the overall sex difference in magnitude of parental care, current evidence shows the strongest support for the paternity uncertainty and mating opportunity cost hypotheses.

Evolved mechanisms of parental care are predicted to be sensitive to at least three contexts: (1) the genetic relatedness of offspring, (2) the ability of the offspring to convert parental care into fitness, and (3) alternative uses of the resources that might be available. Abundant empirical evidence supports the hypothesis that genetic relatedness to offspring affects human parental care. Studies show that stepparents have fewer positive parental feelings than genetic parents. Interactions between stepparents and stepchildren tend to be more conflict-ridden than those between genetic parents and children. Newborn babies are said to resemble the putative father more than the putative mother,

BOX **7.1**

Killing Parents and the Asymmetry of Valuing Parents and Children

On Sunday afternoon, January 2nd, the victim (male, age 46) was killed in his home by a single shotgun blast at close range. The killer (male, 15) was the victim's son, and the circumstance was familiar to the investigating police. . . . The home was a scene of recurring violence, in which the victim had assaulted his wife and sons, had threatened them with the same weapon he eventually died by, had even shot at his wife in the past. On the fatal Sunday, the victim was drunk, berating his wife as a "bitch" and a "whore," and beating her, when their son acted to terminate the long history of abuse (Daly & Wilson, 1988, p. 98).

Assuming certainty in paternity, parents and children are genetically related by an *r* of .50. But it does not follow from an evolutionary perspective that they should value each other equally. Children are the vehicles for their parents' genes, but as the parents age they become less and less valuable to their children precisely as the children become more and more valuable to their parents (i.e., as the parents' other avenues to achieving reproduction diminish). The end result is that by adulthood children are more valuable to their parents than the parents are to the children (Daly & Wilson, 1988). A clear prediction follows from this logic: those who are less valuable will be at greater risk of

being killed, so by adulthood offspring will be more likely to kill their parents than vice-versa.

There is some limited empirical evidence to support this prediction, at least with fathers. In one study conducted in Detroit, of a total of eleven homicides involving parents and adult children, nine parents were killed by their adult children, whereas only two adult children were killed by their parents (Daly & Wilson, 1988). In a larger study of Canadian homicides, ninety-one fathers were killed by their adult sons (82 percent of father-son homicides), whereas only twenty adult sons were killed by their fathers (18 percent of father-son homicides). It should be noted that this sample excluded homicides involving stepfathers, a relationship that as we saw earlier in this chapter carries a special kind of conflict.

These homicide data are preliminary, of course, and do not reveal much about the underlying psychology of parent-offspring conflict as a consequence of the predicted asymmetry of valuation. They do suggest, however, that there are risks associated with being the less valued party in the parent–child relationship. Future research, guided by this reasoning, will undoubtedly reveal a wealth of information about the conflictual nature of this special and close genetic relationship.

suggesting mechanisms to influence the putative father to invest in the child. Investment in children's college education is higher with genetic children than with stepchildren and higher when paternity certainty is high. Children living with one genetic parent and one stepparent are forty times more likely to suffer physical abuse and forty to one hundred times more likely to be killed than children living with both genetic parents. Genetic relatedness of parent to child, in short, appears to be a critical determinant of the quality of parental care.

Evolved parental mechanisms are also predicted to be sensitive to the ability of the offspring to convert parental care into reproductive success. Three lines of research support this theoretical expectation. First, children born with congenital problems such as spina bifida or Down syndrome are commonly institutionalized or given up for adoption; if they are cared for and not given up for adoption, they are far more likely to be physically abused by their parents. Second, a small study of twins found that mothers tend to invest more in the healthy infants than in their less healthy twins. Third, young infants are at greater risk of abuse and homicide than older children.

The third context predicted to affect the quality of parental care is the availability of alternative uses of resources that could be invested in a child. Effort and energy are finite, and effort allocated to one activity must necessarily take away from other activities. Several studies have examined patterns of infanticide on the assumption that such killings are reverse assays of parental care—that is, they indicate the exact opposite of parental care. Studies show that young mothers are more likely than older mothers to commit infanticide, presumably because younger women have many years ahead in which to bear and invest in offspring, whereas older women have fewer years. Unmarried women are more likely than married women to commit infanticide. These trends presumably reflect evolved decision rules in women about the ways in which they allocate effort. Finally, men, who tend to have more opportunities than women to channel effort into mating, tend to provide less direct parental care than do women. Among the Aka, men who are high in status invest less in direct child care than men who are low in status. Presumably high-status Aka men channel their efforts into attracting more wives. In sum, the availability of alternative uses of resources affects decision rules about when to allocate effort to parental care.

The evolutionary theory of parent–offspring conflict suggests that the "interests" of parents and children will not coincide perfectly because they are genetically related by only 50 percent. The theory predicts that each child will generally desire a larger portion of parental resources than the parents want to give. This theory yields some surprising predictions, such as: (1) mother–offspring conflict will sometimes occur in utero, such as over whether the fetus is spontaneously aborted; and (2) parents tend to value their children more than their children value them as both get older. Empirical evidence on pre-eclampsia supports the first prediction—it appears that fetuses secrete large amounts of human chorionic gonadotropin (hCG) into the mother's bloodstream, which prevents the mother from menstruating and allows the fetus to remain implanted, thus subverting any attempts by the mother to spontaneously abort it. Evidence from homicide data supports the second prediction—parents, who are less valuable as they grow older, are more often killed by their older children than the reverse. On the assumption that those who are less valuable are at greater risk of being killed, adult offspring should be more likely to kill their parents than vice versa. The preliminary data suggest that parent–offspring conflict will be an important domain for future empirical studies in evolutionary psychology.

CHAPTER

8

Problems of Kinship

Human beings, wherever we meet them, display an almost obsessional interest in matters of sex and kinship.

—Edmund Leach, 1966

Imagine a world in which everyone loved everyone else equally. There would be no favoritism. You would be just as likely to give your food to a passing stranger as to your children. Your parents would be just as likely to pay for a neighbor's college education as they would be to pay for yours. And when forced by fate to save only one person's life when two were drowning, you would be just as likely to save a stranger as you would your brother or sister.

Such a world is hard to imagine. The evolutionary theory of inclusive fitness explains why it is so difficult to conceive. From the perspective of inclusive fitness theory, people differ in their genetic relatedness to others. As a general rule, we are related by 50 percent to our parents, children, and siblings. We are related by 25 percent to our grandparents and grandchildren, half brothers and half sisters, and uncles, aunts, nieces, and nephews. We are related by 12.5 percent of our genes, on average, to our first cousins, and half as much to our second cousins. We typically are genetically unrelated to strangers.

From the perspective of inclusive fitness theory, an individual's relatives are all vehicles of fitness, but they differ in value. In the last chapter we saw that children differ in their values to their parents; in this chapter we will explore the theory and evidence that kin differ in value to us. Theoretically, if everything else is equal selection will favor adaptations for helping kin in proportion to their genetic relatedness. Selection will favor mechanisms for helping ourselves twice as much as we help a brother, for example. But a brother, in turn, is twice as related to us as a nephew, and so would get twice the help. In life, of course, not everything is equal. Holding genetic relatedness constant, for example, one brother struggling to make it as a songwriter might benefit more from our gifts of aid than another brother who happens to be wealthy. But if there is one straightforward prediction from inclusive fitness theory it is this: Selection will favor the evolution of mechanisms to help close kin more than distant kin and distant kin more than strangers.

This chapter explores the evolutionary psychology of kinship. It differs from the previous chapters, however, in that it is heavy on theory and light on empirical data. There is a reason for this. Despite the tremendous importance of kinship from an evolutionary perspective, the topic has been almost entirely ignored by psychologists (Daly, Salmon, & Wilson, 1997). One reason is that kin are far more difficult to study than strangers, who are readily available in introductory psychology subject pools. Second, in the modern urban context we often live apart from extended kin. People typically grow up in relatively isolated nuclear families and then move away to go to college or live in other towns or cities where typically no kin are present. Third, favoritism toward kin may be so obvious and so common that researchers do not deem it a topic worthy of groundbreaking discoveries. No scientist would make headlines with a publication announcing that research discovers that people help family members more than strangers. A fourth and more speculative reason might be that nepotism (the favoring of relatives) is somewhat embarrassing to people in modern Western societies (Hamilton, 1987) because it appears to contradict the ideals of democracy and egalitarianism. Perhaps for all these reasons, the study of psychological mechanisms surrounding kinship has a relatively impoverished empirical base. But what evidence exists is exciting and points to a rich vein for future exploration.

Theory and Implications of Inclusive Fitness

In this section we first introduce Hamilton's rule—the technical formulation of inclusive fitness theory. From this perspective we will see that the favoritism that parents show their own children can be viewed as a special case of favoritism toward the "vehicles" that contain copies of their genes. We will then explore the profound consequences of this formulation for topics such as cooperation, conflict, risk taking, and grieving.

Hamilton's Rule

According to the theory of inclusive fitness, the ultimate evolutionary fate of a heritable trait is the impact it has on the inclusive fitness of the individuals who carry it. Inclusive fitness is the

> sum of the trait's effects, by any and all causal chains, on the survival and reproduction of the focal individual (its "direct" fitness effects . . .) plus whatever effects it may have on the survival and reproduction of the focal individual's relatives, weighted by the closeness of the relationship ("indirect" fitness effects). (Daly & Wilson, 1997, p. 267)

To understand this formulation of inclusive fitness, imagine a gene that causes an individual to behave altruistically toward another person. Altruism, as used here, is defined by two conditions: (1) incurring a cost to the self to (2) provide a benefit to the other person. The question that Hamilton posed was: Under what conditions would such an altruistic gene evolve and spread throughout the population? Under most conditions, we would expect that altruism would *not* evolve. Incurring costs to the self will hinder personal reproduction, so selection will generally operate against incurring costs for other people, many of whom are competitors. Hamilton's insight, however, was that such altruism could indeed evolve if the costs to the self were outweighed by the benefit to the recipient of the altruism, multiplied by the probability that the recipient carried a copy of that gene for altruism. Hamilton's rule, stated more formally, is that natural selection favors mechanisms for altruism when

$$c < rb$$

In this formula c is the cost to the actor, r is the degree of genetic relatedness between actor and recipient, and b is the benefit to the recipient. Both costs and benefits are measured in reproductive currencies.

This formula means that selection will favor an individual to incur costs (being "altruistic") if the benefits to a .50 kin member are more than twice the costs to the actor; if the benefits to a .25 kin member are more than four times the costs to the actor; or if the benefits to a .125 kin member are more than eight times the costs to the actor. An example will illustrate this point. Imagine you pass by a river and notice that some of your genetic relatives are drowning in a ferocious current. You could jump in the water to save them, but you would pay with your own life. According to Hamilton's rule, selection will favor decision rules that, on average, result in your jumping into the water to save three of your brothers, but not one. The reason is this: By saving three brothers you lose your own life (a loss of 1.0), but the benefit is a gain of 1.5 in genetic currencies, since each brother carries .50 of your genes. You would be predicted not to sacrifice your own life for just one brother, because that would violate Hamilton's rule—you would lose your own life (1.0), but only gain .50. Using the logic of Hamilton's rule, evolved decision rules should lead you to sacrifice your own life for five nieces or nephews (the 1.25 gain outweighs the 1.0 loss), but you would have to save nine first cousins before you would sacrifice your own life.

The key point to remember is not that people's behavior will necessarily conform to the logic of inclusive fitness. Instead, the key is that Hamilton's rule defines the conditions under which aid to kin can evolve. It defines the selection pressure to which genes for altruism—indeed any genes—are subject. Any traits that happen to enter the population through mutation and violate Hamilton's rule will be ruthlessly selected against. Only those genes that code for traits that fulfill Hamilton's rule can spread throughout the population and hence evolve to become part of the species-typical repertoire. This is sometimes called an *evolvability constraint* because only genes that meet the conditions of Hamilton's rule can evolve.

Hamilton's theory of inclusive fitness is the single most important theoretical revision of Darwin's theory of natural selection in this century. Before this theory, acts of altruism were genuinely puzzling from an evolutionary perspective because they appeared to go against the actor's personal fitness. Why might a ground squirrel give an alarm call when encountering a predator, thus making that squirrel vulnerable to the predator? Why would a woman sacrifice a kidney so her brother might live? Hamilton's formulation of inclusive fitness solved all these puzzles in one bold stroke and showed how altruistic behavior far removed from personal reproduction could easily evolve.

Theoretical Implications of Hamilton's Rule

At the most general level, the most important implication of Hamilton's theory of inclusive fitness is that psychological adaptations are expected to have evolved for each particular type of kin relationship. Nothing in Hamilton's theory *requires* that such kinship mechanisms necessarily evolve—after all, in some species members don't even live with their kin, so selection could not fashion specific kin mechanisms. But the theory yields predictions about the general form of such kin mechanisms, if they do evolve. In the previous chapter we saw that there were many specific "problems of parenting," and we reviewed evidence for the evolution of parental mechanisms including the differential favoring of children according to qualities such as the probability of being the child's parent and the reproductive value of the child. The theory of inclusive fitness renders parenting as a special case of kinship, albeit an extremely important special case, because parenting represents just one way of investing in "vehicles" that contain copies of one's genes. Other specific relationships that would have recurred throughout human evolutionary history include sibships, half sibships, grandparenthood, grandchildhood, and so on. Let's consider a few of these to get a sense of the sorts of adaptive problems these kin relationships would have posed.

Sibships.   Brothers and sisters impose unique adaptive problems, and have done so recurrently throughout human evolutionary history. First, a brother or a sister may be a major social ally—after all, your siblings are related to you by 50 percent. But sibs, perhaps more than all other relatives, are also major competitors for parental resources. As we saw in the last chapter, parents have evolved to favor some children over others. As the theory of parent–offspring conflict suggests, what is in the best interests of the parents is not the same as what is in the best interests of a particular child. One consequence is that children historically faced the recurrent adaptive problem of competing with each other for access to parental resources. Given this conflict, it is not surprising that sibling relationships are often riddled with ambivalence (Daly & Wilson, 1997, p. 275).

In an intriguing analysis (Sulloway, 1996) it has been proposed that the adaptive problems imposed by parents on children will create different "niches" for children, depending on their birth order. Specifically, because parents often favor the oldest child, the first born tends to be relatively more conservative and more likely to support the status quo. Second borns, however, have little to gain by supporting the existing structure and everything to gain by rebelling against it. Later borns, and especially middle borns, according to Sulloway, develop a more rebellious personality because they have the least to gain by maintaining the existing order. The youngest, on the other hand, may receive more parental investment than middle children, as parents often let out all the stops to invest in their final direct reproductive vehicle.

The evolutionary psychologist Catherine Salmon (1997) has found some support for these speculations. She discovered that middle borns differ from first and last borns in scoring lower on measures of family solidarity and identity. Middle borns, for example, are less likely to name a genetic relative as the person to whom they feel closest. They are also less likely to assume the role of family genealogist. Clearly, more research is needed on the intriguing effects of birth order on the psychology of kinship solidarity.

Sibs versus Half Sibs.   Another aspect of kinship that is theoretically critical is whether a sib is a full or a half sib. Given a common mother, for example, do you and your sibling share a father? This distinction is theoretically important because full sibs are genetically related by 50 percent on average, whereas half sibs are genetically related by only 25 percent on average. In an intriguing study of ground squirrels, Warren Holmes and Paul Sherman (1982) discovered that full sisters were far more likely than half sisters to cooperate in the mutual defense of their young.

Do humans make similar distinctions? We don't know because no one has examined this issue. However, there are good reasons to believe that the distinction between full and half sibs was a recurrent selection pressure over the course of human evolutionary history. Studies of contemporary tribal societies indicate that mothers do commonly have children by different men, sometimes as result of extramarital affairs and sometimes as a result of serial marriages (Hill & Hurtado, 1996). Daly and Wilson (1997) speculate that it "could well be the case that in human prehistory it was a virtual toss-up whether successive children of the same woman were full or half-siblings, and the distinction between ($r = .5$) and ($r = .25$) is by no means trivial when the decision to cooperate or to compete is a close call" (Daly & Wilson, 1997, p. 277). The conflicts that emerge in stepfamilies containing sibs of different degrees of genetic relatedness would be an ideal context for testing these speculations.

Grandparents and Grandchildren.   Grandparents are related to their grandchildren by an r of .25. The fact that modern women often live well beyond menopause has led to the hypothesis that menopause itself evolved as a means of ceasing direct reproduction to invest in children and then grandchildren, in what has become known as the "grandmother hypothesis" (Hill & Hurtado, 1991). Across cultures, postmenopausal women do contribute substantially to the welfare of their grandchildren (Lancaster & King, 1985). It is reasonable to believe, therefore, that grandparenting has been a recurrent feature of human evolutionary history, so specific psychological mechanisms designed to allocate grandparents' investment may have evolved. As we will see later in this chapter, there is solid evidence for this hypothesis.

Hypotheses about Universal Aspects of Kinship.   Daly, Salmon, and Wilson (1997) outline a set of hypotheses about the universal aspects of the psychology of kinship. First, they suggest that ego-centered kin terminology will be universal. That is, in all societies, all kin will be classified in reference to a focal individual. My parents are not the same people as your parents. My brothers are not the same as your brothers. All kin terms, in short, flow from the ego-centered focal individual.

Second, all kinship systems will make critical distinctions along the lines of sex and generation. Mothers are distinguished from fathers, sisters are distinguished from brothers. This sex discrimination is presumed to occur because the sex of a kin member has a host of reproductive implications. Mothers, for example, have 100 percent certainty in their genetic overlap with children, whereas fathers do not. Sons may become wildly reproductively successful through multiple matings, whereas daughters cannot. The sex of the kin member, in short, is pivotal to the adaptive problems he or she faces, so all kin systems should make discriminations according to sex.

Third, generation is also critical. As we saw in Chapter 7, the relationship between parents and children is often asymmetrical. With advancing age, for example, children become increasingly valuable vehicles for their parents, whereas parents become less and less useful to their children. Therefore, we expect that all kin systems will make distinctions according to generation.

Fourth, kin relations will be universally arrayed on a dimension of "closeness," and closeness will be highly linked with genetic overlap. The emotional (feeling close to someone) and cultural recognitions of "closeness," in short, are predicted to correspond to genetic closeness. This prediction obviously does not require that people be aware of genes, reproduction, or genetic relatedness.

Fifth, the degree of cooperation and solidarity between kin will be a function of their degree of genetic overlap. Close kin will rush to one's aid in times of need, for example, far more readily than will distant kin. Furthermore, imbalances in reciprocity, such as when you give food or gifts with no expectation of return, will be considered acceptable when they occur between close kin, but increasingly unacceptable as the degree of genetic relatedness decreases, and will be least acceptable when there is no genetic relatedness, for example between friends. In sum, cooperation and conflict should be predictable from the degree of genetic relatedness between kin members; people are predicted to turn to close kin rather than distant kin when it really matters; and whatever conflicts of interest exist, they will be mitigated more among close kin than among distant kin.

A sixth implication of inclusive fitness theory is that the elder members of an extended kin family will encourage or pressure the younger members to behave more altruistically and cooperatively toward collateral kin (i.e., kin who are not direct descendants, such as one's brothers, sisters, cousins, nephews, and nieces) than is their natural inclination. Imagine an older man who has a son, a sister, and the sister's son as relatives. From this older man's perspective, his sister's son (his nephew) is genetically related to him by .25, and so constitutes an important fitness vehicle for him. But from his own son's perspective, this person is merely a cousin, and so is only related by him by .125. From his perspective, any sacrifice he makes for his cousin would have to yield eight times the cost, according to Hamilton's rule ($c < rb$). Thus, any act of helping by the older man's son toward his sister's son (the boy's cousin) will be more beneficial to the fitness of the older man than to his son. In sum, a powerful and interesting implication of inclusive fitness theory is that older members of a kin family will encourage younger members to help their cousins and other kin more than they are naturally inclined to do, if they were acting in their own best interest. This is an example of a conflict of interest that may contribute to a "generation gap."

A seventh implication of inclusive fitness theory is that one's position within an extended kin network—one's genealogical links—will be core components of the self-concept. Your beliefs about "who you are" will include kin linkages, such as "son of X," "daughter of Y," or "mother of Z." This is a directly testable proposition that has profound psychological implications for the self-concept (Salmon & Daly, 1996).

An eighth implication of inclusive fitness theory is that despite differences across cultures in the exact kin terms that are employed and their putative meanings, people everywhere will be aware who their "real" relatives are. Consider the Yanomamö Indians of Venezuela. They use the kin term *abawa* to refer to both brothers and cousins. In English, however, we have different words, *brothers* and *cousins*. Does this terminological conflation among the Yanomamö obscure their real kin relationships? Anthropologist Napoleon Chagnon examined this issue by interviewing Yanomamö and showing them photographs of what English speakers would call their brothers and cousins. Although the Yanomamö said "*abawa*" in looking at both of the photographs, when asked "which one is your real *abawa*?" each invariably pointed to his actual blood brother and not to his cousin (Chagnon, 1981; Chagnon & Bugos, 1979). Furthermore, a "real *abawa*" is far more likely to come to a Yanomamö villager's aid in a social conflict. In short, although kin terms differ somewhat from culture to culture, and some appear to blend or conflate different kinship categories, inclusive fitness theory suggests that people everywhere will be keenly aware who are their real kin.

A final implication of inclusive fitness theory is that kinship terms will be used to persuade and influence other people, even when no actual kinship is involved. Consider the panhandler's request: "Hey, brother, can you spare some change?" Precisely why does the panhandler frame the request in this manner? One hypothesis is that he or she is using the kin term "brother" to activate the psychology of kinship in the target. Because we would be more likely to help a brother than a total stranger, the use of the term "brother" may in some small way trigger the psychology of kinship, and hence increase the odds of our actually giving spare change. Similar forms of kin term usage are heard in college fraternities and sororities, where members refer to each other as "brothers" and "sisters." Feminist slogans that invoke "sisterhood" may have similar intents at increasing alliances among women who are not genetic kin. In sum, the invocation of kinship through language is a predicted strategic implication of inclusive fitness theory—a hypothesis that is easily amenable to empirical testing.

Empirical Findings That Support the Implications of Inclusive Fitness Theory

The psychology of kinship has been relatively ignored in scientific literature. There is less research to report, despite the heavy theoretical implications of inclusive fitness theory. Several promising avenues of research have been explored in humans and other animals, however, and suggest that this will be a rich vein for the discovery of evolved psychological mechanisms. In this section we highlight the most important of these empirical investigations.

Alarm Calling in Ground Squirrels

When Belding's ground squirrels detect a terrestrial predator, such as a badger or a coyote, they sometimes emit a high-pitched staccato whistle that functions as an alarm call alerting other ground squirrels in the immediate vicinity to danger. The alerted squirrels then scramble to safety and avoid being picked off by the predator. The alerted squirrels clearly benefit from the alarm call because it increases their odds of survival, but the alarm caller suffers. The whistle makes the alarm caller more easily detectable, and predators are more likely to hone in on the alarm caller for their meal. How can we account for this puzzling finding, which seems so contrary to individual survival?

Several hypotheses have been advanced to explain this apparent act of altruism (Alcock, 1993):

1. *The predator confusion hypothesis:* The alarm call may function to confuse the predator by creating a mad scramble, in which all the ground squirrels rush around for safety. This confusion may help the squirrels, including the alarm caller, to escape.

2. *The predator deterrence hypothesis:* Although we might think that giving the alarm call draws attention to the caller, perhaps it functions instead to deter predators. Once they are detected, perhaps predators give up the hunt, knowing that their odds are better when they can strike undetected. According to this hypothesis, the alarm call functions to increase the survival of the alarm caller.

3. *The reciprocal altruism hypothesis:* The alarm caller may put itself at risk by whistling, but perhaps he or she will benefit subsequently when friends in the group reciprocate at a later date by alarm calling. This hypothesis requires that relationships be somewhat stable, and that ground squirrels remember who did and did not help them in the past, reciprocating only with those who did.

4. *The parental investment hypothesis:* Although the alarm caller is placed at greater risk by sounding the signal, perhaps its children are more likely to survive as a result. In this way the alarm call may function as a form of parental investment.

5. *Inclusive fitness hypothesis:* Although the signaler might suffer in the currency of survival, the squirrel's aunts, uncles, brothers, sisters, fathers, mothers, and cousins all benefit. According to this hypothesis, the signal alerts the "vehicles" that contain copies of the squirrel's genes—providing an inclusive fitness benefit.

To test these hypotheses, biologist Paul Sherman spent many summers in the California woods painstakingly marking, tracking, and studying an entire colony of Belding's ground squirrels (Sherman, 1977, 1981). The results are fascinating. Sherman was able to rule out the first two hypotheses rather quickly. Sounding the alarm indeed puts the signaler at great risk because predators (including weasels, badgers, and coyotes) were observed stalking and killing alarm callers at a far higher rate than noncalling squirrels in the vicinity. So predators are not confused by the alarm call (hypothesis 1); instead, they hone in on the alarm caller directly. Further, predators are not deterred from the hunt (hypothesis 2).

Sherman's second finding was that alarm calling is not at all linked with the length of the relationship a squirrel has had with others in the vicinity, nor with the familiarity between the alarm callers and the squirrels that benefit from the alarm call. This appears to rule out hypothesis 3, which states that reciprocal altruism is the primary function of alarm calls. Stable, long-term alliances are typically required for the evolution of this sort of reciprocity (Axelrod, 1984; Axelrod & Hamilton, 1981).

This leaves us with only two hypotheses—the parental investment hypothesis and the inclusive fitness hypothesis. When male Belding's ground squirrels mature, they leave home and join nonrelated groups. Females, on the other hand, remain with their natal group, and so are surrounded by aunts, nieces, sisters, daughters, and other female relatives. It turns out that females give alarm calls far more often than males—approximately 21 percent more often. This finding, taken alone, is consistent with both the parental investment hypothesis and the inclusive fitness hypothesis because both daughters and other genetic relatives of the alarm caller benefit from the signal.

The critical test comes with female ground squirrels who do not have daughters or other children around but do have other genetic relatives in the vicinity. Do they still emit the alarm calls when they spot a predator? The answer is yes. Females without their own children still sound the alarm, as long as they have sisters, nieces, and aunts in the area. In sum, although parental investment is likely to be one function of the alarm calls, the inclusive fitness hypothesis is also strongly supported because females sound the alarm even when they do not have offspring of their own. Sherman found further support for the inclusive fitness hypothesis in his discovery that female ground squirrels will rush to the aid of genetic relatives—their sisters as well as their daughters—to assist them in territorial conflicts with invaders, but will not help nonrelatives in such conflicts (Holmes & Sherman, 1982). Taken together, these findings support the idea that altruism can evolve through the process of inclusive fitness.

Ground squirrels are one species; humans are another. Can we assume that inclusive fitness likewise predicts altruism among humans?

Patterns of Helping in the Lives of Los Angeles Women

In one early test of inclusive fitness theory applied to humans, two researchers intensively studied a sample of three hundred adult women from Los Angeles ages thirty-five to forty-five. The following are reasons given by these women for receiving help:

> When I needed money to get into the union; When I broke my collarbone and he took over the house; Talking to a friend about her marital problems; picking up a friend's kids the whole time she was sick; When my son was in trouble with the police; She kept the children when my third child was born; When her husband left her; When she had a leg amputated; Loaned us money for a house down-payment. (Essock-Vitale & McGuire, 1985, p. 141)

The women described 2,520 instances of receiving help and 2,651 instances of giving help. Among the predictions in this study were two that are most relevant here: (1) among kin, helping will increase as a function of genetic relatedness; and (2) among kin, helping will increase as the recipient's reproductive value increases.

Figure 8.1 shows the percentage of instances of helping falling into three different categories of kinship—50 percent genetic overlap, 25 percent genetic overlap, and less than 25 percent genetic overlap (e.g., first cousin). As predicted, helping exchanges were

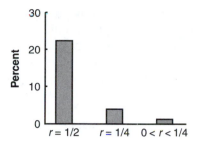

FIGURE 8.1   Percentage of Major Helping by Closeness of Kinship. r = coefficient of relationship (e.g., r of 1/2 = parents, full siblings, children; r of 1/4 = half-siblings, grandparents, aunts, uncles, grandchildren, nieces, nephews; r greater than zero but less than 1/4 = cousins, children of half-siblings, etc.). More acts of helping are directed toward close genetic relatives than toward distant genetic relatives.

Source: Reprinted from *Ethology and Sociobiology, 6,* S. M. Essock-Vitale & M. T. McGuire, Women's lives viewed from an evolutionary perspective. II. Patterns of helping, 143, copyright © 1985, with permission from Elsevier Science.

more likely to occur with close kin than with distant kin, supporting a key prediction from inclusive fitness theory. It is important to note, however, that the total percentage of instances of helping involving kin was only about a third. Many acts of helping were received from, and directed toward, close friends—a topic we will consider in Chapter 9.

The second prediction was that helping among kin will be preferentially channeled to those of higher reproductive potential, a prediction that was also supported. Women were far more likely to help their children, nieces, and nephews than vice versa. Acts of helping apparently flow from the older to the younger, perhaps reflecting the greater future reproductive potential of the younger recipients.

These findings are limited in a variety of ways. They are restricted to one sex (women), one city (Los Angeles), and one method of information gathering (questionnaire). As we will see below, however, kinship exerts a powerful effect on helping when the sample is extended to men, to different populations, and to different methodologies.

Life or Death Helping among Humans

Evolutionary thinking strongly suggests that acts of helping and altruism will be nonrandomly distributed, and that degree of genetic relatedness will be one of the most important determinants of who one helps. Genetic relatives are the vehicles for our fitness, and the closer the relative, the more beneficial an act of help will be to our fitness. We don't think about this, of course, when we help others. Rather, this describes the selection pressures over human evolutionary history that would likely have forged psychological mechanisms or decision rules that lead us to aid close relatives more than distant ones.

One study explored a set of hypotheses derived from inclusive fitness theory to determine these decision rules (Burnstein, Crandall, & Kitayama, 1994). Specifically, the researchers hypothesized that helping others will be a direct function of the recipient's ability to enhance the inclusive fitness of the helper. Helping should decrease linearly, they reasoned, as the degree of genetic relatedness between helper and recipient decreases. Thus helping is predicted to be greater among siblings (who are genetically related by 50 percent on average) than between a person and his or her sibling's children (who are genetically related by 25 percent on average). Helping is expected to be lower still between individuals who are genetically related by only 12.5 percent, such as first cousins. No other theory in psychology predicts this precise helping gradient or specifies kinship as an underlying principle for the distribution of acts of altruism.

Genetic relatedness is important, but it is not the only theoretical consideration that is predicted to affect the decision rules surrounding altruism. Helping should decrease as a function of the age of the recipient, all else being equal, since helping an older relative will have less impact on one's fitness than helping a younger relative because the latter are more likely to produce offspring that carry some of the same genes. In addition to age, genetic relatives higher in reproductive value and those who offer a better return on one's "investment" should be helped more than those of lower reproductive value and those who offer a lower return. Again, no other theory in psychology generates these precise predictions.

In a series of studies (Burnstein et al., 1994) to test these hypotheses, an important distinction was made between two types of helping: (1) helping that is substantial, such as acts that affect whether the recipient will live or die, and (2) helping that is relatively trivial, such as giving a homeless person a little spare change. The predicted patterns of altruism should be stronger under the first type and less so under the second.

To test these hypotheses Burnstein and his colleagues studied two different cultures, America and Japan. Participants were asked questions about what they would do in a scenario in which a house was rapidly burning and they had only enough time to rescue one of the three people in the house. The researchers stressed that only the person who received help would survive—all others would perish. In the less significant form of everyday helping, subjects evaluated scenarios in which they had to indicate which persons they would help by picking up a few small items from a store. As in the more serious burning house scenario, the subject could help only one person. Recipients of the help varied in degree of genetic relatedness to the helper.

Helping in these hypothetical scenarios decreased steadily as the degree of genetic relatedness decreased. The .50 sibling was helped more than the .25 relatives, who in turn were helped more than those with only .125 genetic relatedness. This result proved especially strong in the life-or-death scenario.

Helping in the life-or-death situation also declined steadily as the potential recipient's age increased. One-year-olds were helped more than ten-year-olds, who in turn were helped more than eighteen-year-olds. Least helped were the seventy-five-year-olds. Interestingly, the effects of age on helping were strongest in the life-or-death situation, but actually reversed in the trivial helping condition. For everyday helping such as running an errand, the seventy-five-year-olds were helped somewhat more than the forty-five-year-olds (see Figure 8.2). These findings replicated well across both Japanese and American samples, thus providing some degree of cross-cultural evidence that the effects are not limited to Western cultures.

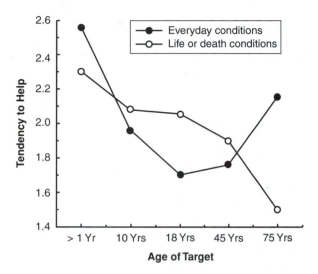

FIGURE 8.2   Tendency to Help as a Function of Recipient's Age under Life-or-Death versus Everyday Conditions.

Source: Some neo-Darwinian decision rules for altruism: Weighing cues for inclusive fitness as a function of the biological importance of the decision by E. Burnstein, C. Crandall, & S. Kitayama, *Journal of Personality and Social Psychology, 67* (1994), 779. Copyright © 1994 by the American Psychological Association. Reprinted with permission.

In sum, Burnstein and his colleagues have documented that helping, when it really matters, increases as a function of genetic relatedness between helper and recipient, and also generally increases as a function of the reproductive value of the relative, as indicated by youthfulness. The one finding that does not accord with the predictions, however, is that one-year-olds are helped more than ten-year-olds, despite the fact that the older children are higher in reproductive value. Further research is needed to clarify this puzzling result. Overall, these findings suggest that selection pressure imposed by inclusive fitness has sculpted human psychological mechanisms that exist in each of us and are designed to make personal sacrifices for those who carry copies of our genes.

Patterns of Inheritance— Who Leaves Wealth to Whom?

Another domain in which to test the theory of inclusive fitness pertains to the inheritance of wealth. When a person writes a will describing who will receive his or her wealth after he or she dies, can the pattern of distribution be predicted from inclusive fitness theory? Do people leave more money to close kin than to distant kin?

Informed by inclusive fitness theory, psychologists Martin Smith, Bradley Kish, and Charles Crawford (1987) tested three predictions about patterns of inheritance based on hypotheses about the evolved psychological mechanisms underlying resource allocation. (1) People will leave more of their estates to genetically related kin and spouses than to unrelated people. The inclusion of spouses in the prediction occurs not because of genetic relatedness, but rather because presumably the spouse will distribute the resources to their mutual children and grandchildren. (2) People will leave more of their estates to close kin than to distantly related kin. (3) People will leave more of their estates to offspring than to siblings, even though the average genetic relatedness is the same in these two types of relationships. The rationale for this prediction is that one's offspring, generally being younger than one's siblings, will on average have higher reproductive value. At the time in the lifespan when wills are typically written or go into effect, siblings are likely to be past their childbearing years, whereas children are more likely to be able to convert resources into future offspring.

To test these predictions, researchers studied the bequests of 1000 randomly selected decedents, 552 men and 448 women, from the Vancouver region of British Columbia, Canada. Only those who left wills were included in the sample (some people do die intestate, or without a will). The researchers recorded the total dollar value of each estate, as well as the percentage of the estate willed to each beneficiary. Beneficiaries were categorized according to their genetic relatedness to the decedent, such as son, daughter, brother, sister, grandson, niece, or cousin. The two categories of nongenetic relationship were spouse and nonfamily. The last category included organizations.

The average estate was $54,000 for men and $51,200 for women. Interestingly, women tended to distribute their estates to a larger number of beneficiaries (2.8) than did men (2.0). Table 8.1 shows the average proportion of the estates bequeathed to each of the different categories of beneficiary.

The first prediction was soundly confirmed. People left only 7.7 percent of their estates, on average, to nonrelatives, and 92.3 percent to spouses or kin. The second prediction was also confirmed. Decedents willed more of their estates to closely related genetic kin than to more distant genetic relatives. Considering only the amount left to kin (excluding the categories of spouse and nonkin), people left 46 percent of their estates to relatives sharing 50 percent of their genes, 8 percent to relatives sharing 25 percent of their genes, and less than 1 percent to relatives sharing only 12.5 percent of their genes. These data support the hypothesis that inclusive fitness has fashioned psychological mechanisms of resource allocation that involve favoring individuals to the degree that they are genetically related.

The third prediction—that people would bequeath more to offspring than to siblings—also was confirmed. Indeed, people left more than four times as much to their children (38.6 percent of the total estate) than to their siblings (7.9 percent of the estate).

In a more recent analysis of wills, Debra Judge (1995) discovered that the finding that women tend to distribute their estates among a larger number of beneficiaries was quite replicable. In particular, a majority of men tended to leave their entire estates to their wives, often with expressed confidence that the wife would pass along the resources to their children. Here are a few examples of the reasons men included in their wills for channeling all of their resources to their wives:

> "... knowing her [wife] to be trustworthy and that she will provide for my boys ... their education and a start in life"

TABLE 8.1   Proportion of Estate Bequeathed to Beneficiary.

Beneficiary Category	Percentage Bequeathed ($\bar{x}$)		
Spouse	36.9		
Kin (excluding spouse)	55.3		
$r = 0.50$ kin		46.5	
Offspring		38.6	
Sons			19.2
Daughters			19.4
Siblings		7.9	
Brothers			3.2
Sisters			4.8
$r = 0.25$ kin		8.3	
Nephews and Nieces		5.1	
Nephews			2.3
Nieces			2.8
Grandchildren		3.2	
Grandsons			1.8
Granddaughters			1.4
$r = 0.125$ kin			
Cousins		0.6	
Male Cousins			0.3
Female Cousins			0.3
Nonkin	7.7		
Total	100[a]		

[a]Rounding error accounts for the discrepancy between tabled values and total.

Source: Reprinted from *Ethology and Sociobiology, 8*, M. S. Smith, B. J. Kish, & C. B. Crawford, Inheritance of wealth as human kin investmant, 175, copyright © 1987, with permission from Elsevier Science.

> "*. . . no provision for my children . . . for the reason that I know she [wife] will make adequate provision for them*"
> "*. . . [wife] can handle the estate to better advantage if the same be left wholly to her and . . . [have] confidence she will provide for her said children as I would have done.*" (Judge, 1995, p. 306)

In sharp contrast to men who commonly expressed confidence and trust in their wives' ability to allocate resources, women who were married when they died did not express such trust. Indeed, when a husband was mentioned at all, it was often with a qualification. For example, six women intentionally excluded their husbands from their wills because they were abandoned by them, or "for reasons sufficient [or "best known"] to me," or because of statements about the husband's "misconduct." In one case a woman left her entire estate to her husband "as long as he lives unmarried" (Judge, 1995, p. 307).

It is difficult to draw direct inferences from this pattern of findings and quotations, but one speculation may be in order. It is known that older men are far more likely than older women to remarry (Buss, 1994). Therefore, widowers may use their previous wife's resources to attract a new mate and perhaps even start a new family. If this is the case resources will be diverted from the original wife's children and other kin to unrelated individuals. In contrast, because older women are unlikely to marry and even more unlikely to have additional children (most will be postmenopausal), the husband can be more confident that his widow will allocate the resources toward their mutual children. If this speculation is correct, it suggests that the psychology of human mating exerts a far-ranging influence on human behavior, to the point of creating a sex difference in the "trust" and "confidence" in the remaining spouse, causing women to allocate fewer of their resources to their husbands than vice versa.

In summary, all three predictions received empirical support from this study. Genetic relatives are bequeathed more than nonrelatives. Close kin receive more than distant kin. Direct descendants, primarily children, receive more than collateral kin such as sisters and brothers.

Given the fact that formal wills are relatively recent inventions, how can we interpret these findings? It is certainly not necessary to postulate a specific "will-making mechanism," since wills are presumably too recent to have constituted a recurrent feature of our environment of evolutionary adaptedness. The most reasonable interpretation is that humans have evolved psychological mechanisms of resource allocation; that genetic relatedness is a pivotal factor in the decision rules of resource allocation; and that these evolved mechanisms operate on a relatively recent type of resources, those accumulated during one's life in the form of tangible assets that can be distributed at will. More generally, these findings lend further empirical support to the theory that inclusive fitness imposes selection pressure on the process that has sculpted human psychological mechanisms.

Investment by Grandparents

The past century has witnessed the gradual disappearance of the extended family, as increased mobility has spread family members to different corners of countries. Despite this departure from the extended kin contexts in which humans evolved, the relationship between grandparents and grandchildren appears to have retained a place of importance (Euler & Weitzel, 1996).

Because today's Western media place a premium on youth, one might think that becoming a grandparent would be marked by great sorrow, a signal of old age and impending death. In fact, precisely the opposite is true. The arrival of grandchildren heralds a time of pride, joy, and deep fulfillment (Fisher, 1983). We have all experienced our elders proudly showing off photographs and memorabilia from the lives of their grandchildren, or had to endure long-winded tales of the grandchildren's exploits and accomplishments.

In humans, grandparents often invest in their grandchildren, and show relationships marked by warmth, frequent contact, and devotion. Specific patterns of grandparental investment are predictable from theories of paternity uncertainty developed by DeKay (1995) and Euler & Weitzel (1996).

There is tremendous variability, however, in how close to or distant from their grandparents grandchildren are. With some the emotional bond is marked by warm feelings, frequent contact, and heavy investment of resources. With others the feelings are distant, contact infrequent, and investment of resources rare. Recently evolutionary psychologists have turned to explaining this variability in grandparental investment—a prime locus for evolved psychological mechanisms because grandchildren represent the crucial vehicles by which their genes are transported into the future.

Theoretically, grandparents are genetically related .25 with each grandchild. So on what basis could we generate predictions about differences in grandparents' investment? Recall the profound sex difference that has cropped up several times—men face the adaptive problem of paternity uncertainty, whereas women are 100 percent certain of their maternity. This applies to grandparents as well as to parents, but here there is a special twist on the theory: We are dealing with two generations of descendants, so from a grandfather's perspective, there are two opportunities for genetic kinship to be severed (DeKay, 1995). First, it is possible he is not the genetic father of his son or daughter. Second, his son might not be the father of his putative grandchildren. This double whammy makes the blood relationships between a grandfather and his son's children the most genetically uncertain of all grandparental relationships.

At the other end of the certainty continuum are women whose daughters have children. In this case, the grandmother is 100 percent certain that her genes are carried by her grandchildren (keep in mind that none of this need be conscious). She is undoubtedly the mother of her daughter, and her daughter is certain of her genetic contribution to her children. In sum, the theoretical prediction from the inclusive fitness theory is clear: From the grandchild's perspective, the mother's mother (MoMo) should invest the most, and the father's father (FaFa) should invest the least, all else being equal.

What about the other two types of grandparents—the mother's father (MoFa) and the father's mother (FaMo)? For each of these cases there was one place in the line of descent where relatedness could be severed. A man whose daughter has a child may not be the actual father of his daughter. A woman with a son may not be related to her son's children, if the son is cuckolded—that is, if the son's wife was inseminated by another man. The investment of these two types of grandparents, therefore, is predicted to be intermediate between the most certain genetic linkage (MoMo) and the least certain genetic linkage (FaFa).

The investment a person makes in grandchildren can take many forms, both behavioral and psychological. Behaviorally one could examine frequency of contact, actual investment of resources, readiness to adopt, or the willing of property. Psychologically one could examine expressed feelings of closeness, magnitude of mourning on the death of a grandchild, and willingness to make sacrifices of various sorts. The hypothesis of "discriminative grandparental investment" predicts that behavioral and psychological indicators on investment should follow the degree of certainty inherent in the different types of grandparental relationships—most for MoMo, least for FaFa, and somewhere in between these two for MoFa and FaMo.

Two separate studies from two different cultures have tested the hypothesis of discriminative grandparental solicitude. In one study conducted in America, evolutionary psychologist Todd DeKay (1995) studied a sample of 120 undergraduates. Each student completed a questionnaire that included information on biographical background and then evaluated each of their four grandparents on the following dimensions: grandparent's physical similarity to self, personality similarity to self, time spent with grandparent while growing up, knowledge acquired from grandparent, gifts received from grandparent, and emotional closeness to grandparent. Figure 8.3 summarizes the results from this study.

The left panel shows the rankings of subjects' emotional closeness to each of their grandparents. Participants indicated the most emotional closeness to their mother's mother and the least emotional closeness to their father's father. A similar pattern emerged for the variables of time spent with the grandparent and the resources (gifts) they received from the grandparent. The sole exception to this perfectly predicted pattern was found with ratings of the knowledge received from the grandparent. Although the least knowledge was gained from the father's father, as predicted, the mother's father and mother's mother were tied for the lead for most knowledge received.

Another interesting pattern emerged for the two grandparents of intermediate relational uncertainty. In each case, for all four variables, the mother's father was ranked higher than the father's mother. How can this pattern be explained, since in each case there is one opportunity for the genetic link to be severed? DeKay (1995) had actually predicted this finding in advance by suggesting that infidelity rates were higher in the younger generation than in the older generation—a suggestion that has some empirical support (Lauman, Gagnon, Michael, & Michaels, 1994). Thus, the relational uncertainty would be higher for the father's mother, since the father would be in the younger generation, than for the mother's father. If this hypothesis receives further empirical support, it would suggest that grandparents may be sensitive to either prevailing rates of infidelity, or to personal circumstances that might jeopardize the genetic link between them, their children, and their grandchildren.

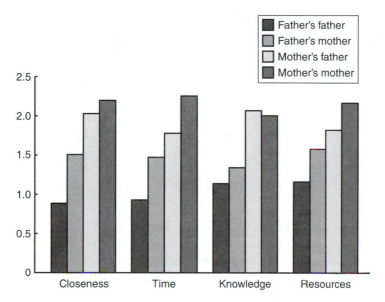

FIGURE 8.3   Grandparental Investment in Grandchildren. Findings show that the mother's mother is closer to, spends more time with, and invests most resources in the grandchild, whereas father's father scores lowest on these dimensions. Findings presumably reflect evolved psychological mechanisms sensitive to the degree of certainty of genetic relatedness.

Source: Grandparental investment and the uncertainty of kinship, by W. T. DeKay, July, 1995, paper presented to Seventh Annual Meeting of the Human Behavior and Evolution Society, Santa Barbara. Reprinted with permission.

A second study of the grandparental investment hypothesis was undertaken by Harald Euler and Barbara Weitzel, who studied a sample of 1,857 participants recruited in Germany (Euler & Weitzel, 1996). Of this sample, 603 cases were selected using the criterion that all four grandparents had to be living at least until the participant reached the age of seven. Subjects were asked how much each grandparent had *gekummert*, a German verb that has both a behavioral and cognitive-emotional meaning. It includes "(1) to take care of, to look after, and (2) to be emotionally and/or cognitively concerned about" (Euler & Weitzel, 1996, p. 55). The results are shown in Table 8.2 on page 240.

The results of the German sample showed precisely the same pattern as the DeKay study of American grandchildren. The maternal grandmother—the relationship showing no relational uncertainty—was viewed as having the most gekummert. The paternal grandfather—the most genetically uncertain of all—was viewed as having the least gekummert. As in the American study, the MoFa showed more investment than the FaMo.

The latter finding is especially interesting because it rules out a potential alternative explanation—that perhaps women in general are more likely to invest than men, a sex difference that might extend to relationships with grandparents. The findings from both studies contradict this alternative. In each study the maternal grandfathers invested more than the paternal grandmothers. In sum, the general expectation of a sex difference in investment cannot account for the fact that grandfathers, at least under some circumstances, invest more than grandmothers.

TABLE 8.2   Grandparent Solicitude. Findings support the hypothesis that greater care is provided by maternal grandmother (most certain of genetic relatedness) than by the paternal grandfather (least certain of genetic relatedness), supporting the idea that paternity uncertainty compounded through the generations affects the psychology of investment.

Grandparent	Parental Certainty	Solicitude		Residential Distance	
		Mean	*SD*	*Mean*	*SD*
Maternal grandmother	+/+	5.16	1.84	3.75	2.26
Maternal grandfather	−/+	4.52	1.98	3.74	2.28
Paternal grandmother	+/−	4.09	2.00	3.83	2.27
Paternal grandfather	−/−	3.70	2.02	3.85	2.32

+ = more care; − = less care

Predictions from Reproductive Strategy and Parental Certainty and Results ($N = 603$); Residential Distance to Grandparent in Logarithmic Kilometers ($N = 207$).

Source: Adapted with permission from: H. A. Euler & B. Weitzel, Discriminative grandparental solicitude as reproductive strategy in *Human Nature* 7:1 (1996) (New York: Aldine de Gruyter) Copyright © 1996 Walter de Gruyter, Inc.

A second possible alternative explanation is that residential distance from the grandparent might account for these findings. To address this Euler and Weitzel evaluated the average residential distance for each of the four types of grandparent relationships in kilometers. As shown in Table 8.2, the mean residential distances for the four types of relationships were virtually identical. Thus this variable cannot account for the findings of differential grandparental investment.

Many questions remain unanswered by this research. How do prevailing rates of infidelity in each generation affect the psychology of grandparents' investment? Do grandparents monitor the likelihood that their sons might be cuckolded and shift their investment accordingly? Do grandparents scrutinize grandchildren for their perceived similarity to them as part of their decision making about investing in those grandchildren?

These questions about the evolutionary psychology of grandparental investment will likely be answered within the next decade. For now we can conclude that findings from two different cultures support the hypothesis that grandparents' investment is sensitive to the varying probability that genetic relatedness might be severed by paternity uncertainty in each generation. (See Box 8.1 on page 241 for a discussion on investment by aunts and uncles.)

Sex Differences in the Importance of Kin Relations

How important are your kin relationships to you? If you are a woman, the odds are that they are quite important. If you are a man, however, the odds are that they are less so. These are the results of a recent pair of studies by two evolutionary psychologists (Salmon & Daly, 1996).

BOX **8.1**

Investment by Aunts and Uncles

According to inclusive fitness theory, selection will favor mechanisms that result in investing in kin as a function of genetic relatedness. Expected relatedness is a function of two factors: (1) genealogical linkage (e.g., sisters are more closely related than uncles and nephews), and (2) paternal certainty caused by extra-pair copulations. In this chapter we have looked at evidence suggesting that as paternal uncertainty increases through the paternal line, investment in grandchildren decreases. Is this effect limited to grandparents' investment, or does the logic extend to other kin relationships, such as aunts and uncles?

According to this logic, maternal aunts (sisters of the mother) should invest more than paternal aunts (sisters of the father). Similarly, maternal uncles (brothers of the mother) should invest more than paternal uncles (brothers of the father). Paternity certainty, and hence genetic relatedness, should be highest on average through the maternal line. Conversely, genetic relatedness should be lowest on average through the paternal line.

To examine this issue, a team of researchers studied 285 American college students, all of

whom reported that both of their biological parents were living (Gaulin, McBurney, & Brakeman-Wartell, 1997). Each participant was asked to rate a series of questions using a seven-point scale: (1) "How much concern does the maternal (paternal) uncle (aunt) show about your welfare?" (2) If you have both a maternal and a paternal uncle (aunt), which one shows more concern about your welfare?" (p. 142). The researchers selected the phrase "concern about your welfare" so participants would think broadly about the various types of benefits they might receive. The results are shown in the table below.

Two main effects are noteworthy. First, there is a main effect for sex—aunts tend to invest more than uncles, regardless of whether they are maternal or paternal. Second, maternal aunts and uncles tend to invest more than paternal aunts and uncles—the predicted laterality effect.

According to the researchers, these two effects are likely to have different causes. They suggest that the sex effects (aunts invest more than uncles) occur because men tend to invest surplus resources into mating opportunities whereas

Concern Rating (and Adjusted Concern Rating) as a Function of Laterality and Sex of Relative. Findings support the hypothesis that maternal aunts invest more than paternal aunts, and maternal uncles invest more than paternal uncles (paternity certainty, and hence genetic relatedness), being highest on average through the maternal line and lowest through the paternal line.

Sex of Relative		Laterality	
		Matrilateral	*Patrilateral*
Aunt	Mean	4.75 (4.71)	3.96 (3.97)
	S.D.	1.84	1.87
Uncle	Mean	3.65 (3.65)	3.28 (3.31)
	S.D.	1.93	1.71

Source: Reprinted with permission from: S. J. C. Gaulin, D. H. McBurney, & S. L. Brademan-Wartell, Matrilateral biases in the investment of aunts and uncles in *Human Nature* 8:2 (1997) (New York: Aldine de Gruyter) Copyright © 1997 Walter de Gruyter, Inc.

(continued)

BOX **8.1** **continued**

women do not. As we saw in the earlier chapters on mating, additional matings historically have paid off more for men than for women in inclusive fitness currencies. Men today presumably carry with them psychological mechanisms that lead them to channel surplus resources into mating, at least more than women do.

The laterality effect, in contrast, has a different explanation, based on the probabilities of paternity uncertainty that occur through the male line. Uncertainty of paternity, and hence a lower likelihood of genetic relatedness, is the best explanation for the evolution of psychological mechanisms that lead to the investment decisions

of aunts and uncles. When paternity certainty is guaranteed, as when you are a sibling of the mother of your niece or nephew, you will invest a lot. When paternity is uncertain, as when you are a sibling of the father of your niece or nephew, you are likely to invest less.

In sum, genetic relatedness, as predicted by inclusive fitness theory, appears to be a major factor in investment in relatives. When genetic relatedness is jeopardized through paternity uncertainty, investment falls off. This effect is robust across different sorts of relationships, including those with aunts, uncles, grandmothers, and grandfathers.

In one study the researchers asked twenty-four adult sibling pairs (one brother and one sister) to reconstruct their kin genealogies as fully as possible using a computerized menu of instructions. Sisters consistently recalled more relatives (an average of 32) than brothers (an average of 27.5), a statistically significant difference. In the sample, twenty women and only two men were able to list more relatives than their opposite sex sibling (in two pairs, the brother and the sister reported an identical number of relatives). This sex difference transcended different categories of kin, whether ascendant (e.g., grandparents, great-grandparents) or collateral genetic relatives that are not in direct line of descent, such as brothers or cousins, whether maternal or paternal.

Can you recall the maiden names of your ascendant kin? If you are a woman, the odds are much better that you can. Whereas 58 percent of the female sample recalled more maiden surnames of their female ascendant kin than did their brothers, not a single brother could recall more of the maiden surnames than his sister (the remainder of the brother–sisters pairs were even in their recall). In sum, women seem to have better recall of kin than do men. This cannot be attributed to a domain-general sex difference in memory because the sexes do not differ overall in their ability to remember things (Salmon & Daly, 1996).

In the second study conducted by Salmon and Daly (1996), three hundred participants (one hundred fifty each of men and women) who were attending a Canadian university completed the "Who Are You" questionnaire: "In the 10 blanks below, please make 10 different statements in response to the question "Who are you?" Write your answers in the order in which they occur to you. Go fairly quickly" (Salmon & Daly, 1996, p. 292).

Although men and women were equally likely to make reference to familial or kinship status (53 percent of women, 51 percent of men), the sexes differed considerably in which aspects of kinship they named. Women were far more likely to mention family roles, especially those labeled with a relationship term. Of those who did use a relationship term, 44 percent of the women described themselves as a "daughter," whereas only 12.5 percent of the men described themselves as a "son." Interestingly, in response to the question about which individual they felt the closest to, both men and women were more likely to name a sister than a brother.

How can we interpret these sex differences in recall and self-description? One explanation is that over the course of human evolutionary history women were more likely to achieve reproductive success through investing in (and receiving investment from) kin members, whereas men were more likely to achieve reproductive success through increased access to potential mates. If this interpretation is correct then we would expect that more of women's cognitive activity would be devoted to thinking about, remembering, and keeping track of kin. According to this interpretation, the above sex differences should be universal across cultures.

Alternatively, these sex differences could be culture specific, reflecting the adaptive problems faced in modern Canadian society or perhaps even Western culture. In these cultures women may be more dependent on kin, whereas men may rely more on nonkin reciprocal relationships such as friendships (Salmon & Daly, 1996). Chagnon (1988), for example, found that among the Yanomamö Indians of Venezuela, men appear to be more skilled than women at classifying kin. The reconstruction of kin lineages among the Yanomamö is apparently critical to men in conforming to rules about who they are permitted to marry.

Only future studies can determine whether the sex differences found by Salmon and Daly (1996) are universal or culture specific. The existing studies, however, suggest the possibility that the sexes may have evolved a somewhat different psychology of kinship, perhaps reflecting the differing nature of adaptive problems men and women have confronted over the long expanse of human evolutionary history, in which kinship was surely a prominent selective force.

A Broader Perspective on the Evolution of the Family

What is a family? Various disciplines define this entity differently, and social scientists have not reached a firm consensus about what constitutes a family (Emlen, 1995). Sociologists often emphasize the childrearing function of the family, defining families as groups of adults living together, bearing the responsibility for producing and raising children. Anthropologists, in contrast, tend to stress kinship, defining families as groups of parents, unmarried children, and sometimes extended kin through which lines of descent can be traced.

Evolutionary biologist Stephen Emlen defines families as "those cases where offspring continue to interact regularly, into adulthood, with their parents" (Emlen, 1995, p. 8092). He distinguishes two types of families: (1) *simple families*, a single parent or conjugal pair in which only one female reproduces (e.g., a mother and her prereproductive offspring); and (2) *extended families*, groups in which two or more relatives of the same sex may reproduce. Notice that the presence of a breeding male is not essential to the definition of family. When the male is present, however, the family is called *biparental* because both the mother and the father share some responsibility for parenting. When the male is absent the family is called *matrilineal* because the female (or the female and her female relatives) are responsible for parenting. One defining feature of all families is that offspring continue to live with their parents past the age at which they are capable of reproducing on their own.

Families are so much a fact of life for humans that we take their existence for granted. The astonishing fact, however, is that a mere 3 percent of all bird and mammalian species form families (Emlen, 1995). Why are families so rare? Why do most offspring throughout the animal world leave the nest as soon as evolution has made them biologically capable of doing so, and so few remain with their parents past sexual maturity? The most likely reason is that remaining in the parental nest (or delaying departure from the nest) carries a tremendous reproductive cost. In simple families offspring do not reproduce while living at home. In extended families, however, parents will often actively suppress the reproduction of their offspring (e.g., by interfering with mating attempts). In both cases, the offspring sacrifice reproduction by delaying departure from the family unit.

Families thus inflict two primary costs on offspring: (1) reproduction is delayed and sometimes directly suppressed (perhaps the heaviest cost); and (2) competition for resources such as food is concentrated rather than dispersed, making life more challenging for both parents and offspring. The only way that families can evolve, in the rare instances in which they do, is when the reproductive benefits of remaining in the family are so great that they outweigh the heavy costs of forgoing early reproduction.

Two major theories have been proposed to explain the evolution of families. The first is the *ecological constraints model*. According to this theory, families emerge when there is a scarcity of reproductive vacancies that might be available to the sexually mature offspring. Under these conditions both the cost of staying within the family and the benefits of leaving are low. The heavy cost of staying within the family—delayed reproduction—vanishes because early reproduction is not possible due to a lack of reproductive vacancies (i.e., resource niches that provide the opportunity for reproduction).

The second theory is the *familial benefits model*. According to this theory, families form because of the bounty of benefits they provide for offspring. These benefits include (1) enhanced survival as a result of aid and protection from family members; (2) an enhanced ability to compete subsequently, perhaps by acquiring skills or greater size and maturity as a result of staying at home; (3) the possibility of inheriting or sharing the family territory or resources as a result of staying at home; and (4) inclusive fitness benefits gained by being in a position to help and be helped by genetic relatives while staying at home.

Emlen (1995) synthesizes these two theories into one unified theory of the origins of the family. His theory of family formation has three premises. First, families form when more offspring are produced than there are available reproductive vacancies to fill. This premise stems from the ecological constraints model. Second, families will form when offspring must wait for available reproductive vacancies until they are in a good position to compete for them. Third, families will form when the benefits of staying at home are large—in the form of increased survival, increased ability to develop competition skills, increased access to familial resources, and increased inclusive fitness benefits. Emlen's theory of the family is thus a synthesis of the ecological constraints and the family benefits models.

Several predictions follow from Emlen's theory. The first set of predictions involves the *family dynamics of kinship and cooperation.*

Prediction 1: Families will form when there is a shortage of reproductive vacancies but will break up when the vacancies become available. Families will be unstable, forming and breaking up depending on the circumstances. This prediction has been tested in several avian species (Emlen, 1995). When new breeding vacancies were created where there previously had been none, mature offspring "flew the coop" and left home to fill those vacancies, thus splitting apart an intact family. This prediction suggests that sexually mature children who are not yet in a position to compete successfully for mates or are not in a resource position to maintain a home on their own will tend to remain with their family unit.

Prediction 2: Families that control many resources will be more stable and enduring than families that lack resources. Among humans, the expectation would be that wealthy families will be more stable than poor families, especially when there is a chance that the children might inherit the parental resources or territory. Children coming from high-resource homes are predicted to be especially choosy about when and under what conditions they decide to leave home. By sticking around mature children may inherit the wealth, so wealthier families should show greater stability over time than poor families. Among many species of familial birds and mammals, offspring do indeed sometimes inherit their parents' breeding position. Davis and Daly (1997) provide empirical support for this prediction by finding that high-income families are indeed more likely to maintain social ties with their extended kin than low-income families.

Prediction 3: Help with rearing the young will be more prevalent among families than among comparable groups lacking kin relatives. A sister or brother, for example, might assist in raising a younger sibling, providing a key inclusive fitness benefit by living with the family. This prediction could easily be tested in humans.

Prediction 4: Sexual aggression will tend to be low in families compared with groups of non-relatives because relatives will evolve to avoid the risks associated with inbreeding. Sexual attraction between siblings will be rare, as will competition between father and son for sexual access to the mother. As a result of reduced sexual competition within families, individuals can avoid incurring the costs of mate guarding. Although family members have many opportunities for sexual contact, incestuous matings are extremely rare among birds and mammals. Among eighteen of the nineteen avian species studied in this regard, mating was almost invariably exogamous—that is, with birds that were outside the family (Emlen, 1995). Among humans incest between genetic relatives is also rare, but it is far more common between stepfathers and stepdaughters (Thornhill, 1992).

Another set of predictions pertains to *changes in family dynamics as a result of the loss or disruption of an existing breeder.*

Prediction 5: When a breeder is lost because of death or departure, family members will get into a conflict over who will fill the breeding vacancy. A core premise of Emlen's theory is that families are an evolved solution to the adaptive problem of a shortage of breeding vacancies. Therefore, the loss of a parent opens up a new vacancy, creating the perfect opportunity for offspring to inherit the natal resources. The higher the quality of the vacancy, the more competition and conflict there should be to fill it. Among Red-cocked woodpeckers, for example, in each of twenty-three cases of the death of a father, one of the sons took over the breeding role and the mother was forced to leave. Among humans an analogous situation might occur if a father died and left behind a large inheritance. Children often engage in lawsuits concerning claims to an inheritance and claims made by genetically unrelated individuals (e.g., a mistress of the father to whom he left resources) are often challenged (Smith, Kish, & Crawford, 1987).

Prediction 6: The loss of an existing breeder and replacement by a breeder who is genetically unrelated to family members already present will produce an increase in sexual aggression. When a mother is divorced, widowed, or abandoned and she remates with an unrelated male, the strong aversions against incest are relaxed. Stepfathers may be sexually attracted to stepdaughters, for example, thus putting mother and daughter in a kind of intrasexual rivalry. Among a variety of avian species aggression between sons and stepfathers is common, since these unrelated males are now sexual competitors (Emlen, 1995). Among humans the prediction of sexual conflict and aggression could easily be tested by comparing stepfamilies with biologically intact families.

Emlen's theory, in sum, generates a rich set of testable predictions. Many of these predictions have received support from avian, mammalian, and primate species, but others remain to be tested. Especially intriguing is their applicability to human families. According to Emlen's theory, we do not expect families to be entirely peaceful and harmonious. Conflict, competition, and even outright aggression are predicted features of family life, stemming from the different "interests" of various family members.

Critique of Emlen's Theory of the Family.

Recently evolutionary psychologists Jennifer Davis and Martin Daly have criticized Emlen's theory, offering several useful modifications as well as empirical tests of a few key predictions (Davis & Daly, 1997). At the most general level Davis and Daly offer three considerations that provide a unique context for examining human families: (1) human families may remain together because of competition from other groups, where remaining in a large kin-based coalition is advantageous in such group-on-group competition; (2) humans engage in extensive social exchange based on reciprocal altruism with nonkin; and (3) nonreproductive helpers, such as postmenopausal women, have little incentive to encourage their offspring to disperse, which may help to stabilize families.

These three considerations may affect the logic of Emlen's predictions. Consider prediction 1, which suggests that families will dissolve when acceptable breeding opportunities become available elsewhere. If a woman is postmenopausal and hence incapable of further reproduction, it would clearly be disadvantageous for her to abandon her family and the help she could provide when a breeding vacancy arose elsewhere. Because she is postmenopausal she is not in a position to exploit the breeding vacancy. Rather, it would be more advantageous for her to remain with her kin and continue to provide help. The relatively early menopause of human women thus may be a unique factor affecting the evolution of human families.

Another modification pertains to the fact that humans engage in extensive social exchange. Consider prediction 3: Help with rearing the young will be more prevalent among families than among comparable groups lacking kin relatives. Women often form friendships with nonkin in which they engage in reciprocal help with childrearing (Davis & Daly, 1997). Prediction 3 could be modified to take into account that *unreciprocated* help with rearing the young will be more prevalent among families than among comparable groups lacking kin relatives. In summary, several of Emlen's predictions could be modified by considering several factors unique to the human animal such as extensive patterns of reciprocal alliances (see Chapter 9) and the prolonged postmenopausal period enjoyed by women.

It is clear from a cross-species comparative analysis that families are exceedingly rare and only emerge under certain conditions, most notably when there is a shortage of breeding vacancies. Given current social interest in "family values," evolutionary psychology has something to offer by illuminating the conditions under which families remain stable or fall apart. In the next decade researchers will undoubtedly test these predictions and the Davis and Daly modifications of them and uncover a rich array of evolved psychological mechanisms—those involving cooperation as well as conflict—designed to deal with the varying adaptive problems posed by families.

Summary

We started this chapter by delving deeper into Hamilton's (1964) theory of inclusive fitness, formalized by Hamilton's rule $c < rb$. For altruism to evolve, for example, the cost to the actor must be less than the benefits provided, multiplied by the genetic relatedness between the actor and the recipient. In one bold stroke this theory offered one answer to the question of how altruism could evolve. It simultaneously extended Darwin's definition of classical fitness (personal reproductive success) to inclusive fitness (personal reproductive success plus the effects of one's actions on the fitness of genetic relatives, weighted by the degree of genetic relatedness).

Next we drew out the profound theoretical implications of inclusive fitness theory for humans. These implications include: (1) that there will be a special evolved psychology of kinship involving psychological mechanisms dedicated to solving the differing adaptive problems confronted when dealing with siblings, half siblings, grandparents, grandchildren, aunts, and uncles; (2) sex and generation will be critical categories differentiating kin because these dimensions define important properties on one's fitness vehicles (e.g., male kin have a higher ceiling on reproduction than female kin; younger kin have higher reproductive value than older kin); (3) kin relations will be arrayed on a dimension from close to distant, with the primary predictor of closeness being genetic relatedness; (4) cooperation and kin solidarity will be a function of genetic relatedness among kin; (5) older kin members will encourage younger kin members to be more altruistic toward genetic relatives such as siblings than younger kin members will naturally be inclined to be; (6) one's position within a family will be central to one's identity; and (7) people will exploit kin terms to influence and manipulate others in nonkin contexts (e.g., "brother, can you spare some cash").

A host of empirical studies has confirmed the importance of kinship as a predictor of helping behavior. One study documented that alarm calling among ground squirrels, a potentially costly endeavor because it draws the attention of predators, occurs when close kin are likely to be nearby. A study of three hundred Los Angeles women found that helping was a function of the genetic relatedness to the individual being helped. Another study showed that in hypothetical life-or-death scenarios, such as risking one's life to pull someone from a burning building, helping was highly predictable from the degree of genetic relatedness between the helper and the person being helped. In studies of inheritance people tend to leave more to genetic relatives (and to spouses who will presumably pass on the resources to genetic relatives) than to nonrelatives. Other studies show that the amount of grief and sorrow that individuals experience is directly related to the degree of genetic relatedness (see Segal, Wilson, Bouchard, & Gitlini, 1995, for empirical evidence; and Archer, 1998, for an extended review of the psychology of grief). All of these empirical studies point to the importance of kinship as a predictor of the allocation of acts of helping.

Grandparental investment is a special arena for testing nonintuitive predictions from inclusive fitness theory. In particular, paternity uncertainty comes into play. A grandfather has double the risk of genetic relatedness being severed: First, he may not be the father of his children. Second, his son may not be the father of his own children. Grandmothers, in contrast, are 100 percent certain that they are the genetic relatives of the children of their daughters. Based on this logic we should expect mothers' mothers to show the heaviest grandparental investment on average, and fathers' fathers to show the least. The other two types of grandparents—fathers' mothers and mothers' fathers—should show investment patterns between these extremes because in each of these cases there is one opportunity for genetic relatedness to be severed.

Empirical evidence from Germany and the United States supports these predictions. In two separate studies by different investigators, it was determined that grandchildren felt closest to their maternal grandmothers and most distant from their paternal grandfathers. Furthermore, grandchildren reported that they received the most resources from their maternal grandmothers and the least from their paternal grandfathers. Although the two other types of grandparents fell in between these extremes, it is interesting to note that in both cases the maternal grandfather invested more than the paternal grandmother. This finding rules out the idea that women invest more than men in kin across the board.

A similar logic applies to investment by aunts and uncles. The siblings of a sister are sure that their sister is the parent of her child, so these aunts and uncles are sure that they are the genetic relatives of their nieces and nephews. The siblings of a brother, in contrast, are not certain because their brother may have been cuckolded. This leads to the prediction of differential investment by aunts and uncles, depending on whether the children are their sister's or brother's. Maternal aunts, for example, would be expected to invest more than paternal aunts.

In a study of investment by aunts and uncles two important predictors of investment by aunts and uncles were determined. First, aunts tended to invest more than uncles, regardless of whether their nieces and nephews were the children of a brother or a sister—a sex effect. Second, the maternal aunts and uncles invested more than the paternal aunts and uncles, supporting the key prediction.

According to several studies, North American women seem to be more invested than men in kin—women are more likely to remember the names of their kin, more likely to identify themselves by their location in their kin network (e.g., "I am the daughter of so-and-so"), and more likely to maintain contact with their extended kin.

The final section of this chapter examined the broader perspective on the evolution of the family. Given the fact that families are exceedingly rare in the animal world—found among roughly 3 percent of all mammals—the very existence of families requires explanation. According to Stephen Emlen, families, consisting of mature offspring continuing to reside at home, occur under two key conditions: (1) when there is a scarcity of reproductive vacancies elsewhere; or (2) when there are distinct benefits of staying at home, such as enhancing survival, improving abilities to compete, and giving aid to (and receiving aid from) genetic relatives.

A host of predictions follow from this theory. The theory predicts, for example, that family stability will be higher when there is more wealth, and hence greater opportunities to benefit from the family and perhaps inherit familial wealth. It predicts that the sudden death of a reproducer within the family will result in a conflict over who will fill the void (e.g., conflict over access to parental wealth). It predicts that stepfathers and stepmothers will invest less than genetic fathers and mothers, and that stepfamilies will be inherently less stable and more conflicted than genetically intact families. Many of these predictions have been tested with nonhuman animals, but most remain to be tested with humans. Emlen's theory has been criticized on several grounds, including (1) that it fails to take into account the fact that postmenopausal women can continue to aid their families and cannot exploit available reproductive vacancies, and (2) people often engage in extensive reciprocal exchange with nonkin. These factors suggest refinements of Emlen's theory that take into account the unique aspects of the human animal.

Genetic relatedness, in sum, is a key predictor of investment by kin. The closer the kin, the heavier the investment. When the genetic relatedness is certain, investment is the highest, other things being equal. When genetic relatedness may be compromised by paternity uncertainty or by the presence of a stepparent, investment decreases. The theory of inclusive fitness has profound consequences for understanding the psychology of kinship and the family that researchers have just begun to explore.

PART FIVE

Problems of Group Living

Group living is a critical part of human adaptation, and evolutionary psychology suggests that the human mind contains many evolved mechanisms dedicated to dealing with the problems of group living. This part contains four chapters, each devoted to a different subset of group living problems.

Chapter 9 focuses on the evolution of cooperative alliances. It introduces the theory of reciprocal altruism, which provides one theoretical solution to the evolution of cooperation. Examples of cooperation in nature, including food sharing in vampire bats and reciprocal alliances among chimpanzees and other nonhuman primates are offered next. The remainder of Chapter 9 explores research on the evolution of cooperative alliance in humans, ending with an evolutionary perspective on the costs and benefits of friendship that includes the psychology of "true friends," who may be deeply engaged in our welfare.

Chapter 10 examines aggression and warfare and comes to the disturbing conclusion that we have accrued many adaptive benefits by inflicting costs on other humans through violence. This chapter introduces the evolutionary logic for why men are more violently aggressive than women in all cultures around the world and provides empirical evidence for particular patterns of aggression, depending on the sex of the perpetrator and the sex of the victim. The end of this chapter explores the evolution of warfare and the controversial question of whether humans have evolved specific adaptations designed to kill other human beings.

Chapter 11 focuses on conflict between men and women. It starts by introducing the logic of strategic interference theory, which provides an overarching framework for understanding conflict between the sexes. The bulk of the chapter summarizes the empirical evidence for particular forms of such conflict, including conflict over sexual access, jealous conflict, conflicts that occur over defections from relationships, and conflict over access to resources.

Chapter 12 deals with a universal feature of human groups—the existence of status or dominance hierarchies. It presents an evolutionary rationale for the emergence of hierarchies, and then focuses on more specific aspects of dominance and status in nonhumans and humans. The human evidence includes a discussion of sex differences in status striving and the behavioral manifestations of dominance and ends with a discussion of strategies of submissiveness.

9

Cooperative Alliances

If thou wouldst get a friend, prove him first, and be not hasty to credit him. For some man is a friend for his own occasion, and will not abide in the day of thy trouble. . . . Again, some friend is a companion at the table, and will not continue in the day of affliction. . . . If thou be brought low, he will be against thee, and will hide from thy face. . . . A faithful friend is a strong defense: and he that hath found such a one hath found himself a treasure. Nothing doth countervail a faithful friend.

—Ecclesiastes 6

A story is told of two friends, one of whom was accused of a robbery he did not commit. Although he was innocent, he was sentenced to four years in jail. His friend was greatly distressed by the conviction so he slept on the floor each night that his friend was in jail. He did not want to enjoy the comfort of a soft bed knowing that his friend was sleeping on a single, musty mattress. Eventually the imprisoned friend was released and the two remained friends for life. How can we explain such puzzling behavior? Why do people form friendships and long-term cooperative alliances?

The Evolution of Cooperation

Personal sacrifices made on behalf of others are not rare among friends. Every day people help their friends in many ways large and small, from giving advice and sacrificing time to rushing to a friend's aid in a time of crisis. Acts of friendship of this sort pose a profound puzzle. Natural selection is competitive. It is selfish because it is a feedback process in which one organism's design features outreproduce those of others in an existing population. Sacrifices are costly to those who make them, yet they benefit the people for whom the sacrifices are made. How could such patterns of friendship and altruism evolve?

The Problem of Altruism

In Chapter 8 we saw how one form of such altruism can evolve when the recipients of the aid are genetic relatives. This sort of altruism is predicted by inclusive fitness theory. Your friends, however, are not usually your genetic relatives. So any cost you incur for a friend results in a loss to you and a gain to the friend. The great puzzle is: How could altruism among nonrelatives possibly evolve, given the selfish designs that tend to be produced by natural selection? This is what evolutionary biologists call the *problem of altruism*. An "altruistic" design feature aids the reproduction of other individuals, even though it causes the altruist (who has this feature) to reproduce less (Cosmides & Tooby, 1992).

The puzzle is complicated further by the findings that altruism is neither new nor unusual. First, there is evidence that social exchange—a form of cooperation—occurs across human cultures and is found frequently in hunter-gatherer cultures that are presumed to closely resemble the ancestral conditions under which humans evolved (Cashden, 1989; Cosmides & Tooby, 1992; Lee & DeVore, 1968; Weissner, 1982). Second, other species far removed from humans, such as vampire bats, engage in forms of social exchange (Wilkinson, 1984). Third, other primates besides humans, such as chimpanzees, baboons, and macaques, also engage in reciprocal helping (De Waal, 1982). Taken together, this evidence suggests a long evolutionary history of altruism, going back millions of years.

A Theory of Reciprocal Altruism

A solution to the problem of altruism has been developed, in increasingly elaborate and sophisticated ways, by the theory of reciprocal altruism (Axelrod, 1984; Axelrod & Hamilton, 1981; Cosmides & Tooby, 1992; Trivers, 1971; Williams, 1966). The theory of reciprocal altruism states that psychological mechanisms for providing benefits to nonrelatives can evolve as long as the delivery of such benefits is reciprocated at some point in the future.

The beauty of reciprocal altruism is that both parties benefit. Consider an example. Two hunters are friends. Their success at hunting, however, is erratic. During the course of a week, only one of the hunters will be successful. The following week, however, the other hunter might be successful. If the first hunter shares his meat with his friend, he incurs a cost of lost meat. This cost, however, may be relatively small because he may have more meat than he or his immediate family can consume before it spoils. The gain to his friend, however, may be large if he has nothing else to eat that week. The following week the situation is reversed. Thus, each of the two hunters pays a small cost in lost meat that provides a larger benefit to his friend. Both friends benefit by the reciprocal altruism more than if each one selfishly kept all the meat from his kill for himself. Economists call this a "gain in trade"—each party receives more in return than it costs to deliver the benefit (Cosmides & Tooby, 1992).

In evolutionary terms these gains in trade set the stage for the evolution of reciprocal altruism. Those who engage in reciprocal altruism will tend to outreproduce those who act selfishly, causing psychological mechanisms for reciprocal altruism to spread in succeeding generations. Reciprocal altruism, in sum, can be defined as "cooperation between two or more individuals for mutual benefit" (Cosmides & Tooby, 1992, p. 169). Approximate synonyms for reciprocal altruism include *cooperation, reciprocation,* and *social exchange.*

One of the most important adaptive problems for the reciprocal altruist is ensuring that the benefits it bestows will be returned in the future. Someone could pretend to be a reciprocal altruist, for example, but then take benefits without responding in kind later. This is called the *problem of cheating*. Later in this chapter we will examine empirical evidence that suggests that humans have evolved specific psychological mechanisms designed to solve the adaptive problem of cheating. First, however, we will examine a fascinating computer simulation that demonstrates that reciprocal altruism can evolve and look at a few nonhuman species to provide concrete examples of the evolution of cooperation.

Tit for Tat

The problem of reciprocal altruism is similar to a game known as the "prisoner's dilemma." The prisoner's dilemma is a hypothetical situation in which two people have been thrown in prison for a crime they are accused of committing together and of which they are indeed guilty. The prisoners are held in separate cells so that they can't talk to each other. Police interrogate both of the prisoners, trying to get each to "rat" on the other. If neither one implicates the other, the police will be forced to set them both free for lack of evidence. This is the cooperative strategy, and from the prisoners' perspective, it is the strategy that would be best for both of them.

In an attempt to get each prisoner to "rat" on (or defect from) the other, however, the police tell each that if he confesses and implicates his partner, he will be set free and given a small reward. If both prisoners confess, however, they will both be sentenced to jail. If one confesses and the other does not, then the implicated partner will receive a stiffer sentence than he would have received if both confessed and the confessor will receive a lighter sentence. The prisoner's dilemma is illustrated in Figure 9.1 on page 256.

In this scheme, R is the reward for mutual cooperation, where neither prisoner tells on the other. P is the punishment each prisoner receives if both confess. T is the temptation to defect—the small reward given in exchange for implicating the other. S is the "sucker's payoff," the penalty one incurs if his partner defects and he does not.

This is called the prisoner's dilemma because the rational course of action for both prisoners is to confess, but that would have a worse outcome for both than if they decided to trust each other (hence the dilemma). Consider the problem of Player A. If his partner does not confess, A will benefit by defecting—he will be set free *and* will receive a small reward for implicating his partner. On the other hand, if his partner defects Player A would be better off defecting as well; otherwise he risks receiving the stiffest penalty possible. In sum, the logical course of action, no matter what one's partner does, is to defect even though cooperation would result in the best outcome for both.

This hypothetical dilemma resembles the problem of reciprocal altruism. Each person can gain from cooperating (R), but each is tempted to gain the benefit of a partner's altruism without reciprocating (T). The worst scenario for each individual is to cooperate and have a partner who defects (S). If the game is played only once, then the only sensible solution is to defect. Robert Axelrod and W. D. Hamilton (1981) showed

Player B

	Cooperation	Defection
Cooperation	$R = 3$ Reward for mutual cooperation	$S = 0$ Sucker's payoff
Defection	$T = 5$ Temptation to defect	$P = 1$ Punishment for mutual defection

Player A

FIGURE 9.1   **The Game of Prisoner's Dilemma.** This is the pay-off matrix used in the tournament run by Robert Axelrod. A game consisted of two hundred match-ups between two strategies. The game is defined by $T > R > P > S$ and $R > (S + T)/2$.

Source: Reprinted with permission from Axelrod, R., & Hamilton, W. D. (1981). The evolution of cooperation. *Science, 211,* 1390–96. Copyright © 1981 American Association for the Advancement of Science.

that the key to cooperation occurs when the game is repeated a number of times but each player does not know when the game will end, as often happens in real life.

The winning strategy in "iterated prisoner's dilemma" games is called *tit for tat.* Axelrod and Hamilton discovered this strategy by conducting a computer tournament. Economists, mathematicians, scientists, and computer wizards from around the world were asked to submit "strategies" for playing two hundred rounds of the prisoner's dilemma. Points were rewarded in accordance with the payoff matrix shown in Figure 9.1. The winner was whoever had the highest number of points. The "strategies" consisted of decision rules for interacting with other players. A total of fourteen strategies were submitted and were randomly paired in competition in a round-robin computer tournament. Some strategies were highly complex, involving contingent rules for modeling the other's strategy and suddenly switching strategies midstream. The most complex had seventy-seven lines of statements in the computer language FORTRAN. The "winner" of the tournament, however, employed the simplest strategy of all, tit for tat, containing a mere four lines of FORTRAN statements. It had two simple rules: (1) cooperate on the first move and (2) reciprocate on every move thereafter. In other words, start by cooperating, and continue cooperating if the other is also cooperating. If the other defects, however, then defect in kind. Trivers (1985) aptly labeled this "contingent reciprocity."

In a second round of the tournament Axelrod solicited a wider range of entries, this time getting sixty-two entries from individuals including physicists, biologists, and computer scientists in six different countries. The second tournament included an indefinite interaction length for each "encounter," rather than the fixed number of two hundred rounds. Tit for tat was resubmitted by its original author, and again it won. When the tournament was conducted to simulate the process of natural selection, with the successful strategies replacing the less successful in succeeding generations, tit for tat again emerged victorious.

Axelrod (1984) identified three features of this strategy that represented the keys to its success: (1) *never be the first to defect*—always start out by cooperating, and continue to cooperate as long as the other player does so; (2) *retaliate only after the other has defected*—defect immediately after the first instance of nonreciprocation; and (3) *be forgiving*—if a previously defecting player starts to cooperate, then reciprocate the cooperation and get on a mutually beneficial cycle. To summarize: "First, do unto others as you wish them to do unto you, but then do unto them as they have just done to you" (Trivers, 1985, p. 392). Strategies for encouraging cooperation that will, in turn, lead to the success of tit for tat are discussed in Box 9.1 on page 258.

The results of this computer tournament suggest that cooperation can evolve fairly easily in nature, but we must keep in mind one critical limitation. The game assumes that the players are equal in their power to reward and punish; yet in everyday life asymmetries in power are quite common. It is not clear how tit for tat would fare under conditions of power asymmetry. Despite this limitation, however, the results clearly demonstrate that contingent cooperation can easily evolve with relatively simple decision rules, and so may be quite prevalent in nature.

Examples of Cooperation in Nature

Each species is unique in many of the adaptive problems it has confronted over the course of its evolution, but different species can arrive at similar solutions to common adaptive problems. It is instructive to examine nonhuman species to see whether they have evolved cooperation. We will start with the fascinating case of vampire bats and then look at baboons and chimps, who are phylogenetically closer to humans.

Food Sharing in Vampire Bats

Vampire bats got their name because their survival depends on the blood of other animals. They live in groups of up to a dozen adult females and associated offspring. The males leave the colony when they are capable of independence. Vampire bats hide during the day, but at night they emerge to suck the blood of cattle and horses. Their victims, of course, are not willing donors. Indeed, the horses and cattle often flick away the bats to prevent them from feeding. The bats' ability to feed successfully apparently increases with age and experience. One study found that 33 percent of the younger bats (under two years old) failed to get blood on any particular evening, whereas only 7 percent of the bats older than two years failed to feed (Wilkinson, 1984).

How do the bats survive failed attempts to find food? Failure at feeding, in fact, can quickly lead to death. Bats can only go without blood for three days. As shown by the statistics above, however, failure is common; all bats fail at one point or another, so the risk of death due to starvation is a constant threat. Wilkinson (1984) discovered that the bats regularly regurgitate a portion of the blood they have sucked and give it to others in the bat colony, but not randomly. Instead, they give regurgitated blood to

BOX **9.1**

Strategies for Promoting Cooperation

According to Axelrod's (1984) analysis of tit for tat as a key successful strategy, several practical consequences follow for the promotion of cooperation. First, *enlarge the shadow of the future*. If the other individual thinks that you will interact frequently in the extended future, he or she has a greater incentive to cooperate. If people know when the "last move" will occur and that the relationship will end soon, there is a greater incentive to defect and not cooperate. Enlarging the shadow of the future can be accomplished by making interactions more frequent and by making a commitment to the relationship, which occurs, for example, with wedding vows. Perhaps one reason that divorces are so often ugly, marred by unkind acts of mutual defection, is that both parties perceive the "last move" and a sharply truncated shadow of the future.

A second strategy that Axelrod recommends is to *teach reciprocity*. Promoting reciprocity not only helps oneself by making others more cooperative, it also makes it more difficult for exploitative strategies to thrive. The larger the number of those who follow a tit-for-tat strategy, the less successful one will be in attempting to exploit others by defecting. Essentially, the cooperators will thrive through their interactions with each other and the exploiters will suffer because of a vanishing population of those on whom to prey.

A third strategy for the promotion of cooperation is to *insist on no more than equity*. Greed is

the downfall of many, perhaps best exemplified by the myth of King Midas, whose lust for gold backfired when everything he touched, even the food he wanted to eat, turned to gold. The beauty of tit for tat as a strategy is that it does not insist on getting more than it gives. By promoting equity tit for tat elicits cooperation from others.

A fourth strategy to promote cooperation is to *respond quickly to provocation*. If your partner defects on you, a good strategy is to retaliate immediately. This sends a strong signal that you will not tolerate being exploited and may prompt future cooperation.

A final strategy for promoting cooperation is to *cultivate a personal reputation as a reciprocator*. We live in a social world in which the beliefs others have about us—our reputations—determine whether they will befriend or avoid us. Reputations are established through one's actions, and word about one's actions spreads. Cultivating a reputation as a reciprocator will make others seek one out for mutual gain. A reputation as an exploiter will lead to intense social shunning. The combined effect of these strategies will create a runaway pattern of cooperation, in which those who were formerly exploiters are forced to rehabilitate their bad reputations by becoming cooperators themselves. In this way cooperation will be promoted throughout the group. These cases will provide important points of comparison for the evolution of cooperation in humans.

their friends, those from whom they have received blood in the past. Wilkinson showed that the closer the association between the bats—the more often they were sighted together—the more likely they were to give blood to each other. Only bats that were sighted in close proximity at least 60 percent of the time received blood from that compatriot. Not a single bat gave blood to another bat with whom he associated for a lesser period of time.

In another part of the study, Wilkinson (1984) used a captive colony of vampire bats to explore additional aspects of reciprocal altruism. He experimentally deprived individual bats of food, and varied the length of time of the deprivation. Wilkinson discovered that the "friends" tended to regurgitate blood more often when their friends were in dire need and close to starvation (e.g., thirteen hours from death) than when they were in mild need (e.g., two days from death). He also found that the starved bats who received help from their friends were more likely to give blood to those who had helped them in their time of need.

In sum, vampire bats show all the signs of having evolved reciprocal altruistic adaptations. Individuals are in frequent contact with one another over long stretches of time. The frequency of association predicts the degree of altruism. The benefits of giving are higher than the costs to the giver. The circumstances are frequently reversed, so that a giver on one day is likely to be the recipient on the next. Finally, individual bats show a preference for giving to those who have recently helped them. Considering these conditions, and the death threat vampire bats continuously face from starvation, it is hard to imagine how bats could survive without reciprocal altruism (Trivers, 1985).

Reciprocity among Nonhuman Primates

Baboons are intensely social. They live in groups and interact frequently. Conflict erupts on a regular basis, often as a result of competition over access to limited resources such as food or sex partners. Anthropologist Craig Packer studied one troop of baboons over a long period of time, enough to witness 140 apparent requests for help in the course of social conflicts (Packer, 1977). During a conflict baboons will solicit help by establishing eye contact with the baboon from whom they seek help and then rapidly shifting eye contact between the prospective helper and their antagonist.

In twenty cases the solicitation involved a conflict between males over sexual access to a female baboon who had entered estrus. Requests for help from a third male baboon in these sexual conflicts tended to elicit aid more often than requests for aid in other contexts. The request for aid yielded success in sixteen of the twenty encounters, and the female then had sex with the baboon who had originally requested help. So in this case, the helper never benefited directly by giving aid—he never received direct sexual access as a consequence of his help. But Packer showed that in subsequent conflicts, when the roles were reversed, the baboon who had previously given help was more likely to receive help. So strong is the pattern of reciprocal altruism among baboons that males who fail to form friendships of this sort rarely gain sexual access to females.

In another study researchers conducted field experiments in which they examined the effects of grooming on proclivities to help at a later time in a sample of vervet monkeys. They first secured tape recordings of females emitting vocal solicitations for help. They then played back these tape recordings to other females who either had or had not been groomed by the solicitor. They found that females who had been groomed recently by the solicitor were far more likely to look around in response to the played-back request for aid. Those who had not been groomed recently simply ignored the request. Interestingly, this effect did not occur if the grooming had been done by a kin member. As shown in Figure 9.2 on page 260, there is a strong tendency to respond to solicitations for help by displaying an attentive response if the caller is a nonkin monkey who

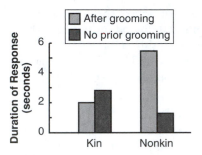

FIGURE 9.2   The Effect of Previous Grooming on Tendency to Respond to Solicitations for Help, in Vervet Monkeys. The duration of attentive response (in seconds) of an individual to playback of the recruitment call of kin or nonkin in the presence or absence of prior grooming by the caller. Attentive response = looking toward the speaker. Duration of looking was measured from a film of the interaction. The difference for nonkin —after grooming or with no prior grooming—is significant. Other comparisons are not.

Source: Reprinted with permission from *Nature.* (Seyfarth, R. M., & Cheney, D. L. [1984]. Grooming, alliances, and reciprocal altruism in vervet monkeys, *308,* 541–543). Copyright © (1984) Macmillan Magazines Limited.

had recently groomed the listener, but recent grooming did not affect the response if the caller was a kin member. Thus helping appears to be a case of reciprocal altruism between nonkin, rather than a case of kin-based helping (Seyfarth & Cheney, 1984).

Several conclusions can be reached from these studies. First, those baboons and vervet monkeys who give help are most likely to receive help. Second, baboons and vervets tend to form stable alliances, so that the friend who "asks" for help is most likely to give help at some point in the future when "asked." Third, these acts of aid are most likely to be the result of reciprocal altruism rather than kinship.

Chimpanzee Politics

Among the chimpanzees at a large zoo colony in Arnhem, the Netherlands, a chimp named Yeroen reigned as the dominant adult male (de Waal, 1982). He walked in an exaggeratedly heavy manner and looked larger than he really was. Only occasionally did he need to demonstrate his dominance, raising the hair covering his body on end and running full speed at the other apes, who scattered in all directions in response to his charge. Yeroen's dominance extended to sexual activity. Although there were four adult males in the troop, Yeroen was responsible for nearly 75 percent of the matings when the females came into estrus.

As Yeroen grew older, however, things began to change. A younger male, Luit, experienced a sudden growth spurt and challenged Yeroen's status. Luit gradually stopped displaying the submissive greeting to Yeroen, brazenly showing his fearlessness. Once Luit approached Yeroen and smacked him hard. Another time Luit used his potentially lethal canines to draw blood. Most of the time, however, the battles were more symbolic, with threats and bluffs in the place of bloodshed. Initially all the females sided with Yeroen, allowing him to maintain his status. Indeed, reciprocal alliances with females are essential to the maintenance of status—males defend the females against attack from other males and act as "peacemakers" in disputes; in return the females support the males, aiding in the maintenance of their status.

One by one, however, the females gradually began to defect and sided with Luit as Luit's increasing dominance became apparent. After two months the transition was complete. Yeroen had been dethroned, and started to display the submissive greeting to Luit. The mating behavior followed suit. Whereas Luit achieved only 25 percent of the matings during Yeroen's reign of power, his copulations jumped to more than 50 percent when he took over. Yeroen's sexual access dropped to zero.

Although ousted from power and lacking sexual access, Yeroen was not ready to retire. Gradually he formed a close alliance with an upcoming male named Nikkie. Neither Yeroen nor Nikkie dared challenge Luit alone but together they made a formidable alliance. Over several weeks the alliance grew bolder in challenging Luit. Eventually a physical fight erupted. Although all the chimpanzees involved sustained injuries, the alliance between Nikkie and Yeroen triumphed. After this victory Nikkie secured 50 percent of the matings. And because of his alliance with Nikkie, Yeroen now secured 25 percent of the matings, up from his previous dethronement level of zero. Although Yeroen never again attained dominant status, his alliance with Nikkie was critical in avoiding total banishment from mating. Reciprocally, Nikkie's alliance with Yeroen was critical in attaining dominance over Luit.

Alliances are central features in the social lives of chimpanzees. Males regularly solicit alliances with females, grooming them and playing with their infants. Without alliances with the females, males could never attain a position of dominance in the troop. As part of the bid for alpha status, a male will bite or chase a female if she is found associating with an opponent. In extreme cases a male will pounce on a female, jumping up and down on her back while she screams. An hour later, when she is no longer associating with the opponent, the male will be extremely friendly, showing great solicitude toward her and her infants. This is a key strategy in the formation of chimpanzee alliances—try to sever the alliances of one's opponents and enlist them.

Through de Waal's fascinating study of chimpanzee politics we catch a glimpse of the complexities of the evolution of reciprocal altruism—alliances that form not just between males, but also between the sexes. With this background we now turn to the evolution of cooperation in humans.

Social Contract Theory

The theory of reciprocal altruism predicts that organisms can benefit by engaging in cooperative exchange. There is one problem, however: many potential exchanges do not occur simultaneously. If I give you a benefit now, I must trust that you will reciprocate and give me a benefit at some later time. If I help you in your time of need, I must trust that you will help me later when I need it. If you fail to reciprocate, then I have incurred a net cost. In short, relationships involving reciprocal exchange are vulnerable to cheating—when people take a benefit without paying the cost of reciprocation (Cosmides & Tooby, 1992).

In nature opportunities for simultaneous exchange sometimes occur. I can give you a piece of fruit that I gathered in exchange for a piece of meat that you hunted. In many contexts there are opportunities for cooperation where simultaneous exchange is simply not possible. If you are being attacked by a wolf, for example, and I rush to your aid, you cannot at the same time repay me for the cost that I incurred. Once the act of helping has been performed, it cannot be undone.

Another reason that simultaneous exchange is sometimes not possible is that the needs and abilities of the interactants are rarely perfectly matched. If I am hungry and you are the only one with an ample food supply, I cannot immediately repay you for preventing me from starving. You must trust that when you are in great need I will rush to your side to help you. Whenever exchanges are nonsimultaneous the window is open for defection—taking the benefit and later cheating by failing to return the favor.

Evolutionary psychologists Leda Cosmides and John Tooby have developed the social contract theory to explain the evolution of cooperative exchange in humans, with special attention to how humans have solved the problem of cheating. The possibility of cheating poses an ever-present threat to the evolution of cooperation. The reason is that cheaters have an evolutionary advantage over cooperators, at least under certain conditions such as the cheating not being detected or punished. If I take the benefits that you offer, but then fail to return the favor at a later time, I benefit twofold—I have gained benefits and avoided incurring the reciprocal costs. For this reason, over evolutionary time cheaters will reproduce more than cooperators until the entire population consists of noncooperators.

The only way reciprocal altruism can evolve is if organisms create a mechanism for detecting and avoiding cheaters. If cooperators can detect cheaters and only interact with like-minded cooperators, reciprocal altruism can gain a toehold and evolve over time. The cheaters will be at a disadvantage because they fail to benefit by entering into cooperative exchanges.

What specific problems do people have to solve to evolve mechanisms that motivate forming social contracts and avoiding the ever-present threat of cheaters? Cosmides and Tooby (1992) outlined five cognitive capacities:

Capacity 1: The ability to recognize many different individual humans. If you give me a benefit and I get lost in a "sea of anonymous others" (Axelrod & Hamilton, 1981), you will be vulnerable to being cheated. You must be able to identify me and remember me as distinct from all other people. The ability to recognize many individuals may seem crashingly obvious, but this is only because humans are so good at it. One study showed that people can identify others whom they have not seen for up to thirty-four years, with a recognition rate over 90 percent (Bahrick, Bahrick, & Wittlinger, 1975). Indeed, there is neurological evidence that this ability is located in a specific area of the brain. People with a lesion in a specific place in the right hemisphere develop a highly specific deficit—an inability to recognize faces called "prosopagnosia" (Gardner, 1974). Humans are also especially good at recognizing other individuals solely by the way they walk (Cutting, Proffitt, & Kozlowski, 1978). In sum, there is good scientific evidence that humans have evolved a proficient ability to recognize many different individuals.

Capacity 2: The ability to remember some aspects of the histories of interactions with different individuals. This capacity breaks down into several different abilities. First, one must be able to remember whether the person with whom he or she has interacted was previously a cooperator or a cheater. Second, one must be able to keep track of who owes what to whom. This requires some sort of "accounting system" for keeping track of the costs you have incurred and the benefits you have received from a specific individual. Failure to keep track of these histories of interaction will make a person vulnerable to being cheated. If you fail to remember who has cheated you in the past then you are vulnerable to being exploited in the future. If you fail to keep track of how much you have given the other person in the past, then you have no way of knowing whether the benefit he or she returns later compensates adequately for the cost you have incurred. Thus far, no research has directly explored this capacity.

Capacity 3: The ability to communicate one's values to others. If your friend fails to understand what you want, how can he or she provide the benefits you need? If you fail to communicate your distress to a defector, you may be vulnerable to future defections. Consider an example from de Waal's (1982) study of chimpanzees. The study concerned Puist and Luit, who had a longstanding relationship of mutual helping when one was under attack.

> This happened once after Puist had supported Luit in chasing Nikkie. When Nikkie later displayed [aggressively] at Puist she turned to Luit and held out her hand to him in search of support. Luit, however, did nothing to protect her against Nikkie's attack. Immediately Puist turned on Luit, barking furiously, chasing him across the enclosure and even hit him. (p. 207)

Puist appears to be communicating to Luit her dissatisfaction with Luit's failure to help in a time of need. Although such chimp communications are nonverbal, among humans language can used to supplement emotional expressions and other nonverbal behavior as the medium of communication of desires, entitlements, and distress about an unfulfilled obligation. The phrases "you owe me," "I need this," "I am entitled to this," and "I want this" represent ways in which humans communicate their values to others.

Capacity 4: The ability to model the values of others. The flip side of the coin to communicating your values is the ability to understand the values of others. If you can detect *when* a person is needy and *how* he or she is needy, the benefit you provide can be tailored to that need. If I provide you with a piece of meat, failing to recognize that you are not hungry and have an ample supply of food, then the benefit I provide will not be worth much to you. By understanding the desires and needs of others you can tailor your exchanges to maximize the benefit you provide, making the other person more indebted to you than if you had failed to model his or her values. This suggests that people may engage in "marketing research" to develop specific understandings of the preferences, needs, and motivations of each person with whom they interact—a proposition that has yet to be examined empirically.

Capacity 5: The ability to represent costs and benefits, independent of the particular items exchanged. Cosmides and Tooby (1989) argue that many animals exchange a delimited set of items, such as food and sex. Humans, however, can and do exchange an astonishing array of items—knives and other tools, meat, berries, nuts, fish, shelters, protection, status, stone axes, assistance in fights, sexual access, money, blow guns, information about enemies, help on term papers, and computer programs, to name but a few. For this reason, Cosmides and Tooby argue, evolved mechanisms of social exchange cannot be prewired to represent (conceptualize) and negotiate for specific items. We must be able to understand and cognitively represent the costs and benefits of a wide range of items. It is our general ability to represent costs and benefits of exchanges, not a specific ability tied to particular items, that has evolved in humans.

In sum, social contract theory proposes the evolution in humans of five cognitive capacities to solve the problem of cheaters and engage in successful social exchange. Humans must be able to recognize other individuals; remember the history of interactions with them; communicate values, desires, and needs to others; recognize them in others; and represent the costs and benefits of a variety of items of exchange.

To test social contract theory Cosmides and Tooby conducted more than a dozen empirical studies on people's responses to logical problems. Logic refers to the inferences one can make about the truth of one statement from the truth of other statements, independent of their form. If I assert "if P, then Q," then once you find out that P is true, you logically infer that Q must also be true. This applies to all statements, such as "if I go to the grocery store, it means that I am hungry" or "if you are sexually unfaithful to me, then I will leave you."

Unfortunately, humans do not seem to be very good at solving logical problems. Imagine that in one room are a few archeologists, biologists, and chess players (Pinker, 1997, p. 334). None of the archeologists are biologists, but all of the biologists are chess players. What follows from this knowledge? More than 50 percent of college students surveyed conclude from this that none of the archeologists are chess players—clearly an invalid inference because the statement "all biologists are chess players" does not imply that no archeologists play chess. No participants in this study concluded that some chess players in the room are nonarcheologists, which is logically derivable from the premises. And roughly 20 percent claimed that no valid inferences can be drawn at all from the above premises, which is clearly wrong.

Consider one type of logic problem (Wason, 1966). Imagine four cards are lying on a table. Each card has a letter on one side and a number on the other, but you can see only one side. Now consider this: Which cards would you need to turn over to test the following rule: "If a card has a vowel on one side, then it has an even number on the other side." Turn over only those cards you would need to turn over to test the truth value of this rule:

If you are like the majority of people in most studies you would turn over the card with the "a," or the "a" and the "2." The "a" card is certainly correct. Because it is a vowel, if it had an odd number on the back it would mean the rule is false. The "2" card, however, yields no information relevant to testing the rule. Because the rule does *not* state that all cards with an even number on one side must have a vowel on the other, it doesn't matter whether a vowel or a consonant is on the back of the "2." In contrast, turning over the "3" card would yield a powerful test of the rule. If the back side of the "3" is a vowel, then the rule is definitively falsified. So the logically correct answer is to turn over cards "a" and "3" (the "b" card also provides no information relevant to the hypothesis, since the rule does not make any statements about what the back side of a consonant card must contain). Why are people—including those who have taken college courses in logic—so bad at solving problems of this sort?

According to Cosmides and Tooby (1992), the answer is that humans have not evolved to respond to abstract logical problems; they have, however, evolved to respond to problems structured as social exchanges when they are presented in terms of costs and benefits. Consider this problem: You are a bouncer at a local bar and your job is to make sure that no one who is underage drinks alcohol. You have to test this rule: "If a person is drinking alcohol, then he or she must be twenty-one years old or older." Which of the following four people do you have to check out to do your job: someone drinking beer, someone drinking soda, a twenty-five-year-old, or a sixteen-year-old? In contrast to the abstract logic problem above, the vast majority of people correctly select the beer drinker and the sixteen-year-old. The logic of the problem is identical to the above abstract problem involving vowels and even numbers. So why are people good at solving this problem but not the abstract problem?

According to Cosmides and Tooby, people reason correctly when the problem is structured as a social contract. If you drink beer but are not over twenty-one years old, then you have taken a benefit without meeting the requirement (cost) of being of age. In other words, people do well when they are "looking for cheaters," those people who have taken a benefit without paying the cost.

For people to succeed at this task, it need only be structured such that they will construe the problem in terms of taking benefits and paying costs. Cosmides and Tooby were able to rule out a number of alternative hypotheses. The effect does not depend on being familiar with the content of the problem, for example. When strange and unfamiliar rules were used, such as "if you get married, you must have a tattoo on your forehead" or "if you eat mongongo nuts, you must be over six feet tall," roughly 75 percent of the subjects still answered correctly (in contrast to the fewer than 10 percent who got it right in the abstract version). According to these studies, the human mind has an evolved psychological mechanism specifically designed to detect cheaters. These findings have been replicated in other cultures, such as the Shiwiar, a foraging tribe in Equador.

The cheater detection mechanism appears to be highly sensitive to the perspective one adopts (Gigerenzer & Hug, 1992). Consider the following rule: "If an employee gets a pension, he has worked for ten years." What would constitute a violation of the social contract? It depends on who you ask. When participants are instructed to take the employee's point of view, they seek out workers who have put in more than ten years but have not received a pension. This would constitute a violation of the social contract by the employer, who failed to grant the pension when it was deserved. On the other hand, when participants are instructed to take the perspective of the employer they seek out workers who have worked for fewer than ten years but who nonetheless have taken a pension. This would constitute a violation of the social contract by the employee, who would be taking a pension without having put in the full ten years of service. Perspective, in short, appears to govern the sorts of cheaters one looks for—if you are an employee you are sensitive to being cheated by your employer; if you are an employer you are sensitive to being cheated by your employees.

Further research is clearly needed to explore social contract theory generally, and the cheater detection mechanism in particular. Recall the basic definition of psychological mechanisms as involving "input, decision rules, and output." We know little about whether people are sensitive to certain items of input—do men and women have special sensitivities to certain types of cheating, such as to sexual infidelity in the context of a marriage social contract? It seems intuitively obvious that people get mad, tell others the person has cheated, and avoid contact in the future, but we know little formally about the "output" side—what specific actions do people take when they detect a cheater and how do those actions differ depending on contexts such as status discrepancies and genetic relatedness? Nonetheless, this research is ground breaking in showing that people do appear to have evolved psychological mechanisms designed to detect cheaters—mechanisms that are activated whenever exchanges are structured in terms of costs and benefits. As Cosmides and Tooby conclude: "The results showed that we do not have a general-purpose ability to detect violations of conditional rules. But human reasoning is well designed for detecting violations of conditional rules when these can be interpreted as cheating on a social contract" (Cosmides & Tooby, 1992, p. 205).

The Psychology of Friendship

Thus far we have considered two primary routes to the evolution of cooperation and altruism. In Chapter 8, we examined Hamilton's Rule, which predicts that adaptations for delivering altruism to others can evolve as long as the cost to the self is lower then the benefits provided to others multiplied by their degree of genetic relatedness (on average over evolutionary time). In other words, one path to the evolution of altruism is through kin selection.

The second route to the evolution of altruism was developed earlier in this chapter —the theory of reciprocal altruism. According to this theory, altruism can evolve through reciprocity—when the delivery of benefits to another person results in reciprocation by that person at a later point in time. This route to cooperation occurs when a person incurs a cost to the self that is offset by a benefit received later.

But do these two routes to cooperation exhaust the theoretical possibilities? Tooby and Cosmides (1996) suggest a third potential avenue for the evolution of cooperation and altruism in the context of friendship. They ask us to consider human intuitions— many people become angry when they hear the evolutionary explanation that their friendships are based solely on explicit reciprocity. People report feeling pleasure when they help others in need without insisting on, or expecting, any future reward. In fact, when a person insists on immediately repaying us for a favor we have performed, we interpret this as a sign of a *lack* of friendship (Shackelford & Buss, 1996). We want to help out our friends, we feel, just because they are our friends, not because we will reap some later reward. Furthermore, in a marriage, which can be considered another type of cooperative relationship, an immediate reciprocal exchange orientation is typically linked with marital dissatisfaction and the expectation that the marriage might dissolve (Hatfield & Rapson, 1993; Shackelford & Buss, 1996). Are people deceiving themselves? Do we really want reciprocal rewards, but fool ourselves into believing that we help our friends out of the goodness of our hearts? Tooby and Cosmides (1996) argue that we should attend to people's intuitions in these matters, for they provide a signal that friendships might in fact not be based on reciprocal exchange.

Should Altruism Be Defined According to the Cost Incurred?   According to the two primary evolutionary theories about the evolution of altruism, altruism is not considered to have occurred unless the individual who is the altruist incurs a cost. In kin selection the person incurs a cost to the self that is offset by the benefit gained by a genetic relative. In the case of reciprocal altruism the person incurs a cost to the self that is later offset by a benefit gained by the self when the friend returns the favor. In short, altruism has been defined by the costs the altruist incurs.

What happens when we reframe the definition? Rather than focusing on whether a person incurs costs, why not focus on the evolution of mechanisms designed to deliver benefits to others? In fact, it is the existence of mechanisms designed to deliver benefits to others that we are trying to explain to begin with, regardless of whether they turn out to be costly to the altruist. Let's consider a simple example. Imagine that you are about to drive to your favorite grocery store to stock up on food for the week and a friend asks if he can come along to pick up a few items. By letting your friend come along in your car you incur no additional cost—you were going to the store regardless. So according to the two classical theories of the evolution of altruism this act would *not* be defined as altruism because you are not incurring a cost. Common sense, of course, tells us that you are certainly delivering a benefit to your friend, and this is true whether the act of helping your friend is beneficial to you, doesn't have any effect, or is costly. Tooby and Cosmides (1996) suggest that we need to understand the evolution of mechanisms designed to deliver benefits to others, regardless of whether they are costly to the person doing the delivering.

From an evolutionary perspective, in fact, the greater the cost to a person of delivering benefits to others, the less widespread delivering such benefits will be. The less costly it is to deliver benefits to others, the more widespread they will be. Once adaptations for delivering benefits to others have evolved, further evolution will act to minimize their costs, or even make it beneficial to the actor to deliver such benefits. This reasoning suggests there is a large class of altruistic mechanisms that have gone unexplored—mechanisms designed to deliver benefits to others when actions stemming from them are least costly and most beneficial to the actor. This takes us out of the realm of kin selection and reciprocal altruism and brings us to the "banker's paradox."

The Banker's Paradox.   Bankers who loan money face a dilemma—a larger number of people seek loans than any bank has money to lend. Bankers must make hard decisions about to whom they should loan money. Some people are good credit risks and demonstrate a high likelihood of paying back the money. Others are poor credit risks, and may not be able to pay the money back. The "banker's paradox" (Tooby & Cosmides, 1996) is this: Those who need money most desperately are precisely the same people who are the lousiest credit risks; those who need money less are far better credit risks, so the bank ends up loaning money to those who need it least, while refusing to loan money to those who need it most.

This dilemma is similar to a profound adaptive problem faced by our ancestors. Each person has a limited amount of help to dispense to others. When someone most urgently needs help, however, is precisely the time when they are the worst "credit risk" and are least likely to be able to reciprocate. If one of our ancestors became injured or diseased, for example, that is precisely the time when he or she most needed help, but was least likely to be a good person on whom to spend one's limited time helping. Our ancestors thus faced a dilemma similar to that of bankers—they had to make critical decisions about *to whom* to "extend credit" and *when* to extend credit to other individuals. Just as some people are better "credit risks" for banks some people are more attractive as objects of our naturally limited ability to assist.

What sorts of adaptations might regulate these crucial decisions? First, people should be able to evaluate whether a person to whom they extend credit will be *willing* to repay in the future. Is this person someone who commonly exploits others for their resources, or someone who appreciates the help he or she receives and tries to bestow benefits on others? Second, people should be able to evaluate whether the person will be in a position to repay in the future. Is this person's fortune likely to change for the better in the future, or will the dire current circumstances continue? And third, is helping this particular person the best use of one's limited capacity to help, relative to other people who might be more attractive objects of investment?

If the recipient of the help dies, suffers a permanent loss of status within the group, or becomes severely impaired, then one's investment might be lost. If a person is in dire straights, then he or she becomes less desirable as an investment relative to individuals whose circumstances are more favorable. This might lead to adaptations that cause a person to callously abandon a friend precisely when he or she most needs help. On the other hand, if the person's trouble is temporary, such as an unusual failure at hunting, then the person might be an especially attractive object for help. Indeed, helping someone whose need is temporary might be promising because the help would be greatly appreciated by the person in need. In sum, selection should favor adaptations that motivate good decisions about when and to whom to extend one's help. Yet the problem remains: Evolution should favor psychological mechanisms that caused people to desert you precisely when you most needed help. How can selection get us out of this predicament? How might we evolve to induce others to help us when we need it most?

Becoming Irreplaceable.   Tooby and Cosmides (1996) propose one solution to this adaptive problem: becoming irreplaceable or indispensable to others. Consider a hypothetical example. Suppose two people are in need of your assistance, but you can only help one of them. Both are your friends and both provide you with benefits that are roughly equal in value to you (e.g., one helps you with your math homework, the other helps you by providing notes from classes you miss). Both fall ill at the same time but you can only nurse one of them back to health. Which one do you help? One factor that might influence this decision is which friend is more irreplaceable. If you know of several other people who might provide you with notes from classes that you miss, for example, but you don't know anyone who is willing or able to help you with your math homework, then your math friend is more difficult to replace. A replaceable person—someone who provides benefits that are readily available from others—in short, is more vulnerable to desertion than someone who is irreplaceable, even if these two friends provide benefits to you that are equal in value. The loyalty of your friendship, according to this reasoning, should be based in part on how irreplaceable each friend has become.

How might a person act to increase the odds that he or she becomes irreplaceable, and thus is an attractive object of investment for other people? Tooby and Cosmides (1996) outline several strategies. One can

1. promote a reputation that highlights one's unique or exceptional attributes;
2. be motivated to recognize personal attributes that others value but that they have difficulty getting from other people;
3. cultivate specialized skills that increase irreplaceability;
4. preferentially seek out people or groups that most strongly value what one has to offer and what others in the group tend to lack—that is, where one's assets will be most appreciated;
5. avoid social groups where one's unique attributes are not valued, or where one's unique attributes are easily provided by others; or
6. drive off rivals who threaten to offer benefits to others that that person alone formerly provided.

No empirical studies have been conducted thus far to test the effectiveness of these strategies, all of which are based on becoming irreplaceable as a solution to the banker's paradox. However, these strategies appear to capture many aspects of what people actually do. People preferentially choose professions that make use of their unique talents, whether in the form of athletic ability, manual dexterity, spatial ability, facility with languages, or musical talent, for example. We continually split into smaller local groups—churches splinter off into different denominations and sects; psychologists splinter off into different "schools" of thought. We do feel threatened when the "new kid in town" has talents that are similar to, or exceed, the talents that formerly we alone offered. In sum, people appear to act in many ways to cultivate a sense of individuality and uniqueness that would facilitate becoming irreplaceable—methods that encourage others to deliver benefits through thick and thin.

Fair-Weather Friends, Deep Engagement, and the Dilemmas of Modern Living.
It's easy to be someone's friend when times are good. It's when you are really in trouble that you find out who are your true friends. Everyone has experienced fair-weather friends who are only there when times are good. But finding a "true friend," someone you know in your heart you can rely on when the going gets tough, can be a challenge.

A profound adaptive problem for humans is distinguishing "true friends" who are deeply engaged in our welfare from "fairweather friends."

The problem is that when times are good, fair-weather friends and true friends act pretty much alike. It's difficult to know who are your true friends when the sailing is smooth. Fair-weather friends can mimic true friends, so the adaptive problem becomes how to differentiate true friends, who are deeply engaged in your welfare from fairweather friends, who will disappear at your hour of deepest need (Tooby & Cosmides, 1996). Selection should fashion in humans assessment mechanisms to make these differentiations. The strongest tests, the most reliable evidence of friendship, come from the help you receive when you are desperately in need. Receiving help during this time will be a far more reliable litmus test than help received at any other time. Intuitively, we do seem to have special recall for precisely these times. We take pains to express our appreciation, communicating that we will never forget the person who helped us when we needed it most.

Modern living creates a paradox, however (Tooby & Cosmides, 1996). Humans generally act to avoid episodes of treacherous personal trouble, and many of today's "hostile forces of nature" that would have put our ancestors in jeopardy have been harnessed or controlled. We have laws to deter robbery, assault, and murder. We have police to perform many of the functions previously performed by one's friends. We have medical knowledge that has eliminated or reduced many sources of disease and illness. We live in an environment that is in many ways safer and more stable than that inhabited by our ancestors. Paradoxically, therefore, we suffer from a relative scarcity of critical events that would allow us to accurately assess those who are deeply engaged in our welfare and discriminate them from our fair-weather friends. It is possible that the loneliness and sense of alienation many feel in modern living—a lack of a feeling of deep social connectedness despite the presence of many seemingly warm and friendly interactions—may stem from the lack of critical assessment events (e.g., times of trouble) that tell us who is deeply engaged in our welfare (Tooby & Cosmides, 1996).

Limited Niches for Friendships.   According to the Tooby and Cosmides theory of the evolution of friendship outlined above, each person has a limited amount of time, energy, and effort. Just as you cannot be in two places at one time, the decision to befriend one person is simultaneously a decision not to befriend another. According to this theory each person has a limited number of *friendship niches,* so the adaptive problem is deciding who will fill these slots. The implications of this theory are different from the implications of the standard theory of reciprocal altruism, in which you bestow benefits in the expectation that they will be returned at a later time. Tooby and Cosmides (1996) suggest instead that several other factors should determine your choice of friends.

1. *Number of slots already filled.* How many friends do you already have, and are they true friends or fair-weather friends? If they are few in number, then psychological mechanisms should motivate actions such as recruiting new friends, consolidating or deepening existing friendships, or making yourself more appealing to prospective friends, should you be so inclined.

2. *Evaluate who emits positive externalities.* Let's say that someone who is physically formidable lives in your neighborhood—perhaps someone built like Arnold Schwarzenegger. His mere existence in your neighborhood deters muggers and other criminals, so you benefit, because fewer criminals prey on you and your family as a result of this person's presence. Some people provide benefits that are properly regarded as side effects of their existence or actions—benefits to you that are not really intentional acts of altruism. Your physically formidable neighbor did not become muscular so as to bestow benefits on you. Instead, your neighbor provides benefits that are side effects or incidental consequences, rather than intentional acts of altruism. Economists call these beneficial side effects *positive externalities.*

People who have special talents or abilities—such as speaking others' dialects or being better at locating berries, game, or water—may provide benefits to those with whom they associate, regardless of whether they help intentionally. Those who radiate many such positive externalities are more attractive as potential friends than those who emit fewer, above and beyond any intentional acts of helping the person performs. Therefore, we would expect selection to have fashioned assessment mechanisms to identify and value such individuals and to motivate us to fill our friendship niches with them.

3. *Select friends who are good at reading your mind.* Helping someone is easier if you can read his or her mind and anticipate needs. A friend who can read your mind and understand your desires, beliefs, and values can help you in ways that are beneficial to you, as well as less costly to him or her. Someone who fails to recognize when you need something, for example, could miss an opportunity to help you. Everyone has known someone who intuitively seemed to "know" what they were thinking, sometimes even before they thought it. These people make good companions.

4. *Select friends who consider you to be irreplaceable.* A friend who considers you irreplaceable has a stronger stake in your well being than someone who considers you expendable. Filling your life with friends who consider you irreplaceable, all else being equal, should result in a greater flow of benefits.

5. *Select friends who want the same things that you want.* Hanging around with friends who value the same things you do will have a wonderful consequence: in the process of changing their local environments to suit their own desires they will simultaneously change your environment as you might like because the two of you desire the same things. Let's take a trivial example. Suppose you like wild parties and you have a friend who also likes wild parties. Your friend seeks out, gets invited to, and frequently attends such parties. Because you are friends with this person, you get to tag along some of the time. Thus at little or no cost your friend provides you with benefits, merely because you happen to want the same things. In the same way, you provide your friend with benefits because you arrange your environment in ways to suit your own desires— because your friend shares those desires, he or she benefits from your arrangements. In sum, selecting a friend who wants the same things you want creates a mutual benefit flow of benefits.

Because we all have a limited number of "friend slots" to fill, selection should favor psychological mechanisms designed to monitor the flow of benefits from each friend—benefits not limited to those the friend intentionally delivers, but also those that flow as a result of shared values and positive externalities, and the degree to which these benefits are irreplaceable. According to Tooby and Cosmides (1996) the primary risk in friendship is not being cheated, as would be the case if friendship were based solely on reciprocal exchange. Rather, the primary risk is failing to form friendships characterized by mutual deep engagement, or being surrounded by fair-weather friends instead of true friends. The psychological mechanisms that monitor friendships, therefore, should include signals that a friend's affection might be declining, signals that another person might be better suited to filling our precious and limited friendship slots, and signals about the degree to which we are regarded as irreplaceable by our friends.

Deep Engagement versus Reciprocal Exchange.   The modern world is filled with social interactions involving reciprocal exchange. Every time you buy something at a store you are exchanging money for goods. Every time you buy lunch for someone and that person reciprocates by buying you lunch the next time, you are engaging in reciprocal exchange. But these exchanges typically do not characterize true friendships. Indeed, the explicit expectation that someone will return each favor in the form of a similar favor characterizes weak friendships, which lack true genuine trust (Tooby & Cosmides, 1996).

What characterizes true friends is another constellation of emotions and expectations entirely. We feel pleasure in the company of our friends, and experience pleasure rather than envy when they are successful. We derive deep satisfaction from shared values and common world views. We are moved to help our friends when they separately need our assistance, even without any explicit expectation that our efforts will be repaid immediately. The widespread sense of social alienation, according to Tooby and Cosmides (1996), occurs because the modern world is filled with explicit contingent exchanges at an unprecedented level, compounded by the relative absence of deep engagement that characterizes true friendship. Future research in evolutionary psychology will undoubtedly document the complex constellation of psychological mechanisms dedicated to the formation of deep engagement.

Costs and Benefits of Friendship

In principle, friendships can provide a bounty of benefits that may be linked directly or indirectly to reproduction. Friends may offer us food and shelter or take care of us when we are ill, thus helping solve adaptive problems of survival. Friends may introduce us to potential mates, thus helping solve an adaptive problem of reproduction. Despite the potential benefits, however, friends may also become our competitors or rivals. They may inflict costs on us by revealing our personal information to our enemies, competing for access to the same valuable resources, or even competing for the same mates. Little is known about the precise benefits and costs of friendships.

Friendships vary on a number of dimensions. One dimension is gender. Friendships may be of the same or the opposite sex; the potential benefits and costs may differ dramatically for these two types of friendship. A same-sex friendship, for example, carries the potential for intrasexual rivalry. An opposite-sex friendship does not. An opposite-sex friendship, however, offers a benefit that a same-sex friendship generally lacks, namely, the potential for mating. Bleske and Buss (under review) tested a number of hypotheses about the benefits and costs of friendship by gathering two sources of information from participants: (1) perceptions of *how beneficial* (or costly) various items would be if they received them from a friend, and (2) reports of *how often* they received these benefits (or costs) from their friends.

The first hypothesis was that for men more than women, one function of opposite-sex friendship is to provide short-term sexual access. This hypothesis follows from the logic of the theory of parental investment (Trivers, 1972). Over the course of human evolutionary history men have been the less investing sex, with their relative reproductive success constrained primarily by the number of women with whom they have sexual intercourse. Thus men may have evolved a powerful desire for sexual access to a large number of women, including their opposite-sex friends.

As predicted, men evaluated the potential for sexual access to their opposite-sex friends as significantly more beneficial than did women, as shown in Figure 9.3 on page 274. Men also reported experiencing unreciprocated attraction toward their opposite-sex friends more often than did women. Women more often than men reported having an opposite-sex friendship in which their friend was romantically attracted to them but not vice versa (Figure 9.4 on page 274). Moreover, men were denied sexual access to their opposite-sex friends more frequently than women. In sum, the evidence supports the hypothesis that men more than women view sexual access as a benefit of opposite-sex friendship.

The second hypothesis was that for women more than for men, a function of opposite-sex friendship is to provide protection. Over the course of our evolutionary history, those women who were able to secure resources (e.g., food and material goods) and protection from men were more reproductively successful than those women who were unable to secure resources and protection for them and their potential offspring. Bleske

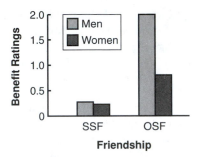

FIGURE 9.3   Benefits of Friendship: Potential for Sexual Access. Results show that men evaluated the potential for sexual access as significantly more beneficial than did women.

SSF = same-sex friendship; OSF = opposite-sex friendship.

Data from Bleske, A., & Buss, D. M. (June 1997). *The evolutionary psychology of special "friendships."* Paper presented at the ninth annual meeting of the Human Behavior and Evolution Society, University of Arizona, Tucson.

and Buss (under review) hypothesized that women have an evolved preference for men who are able and willing to offer them resources and protection, or who have future prospects of an ability to offer such benefits. In support of this hypothesis, women reported that they received protection from their opposite-sex friends. On a scale of 0 to 6, women's reports of receiving protection from their opposite-sex friends averaged 3.06, whereas men's reports averaged only 1.68—a statistically reliable difference.

A third hypothesis was that opposite-sex friendships function to provide information about the opposite sex. Given that opposite-sex friends may be more likely to have information about their own gender, men and women should perceive such information

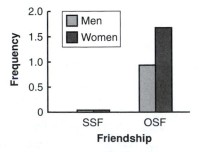

FIGURE 9.4   Experiencing Romantic Attraction from a Friend. Women more often than men reported having an opposite-sex friendship in which their friend felt romantically attracted to them, but in which they were not romantically attracted to their friend.

SSF = same-sex friendship; OSF = opposite-sex friendship.

Data from Bleske, A., & Buss, D. M. (June 1997). *The evolutionary psychology of special "friendships."* Paper presented at the ninth annual meeting of the Human Behavior and Evolution Society, University of Arizona, Tucson.

as a benefit of opposite-sex friendship more than of same-sex friendship. If gaining knowledge about what the opposite sex prefers in a short-term or a long-term mate has helped men and women solve the many adaptive problems of human mating, for example, men and women should perceive such information as highly beneficial. In support of this hypothesis, men and women did report receiving information about the opposite sex from their opposite-sex friends ($M = 2.84$) more often than from their same-sex friends ($M = 1.86$). In same-sex friendships women received information about the opposite sex more often ($M = 2.15$) than did men ($M = 1.48$). This type of information appears to be a more characteristic benefit to women than to men of same-sex friendships. Moreover, men and women reported that receiving information about the opposite sex from an opposite-sex friend ($M = 4.15$) was more beneficial than receiving such information from a same-sex friend ($M = 3.12$). In sum, the empirical tests conducted as part of this study support the contention that friendships provide information about members of the opposite sex.

A fourth hypothesis was that men and women will perceive intrasexual rivalry as a potential cost of same-sex friendship. If same-sex friends are more likely to have similar interests, personalities, and desirability to mates than two same-sex individuals taken at random, same-sex friends may find themselves in competition with each other to attract a long-term mate. As predicted, men and women reported intrasexual rivalry over mates in their same-sex friendships ($M = 1.03$). The reported rate of competition was relatively low, but significantly higher than rates of sexual rivalry in opposite-sex friendships ($M = 0.14$). Further, men and women evaluated the potential for sexual rivalry as *more costly* in a same-sex friendship ($M = 2.12$) than in an opposite-sex friendship ($M = 0.71$). These data suggest that sexual rivalry is not unique to interactions between same-sex strangers and enemies. Interestingly, men reported more frequent intrasexual rivalry in their same-sex friendships ($M = 1.35$) than did women ($M = .79$). It is likely that this greater sexual rivalry stems from men's greater desire for short-term casual sex—an interpretation supported by the finding that men view short-term sexual access as an important benefit of opposite-sex friends. In sum, the results suggest that sexual rivalry does sometimes occur in same-sex friendships, especially for men, and it is perceived to be a cost of such friendships.

Distinguishing between Benefits and Functions of Friendship.   An evolutionary perspective requires a conceptual distinction between *beneficial effects* and *functions*. One benefit of having opposable thumbs, for example, is the ability to use scissors or to operate a joystick on a computer game, but clearly these modern benefits are not considered proper functions of opposable thumbs—the adaptive problems they were designed to solve (unless, perhaps, one wants to consider a more abstract function, such as tool use). Similarly, modern friendships may provide many benefits—such as help with homework or assistance with computer programming—that are not considered proper functions of friendship. The hypothesis that something is a proper function of friendship carries a conceptual assertion—that friendship evolved in part because it contributed recurrently to the solution of a particular adaptive problem over human evolutionary history.

The Bleske and Buss studies cannot definitively distinguish between beneficial effects and evolved functions of friendship. The hypothesis that one function of friendship for women is physical protection, for example, would ideally require the following sources of evidence: (1) Do women desire friends who can offer this benefit? (2) Do they select friends preferentially using this criterion? (3) Do women break off friendships that fail to provide this benefit when the situation calls for it, such as when they are threatened? (4) Do women perceive that protection is an important benefit derived from friendship? (5) Do the sexes differ in their perceptions of the importance of this benefit? (6) Do the above design features appear cross-culturally?

These studies do provide evidence bearing on only some of these standards, such as perceptions of benefit, frequency of receiving benefit, and sex differences in perceptions and reported frequencies. Although the current studies cannot definitively differentiate between benefits and functions of friendship, they do identify benefits that are reasonable candidates for further examination as possible functions of friendship.

Summary

We started this chapter by considering the problem of altruism: design features that aid the reproduction of other individuals, even though the altruist who has this feature incurs a cost. The puzzle is how such altruism could have evolved, given that it seems to go against Hamilton's Rule. One solution came from the theory of reciprocal altruism, which states that psychological mechanisms for providing benefits to nonrelatives can evolve as long as the delivery of those benefits causes the recipient to reciprocate at some point in the future. The most important adaptive problem the reciprocal altruist faces, however, is the threat of cheaters—people who take benefits without reciprocating at a later time.

One solution to this problem emerged from a computer tournament conducted by Robert Axelrod. He discovered that tit for tat—a strategy in which an individual cooperated on the first move but reciprocated in kind thereafter—was highly successful. It tended to promote cooperation, but also helped to solve the problem of cheating by punishing defectors immediately.

Examples of reciprocal altruism are abundant in the animal world. Vampire bats share their blood with "friends" who were unsuccessful on any given night; at a later point the friends reciprocate the favor, giving blood preferentially to those who have recently helped them. Baboons, vervet monkeys, and chimpanzees also form reciprocal alliances. Baboons and vervets who give help are most likely to receive help. Baboons and vervets tend to form stable alliances, so that the friend who "asks" for help is most likely to give help at some point in the future when "asked." These acts of aid are most likely to be the result of reciprocal altruism rather than kinship. Among chimpanzees, reciprocal alliances form among males, among females, and among males and females.

Social contract theory proposes the evolution of five cognitive capacities in humans to solve the problem of cheaters and engage in successful social exchange. Humans must be able to recognize other individuals; remember their mutual history of interactions; recognize the values, desires, and needs of others; communicate the values, desires, and needs of others; and represent the costs and benefits of a large variety of items of exchange. Researchers have demonstrated that people have cheater-detection mechanisms, which were revealed by showing a special ability to reason when logic problems are phrased in the form of social contracts. People tend to be especially vigilant about searching for those who have taken benefits without paying the expected costs.

The evolution of friendship poses a special problem that is captured by the banker's paradox: Although banks are in the business of loaning money to people who need it, the people who most need money are the worst credit risks, so banks end up loaning money to people who need it least while denying loans to those who need it most. Similarly, when we most need help from our friends likely coincides with the time when we are the poorest "credit risk," unable to return benefits to those who help us. One solution to this paradox is to become irreplaceable—if we provide benefits that no one else offers, our friends have a tremendous stake in our welfare and will therefore want to help when we most need it. A key distinction is between fair-weather and true friends. We tend to know who are our true friends from their behavior toward us when we most need their help. It is possible that the sense of alienation many people feel stems from the fact that humans have conquered many "hostile forces of nature," and so are less likely to face life-threatening events that allow us to know who are our true friends—those who are deeply engaged in our welfare. Although people may have many significant friendships, many feel that others are not deeply involved in their lives.

Some work has been conducted on the functions of friendship by exploring the perceived benefits (and costs) of friendships. Men and women form same-sex friendships as well as opposite-sex friendships, but the evidence points to sex differences in the functions of friendship. Men more than women perceive short-term sexual access as a benefit of opposite-sex friendships. Women more than men perceive protection as a benefit of opposite-sex friendships. Both sexes perceive information about the opposite sex to be an important benefit of opposite-sex friendship.

One cost of same-sex friendship is the potential for sexual rivalry. Sexual rivalry appears to be more prevalent among male friends than among female friends, perhaps because of men's stronger desire for short-term mating, which would throw them into conflict more often.

10 Aggression and Warfare

From an evolutionary point of view, the leading cause of violence is maleness.
—Robert Wright, 1995

One afternoon in January 1974, a group of eight chimpanzees in the Gombe National Park in Tanzania formed a fighting party and traveled south (Wrangham & Peterson, 1996). They appeared to take pains to maintain silence and stealth as they traveled toward the border of their usual home range. They crossed that border, followed by Hillali Matama, a researcher from Jane Goodall's Gombe team. A short distance away was Godi, a young male roughly twenty-one years old, who was feasting peacefully on the ripe fruit of a tree. Godi usually ventured out for food with his comrades, the six other males in the Kahama chimpanzee community, but this day he had chosen to travel alone.

By the time Godi spotted the eight trespassers, they had already reached his feeding tree. Godi made a mad dash to elude them but they gave chase, caught up with him, and tackled him by grabbing his legs. Humphrey, one of the leading chimps in the fighting party, pinned two of Godi's limbs, holding him immobile while the others gathered around. With Godi's face pushed into the dirt, the other males attacked—in a frenzy of screaming, charging, biting, and striking, Godi's attackers looked like a human gang of adolescents beating up a lone victim who happened to be in the wrong place at the wrong time. After ten minutes the pummeling and biting stopped, and Godi watched as his attackers left to return to their home range. Godi bled from more than a dozen wounds, his body a bruised mess from the vicious attack. The researchers never saw Godi again. Although he did not die immediately from the attack, they speculated that he almost surely died within a few days or a week.

This attack is remarkable not for its viciousness, nor for the coordinated manner in which the intruders rendered their victim helpless. It is remarkable because it was the first time a human observer had witnessed a chimpanzee raid a neighboring territory to assault an enemy with lethal results. Further, it led researchers to question their long-held assumption that other primates are peaceful and harmonious, and that only humans kill their own. It also caused researchers to question the long-held assumption that chimpanzees represented an "arcadian existence of primal innocence" or the peaceful "paradise that man had somehow lost" (Ardry, 1966, p. 222). On the contrary, leading researchers have concluded that the "male violence that surrounds and threatens chimpanzee communities is so extreme that to be in the wrong place at the wrong time from the wrong group means death" (Wrangham & Peterson, 1996, p. 21).

Humans are not chimpanzees, of course, and we must be wary of superficial comparisons between humans and other species. Evidence for extreme aggression in chimpanzees, by itself, may say nothing about aggression in humans. Wrangham and Peterson (1996), however, make a remarkable observation. Of the more than ten million animal species that exist, including four thousand mammals, only two species have been documented to show intense male-initiated territorial aggression, including coordinated coalitions that raid neighboring territories and result in lethal attacks on members of their own species: chimpanzees and humans.

Humans, like chimpanzees, form aggressive male-bonded coalitions in which members support each other in a mutual quest to aggress against others. Human recorded history is filled with such rivalries: the Spartans and the Athenians, the crusades, the Hatfields and the McCoys, the Palestinians and the Israelis, and the Tutsis and the Hutus. In all cultures men commonly have bonded together to attack other groups or to defend their own. Humans and chimpanzees share this unique pattern of aggression and with no other known species (Wrangham & Peterson, 1996).

From these observations we can ask: What is the source of human aggression? What are the major patterns of human aggression—who is aggressive and under what circumstances? Why does it exist in the forms that it does? These are the questions that will be the focus of this chapter.

The Demise of Instinct Theory

Contemporary psychological theories of aggression often invoke general learning mechanisms combined with explanations specifying the plagues of modern living—violence in movies and television, teachings in Western society, the purchase by parents of toy weapons for their children (Berkowitz, 1993). By watching aggressive models on television, for example, children are said to acquire aggressive dispositions through observational learning (Berkowitz, 1993; Eron, 1982; Huesmann & Eron, 1986). Although these factors undoubtedly play a causal role in the development of aggression, they run aground as *complete* explanations when confronted with historic and cross-cultural records. These factors don't explain the paleontological findings, which reveal a long history of human violence thousands of years before the invention of guns or television, or even the rise of Western civilization (Trinkaus & Zimmerman, 1982). They don't explain the prevalence of violence among traditional societies uninfluenced by Western civilization and entirely lacking exposure to television (e.g., Chagnon, 1983). Among the Yanomamö of Venezuela, for example, 30 percent of the males die at the hands of other humans, either from within their local tribe or as a result of wars with neighboring tribes

(Chagnon, 1988). Although the Yanomamö may be unusually violent as a group, rates of homicide are commonly high among traditional societies, such as the Ache of Paraguay (Hill & Hurtado, 1996) and the Tiwi of northern Australia (Hart & Pilling, 1960). Even in the relatively peaceful !Kung San of Botswana, homicide rates exceed those of the city of Detroit (Daly & Wilson, 1988). So another set of explanatory principles is needed, one that does not rely primarily on modern phenomena such as violence on television, the mass media, Western society, toys, crowding, or the alienation of modern living.

Most social psychology textbooks include chapters on aggression that examine various explanations for its occurrence (e.g., Myers, 1995; Sabini, 1995). Among the explanations considered, one often finds a section on the "instinct theory of aggression," usually attributed to Sigmund Freud and ethologist Konrad Lorenz that is selected to represent a class of "biological explanations." According to these accounts, aggressive energy is said to be an instinctual drive that builds up until it explodes. It may be "released" by external stimuli, but its internal building quality guarantees that it will be "pushed out" one way or another.

This depiction of instinct theory is usually dismissed with dispatch. According to Myers (1995), for example, "the idea that aggression is an instinct collapsed as the list of supposed human instincts grew to include nearly every conceivable human behavior . . . what the social scientists had tried to do was to *explain* social behavior by *naming* it" (p. 438; emphasis in the original). The second argument for dismissal is that "instinct theory . . . fails to account for the variation in aggressiveness, from person to person and culture to culture" (Myers, 1995, p. 439). According to this argument, "biological" represents those things that are invariant, and so evidence of cultural or individual variability requires "nonbiological" explanations.

Berkowitz (1993) provides a more detailed critique. He dismisses the instinct idea on the following grounds: (1) scientists have not discovered in the brain or body any reservoirs of aggressive energy; (2) research rarely reveals spontaneous aggression, but commonly finds that aggressive behavior occurs in response to external stimuli; and (3) there are different types of aggression, not one single type. Following these dismissals textbook writers proceeded to spend the bulk of the coverage of theories invoking environmental conditions, such as observational learning as a result of media exposure to violence.

Perhaps the dismissal was too hasty. During the domination of learning theory, which reigned over psychology for the bulk of this century, biological explanations were commonly ridiculed. The dichotomies drawn between instincts and learning, biology and environment, or nature and nurture, however, are inherently false, as we have discussed in previous chapters (Tooby & Cosmides, 1992). These dichotomies obscure more than they reveal.

The fact that humans show such behavioral flexibility and context sensitivity is certainly enough to discard notions of inflexible aggressive instincts invariably getting "pushed out" into behavior regardless of circumstances. But neither are humans passive receptacles for environmental forces, unformed lumps of clay until they are molded by reinforcement contingencies. A more complex model is needed—a model anchored in evolutionary psychology.

Aggression as a Solution to Adaptive Problems

An evolutionary psychological perspective does not yield a single hypothesis about the origins of aggression or any other behavioral phenomenon. Within evolutionary psychology several hypotheses are sometimes proposed and put into scientific competition with each other. Below we detail several leading candidates for adaptive problems to which aggression might be an evolved solution (Buss & Shackelford, 1997b).

Co-Opt the Resources of Others

Humans, perhaps more than any other species, stockpile resources that historically have been valuable for survival and reproduction. These include fertile land and access to fresh water, food, tools, and weapons. There are many means for gaining access to the valuable resources held by others, such as engaging in social exchange, stealing, or trickery. Aggression is also a means of co-opting the resources of others.

Aggression to co-opt resources can occur at the individual or the group level. At the individual level one can use physical force to take resources from others. Modern-day forms include bullies at school who take the lunch money, books, leather jackets, or designer sneakers from other children (Olweus, 1978). Childhood aggression is commonly about resources such as toys and territory (Campbell, 1993). Adult forms include muggings and beatings as a means to forcibly extract money or other goods from others. The *threat* of aggression may be enough to secure resources from others, as when a child

In humans, males more than females resort to physical aggression to co-opt the resources of others. The sex difference in the use of physical aggression emerges as early as three years of age.

gives up his lunch money to prevent a beating or a small store owner gives mobsters money for "protection" to prevent his or her business from being ruined.

People, particularly men, often form coalitions for the purposes of forcibly co-opting the resources of others. Among the Yanomamö, for example, male coalitions raid neighboring tribes and forcibly take food and reproductive-aged women (Chagnon, 1983). Throughout recorded human history warfare has been used to co-opt the land possessed by others, and to the victors go the spoils. The acquisition of reproductively relevant resources through aggression is one evolutionary hypothesis. Selection could have favored aggressive strategies when the benefits, on average, outweighed the costs in the currency of fitness.

Defend against Attack

The presence of aggressive conspecifics poses a serious adaptive problem to would-be victims: they stand to lose the valuable resources that are co-opted by their aggressors. In addition, victims may suffer injury or death, impeding both survival and reproduction. Victims of aggression may also lose in the currency of status and reputation. The loss of face or honor entailed by being abused with impunity can lead to further abuse by others, who may select victims in part based on the ease with which they can be exploited or their unwillingness to retaliate.

Aggression, therefore, can be used to defend against attack. Aggression may be an effective solution to this adaptive problem by preventing one's resources from being taken forcibly. It can be used to cultivate a reputation that deters other would-be aggressors. And it can be used to prevent the loss of status and honor that would otherwise follow from being victimized with impunity. Defense against attack, in summary, is a second evolutionary hypothesis for the origins of human aggression.

Inflict Costs on Intrasexual Rivals

A third adaptive problem is posed by same-sex rivals who are vying for the same resources. One such resource consists of access to valuable members of the opposite sex. The image of the bully kicking beach sand in the face of a weaker man and walking away with that man's girlfriend is a stereotyped notion of intrasexual competition, but the notion underlying it is powerful.

Aggression to inflict costs on rivals can range from verbal barbs to beatings and killings. Men and women both derogate their same-sex rivals, impugning their status and reputation to make them less desirable to members of the other sex (Buss & Dedden, 1990). At the other end of the spectrum, men sometimes kill their same-sex rivals in duels. Bar fights that start as trivial altercations can escalate to the point of death (Daly & Wilson, 1988). And men sometimes kill other men they find out have had sex with their wives or girlfriends (Daly & Wilson, 1988).

Because evolution operates according to *differences* in designs, a cost inflicted on a rival can translate into a benefit for the perpetrator. According to this third evolutionary hypothesis, a key function of verbal and physical aggression is to inflict costs on same-sex rivals.

Negotiate Status and Power Hierarchies

A fourth evolutionary hypothesis is that aggression functions to increase one's status or power within existing social hierarchies. Among the Ache of Paraguay and the Yano-mamö of Venezuela, for example, men engage in ritual club fights with other men. Men who have survived many club fights are admired and feared, and so attain status and power (Chagnon, 1983; Hill & Hurtado, 1996). Modern societies have ritualized aggression in the form of boxing matches, for example, after which the victor experiences status elevation and the loser a status loss.

Men who expose themselves to danger in warfare to kill enemies are regarded as brave and courageous, and consequently experience an elevation in their status within the group (Chagnon, 1983; Hill & Hurtado, 1996). Within street gangs, men who display ferocity in their beatings of fellow or rival gang members experience status elevation (Campbell, 1993).

The hypothesis that aggression sometimes serves the adaptive function of status elevation does not imply that this strategy works in all groups. Aggression within many groups may result in a status decrement. A professor who punched another professor at a faculty meeting or in a crowded hall or class, for example, would almost certainly experience a decline in status. The key to the status elevation hypothesis is to specify the evolved psychological mechanisms that are sensitive to the *social contexts* in which aggression pays.

Deter Rivals from Future Aggression

Cultivating a reputation as aggressive may function to deter aggression and other forms of cost infliction from others. And most would think twice about stealing from a Mafia hit man or tangling with Mike Tyson. And most people would hesitate to flirt with the girlfriend of a member of the Hell's Angels motorcycle gang. Aggression and the reputation for aggression thus can act as deterrents, helping to solve the adaptive problem of others attempting to co-opt one's resources and mates.

Deter Long-Term Mates from Sexual Infidelity

A sixth hypothesis is that aggression and the threat of aggression function to deter long-term mates from sexual infidelity. Much empirical evidence suggests that male sexual jealousy is the leading cause or precipitating context of spousal battering (Daly, Wilson, & Weghorst, 1982). Studies of shelters for battered women, for example, document that in the majority of cases women cite extreme jealousy on the part of their husbands or boyfriends as the key cause of the beating (Dobash & Dobash, 1984). As repugnant as this may be, some men do beat their wives to deter them from consorting with other men.

The Context-Specificity of Aggression

This account of six key adaptive problems that might be solved by a strategy of aggression strongly suggests that aggression is not a unitary, monolithic, or context-blind strategy. Rather, aggression is likely to be highly context specific, triggered only in contexts that resemble those in which our ancestors confronted certain adaptive problems and reaped particular benefits.

Consider the use of spousal battering to solve the adaptive problem of a partner's potential infidelity. This problem is more likely to be confronted by men who are lower in relative mate value than their wives, for example, or who experience a decrement (e.g., loss of a job) in the resources that women value (Buss, 1994). Under these conditions, the probability that a woman might commit infidelity or defect from the relationship altogether is likely to be higher, so the adaptive problem is confronted more aggressively. Men in these conditions are predicted to be more aggressive than men whose partners are less likely to commit infidelity or to leave the relationship.

Adaptive benefits must also be evaluated within the context of *costs*. Aggression, by definition, inflicts costs on others, and those others cannot be expected to absorb the costs passively or with indifference: "Lethal retribution is an ancient and cross-culturally universal recourse for those subjected to abuse" (Daly & Wilson, 1988, p. 226). One of the most robust findings in aggression research is that aggression tends to cause retaliatory aggression (Berkowitz, 1993; A. Buss, 1961). This can sometimes cause escalating cycles of aggression and counteraggression, as in the fabled family feud between the Hatfields and the McCoys (Waller, 1993).

One critical context for costs pertains to the reputational consequences of aggression. Cultures and subcultures differ in whether aggression enhances or diminishes status. Among "cultures of honor," for example, failure to aggress when insulted can lead to status loss (Nisbett, 1993). A daughter who has brought shame on the family name by engaging in premarital sex, for example, may be killed as an "honorable" solution to the problem of restoring the status of the family (Daly & Wilson, 1988). The failure to kill such a daughter may result in a lowering of status of the rest of her family in these cultures.

Another dimension of cost pertains to the ability and willingness of the victim to retaliate. Among schoolchildren, bullies typically select victims or "whipping boys" who cannot or will not retaliate (Olweus, 1978). Similarly, the husband of a woman with four strapping brothers and a powerful father living nearby will think twice before beating her for flirting with someone else. The presence of extended kin, therefore, is one context of cost that should moderate the manifestation of spousal violence. Recent empirical evidence supports this prediction. In a study of domestic violence in Madrid, Spain, it was found that women with higher densities of genetic kin both inside and outside Madrid experienced lower levels of domestic violence (Figueredo, 1995). A higher density of genetic kin within Madrid appears to have exerted an even larger protective effect than kin outside Madrid, supporting the importance of kin's proximity.

In some contexts aggressors will suffer reputational damage because of their aggression. In academic circles, for example, physical aggression is shunned, and those who engage in it can suffer ostracism. Among members of some street gangs, the failure to engage in aggression when provoked will result in an irreparable loss of status (Campbell, 1993).

The key point is that an evolutionary psychological perspective predicts that evolved mechanisms will be designed to be sensitive to context, not the rigid invariant expression of aggression depicted in earlier instinct theories. Thus, findings of variability of aggression across contexts, cultures, and individuals in no way falsify particular evolutionary hypotheses. Indeed, that very context sensitivity is a critical lever for testing evolutionary hypotheses (Dekay & Buss, 1992).

Earlier researchers in this area concluded that variability simultaneously falsified "biological" theories and confirmed "learning" theories. Evolutionary psychology jettisons this false dichotomy by proposing a specific interactional model—aggression as evoked by particular adaptive problems confronted in particular cost-benefit contexts. In principle, the mechanisms producing aggression could remain dormant for the entire life of an individual, if the relevant contexts are not encountered. Aggression, on this account, is based on evolved psychological mechanisms, but is not rigid or invariant and does not get "pushed out" regardless of circumstances.

Why Are Men More Violently Aggressive Than Women?

In homicides committed in Chicago between 1965 and 1980, 86 percent were committed by men (Daly & Wilson, 1988). Of these, 80 percent of the victims were also men. Although the exact percentages vary from culture to culture, cross-cultural homicide statistics reveal strikingly similar findings. In all cultures studied to date, men are overwhelmingly more often the killers and the majority of their victims are other men. Any reasonably complete theory of aggression must provide an explanation for both facts— why men engage in violent forms of aggression so much more often than women and why other men comprise the majority of their victims.

An evolutionary model of intrasexual competition provides the foundation for such an explanation. It starts with the theory of parental investment and sexual selection (see Chapter 4). In species in which females invest more heavily in offspring than males, females are a valuable limiting resource on reproduction for males. Males are constrained in their reproduction not so much by their ability to survive but by their ability to gain sexual access to the high-investing females.

The sex difference in minimum obligatory parental investment (e.g., mammalian females bear the burdens of internal fertilization, and gestation) means that males can sire more offspring than females can (see Chapter 4). Stated differently, the ceiling on reproduction is much higher for males than for females. This difference leads to differences in the *variances* in reproduction between the sexes. The differences between the haves and the have-nots, therefore, are greater for males than for females.

The greater the variance in reproduction, the more selection favors riskier strategies (including intrasexual competition) within the sex that shows the higher variance. In an extreme case, such as the elephant seals off the coast of northern California, 5 percent of the males sire 85 percent of all offspring produced in a breeding season (Le Boeuf & Reiter, 1988). Species that show higher variance in the reproduction of one sex compared to the other tend to be highly sexually dimorphic (i.e., different in size and shape) across a variety of physical characteristics. The more intense the effective polygyny, the more dimorphic the sexes are in size and form (Trivers, 1985). Elephant seals are highly sexually dimorphic in weight, for example, with males weighing four times what females weigh (Le Boeuf & Reiter, 1988). Chimpanzees are less sexually dimorphic in weight, with males having roughly twice the weight of females. Humans are mildly dimorphic in weight, with males roughly 12 percent heavier than females. Within primate species, the greater the effective polygyny the more pronounced the sexual dimorphism, and the greater the reproductive variance between the sexes (Alexander, Hoodland, Howard, Noonan, & Sherman, 1979).

Effective polygyny means that some males gain more than their "fair share" of copulations while other males are shut out entirely, banished from contributing to the ancestry of future generations. Such a system leads to more ferocious competition within the high-variance sex. In essence, polygyny selects for risky strategies, including those that lead to violent combat with rivals and those that lead to increased risk taking to acquire the resources needed to attract members of the high-investing sex. Members of one's own sex are primary competitors for valuable members of the opposite sex.

Violence can occur at the top as well as the bottom of the hierarchy. Given an equal sex ratio, for each man who monopolizes two women, another man is consigned to bachelorhood (Daly & Wilson, 1996b). For those facing reproductive oblivion, a risky, aggressive strategy may represent a last resort. Homicide data reveal that men who are poor and unmarried are more likely to kill compared with their more affluent and married counterparts (Wilson & Daly, 1985). In short, there are two sides to the use of aggression in competitive contexts marked by some degree of polygyny: (1) aggression by a male to "win big," thereby gaining access to multiple mates, and (2) aggression to avoid total reproductive failure by being shut out of mating altogether.

To understand why men would take large risks in mating contexts, let's consider an analogy: foraging for food. Consider an animal who is able to secure a foraging territory that provides just enough food to stay alive but not enough food to breed. Outside this territory are risks, such as predators who may make the animal their next meal if he leaves his home territory. In this situation the only males who succeed in breeding are those willing to take risks to venture outside their secure territory to get food. Some will be killed by the predator, of course, and that's why venturing outside is risky. But others will manage to avoid the predator, secure the additional food, and thereby successfully breed. Those who fail to take the risks to venture outside their territory will fail to breed entirely. This situation selects for risk taking as a strategy for breeding. Selection in this context acts as a sieve, filtering out those who fail to take risks.

As Daly and Wilson noted, "sexual dimorphism and violent male–male competition are ancient and enduring elements of our human evolutionary history" (1988, p. 143). Current levels of sexual dimorphism among humans are roughly the same as those of our ancestors living 50,000 years ago. Male–male combat among humans, as among other sexually dimorphic mammals, is a leading cause of injury and death among males.

Modern humans have inherited the psychological mechanisms that led to our ancestors' success. This does *not* imply that men have a conscious or an unconscious desire to increase their reproductive success. Nor does it imply that men have an "aggression instinct" in the sense of some pent-up energy that must be released. Rather, men have inherited from their ancestors psychological mechanisms sensitive to contexts in which aggression probabilistically leads to the successful solution of a particular adaptive problem.

This account provides a parsimonious explanation for both facts revealed in the cross-cultural homicide record. Males are more often the perpetrators of violence because they are the products of a long history of mild but sustained effective polygyny characterized by risky strategies of intrasexual competition for access to the high-investing sex. The fact that men die on average seven years earlier than women is but one of the many markers of this aggressive intrasexual strategy (Trivers, 1985).

Men are the victims of aggression far more than women because men are in competition primarily with other men. It is other men who form the primary sources of strategic interference, other men who impede their access to resources needed to attract women, and other men who try to block their access to women. To the victors go the spoils. The losers remain mateless and sustain injury or even early death.

Women also engage in aggression, and their victims are also typically members of their own sex. In studies of verbal aggression through derogation of competitors, for example, women slander their rivals by impugning their physical appearance and hence their reproductive value (Buss & Dedden, 1990; Campbell, 1993). The forms of aggression committed by women, however, are typically less florid, less violent, and hence less risky than those committed by men—facts accounted for by the theory of parental investment and sexual selection (see Campbell, 1995).

Empirical Evidence for Distinct Adaptive Patterns of Aggression

With this theoretical background in mind, we now turn to the empirical evidence on aggression in humans. First, we consider evidence for the most straightforward prediction from the evolutionary theory of aggression—that men will be more likely than women to use violence and aggression. Then we consider in detail each of the four possible pairings of sex of perpetrator crossed with sex of victim, starting with men's aggression toward other men.

Evidence for Sex Differences in Same-Sex Aggression

In this section we will consider evidence for sex differences in aggression. Several sources of evidence are available: meta-analyses of sex differences in aggression, homicide statistics, studies of bullying in the classroom, and ethnographic evidence from aboriginal communities.

A Meta-Analysis of Sex Differences in Aggression.   Psychologist Janet Hyde conducted a meta-analysis of studies of the effect sizes for sex differences in different forms of aggression (Hyde, 1986). An effect size, in this context, refers to the magnitude of the sex difference. An effect size of .80 may be considered large, .50 medium, and .20 small.

The following are the effect sizes, averaged across dozens of studies, for various forms of aggression: aggressive fantasies (.84), physical aggression (.60), imitative aggression (.49), and willingness to shock others in an experimental setting (.39). All show greater male scores on aggression. Interestingly, Hyde found no evidence for a sex difference in scores on the Hostility Scale (.02). In summary, the results of this meta-analysis support a key prediction from the above evolutionary analysis of aggression—men use aggression more than women in a variety of forms, and the effect sizes tend to range from medium to large.

Same-Sex Homicides.   Homicides are statistically rare, but they provide one assay for examining patterns of aggression. Daly and Wilson (1988) compiled same-sex homicide statistics from thirty-five different studies representing a broad span of cultures from downtown Detroit to the BaSoga of Uganda. Although homicide rates vary widely from culture to culture, the most useful way to compare the sexes is to calculate the proportion of same-sex homicide committed by males (i.e., the percentage of same-sex homicides that are male–male homicides). A subset of these statistics is shown in Table 10.1.

The statistics listed in Table 10.1 are overwhelmingly consistent. In every culture for which there are data, the rate at which men kill other men far exceeds the rate at

TABLE 10.1   Same-Sex Homicides in Various Studies.

Location	Male	Female	Proportion Male
Canada, 1974–1998	2,965	175	.94
Miami, 1925–1926	111	5	.96
Detroit, 1972	345	16	.96
Pittsburgh, 1966–1974	382	16	.96
Tzeltal Mayans, Mexico, 1938–1965	37	0	1.00
Belo Horizonte, Brazil, 1961–1965	228	6	.97
New South Wales, Australia, 1968–1981	675	46	.94
Oxford, England, 1296–1398	105	1	.99
Scotland, 1953–1974	172	12	.93
Iceland, 1946–1970	10	0	1.00
Denmark, 1933–1961	87	15	.85
Bison-Horn Maria, India, 1920–1941	69	2	.97
!Kung San, Botswana, 1920–1955	19	0	1.00
Congo, 1948–1957	156	4	.97
Tiv, Nigeria, 1931–1949	96	3	.97
BaSoga, Uganda, 1952–1954	46	1	.98
BaLuyia, Kenya, 1949–1954	88	5	.95
JoLuo, Kenya	31	2	.94

Source: Reprinted with permission from: Daly, Martin & Wilson, Margo. *Homicide.* (New York: Aldine de Gruyter) Copyright © 1988 by Aldine de Gruyter.

which women kill other women. However, various news stories have suggested an alarming increase in violence and crimes committed by women (Daly & Wilson, 1988). Some suggest that this represents the "dark side" of women's liberation, as women progress toward equality with men. In fact, the increase in crime is caused entirely by an increase in the arrests of women for petty theft. There is no evidence that the proportion of women committing violent crimes such as homicide has increased at all. As Daly and Wilson (1988) concluded: "Indeed there is no evidence that the women in *any* society have *ever* approached the level of violent conflict prevailing among men in the same society" (p. 149; emphasis in original).

Same-Sex Bullying in Schools.   Homicides represent the most extreme form of aggression, but similar sex differences show up in milder forms of aggression, such as bullying in middle and high schools. In one study (Ahmad & Smith, 1994) researchers looked at 226 middle-school (eight to eleven years old) and 1,207 high-school (eleven to sixteen years old) students. Using an anonymous questionnaire, they asked each student how often he or she had been bullied, how often he or she had joined others in bullying others at school, and the particular forms the bullying took. The researchers found significant sex differences on all measures. In reports of bullying others, for example, 54 percent of the middle-school boys reported engaging in bullying, whereas the comparable figure for same-age girls was 34 percent. In high school, 43 percent of the boys but only 30 percent of the girls reported bullying.

These sex differences, however, underestimate the rates of violent aggression. When the type of bullying is examined, a larger sex difference emerges. In the high-school sample 36 percent of the boys but only 9 percent of the girls reported being physically hurt, such as being hit or kicked, by a bully. Furthermore, 10 percent of the boys but only 6 percent of the girls reported having had their belongings taken away from them—a finding that supports the hypothesis that one function of aggression is to co-opt the resources of others. On two measures of bullying, however, girls scored higher than boys. A full 74 percent of the girls reported that others had called them nasty names, whereas only 57 percent of the boys reported this form of bullying. Even more striking was the item "I have had rumors spread about me," which 30 percent of the girls but only 17 percent of the boys reported having experienced.

The content of the verbal forms of aggression is revealing. The most frequently used nasty names and rumors spread by girls about other girls involved terms such as "bitch," "slag," "hussy," and "whore." These kinds of bullying were common among high-school girls but virtually absent among the middle-school students, suggesting a rise in intrasexual mate competition, where the adaptive problems of mating begin to be encountered.

Similar sex differences have been observed in other cultures. In a study conducted in Turku, Finland, 127 fifteen-year-old schoolchildren were assessed through both peer nomination techniques and self-report (Bjorkqvist, Lagerspetz, & Kaukiainen, 1992). Boys showed more than three times the rates of direct physical aggression than girls. Direct physical aggression involved tripping, taking things from another, kicking and striking, seeking revenge in games, and pushing and shoving. Indirect aggression, in contrast, was measured with items such as gossiping, shunning another person, spreading vicious rumors as revenge, breaking contact with the person, and be-friending someone else as revenge. The fifteen-year old girls showed approximately 25 percent higher rates of indirect aggression than the same-age boys.

In sum, studies of bullying support the prediction of a sex difference in the use of violent and risky forms of aggression. Males engage in these forms of aggression more frequently than females. These sex differences show up in college samples (Gladue, 1991), as well as in patterns of aggressive driving—men drive faster than women, are more likely to tailgate, and more frequently displace other cars when changing lanes (Atzwanger, 1995). When females aggress—which they do—they tend to use less vio-lent methods, such as the verbal derogation of their competitors.

Aggression in an Australian Aboriginal Community.

Anthropologist Victoria Burbank spent several months studying a community she calls Mangrove, a southeast Arnhem Land community of roughly six hundred Australian aborigines. She used an unusual method, but one perhaps no less valid than any of the other methods used by social scientists. Burbank recorded 793 cases of aggressive behavior. Many were ver-bally conveyed to her by residents, often females. In roughly one third of the cases two or more informants conveyed information about the same aggressive episode. In fifty-one cases Burbank recorded her own observations of what happened in the aggressive interactions.

Here is one sample of what Burbank (1992) recorded:

> Near here when [a man] was with two of his wives, a "brother" tried to pull them out. "You can't have them," he said. "We'll fight in camp." There the husband stabbed the young man in the side and his guts spilled out. He did this when some men had grabbed the young man but not him. He then gave him a spear and said, "Here [offering his chest] kill me and we'll die together." But everyone called out, "Not in the guts," so the dying man stabbed [the husband] in the shoulder. Then he died. (pp. 254–255)

Burbank coded the 793 aggressive episodes into categories and examined sex dif-ferences in the frequency within each category. Men overwhelmingly resorted to more dangerous aggression than women. Of the ninety-three episodes in which a dangerous weapon was used, in twelve a gun was fired, in sixty-four a spear was thrown, and in fourteen a knife was used, all by men. In contrast, there were only two cases in which a woman used a knife and one in which a woman used a spear. In all, ninety of the aggres-sive episodes in which a dangerous weapon was used were committed by men and only three by women. Men, in sum, accounted for 97 percent of the aggressive episodes in which a dangerous weapon was used.

These aboriginal men were also more likely than women to put on aggressive displays—dramatic and potentially dangerous actions in which no physical harm was committed, but perhaps their reputations were enhanced. In these displays, ninety men picked up a dangerous weapon but did not use it, fourteen drove a vehicle around the settlement at high speeds, thirty-five attacked an object, and five threatened to attack.

These totaled 144 instances of aggressive display, in contrast to only 57 instances in which women performed similar aggressive displays.

There were only a few categories in which women's rates of aggression exceeded those of men. The first was in the use of sticks—sixty-three women compared with twenty-five men. Sticks did considerably less damage to the victims than dangerous weapons such as knives, spears, or guns. Women's preference for sticks is all the more striking because other weapons, such as knives, were readily available to them from cooking and other activities. We can surmise that women intend to do less physical damage than men, and this in part determines their choice of weapons. The second category in which women's aggression exceeded men's was verbal. A total of 221 episodes of verbal aggression were performed by women, in contrast to 141 episodes of verbal aggression by men.

In sum, these sex differences are strikingly similar to those reported in the studies of bullying in England and Finland discussed earlier. Based on the available data we can conclude that sex differences in the use of physical aggression are large and consistent, with males in every study emerging as more physically aggressive than females. A classic work on sex differences noted: "We have seen that the greater aggressiveness of the male is one of the best established, and most pervasive, of all psychological sex differences" (Maccoby & Jacklin, 1974, p. 368). This conclusion does not extend, however, to verbal aggression.

The "Young Male Syndrome." The evolutionary logic of same-sex aggression predicts that men will be more willing than women to engage in risky and violent tactics. Not all men, however, engage in such tactics, and this within-sex variation must also be explained. In particular, young men appear to be the most prone to engaging in risky forms of aggression—aggression that puts them at risk of injury and death. Wilson and Daly (1985) call this the "young male syndrome."

An empirical illustration of the young male syndrome is shown in Figure 10.1 on page 292, which gives homicide rates by age and sex of the victim for a large sample drawn from the United States in 1975 (results for other years show the same shape and distribution). Through age ten, males and females do not differ in the likelihood of becoming homicide victims. At adolescence, however, killings of males start to skyrocket, reaching a peak when they are in their mid-twenties. At that age men are six times more likely than women to become the victims of homicide. From the mid-twenties on, men's victimization rates start to drop sharply, suggesting that men then begin to avoid physically risky tactics. By age seventy-five, the sexes have virtually converged, showing little difference in homicide rates. In sum, homicides are indeed disproportionately concentrated among young men—the young male syndrome.

Why would young men, at the peak of their physical prowess and at the age at which death from disease is the lowest, be the most prone to place their lives at risk by engaging in violence? Daly and Wilson offer an explanation based on an evolutionary analysis of mate competition in an ancestral environment with some degree of polygyny: "Young men are both especially formidable and especially risk-prone because they constitute the demographic class upon which there was the most intense selection for confrontational

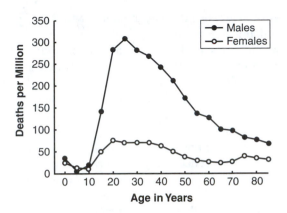

FIGURE 10.1   Homicide Victimization Rates by Age and Sex for the United States in 1975. The figure shows evidence for the "young male syndrome," in which young men entering the mating arena show the greatest degree of risk-taking and violent strategies. Data from U.S. Department of Health, Education, and Welfare (1979) and U.S. Bureau of the Census (1977).

Source: Reprinted from *Ethology and Sociobiology, 6,* M. Wilson & M. Daly, Competitiveness, risk-taking, and violence: The young male syndrome, 59–73, copyright © 1985, with permission from Elsevier Science.

competitive capabilities among our ancestors" (Daly & Wilson, 1994, p. 277). Specifically, they argue that over the course of human evolutionary history a young man seeking a wife had to display formidable physical prowess in hunting, tribal raids, tribal defense, and the ability to defend his interests. These displays were designed to impress not only women but also other men, to deter rival men from hindering the man in his quests.

This argument, by itself, can be applied to many mammals. What makes humans unique, according to Daly and Wilson, is the importance of cultivating a *reputation*, which can have a long-lasting effect. Competitive success or failure early in life may have been a strong determinant of reputation, which could affect a man's total lifetime survival and reproductive success. Demonstrations of bravery in the face of danger, for example, might have had reputational consequences that lasted a lifetime. The finding that displays of violence by young men are almost invariably performed in the presence of an audience suggests that they are designed not merely to vanquish a rival, which after all could be done in the dead of night, on a lonely bend in the path, or under the protective cover of a hideout. The presence of an audience suggests that risky displays are also designed to impress peers and cultivate a formidable social reputation.

This explanation also accounts for why we bestow prestige and status on those who take risks and succeed in spite of the risks (Zahavi & Zahavi, 1996). If past success in these dangerous ventures predicts future success, and if past failure likewise predicts future failure, then it is important for people to track the outcomes of these risky ventures—information that must be encoded and passed on to others in the form of one's reputation. In Chapter 12 we will return to this topic in greater depth when we consider the evolutionary psychology of prestige, status, and reputation.

The young male syndrome explanation also accounts for fascinating findings from a large-scale study of episodes of violent conflicts from collective aggression (e.g., riots, gang fights) that result in death (Mesquida & Wiener, 1996). Across a variety of states and countries, they discovered that the higher the percentage of males in the age group of 15 to 29, relative to the percentage of males 30-years-old or older, the higher the levels of coalitional aggression. This link is so strong that the proportion of young males in a population may be the best, or one of the best, predictors of violent aggression.

In sum, the evolutionary explanation of the "young male syndrome" can account for a host of empirical findings, including variations in collective aggression, the sudden surge in muscle strength in males from puberty through the mid-twenties, the surge in aerobic capacity in adolescence and the mid-twenties, and especially the surge in measures of quick energetic bursts that might be needed for risky forms of aggression (Daly & Wilson, 1994). All of these changes appear to be linked with the emergence of a physically risky competitive strategy.

Contexts Triggering Men's Aggression against Men

Homicide represents the most extreme form of aggression, and homicide statistics worldwide reveal that the majority of killers are men, as are the majority of victims. Several causal contexts surround male–male homicides.

Marital and Employment Status.   First, killers and victims often share similar characteristics, such as being unemployed and, perhaps relatedly, unmarried. In a study of Detroit homicides in 1982, for example, although only 11 percent of the adult men in Detroit were unemployed that year, 43 percent of the victims and 41 percent of the perpetrators were unemployed (Wilson & Daly, 1985). The same study revealed that 73 percent of the male perpetrators and 69 percent of the male victims were unmarried, as contrasted with only 43 percent of the same-age men in the Detroit area. Thus, lacking resources and being unable to attract a long-term mate appear to be social contexts linked with male–male homicides. This is especially true among young men, who are new and not established entrants into the fiercely competitive arena for status and mating. When one is on a path to reproductive oblivion, it sometimes seems to pay off to take large and dangerous risks.

Status and Reputation.   One of the key motives of male–male homicide is the defense of status, reputation, and honor in the local peer group. Here is what one man said about his early gang fights, invoking both reputation and deterrence as motives for aggression: "The one giving out the most stitches got the reputation. It also made others think twice before coming near you" (Boyle, 1977, p. 67). Naively, these are often classified as "trivial altercations" in the police records. A typical case is the barroom verbal altercation that escalates out of control. The combatants, sometimes unable to back down and fearing humiliation in the eyes of their peers, break a bottle, pull a knife, or open fire. The seemingly trivial nature of the arguments sometimes puzzles police. A Dallas homicide detective noted, "Murders result from little ol' arguments over nothing at all. Tempers flare. A fight starts, and someone gets stabbed or shot. I've worked on cases where the principals had been arguing over a 10 cent record on a juke box, or over a one dollar gambling debt from a dice game" (Mulvihill, Tumin, & Curtis, 1969, p. 230).

Status, reputation, and honor are far from trivial, however. Because humans evolved in the context of small groups (e.g., Alexander, 1987; Tooby & DeVore, 1987), a loss of status could have been catastrophic in the currency of survival and reproduction. We carry with us ancient psychological mechanisms for aggression designed for a time and a place long past but not forgotten. These mechanisms operate in the modern context, triggered by cues to a loss of status. They may be maladaptive today, just as our taste for fat may be maladaptive in a modern environment characterized by fast-food restaurants at every street corner. The Stone Age mechanisms nevertheless continue to operate in todays' Information Age, triggered by events that would have activated them in our ancestral past.

One final indicator of the links between aggression and status comes from a study of two tribes in the Ecuadorian Amazon by evolutionary anthropologist John Patton (1997). Patton took photographs of every man in each of the tribes. Forty-seven informants were used, twenty-six from the Achuar coalition and twenty-one from the Quichua coalition. Each informant ranked each of thirty-three married men in terms of status. Patton presented three pictures at a time and informants indicated who in that grouping had the highest status, who had the second highest status, and who had the least status. Status scores were calculated by summing across all the informants. In a separate task informants judged the "warriorship" of each man: "If there was a war to-

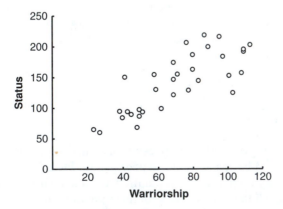

FIGURE 10.2   Status by Warriorship. The figure shows that men judged to be the "best warriors" are largely the same men who enjoy the highest social status.

Source: Are Warriors Altruistic? Reciprocal Altruism and War in the Ecuadorian Amazon by J. Q. Patton, June 4–8, 1997. Paper presented at the Human Behavior and Evolution Society Meetings, University of Arizona, Tucson. Reprinted with permission.

day, which of these men would be the best warrior?" (Patton, 1997, pp. 12–13). Warriorship scores were calculated by summing across the informants.

The results are shown in Figure 10.2. Status and warriorship are highly correlated. For the Quichua men status and warriorship are correlated +.90. For the Achuar men they are correlated +.77. In short, ferocity as a warrior appears to be closely linked with one's social status within the group.

Sexual Jealousy and Intrasexual Rivalry. Sexual jealousy appears to be another key context triggering same-sex aggression and homicide. It is predominantly men who do the killing and other men who are the victims. A summary of eight studies of same-sex killings involving "love triangles" documented that 92 percent were male–male homicides and only 8 percent were female–female homicides (Daly & Wilson, 1988, p. 185).

Rivalry and competition over women can trigger nonlethal aggression as well. In a study of mate guarding (tactics used to keep a mate and fend off rivals), for example, men more than women picked a fight with the rivals who showed interest in their mates and threatened to hit rivals who were making moves on their mates (Buss, 1988c). Thus, male aggression against rivals is manifest in a very specific context—dealing with the adaptive problem of mate retention.

In a study of competitor derogation, men were far more likely than women to physically dominate their rivals and render them less desirable to the opposite sex (Buss & Dedden, 1990). Furthermore, committing such acts of aggression was judged to be more effective for men than for women in lowering the victim's desirability in the eyes of the opposite sex.

At the other end of the spectrum is warfare—coalitions of males aggressing against each other. In the recorded history of humans, there is not a single instance of women forming a war party to raid a neighboring village. Tribal warfare, however, is common among male coalitions (e.g., Chagnon, 1983). Later in this chapter we will explore tribal warfare, but first we will turn to the contexts that trigger aggression among women.

Contexts Triggering Women's Aggression against Women

Women's physical same-sex aggression, compared with that of men, is less frequent, less violent, and less showy (Campbell, 1995). In a sample of forty-seven Detroit homicides in 1972 involving sexual jealousy, only three were committed by women against a same-sex rival (Daly & Wilson, 1988, p. 184). The low levels of risky physical aggression, however, do not translate into no aggression at all.

Intrasexual Rivalry. If aggression is defined as inflicting costs on someone else, women's aggression can be quite potent. In a study of derogation of competitors, women engaged in as much verbal aggression against their rivals as did men (Buss & Dedden, 1990). The *content* of the derogation, however, was different. Women exceeded men in derogating their rivals on the basis of physical appearance and sexual promiscuity, for example. They were more likely than men to call their competitors fat and ugly, mention that the rival's thighs were heavy, make fun of the size and shape of their rival's body, and call their rival physically unattractive (Buss & Dedden, 1990). Women seem to be extraordinarily observant about the physical imperfections in other women's appearances, and take pains in the context of intrasexual competition to point them out publicly, thereby drawing attention to them and amplifying their importance in men's attentional field.

In the domain of sexual conduct, women were more likely than men to say that their rivals slept around a lot, had many past boyfriends, were sexually promiscuous, and would sleep with practically anyone (Buss & Dedden, 1990). Furthermore, this derogation tactic was context dependent. When the man sought a short-term mate, derogating a competitor by implying promiscuity was not at all effective, presumably because men are relatively indifferent to this quality in a short-term mate, and might even value it because it signals an increased likelihood of sexual intercourse (Schmitt & Buss, 1996). When the man sought a long-term mate, in contrast, derogating a rival on the promiscuity dimension was extremely effective, presumably because men seeking long-term mates place a premium on sexual fidelity (Buss & Schmitt, 1993).

In sum, women derogate other women as often as men derogate other men in the context of competition for mates. This is not an invariant aggressive instinct, nor does it get "pushed out" regardless of context. Rather, women seem to be aware of what men desire in both short-term and long-term mating contexts, and shift their derogation tactics accordingly.

Contexts Triggering Men's Aggression against Women

Much of men's nonsexual violence against women is directed at spouses, mates, or girlfriends, and sexual jealousy appears to be the major cause. In one study of Baltimore spousal homicides, twenty-five of thirty-six were attributed to jealousy, and the wives were victims in twenty-four of these cases (Guttmacher, 1955). In a study of battered women at safe houses or shelters, two-thirds reported that their husbands were extremely jealous (Gayford, 1975). In another study, fifty-seven of sixty battered women reported extreme jealousy and possessiveness on the part of their husbands (Hilberman & Munson, 1978). In yet another study, in the majority of one hundred cases of spousal violence investigated the husbands reported frustration over their inability to control their wives, with accusations of infidelity the most common complaint (Whitehurst, 1971).

Sexual jealousy is also a key context for spousal homicide, and apparently the most common cause across cultures (Daly & Wilson, 1988). Men who kill their wives or girlfriends typically do so under one of two key conditions—the observation or suspicion of a sexual infidelity or when the woman is terminating the relationship. The first represents cuckoldry, which places a man at risk of investing his limited resources in an offspring to whom he is not genetically related. The second represents the loss of a reproductively valuable woman to a rival—also a direct loss in the currency of fitness. This adaptive logic, of course, is not present in men's minds. But men carry with them the psychological mechanisms that led to their ancestors' successes, and one collection of such mechanisms fuels sexual jealousy and proprietariness over mates, both of which can lead to aggression.

One characteristic of female victims glaringly stands out—their age. Young wives and girlfriends are far more likely to be killed than older ones (Daly & Wilson, 1988). Because youth is a powerful cue to a woman's reproductive value, it follows that male sexual jealousy would be especially targeted toward young mates. It is also likely that younger women are more often the objects of desire by other men, so male sexual jealousy might be triggered by the presence of rivals attempting to attract these women.

To more explicitly test the hypothesis that men use violence against their mates as a means of controlling their sexuality, one study (Wilson, Johnson, & Daly, 1995) looked at 8,385 women, of whom 277 had been assaulted by their husbands over the past year. Two forms of violence were assessed: "nonserious" and "serious." The assessment of nonserious violence included questions such as these: "Has your husband/partner ever threatened to hit you with his fist or anything else that could hurt you?" "Has he ever thrown anything at you that could hurt you?" "Has he ever pushed, grabbed, or shoved you?" "Has he ever slapped you?" "Has he ever kicked, bit, or hit you with his fist?" "Has he ever hit you with something that could hurt you?" The items assessing serious violence included: "Has he ever beaten you up?" "Has he ever choked you?" "Has he ever threatened to use or has he ever used a gun or knife on you?"

At a different point in the interview the women were asked about the jealousy and controlling behaviors of their husbands with the following items: "He is jealous and doesn't want you to talk to other men;" "He tries to limit your contact with your family or friends;" "He insists on knowing who you are with and where you are at all times;" "He calls you names to put you down or make you feel bad;" "He prevents you from knowing about or having access to the family income, even if you ask."

The "autonomy-limiting" items were positively linked with violence perpetrated by husbands against their wives. In general, men who commit violence against their wives also display an inordinate amount of jealousy and controlling behavior. The more serious forms of violence are linked with greatly elevated scores on jealousy and autonomy-limiting behavior. These findings lend support to the hypothesis that violence by men is used as a strategy for controlling their mates, with the goal of preventing sexual access to other men or a defection from the relationship.

The key point is not that violence against women is produced by some sort of invariant instinct. Rather, its patterning—the contexts in which it emerges and the nature of the targets—is highly dependent on the specific adaptive problem being faced.

Contexts Triggering Women's Aggression against Men

It may seem that women rarely inflict violent aggression against men. In reports of spousal abuse, such as slapping, spitting, hitting, and calling nasty names, however, the percentages of male and female victims often are roughly the same (e.g., Buss, 1989b; Dobash, Dobash, Wilson, & Daly, 1992).

Defense against Attack.   Extreme aggression such as spousal homicide is less frequently perpetrated by women, but it does occur. The contexts are almost always linked with one of two factors—the woman is defending herself against a husband who is enraged over a real or suspected infidelity and after a prolonged history of physical abuse, when the woman sees no way out of the coercive grip of her husband (Daly & Wilson, 1988; Dobash et al., 1992). Male sexual jealousy, in short, appears to be at the root of women killing their husbands, as well as at the root of the more common case of men killing their wives.

Warfare

Human recorded history, including hundreds of ethnographies of tribal cultures around the globe, reveals male coalitional warfare to be pervasive across cultures worldwide (e.g., Chagnon, 1988; Tooby & Cosmides, 1988). So warfare is an activity pursued exclusively by men. The intended victims are most often other men, although women frequently suffer as well. Although few wars are initiated solely with the stated intent of capturing women, gaining more copulations is almost always viewed as a desired benefit of successfully vanquishing an enemy. Box 10.1 on page 299 provides a description of one specific tribal war.

Among the more than 4,000 species of mammals, only two have been observed to form coalitions that kill conspecifics—chimpanzees and humans. Human warfare is nearly exclusively a male activity. Theoretical analyses suggest that there can be profound adaptive benefits to engaging in warfare that, under certain circumstances, can outweigh the risk of dying.

BOX **10.1**

Yanomamö Warfare

Evolutionary anthropologist Napoleon Chagnon offered a vivid description of one specific war conducted by one Yanomamö tribe against another. The conflict started with Damowa, a head man of the Monou-teri, one of the Yanomamö villages. Damowa had a habit of seducing other men's wives—an activity that led to frequent club fights within the village. When a neighboring tribe, the Patanowa-teri, raided the Monou-teri, they succeeded in capturing five women. Damowa expressed anger and convinced his tribe to declare war on the Patanowa-teri.

During the first raid the Monou-teri surprised one of their enemies, a man named Bosibrei, who was climbing a rasha tree to get fruit. He made a fine target silhouetted against the azure sky. Damowa and his coalition sent a round of arrows at Bosibrei, killing him instantly and immediately retreated, returning home.

Aggression often provokes retaliatory aggression, and the Patanowa-teri set their sights on vengeance. They managed to catch Damowa while he was outside his garden searching for honey. He had two wives with him. Five arrows hit their mark in Damowa's stomach. Still alive, he cursed his enemies and managed to shoot one of his arrows. But a final arrow struck Damowa's neck, killing him. This time the raiders did not try to abduct more women, because they feared Damowa's comrades. So they retreated to safety, as Damowa's wives ran back to camp to alert the others. The killers escaped and the Monou-teri themselves fled into the cover of the jungle, fearful that the raiders might return.

With their leader dead, the Monou-teri were demoralized. But soon a new leader, Kaobawa, stepped forward and stirred the tribe into seeking revenge for Damowa's death. Failure to retaliate can lead to reputational damage—the defeated group will be perceived by others as easily exploitable, so the Monou-teri felt they had to take action to prevent further raids.

The night before the raid, Kaobawa stirred the men into an emotional frenzy. He began to sing "I am meat hungry! I am meat hungry!" (Chagnon, 1983, p. 182). The other raiders echoed this phrase, and concluded in a high-pitched scream that sent chills down Chagnon's spine. The screaming became more and more enraged as the raiding party worked itself into a frenzy of vengeance.

At dawn the next morning the women presented the raiders with a large cache of plantains as food for their raid. The men covered their faces and bodies in black paint. The mothers and sisters of the warriors offered parting advice, such as "Don't get yourself shot up" and "You be careful now!" (p. 183). The women then wept, fearful for the safety of their men.

After they had been gone for five hours, one of the raiders reappeared at the camp, complaining that a sore foot prevented him from keeping up with the others. He had enjoyed the pomp and ceremony of the previous evening, which impressed the women. But he, like many of the Yanomamö who go into battle, was deeply afraid.

The trek to reach their enemies was long and took several days. At night the raiding party built fires to keep warm, but on the last night this luxury had to be eliminated for fear of alerting the enemy to their presence. On the evening before the raid, several more men developed sore feet and belly aches, and turned to go back to their home camp. The remaining warriors finalized their plan of attack. They decided to break into smaller groups, each consisting of four to six men. This grouping allowed them to retreat under protection—two men from each group would lie in wait to ambush potential pursuers.

Among the raiding party was the twelve-year-old son of Damowa, who had been brought along for the chance to avenge his father's death. This was his first raid, so the older men kept him in the middle of the group to minimize his exposure to danger.

Meanwhile, back at the home camp of the Monou-teri, the women grew nervous. Unprotected women risk being kidnapped by neighbor-

(continued)

BOX **10.1** continued

ing tribes, and even allies cannot always be trusted. Their nervousness turned to irritability, and squabbles broke out among them. One woman hit another with a stick, knocking her out cold. For the most part the women just waited.

The raiding party managed to shoot and kill one enemy before fleeing. They extracted their vengeance, but were themselves now in great danger. The Patanowa-teri gave chase, managing to get ahead of the Monou-teri as they retreated, and ambushed them. One Monou-teri was wounded by a bamboo-tipped arrow that pierced his chest. The next morning the Monou-teri raiding party arrived home carrying their injured comrade. Although seriously injured, he survived to go on a future raid.

When Napoleon Chagnon returned to the Yanomamö a year later, the war among the Monou-teri and Patanowa-teri was still going strong, with repeated cycles of raids and counterraids. The Monou-teri had managed to kill two Patanowa-teri and capture two of their women, and the Patanowa-teri had managed to kill one Monou-teri. At this brief juncture, then, the Monou-teri were ahead, as it were. The Patanowa-teri will not stop their raids until they have avenged the deaths of their comrades and the losses of their women, however. And when they do, the Monou-teri will be forced to retaliate in kind.

Yanomamö warfare highlights several key themes in the evolution of human aggression: warfare is primarily a male activity; sexual access to women is often a central resource that flows to the victors of wars; retaliation and revenge are critical to maintaining credible reputations; and men and women are often genuinely afraid of the deadly consequences of violent tribal combat.

The Evolutionary Psychology of War.   In a brilliant analysis of the logic of warfare, Tooby and Cosmides (1988) drew attention to a fact that is often overlooked: War is an intensely *cooperative* venture. It could not occur without the formation of cooperative alliances among men on either side. The men must come together and function as a cooperative unit. So formidable is this requirement that only two species of mammals have ever been observed to form aggressive coalitions against other members of their own species: chimpanzees and humans.

The evolution of warfare has to overcome another major obstacle—the benefits, in fitness currencies, have to be sufficiently high to overcome the devastating risks of injury and death to those who participate. War is an extremely costly venture for everyone involved. As Tooby and Cosmides noted: "It is difficult to see why any sane organism, selected to survive and genetically propagate, should seek so actively to create conditions of such remarkable personal cost and danger" (1988, p. 2). So how could evolution select for psychological mechanisms that predisposed men to incur such risks? How can we account for the fact that throughout recorded human history wars have been initiated with regularity and warriors prized and glorified by the members of their groups?

The evolutionary theory of warfare proposed by Tooby and Cosmides (1988) has four essential conditions that must be met for adaptations to evolve for initiating coalitional aggression.

1. *The average long-term gain in reproductive resources must be sufficiently large to outweigh the reproductive costs of engaging in warfare over evolutionary time.* What reproductive resource could be sufficiently large? An increase in copulations with females is the most likely candidate—the resource that imposes the greatest limit on male reproduction. Sexual access, in contrast, does not impose the same limit on women's reproduction, as noted in the discussion of the theory of parental investment and sexual selection. The fact that women's obligatory investment in offspring is so great is what makes them such a valuable yet limited resource for men. This asymmetry between the sexes means that women have little to gain by going to war for increased access to men. Sperm are cheap, and there has never been a lack of men willing to contribute them in the quantities women need for successful fertilization. In sum, men have a great deal to gain by warfare if it results in a substantial increase in sexual access to women—this is the scarce reproductive resource that might make it worth the risk.

2. *Members of coalitions must believe that their group will emerge victorious.* This means not merely the belief that one's coalition will win the battle, but also that the collective resources of one's coalition will be greater after the aggressive encounter than before it.

3. *The risk that each member takes and the importance of each member's contribution to the success must translate into a corresponding share of the benefits.* This is a form of the "cheater detection" criterion for the evolution of cooperation that we discussed in Chapter 9. Men who do not take risks by fighting must be excluded from taking the spoils of victory. Men who take more risks—as leaders do when they take their men into battle—get a proportionately larger share of the spoils of war. Similarly, men whose contribution to the success of the battle is larger get a proportionately larger share of the resulting reproductive resources.

4. *Men who go into battle must be cloaked in a "veil of ignorance" about who will live or die.* The likelihood of death, in other words, must be more or less randomly distributed among the coalition members. If you know that death is certain before you go into battle, you have nothing to gain by doing so. Selection would operate strongly against any psychological propensity to go into battle when death is certain. Indeed, the "battlefield panic" that causes some men to defect might reflect the operation of a psychological mechanism that propels a man out of harm's way when the likelihood of death approaches certainty. If the risk is shared with others, however, and no one knows who will survive and who will die, then selection can favor, on average, a psychological propensity to engage in coalitional warfare.

These conditions, which Tooby and Cosmides (1988) call "the risk contract of war," yield some surprising predictions. The most important pertains to the effects of some degree of mortality on evolutionary selection pressures for psychological mechanisms designed to lead men to war. Recall that natural selection operates on genes for particular design features based on their *average* reproductive consequences, totaled over evolutionary time. In Chapter 3, for example, we explored the evolution of men's propensities to take risks that lead to greater on-average reproductive success, but at a cost of a shorter life span.

Let's apply this logic to warfare. Suppose ten men form a coalition to raid a neighboring tribe. During the raid, five fertile women are captured. If all of the men survive, then the average gain in sexual access is .50 of a fertile woman per man (five women divided by ten men equals .50 average per man). Now suppose five of the men die in the battle and the same five fertile women are captured. Now the gain for each of the five surviving men is a gain in sexual access of 1.0 fertile woman (five women divided by five men equals 1.0). The *average* gain across all the men who went into battle, however, has remained unchanged at .50 (five women divided by the ten men who went into battle still equals .50). In other words, the average reproductive gains of the *decision* to go into battle are identical across the two conditions, even though in one case no men died and in the other five men died.

For those who die, of course, the battle results in a total loss. But the resources those men would have gained are simply allocated to those in the coalition who survive. As a result, the reproductive gains of those who survive are exactly equal to the reproductive losses of those who died. This means that the *average* reproductive gain has not changed one bit as a consequence of half the men dying. In sum, because it operates on average reproductive effects across individuals over evolutionary time, selection can favor psychological mechanisms that lead men into war, even if those mechanisms expose men to some risk of death.

This evolutionary theory of warfare leads to some specific predictions: (1) men, but not women, will have evolved psychological mechanisms designed for coalitional warfare; (2) sexual access to women will be the primary benefit that men gain from joining male coalitions; (3) men should have evolved psychological mechanisms that lead them to panic and defect from coalitions when death appears to be an imminent result of remaining; (4) men should be more likely to go to war when their odds of success appear high, as when the number of men in their coalition greatly exceeds the number of men in the opposing coalition; (5) men should have evolved psychological mechanisms designed to enforce the risk contract—that is, to detect and punish cheaters, defectors, and traitors; and (6) men should have evolved psychological mechanisms designed to detect, prefer, and enlist men in the coalition who are willing and able to contribute to its success. Given the recent proposal of this theory of the evolution of war, empirical research bearing on these predictions is relatively sparse. Nonetheless, several lines of evidence examined below provide support for these predictions.

Men Engage in Warfare.   The fact that men across cultures form coalitions whose purpose is to kill men in other coalitions is observed across cultures (Alexander, 1979; Chagnon, 1988; Otterbein, 1979; Wrangham & Peterson, 1996). In some cultures such as the Yanomamö, tribes appear to be constantly at war. In no culture have women ever been observed forming coalitions designed to kill other human beings. These facts may seem obvious, and were certainly widely known prior to the Tooby and Cosmides (1988) theory of the evolution of war. But they remain consistent with this theory, and call into question alternative theories such as that war is an arbitrary social construction (van der Dennen, 1995).

Men Are More Likely to Spontaneously Assess Their Fighting Ability.   If men recurrently engaged in violent aggression more than women over the course of human evolutionary history, one would expect that men have evolved distinct psychological mechanisms that lead them to evaluate the conditions under which it is wise to engage in combat. One such mechanism is the self-assessment of one's fighting ability relative to other men. Evolutionary psychologist Adam Fox (1997) predicted that men have evolved mechanisms for assessing fighting ability, specifically that men will assess fighting ability more frequently than women.

To test these predictions Fox asked a sample of college students to report how often they imagined the probable outcomes of fights involving themselves and others. The results are shown in Figure 10.3. The sex differences are dramatic. The majority of men reported imagining the probable outcomes of such fights at least once a month, with the most common response being once a week. The majority of women, in contrast, reported only occasionally imagining the outcomes of fights. The most common response of women was "never." These findings support the prediction that men assess their own fighting ability more often than women—a possible evolved psychological mechanism designed to gauge whether it is worthwhile to enter into combat.

Sexual Access as a Recurrent Resource That Flows to Victors.   Two evolutionary psychologists, Craig Palmer and Christopher Tilley, tested the proposition that sexual

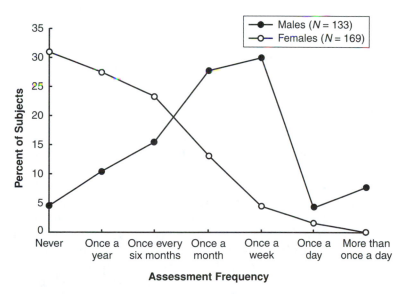

FIGURE 10.3   Assessment of Fighting Ability. The figure shows that men tend to spontaneously assess their own fighting ability more than women do, suggesting a possible psychological adaptation to warfare.

Source: The Assessment of Fighting Ability in Humans by A. Fox, 1997. Paper presented to the Ninth Annual Meeting of the Human Behavior. Reprinted with permission.

access to women is the primary motivation for males to join gangs (Palmer & Tilley, 1995). A gang may be defined as a "self-formed association of peers, bound together by mutual interests, with identifiable leadership, well-developed lines of authority . . . who act in concert to achieve a specific purpose or purposes" (Miller, 1980, p. 121). Gang warfare is common across America, especially in large cities such as Los Angeles, and death is a common outcome. Why do males join gangs in which they risk death?

As one gang member explained: "The gang seemed to control the things I wanted. I was kind of a dork when I was in elementary school. I was really into my studies, and I didn't get involved in any stuff that the gang was doing. But then I began to see that they had the girls." (Padilla, 1992, p. 68).

Palmer and Tilley (1995) were interested in testing the prediction with empirical data, not merely individual testimonials and anecdotal evidence. They studied a sample of fifty-seven reported gang members in Colorado Springs, Colorado, and compared them with sixty-three same-age males from the same community who were not affiliated with gangs. Data on the number of sex partners during the previous thirty-day period were collected. The results: Gang members reported a significantly greater number of sex partners during the past month (average, 1.67 partners) than did nongang members for the same time period (average, 1.22). The two subjects in the study with the largest numbers of sex partners were both gang leaders, who reported eleven and ten partners within the previous ninety days. Not a single nongang member in the study reported having more than five sex partners during that same three-month interval.

Palmer and Tilley (1995) note that data from a random sample of the population found that 55 percent of men of comparable ages had only one or fewer sex partners during the previous year, and only 14 percent reported more than four sex partners during that time (Laumann et al., 1994). If this is used as a comparison we can conclude that many gang members have more sex partners during a single month than the average man has over the course of an entire year. Further evidence is needed, however, because it is possible that gang members may exaggerate numbers of sex partners more than nongang members.

Additional empirical evidence for an increased number of sex partners among coalitional leaders comes from Chagnon's (1988) study of the Yanomamö. Among the Yanomamö, the most frequently cited explanation for going to war with another tribe is revenge for a previous killing, and the most common account of the initial cause of the fighting was "women." The Yanomamö make a social distinction between *unokais* (those who have killed) and *non-unokais* (those who have not killed). This distinction is critical to a man's reputation, and it is apparently widely known throughout each village who are the *unokais*. The victims of the *unokai* men are primarily other men killed during raids against one of their enemies, although some of the killings took place within the group because of sexual jealousy. The number of living *unokais* in the population at the time of the study was 137. Most *unokais* have killed only once, but the few who have killed many times (the local record was then sixteen killings) develop a special reputation for being *waiteri*, or fierce.

When the *unokais* were compared with the *non-unokais* of the same age, one statistical difference stood out: the *unokais* had more wives. As young as twenty to twenty-four years, the *unokais* average 0.80 wives, almost four times as many as the *non-unokais*, who averaged only 0.13 wives. From the sample of men over the age of forty-one, the *unokais* averaged 2.09 wives and the *non-unokais* only 1.17 wives. Thus, the *unokais* clearly have more sex partners through marriage to more women. Anecdotal evidence suggests that *unokais* also have more extramarital affairs (Chagnon, 1983). In sum, if having killed is viewed as a reasonable proxy for having participated and contributed importantly to coalitional warfare, this evidence supports the hypothesis that sexual access to women is an important reproductive resource gained through coalitional aggression.

What Qualities Do Men and Women Seek in Coalitional Allies? Three researchers explored this question by asking sixty men and fifty-three women to evaluate how desirable 148 potential characteristics were in a coalition member. A coalition was defined as "a group of people with whom you identify because you pursue common goals" (DeKay, Buss, & Stone under review, ms. p. 13). Each characteristic was rated on a scale ranging from −4 (extremely undesirable in a coalition member) to +4 (extremely desirable in a coalition member). The list of 148 characteristics was derived from three sources: (1) nominations of acts and events that might increase the status and reputation of a person; (2) markers of the major personality variables of dominance, agreeableness, conscientiousness, emotional stability, and openness; and (3) theoretical characteristics derived from evolutionary predictions about the functions of coalitions. For example, the item "being brave in the face of danger" was included to test the hypothesis that one function of male coalitions (and hence the basis on which men select coalition partners) is *aggression* against other coalitions or *defense* of one's group.

Both men and women rated the following characteristics as highly desirable in a coalition member: being hardworking, being intelligent, being kind, being openminded, being able to motivate people, having a wide range of knowledge, having a good sense of humor, and being considered dependable. There were notable sex differences, however, that point to the distinct functions of men's coalitions. Men more than women found the following characteristics desirable: being brave in the face of danger (2.40 vs. 1.66, men vs. women), being physically strong (1.07 vs. 0.43), being a good fighter (1.30 vs. 0.42), being able to protect others from physical harm (1.37 vs. 0.89), being able to tolerate physical pain (0.75 vs. 0.36), being able to defend oneself against physical attack (1.90 vs. 1.43), and being physically able to dominate others (0.35 vs. −0.42). Similarly, men evaluated the following qualities in a coalition member as more undesirable than did women: being poor at athletic activities (−0.68 vs. −0.23) and being physically weak (−1.08 vs. −0.55).

This is merely one study using a restricted sample of American undergraduates, so no grand conclusions can be drawn. Certainly it would be useful to replicate this study in different cultures. Nonetheless, it is interesting to note that even in the modern context of American universities, seemingly so distant from the tribal warfare of human ancestral past, men seem to select coalition members in part based on qualities that will help the coalition succeed in group-on-group aggression and physical defense.

Summary of Warfare. The theory of warfare developed by Tooby and Cosmides (1988) points to an often overlooked conclusion—that warfare requires elaborate cooperation among members of one group to coordinate their aggressive actions against another group. The theory also proposes that sexual access to women would have been the key reproductive resource that selected for men to evolve a psychology of warfare. The theory leads to some surprising predictions—for example, that as long as there exists a "veil of ignorance" about who will be killed, the mortality rate will not affect the average reproductive benefits of a strategy of entering battle.

A variety of sources of empirical evidence support some of the key predictions of this theory of warfare. First, men have recurrently engaged in warfare over recorded human history, whereas there is not a single documented case of women forming same-sex coalitions to go to war. Second, men spontaneously assess their fighting ability more than women, suggesting the existence of evolved mechanisms to evaluate the propitiousness of entering an aggressive confrontation. Third, studies of gangs and ethnographic evidence on warfare both suggest that warfare leads to increased sexual access to women. Finally, men prefer coalition members who are brave in the face of danger, are physically strong, have good fighting ability, and have the ability to protect others—qualities that appear to make for a good comrade in battle. Although more research on this fascinating area is needed, the available empirical evidence supports the theory that men have evolved specific psychological mechanisms for engaging in warfare.

Do Humans Have Evolved Homicide Modules?

> Then she said that since she came back in April she had f___ed this other man about ten times. I told her how can you talk love and marriage and you been f___ing with this other man. I was really mad. I went into the kitchen and got the knife. I went back to our room and said were you serious when you told me that. She said yes. We fought on the bed, I was stabbing her and her grandfather came up and tried to take the knife out of my hand. I told him to go and call the cops for me. I don't know why I killed the woman, I loved her. (Carlson, 1984, p. 9)

More than 18,000 homicides are committed in the United States, each year, according to FBI crime statistics (Kenrick & Sheets, 1993). Of these, more than 80 percent are committed by men (Daly & Wilson, 1988). Mainstream social scientists often explain the sex differences in homicide rates in the United States by invoking "culture-specific gender norms" (e.g., Goldstein, 1986). This theory encounters an empirical problem: The sex difference is found in *every culture* across the globe for which homicide statistics are available (Daly & Wilson, 1988). Theories that invoke local cultural norms obviously cannot satisfactorily explain a universal human pattern.

Actual homicides are statistically rare, and thus difficult to study. For every homicide that is actually committed, however, there may be dozens or hundreds of *thoughts* or *fantasies* that individuals entertain about killing another human being. Consider this homicidal fantasy reported by a male undergraduate: "I wanted to kill my old girlfriend. She lives in (another city) and I was just wondering if I could get away with it. I thought about the (price of) airfare and how I might set up an alibi. I also thought about how I would kill her in order to make it look like a robbery. I actually thought about it for about a week and never did come up with anything" (Kenrick & Sheets, 1994, p. 15). This man did not kill his girlfriend. But the recurrence of thoughts about homicide opens up a window for investigation into the psychology of homicide.

Evolutionary psychologists Doug Kenrick and Virgil Sheets have capitalized on this opportunity, conducting two studies on a total of 760 undergraduates. Their methods were simple. They asked subjects to provide demographic information, including their age and sex, and then describe the last time they had thoughts about killing someone. They inquired about the circumstances that triggered the violent thoughts as well as the content of those thoughts: "who you wanted to kill, how you imagined doing it, etc." (Kenrick & Sheets, 1993, p. 6). They queried subjects about the frequency of fantasies, the specific relationship with the person they thought of killing, and whether the fantasy had been triggered by a physical attack, a public humiliation, or any on a list of other provocations.

The two studies revealed similar results, so we will focus only on the second study, which was larger and more detailed in scope. First, more men (79 percent) than women (58 percent) reported experiencing at least one homicidal fantasy (see Figure 10.4). Second, 38 percent of the men, but only 18 percent of the women, reported having had several homicidal fantasies. Third, men's fantasies tended to last longer than women's fantasies. Most women (61 percent) reported that their homicidal thoughts typically lasted only a few seconds. Most men reported that their homicidal thoughts lasted a few minutes, with 18 percent reporting that their fantasies lasted a few hours or longer. These findings support the hypothesis that men are psychologically more disposed to homicide than women—a finding also supported by the actual homicide statistics.

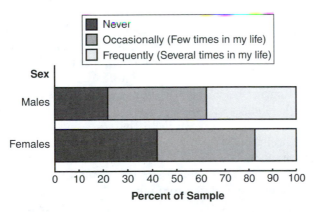

FIGURE 10.4   The Frequency of Homicidal Fantasies. The figure shows that a larger percentage of men than women engage in homicidal fantasies, and that men also tend to have more frequent homicidal fantasies than do women.

Source: Reprinted from *Ethology and Sociobiology, 14,* D. T. Kenrick & B. Sheets, Homicidal fantasies, 231–246, copyright © 1993, with permission from Elsevier Science.

Sex differences were also apparent in the triggers of homicidal thoughts. Men were more likely than women to have homicidal thoughts in response to a personal threat (71 percent versus 52 percent), the fact that someone stole something from them (57 percent versus 42 percent), a desire to know what it is like to kill (32 percent versus 8 percent), a conflict over money (27 percent versus 10 percent), and public humiliation (59 percent versus 45 percent).

Men and women also differed in the targets of their homicidal fantasies. Men were more likely to fantasize about killing a stranger (53 percent versus 33 percent), a national leader (34 percent versus 17 percent), a boss (35 percent versus 21 percent), or a room-mate (34 percent versus 23 percent).

The evolutionary logic of inclusive fitness theory predicts greater conflicts between children and their stepparents than between children and their genetic parents, and the homicidal fantasy evidence bears this out. Of those who lived with a stepparent, fully 44 percent reported fantasies about killing them. Among those who lived for longer than six years with a stepparent, an even larger number—59 percent—reported such homicidal fantasies. In contrast, the figures for killing a mother or a father were lower—31 percent and 25 percent, respectively.

How can these findings be explained from an evolutionary perspective? There are two distinct possibilities. The one adopted by Kenrick and Sheets (1993), and also by Daly and Wilson (1988), may be called the "slip-up hypothesis." According to this hypothesis, males have evolved a psychological propensity for violence as a means of coercive control and eliminating sources of conflict. This propensity typically results in threats of violence or sublethal violence as a behavioral output. Occasionally, how-ever, there is a "slip," such that the violence accidentally bubbles over into a homicide: "There is brinkmanship in any such contest, and the homicides by spouses of either sex may be considered slips in this dangerous game" (Daly & Wilson, 1988). The same slip-ups may occur in other forms of homicide, such as male–male homicide.

An alternative is the "evolved homicide module hypothesis" (Buss & Duntley, 1998; Duntley & Buss, 1998). According to this hypothesis humans—especially men—have evolved specific psychological mechanisms that predispose them to kill conspecifics under certain predictable circumstances such as warfare, intrasexual rivalry, or spousal infidelity or defection. Humans presumably have homicidal fantasies as one component of these evolved homicide modules that allow a person to build and work through the homicidal scenario in his or her mind, evaluate the costs and benefits of various courses of action, and then choose to kill when the benefits outweigh the costs. In many circumstances the costs are too great—in all societies the person risks the wrath of kin and punishment from other interested members of the group (Daly & Wilson, 1988). These costs are weighted and deter many from killing. The proposal is *not* that men have a "killer instinct" whereby they are impelled to kill regardless of circumstances. Rather, it is that acts of killing are one part of the behavioral output of evolved homicide modules whose activation is triggered by particular forms of input, and then costs and benefits are evaluated.

These competing evolutionary hypotheses—the slip-up hypothesis and the evolved homicide modules hypothesis—have not yet been pitted against each other in empirical tests. The high prevalence of homicidal fantasies, the predictability of the circumstances that trigger them, the evidence of sex differences, and the premeditated quality of many homicides, however, do not accord well with the slip-up hypothesis. Research designed to test these hypotheses is underway. Within the next decade we can expect a resolution to the debate about whether humans have evolved specific homicide modules.

Summary

From the perspective of evolutionary psychology aggression is not a singular or a unitary phenomenon. Rather, it represents a collection of strategies that are manifest under highly specific contextual conditions. The mechanisms underlying aggression have emerged, on this account, as solutions, albeit repugnant ones, to a host of distinct adaptive problems such as resource procurement, intrasexual competition, hierarchy negotiation, and mate retention.

From this perspective variability in aggression—between the sexes, among individuals, over the life span, and across cultures—is predicted. This contrasts markedly from earlier instinct theories in which aggression was presumed to be manifest invariantly, "pushed out" in all people one way or another. It also contrasts with domain-general learning accounts in that it suggests specific dedicated psychological mechanisms that have evolved over thousand of generations in response to particular adaptive social problems. Simultaneously, however, it illustrates the point that documented variability does not imply that biology is irrelevant. An evolutionary psychological perspective is truly interactionist—it specifies a set of causal conditions in which particular features of the perpetrator, victim, social context, and adaptive problem are likely to evoke aggression as a strategic solution.

An evolutionary perspective suggests at least six classes of benefits that would have accrued to ancestors who used an aggressive strategy: co-opting the resources of others, defending oneself and one's kin against attack, inflicting costs on intrasexual rivals, negotiating status and power hierarchies, deterring rivals from future aggression, and deterring long-term mates from infidelity or defection.

Sound evolutionary arguments predict that aggression is likely to emerge more strongly among men, with both aggressors and victims being men. Given a mating system of some degree of polygyny, selection will favor "risky tactics" among men both to gain sexual access to more women than their "fair share" and to avoid being excluded from mating entirely. The empirical evidence strongly suggests that most physical aggression is perpetrated by men and that most of the victims are men. This evidence includes the incidence of same-sex homicides across cultures, the frequency of bullying in school, and ethnographic evidence of physical violence from Australian aboriginal communities.

A variety of contexts are linked with aggression occurring within each sex-of-perpetrator by sex-of-victim combination. Contexts triggering men's aggression against other men include being unemployed and unmarried—contexts that suggest that men are on a path to being excluded from mating, which may trigger a risky aggressive strategy. Men also aggress against other men when their status and reputation are threatened and when they observe or suspect a rival of sexually "poaching" on their mate.

Women aggress against other women primarily in the context of intrasexual competition. Women, however, are far less likely to use physical aggression, preferring instead to derogate their competitors verbally. Two prominent derogation tactics are calling their rivals promiscuous and impugning their rival's physical appearance—both of which attain their effectiveness because they violate men's desires in a long-term mate.

Men aggress against women primarily in the context of controlling their sexuality. Sexual jealousy is a key context triggering men's aggression against their mates. Presumably such aggression historically functioned to deter a mate from further infidelity or from defecting from the relationship entirely. Younger women who are therefore higher in reproductive value are more vulnerable to aggression from their partners, presumably because ancestral men had a greater incentive to maintain exclusive sexual access to more desirable reproductive women.

Women kill men rarely, but when they do, it is typically in self-defense. The context usually involves a woman defending herself against a mate who is enraged about a real or suspected infidelity.

Warfare, defined as aggression by a cooperative coalition against another cooperative coalition, is extraordinarily rare in the animal world. Only two mammalian species have been observed to engage in warfare—chimpanzees and humans. An evolutionary perspective leads to the prediction that warfare will be practiced primarily by men, with the primary reproductive benefit being increased sexual access to women. Empirical evidence supports this theory: Men have engaged in warfare throughout human recorded history; sexual access to women appears to be a recurrent benefit that flows to victors of warfare; men more than women spontaneously assess their fighting ability relative to others; and men more than women value coalition members who are strong, are brave in the face of danger, and have good fighting abilities. Although more research is needed, the available evidence supports the evolutionary theory of warfare and suggests the evolution in men of specific psychological mechanisms designed to wage war.

The final section of the chapter considered two contrasting hypotheses designed to explain the evolution of the killing of other human beings. The first hypothesis suggests that killings are "slip-ups" that result from the use of violence and the threat of violence as a means of coercively controlling others. The second hypothesis suggests that humans, especially men, have evolved specific "homicide modules" that are designed to motivate killing other humans under specific circumstances when the benefits outweigh the costs. The high prevalence of homicidal fantasies, the predictability of the circumstances that trigger them, the evidence of gender differences, and the premeditated quality of many homicides all seem to support the homicide modules hypothesis, although further research is needed to compare predictions from the two theories directly.

An evolutionary psychological perspective on human aggression has many limitations. This perspective currently cannot account, for example, for why three men confronted with their wive's infidelity will result in a beating in one case, a homicide in the second, and drunkenness in the third. It currently cannot account for why some cultures, such as the Yanomamö, seem to require male violence to attain a position of status, whereas in other cultures aggression leads to irreparable reputational damage. The current evolutionary psychological account of aggression is limited in these and many other respects.

Even at this preliminary stage of inquiry, however, an evolutionary psychological account of aggression provides a guide suggesting particular lines of investigation not examined by other approaches. It can account parsimoniously for a host of otherwise inexplicable findings, such as the universally greater prevalence of aggression by men against other men, the ubiquity of male sexual jealousy as a cause of spousal violence and spousal homicide, and the identification of stepparenting as a causal context putting children at risk of aggression. As such, an evolutionary psychological account brings us one step closer to a complex interactionist theory of human aggression.

11 Conflict between the Sexes

There will always be a battle between the sexes because men and women want different things. Men want women and women want men.

—George Burns

In every age the battle of the sexes is largely a battle over sex.

—Donald Symons, 1979

In a recent study of high school students 36 percent of the girls reported having experienced physical violence in dating relationships (DeGroat, 1997). The same study found that 44 percent of those who had suffered moderate levels of violence—being kicked, pinched, scratched, slapped, or pulled—remained in the abusive relationship. And 36 percent of those who had experienced severe violence—being choked, punched, or threatened with a weapon—also remained in the relationship. That study is just the tip of the large iceberg of conflict between the sexes. This chapter will explore the evolutionary basis for conflicts between the sexes and the empirical research surrounding it.

When evolutionary psychologists first started to explore conflict between the sexes, relatively little was known about the topic. One evolutionary psychologist started simply by asking men and women to list all the things members of the opposite sex did that upset, annoyed, angered, or irritated them (Buss, 1989b). The college participants listed 147 distinct sources of conflict ranging from condescension, insults, and physical abuse to sexual aggression, sexual withholding, sexism, and sexual infidelity. This list was then used to test a series of evolutionary psychological hypotheses based on the theory of strategic interference.

Strategic Interference Theory

Human conflict is a universal feature of social interaction, and it occurs in many forms. In Chapter 10 we examined the many manifestations of same-sex conflict, including derogation of competitors, physical violence, and warfare. These are conflicts that were predictable from evolutionary accounts. Members of the same sex are often in competition with each other for precisely the same resources: members of the opposite sex and the resources needed to attract them.

Evolutionary psychologists have predicted conflict between the sexes, but not because men and women are in competition for the same reproductive resources. Rather, many sources of conflict between the sexes can be traced to evolved differences in sexual strategies. As we saw in Chapters 4, 5, and 6, both sexes have evolved short-term and long-term mating strategies. But the nature of these strategies differs for the sexes. One of the most important differences pertains to short-term mating strategies. Men, far more than women, have evolved a deeper desire for sexual variety. This desire manifests itself in many forms, including seeking sexual access sooner, more persistently, and more aggressively than women typically desire. Conversely, women have evolved to be more discriminating in short-term mating, typically delaying sexual intercourse beyond what men usually desire. Clearly the sexes cannot simultaneously fulfill these conflicting sexual desires. This is an example of a phenomenon called strategic interference.

Strategic interference may be defined as when a person employs a particular strategy to achieve a goal and another person blocks or prevents the successful enactment of that strategy or the fulfillment of the desire. If a woman adopts a strategy of delaying sexual intercourse until she feels some emotional involvement or commitment from a man, for example, and the man persists in his sexual advances even after the woman has indicated her desire to wait, then the result is interference with the woman's sexual strategy. At the same time, however, the delays imposed by the woman interfere with the man's short-term mating strategy of seeking sex sooner. In sum, men and women come into conflict not because they are competing for the same resources, as occurs in same-sex strategic interference, but rather because the strategy of one sex can interfere with the strategy of the other.

The theory of strategic interference applies not just to conflicts about the timing of sexual intercourse. Conflict can pervade all relations between the sexes, from contact in the workplace and on the dating scene to skirmishes that occur over the course of a marriage. Sexual harassment is a form of strategic interference in the workplace. Deception on the dating scene is another form of strategic interference. A man who deceives a woman about his marital status and a woman who deceives a man about her age both violate the desires of the opposite sex and so represent forms of strategic interference. Within a marriage, sexual infidelity represents another form of strategic interference because it violates the desires of the spouse. Coercive control, threats, violence, insults, and attempts to lower a partner's self-esteem constitute other forms of strategic interference in long-term relationships. The key point is that strategic interference—blocking the strategies and violating the desires of someone else—is predicted to pervade interactions between the sexes, from strangers to intimate partners.

The second component of strategic interference theory postulates that the "negative" emotions such as anger, distress, and upset are key human psychological solutions that have evolved in part to solve the adaptive problems posed by strategic interference. There are quotation marks around *negative* because although these emotions are generally painful to experience, they are hypothesized to be functional in solving the adaptive problems of strategic interference in several ways. First, they point out problematic events, focusing our attention on them and momentarily screening out less relevant events. Attention, after all, is a scarce resource, and must be allocated judiciously. When a person experiences anger or distress, these emotions guide their attention to the sources of the distress. Second, the emotions mark those events for storage in memory and easy retrieval from memory. Third, emotions lead to action, causing people to strive to eliminate the source of strategic interference.

In summary, the theory of strategic interference has two main postulates. First, strategic interference is predicted to occur whenever members of one sex violate the desires of members of the opposite sex; historically such interference would have prevented our forebears from successfully carrying out a preferred sexual strategy and hence would have reduced their reproductive success. Second, "negative" emotions such as anger, rage, and distress represent evolved solutions to the problems of strategic interference, alerting people to the sources of interference and prompting action designed to counteract it.

Before proceeding to the empirical studies that test this theory, we must note two important qualifiers. First, conflict per se serves no adaptive purpose. It is generally not adaptive for individuals to get into conflict with the opposite sex as an end in and of itself. Rather, conflict is more often an undesirable outcome of the fact that the sexual strategies of men and women differ in profound ways. This means that men and women cannot simultaneously reach their goals or pursue their desired sexual strategies without coming into conflict, at least some of the time.

A second qualification is that the metaphor of the "battle between the sexes" can be misleading. The phrase implies that men as a group are united in their interests and women are likewise united in their interests, and the two groups are somehow at war with each other. Nothing could be farther from the truth. An evolutionary perspective helps us to understand why. Men cannot be united with all other men as a group for the fundamental reason that men are in competition primarily with members of their own sex. The same is true for women. Therefore, a unification or a "confluence of interests" cannot occur between all members of one sex. Of course, men and women can form specific alliances with particular members of their own sex, but this in no way contradicts the fundamental principle that individuals are primarily in competition with members of their own gender. With these qualifications in mind, let's turn to the empirical evidence that bears on the evolution of conflict between the sexes.

Conflict about the Occurrence and Timing of Sex

Disagreements about the occurrence and timing of sex may be the most common sources of conflict between men and women. In a study of 121 college students who kept daily diaries of their dating activities for four weeks, 47 percent reported one or more disagreements about their desired level of sexual intimacy (Byers & Lewis, 1988). These disagreements always show a predictable sex difference. In one study of Australian undergraduate students, for example, 53 percent of the 217 women in the study reported that at least one man had "overestimated the level of sexual intimacy . . . desired," whereas 45 percent of the 72 men reported that at least one woman had "underestimated the level of sexual intimacy . . . desired" (Paton & Mannison, 1995, p. 447).

Men sometimes seek sexual access with a minimum of investment. Men often guard their resources and are extraordinarily choosy about who they invest those resources in. They are "resource coy" and often preserve their investment for long-term mates. Because women often pursue a long-term sexual strategy they often seek to obtain investment, or signals of investment, before consenting to sex. Yet the investment that women covet is precisely the investment that men most vigorously guard. The sexual access that men seek is precisely the resource that women are so selective about giving.

Conflict over Sexual Access

Inferences about Sexual Intent.   A major psychological source of these conflicts is the fact that men sometimes infer sexual interest on the part of a woman when it does not exist. A series of experiments have documented this phenomenon (Abbey, 1982; Saal, Johnson, & Weber, 1989). In one study 98 male and 102 female college students viewed a ten-minute videotape of a conversation in which a female student visits a male professor's office to ask for more time to complete a term paper. The actors in the film were a female drama student and a professor in the theater department. Neither the student nor the professor acted flirtatious or overtly sexual, although both were instructed to behave in a friendly manner. People who witnessed the tape then rated the likely intentions of the woman using a seven-point scale. Women watching the interaction were more likely to say that she was trying to be friendly, with an average rating of 6.45, and not sexy (2.00) or seductive (1.89). Men, also perceiving friendliness (6.09), were significantly more likely than women to infer seductive (3.38) and sexual intentions (3.84). Similar results were obtained when 246 university students rated the intentions of women in photographs of a man and a woman studying together (Abbey & Melby, 1986). Men rated the photographed women as showing moderate intent to be sexy (4.87) and seductive (4.08), whereas women rating identical photographs saw considerably less sexual intent (3.11) and less seductive intent (2.61). Men interpret simple friendliness and mere smiling by women as indicating more sexual interest than women viewing exactly the same events.

Thus far there has been only one cross-cultural test of this sex difference in perceptions of sexual intent. A sample of 196 Brazilian college students, 98 men and 98 women, evaluated four hypothetical scenarios presented in Portuguese (DeSouza, Pierce, Zanelli, & Hutz, 1992). A parallel sample of 204 American college students evaluated the scenarios in English. In each scenario a man and a woman spent time together at a party. The scenarios differed in whether the participants had been drinking alcohol and in whether the woman agreed to go back to the man's dorm room with him. After viewing each scenario participants rated four questions on a seven-point scale, assessing the degree to which each character had communicated either a willingness to have sex or an expectation of having sex. Responses to the four questions were summed to yield a composite index of perceived sexual intent.

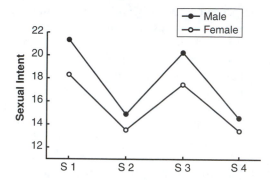

FIGURE 11.1   Average Judgments of Sexual Intent in Brazil and the United States. The figure shows that men tend to infer more sexual intent than women in response to the same scenario.

Source: Perceived sexual intent in the United States and Brazil as a function of nature of encounter, subjects' nationality, and gender by E. R. DeSouza, T. Pierce, J. C. Zanelli, & C. Hutz, *Journal of Sex Research, 29* (1992), 251–260. Reprinted with permission.

The results are shown in Figure 11.1. Brazilian college students consistently perceived more sexuality in the characters' behavior than did the American college students, with mean scores of 18.77 and 14.27, respectively. Gender differences were also highly significant, as shown in Figure 11.1. Men across both cultures perceived more sexual intent in the characters' actions than did women, with mean scores of 17.53 and 15.50, respectively. Separate analyses of each culture showed that the sex differences in inferences about sexual intent remained robust, especially for the scenarios in which the characters consumed alcohol. The differences by sex, however, were smaller in the Brazilian sample than in the American sample, perhaps suggesting that conflicts over differences in the perceptions of sexual interest may be a bit less likely to occur in Brazil.

When in doubt men infer sexual interest. Men act on their inferences, occasionally opening up sexual opportunities. If over evolutionary history even a tiny fraction of these led to sex, men would have evolved lower thresholds for inferring women's sexual interest. It is impossible to state unequivocally that males misperceive women's sexual interest because it is impossible to determine with certainty what someone's interests and intentions actually are. But we can say with certainty that men have lower thresholds for perceiving sexual interest than women.

This male mechanism is susceptible to manipulation. Women sometimes use their sexuality as one such tactic. In one study of two hundred university students, significantly more women than men reported using smiling and flirting as a means for eliciting special treatment from members of the opposite sex, even though they had no interest in having sex with those men (Buss, 1994).

The fact that men are likely to perceive that women are interested in them sexually when they really aren't, combined with women's intentional exploitation of this psychological mechanism, creates a potentially volatile mix. The differing sexual strategies of men and women lead to conflicts over desired levels of sexual intimacy, over men's feelings that women lead them on, and over women's feelings that men are too pushy about having sex.

Deception about Commitment.   Another manifestation of conflict over sexual access comes from research on deception between the sexes. Men report intentionally deceiving women about emotional commitment. When 112 college men were asked whether they had ever exaggerated the depth of their feelings for a woman to have sex with her, 71 percent admitted to having done so, compared with only 39 percent of the women (Buss, 1994). Each woman was asked whether a man had ever deceived her by exaggerating the depth of his feelings to have sex with her and 97 percent of the women admitted that they had experienced this tactic, in contrast to only 59 percent of the men.

In human courtship the costs of being deceived about a potential mate's resources and commitment are shouldered more heavily by women. An ancestral man who made a poor choice of a sex partner risked losing only a small portion of his time, energy, and resources, although he may also have evoked the rage of a jealous husband or a protective father. An ancestral woman who made a poor choice of a casual mate, allowing herself to be deceived about the man's long-term intentions or willingness to devote resources to her, however, risked pregnancy, childbirth, and child rearing unaided.

Because the deceived can suffer severe losses, there must have been tremendous selection pressures for the evolution of a form of psychological vigilance to detect cues to deception and to prevent its occurrence. The modern generation is merely another cycle in the endless spiral of an evolutionary arms race between deception perpetrated by one sex and detection accomplished by the other. As the deceptive tactics grow more subtle and refined, the ability to penetrate deception becomes more acute.

Women have evolved strategies to guard against deception. When a woman seeks a committed relationship, the first line of defense is imposing courtship costs by requiring extended time, energy, and commitment before consenting to sex. More time buys the advantage of more assessment. It allows a woman greater opportunity to evaluate a man, to assess how committed he is to her, and to detect whether he is burdened by prior commitments to other women and children. Men seeking to deceive women about their intentions typically tire of extended courtship. They go elsewhere for sex partners who are more readily accessible.

To guard against deception women spend hours discussing with their friends the details of interactions they have had with their mates or with potential mates. Conversations are recounted and scrutinized. When asked, for example, whether they talk with their friends to try to figure out the real intentions of someone they have gone out with, most women admit that they do. Men, in contrast, are significantly less inclined to devote effort to this problem of assessment (Buss, 1994). Women must separate men seeking casual sex from those seeking marriage. Ancestral men generally had less need than women to channel time and effort into assessing a potential mate's temporal intentions.

Sexual Harassment.   Disagreements over sexual access occur not just in the context of dating and marital relationships, but also in the workplace, where people commonly seek casual and permanent mates. When such advances are unwelcome, this crosses a line and

becomes sexual harassment, which is defined as "unwanted and unsolicited sexual attention from other individuals in the workplace" (Terpstra & Cook, 1985). Sexual harassment can range from mild forms, such as unwanted staring and sexual comments, to
physical violations, such as the touching of breasts, buttocks, or crotch. Sexual harassment produces obvious conflict between the sexes and is the result of differences between
men's and women's evolved psychologies.

Sexual harassment is typically motivated by the possibility that such a come-on
might lead to a short-term sexual encounter, although this does not exclude the possibility that it is sometimes motivated by the desire to exercise power or to seek lasting
romantic relationships. The view that sexual harassment is a product of the evolved sexual strategies of men and women is supported by the profiles of typical victims, including
such elements as gender, age, marital status, and physical attractiveness; their reactions to
unwanted sexual advances; and the conditions under which they were harassed.

Victims of sexual harassment are not random with respect to sex. In one study of
complaints filed with the Illinois Department of Human Rights over a two-year period,
women filed seventy-six complaints whereas men filed only five. Another study of 10,644
federal government employees found that 42 percent of the women, but only 15 percent
of the men, experienced sexual harassment at some point (Gutek, 1985). Of the sexual
harassment complaints filed in one Canadian province, ninety-three cases were filed by
women and only two by men. In both of the latter cases the harassers were men. It seems
clear that women are generally the victims of sexual harassment and men are generally
the perpetrators. Nonetheless, given the tendency of women to experience greater
distress to acts of sexual pushiness or aggressiveness, it is likely that women would
be more upset than men by the same acts of sexual harassment. Hence, women might be
more likely than men to file official complaints when harassed.

Although any woman may be the target of sexual harassment, the victims are disproportionately concentrated among young, physically attractive, and single women.
Women over forty-five are far less likely than younger women to have experienced sexual harassment of any type (Studd & Gattiker, 1991). One study found that women
between the ages of twenty and thirty-five filed 72 percent of the complaints of harassment, although they represented only 43 percent of the labor force at the time. Women
over forty-five, who represented 28 percent of the workforce, filed only 5 percent of the
complaints. In none of the many studies of sexual harassment have older women been at
equal or increased risk of harassment compared to younger women. The targets of sexual harassment are relatively young, which jibes with the general manifestations of male
sexual interest.

Single and divorced women are subjected to sexual harassment more than married
women. In one study, 43 percent of women filing complaints were single, although they
represented only 25 percent of the labor force; married women, comprising 55 percent
of the labor force, filed only 31 percent of the complaints. There may be several reasons
for this phenomenon. Married women are generally less receptive to sexual advances
from male co-workers than are single or divorced women because they risk losing the
commitment and resources of their husbands. Moreover, the costs that might be imposed on a sexual harasser by a jealous husband are nonexistent when the victim is single. Single women are thus more attractive targets.

Reactions to sexual harassment tend to follow the logic predicted by evolutionary psychology. When men and women were asked how they would feel if a coworker of the opposite sex asked them to have sex, 63 percent of the women said they would be insulted, whereas a minority, 17 percent of the women, said they would feel flattered. Men's reactions were just the opposite—only 15 percent said they would be insulted, whereas 67 percent said they would feel flattered. These reactions fit with the evolutionary logic of human mating, with men having positive emotional reactions to the prospect of casual sex and women having more negative reactions to being treated as sex objects. These results support strategic interference theory.

The degree of chagrin that women experience after sexual advances, however, depends in part on the status of the harasser. In one study 109 college women rated how upset they would be if a man they did not know, whose occupational status varied from low to high, persisted in asking them out on a date despite their repeated refusals (Buss, 1994). On a seven-point scale, women would be most upset by persistent advances from construction workers (4.04), garbage collectors (4.32), cleaning men (4.19), and gas station attendants (4.13), and least upset by persistent advances by premedical students (2.65), graduate students (2.80), or successful rock stars (2.71). When 104 different women were asked how flattered they would feel by outright sexual propositions from men with various occupations, the responses were similar. The emotions in the sexually harassed that signal strategic interference on the part of the person doing the harassing apparently are sensitive to the status of the sexual harasser.

Women's reactions to sexual harassment also depend heavily on whether the motivation of the harasser is perceived to be sexual or romantic. Sexual bribery, attaching job promotions to sex, and other cues that the person is interested only in casual sex, are more likely to be labeled harassment than are signals of potential interest that may transcend the purely sexual, such as nonsexual touching, complimentary looks, or flirting (Studd, 1996). When 110 college women used a seven-point scale to rate how sexually harassing a series of actions were, acts such as a fellow coworker putting his hand on a woman's crotch (6.81) or trying to corner a woman when no one else was around (6.03) were seen as extremely harassing (Buss, 1994). In contrast, acts such as a coworker telling a woman that he sincerely liked her and would like to have coffee with her after work was judged to be only 1.50, where a 1 signified no harassment at all. Clearly short-term sexual overtures and coercive intentions are seen as more harassing than sincere romantic intentions. Future studies might seek to cleanly separate coercive sexual overtures from those that are not coercive.

Not all women, however, label even coercive behavior harassment. For example, 17 percent of the women in a study of sexual harassment in the workplace did not consider sexual touching to be harassment (Studd & Gattiker, 1991). Women's evolved sexual strategy may be conditional in that women sometimes can benefit from, or take advantage of, men's sexual advances. It is clear, for example, that women as well as men often seek and find romantic and sexual relationships in the workplace. Some women are even willing to exchange sex for good positions and privileges at work. One woman reported that she did not consider the expectation that she would have sex with her foreman harassment because "all the women were treated the same way" and because she was able to get "easy work" that way (Quinn, 1977). Just as women may gain material benefits from casual mating outside the workplace, there may be circumstances in which women gain benefits from casual mating inside the workplace.

The findings about the profiles of sexual harassment victims, the sex differences in emotional reactions to sexual harassment, and the importance of the status of the harasser follow from the evolutionary logic of sexual strategies and strategic interference theory. Men have evolved lower thresholds for seeking casual sex without commitment and lower thresholds for perceiving sexual intent in others, and these evolved sexual mechanisms operate in the work context no less than in any other social context. Women appear to have evolved psychological patterns of anger and distress in reaction to acts of sexual harassment—emotions that presumably neutralize the strategic interference or lower the likelihood of it occurring in the future.

Sexual Aggressiveness.   Sexual aggressiveness, the vigorous pursuit of sexual access despite a woman's reluctance or resistance, can take many forms other than sexual harassment. Sexual aggressiveness is one strategy men use to minimize the costs they incur for sexual access, although this strategy carries its own costs in the form of retaliation and damage to their reputation. Acts of sexual aggression are exemplified by the man's demanding or forcing sexual intimacy, failing to get mutual agreement for sex, and touching a woman's body without her permission. In one study college women were asked to evaluate 147 potentially upsetting actions that men could do to them on a scale ranging from 1 (not at all upsetting) to 7 (extremely upsetting) (Buss, 1989b). Women rated sexual aggression on average to be 6.5. No other kinds of acts that men could perform, including verbal abuse and nonsexual physical abuse, were judged by women to be as upsetting as sexual aggression. Contrary to the view held by some men, women do not want forced sex.

Men, in sharp contrast, seem considerably less bothered if a woman is sexually aggressive; they see it as relatively innocuous compared with other sources of discomfort. On the same seven-point scale, for example, men judged the group of sexually aggressive acts to be 3.02, or only slightly upsetting, when performed by a woman. A few men spontaneously wrote in the margins of the questionnaire that they would find such acts sexually arousing if a woman were to perform them. Other sources of distress, such as a mate's infidelity and verbal or physical abuse, were potentially far more upsetting to the men—6.04 and 5.55, respectively—than sexual aggression by a woman.

One disturbing difference between men and women is that men consistently underestimate how unacceptable sexual aggression is to women. When asked to judge its negative impact on women, men rate it only 5.8 on a seven-point scale, which is significantly lower than women's own rating of 6.5. This is an alarming source of conflict between the sexes as it implies that some men will be inclined to use sexually aggressive acts because they fail to appreciate how distressing that is to women. In addition to creating conflict between individuals in their heterosexual interactions, men's failure to correctly understand the psychological pain that women experience as a result of sexual aggression may be one of the mechanisms causing men to lack empathy for rape victims (Thornhill, 1996).

Women, in contrast, overestimate how upsetting sexual aggression by a woman is to a man, judging it to be 5.13, or moderately upsetting, in contrast to men's rating of only 3.02 (Buss, 1989b). Men and women both fail to evaluate correctly how serious this source of conflict is for the other sex. This sex-linked bias in perception may result from erroneous beliefs about the other sex based on one's own reactions. That is, men think women are more like them and women think men are more like them in their reactions to sexual aggression; both are off the mark.

Individual Differences in Sexual Aggression: The Mate Deprivation Hypothesis.

Not all men inflict costs of sexual aggression on women. Indeed, evolutionary psychologists including Neil Malamuth have conducted research designed to identify the characteristics of men who are sexually aggressive (Malamuth, 1996; Malamuth, Sockloskie, Koss, & Tanaka, 1991). These researchers have identified two paths to sexual aggression. The first is the *impersonal sex path*. This includes males who place a high emphasis on sexual conquest as a source of peer status and self-esteem. Not all males who pursue impersonal short-term mating, of course, use sexual aggression, but this proclivity is statistically linked with the use of sexual aggression.

The second is called the *hostile masculinity path*. This path combines two interrelated components: (1) an insecure, defensive, hypersensitive, hostile, and distrustful orientation, especially toward women; and (2) pleasure in dominating and controlling women. Men who score high on measures of hostile masculinity tend to have a history of experiencing rejection by women. They endorse items such as "I have been rejected by too many women in my life" and "I am sure I get a raw deal from the women in my life" (Malamuth, 1996). These men feel that they have been hurt, deceived, betrayed, and manipulated by women. Malamuth suggests that hostile masculinity might allow men to avoid feeling sympathy or empathy for the victim that might otherwise inhibit the use of sexual aggression.

The most important finding of this research is that the *combination* of paths is most predictive of sexual aggression. Men who have both an impersonal orientation toward sex and display hostile masculinity are most at risk for sexually aggressing against women. This research has led to a specific evolutionary psychological prediction: Men who have experienced deprivation of sexual access to women will be more likely to use sexually aggressive tactics (Lalumiere, Chalmers, Quinsey, & Seto, 1996). This has been called the *mate deprivation hypothesis* (see Lalumiere & Quinsey, 1996; Quinsey & Lalumiere, 1995; Thornhill & Thornhill, 1983, 1992). According to this hypothesis, men have evolved a conditional mating strategy—when they cannot secure mates through the means of attraction they experience deprivation, which prompts them to use sexually aggressive tactics to avoid being excluded entirely. In the extreme this might be manifest as rape: "Rape may be engaged in by men who are relatively unsuccessful in competition for the resources and status necessary to attract and reproduce successfully with desirable mates" (Thornhill, Thornhill, & Dizinno, 1986, p. 103).

This hypothesis was tested on a sample of 156 heterosexual males with a mean age of twenty (Lalumiere et al., 1996). The measures of sexual coercion included both nonphysical (e.g., "Have you ever had sexual intercourse with a woman even though she didn't really want to because she felt pressured by your continual arguments?") and physical coercion (e.g., "Have you ever had sexual intercourse with a woman when she didn't want to because you used some degree of physical force?"). The measure of mating success was assessed by the Self-Perceived Mating Success Scale, which included items such as "Members of the opposite sex that I like tend to like me back"; "I receive many compliments from members of the opposite sex"; "I receive sexual invitations from members of the opposite sex"; and "Members of the opposite sex are attracted to me." Background socioeconomic status and perceived future income potential were also assessed.

The results contradicted the predictions the authors derived from the mate deprivation hypothesis of sexual aggression. Men who scored high on self-perceived mating success also tended to score high on the measures of sexual aggression, as shown in Figure 11.2. Furthermore, men who evaluated their future earning potential as high tended to use more physical coercion than men who perceived their future earning potential as low. In summary, the results failed to support the mate deprivation hypothesis, showing that evolutionary psychological hypotheses can be falsified.

The men who tended to be sexually aggressive did, however, endorse and pursue a short-term sexual strategy. They expressed a greater preference for partner variety and casual sex, supporting the Malamuth (1996) finding that one path to sexual aggression is impersonal sex. Indeed, sexually aggressive men in this sample reported having more mating opportunities, more frequent sexual intercourse, and more extensive sexual histories than men who tended not to use sexually aggressive tactics.

The authors offer one possible avenue for saving the mate deprivation hypothesis. They suggest a "micro mate deprivation hypothesis," whereby men who adopt a

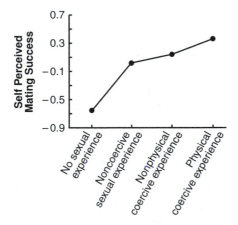

FIGURE 11.2   Self-Perceived Mating Success and Sexual Aggression. The figure shows that men who score high on self-perceived mating success tend to score higher on sexual coercion, contrary to mate deprivation hypothesis.

Source: Reprinted from *Ethology and Sociobiology, 17,* M. L. Lalumiere, L. J. Chalmers, V. L. Quinsey, & M. C. Seto, A test of the mate deprivation hypothesis of sexual coercion, 299–318, copyright © 1996, with permission from Elsevier Science.

short-term mating strategy suffer *periodic* difficulty in securing sexual access, and so resort to aggressive tactics in these contexts. Future research must assess directly the proportion of copulations that are attained through coercive and noncoercive means to test this modification of the mate deprivation hypothesis.

Sexual Withholding. The flip side of the coin of sexual aggression is sexual withholding. Men consistently complain about women's sexual withholding, defined by such acts as being sexually teasing, saying no to intercourse, and leading a man on and then stopping him. On a seven-point scale men judged sexual withholding to be 5.03, whereas women judged it 4.29 (Buss, 1989b). Both sexes are bothered by sexual withholding, men significantly more than women.

For women sexual withholding fulfills several possible functions. One is to preserve their ability to choose men of high quality who are willing to commit emotionally and invest materially. Women withhold sex from certain men and selectively allocate it to others of their own choosing. Moreover, by withholding sex women increase its value. They render it a scarce resource. Scarcity increases the price that men are willing to pay for it. If the only way men can gain sexual access is by heavy investment, then they will make that investment. Under conditions of sexual scarcity, men who fail to invest fail to secure copulations. This creates another conflict between a man and a woman— her withholding interferes with his strategy of gaining sexual access sooner and with fewer emotional strings attached.

Another function of sexual withholding is to manipulate men's perception of a woman's value as a mate. Because highly desirable women are more sexually inaccessible to the average man by definition, women sometimes exploit men's perceptions of their desirability by withholding sexual access (Buss, 1994). A final possible function of sexual withholding, at least initially, is to encourage a man to evaluate a woman as a permanent rather than a temporary mate. Granting sexual access early and often causes men to see a woman as a casual mate. They may perceive her as too promiscuous and too sexually available, characteristics that men avoid in committed mates.

Because men sometimes pursue casual sex with a variety of women, yet typically commit only to one, women's sexual withholding can create conflict by interfering with men's sexual strategies. By withholding sex women impose a cost on men. They circumvent the component of men's mating strategy that involves obtaining low-cost sex. Certainly women have a right to choose when and where they want to have sex. Unfortunately, the exercise of that choice interferes with one of men's deep-seated sexual strategies, and is therefore experienced by men as upsetting; hence it is one of the key sources of conflict between the sexes.

In sum, there is substantial empirical evidence that strategic interference occurs around the issue of sexual access. Men pursue sexual access sooner, more persistently, and more aggressively than women want, and infer that women are more interested in having sex with them than they likely are. Women experience anger and upset about these forms of sexual persistence, which may represent an evolved psychological solution to the adaptive problem of strategic sexual interference by men. Men, on the other hand, appear to experience strategic interference as a result of women's sexual withholding, which makes them angry and distressed.

Jealous Conflict

In Chapter 5 we explored men's long-term mate preferences, one of which was a desire for a partner who indicated she would be sexually faithful during the course of the marriage. This mate preference is presumably designed to solve—at least in part—the adaptive problem of paternity uncertainty. This provides a clue that men are deeply concerned about the sexual contact their mates might have with other men. Indeed, as we saw in Chapter 6 there are many potential benefits that women can accrue from extramarital affairs, such as resources, good genes, and the potential for a better mate. These considerations point to a profound source of conflict between the sexes—conflict between a husband's desire for exclusive sexual access to his partner and the wife's desire for potential sexual contact with other men. In short, there is the potential for conflict between the sexes over cuckoldry.

The potential for cuckoldry creates a serious adaptive problem for men that is magnified in humans because of the tremendous investment that men often channel toward their children. If a man is cuckolded he must consider the possibility that he is investing all of his resources in another man's children. But the problem is even more severe than that. Not only does he "lose" his own investment, he also stands to lose the investment of his partner, who would now be investing her efforts in another man's child. In addition, the cuckolded man stands to lose all of the energy and effort he devoted to selecting, attracting, and courting his partner.

Ancestral men who failed to solve this adaptive problem not only risked suffering direct reproductive losses, they also risked losing status and reputation, which could have seriously impaired their ability to attract other mates. Consider the reaction in Greek culture to cuckoldry:

> The wife's infidelity . . . brings disgrace to the husband who is then a Keratas—the worst insult for a Greek man—a shameful epithet with connotations of weakness and inadequacy. . . . While for the wife it is socially acceptable to tolerate her unfaithful husband, it is not socially acceptable for a man to tolerate his unfaithful wife and if he does so, he is ridiculed as behaving in an unmanly manner. (Safilios-Rothschild, 1969, pp. 78–79)

Evolutionary psychologists have hypothesized that sexual jealousy is one psychological mechanism that has evolved in men to combat the manifold potential costs of being cuckolded (Daly, Wilson, & Weghorst, 1982; Symons, 1979).

Jealousy in men might help solve this adaptive problem in several ways. First, it might sensitize a man to circumstances in which his partner might be unfaithful, thus promoting vigilance. Second, it might prompt actions designed to curtail his partner's contact with other men. Third, it might cause him to increase his own efforts to fulfill his partner's desires so that she would have less reason to stray. And fourth, jealousy might prompt a man to threaten or otherwise fend off rivals who showed sexual interest in his partner. One clear prediction from this line of reasoning is that a man's jealousy should focus heavily on the potential *sexual* contact that his partner might have with another man. The hypothesis is that sexual jealousy evolved in men in response to the heavy costs imposed by cuckoldry.

Women also face a profound adaptive problem because of a partner's infidelity, but it is not defined by a compromise in a woman's certainty that she is the mother of her children. Recall that maternity certainty is always 100 percent because fertilization occurs in the woman's body. If an ancestral woman's partner committed an infidelity, however, this could have posed a profound adaptive problem. Because men tend to channel investments and resources to women with whom they have sex, a husband might devote time, attention, energy, and effort to another woman and her children rather than his wife and children. For these reasons evolutionary psychologists have predicted that women's jealousy would be more likely to focus on cues to the long-term diversion of a man's commitments, such as his becoming *emotionally* involved with another woman (Buss, Larsen, Westen, & Semmelroth, 1992).

Sex Differences in Jealousy

Prior to studies by evolutionary psychologists, dozens of empirical studies explored the psychology of jealousy. The most common finding was that men and women do not differ in either the frequency or the magnitude of the jealousy they experience. In one study 300 participants, partners in 150 romantic relationships, rated how jealous they were in general, how jealous they were of their partner's relationships with members of the opposite sex, and the degree to which jealousy was a problem in their relationship. Men and women reported equal amounts of jealousy, confirming that the sexes experience jealousy roughly equally and with equal intensity (White, 1981).

This lack of a sex difference in jealousy has been replicated in a sample of more than two thousand individuals from Hungary, Ireland, Mexico, the Netherlands, Russia, the former Yugoslavia, and the United States (Buunk & Hupka, 1987). Participants expressed their reactions to a variety of different sexual scenarios. Men and women in all seven countries expressed almost identical negative emotional reactions to thoughts of their partners flirting with someone else. The sexes were also identical in their jealous reactions to a partner hugging or dancing with someone else, although their response to these events was less negative than to flirting. Across cultures, apparently, both men and women get jealous when a romantic relationship is threatened.

According to an evolutionary psychological analysis, all these studies, although informative about the equality of the sexes in experiencing jealousy, had posed the question in too global a manner. An evolutionary analysis leads to the prediction that although both sexes will experience jealousy, they will differ in the weight they give to the cues that trigger jealousy. Men are predicted to give more weight to cues to *sexual* infidelity, whereas women are predicted to give more weight to cues to a long-term diversion of investment, such as *emotional* involvement with another person (Buss et al., 1992).

In a systematic test of the hypothesized sex differences, 511 college students were asked to compare two distressing events: (a) their partner having sexual intercourse with someone else, or (b) their partner becoming emotionally involved with someone else (Buss et al., 1992). Fully 83 percent of the women found their partner's emotional infidelity more upsetting, whereas only 40 percent of the men did. In contrast, 60 percent of the men experienced their partner's sexual infidelity as more distressing, whereas only 17 percent of the women did. This constitutes a huge 43 percent difference between the sexes in their responses, large by any standard in the social sciences. By posing a more precise question—not whether each sex experiences "jealousy," but rather which precise triggers of jealousy are more distressing—the evolutionary psychological hypothesis was able to guide researchers to discover a sex difference that had previously gone unnoticed.

Verbal reports are reasonable sources of data, but ideally, converging evidence from other data sources is more scientifically compelling. To explore the generality of the above findings across different scientific methods, thirty men and thirty women were brought into a psycho-physiological laboratory (Buss et al., 1992). To evaluate physiological distress from imagining the two types of infidelity the experimenters placed electrodes on the corrugator muscle on the brow of the forehead, which contracts when people frown; on the first and third fingers of the right hand to measure electrodermal response, or sweating; and on the thumb to measure pulse or heart rate. Participants were asked to imagine either a sexual infidelity ("imagining your partner having sex with someone else . . . get the feelings and images clearly in mind") or an emotional infidelity ("imagining your partner falling in love with someone else . . . get the feelings and images clearly in mind"). Subjects pressed a button when they had the feelings and images clearly in mind, which activated the physiological recording devices for twenty seconds.

The men became more physiologically distressed by the sexual infidelity. Their heart rates accelerated by nearly five beats per minute, which is roughly the equivalent of drinking three cups of strong coffee at one time. Their skin conductance increased 1.5 units with the thought of sexual infidelity, but showed almost no change from baseline in response to the thought of emotional infidelity. And their corrugator frowning increased, showing 7.75 microvolt units of contraction in response to sexual infidelity, as compared with only 1.16 units in response to emotional infidelity.

Women tended to show the opposite patterns. They exhibited greater physiological distress at the thought of emotional infidelity. Women's frowning, for example, increased to 8.12 microvolt units of contraction in response to emotional infidelity, as compared with only 3.03 units of contraction in response to sexual infidelity. The convergence of psychological reactions of distress with physiological patterns of distress in men and women strongly supports the hypothesis that humans have evolved mechanisms specific to the sex-linked adaptive problems they recurrently have faced over evolutionary history.

These sex differences have been replicated in Germany, the Netherlands, Korea, and Japan (Buunk, Angleitner, Oubaid, & Buss, 1996). Figure 11.3 shows reactions from individuals in these cultures to which jealousy scenario is more distressing, sexual or emotional infidelity. The magnitude of the sex difference varies somewhat from culture to culture—significant in Korea and Japan and smaller in the Netherlands—but the sex difference remains robust across cultures. In sum, men's jealousy appears to be more sensitive to cues of sexual infidelity and women's jealousy more sensitive to cues to emotional infidelity—results that were found across both psychological and physiological methods, as well as across cultures.

The evolutionary interpretation of this sex difference in jealousy has been challenged (DeSteno & Salovey, 1996). These psychologists have proposed that sexual and

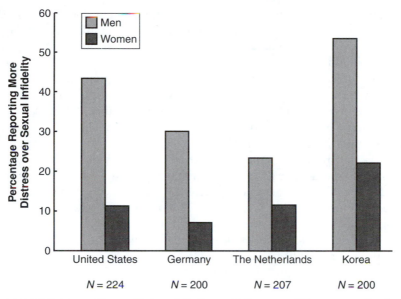

FIGURE 11.3   Cross-Cultural Jealousy Dilemmas. Men across all cultures report greater distress than do women in response to sexual infidelity scenario; women across all cultures report greater distress than do men in response to emotional or love infidelity.

N = sample size.

Source: Buunk, B. P., Angleitner, A., Oubaid, V., & Buss, D. M. (1996). Sex differences in jealousy in evolutionary and cultural perspective: Tests from the Netherlands, Germany, and the United States. *Psychological Science*, 7, 359–363. Reprinted with permission.

emotional infidelity are often correlated. People tend to get emotionally involved with those with whom they have sex, and conversely tend to become sexually involved with those with whom they are emotionally close. But men and women might differ in their beliefs about the correlation. Perhaps women get more upset about a partner's emotional involvement because they think it implies that their partner will also become sexually involved. Women might believe that men can have sex, in contrast, without getting emotionally involved, and so imagining a partner's sexual involvement is less upsetting. Men's beliefs might differ. Perhaps men get more upset about a partner's sexual involvement because they think that a partner is likely to have sex only if also emotionally involved, whereas they think a woman can easily become emotionally involved without having sex with a man. In sum, because men and women might hold different beliefs about the links between sexual and emotional infidelity, they might respond differently to which one is more upsetting when forced to choose.

Four empirical studies were conducted in three different cultures to test predictions from the competing hypotheses (Buss et al., 1999). The first study involved 1,122 undergraduates at a liberal arts college in the southeastern United States. The original infidelity scenarios (Buss et al., 1992) were altered to render the two types of infidelity mutually exclusive. Participants reported their relative distress in response to a partner's sexual infidelity with no emotional involvement, and emotional involvement with no sexual infidelity. As shown in Figure 11.4, a notable gender difference emerged, as predicted by the evolutionary model. If the belief hypothesis were correct, then the sex difference should have disappeared. It did not.

A second study provided four additional tests of the predictions from the two models using three strategies and American undergraduates. One strategy employed three different versions of rendering the two types of infidelity mutually exclusive. A second strategy involved positing that both types of infidelity had occurred, and requested that participants indicate *which aspect* they found more upsetting. A third strategy used a statistical procedure to test the independent predictive value of sex and beliefs in accounting for which form of infidelity would be more distressing. The results were conclusive: Large gender differences were discovered, precisely as predicted by the evolutionary model (see Figure 11.4). No matter how the questions were worded, no matter which methodological strategy was employed, and no matter how stringently the conditional probabilities were controlled, the sex differences remained.

A third study replicated the six infidelity dilemmas in a non-Western sample of native Koreans. The original sex differences (Buss et al., 1992) were replicated, show-

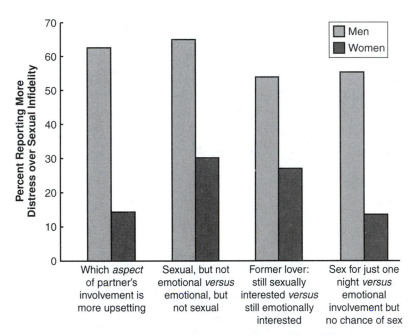

FIGURE 11.4   Four Critical Tests of Competing Hypotheses. The figure shows that sex differences in response to sexual versus emotional infidelity remain strong, even when requesting subjects to indicate which aspect of the infidelity was more distressing when both had occurred, and when the infidelity types are rendered mutually exclusive.

Source: Buss, D. M., Shackelford, T. K., Kirkpatrick, L. A., Choe, J., Hasegawa, M., Hasegawa, T., & Bennett, K. (1999). Jealousy and the nature of beliefs about infidelity: Tests of competing hypotheses about sex differences in the United States, Korea, and Japan. *Personal Relationships.* Reprinted with permission of the author.

ing that women indicated more distress than men to emotional infidelity, whereas men more than women found sexual infidelity distressing. With two strategies to control for conditional probabilities, the gender differences again remained robust. The evolutionary hypothesis survived this empirical hurdle. A fourth study tested the predictions about jealousy and about the nature of beliefs in a non-Western Japanese sample. The results again provided support for the evolutionary hypothesis (Buss et al., 1999).

This hypothesis about the psychology of jealousy has withstood several strong attempts at disproving it and parsimoniously accounts for a constellation of empirical findings. It can account for the original findings of sex differences in infidelity (Buss et al., 1992). It can account for sex differences in jealousy, even when conditional probabilities are controlled. It can account for sex differences in which one aspect of infidelity is more upsetting when both have occurred. And it can account for the cross-cultural robustness of these sex differences, now documented in Western cultures such as the Netherlands and Germany and in the non-Western cultures of Korea and Japan.

From Vigilance to Violence: Tactics of Mate Retention

Evidence that men have evolved a powerful psychological mechanism that creates in them feelings of jealousy helps us to understand how they might have solved the adaptive problem of the partial or total loss of a partner. Psychological mechanisms, however, can evolve only if they produce behavioral output that actually solves the adaptive problem. In the case of jealousy, the behavioral output would have to (1) deter a partner from committing infidelity, or (2) lower the odds that the partner will defect from the relationship. Two studies (Buss, 1988c; Buss & Shackelford, 1997c) explored the behavioral output of jealousy in the form of mate retention tactics ranging from vigilance to violence.

The first step in this program of research was to secure a list of acts designed to solve the adaptive problems of infidelity and relationship defection. Toward this end 105 participants were asked to list acts they believed would be directed toward these adaptive problems. The instructional set read as follows: "In this study, we are interested in the things that people do when they want to prevent their partner from getting involved with someone else. . . . Please think of three people you know who have done things to prevent their partner from getting involved with someone else and list them" (Buss, 1988c, p. 296). Table 11.1 on page 330 shows a sample of these acts. Once this list of acts of mate retention was established, studies of dating and married couples were carried out to test several evolutionary psychological hypotheses about the context-specific determinants of mate retention.

Sex Differences in the Use of Mate-Retention Tactics

The results of these studies revealed that men were more likely than women to use several tactics of mate retention, as predicted. A man would be more likely to conceal his partner, such as by not taking her to a party where other men would be present and insisting that she spend all of her free time with him. Men were also more likely to resort to

TABLE 11.1   Sample Tactics and Acts of Mate Retention. Tactics of mate retention range from vigilance to violence. These are used to keep a mate and fend off intrasexual rivals.

Vigilance

1. He called her at unexpected times to see who she was with.
2. He called her to make sure she was where she said she would be.

Concealment of Mate

1. He did not take her to the party where other men would be present.
2. He did not let her talk to other men.

Monopolize Mate's Time

1. He insisted that she spend all of her free time with him.
2. He would not let her go out without him.

Jealousy Induction

1. He talked to another woman at the party to make her jealous.
2. He showed interest in other women to make her jealous.

Emotional Manipulation

1. He threatened to harm himself if she ever left him.
2. He made her feel guilty about talking with other men.

Derogation of Competitors

1. He told her that the other guy was stupid.
2. He cut down the other guy's strength.

Resource Display

1. He spent a lot of money on her.
2. He bought her an expensive gift.

Love and Care

1. He told her that he loved her.
2. He was helpful when she really needed it.

Submission and Self-Abasement

1. He told her that he would change in order to please her.
2. He became a "slave" to her.

Physical Signals of Possession

1. He held her closer when another man walked into the room.
2. He put his arm around her in front of the others.

Intrasexual Threats

1. He stared coldly at the other guy who was looking at her.
2. He threatened to hit the guy who was making moves on her.

Violence toward Partner

1. He yelled at her after she showed an interest in another man.
2. He hit her when he caught her flirting with someone else.

Violence toward Rivals

1. He hit the guy who made a pass at her.
2. He got his friends to beat up the guy who had made a pass at her.

From Buss, D. M. (1996, June). *Mate retention in married couples.* Paper presented to the Annual Meeting of the Human Behavior and Evolution Society. Evanston, IL.

threats and violence, especially against rivals, such as threatening to hit a guy who was making moves on his partner or picking a fight with a guy who was interested in her. Men were also more likely to use *resource display*, buying the partner jewelry, giving her gifts, and taking her out to expensive restaurants. Interestingly, and not predicted, was the finding that men in both dating and married couples tended to use acts of submission and self-abasement more than women. For example, more men than women reported groveling and saying that they would do anything their partner wanted to get the partner to stay in the relationship.

Women performed some acts of mate retention more than men. As predicted, women tended to enhance appearance as a tactic of mate retention—making up their faces, wearing the latest fashions, and making themselves "extra attractive" for their mates.

Women also tended to induce jealousy in their partners by flirting with other men in front of them, showing interest in other men to make their partners angry, and talking with other men to make their partners jealous. One study identified a key context in which women intentionally elicit jealousy. It examined discrepancies between a man's and a woman's admitted involvement in a relationship. These discrepancies in how involved each partner admits to being usually signal differences in the desirability of the partners; the less involved person is generally more desirable (Buss, 1994). Although women admit to inducing jealousy overall more than men, not all women use this tactic. Whereas 50 percent of the women who view themselves as more involved than their partners in the relationship intentionally provoke jealousy, only 26 percent of the women who are equally or less involved resort to provoking jealousy (White, 1980).

Women acknowledge that they are motivated to elicit jealousy to increase the closeness of their relationship, to test the strength of their relationship, to see if their partner still cares, and to motivate their partner to be more possessive of them. Discrepancies between partners in desirability, as indicated by differences in involvement in the relationship, apparently cause women to provoke jealousy as a tactic to gain information about, and to increase, a partner's level of commitment.

In sum, men are more likely than women to conceal their mates, display resources to their mates, submit to their mates, and use violence against rivals as tactics to prevent their mates from getting involved with other men. Women are more likely than men to enhance appearance, thus fulfilling an evolved desire that men have for physically attractive partners. Women are also more likely to induce jealousy in their partners—perhaps as a strategy of indicating to their partners that they have other mating possibilities, and thus communicating information about their desirability.

Contexts Influencing the Intensity of Mate-Retention Tactics

Jealousy and its behavioral output in the form of mate retention are predicted to be highly sensitive to certain features of the relationship. Buss and Shackelford (1997c) tested a series of context-specific hypotheses using a sample of newlywed couples. These hypotheses included the following: (1) perceived likelihood of partner infidelity will be linked with an increase in mate-retention tactics, (2) youthfulness and physical attractiveness of the wife will be positively linked with men's mate-guarding tactics, (3) high income and status striving of the husband will be linked with higher levels of mate-retention tactics performed by women, and (4) the larger the perceived mate value discrepancies between husband and wife, the more intense the mate-retention efforts.

Perceived Likelihood of Infidelity.   One of the most important cues that signal the adaptive problem of a failure of mate retention is the perception or suspicion of spousal infidelity. From a man's perspective sexual infidelity could jeopardize his certainty in paternity, thus risking the loss of all the effort he has expended in selecting, courting, and attracting his mate. He further risks investing in offspring sired by rival men, as well as incurring opportunity costs by forgoing other mating opportunities. Individuals who suspect that their partners are likely to be unfaithful were hypothesized to devote more effort toward the adaptive problem of mate retention than individuals who do not suspect their partners will be unfaithful.

To test this hypothesis, a sample of 107 newlywed couples reported on the perceived probability of infidelity by their partners. Participants estimated on a scale ranging from 0 to 100 percent the probability that their spouse would flirt with a member of the opposite sex within the next year, as well as passionately kiss, go out on a romantic date, or have a one-night stand, a brief affair, and a serious affair with a member of the opposite sex within the next year. In a separate testing session participants also completed an itemized "act report" in which they indicated how often they had performed each of 104 acts of mate retention within the past year. The rating scale ranged from "never" to "often."

Statistical analyses revealed that men's, but not women's, mate-retention efforts were positively linked with the perceived probability of their spouse being unfaithful within the next year. Men who perceived infidelity as more likely were especially prone to report concealing their partner, committing violence toward rivals, and derogating rival men. These relationships remained statistically significant even after controlling for the effects due to the husband's age, the wife's age, and the length of the relationship. In sum, men's, but not women's, mate-retention efforts appear to be sensitive to the context of the perceived likelihood of infidelity.

Reproductive Value of the Wife: Effects of Age and Physical Attractiveness.   As discussed in Chapter 5, two powerful cues to a woman's reproductive value and fertility are her youth and her physical attractiveness—qualities known to be highly desirable to men across cultures (Buss, 1989a; Kenrick & Keefe, 1992). Men married to women of higher reproductive value—those who are younger and more physically attractive—were hypothesized to devote more effort to mate guarding than men married to women of lower reproductive value. To test this hypothesis men's mate-retention efforts were correlated with the ages and physical attractiveness of their wives. A sample of these results is shown in Figure 11.5.

Men married to younger women reported devoting greater effort to the adaptive problem of mate retention. Further, they reported greater partner concealment, emotional manipulation, verbal signals of possession (e.g., indicating that the woman was "my wife"), possessive ornamentation (e.g., insisting that she wear his ring), intrasexual threats, and violence against rival men than did men with older wives. These results held even after statistically controlling for other variables, such as the length of the relationship and the age of the husband.

Men's mate-retention tactics were also linked with their perceptions of their partner's physical attractiveness. Men married to women they perceived to be physically attractive reported greater resource display, appearance enhancement, verbal signals of possession, and intrasexual threats than did men married to women they perceived to be less physically attractive. Interestingly, these links were not obtained for ratings made by

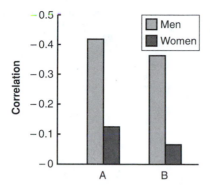

FIGURE 11.5   Mate Retention as a Function of Age of Spouse. The figure shows that men married to younger women devote more effort to mate retention than men married to older women, even after controlling for men's own age and the length of the relationship. (A) shows the correlation between the intensity of mate retention and the age of spouse. (B) shows the correlation between the intensity of mate retention after controlling for own age and the length of the relationship. Data from Buss & Shackelford (1997c).

the interviewers of women's physical attractiveness. Men's mate-retention efforts appear to be more a function of their subjective perceptions of their partner's attractiveness than of independently assessed interviewer judgments of their partner's attractiveness.

Income and Status Striving of the Husband.   Women's mate-retention tactics, in contrast to those of men, were *not* hypothesized to be a function of the husband's age or physical attractiveness, and indeed they were not. Women's efforts at mate retention, however, were hypothesized to be linked with the value of their mates on the dimensions of income and status striving—the degree to which the husband devotes effort to getting ahead in the status and work hierarchy (Buss & Shackelford, 1997). These are sex-linked components of mate value that women across cultures desire in long-term mates (see Chapter 4).

To test this hypothesis Buss and Shackelford (1997) correlated mate retention tactics with the partner's income and with four measures of status striving. These measures include the degree to which a person uses deception or manipulation to get ahead, industriousness and hard work, social networking, and ingratiating oneself with superiors. Six of the nineteen tactics of mate retention performed by women were significantly and positively correlated with the husband's income. Women married to men with higher incomes reported greater vigilance, violence toward partner, appearance enhancement, possessive ornamentation, and submission and self-abasement.

Women married to men who devoted more effort to status striving reported significantly more emotional manipulation, resource display, appearance enhancement, verbal signals of possession, and possessive ornamentation than women married to men low on status striving. These correlations remained significant even after statistically controlling for other factors, such as the ages of the spouses and the length of their relationship. A sample of these findings is shown in Figure 11.6 on page 334.

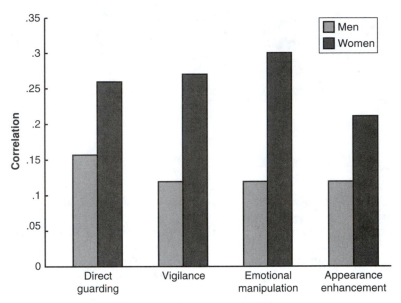

FIGURE 11.6   Mate Retention and Spouse's Status Striving. The figure shows that women married to men high in status striving devote more effort to mate retention than do women married to men lower in status striving. The effects of women's status striving on men's mate retention efforts are smaller and do not reach statistical significance. Data from Buss & Shackelford (1997c).

In summary, research has confirmed several key evolutionary psychological hypotheses about the contexts in which men and women will devote more effort to the adaptive problem of mate retention. Men devote more effort when they perceive that their partners might be unfaithful within the next year and when their partners are young and physically attractive, two important cues to a woman's reproductive value. Women devote more effort to mate retention when their husbands have higher income and when their husbands channel a lot of effort toward getting ahead in the status and work hierarchies. These tests are especially important in demonstrating the heuristic value of evolutionary psychology—generating hypotheses and predictions that simply have never been generated by more mainstream psychological theories. Indeed, prior to the work of evolutionary psychologists no one had examined the effort people devote to solving the adaptive problem of mate retention.

Violence toward Partners

Mate retention has an extremely destructive side: the use of violence against partners. The following is a frightening description of such violence among the Yanomamö:

> I was told about one young man in Monou-teri who shot and killed his wife in a rage of sexual jealousy, and during one of my stays in the villages a man shot his wife in the stomach with a barbed arrow. . . . Another man chopped his wife on the arm with a

machete; some tendons to her fingers were severed. . . . A club fight involving a case of infidelity took place in one of the villages just before the end of my first field trip. The male paramour was killed, and the enraged husband cut off both of his wife's ears. (Chagnon, 1992, p. 147)

Why would anyone ever commit violence against a partner? Wilson and Daly (1996) provide a compelling hypothesis. Men use violence and threats as a strategy to limit a partner's autonomy, thus decreasing the odds that the partner will commit infidelity or defect from the relationship. Indeed, women who actually leave their husbands are frequently pursued, threatened, and assaulted. Wives who have left their husbands are at a substantially higher risk of being killed than women who remain with their husbands, as shown in Figure 11.7. These spousal homicides often follow from threats to pursue and kill wives if they ever leave, and the murderers often explain their violent behavior as "a response to the intolerable stimulus of their wives' departure" (Wilson & Daly, 1996, p. 5).

Intuitively, however, this homicidal behavior seems bizarre and maladaptive. Killing a wife imposes a cost on the perpetrator as well as the victim, as the husband has essentially destroyed any access to a reproductively valuable commodity. Killing a wife, therefore, seems genuinely puzzling from an evolutionary perspective. Wilson and Daly (1996) explain this puzzle by proposing that violence is a means of deterrence:

> A threat is an effective social tool, and usually an inexpensive one, but it loses its effectiveness if the threatening party is seen to be bluffing, that is to be unwilling to pay the occasional cost of following through when the threat is ignored or defied. Such vengeful follow-through may appear counterproductive—a risky or expensive act too late to be useful—but effective threats cannot "leak" signs of bluff and may therefore have to be sincere. Although killing an estranged wife appears futile, threatening one who might otherwise leave can be self-interested, and so can pursuing her with further threats, as can advertisements of anger and ostensible obliviousness to the costs. (pp. 2–7).

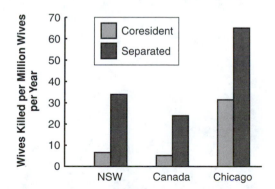

FIGURE 11.7   **Rates of Uxoricides Perpetrated by Registered-Marriage Husbands, for Coresiding versus Estranged Couples in New South Wales (NSW), Australia (1968–1986); Canada (1974–1990); and Chicago (1965–1989).**

Source: Male sexual proprietariness and violence against wives by M. Wilson & M. Daly, *Current Directions in Psychological Science*, 5, 1996, 5. Reprinted with permission.

In short, the willingness to resort to extreme violence, according to this hypothesis, represents a risky strategy of deterring the wife from leaving and deterring sexual rivals—a strategy that sometimes has to be acted out to be effective.

As with the hypothesis about the intensity of mate retention as a function of the woman's reproductive value, young and attractive women may be more vulnerable to violence from their partners. As Wilson and Daly (1993) noted: "Young wives may be more likely than older wives to terminate an unsatisfactory marriage, more likely to be approached by sexual rivals of the husband, and more likely to form new sexual relationships. Hence, we hypothesize that men will be especially jealous, proprietary and coercive toward younger wives" (Wilson & Daly, 1993, p. 285).

This hypothesis is confirmed by the spousal homicide data. The wives who are at greatest risk of being killed by their husbands are in their teenage years; the lowest rates of spousal homicide are among postmenopausal women (Daly & Wilson, 1988). Part of this finding may be attributed to the fact that young women are often married to young men, and young men are known to commit violence of all sorts more frequently than older men. The age of the man, however, cannot completely account for the findings, because young women married to older husbands are actually at greater risk of being killed than young women married to young men (Wilson & Daly, 1993).

Another context that may provoke violence occurs when a man lacks the resources to provide positive incentives for a mate to remain in the relationship. As we saw in Chapter 6, women whose partners lose their jobs or otherwise fail to provide economic resources indicate that they are more likely to have affairs. This leads to a specific prediction: Men who experience a relative lack of economic resources will be more likely to use violence as a mate-retention tactic than will men who have economic resources, and who therefore can retain a mate with positive incentives (Wilson & Daly, 1993).

Men sometimes use violence, or threats of violence, as a strategy of mate retention and infidelity prevention. Research suggests that these coercive tactics are used more often by men married to young and physically attractive partners.

The empirical findings appear to support this hypothesis. One study examined 1,156 women sixteen or older who were killed in New York City over the five-year period 1990 through 1994 (Belluck, 1997). Nearly half were killed by husbands or boyfriends, either current or former. Roughly 67 percent, however, were killed in the poorest boroughs of New York—the Bronx and Brooklyn. These findings contradict the common belief that "domestic violence knows no class." The findings show higher rates of spousal homicide among men who are poor and unemployed—circumstances that prevent men from using positive incentives such as resource provisioning to keep a mate.

The use of violence, of course, does not always or even usually result in the wife's being killed. For every spousal homicide there may be hundreds of cases of sublethal violence that husbands use to control their wives. In one study of one hundred court cases involving litigation over actual violence within marital relationships, the authors concluded: "At the core of nearly all the cases involving physical violence, the husband responded out of frustration at being unable to control the wife, often accusing her of being a whore or of having an affair with another man" (Whitehurst, 1971, p. 686).

Several contexts might protect women from being victimized by violence from their partners. One is the presence of the woman's extended kin, who might deter a partner from committing violence against her. This is precisely what evolutionary psychologist A. J. Figueredo found in his study of domestic violence in Spain (Figueredo, 1995). He constructed a single measure of domestic violence that included verbal abuse, physical abuse, escalated life-threatening violence, and sexual violence and conducted a telephone survey of battered and nonbattered women in Madrid. The principal hypothesis was that a woman's extended kin network would protect her against spousal abuse. Results confirmed the hypothesis: The higher the density of genetic kin both inside and outside Madrid, the lower the rates of domestic violence against women. The density of kin within Madrid had an especially strong effect, whereas having more distant kin had a weaker effect on reducing spousal abuse.

In sum, male sexual jealousy appears to be one of the central causes of violence against women within relationships. According to one hypothesis, violence is used as a coercive tactic designed to keep a mate faithful, prevent future infidelity, and prevent defection from the relationship. Not all men use violence for these goals, and not all women are equally vulnerable. Men lacking the economic resources that might otherwise keep a woman in a relationship voluntarily are more prone to using violence. Women who are young, and hence high in reproductive value and attractive to other men, appear to be especially vulnerable to violent victimization by their partners. Two factors appear to reduce a woman's risk of violence—selecting a mate who has a reliable source of economic resources and the number and density of kin living in close proximity to her.

Conflict over Access to Resources

Scientists have tried for years to discover a culture in which men did not dominate women in the domains of overt political power and material resources. Although many people have heard rumors about cultures in which women dominate men, none have ever been documented in the literature. Feminist anthropologists who have spearheaded the search have concluded that such cultures do not exist (Ortner, 1974). Societies differ, of course, in the degree of social and economic inequality between the sexes.

The generalization that men tend to wield power and control resources, however, should not obscure the fact that in nearly every culture women contribute substantially to the accrual of economic resources. In hunter-gatherer societies, for example, women sometimes contribute 60 to 80 percent of the calories through gathering food from plants (Tooby & DeVore, 1987). Furthermore, women often exert considerable power through various means including exerting preferential mate choice; divorcing men under certain conditions; controlling or regulating men's access to their sexuality; and influencing their sons, lovers, fathers, husbands, sisters, mothers, and grandchildren (Buss, 1994).

It cannot be disputed that men often use resources to control or influence women. If men possess the resources that women need, then they can use those resources to control women. In the mating domain men use their resources to attract women, as we saw in Chapter 4. Furthermore, once in relationships, women lacking resources often feel at the mercy of their partners for fear of the loss of those resources (Wilson & Daly, 1992). These key points—men's control of resources and men's use of resources to control women—appear to be issues of agreement between feminists and evolutionary psychologists (Buss, 1996a).

Feminist scholars often trace the roots of women's oppression by men to *patriarchy*, a term referring to men's dominance over women in the family specifically and in society more generally (Smuts, 1995). A reasonable scientific question pertains to the origins of the phenomena subsumed under this term. Although historically some feminists have offered speculation about the origins of male control and domination—for example, by tracing it to the fact that men are larger and stronger than women—no consensus has been reached on this issue (Faludi, 1991; hooks, 1984; Jagger, 1994; Smuts, 1995). Most feminists simply take male domination and control as a starting point or a given (Smuts, 1995).

Women's Mate Preferences and Men's Competitive Tactics as Causes of Resource Inequality

An evolutionary perspective offers insights into the origins and history of men's attempts to control women (Buss, 1996a; Smuts, 1995). First, women's preferences for men with resources, as documented in Chapter 4, are hypothesized to play a critical role in human evolution. These preferences, operating repeatedly over thousands of generations, have led women to favor as mates men who possess status and resources and to disfavor men who lack these assets. In human evolutionary history men who failed to acquire resources were more likely to have failed to attract women as mates.

Women's preferences, according to this view, thus established an important set of ground rules for men in their competition with one another. Based on sexual selection theory, the desires of one sex establish the critical dimensions along which members of the opposite sex compete. Because ancestral men tended to place a premium on women's physical appearance, for example, attractiveness was established as a major dimension along which women compete with one another. The $53 billion dollar cosmetics industry in the United States, overwhelmingly a female consumer industry, is testament to the magnitude of this form of intrasexual competition among women.

Analogously, women's desires for men with resources established the acquisition of resources as a major dimension of men's competition with each other. Modern men have inherited from their ancestors psychological mechanisms that not only give priority to resources and status, but also tend to lead men to take risks to attain resources and status (see Chapter 10). Men who failed to give the goals of status and resources high personal priority and failed to take calculated risks to best other men likewise failed to attract mates. This sort of competition carries a large price tag in male–male violence and homicide, as well as an earlier death, on average, than women.

Women's preferences and men's strategies of intrasexual competition coevolved, as did men's preferences and women's strategies of intrasexual competition. Men may have started controlling resources to attract women, and women's preferences may have followed. Alternatively, women's preferences for successful, ambitious, and resourceful mates may have selected for men's competitive strategies of risk taking, status striving, and derogation of competitors along the dimensions of status and resources. Women's preferences may have imposed selection pressure on men to form coalitions to gain resources and engage in individual efforts aimed at besting other men to acquire the resources that women desire. Most likely, however, men's competitive strategies and women's mate preferences coevolved. The intertwining of these coevolved mechanisms created the conditions in which men could dominate in the domain of resources.

The hypothesis that women have played a role in men's control of resources through the influence of their mate preferences on men's competitive strategies strikes some as "blaming the victim." Not only do women suffer from men's control over resources, now it seems that they are getting blamed for it as well. The inference of blame, however, does not follow from the identification of women's participation in one aspect of history. From the vantage point of evolutionary psychology, neither sex deserves blame. Instead, modern humans are the end products of a long process that involved the coevolution of women's preferences and men's intrasexual competition tactics. As products of this process men and women are equally blameworthy or blameless. Issues of blame are irrelevant in the evolutionary psychological analysis of the origins of men's control over resources.

The evolutionary origin of men's monopolization of resources is not simply an incidental historical footnote of passing curiosity. Rather, it has a profound bearing on the present because it reveals some of the primary causes of men's continuing control of resources. Women today continue to want as mates men who have resources as they continue to reject men who lack resources (Buss, 1994). In any given year, the men women choose to marry earn more money than men of the same age who women overlook as mates. Women who earn more than their husbands divorce at double the rate of women whose husbands earn more than they do. Furthermore, men continue to form alliances and compete with other men to acquire the status and resources that make them desirable to women. The forces that originally caused the resource inequality between the sexes—women's preferences and men's competitive strategies—contribute to the maintenance of resource inequality today.

This analysis of resource inequality does not deny the existence of other contributing causes such as the sexist practice of giving women and men unequal pay for the same work. Nor does this analysis imply that men's greater control of resources is inevitable (see Smuts, 1995). It does suggest that evolutionary psychology is critical in identifying the causes of resource inequality. See Box 11.1 for further discussion of conflict and cooperation between the sexes.

BOX **11.1**

Are All Men United to Control Women?

Feminist writers sometimes portray all men as united for the common goal of oppressing all women (Dworkin, 1987; Faludi, 1991). Evolutionary psychological analyses suggest that this cannot be true because men and women compete mainly against members of their own sexes. Men strive to control resources at the expense of, and to the exclusion of, other men. Men deprive other men of resources, exclude other men from positions of power and status, and derogate other men to make them less desirable to women. The fact that roughly 70 percent of all homicides involve men killing other men is just the tip of the iceberg of costs that men incur as a result of their intrasexual competition (Daly & Wilson, 1988).

Women do not escape the damage inflicted by members of their own sex. Women compete with each other for access to high-status men, have sex with other women's husbands, and lure men away from their wives. Women slander and denigrate their rivals, especially those who pursue short-term mating strategies (see Chapter 10). Women and men are both victims of the sexual strategies of their own sex and so cannot be said to be united with all members of their own sex for some common goal such as oppressing the opposite sex.

The primary exception to this is when men form coalitions that function as subgroups, as we saw in Chapter 10. These coalitions are sometimes used to gain access to women's sexuality, as

in a brutal gang rape or a raid on a neighboring village to capture women (Smuts, 1992). Furthermore, men's coalitions may sometimes be used to exclude women from power—for example, when exclusive men's clubs or lodges in which business is transacted explicitly prevent women from joining. These same coalitions, however, are also directed against other men and their coalitions. In business, politics, and warfare men form coalitions for their own benefit at the expense of other coalitions of men.

It must also be recognized that both men and women benefit from the strategies of the opposite sex. Men provide resources to certain women, such as their wives, mistresses, sisters, daughters, and mothers. A woman's father, brothers, and sons all can benefit from her selection of a mate with status and resources. Contrary to the view that men and women are united with all members of their own sex for the purpose of oppressing the other sex, evolutionary psychology points to a different conclusion: Each individual is united in interests with some members of each sex and is in conflict with some members of each sex. Simple-minded views of same-sex conspiracies by one sex defy evolutionary logic. This evolutionary analysis points to two important implications for conflict between the sexes: the link between same-sex competition and conflict between the sexes and the exploitation of the desires of one sex by the other.

Same-Sex Competition Is Intimately Linked with Conflict between the Sexes

It should be clear from this analysis that conflict between the sexes cannot be separated from same-sex competition. Consider, for example, the fact that women tend to compete with one another in the realm of physical appearance. This no doubt harms women in many ways. As feminist Naomi Wolf (1991) observed, the constant bombardment of women with images of flawless airbrushed models may create unrealistic expectations all around and may damage women's self-esteem (see also Kenrick, Guttieres, & Goldberg, 1989). This phenomenon, according to an evolutionary psychological analysis, can ultimately be traced to men's preferences. Over human evolutionary history men have imposed their desire for attractiveness on women because physical attractiveness provides cues to health and youth, and hence to fertility and reproductive value. Men with these preferences outreproduced other men who lacked such preferences, or who had alternative preferences, such as for women who were prepubescent or postmenopausal. Because men today are the descendants of men who carried genes for this mate preference, they continue to impose this pressure on women.

The same analysis, however, suggests that women are competing primarily with other women. A woman enhances her own beauty at the expense of other women because she improves her odds of attracting a desirable man at the expense of her same-sex rivals. The tactic of appearance enhancement, although traceable to men's mate preferences, is carried out by women at a cost to other women. The same logic applies to men, as just discussed in the context of competition for the status and resources that make men desirable to women. Conflict between the sexes, in short, is intimately linked with same-sex competition.

Women and Men Exploit the Desires of the Opposite Sex

Prostitution provides a good example of the exploitation of the desires of others. From one perspective prostitution exists because of a powerful evolved male desire for sexual variety, which, combined with the inability of some men to attract women, creates a powerful demand for the sexual services of women. Some women are able to pursue a strategy of exploiting men's sexual desires to extract money and other resources in exchange for sex. In countries and states where prostitution is legal, women choose to pursue this profession (Burley & Symanski, 1981). Some Malay women in Singapore, for example, said that they became prostitutes to avoid the hard work expected of wives, which includes gathering firewood and laundering clothes. Among the Amhara and Bemba, prostitutes earn enough through casual sex to hire men to do the work that is normally expected of wives. A woman who chooses prostitution may do so because of restricted alternative strategies of resource acquisition, such as an inability to secure other forms of lucrative employment or a failure to attract a sufficiently investing mate. Alternatively, some women choose prostitution because it provides a quick and lucrative source of income and hence may be seen as a desirable alternative to a nine-to-five job or a demanding husband. The fact that some women choose prostitution voluntarily, of course, does not negate the fact that others are forced or coerced into prostitution.

Some people are adamantly against prostitution and argue that it is a patriarchal institution designed to oppress women (MacKinnon, 1987). Alternatively, some feminists are strong advocates of a woman's right to engage in prostitution (Wolfe, 1975). One perspective is that women who oppose prostitution can be viewed as engaging in a battle with other women about what strategies of resource acquisition are acceptable (Symons, 1979). Typically, women who oppose prostitution are in a better position to pursue alternate means of acquiring resources, either through their careers or through marrying men with resources.

Prostitutes, like women who pursue short-term sexual strategies, pose a threat primarily to other women by exploiting the desires of men. Their presence may deter some men from pursuing marriage, which entails a long-term commitment of resources to one woman. As Symons observed: "To the extent that heterosexual men purchase the services of prostitutes and pornographic masturbation aids, the market for the sexual services of non-prostitute women is diminished and their bargaining power vis-à-vis men is weakened. . . . In fact, feminist prostitutes and many non-prostitute, heterosexual feminists are in direct competition, and it should be no surprise that they are often to be found at one another's throats" (1979, pp. 259–260). The presence of prostitutes, of course, does not prevent men from marrying, and men's desire for long-term mating is just as strong as women's (Buss & Schmitt, 1993). Nonetheless, prostitutes may siphon off resources that might otherwise go to a man's wife and children. Movements to eliminate prostitution may have the effect of depriving some women of one strategy of resource acquisition—that of exploiting men's desire for sexual variety.

This evolutionary analysis, of course, does not speak to the value issue of whether prostitution is desirable or undesirable for a particular society or its members. Rather, it provides some of the critical ingredients for understanding the underlying dynamics of conflicts within and between the sexes.

Summary

Conflict between men and women pervades social living, from disagreements on dates to emotional distress within marriages. Evolutionary psychology provides several key insights into why such conflicts occur and the particular forms they take. The first insight comes from strategic interference theory, which holds that conflict results from a person blocking or impeding the successful enactment of a strategy designed to reach a particular goal. If a woman happens to be pursuing a strategy of long-term mating and a man a strategy of short-term mating, they will interfere with the successful attainment of the goal of each other's strategies. Negative emotions such as anger, distress, and jealousy are hypothesized to be evolved solutions that alert individuals to strategic interference.

Conflict over sexual access is one of the largest spheres of conflict between the sexes and takes many forms. First, studies document that men consistently infer greater sexual intent than do women, especially in response to ambiguous signals such as a smile. Second, men sometimes deceive women, notably about their emotional involvement and long-term intentions, as a strategy for gaining short-term sexual access to women. A third manifestation of conflict over sexual access occurs in the form of sexual harassment in the workplace. Men are overwhelmingly the perpetrators of sexual harassment, women overwhelmingly the victims. The victims also tend to have a particular profile—they are often young, single, and physically attractive. Women tend to get more upset about sexual harassment than do men in response to the same acts, supporting the postulate that this negative emotion serves as a signal of strategic interference. For any particular act of harassment, women's upset tends to be greater if the harasser is low in status, such as a garbage collector or a construction worker, and less if the harasser is high in status.

Sexual aggressiveness occurs outside the workplace as well. As with sexual harassment, women tend to be more upset than men by the same acts of sexual aggression, such as touching their bodies without their permission and persisting in sexual advances even if they have said no. Studies show that men tend to underestimate how upset women get about acts of sexual aggression. Men differ in whether they use sexually aggressive tactics, and evolutionary psychologists have attempted to predict which men will use these tactics. The mate deprivation hypothesis, the idea that men who fail to attract women through other means use sexual aggression, has been advanced to explain why some men use sexually aggressive tactics. The available evidence points to the opposite conclusion —men who use sexual aggression tend to rate themselves very attractive to women and indicate a history of better success in gaining sexual access to women than do men who do not use sexually aggressive tactics. Although we do not currently have a clear understanding of why some men but not others use sexual aggression, a consistent pair of findings may provide important clues: Men who use sexual aggression tend to be characterized by (1) an orientation toward short-term impersonal sex, and (2) a psychology of hostile masculinity.

Jealous conflict defines another large category of conflict between the sexes. Evolutionary psychologists have suggested that jealousy is an evolved solution to the problem of mate defection. They predict that men's jealousy will focus heavily on the sexual infidelity of a partner, since historically that would have compromised a man's paternity certainty. Women's jealousy, in contrast, is predicted to focus more on the long-term diversion of a mate's investment and commitment. A large body of empirical evidence supports these predictions—men tend to get more jealous about sexual infidelity, women about emotional infidelity. These sex differences are large, show up in psychological and physiological data, and have been replicated across a half-dozen cultures. Moreover, when men and women are asked to imagine that a partner has been both sexually and emotionally unfaithful, men continue to get more upset about the sexual aspect of the infidelity and women about the emotional aspect.

The psychology of jealousy produces behavioral output that is presumably designed to deter a romantic partner from leaving or committing an infidelity—behavior that ranges from vigilance to violence. Men tend to engage in intense mate-retention efforts when they are married to partners who are young and physically attractive, two known cues to a woman's reproductive value. Women tend to engage in intense mate-retention efforts when they are married to men who have higher incomes and who devote a lot of effort to status striving. Violence toward partners is an extreme and destructive mate-keeping tactic. It is used by more men than women, and tends to be used most by men who lack the economic means to keep a mate through positive incentives.

Men and women also conflict over access to resources. Evolutionary psychology sheds light on the pervasive finding that men tend to control economic resources worldwide, although there are individual and cultural differences. This is one aspect of what has been called patriarchy. The sex difference can be traced to the coevolution of women's preferences and men's competitive mating strategies. Women throughout evolutionary history have preferentially selected men who were able to accrue and control resources, and men have competed with one another to attract women by acquiring such resources. An evolutionary analysis also suggests that men cannot be united with all other men in their desire to keep women from gaining access to these resources. Men are in competition primarily with other men, not with women. Furthermore, men are aligned in their interests with many specific women, such as their friends, sisters, wives, lovers, nieces, and mothers.

Each sex has evolved to exploit the desires of members of the opposite sex and evolutionary psychology provides insights into the particular forms such exploitation takes. Prostitution, for example, exploits men's evolved desires for short-term casual sex and sexual variety. Conflict between the sexes will be hard to eliminate, but understanding the evolved psychological dynamics that underlie the conflict may help reduce it.

12 Status, Prestige, and Social Dominance

All animals are equal. But some animals are more equal than others.
—George Orwell

We come into the world equipped with a nervous system that worries about rank.
—Robert Frank, 1985

In 1996 Admiral Jeremy Boorda, chief of operations for the United States Navy, was about to be interviewed about the combat medal "V" for valor that he then displayed proudly on his chest of ribbons (Feinsilber, 1997). In fact, Admiral Boorda had never been awarded this medal. So rather than face the shame of being exposed for the false display, he committed suicide. A year later, Federal Judge James Ware of San Jose, California, was exposed for falsely claiming to be the older brother of Virgil Ware, a young boy who had been killed by white teenagers in a racial attack in 1963 in Birmingham, Alabama, the same day four girls were killed in the bombing of a Black church. Ware had frequently used the claim to assert that he was fueled by a "hunger for justice," and his rise to fame as a judge was sometimes linked with this false claim, which gave him social status. When the deception surfaced he was forced to withdraw from consideration for an appointment to a high-level appeals court. These are just two events from among hundreds like them that have come to light over the past decade. Why would people falsify their credentials and risk being exposed as frauds merely to enhance their status and social position?

Status, prestige, esteem, honor, respect, and rank are accorded differentially to individuals in all known groups. People devote tremendous effort to avoiding disrepute, dishonor, shame, humiliation, disgrace, and loss of face. Empirical evidence suggests that status and dominance hierarchies form quickly. In one study of fifty-nine three-person groups of individuals who had previously been unknown to each other, a clear hierarchy emerged within *one* minute in 50 percent; a clear hierarchy emerged within the first *five* minutes in the other 50 percent (Fisek & Ofshe, 1970). Even more striking, group members could accurately evaluate their own future status within a new group after they had merely seen the other members and before anyone had uttered a single word (Kalma, 1991). If there were ever a reasonable candidate for a universal human motive, status striving would be at or near the top of the list (Barkow, 1989; Frank, 1985; Maslow, 1937; Symons, 1979).

The Emergence of Dominance Hierarchies

Crickets remember their history of successes and failures in fights with other crickets (Dawkins, 1989). If a cricket tends to win a lot of fights, it becomes more aggressive in subsequent fights. On the other hand, if it loses a lot of fights it will become submissive, avoiding confrontations in the future. This phenomenon was documented experimentally by the evolutionary biologist Richard Alexander (Alexander, 1961), who introduced a "model" cricket that overpowered other crickets. After being beaten up by the model, the crickets were more likely to lose subsequent fights when battling real crickets. It is as though each cricket formed an estimate of its own fighting ability relative to others, and behaved accordingly. Over time a dominance hierarchy emerged, whereby each cricket could be assigned a rank order, with crickets lower in the hierarchy giving in to those higher up.

Interestingly, male crickets who have recently emerged victorious are more likely to seek the sexual favors of female crickets. Dawkins (1989) suggests that this should be labeled the "Duke of Marlborough Effect," based on that man's appearance in the diary of the Duchess of Marlborough: "His Grace returned from the wars today and pleasured me twice in his topboots" (Dawkins, 1989, p. 286). Studies of humans provide circumstantial support for this effect. In a study of tennis players, testosterone levels doubled the day before important matches. After the matches, the testosterone levels of the losers dropped dramatically, whereas those of the winners remained high (Mazur & Booth, in press).

Similar phenomena occur throughout the animal world. The phrase "pecking order" comes from the behavior of hens. When hens first come together they fight frequently. Over time, however, the fighting subsides because each hen learns that she is dominant to some hens but subordinate to others. This pecking order tends to be stable over time, and has advantages for each individual hen. Dominant hens gain because they do not have to engage in continuous costly combat to defend rank. Subordinate hens gain because they avoid injury that would occur from challenging the dominant hens. It is important to bear in mind that this pecking order, or dominance hierarchy, does not have a function per se. The hierarchy is a property of the group, not the individual. Instead, the strategies of each individual hen have a function, and in the aggregate they produce a stable hierarchy. This means that we have to consider the functions of being submissive, as well as the functions of being dominant.

All-out fighting in every encounter with another individual is a foolish strategy. The loser risks injury and death, and so would have been better off giving in—relinquishing its territory, food, or mate—from the start. Fighting is also costly for the victor. In addition to the risk of injury from battle, victors allocate precious energetic resources, time, and opportunities in battle. So both losers and winners would have been better off if each could determine who would win in advance and simply declare a winner without suffering the costs of fighting. By submitting the loser is able to walk away alive and injury free.

Although he has relinquished a resource for the moment, a loser can venture elsewhere when opportunities might be better, or he might lie low, waiting for a more opportune moment to challenge (Pinker, 1997).

In sum, selection will favor the evolution of assessment abilities—psychological mechanisms that include assessment of one's own fighting abilities relative to those of others. In humans these assessment mechanisms are likely to be complex, transcending mere physical brawn to include the ability to enlist powerful friends and allies, the network of social connections, and the extensiveness of the kin group of each combatant. Following assessment, strategies of dominance and submissiveness can both have functions. The primary function of each is to avoid costly confrontations when the outcomes of conflict can be determined in advance. Of course, there is sometimes uncertainty about the outcome. The various bluffs and bellows and hairs-on-end may be designed to exaggerate participants' prowess and get another to back down prematurely. But selection would also favor seeing through these bluffs, since animals that submitted prematurely or needlessly would lose access to precious resources. The key point is that dominant and submissive strategies both have functions for the individual. In the aggregate they produce a dominance hierarchy.

In functional terms, a *dominance hierarchy* refers to the fact that some individuals within a group reliably gain greater access than others to key resources—resources that contribute to survival or reproduction (Cummins, 1998). Those who are ranked high in the hierarchy secure greater access to these resources; those who are low ranking or subordinate have less access to these resources. In the simplest form, dominance hierarchies are *transitive*, meaning that if A is dominant over B, and B is dominant over C, then A will be dominant over C. Dominance hierarchies have been documented in a wide variety of nonhuman animals, from crayfish to chimpanzees.

Dominance and Status in Nonhuman Animals

More than one male crayfish cannot inhabit the same territory without determining who is the boss (Barinaga, 1996). The crayfish circle each other cautiously, sizing up their rivals. They then plunge into a violent fray, trying to tear each other apart. The crayfish who emerges victorious becomes dominant, strutting around "his" territory. The loser slinks away to the periphery, avoiding further contact with the dominant male.

The subsequent behaviors of the winners and the losers are so different that researchers suspected that changes must occur in their nervous systems. Researcher Donald Edwards and his colleagues discovered a specific neuron in crayfish that responds differently to the neurotransmitter serotonin, depending on the animal's status. In dominant crayfish the presence of serotonin makes the neuron more likely to fire. In the losers serotonin inhibits the neuron from firing. This is the "first time that one has been able to link a social phenomenon to a change in a particular identified synapse" (Barinaga, 1996, p. 290).

One battle, however, rarely consigns an animal to a permanent position as dominant or subordinate. When researchers put two subordinate crayfish in the same territory together, one would inevitably shift from subordinate to dominant status. When

the neurons were tested two weeks later, the researchers found that in the dominant animal the crucial neuron was excited by serotonin, rather than inhibited by it. Thus, subordinate crayfish readily make the shift to dominant status when circumstances change.
The same is not true of dominant crayfish, however. When researchers paired two previously dominant crayfish in the same territory, one was inevitably forced into subordinate status. But the loser, who previously had been dominant, continued to be aggressive,
forcing fights with the dominant crayfish even to the point of getting itself killed. It is as
if "the animals are reluctant to go from being dominant to being subordinate" (Barinaga,
1996, p. 290).

Chimpanzees also battle for dominance status (de Waal, 1982). Dominant male
chimps strut around, making themselves look deceptively large and heavy. The most
reliable indicator of dominance status among chimps is the number of submissive
greetings an animal receives from others. Submissive greetings are a short sequence of
pant-grunts that are accompanied by a lowering of the body so the submissive male is
literally looking up at the dominant male. This lowering is often accomplished while
making a series of quick, deep bows. Sometimes the submissive chimp brings objects to
greet the dominant chimp, such as a leaf or a stick, which he presents while kissing
the feet, neck, or chest of the dominant chimp. The dominant male, in turn, reacts by
stretching to full height and making his hair stand on end so he appears even larger. An
observer might conclude that the two chimps are substantially different in size, even if
they are in fact the same size. One male chimp grovels while the other struts, sometimes leaping over the submissive animal. The females, in contrast, usually present
their rear ends to the dominant chimp for inspection. The occasional failure to display
the submissive greeting by either a male or a female is a direct challenge to the dominant chimp's status, and may provoke aggressive retaliation.

Dominance status among male chimps comes with a key perk—increased sexual
access to females (de Waal, 1982). The dominant chimp in a colony typically secures at
least 50 percent of the copulations, and sometimes as many as 75 percent, even when
there are a half-dozen other males in the colony. A survey of seven hundred studies
concluded that middle- to high-ranking males typically have a reproductive advantage
over the lowest-ranking males (Ellis, 1995), although there are some species in which
females mate surreptitiously with subordinate males, such as the rhesus macaques (Manson, 1992).

Increased sexual access by dominant male chimps seems to be especially pronounced when the females enter estrus (Ellis, 1995). Three of the four studies that
examined this link found that dominant males experienced greater sexual access when
females entered estrus, and were thus most likely to conceive, suggesting that subordinate sexual access may occur when the females are less likely to conceive. One study
using DNA fingerprinting supported this conclusion, finding that high-ranking males
had indeed sired a disproportionate number of offspring (relative to lower-ranking
males). Similar results on the links between dominance, sexual access, and reproductive
outcomes have been found with orangutans and baboons (Ellis, 1995).

Two other key features of primate dominance hierarchies have been noted (Cummins, 1998). First, these hierarchies are not static. Individuals continually compete for
elevated position and sometimes usurp a dominant male. Ousted males sometimes re-

gain a measure of their former dominance. Deaths and injuries of a dominant animal can result in a period of instability in which others rush to fill the void at the top of the hierarchy. Individuals continuously jockey for position in the hierarchy, rendering it a dynamic form of social organization. Second, the physical size of a primate is not the primary determinant of rank. Rising in primate hierarchies instead depends heavily on social skills, notably the ability to enlist allies on whom one can rely for support in contests with other individuals. For example, there was one documented case in which a subordinate male ended his alliance with an alpha male because the alpha had refused to support him in contests with another male over sexual access to a particular female (de Waal, 1992).

Increased sexual opportunities with females provides a powerful adaptive rationale for the evolution of dominance-striving mechanisms. It also suggests an evolutionary basis for the sex difference in the dominance-striving motive.

Evolutionary Theories of Dominance and Status

An evolutionary theory of dominance and status must specify the adaptive problems that are solved by ascending status hierarchies, as well as grapple with superior or subordinate positions within such hierarchies. Ideally, a good theory should be able to predict which tactics people will use to negotiate hierarchies. Academics, for example, jockey for position, but in different ways than might occur in an inner-city neighborhood: "Brandishing a switchblade at a scholarly conference would somehow strike the wrong note, but there is always the stinging question, the devastating riposte, the moralistic outrage, the withering invective, the indignant rebuttal, and the means of enforcement in manuscript reviews and grant panels" (Pinker, 1997, p. 498).

A good theory would also have to account for why status striving appears to be so much more prevalent among males than among females. Ideally, such a theory would also account for the behavior of those consigned to subordinate status. Thus far, no complete theories of human status hierarchies have been proposed that answer all these key questions. But important inroads have been made. Let's start by considering an evolutionary explanation for sex differences in the motive for status striving.

An Evolutionary Theory of Sex Differences in Status Striving

As discussed in earlier chapters, human males and females differ dramatically in the extent to which their reproductive outputs can vary. Because sperm are relatively abundant and males are not obligated to invest heavily in their offspring, the ceiling for male reproduction is much higher than for female reproduction. Stated differently, male reproductive success is typically much more *variable* than female reproductive success. Nearly all fertile females will succeed in reproducing, regardless of their social status, but the same cannot be said of all fertile males. For each male who gains reproductive access to a disproportionate share of women, other men are consigned to bachelorhood and reproductive oblivion. This suggests that the more polygynous the mating system—that is, the more variance there is in male sexual access to women—the stronger the selection pressure on males to become one of the few who succeed in reproduction. Furthermore, selection will favor strategies that don't exclude an individual from reproducing entirely.

Elevated dominance and status can give males greater sexual access along two paths. First, dominant men may be preferred as mates by women (Kenrick et al., 1990). High-status men can offer women greater protection, increased access to resources that can be used to help support them and their children, and perhaps even better health care (Buss, 1994; Hill & Hurtado, 1996). Women in polygynous societies often prefer to share with other cowives a bounty of resources that a high-ranking man can provide, rather than have all of the smaller share of resources held by a lower-ranking man (Betzig, 1986). So one potential benefit of being a high-ranking man is preferential selection by women as a mate. This preferential choice can occur when women choose long-term or short-term mates, since women in many cultures preferentially select high-status men as partners for affairs (Baker & Bellis, 1995; Buss, 1994; Hill & Hurtado, 1996).

A second path through which dominant men gain increased access to women is through intrasexual domination. Dominant men may simply usurp the mates of subordinate men, leaving these low-ranking men helpless to retaliate. As Daly and Wilson noted: "Men are known by their fellows as 'the sort who can be pushed around' and 'the sort who won't take any shit,' as people whose word means action or people who are full of hot air, as guys whose girlfriends you can chat up with impunity or guys you don't want to mess with" (1988, p. 128). Napoleon Chagnon reported this example of an interaction between two Yanomamö brothers. The higher-status brother (Rerebawa) had an affair with the wife of his lower-status brother. When the cuckolded brother found out he attacked Rerebawa, but received a sound thrashing with the blunt side of an ax. When Rerebawa gave Chagnon a tour of the village, he made it a point to introduce him to his lower-status brother by grabbing him by the wrist and dragging him to the ground, announcing, "This is the brother whose wife I screwed when he wasn't around!" (Chagnon, 1983, p. 29). This was a deadly insult that might otherwise have provoked a bloody club fight if the two Yanomamö men were of equal status. However, the subordinate brother just slunk away in shame, relieved not to have to battle his brother.

Status and Sexual Opportunity.   Is there evidence that elevated status in men actually leads to more sexual opportunities with women? Kings, emperors, and despots throughout recorded history have routinely collected women in harems, choosing the young, the fertile, and the attractive. The Moroccan emperor Moulay Ismail the Bloodthirsty, for example, had a harem of 500 women with whom he sired 888 children. Evolutionary anthropologist Laura Betzig assembled systematic data from the first six civilizations—Mesopotamia, Egypt, Aztex Mexico, Incan Peru, imperial India, and imperial China (Betzig, 1993). These civilizations spanned four continents and roughly four thousand years, beginning in about 4,000 B.C.

All six civilizations show a remarkably consistent pattern. In India, Bhupinder Singh housed 332 women in his harem. These included ten high-ranking Maharanis, fifty middle-ranking Ranis, and other assorted mistresses and servants without rank: "All of them were at the beck and call of the Maharaja. He could satisfy his lust with any of them at any time of day or night" (Dass, 1970, p. 78). This extravagant sexual access to women was restricted to those high in status and power. Many men could afford only a single wife, and some were so poor they could not afford even one. The rich nobles, on the other hand, could easily afford harems, and until very recently, in India, many did (Betzig, 1993).

In imperial China, a similar story unfolded. By the end of the Chou dynasty in 771 B.C., kings kept "one queen (*hou*), three consorts (*fu-jen*), nine wives of the second rank (*pin*), twenty-seven wives of the third rank (*shih-fu*), and eighty-one concubines (*yu-chi*)" (van Gulik, 1974, p. 17). Palace agents were required to scour the land for young, beautiful, and accomplished women, who were then transported back to the palace. The least attractive were given menial work at the palace, while the most attractive were chosen for the imperial harem. The number of women corresponded closely to the status of the man. The emperor Huang-ti was said to have had intercourse with 1,200 women. The deposed emperor Fei-ti kept six palaces stocked with more than 10,000 women. Great princes were restricted to hundreds of women, great generals had thirty or more, upper-class men housed six to twelve, and middle-class men kept only three or four (Betzig, 1993).

Across the globe, in Incan Peru, there were "houses of virgins" with 1,500 women, although no upper limit was set on the number. The women waited in these houses until receiving a summons from the king, at which point they were brought to wherever the king happened to be. As in China, the number of women kept depended on the status and rank of the man. The emperors kept the most women, numbering in the thousands. Inca lords kept a minimum of seven hundred "for the service of his house and on whom to take his pleasure" (Cieza de Leon, 1959, p. 41). According to Incan law and custom, "principal persons" were given fifty young women; leaders of vassal nations, thirty; heads of provinces of more than 100,000 people were given twenty; governors of 100, eight; petty chiefs, seven; smaller chiefs, five; and so on. Women were distributed strictly according to the status and rank of the man.

The story is repeated again in Egypt judging by historical records from 1416 to 1377 B.C.; "The constant demand of the king of his provincial governors was for more beautiful servant girls" (Redford, 1984, p. 36). The records fail to show the specific numbers of women, but it is clear that the Mesopotamian kings at Sumer, Assyria, and Babylon sired many children by numerous wives, concubines, and slave women, sometimes in the thousands of women (Betzig, 1993). Status and rank, it appears, afforded men great sexual access to women in each of the six first recorded human civilizations.

This linkage appears to hold in modern times as well, although undoubtedly not to the same extent. Legally enforced monogamy in modern Western cultures places serious restrictions on the number of women a man can marry. The elimination of harems coincided with the end of the prevelance of despots and kings. Nonetheless, one recent study showed that men who were high in status indeed gained greater sexual access to a larger number of women (Perusse, 1993). Because this access occurs in the context of legally enforced monogamy, the increased sexual access of high-status men comes entirely from short-term sex partners and extramarital affairs. Furthermore, men who are high in status are able to marry women who are considerably more physically attractive than men

Alex Joseph, surrounded by his nine wives, living in a small town in Arizona. Historically and cross-culturally, high-status men often become effectively polygynous, gaining sexual access to multiple women in the form of wives, mistresses, or concubines.

who are lower in status (Elder, 1969; Taylor & Glenn, 1976; Udry & Eckland, 1984). High-status men also seek out women who are younger and hence more fertile (Grammer, 1992). Although the structure of modern civilization has changed considerably from that typifying the earliest civilizations, the link between a man's status and sexual access to young, attractive women has remained more or less the same.

In sum, empirical evidence supports the evolutionary rationale for predicting a sex difference in the strength of the motivation to achieve high status. All available evidence suggests that high status in men leads directly to increased sexual access to a larger number of women. Elevated status in women, of course, also could confer many reproductive advantages. But the direct increase in sexual access afforded men high in status suggests a more powerful selective rationale for a status-striving motive in men.

Are Men Higher in Status Striving?   Is there any direct evidence that men are higher than women in dominance or status striving? Surprisingly few studies have been devoted to this question, but there are some hints. In one six-culture study Whiting and Edwards (1988) discovered that boys were more likely than girls to engage in rough-and-tumble play, assaults and other aggressive actions, displays of "egoistic" dominance, and acts of seeking attention. Boys in all six cultures were more likely than girls to issue dominance challenges to same-age peers. Girls, in contrast, tended to display nurturance and pleasing sociability more than boys.

Psychologist Elenor Maccoby (1990) has done perhaps more than any other psychologist in reviewing the evidence for sex differences in children across literally thousands of studies. She described two of the most robust sex differences in the preschool years:

> The first is the rough-and-tumble play style characteristic of boys and their orientation toward the issues of competition and dominance. . . . A second factor of importance is that girls find it difficult to influence boys. . . . Among boys, speech serves largely egoistic functions and is used to establish and protect an individual's turf. Among girls, conversation is a more socially binding process. (p. 516)

A sex difference in dominance motivation thus appears to emerge at an early age.

Another source of evidence about sex differences comes from an extensive program of research by psychologists Felicia Pratto and Jim Sidanius on what they call social dominance orientation (SDO) (Pratto, Sidanius, & Stallworth, 1993). They developed a scale to measure SDO, which they describe as a preference for social hierarchies. Those high on this orientation endorse an ideology involving the legitimacy of one group's domination over another, the deservingness of discrimination and subordination of one group by another, and the allocation of more perks to one group than another. Some of the items on the SDO scale are "To get ahead in life, it is sometimes necessary to step on others"; "Rich people have their money because they are simply better people"; "Some people are just inferior to others"; "Some groups are simply not the equals of others"; "Only the best people [for example, the smartest, richest, most educated, and so on] should get ahead in this world"; "Winning is more important than how the game is played"; "[It is OK to get] ahead in life by almost any means necessary" (Pratto 1996, p. 187).

These psychologists argue that SDO should be higher in men than in women because such an orientation led ancestral men to greater control of, and access to, women. Furthermore, they propose that women would have been selected to choose men high in SDO, since this would have lead to a greater bounty of benefits for themselves and their children. Taken together, both rationales suggest an evolutionary basis for predicting a sex difference in SDO. Indeed, men consistently score higher than women on SDO scales. In one study of one thousand Los Angeles adults, men scored higher on SDO scales—a sex difference that proved consistent across culture of origin, income, education, political ideology, and several other variables (Pratto, 1996). The sex difference in social dominance orientation has also been documented in other cultures, most notably in Sweden, which is one of the most egalitarian cultures on earth (Buss, 1994). In sum, men appear to score higher on attitudes endorsing getting ahead, including those that justify one person's higher status than another and one group's dominance over another. These findings support the evolutionary theory of a sex difference in motivation to gain dominance or status, although more research is needed.

Men and Women Express Their Dominance through Different Actions. Another source of evidence for a sex difference in dominance comes from the acts through which men and women express their dominance. In one study one hundred acts previously mentioned as dominant were listed (Buss, 1981). Examples include: "I took command of the situation after the accident"; "I talked a great deal at the meeting"; "I demanded a back rub"; "I decided which programs the group would watch on TV"; "I hung up the phone on my lover." The first study asked men and women to rate each act for its social desirability, or how worthwhile it was in their eyes. Profound sex differences emerged. Women more than men tended to rate *prosocial dominant acts* as more socially desirable, including: "Taking charge of things at the committee meeting"; "Taking a stand on an important issue without waiting to find out what others thought"; "Soliciting funds for an important cause"; and "Being active in many community and campus activities."

In sharp contrast, men more than women tended to rate *egoistic dominant acts* as more socially desirable, including: "Managing to get one's own way"; "Flattering to get one's own way"; "Complaining about having to do a favor for someone"; "Blaming others when things went wrong." Men appear to regard more selfish dominant acts as more desirable, or less undesirable, than do women.

Do these sex differences emerge in the actual behaviors of men and women? To test for this sex difference, forty-three women and forty men were administered the California Psychological Inventory Dominance Scale (Gough, 1964) and the Personality Research Form Dominance Scale (Jackson, 1967). A week later participants completed a self-report version of how often they had performed each of the one hundred dominant acts on the scales (Buss, 1981). The dominance scores on the personality scales were then correlated with the dominant act performance for each sex. Dominant men and women alike tended to perform many dominant acts, such as: "I was highly involved in a political campaign"; "I took the lead in livening up a dull party"; "I addressed a public gathering"; "I told a long story to entertain others;" "I took command of the situation after the accident."

Despite these similarities, dominant men and women also tended to perform somewhat different dominant acts. Dominant men, but not dominant women, reported performing the following acts: "I told others to perform menial tasks rather than doing them myself"; "I managed to get my own way"; "I told him which of two jobs he should take"; "I managed to control the outcome of the meeting without the others being aware of it"; "I demanded that someone else run the errand." Dominant men, in other words, appear to perform a relatively high frequency of egoistic dominant acts, in which others are influenced for the direct personal benefit of the dominant individual.

Dominant women, in contrast, tended to perform a higher frequency of prosocial dominant acts, such as: "I settled a dispute among the members of the group"; "I took the lead in organizing a project;" "I introduced a speaker at the meeting." Dominant women appear to express their dominance primarily through actions that facilitate the functioning and well-being of the group.

This sex difference in the expression of dominance has also been revealed through a subtle psychological experiment by personality psychologist Edwin Megargee (1969). Megargee wanted to devise a laboratory test situation in which he could examine the effect of dominance on leadership. He first administered the California Psychological

Inventory Dominance Scale to a large group of men and women who might serve as potential subjects. He then selected only those men and women who scored either high or low on dominance.

Upon completion of this selection procedure, Megargee (1969) brought pairs of individuals into the laboratory, in each case pairing a high-dominant subject with a low-dominant subject. He created four conditions: (1) a high-dominant man with a low-dominant man; (2) a high-dominant woman with a low-dominant woman; (3) a high-dominant man with a low-dominant woman; and (4) a high-dominant woman with a low-dominant man.

Megargee presented each of these pairs with a large box containing many red, yellow, and green nuts, bolts, and levers. Subjects were told that the purpose of the study was to explore the relationship between personality and leadership under stress. Each pair of subjects was to work as a team of troubleshooters and repair the box as quickly as possible by removing nuts and bolts of certain colors and replacing them with other colors. However, one person from the team had to be the leader, a position that entailed giving instructions to his or her partner. The second person was to be the follower, and must carry out the menial tasks requested by the leader. The experimenter then told the subjects that it was up to them to decide who would be the leader and the follower.

The important question for Megargee was who would become the leader and the follower. He simply recorded the percentage of high-dominant subjects within each condition who became leaders. He found that 75 percent of the high-dominant men and 70 percent of the high-dominant women took the leadership role in the same-sex pairs. When high-dominant men were paired with low-dominant women, however, 90 percent of the men became leaders. The most startling result occurred when the woman was high and the man low in dominance. Under these conditions, only 20 percent of the high-dominant women assumed the leadership role.

From these laboratory findings alone, one might conclude that the women in this condition were suppressing their dominance, or that the men, despite being low in dominance, felt compelled to assume a standard sex role by taking charge. It turns out, however, that neither conclusion is warranted. Megargee had recorded the conversations between each pair of subjects while they were deciding who would be the leader. When he analyzed these tapes, he made a startling finding: the high-dominant women were *appointing* their low-dominant partners to the leadership position. In fact, the high-dominant women actually made the final decision about the roles 91 percent of the time! This finding suggests that women express their dominance in a different manner than the men in the mixed-sex condition. This basic sex difference in the expression of dominance has been found repeatedly by subsequent investigators (e.g., Carbonell, 1984; Davis & Gilbert, 1989; Nyquist & Spence, 1986).

Megargee's study highlights a key sex difference—men tend to express their dominance through acts of personal ascension whereby they elevate themselves to positions of power and status. Women tend to be less oriented toward personal striving for status over others, opting instead to express their dominance for group-oriented goals. These studies, taken together, support the hypothesis that the sexes differ in status striving.

In sum, a variety of sources of evidence support the evolutionary rationale for a sex difference in dominance. Men who attain positions of status and dominance tend to use these positions to gain increased sexual access to women. Men score higher on social dominance orientation scales, tending to endorse attitudes justifying their superiority to other individuals and groups. Men tend to express their dominance through egoistic acts that involve personal benefit and the subordination of others, whereas women tend to express their dominance through more prosocial actions that do not necessarily elevate themselves over others.

Dominance Theory

Evolutionary psychologist Denise Cummins (1998) recently proposed a dominance theory as a framework to account for many human cognitive capacities that are otherwise puzzling. She started with the proposal that the struggle for survival in human (and chimpanzee) groups was often characterized by conflicts between those who were dominant and those who were trying to outwit those who were dominant: "The evolution of mind emerges from this scene as a strategic arms race in which the weaponry is ever-increasing mental capacity to represent and manipulate internal representations of the minds of others" (Cummins, 1998, p. 37). Selection will favor strategies that cause one to rise in dominance, but also will favor the evolution of subordinate strategies to subvert the access of the dominant individual to key resources. These strategies include deception, guile, false subordination, friendship, and manipulation to gain access to the resources needed for survival and reproduction. Among chimpanzees, for example, subordinate males attempt to conceal their erections when their "illicit" sexual activity with a female is discovered by a dominant male, suggesting a subordinate's capacity for "reading" and deceiving a dominant male (de Waal, 1988). Cummins (1998) proposed that these cognitive capacities to reason about the minds of others have evolved in primates, including humans, to thwart the primary or exclusive access to resources by those high in dominance.

Dominance theory has two key propositions (Cummins, 1998). First, it proposes that humans have evolved domain-specific strategies for reasoning about social norms involving dominance hierarchies. These include understanding aspects such as permissions (e.g., who is allowed to mate with whom), obligations (e.g., who must support who in a social contest), and prohibitions (e.g., who is forbidden to mate with whom). Second, dominance theory proposes that these cognitive strategies will emerge prior to, and separate from, other types of reasoning strategies.

Cummins (1998) marshals several forms of evidence to support the dominance theory. The first pertains to the early emergence in a child's life of reasoning about rights and obligations, called *deontic reasoning*. Deontic reasoning is reasoning about what a person is permitted, obligated, or forbidden to do (e.g., Am I old enough to be allowed to drink alcoholic beverages?). This form of reasoning contrasts with *indicative reasoning*, which is reasoning about what is true or false (e.g., Is there really a tiger hiding behind that tree?). A number of studies find that when humans reason about deontic rules, they spontaneously adopt a strategy of seeking rule violators. For example, when evaluating the deontic rule "all those who drink alcohol must be 21 years old or older," people spontaneously look for others with alcoholic drinks in their hands who might be underage. In marked contrast, when people evaluate indicative rules, they spontaneously look for confirming instances of the rule. For example, when evaluating the indicative rule "all polar bears have white fur," people spontaneously look for instances of white-furred polar bears, rather than falsifying instances of bears that might not have white fur. In short, people adopt two different reasoning strategies, depending on whether they are evaluating a deontic or an indicative rule. For deontic rules people seek out rule violations; for indicative rules people seek out instances that conform to the rule. These distinct forms of reasoning have been documented in children as young as three years old, suggesting that they emerge reliably early in life (Cummins, 1998). Perhaps not coincidentally, at age three children organize themselves into transitive dominance hierarchies (that is, hierarchies in which if A is dominant to B, and B is dominant to C, then A is dominant to C). Moreover, young children also can reason about transitive dominance hierarchies earlier in life than they can reason transitively about other stimuli (Cummins, 1998).

Dominance theory predicts that human reasoning will be strongly influenced by rank, and there is some empirical support for this proposition. Evolutionary psychologist Linda Mealey showed study participants pictures of men along with biographical information that revealed each man's social status (high versus low) and character (history of cheating, irrelevant information, or history of trustworthiness) (Mealey, Daood, & Krage, 1996). A week later participants returned to the lab and were asked to report which of the photographs they remembered from the previous week. Several important results emerged. First, the "cheaters" were remembered far more frequently than the noncheaters. Second, memory for cheaters was especially enhanced if the cheaters were low in status, whereas the memory bias for cheaters was diminished if the cheaters were high in status. Third, the memory bias for cheaters was stronger for men than for women participants. These results support the proposal that humans have evolved selective attention and memorial storage mechanisms designed for processing important social information—mechanisms that are especially sensitive to who has cheated and the status of who has cheated. These results also support Cummins's (1998) dominance theory, which proposes that human social reasoning will be strongly affected by rank.

Other studies offer more circumstantial support for this proposition. When people are angered or frustrated they experience an increase in blood pressure. If they are given a chance to aggress against the person who caused their anger or frustration, their blood pressure returns to normal, but only if the "target" of their aggression is lower in status. When the target of the aggression is higher in status, blood pressure remains high (Hokanson, 1961).

In the most direct test of the effects of status on social reasoning, Cummins had subjects test for the rule "if someone was assigned to lead a study session, that person was required to tape record the session" (Cummins, 1998, p. 41). The reasoner's task was to test for compliance with the rule by selecting which study session records to inspect. Here was the crucial manipulation: Half the participants were told to adopt the perspective of the high-ranking individual, in this case a dormitory resident assistant, and to check on the students under their care. The other half were told to adopt the perspective of a student (low ranking), and to check on possible violations by the dormitory resident assistant. The results showed a compelling link between status and social reasoning: 65 percent looked for potential rule violations when they were checking on people lower in status than themselves, whereas only 20 percent looked for potential rule violations when they were checking on people of equal or higher status than themselves.

These studies all provide support for dominance theory. Deontic reasoning strategies appear to emerge early in life. People are especially sensitive to social information about what is permitted, obligatory, or forbidden. People spontaneously check for violations of deontic rules, and do so more for people lower in status than those higher in status. Cummins concludes: "If one were to guess at which problems cognition evolved to solve, one would be hard pressed to come up with a better candidate than dominance" (Cummins, 1998, p. 46).

Social Attention-Holding Theory

Whereas Cummins stresses the information-processing strategies that might follow from the recurrent adaptive problems posed by dominance hierarchies, another theory developed by evolutionary psychologist Paul Gilbert (1990) emphasizes the emotional components of dominance. Gilbert bases his theory in part on the concept of *resource holding potential* (RHP) stemming from work conducted on nonhuman animals (Archer, 1988; Parker, 1974; Price & Sloman, 1987). RHP refers to an evaluation that animals make about themselves relative to other animals regarding their relative strengths and weaknesses. Losers of contests and those that determine before contests that they are inferior have low RHP. Winners of contests and those who determine that they are likely to win contests are superior in RHP. The behaviors that follow from these relative assessments give rise to dominance hierarchies.

After evaluations of RHP are made, three types of behavior follow. First, the animal might *attack* the other, especially if it perceives itself to be superior in RHP. Second, the animal might *flee*, especially if it perceives itself to be inferior in RHP. Third, the animal might *submit*—relinquishing critical resources to those higher in RHP. In this analysis, dominance is not a property of an individual per se, but rather is a description of the relationship between two or more individuals. When these relationships are aggregated across many relationships, they can be described as a dominance hierarchy.

According to Gilbert (1990), humans have co-opted RHP for another mode— *social attention-holding potential* (SAHP). SAHP refers to the quality and quantity of attention others pay to a particular person. According to this view, humans compete with each other to be attended to, and valued by, others in the group. When group members bestow a lot of quality attention on an individual, that individual rises in status. Ignored individuals are banished to low status. Differences in rank, according to this theory, stem not from differences in threat or coercion, but from differences in attention conferred by others.

Why would anyone bestow status on one person and ignore another? This is a crucial question, and Gilbert offers a few suggestions that require further exploration.

He suggests that humans bestow attention on those who perform a function that is valued by the bestowers. A doctor who helps aid someone when he is sick, for example, receives high-quality attention from the sick person. People compete to bestow benefits on others, in this view, to rise in SAHP. Those who fail to bestow benefits are shunned and cut off from attention and resources.

The most novel theoretical contribution of Gilbert's (1990) theory comes from hypotheses about the role of mood or emotion as a consequence of changes in rank. Going up in rank produces two hypothesized consequences—*elation* and an increase in *helping*. Winning competitive encounters tends to produce an elevated mood, or what might be called "winner's elation." Those who witness the faces of the winners and losers after an athletic contest can easily identify differences in elation. Presumably a positive mood increases the likelihood of seeking out future competitions, along with an increased assessment of one's probabilities of winning. The second and related change is an increase in helping. Psychologists have documented that those who experience a rise in status are more likely to behave in a friendly and helpful manner (Eisenberg, 1986). Interestingly, some people avoid seeking help from others because they believe doing so will reduce their perceived status (Fisher, Nadler, & Whitcher-Alagna, 1982). Furthermore, there is evidence that higher-status individuals help more than lower-status individuals at hospital emergency wards (Brewin, 1988). In sum, elevations in rank appear to be linked with elevations in mood and helpful behavior.

Plummeting in status has a different set of consequences for mood and emotion according to SAHP theory—the onset of social anxiety, shame, rage, envy, and depression. In public speaking, the greater the potential consequences for status, the greater the *social anxiety*. Giving a talk to a group of undergraduates, for example, is generally not as

According to one theory, winning results in an elevated mood, producing an increase in helping behavior and an increase in the probability of winning future competitions (left). Losing can produce depression, social anxiety, and envy (right).

anxiety-provoking for professors as giving a talk at an international conference of experts. Social anxiety presumably functions to motivate efforts to avoid status loss. *Shame* is a related emotion. Shame typically comes about when a public appraisal results in one's being the object of scorn or disdain, with the attendant decrease in perceived status. A shamed individual perceives him- or herself to be small, inferior, or contemptible. Bodily movements coincide with this self-evaluation, including avoiding eye contact with others, lowering one's chin, and hunching one's body posture (Wicker, Payne, & Morgan, 1983). Shame presumably motivates an individual to avoid being the object of scorn, either at present or in the future.

Rage is another hypothesized reaction to the loss of status. Rage may function to motivate an individual to seek revenge on the person who caused the status loss. The often-quoted remark "no one makes me look stupid and gets away with it" may represent an example of the rage and consequent revenge that follow the loss of status, and may be used to justify retaliatory aggression (Gilbert, 1990).

Envy is one of the least studied emotions in psychology but may be extraordinarily important, according to SAHP theory. Envy is linked with rank in that people experience envy when someone else has resources, houses, mates, or prestige that they want but fail to possess. Envy may function to motivate us to imitate those who have what we want. Hero worship and the idealization of others may reflect positive manifestations of the emotion of envy. On the negative side, envy may prompt actions designed to tear down those who have more than we do, such as derogating their achievements or spreading false rumors about them. Envy may prompt a husband to belittle his wife's achievements to maintain his superior rank in the marriage (Horung, McCullough, & Sugimoto, 1981). Envy can be extremely destructive in organizations, as when a manager undermines the efforts of his or her workers to prevent them from outshining him or her (Gilbert, 1990).

Depression is the final hypothesized emotional reaction to the loss of status, although depression can arise from many other factors as well, including the loss of attachment bonds (Gilbert, 1990). Depression from the loss of rank can occur when a person loses his or her looks, is fired from a job, perceives him- or herself to be a burden on others, or fails in some socially visible manner. There is empirical evidence that depression prompts submissive behavior designed to appease others and to prevent the onslaught or continuation of aggression from them (Forrest & Hokanson, 1975). People bounce back from depression when they find employment again or otherwise discover a way to bestow value on others and hence increase their social attention-holding potential (Gilbert, 1990).

In summary, SAHP theory proposes that many aspects of human emotional life, from elation to depression, are evolved features of psychological mechanisms designed to deal with the adaptive problems of status hierarchies. Little research has been conducted to test the various hypotheses about the specific functions of emotions, but the theory has intuitive appeal and shows much promise.

Determinants of Dominance

A variety of verbal and nonverbal characteristics signal high dominance and status. These range from time spent talking to testosterone. This section summarizes the most important correlates of dominance and status. In many cases causation cannot be inferred from the correlational data. If testosterone is correlated with dominance, for example, does it mean that high testosterone leads to high dominance, or does high dominance lead to high testosterone, or both? If high-status people tend to stand taller than low-status people, does standing tall lead to status, or does status lead to standing tall, or both? We cannot answer these causal questions in most cases. Nonetheless, the correlates of dominance and status provide a fascinating portrait of what goes along with relative rank.

Verbal and Nonverbal Indicators of Dominance.   In summarizing this literature Argyle (1994) concluded that dominant individuals tend to stand at full height, often facing the group, with hands on hips and an expanded chest; they gaze a lot, looking at others while talking; they do not smile much; they touch others; they speak in a loud and low-pitched voice; and they gesture by pointing to others. The behaviors of low-ranking or submissive individuals are typically the opposite: their body posture is often bent rather than straight; they smile a lot; they speak softly, look while the other is speaking, and give many deferential head nods; they speak less than those higher in status; they don't interrupt others who are speaking; and they address the high-status persons in the group rather than the group as whole.

What about walking tall? Walking fast? Schmitt and Atzwanger (1995) predicted that a link between pace and status would occur for men, but not for women. Their reasoning: Males over the course of human evolutionary history have competed for females by impressing them with signs of their hunting skills, including locomotory speed and perseverance. In a busy location in Vienna, Austria, one observer measured the pace of pedestrians. Later, a second observer interviewed each individual about his or her age, body height, and socioeconomic status. The results are shown in Figure 12.1.

Significant positive correlations were found between walking speed and socioeconomic status for men. For women, in contrast, there were no significant positive correlations. The results support the author's hypothesis that walking speed is a sex-linked status display for men but not for women.

Size and Dominance.   Given the complexity of human status hierarchies, and the many paths to gaining attention from others, it comes as a surprise that sheer size still counts. Indeed, the term "big man" has a dual meaning in most cultures, referring to both a man of large physical stature and a man of importance, influence, power, and authority (Brown & Chia-yun, n.d.). In some cultures the word for "leader" literally means "big man." Many status metaphors refer to physical stature, such as "being on *top*" and "being *under* someone's control," "walking *tall*," and "being *crestfallen*." Indeed, in reviewing the ethnographic evidence from a variety of cultures, Brown and Chia-yun conclude that " 'big man' is a reflection or recognition in culture of a pervasive feature of nature: The tendency among humans (and other animals) for rank or social stature to correlate with physical stature" (Brown & Chia-yun, n.d., p. 10). The preference that people express for leaders who are tall is found among cultures as diverse as the Aka pygmies in Africa and the Mehinaku in the Amazon rainforests of Brazil.

The link between physical and social stature has been explored experimentally (Wilson, 1968). In one study the same man was introduced to different audiences, but was identified to each audience as having a different rank—professor, graduate student,

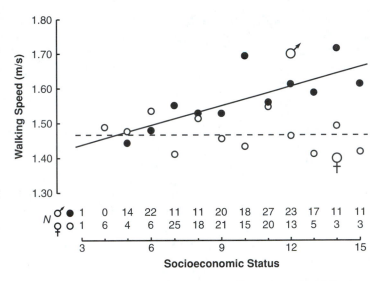

FIGURE 12.1 Association between Walking Speed and Socioeconomic Status (SES, high numbers indicate high SES) of Pedestrians. Men ($N = 167$) walk faster, the higher their SES, whereas the pace of women ($N = 159$) is independent of their SES.

Source: Reprinted from *Ethology and Sociobiology, 16,* A. Schmitt & K. Atzwanger, Walking fast—ranking high: A sociobiological perspective on pace, 451–462, Copyright © 1995, with permission from Elsevier Science.

and so on. The audiences were subsequently asked to estimate the height of the man. Audiences to whom the man was described as being high in status recalled him as being taller than audiences to whom the man was described as being lower in status. Even with people we know personally, our mental image of their height is exaggerated if we know them to be high in social status (Dannenmaier & Thumin, 1964).

In studies in the United States, tall men have an advantage in being hired, promoted, paid, and elected (Gillis, 1982). Tall men earn higher salaries, averaging roughly six hundred dollars more per year for each inch above the mean of 5 feet, 8 inches. In presidential elections in the twentieth century, the taller of the two candidates won 83 percent of the time. Although humans may have the most complex and elaborate prestige hierarchies, sheer size remains an important factor.

Testosterone and Dominance. Testosterone is an androgen, perhaps the most important class of hormones that contribute to developing and maintaining "masculine" features in a variety of animals (Mazur & Booth, in press). Castrated male chicks, for example, typically fail to develop the red comb and wattles that signal the rooster's reproductive competence, fail to crow and court hens, and avoid confrontations with other cocks. Among humans, sex differences in testosterone are striking. Men average one hundred-thousandth of a gram of testosterone per liter of blood, fully seven times the average for women (Mazur & Booth, in press). Although testosterone is produced in the adrenal cortex, as well as in the ovaries in women, the Leydig cells of men's testes produce a much larger amount, accounting for the large sex difference. Testosterone can be measured through blood or saliva samples.

At puberty the male testes dramatically increase their production of testosterone, resulting in a tenfold increase over prepubescent levels. This surge in testosterone brings about the changes we associate with puberty—penis growth, deepening of the voice, increased muscle mass, facial and bodily hair, and an increased interest in sex (see Box 12.1 on page 364 for a brief look at the effects of facial dominance on status and sexuality).

Scientists have long suspected that testosterone is closely connected with dominance and status in a variety of animal species. In one study, for example, low-ranking cows were treated with testosterone (Bouissou, 1978). Subsequently, the treated cows rose in rank among the other cows. When testosterone was withdrawn, they sank to their previous low ranks. A similar effect was documented for low-ranking roosters who were injected with testosterone—their comb sizes increased and they rose in the status hierarchy, sometimes to the top position (Allee, Collias, & Lutherman, 1939).

The causal effects of testosterone on rises in status among humans are more difficult to document, in part because ethical issues make it more difficult to experimentally manipulate testosterone levels in humans. Higher testosterone levels have been correlated with a variety of dominating behaviors among both prisoners and nonprisoners. High testosterone levels are also correlated with a diverse array of rebellious and antisocial acts, especially among young males (Mazur & Booth, in press). Because these studies are all correlational, it cannot be concluded that high testosterone levels cause these dominating behaviors. In fact, there is evidence for precisely the reverse causality.

One of the most well-documented effects with humans is that changes in status result in changes in testosterone (Mazur & Booth, in press). The testosterone levels of athletes rise just prior to their matches, perhaps making individuals more willing to take risks. Perhaps more important, winners of the matches show a rise in testosterone for up to two hours after the match, whereas the losers show a decline in testosterone. Mood changes accompany testosterone changes, as the high testosterone winners display an elevated mood relative to the low testosterone losers. These effects are most pronounced when the athletes regard the match as important.

Similar effects have been documented away from the athletic arena in competitions involving games of chess (Mazur, Booth, & Dabbs, 1992), reaction time "contests" in the laboratory (Gladue, Boechler, & McCaul, 1989), and symbolic challenges via verbal insults (Nisbett, 1993). Winners show elevated testosterone levels, losers depressed testosterone levels. The effects of winning and losing extend even to sports fans who do not participate in the competition. When Brazil beat Italy in the 1994 World Cup in soccer, the Brazilian fans who watched the match on TV showed a rise in testosterone, whereas the Italian fans who watched the match showed a decline (Fielden, Lutter, & Dabbs, 1994).

The evolutionary function of these changes in testosterone are not known, but one speculation is that winners are soon likely to face other challengers, so the elevated levels of testosterone may prepare them for further contests. The decrease in testosterone among losers may function to prevent injury by discouraging them from further confrontations until a more opportune time (Mazur & Booth, in press). Alternatively, the

BOX **12.1**

Facial Dominance

A dominant-looking face may be another signal of status. Facial dominance is indicated by qualities such as a prominent chin, heavy brow ridges, and a muscular face; low dominance is indicated by the opposite qualities—a weak chin, slight brow ridges, and a fleshy face. The evolutionary psychologists Ulrich Mueller and Allan Mazur (1996) rated the facial dominance of 434 West Point cadets, and then followed them through their military careers. They discovered that those with dominant-looking faces obtained higher ranks at the military academy. Facial dominance was also positively linked with their ranks at midcareer, as well as with promotions in late career, more than twenty years after the initial photographs were taken.

In another study the facial dominances of fifty-eight high school boys were rated along with physical attractiveness and pubertal development (Mazur, Halpern, & Udry, 1994). Subsequently, these boys completed questionnaires that requested information about their sexual experiences. All three predictors—facial dominance, physical attractiveness, and pubertal development—were positively correlated with having experienced sexual intercourse and with the total number of sex partners. After statistically controlling for attractiveness and pubertal development, however, facial dominance still significantly predicted sexual experience. The authors concluded that a dominant facial appearance leads to increased sexual access among males.

---

elevated testosterone levels of winners may function to elevate self-confidence, fostering the assumption of a higher status role, perhaps even fostering an increase in sexual access to women. These functional speculations remain to be tested by future research.

Much less research has been conducted on the links between testosterone and dominance and status among women. The scant research there is, however, has failed to uncover the same links found in men. A few studies report a positive correlation between testosterone in women and levels of unprovoked violence in prisoners, but other studies have failed to confirm this link (Mazur & Booth, in press). In one study, researchers found that status, as assessed through peer judgments, was lower among the women with high testosterone levels, suggesting the opposite effect from that observed with men (Cashden, 1995). Interestingly, women with high testosterone levels tended to overestimate their own status. Thus, high testosterone levels in these women were linked with high self-assessments of status, but with low peer assessments of status. Further research is needed to clarify the links between testosterone and status in women.

The overall conclusion from this research must be confined to men and points to a reciprocal model of causation (Dabbs & Ruback, 1988; Mazur & Booth, 1997). High testosterone levels in men may lead to dominating behaviors that lead to high status in some subcultures, but reciprocally, elevations in status appear to lead to rises in testosterone levels (Bernhardt, 1997). Future research can be expected to clarify more precisely the evolutionary functions of these reciprocal causal links.

Serotonin and Dominance.   Recently the neurotransmitter serotonin has been explored in relation to dominance (Cowley & Underwood, 1997). Prozac, a drug commonly used in fighting depression and anxiety, works by increasing serotonin in the brain.

Evolutionary scientists Michael McGuire and Michael Raleigh conducted experiments with vervet monkeys and found that males with high social rank had almost twice as much serotonin in their blood as the low-ranking monkeys (McGuire & Troisi, 1998). Like testosterone, however, the causal paths can run in both directions. When alpha males were overthrown, their serotonin levels plummeted. When a lower-ranking male ascended to power, his serotonin levels swelled. In one fascinating study McGuire and Raleigh discovered that they could dramatically reduce the serotonin levels of an alpha male simply by keeping him behind a one-way mirror so the other monkeys could not see him and thus failed to perform the submissive displays. Apparently the alpha males interpreted the failure of others to submit as a sign of lost status, so their serotonin levels plummeted.

In another study McGuire and Raleigh studied forty-eight students in a university fraternity, including officers and regular members. They discovered that the officers' serotonin levels were 25 percent higher than those of the regular members. In an amusing small-sample test the researchers then analyzed their own serotonin levels and found that McGuire (the lab director) had 50 percent more serotonin than Raleigh (the research assistant). In sum, the neurotransmitter serotonin joins testosterone as one of the brain chemicals responsible for mediating one's position in the status hierarchy.

Needed: A Theory of the Determinants of Dominance. The above brief review covers merely a few of the qualities that are correlated with dominance and social status. Lacking is a broad theory that can explain precisely what people value in others, why they value those things, and precisely why humans hold some people in esteem and awe while others remain ignored or are humiliated. Are the qualities that lead to high status the same in men and women? Are they the same for children as for adolescents and adults? Why do some subcultures give status to physical strength and toughness, while others derogate individuals with such qualities as thugs? How culturally variable are prestige criteria? What is the collection of psychological mechanisms that has evolved to grapple with getting ahead? Are there universals in prestige criteria, and can they be predicted in advance from an evolutionary psychological analysis? These and other key questions are being answered by cross-cultural research on prestige, status, and reputation (Buss, 1995b).

Strategies of Submissiveness

We have spent most of this chapter exploring the high end of dominance and status—the signals of status, the sexual access that high-status men attain, and the fact that high-status people walk tall and fast. Perhaps our attention is naturally drawn to focus on those high in status. Indeed, we have explored one theory that proposes that social attention defines high status. But there is another side that requires exploration—the adaptive problems posed by being low in status. This section is speculative because the low end of the status totem pole has received little research attention.

Deceiving Down. Evolutionary biologist John Hartung asks us to consider people who are stuck in a position they might otherwise perceive as unfair, or beneath their station

(Hartung, 1987). Consider a man who holds a job that he knows does not take full advantage of his talents, or a wife who knows she is more intelligent than her husband. Acting like your job or your spouse is beneath you could put your employment or your marriage in jeopardy. Your boss might fire you for insubordination. Your spouse might seek someone with whom he or she feels more comfortable and less threatened. The adaptive solution that Hartung proposes is called *deceiving down*. Deceiving down is not "playing dumb," or pretending to be less than you are. Instead, it involves an actual reduction in self-confidence to facilitate acting in a submissive, subordinate manner.

The evolutionary logic is that situations have commonly existed in which it was adaptive to convincingly portray oneself as subordinate, and hence nonthreatening. Those who are real threats risk incurring the wrath of the dominant, who may seek to vanquish anyone perceived as a rival. By truly acting subordinate one avoids incurring this wrath, continuing to occupy a position within the group. It also permits one to bide one's time until a more opportune moment arises in which to seek dominant status. Whether this hypothesis pans out empirically, such that people forced to occupy positions beneath them actually reduce their self-esteem so that they can more convincingly display subordination, remains a question for future research.

The Downfall of "Tall Poppies."

The *Oxford English Dictionary* defines *tall poppy* as "an especially well-paid, privileged, or distinguished person" (Simpson & Weiner, 1989). The *Australian National Dictionary* defines *tall poppy* as "a person who is conspicuously successful" and "one whose distinction, rank, or wealth attracts envious notice or hostility" (Ramson, 1988). Psychologist Norman Feather (1994) has explored people's reactions to the fall of tall poppies, finding that they depend on a variety of factors. One common reaction is captured by the German word *Schadenfreude*, which means experiencing pleasure in another's misfortunes. Although there is no strict equivalent word in English, when English speakers hear the definition for the first time, "their reaction is not, 'Let me see . . . Pleasure in another's misfortunes . . . What could that possibly be? I cannot grasp the concept; my language and culture have not provided me with such a category.' Their reaction is, 'You mean there's a *word* for it? Cool!' " (Pinker, 1997, p. 367).

Occupying a subordinate position carries costs. Because high-status individuals are known to gain preferential access to key resources that enhance survival and reproduction, subordinate individuals are often left with the scraps. A study of subordinate behavior illustrates the potential strategies of subordinates (Salovey and Rodin, 1984). The researchers provided participants with feedback that their standing on a self-relevant characteristic was worse than that of a successful peer on the exact same characteristic. After receiving this feedback participants were found to verbally derogate the successful other, were less likely to seek friendship with that person, and reported feeling more anxious and depressed about interacting with this successful other. Disparaging a successful competitor may make a person feel better, but simply making oneself feel better hardly qualifies as an evolutionary function of envy. Disparaging a more successful competitor may lead to other outcomes, such as reputational damage to the competitor or the redirection of one's efforts toward a different arena, both of which could qualify as proper evolutionary functions.

Feather (1994) conducted a series of studies in which participants read scenarios about the falls of various tall poppies. An academic superstar, for example, might plunge in performance on a critical final exam. Feather varied features of the scenarios, such as whether the person's initial success was deserved, whether the fall was large or small, and whether the fall was due to some mistake made by the tall poppy. He also tested participants in Japan and Australia to assess the cross-cultural generality of reactions to the fall of a tall poppy. One of the dependent measures was the Tall Poppy Scale, which contains items such as: "It's good to see very successful people fail occasionally"; "Very successful people often get too big for their boots"; "Very successful people who fall from the top usually deserve their fall from grace"; "Those who are very successful ought to come off their pedestals and be like other people"; "People who are 'tall poppies' should be cut down to size"; "Very successful people sometimes need to be brought back a peg or two, even if they have done nothing wrong" (Feather, 1994, p. 41).

Across a series of studies, Feather discovered several important conditions under which people take pleasure in the fall of a tall poppy. First, when the high status of a tall poppy was made salient, participants reported more happiness with the fall from grace. Second, when the success of a tall poppy was not perceived to be deserved, participants reported more pleasure with his or her fall than when it was perceived as deserved. Third, *envy* was the most common emotional experience participants felt toward a tall poppy, especially if the other person's success was in a domain that was important to the participant, such as academic achievement among students. Fourth, Japanese subjects reacted more favorably to the fall of tall poppies than did Australian subjects, suggesting some cultural variation in *Schadenfreude*. Fifth, subjects with low self-esteem reported more delight with the fall of tall poppies than did subjects with high self-esteem.

Although more research needs to be conducted on this topic, the available evidence suggests that one submissive strategy is to facilitate the fall of those with greater status, and to take delight in their fall. The pleasure people feel in a rival's misfortunes may act as a motivational mechanism to promote those misfortunes. Because evolution by selection always occurs on a relative basis—one's success relative to others—we expect two general strategies of getting ahead in status and dominance hierarchies. One is self-enhancement, or attempting to achieve something relative to one's competitors. The second is to promote the downfall of others. It appears from the research that humans use both strategies.

Summary

This chapter explored the evolutionary psychology of status and social dominance, phenomena observed widely throughout the animal world from crayfish to humans. A *dominance hierarchy* refers to the fact that some individuals within a group reliably gain greater access than other individuals to key resources—resources that contribute to survival or reproduction. The existence of such hierarchies poses a series of adaptive problems to which animals have evolved solutions, including motivation to get ahead and strategies to cope with subordination. Size is an important determinant of dominance in some species, but in primate species such as chimpanzees and humans, social skills at enlisting allies become critical to attaining high status. High-ranking animals often, although not always, gain preferential access to key resources needed for survival and reproduction.

A strong argument can be made that selection has favored the evolution of greater motivation for status striving in men than in women. The more polygynous the mating system, the more it has paid in reproductive success for men compared to women to take risks to ascend the status hierarchy. Ascent in these systems is linked with increases in the number of wives historically and the number of sex partners currently. The empirical evidence supports this evolutionary hypothesis. Across cultures and over human recorded history going back to 4000 B.C., high-status men consistently have acquired sexual opportunities with a large number of wives, mistresses, and concubines. Across cultures, males form hierarchies as early as age three. Empirical evidence supports the hypothesis that men are higher in social dominance orientation—the endorsement of beliefs that it is justified that some people are superior to others. Women tend to be more egalitarian, men more hierarchical. Men and women also differ in the actions through which they express dominance. Whereas women tend to express dominance through pro-social actions (e.g., settling disputes among others in the group), men tend more often to express dominance for personal gain and ascension (e.g., getting others to do menial tasks rather than doing them themselves). When given a choice of roles to take, dominant women tend to appoint men as leaders, whereas dominant men take the leadership role for themselves.

Dominance theory was proposed by Denise Cummins to explain the cognitive mechanisms that might have evolved to negotiate dominance hierarchies. Dominance theory has two key propositions. First, humans have evolved domain-specific strategies for reasoning about social norms involving dominance hierarchies. These include understanding aspects such as permissions (e.g., who is allowed to mate with whom), obligations (e.g., who must support who in a social contest), and prohibitions (e.g., who cannot join the ceremonial war dance). Second, these cognitive strategies are predicted to emerge prior to, and separately from, other types of reasoning strategies. Among the empirical evidence to support this theory are the following: (1) children as young as age three appear to reason about dominance hierarchies, including the property of transitivity; (2) people tend to remember the faces of cheaters more if the cheaters are lower in status than if they are higher in status; and (3) people tend to look for violations of rules among lower-status individuals when they are asked to assume the perspective of a higher-status individual.

Whereas dominance theory emphasizes the reasoning mechanisms that underlie dominance, social attention-holding potential (SAHP) theory proposes a variety of emotional mechanisms designed to solve the various adaptive problems posed by living in social hierarchies. These include elation after a rise in status, social anxiety in contexts in which status could be gained or lost, shame and rage as a consequence of status loss, envy to motivate the acquisition of what others have, and depression to facilitate submissive posturing to avoid further attacks from superiors.

Dominance is determined and indicated by a variety of factors, including upright posture, low resonant voice, direct eye contact, a fast-paced stride, facial features such as a strong jaw, and physical size. The hormone testosterone and the neurotransmitter sero-tonin have both been linked with dominance, although the direction of causality is uncer-tain in both cases. There is some evidence that testosterone increases after winning and decreases after losing. In chimps serotonin plummets following a loss of status, as when others fail to emit a submissive greeting. The precise evolutionary functions of testos-terone and serotonin remain to be clarified, but increases may play a role in maintaining dominance and decreases may help animals to avoid dangerous challenges.

Although most of this chapter focused on the high end of dominance, it is impor-tant not to neglect the low end. Ancestral humans recurrently confronted situations in which they were subordinate, so it would be surprising if selection had not favored the evolution of mechanisms designed to deal with the adaptive problems posed by subordi-nation. Although little research has been directed at this issue, two hypothesized submis-sive strategies are deceiving down (lowering one's self-esteem to avoid confrontation and to better carry out the subordinate role without incurring wrath from the dominant) and derogating tall poppies. Cross-cultural research is needed to test these various hypothe-ses and speculations and to provide a firmer foundation for a more complete evolution-ary theory of status, prestige, and social dominance.

PART SIX

An Integrated Psychological Science

This concluding part reviews the entire field of psychology from an evolutionary perspective. Chapter 13 reveals how an evolutionary perspective can provide key insights into each of the major branches of psychology, including cognitive, social, developmental, personality, clinical, and cultural. This chapter concludes that these current disciplinary boundaries within psychology may be somewhat artificial. Evolutionary psychology cuts across these boundaries and suggests that the field of psychology would be better organized around the adaptive problems that humans have faced over the long expanse of evolutionary history.

13 Toward a Unified Evolutionary Psychology

*Many sciences develop for a time as exercises in description and empirical general-
ization. Only later do they acquire reasoned connections within themselves and with
other branches of knowledge. Many things were scientifically known of human
anatomy and the motions of the planets before they were scientifically explained.*
—George Williams, 1966

Imagine you are a Martian visiting Earth to study the most commonly encountered large
mammal—human beings. You discover that there exists a scientific discipline devoted to
studying humans called *psychology*, so you visit a university to spy on some psychologists
to see what they have discovered. The first thing you notice is that there are many different types of psychologists who go by different names. Some call themselves "cognitive
psychologists," and study how the mind processes information. Some call themselves
"social psychologists," and study interpersonal interactions and relationships. Some call
themselves "developmental psychologists," and study how humans change psychologically throughout their life spans. Some call themselves "personality psychologists," and
focus mainly on the differences between people, although some study human nature.
Some call themselves "cultural psychologists," and highlight some astonishing differences such as between the highly individualistic cultures such as America and the more
collective cultures such as Japan. And some call themselves "clinical psychologists" and
study ways the mind malfunctions.

As a Martian, these disciplinary divisions might strike you as odd. Social behavior, for example, certainly requires the processing of information, so why is social psychology separate from cognitive psychology? Individual differences, another example,
certainly develop over time and many of the most important individual differences are
social in nature, so why is personality psychology separate from developmental and
social psychology? Understanding the malfunctioning of the mind certainly requires
an understanding of how the mind is supposed to function, so why is clinical psychology separate from the rest of psychology?

Despite this strange division of labor among psychologists, when you examine what
they have discovered, you might come away at least somewhat impressed. Cognitive

psychologists, for example, have documented a fascinating array of cognitive biases and heuristics that suggest the human mind fails to function according to formal rules of logic (Tversky & Kahneman, 1974). Social psychologists have discovered an array of fascinating phenomena—the facts that people tend to loaf by failing to pull their fair share of the load when the group they are in gets large (Latané, 1981); that people tend to take credit for successful outcomes but blame others for unsuccessful outcomes (Nisbett & Ross, 1980); and that people tend to obey an authority figure, even if it means delivering harmful electric shocks to other people (Milgram, 1974). Developmental psychologists have discovered that children develop an understanding that other people have desires at age three, don't understand that other people have beliefs until age four, and don't understand that people have sexual desires until puberty. Personality psychologists have documented some fascinating individual differences—some people are consistently more Machiavellian or manipulative than others. And clinical psychology has uncovered an array of disorders and some of their properties—twice as many women as men suffer from depression, schizophrenia shows substantial heritability and is nearly impossible to cure, and common phobias of heights and snakes can be easily cured through systematic desensitization treatment.

You want to convey to your Martian colleagues an integrated understanding of this strange species called Homo sapiens. You want to retain all the important insights the psychologists have discovered, but you don't want to cling to the disciplinary divisions that strike you as somewhat arbitrary. Because evolution by selection is the only known process capable of generating complex organic design, such as that in the human mind, evolutionary psychology appears to be the only viable meta-theory powerful enough to integrate all these subdisciplines. This is the meta-theory that seeks to present a unified understanding of the mechanisms of the mind that characterize this strange species of bipedal primates.

This chapter is devoted to panning back from the details and getting a larger, more macroscopic view of human psychology. The first section examines each of the subdisciplines of psychology and illustrates some ways in which evolutionary psychology can inform them. The second section presents an argument that the future of an integrated psychology rests with dissolving traditional disciplinary boundaries.

Evolutionary Cognitive Psychology

All psychological mechanisms entail, by definition, information-processing devices that are tailored to solving adaptive problems. Because many of the adaptive problems that humans have confronted over the course of evolutionary history are intrinsically social, cognitive psychology must deal with the ways in which we process information about other people. The entire cognitive system, according to an evolutionary psychological perspective, is a complex collection of interrelated information-processing devices, functionally specialized for solving specific classes of adaptive problems.

Traditional cognitive psychology is anchored by several core assumptions that evolutionary psychology challenges (Cosmides & Tooby, 1994a). First, mainstream cognitive psychologists tend to assume that cognitive architecture is *general purpose* and *content free*. This means that the information-processing devices that are responsible for food selection are assumed to be the same as those for mate and habitat selection. These general-purpose mechanisms include the abilities to reason, learn, imitate, calculate means–ends relationships, compute similarity, form concepts, and remember things. Evolutionary psychologists, as documented throughout this book, make precisely the opposite assumption—that the mind is likely to consist of a large number of specialized mechanisms, each tailored to solving a different adaptive problem.

One consequence of the mainstream cognitive assumption of a general-purpose information-processing device is that little attention has been given to the sorts of stimuli used in cognitive experiments. Cognitive psychologists tend to select stimuli based on ease of both presentation and experimental manipulability. This leads to categorization studies that use triangles, squares, and circles rather than anything corresponding to "natural" categories such as kin, mates, enemies, or edible objects. Indeed, many cognitive psychologists have intentionally used artificial stimuli precisely because they want to get rid of the messy "content" with which subjects might have had prior experience. Literally hundreds of experiments were conducted using "nonsense syllables" to study memory processes because researchers believed that actual words with understandable content would "contaminate" the results. The use of artificial content-free stimuli makes sense if the mind is indeed a general-purpose information processor. It makes less sense if cognitive mechanisms are specialized to process information about particular tasks.

As discussed in Chapter 2, there are at least two major problems with the assumption of general processing mechanisms: (1) what constitutes a successful adaptive solution differs from domain to domain—the qualities needed for successful food selection, for example, differ from those needed for successful mate selection; (2) the number of possible behaviors generated by unconstrained general mechanisms approaches infinity, so the organism would have no way of determining the successful adaptive solutions from among the blizzard of unsuccessful ones (the problem of combinatorial explosion discussed in Chapter 2).

A second core assumption of traditional cognitive psychology is *functional agnosticism* —the view that information-processing mechanisms can be studied in ignorance of the adaptive problems they were designed to solve. Evolutionary psychology, in contrast, infuses the study of human cognition with functional analysis. Just as we cannot understand the human liver without knowing what it is designed to do (filter toxins), evolutionary psychologists contend that we cannot understand how humans categorize, reason, make judgments, and store and retrieve specific things from memory without understanding the functions of the cognitive mechanisms on which these activities are based.

In sum, evolutionary psychologists replace the core assumptions of mainstream cognitive psychology—general-purpose and content-free mechanisms along with functional agnosticism—with a different set of assumptions that permits integration with the rest of life science (Tooby & Cosmides, 1992):

1. The human mind consists of a set of evolved information-processing mechanisms embedded in the human nervous system.

2. These mechanisms, and the developmental programs that produce them, are adaptations produced by natural selection over evolutionary time in ancestral environments.
3. Many of these mechanisms are functionally specialized to produce behavior that solves particular adaptive problems, such as mate selection, language acquisition, and cooperation.
4. To be functionally specialized, many of these mechanisms must be richly structured in content-specific ways.

Based on the work of David Marr (1982), Cosmides and Tooby (1994a) argue that cognitive psychology should be anchored in *computational theories:* "A computational theory specifies what that problem is and why there is a device to solve it. It specifies the *function* of an information processing device" (p. 44). Computational theory is based on the following arguments:

(1) Information processing devices are designed to solve problems.
(2) They solve problems by virtue of their structure.
(3) Hence to explain the structure of a device, you need to know
   (a) *what* problem it was designed to solve, and
   (b) *why* it was designed to solve that problem. (p. 44)

By itself, computational theory is not enough to establish precisely *how* a mechanism goes about actually solving an adaptive problem because any particular adaptive problem will have many solutions. Warm-blooded animals must solve the adaptive problem of thermal regulation, for example. But dogs do it through evaporation from a protruding tongue, whereas humans do it through hundreds of thousands of sweat glands contained in the skin. Computational theories don't provide a shortcut to conducting the scientific experiments to test hypotheses about how organisms actually solve problems. They do, however, constrain the search space by describing what counts as a successful solution. Computational theories are therefore able to exclude from consideration the thousands of possibilities that fail, in principle, to solve an adaptive problem. One such constraint in humans, for example, is that the relevant information for solving the adaptive problem must have been a recurrent feature of human ancestral environments.

Several programs of cognitive research have been based on these new assumptions about the nature of human cognition that promise to revolutionize thinking about entire domains of cognitive functioning. Below we discuss a few examples.

Problem Solving: Heuristics, Biases, and Judgment under Uncertainty

Much of so-called "higher cognition" concerns problem solving and judgment under conditions of uncertainty. According to many modern judgment researchers, humans are prone to errors when problem solving and making decisions under conditions of uncertainty (e.g., Nisbett & Ross, 1980; Tversky & Kahneman, 1974). Indeed, a major cottage industry has sprung up in cognitive psychology to document the various errors and biases to which humans are predisposed. Following are two examples:

1. *Base-rate fallacy:* People tend to ignore base-rate information when presented with compelling individuating information. Base rates refer to the overall proportion of something in a sample or population. Consider this example. Imagine there is a roomful of people, 70 percent of whom are lawyers and 30 percent of whom are engineers. One is a man named George who dislikes novels, likes to do carpentry on weekends, and wears a pocket protector in his shirt pocket to carry his pens. His own writing is dull and rather mechanical, and he has a great need for order and neatness. What is the probability that George is (A) a lawyer, or (B) an engineer. Most people tend to ignore the base-rate information, which suggests that it is more likely that George is a lawyer (70 percent of the people in the room are lawyers). Instead, they give too much weight to the individual information, which is highly salient, and declare that George is likely to be an engineer. This error, called the base-rate fallacy because people tend to ignore the actual mathematical proportion (of lawyers, in this sample), violates mathematical formulas by which base rate and individuating information should be combined appropriately.

2. *The conjunction fallacy:* If I tell you that Linda wears tie-dyed shirts and buttons asserting that "men are slime," and frequently tries to organize the women in her workplace, is it more likely that (A) Linda is a bank teller, or (B) Linda is a feminist bank teller? A majority of people believe that (B) is more likely, despite the fact that this violates the cannons of logic (see Figure 13.1): B (feminist bank tellers) is a subset of A (bank tellers), so the likelihood of A must be greater than B. Stated differently, the *conjunction* of "feminist" and "bank teller" must be lower in likelihood than bank teller alone, because conjunctive events can never exceed the likelihood of their individual elements. Because the description of Linda seems so representative of a feminist, however, most people ignore logic and go with what seems obvious.

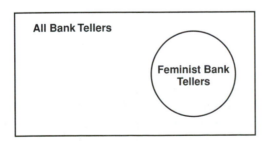

FIGURE 13.1   Venn Diagram of Bank Tellers and Feminist Bank Tellers. Feminist bank tellers are logically a subset of all bank tellers; therefore, the likelihood of someone being a feminist bank teller cannot be higher than the likelihood of someone being a bank teller. Yet most participants in a study say that it is more likely that "Linda" is a feminist bank teller.

The extensive literature showing how foolish people are is, of course, great fun. But is the model of the mind it portrays accurate? Is human cognition riddled with biases and errors, simply because humans use crude and error-prone short cuts to make judgments under uncertainty? An evolutionary perspective would give one pause before accepting this conclusion, if only because human ancestors had to do some pretty impressive problem solving to deal with the hundreds of adaptive problems necessary to survive and reproduce.

Tooby and Cosmides (under review) argue that an evolutionary perspective presents something of a paradox when contrasted with the view of humans as riddled with cognitive biases. Humans routinely solve complex natural tasks, many of which have defied attempts to be modeled in artificial intelligence systems. In vision, object recognition, grammar induction, and speech perception, people easily surpass the performance of all artificial systems, even though scientists are equipped with all the tools of modern logic and formal statistical decision theories (Tooby & Cosmides, under review). The paradox is this: If humans are so riddled with cognitive mechanisms that commonly cause errors and biases, how can they routinely solve complex problems that surpass any system that can be developed artificially?

Tooby and Cosmides argue that the paradox can be resolved by a careful evolutionary psychological analysis: "Just as in classic times, Greeks judged non-Greeks to be 'barbarians' because they spoke Greek poorly (their speech sounding to Greek ears like 'ba-ba-ba'), so now we may be judging human reason harshly because our criteria for recognizing sophisticated performance have been parochial" (Tooby & Cosmides, under review, ms. p. 4). They argue for an evolutionary theory of cognitive mechanisms called *ecological rationality*. Over evolutionary time, the human environment has had certain statistical regularities—rain often followed thunder; violence sometimes followed angry shouts; sex sometimes followed prolonged eye contact; dangerous bites often followed getting too close to a snake; and so on. These statistical regularities are called *ecological structure*. Ecological rationality consists of evolved mechanisms containing design features that utilize this ecological structure to facilitate adaptive problem solving.

The shape and form of cognitive mechanisms, in other words, coordinate with the recurring statistical regularities of the ancestral environments in which humans evolved. We fear snakes and not electrical outlets, for example, because of a recurrent statistical regularity between snakes and debilitating or lethal consequences; electrical outlets are too recent an invention to have recurrently produced debilitating or lethal outcomes. Problem-solving strategies, in short, may be exquisitely designed for solving one set of problems—those that recurred over evolutionary time—but very poor at solving artificial or novel problems. When there is a mismatch between the problem presented and the problem the mechanism was designed to solve, errors will result.

Tooby and Cosmides (under review) take the argument further. Theories of formal logic that are content independent—the theories that the researchers of cognitive biases claim humans should use—are exceptionally poor at solving real adaptive problems. The world is full of logically arbitrary relationships—dung happens to be potentially dangerous to humans, for example, but provides a hospitable home for dung flies. So applying formal logic cannot in principle solve the adaptive problem for humans of avoiding the consumption of dung. The only thing that can solve it is a content-specific mechanism, one that has been built over evolutionary time to capitalize on the recurring statistical regularities associated with dung as it interacted with our hominid ancestors. To judge human performance by comparing it to outcomes generated by formal mathematical and statistical theories, Tooby and Cosmides argue, is like judging the winners in an archery contest "not by who actually hit the target most often but by who displayed the judges' idea of the best form while aiming" (under review, ms. p. 14).

Human adaptive problem solving—which our ancestors must have done reasonably well or else they would have failed to become our ancestors—always depends on three ingredients: (1) the specific *goal* being sought (the problem that must be solved), (2) the *materials* at hand, and (3) the *context* in which the problem is embedded. Finding a single "rational" method for solving all problems that is independent of content is impossible. The criterion by which the "correctness" of solutions is evaluated is evolutionary: The decisions made by the cognitive mechanism led, on average, to better survival and enhanced reproduction in ancestral environments relative to alternative designs present at the time. What matters in the eyes of selection is not truth, validity, or logical consistency, but simply what works in the currency of replicative success: "Ancestral environments and lifeways were the engineering proving ground within which alternatively designed cognitive devices were tested against one another" (Tooby & Cosmides, under review, ms. p. 29).

Before we conclude that human cognitive mechanisms are riddled with biases and errors of judgment, we need to ask which adaptive problems human cognitive mechanisms evolved to solve and what would compose "sound judgment" or "successful reasoning" from an evolutionary perspective. If humans have trouble locating their cars by color at night in parking lots illuminated with sodium vapor lamps, we would not conclude that our visual system is riddled with errors. Our eyes were designed to perceive the color of objects under natural, not artificial light (Shepard, 1992).

Many of the research programs that have documented "biases" in judgment, it turns out, have used artificial, evolutionarily unprecedented experimental stimuli analogous to sodium vapor lamps. Many, for example, require subjects to make probability judgments based on a single event (Gigerenzer, 1991; 1998). "Reliable numerical statements about the probability of a single event were rare or nonexistent in the Pleistocene—a conclusion reinforced by the relative poverty of number terms in modern band level societies" (Tooby & Cosmides, under review, ms. p. 40). A specific woman cannot have a 35 percent chance of being pregnant—she either is pregnant or is not, so probabilities hardly make sense when applied to a single case.

The human mind, however, may have been well designed to record the *frequencies* of events: I went to the valley eight times; how many times did I find berries? The last three times I put my arm around a potential mate, how many times was I rebuffed? If some mechanisms of the human mind are designed to record event frequencies rather than single-event probabilities, then experiments that require subjects to calculate probabilities from single events may be presenting artificial and evolutionarily novel stimuli, analogous to testing vision under the illumination of sodium vapor lamps. Let's now briefly examine two programs of research based on evolutionary cognitive psychology.

Frequency Representations and Judgment under Uncertainty.   Is there evidence that human cognitive mechanisms are designed to record event frequencies? Cosmides and Tooby (1996) advance the *frequentist hypothesis*, the proposition that some human reasoning mechanisms are designed to take as input frequency information and produce as output frequency information. Some advantages of operating on frequentist representations are that: (1) they allow a person to preserve the number of events on which the judgment was based (e.g., How many times did I go to the valley to search for berries over the past two months?); (2) they allow a person to update his or her database when new events and information are encountered (e.g., adding information from a third month of trips to the valley to search for berries); and (3) they allow a person to construct new reference classes after the events have been encountered and remembered, allowing a person to reorganize the database as needed (e.g., remembering that the frequency of encountering berries differed depending on whether the trips to the valley were made in the spring or the fall). Frequency representations can provide crucial input into problem-solving and decision-making mechanisms.

Consider the following, which has been called the medical diagnosis problem: "If a test to detect a disease whose prevalence is 1/1000 has a false positive rate of 5% [that is, the test indicates that 5% of those tested have the disease, even though they do not], what is the chance that a person found to have a positive result actually has the disease, assuming that you know nothing about the person's symptoms or signs? _____%" (Cosmides & Tooby, 1996, p. 21). Of a sample of experts at Harvard Medical School, only 18 percent answered 2 percent, which is the "correct" answer according to most interpretations of the problem. A whopping 45 percent of the experts answered 95 percent, which suggests that they ignored the base-rate information about false positives.

But what if the same problem is presented using frequency information? That is precisely what Cosmides and Tooby (1996) did.

> 1 out of every 1000 Americans has disease X. A test has been developed to detect when a person has disease X. Every time the test is given to a person who has the disease, the test comes out positive (i.e., the "true positive" rate is 100%). But sometimes the test also comes out positive when it is given to a person who is completely healthy. Specifically, out of every 1000 people who are perfectly healthy, 50 of them test positive for the disease (i.e., the "false positive" rate is 5%).
>
> Imagine that we have assembled a random sample of 1000 Americans. They were selected by a lottery. Those who conducted the lottery had no information about the health status of any of these people. Given the information above: On average, how many people who test positive for the disease will actually have the disease? ____ out of _____. (p. 24)

The correct answer is roughly 2 percent.

In sharp contrast to the original medical diagnosis problem, 76 percent of the subjects (Stanford undergraduates) gave the correct answer, as opposed to only 12 percent who got the answer right when the problem was presented in its original format. When the information is presented in a format using frequencies, performance improves dramatically. But does 76 percent represent some sort of upper limit on good performance for problems of this sort?

One reason to suspect that performance could be improved further pertains to the fact that the information in the problem was conveyed in writing, which has only been used by humans for roughly the past five thousand years. What if the same problem required subjects to visually depict the information?

To test whether subjects' performances would get better if information was represented visually, Cosmides and Tooby (1996) used a problem almost identical to the one above but added visual representations of the random sample of people who were tested for the disease and the following instructions about how to interpret them:

> The 100 squares pictured below represent this random sample of 100 Americans. Each square represents one person.
>
> Using these squares, we would like you to depict the information given above. To indicate that a person actually has the disease, *circle* the square representing that person. To indicate that a person has tested positive for the disease, *fill in* the square representing that person. Given the information above: On average, (1) Circle the number of people who will have the disease. (2) *Fill in* squares to represent the people who will test positive for the disease. (3) How many people who test positive for the disease will *actually* have the disease? _____ out of _____. (p. 34).

The results from this study are shown in Figure 13.2, along with the results from the previous study. Astonishingly, 92 percent of the subjects got the correct answer when instructed to depict the information pictorially. In summary, presenting the information

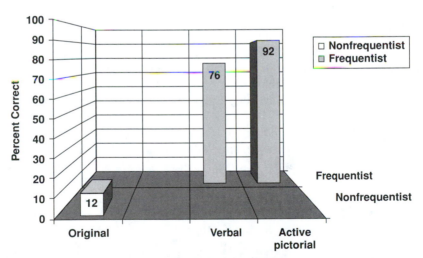

FIGURE 13.2   Comparing the Percent of Correct Answers for the Original, Nonfrequentist Version to the Percent Correct for the Two Frequentist Versions. In the active pictorial condition, which elicited the highest levels of performance, subjects were required to form a frequentist representation.

Source: Reprinted from *Cognition, 58,* L. Cosmides & J. Tooby, Are humans good intuitive statisticians after all? Rethinking some conclusions from the literature on judgment under uncertainty. 1–73, Copyright © 1996, with permission from Elsevier Science.

in frequentist terms verbally allows three quarters of the subjects to get it right, but adding a visual frequentist representation allows almost all the subjects to get it right.

These results suggest that people do *not* ignore base-rate information in making judgments, as long as the base-rate information is presented in a manner that maps more closely onto the sorts of input that humans would have been likely to process in ancestral times. Cosmides and Tooby (1996) are not arguing that all cognitive mechanisms are designed to process information about the frequencies of events. Rather, they argue that some forms of decision making that occur under conditions of uncertainty require the processing of frequency information. The domains most likely to require processing about event frequency are those in which information changes rapidly over a person's life span or across generations—domains such as the locations of game animals, the distribution of edible plants, and the locations of predators. Local sampling of events during a person's life is necessary in these domains because local frequencies provide the most reliable basis for making predictions.

In sum, these results offer a challenge to the mainstream cognitive view that the problem-solving abilities of humans are riddled with errors and biases (Cummins & Allen, 1998). Evolutionary psychological analysis is helpful in identifying the sorts of adaptive problems the human mind was designed to solve. This includes an understanding of the format of the information humans are designed to process. Conducting experiments that more closely mimic the formats of the information that humans were designed to process provides a different picture of the cognitive capabilities of humans when engaged in making judgments under uncertainty (see also Wang, 1996).

The portrait of human cognitive mechanisms afforded by this line of thinking offers a marked contrast to the mainstream portrait of general mechanisms and crude heuristics. Rather than a single general intelligence, humans possess multiple intelligences. Rather than a general ability to reason, humans have many specialized abilities to reason, depending on the nature of the adaptive problems they were designed by selection to solve. Rather than general abilities to learn, imitate, calculate means–ends relationships, compute similarity, form concepts, remember things, and compute representativeness, evolutionary psychology suggests that the human mind is filled with complex and problem-specific cognitive mechanisms, each designed to solve a different adaptive problem. Because many of the most important adaptive problems human ancestors had to confront were social in nature, the study of human cognition cannot be divorced from the study of human social interaction: "Mechanisms describable at the cognitive level underlie and organize all of human thought and behavior—not just knowledge acquisition—and so cognitive psychology needs to broaden its scope to include them" (Cosmides & Tooby, 1994b, p. 105).

Female Superiority in Spatial Location Abilities

Another fascinating new line of cognitive research, guided by evolutionary psychological thinking, pertains to spatial abilities. It has long been known that men show superior performance, on average, on tasks of spatial ability that require mental rotation, map reading, and maze learning. These and related sex differences in skills such as geometry are hypothesized to have originated through sexual selection (Geary, 1996). The evolutionary psychologist Irwin Silverman and his colleagues (Silverman & Eals, 1992; Silverman & Phillips, 1998) argued that these particular forms of spatial ability are precisely those that would have facilitated skill at hunting—a task performed mainly by men over the course of human evolutionary history (Tooby & DeVore, 1987).

Women, in contrast, have specialized in gathering, so Silverman and his colleagues proposed that contrary to all published studies on spatial ability, women would display superiority in particular forms of spatial tasks—those that would have facilitated gathering. Remembering where plants are located in geographical space is one such ability. The researchers conducted a variety of empirical studies using both artificial and natural stimuli to test this hypothesis. The results were consistent across studies—women outperformed men on spatial tasks involving location memory and object memory such as those shown in Figure 13.3 (Silverman & Phillips, 1998).

Although clearly more research is needed, the implications of these studies are far reaching. First, they imply that there may be several distinct abilities that are included

FIGURE 13.3   The Stimulus Array Used for Tests of Object and Location Memory. Women tend to score higher than men on tests of location memory, a sex difference hypothesized to be an adaptation to gathering.

Source: From *The Adapted Mind: Evolutionary Psychology and the Generation of Culture,* edited by Jerome H. Barkow, L. Cosmides, and John Tooby. Copyright © 1992 by Oxford University Press, Inc. Used by permission of Oxford University Press, Inc.

within the domain of "spatial" and that these are far more domain specific in nature than previously believed. Second, they suggest that studies of sex differences in cognitive abilities benefit by examining the nature of the adaptive problems men and women have faced over human evolutionary history. Sex differences cannot be explained by global and hence inaccurate characterizations of spatial abilities that ignore more modular processes.

In sum, the work on spatial abilities supports the general conclusion about human cognition that is emerging from the research on problem solving under conditions of uncertainty. The human cognitive system appears to be multimodular, consisting of a large number of specialized information-processing mechanisms, each designed to solve a different adaptive problem.

Evolutionary Social Psychology

Many of the most important adaptive problems humans have faced over the past several million years are inherently social in nature: negotiating social hierarchies, forming long-term social exchange relationships, using language to communicate and influence others, forming short-term and long-term mateships, managing social reputations amidst a landscape of shifting allies and rivals, and dealing with kin of varying and uncertain degrees of genetic relatedness. Because so many adaptive problems are likely to have been social, the human mind should be heavily populated with psychological mechanisms dedicated to social solutions. Much of evolutionary psychology, therefore, will be evolutionary social psychology (Simpson & Kenrick, 1997).

Evolutionary social psychology offers the promise of answering some of the most profound questions about the human animal. Why do people live in groups? Why do people form relationships—mateships, friendships, coalitions, and kin ties—that endure over years and decades? Why do we select mates and friends preferentially, and what selection criteria do we use? Why do people cooperate with some, yet compete with others? Why are social relationships sometimes riddled with conflict and strife, but other times characterized by love and cooperation? Is love, as The Beatles suggested, all we need? Because most human social interaction has taken place within the context of enduring relationships, questions about the psychology of relationships should form the core of the field of social psychology.

This focus on relationships is in sharp contrast to the current field of mainstream social psychology, which tends to be "phenomenon" oriented. Typically, some interesting, counterintuitive, or anomalous observation is noticed and empirically documented. Examples include (1) *the correspondence bias*, the tendency to explain a person's behavior by invoking enduring dispositions, even when it can be shown that situational causes are responsible (Gilbert & Malone, 1995; Ross, 1981); (2) *the social loafing effect*, the tendency for individuals to perform less work toward a joint outcome as group size increases (Latané, 1981); (3) *self-handicapping*, the tendency to present publicly a purported weakness about oneself to provide an excuse in the event one fails at a task (Leary & Shepperd, 1986); (4) *the self-serving bias*, the tendency to make attributions that make oneself look better than others in the group (Nisbett & Ross, 1980); (5) *the confirmation bias*, the tendency to selectively seek out information that affirms (rather than falsifies) an already-held hypothesis (Hansen, 1980); and many others.

Social psychology has thus amassed a number of interesting descriptions of empirical phenomena of considerable importance. But it has not yet developed a theory powerful enough to explain the origins of these phenomena or to show how they fit within a larger understanding of human psychology. Evolutionary psychology provides the missing framework to theoretically anchor the empirical discoveries of social psychologists. Two major routes to evolutionizing social psychology will be (1) capitalizing on evolutionary theories about social interactions, and (2) using evolutionary psychology as a heuristic or guide to discovering important social problems.

Capitalizing on Evolutionary Theories about Social Phenomena

Most of the major theoretical advances in evolutionary biology have been about social phenomena, yet these important theories have been almost entirely ignored by mainstream social psychologists. The first is *inclusive fitness theory* (Hamilton, 1964). This theory, which expanded classical fitness to include the actions of an organism that have fitness effects on other organisms that carry copies of its genes, was the first to solve many of the issues surrounding social altruism. A direct implication is that altruistic acts should be heavily directed toward other organisms that (1) are likely to have copies of the helper's genes, and (2) have the ability to convert such help into increased survival or reproduction. Social psychologists who have begun to test the implications of this theory for humans have come away with new and exciting results. The self-reported likelihood of risking one's life to save another's life, for example, is directly a function of the degree of genetic relatedness to the helper (Burnstein et al., 1994). The theory of inclusive fitness has profound consequences for the social psychology of the family, altruism, helping, coalitions, and even aggression. Future research should uncover a fascinating array of other psychological mechanisms that follow from inclusive fitness theory.

The second important evolutionary theory for social psychology is *sexual selection*—the theory that evolution can occur through mating advantage accrued through (1) besting intrasexual competitors, and (2) being preferentially chosen as a mate by members of the opposite sex (Darwin, 1871). This theory has already proved invaluable to discovering key psychological mechanisms in same-sex competition, homicide and other forms of violence, risk taking, mate choice, conflict between the sexes, sex differences in status striving, and even sex differences in the risk of dying. Indeed, the theory of sexual selection provides the most promising theory for integrating many of the sex differences found in humans and other primates (Buss, 1996a).

The third important theory is *parental investment theory*, which provided a theoretical prediction about the operation of the two components of sexual selection (Trivers, 1972). Specifically, the sex that invests more in offspring is predicted to be more choosy in mate selection. The sex investing less in offspring is predicted to be less choosy in mate selection and more competitive with its own sex for sexual access to the high-investing sex. This theory has led to many important discoveries about strategies of human mating (Buss, 1994; Ellis & Symons, 1990; Kenrick & Keefe, 1992), and promises many more discoveries.

The theory of *reciprocal altruism* provides a fourth theoretical anchor for social psychology (Axelrod & Hamilton, 1981; Trivers, 1971; Williams, 1966). This theory offers an evolutionary explanation for many important social phenomena, such as friendship, cooperation, helping, altruism, and social exchange. It also provides a source of insights for the analysis of close relationships, including friendships and cooperative coalitions. Social exchange has been an enduring topic within mainstream social psychology. Evolutionary theories of reciprocal altruism and related theories offer an evolutionary explanation for its importance and further predictions about its form (e.g., Cosmides & Tooby, 1992).

Fifth, the theory of *parent–offspring conflict* provides another conceptual anchor for social psychology (Trivers, 1974). This theory furnishes precise predictions about family dynamics. Whereas conflict within families is often viewed as a symptom of malfunctioning, the theory of parent–offspring conflict predicts that such conflicts will be common in most families. It supplies an explanation for sibling rivalry. It accounts for the more frequent incidence of child abuse in stepfamilies. It predicts conflict between mother and child over the timing of weaning. "The theory of parent–offspring conflict also predicts conflict between children and their parents over activities such as extramarital involvement, which may be beneficial to the parent but costly for the child" (Friedman & Duntley, 1998). And it offers a framework for a host of other phenomena that no existing theory within social psychology has yet attempted to predict or explain.

In sum, theoretical advances in evolutionary biology offer social psychology a powerful set of tools for anchoring and integrating social phenomena. They also provide a guide to important domains of inquiry, as outlined below.

Heuristic Value of Evolutionary Social Psychology

Evolutionary social psychology begins with providing a guide to important domains of inquiry that have been relatively neglected in mainstream social psychology. The first such guide is that events surrounding reproductive activity should be prime targets for the discovery of evolved social psychological mechanisms. Because the engine that drives the evolutionary process is differential gene replication, activities surrounding reproduction should be especially likely loci for the evolution of specific psychological mechanisms. One of the most obvious such domains is mating, and for this reason three of the chapters in this book were devoted to the topic (Chapters 4, 5, and 6).

Mating may be the most obvious domain linked with reproduction, but it is not the only one. Another critical domain is the evolutionary social psychology of status, prestige, and reputation. Humans are a group-living species with well-articulated social hierarchies that occur universally across cultures and subcultures. People's prestige, status, and reputation determine a host of evolutionarily important events such as survival and access to mates. Evolutionary psychology suggests that this topic is central to social psychology, and thus an entire chapter (12) was devoted to it despite the relative lack of research in the domain.

A second guide provided by evolutionary psychology pertains to kinship and family relations, which should be prime targets for the discovery of evolved psychological mechanisms. Inclusive fitness theory directs attention not just to events surrounding individual reproduction. Momentous events such as patterns of parental investment, parental favoritism, parent–child conflict, brotherly and sisterly love, sibling conflict, and grandparental investment become important loci for potential evolved psychological mechanisms. The theory of inclusive fitness guides researchers to these topics and to specific predictions about what sorts of evolved mechanisms might be predicted based on genetic relatedness among individuals.

Evolutionary psychology, in short, provides a powerful metatheory (Buss, 1995a) for why humans are so profoundly fascinated by the plays of Shakespeare and the stories on soap operas and in tabloid newspapers: mating, divorce, pregnancy, revelations about paternity, deceit, manipulation, power, sibling rivalries, parental manipulations, and extramarital affairs. These are the social events that have affected the reproductive fates of our forbears, and should assume a proper role in evolutionary social psychology.

Mating relationships have obvious and direct connections with reproduction. Kin have provided over evolutionary time obvious opportunities for investing in vehicles that carry copies of one's genes. Other social relationships, however, are critical in securing mateships and in acquiring the resources that can be used to invest in kin. These include casual friends, true friends, reciprocal exchange partners, and coalitional allies. Relationships, in short, should form the core of evolutionary social psychology. Through the metatheory of evolutionary psychology, each of the fascinating discoveries made by social psychologists can be positioned within a larger framework.

The Return of Group Selection as Multilevel Selection Theory.   In Chapter 1, we discussed the demise of the theory of group selection, the idea that there are group–level adaptations that evolved through the differential reproduction and extinction of groups. After the publication of George Williams's (1966) critique of group selection, nearly all evolutionary biologists relinquished their subscriptions to that idea. They did so not because group selection was theoretically impossible. In fact, Williams showed that group selection *is* theoretically possible, and may indeed have occurred for some species such as honeybees. The conclusion, rather, was that the conditions that make group selection likely—such as (a) a high degree of "shared fate" of members within the group, (b) low levels of reproductive competition within the group, and (c) recurrent patterns of differential reproduction and extinction of groups—are rarely seen in nature, and unlikely to have been a strong force for most species.

Recently, the evolutionary biologist David Wilson and the evolutionary philosopher Elliot Sober have argued that group selection is far more viable than most biologists had concluded (Sober & Wilson, 1998; Wilson & Sober, 1994). The argument centers on the issue of whether groups can have functional organization in the same way that individuals have functional organization. Just as individuals can be "vehicles" of selection, so groups too can be "vehicles" of selection. They suggest, for example, that humans do many things to reduce reproductive differences within the group, such as passing laws that restrict men and women to one spouse. Groups whose members cooperate with each other better, to take another example, may have out-reproduced groups composed of more selfish individuals. This resurrection of group selection is sometimes called *multilevel selection theory* to acknowledge that selection can operate on many levels, including individuals, groups within species, and even larger entities such as multispecies ecosystems.

If multiselection theory has any merit, it will have profound implications for evolutionary social psychology in pointing to group–level adaptations that may have been entirely missed by those focusing on adaptations at the level of the individual organism (e.g., altruism for self-sacrifice for the group, even when the group members are not kin). Many biologists and evolutionary psychologists remain skeptical of this new group selection (e.g. Cronk, 1994; Dawkins, 1994; Dennett, 1994). They argue that the conditions required to make group selection a powerful force are rarely met, especially with humans. Given that humans within groups compete heavily with each other and groups often show high fluidity, with members defecting from one group to another and forming new groups with new combinations, individuals rarely have the high levels of "shared fate" within the group that would faciliate group selection.

Fortunately, whether Wilson and Sober or their critics are right about the power and importance of group selection is ultimately an empirical issue. At a minimum, posing questions and group selection may indeed lead to new discoveries about human social psychology, even if in the long run group selection turns out to be the "weak force" that George Williams envisioned.

Evolutionary Developmental Psychology

Developmental psychology is not a branch of psychology with a particular content attached to it. Rather, it is an approach to psychological phenomena of any sort that incorporates a temporal, life-span, or ontogenetic perspective. One can study personality development, social development, moral development, perceptual development, cognitive development, or developmental psychopathology. Thus, developmental psychology cuts across the other traditional branches of psychology and is defined by its temporal perspective rather than its psychological content. Because few psychological mechanisms emerge at birth fully developed, a developmental perspective will necessarily be an essential part of the proper description and understanding of nearly every psychological mechanism.

But can evolutionary psychology shed any light on how these mechanisms develop during the course of an individual's life? One key insight currently missing from mainstream developmental psychology is this: *human beings face predictably different adaptive problems at various points in their lives.* Infants face the problem of survival, but not the problem of mating. Problems of mating are faced predictably before problems of parenting. Problems of parenting are faced predictably before problems of grandparenting. As a general rule, the evolutionary psychology meta-theory predicts that new adaptive mechanisms will develop or become activated in an individual's life as he or she faces cues to each new adaptive problem—cues that correspond to the adaptive problems our ancestors faced over the course of their development. To the degree that these adaptive problems have a specieswide temporal sequence or progression, evolutionary psychologists will be able to formulate a developmental theory of human nature. At a minimum, an evolutionary perspective will provide heuristic value by posing questions that would not otherwise be posed, guiding researchers to areas they might not otherwise consider, causing them to note certain observations they might have missed when human behavior is examined without the corrective lens of evolutionary psychology. This section provides a few examples of this heuristic value for developmental psychology (see MacDonald, 1988; Segal, Weisfeld, & Weisfeld, 1997; and Surbey, 1998, for more comprehensive treatments).

Theory of Mind Modules

Recent work by the psychologists Allen Leslie (1991) and Henry Wellman (1990), and others has documented that at roughly three years of age children develop a "theory of mind." This entails inferences about the *beliefs* and *desires* of other individuals inhabiting each child's social world. Combining inferences about beliefs and desires enables a child (and presumably adults) to predict the behavior of others. When asked to "explain" why James went to the school cafeteria, for example, a child will invoke the notion that James had a desire (hunger) and a belief (that food can be obtained in the cafeteria). Prior to the age of three (two in some studies) children do not make inferences that others have beliefs and desires. Presumably, the ability to better predict other people's behavior from knowledge of their beliefs and desires helped early humans solve adaptive problems such as anticipating hostile attacks, enlisting aid from those who might be inclined to give it, pacifying conflicting parents, making threats more credible, forming coalitions, and so forth.

The inferential procedures by which theory of mind modules operate are different from those by which inferences about physical entities operate. Studies support the emergence of theory of mind modules at roughly the same age in different cultures (Avis & Harris, 1991). Evidence from cognitive neuroscience suggests localization of this module, as indicated by the fact that it can be selectively damaged. Many of the features of autism, for example, appear to be caused by the localized impairment of the module (Baron-Cohen, Leslie, & Frith, 1985).

In short, solid evidence is converging from a variety of sources to point to the development in children of cognitive mechanisms specialized for making inferences about the minds of others. These mechanisms are designed to solve the adaptive problems of predicting and explaining the behavior of others and they operate on principles different from mechanisms dealing with physical entities. There is evidence that these mechanisms emerge across different cultures at roughly the same age. Selective damage to particular areas of the brain provides neurological evidence that also points to a modular mechanism.

The developmental story of theory of mind mechanisms, however, may turn out to be more complex than this. Some have speculated that theory of mind modules are far more content saturated than has yet been proposed or discovered (Buss, 1996b). This speculation is based on the idea that theories of mind must solve very different sorts of social adaptive problems. Women, for example, might have a "theory of men's minds" that differs from their "theory of women's minds" because the sorts of adaptive problems confronting women differ depending on whether they are interacting with a man or with a woman (e.g., inferences about the other's sexual desires; Haselton & Buss, 1997).

Developmentally, puberty might bring on line for females reliable ideas about the specific desires and beliefs of men—for example, that some men "just want one thing" in the domain of sexuality and relationships. Part of the postpubescent woman's theory of men's minds, based on this hypothesis, involves attributing or inferring men's desire for casual sex without commitment. The content-saturated theory of men's minds, in this speculative example, is not part of women's theories of men's minds before they reach puberty, is not part of women's theories of other women's minds, and is not part of men's theories of women's minds. One prediction based on this hypothesis is that this content-specific feature of women's theory of mind shows the properties it does—specific developmental emergence and a specific class of humans to which it is applicable—because it helped ancestral women solve a specific social adaptive problem: guarding against premature sexual involvement, which in ancestral environments could have resulted in an unwanted or an untimely pregnancy without a man around to contribute parental investment.

The social world contains an infinite number of events and properties to which one could potentially attend. Women could form theories of men's minds with respect to their desires for sugar, fat, salt, and protein or their preferences for oak trees as opposed to maples. An evolutionary psychological analysis, however, suggests that women's theories of men's minds are likely to be predisposed to learn particular classes of men's desires and beliefs—those that are especially relevant for solving adaptive problems involved in dealing with men. The psychological mechanisms of women, in short, determine the features of their social environment to which they selectively attend and about which they generate inferences and formulate theories.

The theoretical rationale for the development of theories of mind is to aid in the prediction of other people's behavior. Accurate inferences about the desires and beliefs of others enables a person to predict behavior more successfully than failing to make such inferences. Because men and women in fact do have different desires and beliefs, at least in the realm of sexuality and mating, it would be astonishing if our theories of mind were insensitive to such important differences. Because men and women have confronted different adaptive problems in dealing with members of the opposite sex, it would further be astonishing if they shared identical theories of mind about the opposite sex. Because postpubescent women face different adaptive problems in dealing with men compared to prepubescent girls, it would be equally astonishing if theories of mind were insensitive to these important developmental shifts.

Attachment and Life-History Strategies

Individuals who share a common evolved psychology can experience different early environmental events that channel them into alternative strategies. According to this notion, each person comes equipped with two or more potential strategies in his or her repertoire. From this species-typical menu, one strategy is selected based on early environmental experiences. These early experiences, in essence, "lock in" a person to one strategy to the exclusion of others that could have been pursued had the environmental input been different.

An Evolutionary Theory of Socialization. Psychologists Belsky, Steinberg, and Draper, (1991), for example, propose that a father's presence or absence early in a child's life can calibrate the kind of sexual strategy he or she adopts later in life. Individuals growing up in fatherless homes during the first five to seven years of life, according to this theory, develop the expectations that parental resources will not be reliably or predictably provided and that adult pair bonds will not be enduring. Accordingly, such individuals cultivate a sexual strategy marked by early sexual maturation, early sexual initiation, and frequent partner switching—a strategy designed to produce a large number of offspring, with low levels of investment in each. Extraverted and impulsive personality traits may accompany this strategy. Other individuals are perceived as untrustworthy, relationships as transitory. Resources sought from brief sexual liaisons are opportunistically attained and immediately extracted.

Individuals who have a reliably investing father during their first five to seven years of life, according to the theory, develop a different set of expectations about the nature and trustworthiness of others. People are seen as reliable and trustworthy, and relationships are expected to be enduring. These early environmental experiences channel individuals toward a long-term mating strategy marked by delay of sexual maturation, later onset of sexual activity, search for long-term securely attached adult relationships, and heavy investment in a small number of children.

All theories of environmental influence, including this one, ultimately rest on a foundation of evolved psychological mechanisms, whether or not they are acknowledged as such (Tooby & Cosmides, 1990). Contrary to views that perpetuate the false dichotomies of nature versus nurture or genetic versus environmental, evolved psychological mechanisms are made necessary by theories of environmental influence (Tooby & Cosmides, 1990). In this particular case the implicit psychological mechanisms are specifically designed to take as input information about the presence and reliability of paternal resources, process that input through an evolved set of decision rules, develop one of two possible psychological models of the social world, and pursue one of two alternative mating strategies as output of the mechanisms.

There are two key points to draw from this developmental theory (Belsky et al., 1991). First, the individual variation lies not on a single dimension or trait, but rather represents a coherent constellation of covarying qualities, including reproductive physiology (e.g., early age of menarche), psychological models of the social world (e.g., others as untrustworthy), and overt behavior (e.g., transitory sexual liaisons).

Second, the individual differences that result from early experiential calibration are adaptively patterned, the result of evolved mechanisms that assess the social environment and select one strategy from the menu. In one case reproductive success historically was attained through a high reproductive rate with perhaps a concomitant decrease in the survival and reproduction of any one offspring. In the other case reproductive success historically was attained through a lower reproductive rate marked by heavy investment in the survival and reproduction of fewer offspring. Different individuals confronted radically different rearing environments. Environmental variation over human evolutionary history presumably selected for developmentally flexible mechanisms that take as input the nature of the rearing environment as a key cue to the expected adult environment. See Hirsch, 1996, for a more complete view of socialization and fathering.

Attachment and Life-History Theory.   The evolutionary psychologist James Chisholm (1996) and Jay Belsky (1997) both propose an integration of life-history theory (Levins, 1968) and attachment theory (Bowlby, 1969) that suggests that these individual differences are adaptively patterned and likely to reflect the high variability of ancestral childrearing environments. Chisholm's argument starts with life history theory, the insight that life cycles constitute evolved adaptive strategies. A core principle of life-history theory is effort allocation (Levins, 1968). Individuals have finite time and resources, and decisions must be made about their allocation to different components of fitness. The components of reproductive success such as survival, growth, mating, and parenting are often in conflict. Effort allocated to one component often precludes effort allocated to the other—there are necessary trade-offs. The effort used to court additional mates, for example, conflicts with the time and energy invested in parenting. According to this theory, natural selection would have fashioned decision rules for changing the allocation of effort to these different components, depending on specific features of context. Strategies are thus "suites of functionally integrated anatomical, physiological, psychological, and developmental mechanisms for optimizing the trade-offs among the components of fitness throughout the life cycle" (Chisholm, 1996; see also Charnov, 1993; Hill, 1993; Stearns, 1992).

One of the most important trade-offs is between current and future reproduction. Increased immediate reproduction occurs at the expense of future reproduction. According to Chisholm, when resources are limited or unpredictable it may pay to increase fertility and decrease investment in any particular offspring, at least under some conditions. Chisholm further argues that the psychology of attachment constitutes an evolved set of mechanisms for making these allocation decisions.

The ancestral environments in which these mechanisms evolved, according to Chisholm, were neither as rosy nor as secure as many attachment theorists have suggested. Risk and uncertainty historically came from many sources: unpredictable food supplies, vagaries of climate and weather, diseases, parasites, predators, and, perhaps most important, other conspecifics such as one's parents. Chisholm argues that the parents' sexual strategy, including the quantity and quality of their investment in offspring, may have provided the most adaptively significant dimension of children's environments.

Variations from *secure attachment,* in this view, represent early experiential calibrations to recurrent threats to the child's survival and growth—the parent's inability or unwillingness to invest heavily in offspring. *Avoidant attachment* (the child shows indifference to the parent) represents an adaptation to parental *unwillingness* to invest, as when the parent is pursuing a short-term mating strategy rather than investing heavily in his or her offspring. *Anxious/ambivalent attachment* (in which the child shows nervousness, fearfulness, and insecurity), in contrast, represents an adaptation to parental *inability* to invest—as when the mother herself is irritable, preoccupied, fearful, hungry, or exhausted. According to Belsky (1997), the secure attachment functioned to promote a strategy of high-investment parenting; the avoidant attachment functioned to promote an opportunistic interpersonal style marked by low-investment parenting; and anxious/ambivalent attachment evolved to foster a "helpers at the nest" style, whereby children remained at home to aid the rearing of their parents' other children.

Given the early stage of theory building, the precise nature of the underlying psychological mechanisms has not been articulated (see Simpson, in press, for a review). Chisholm presumably does not mean to imply that an infant can literally draw inferences that distinguish between parental intent (unwillingness to invest) and capacity (ability to invest). Rather, the infant presumably detects parental behaviors that are probabilistically linked with these differing states, upon which different attachment styles are activated from the triadic menu. The next decade of research should witness more direct focus on the precise nature of the psychological mechanisms underlying different attachment styles.

Do attachment styles represent early environmental calibration, or do they reflect heritable individual differences, as suggested by some research (Goldsmith & Harmon, 1994)? Are individual differences in attachment stable over the life course? Do the underlying psychological mechanisms of attachment coordinate with the specific features of adaptive problems posed by each alternative strategy? These questions await further conceptual and empirical work. Nonetheless, recent studies have demonstrated that early age of menarche is indeed linked with parental marital unhappiness and more rejection from the father, as well as with an earlier age of dating men, suggesting much promise for the theory of early attachment in promoting different adult sexual strategies (Kim, Smith, & Palermiti, 1997), although it is not inconsistent with a pure heritability interpretation.

In summary, theory of mind, parental socialization, language development, and attachment styles represent a small sampling of the ways in which evolutionary developmental psychologists approach changes over time in the human life course. Others include the role of prolonged immaturity and play in human development (Bjorklund, 1997), children's motivations to join peer groups (MacDonald, 1996), the development of inhibitory mechanisms such as the delay of gratification and sexual restraint (Bjorklund & Kiel, 1996), the evolutionary aspects of adolescence such as mate competition and puberty rites (Surbey, 1998; Weisfeld, 1997; Weisfeld & Billings, 1988), sex-linked socialization practices (Low, 1989), and attachment styles as they affect adult romantic relationships (Kirkpatrick, 1998). Ultimately, a comprehensive evolutionary developmental psychology will include an account of the species-typical, sex-differentiated, and individually differentiated transformations over the life span of the adaptive problems faced and the psychological mechanisms activated.

Evolutionary Personality Psychology

Personality psychology may be the broadest and most encompassing branch of psychology. Historically, all "grand" theories of personality have hypotheses about the contents of human nature at their core, such as motives for sex and aggression (Sigmund Freud), self-actualization (Abraham Maslow), striving for superiority (Adler), or striving for status and intimacy (David McClelland; Henry Murray; Jerry Wiggins). Hypothesized psychological features of human nature have provided much of the "core" around which these grand theories of personality have been constructed.

On the other hand, personality psychology has also been centrally concerned with the enduring ways in which individuals differ. Much current personality research explores questions such as: What are the most important ways individuals differ? What are the origins of individual differences? What are the psychological and physiological correlates of individual differences? What are the consequences of particular dimensions of individual differences for social interaction, psychopathology, well-being, and the life course?

Most research and theory in evolutionary psychology has focused on species-typical psychological mechanisms, as discussed throughout this book. Individual differences, in contrast, have been relatively neglected and pose a greater challenge for evolutionary psychologists (Buss & Greiling, 1999; MacDonald, 1995; Tooby & Cosmides, 1990; Wilson, 1994). Evolutionary biologists, as a general rule, have tended to focus on species-typical adaptations, ignoring individual differences except in their role of providing the raw materials on which natural selection operates. Individual differences, particularly those that are heritable, are often relegated to secondary status because they are thought to originate primarily through nonselection forces such as random mutation (Tooby & Cosmides, 1990; Wilson, 1994). Genetic differences are sometimes viewed as "noise" or "genetic junk" maintained within a population precisely because they are presumed to be *unrelated* to the core of the evolutionary process—adaptation and natural selection (Thiessen, 1972). Heritable individual differences are to species-typical adaptations, in this view, as differences in the colors of the wires in a car engine are to the engine's functional working components—one can vary the coloring of the wires without affecting the functioning of the engine (Tooby & Cosmides, 1990).

If unity of science is taken to be a reasonable goal (Wilson, 1998), these different conceptualizations are difficult to reconcile. Because natural selection tends to reduce genetic variability within populations by favoring some genes and weeding out others, why do behavioral genetic studies consistently find moderate heritability for personality dispositions (Plomin et al., 1997)? If individual differences really are independent of adaptation and natural selection, why are individual differences reliably linked to activities closely connected with reproductive success, such as survival and sexuality? Individual differences in extraversion, for example, are linked with differences in sexual access to partners (Eysenck, 1976). Conscientiousness is known to be correlated with work and status attainment (Kyl-Heku & Buss, 1996). Impulsivity is linked with extramarital affairs (Buss & Shackelford, 1997a) and higher mortality rates (Friedman et al., 1995). If the individual differences studied by personality psychologists are reliably linked with reproductively relevant phenomena such as status, sexuality, and even survival, perhaps they play a more important role in human evolutionary psychology than previously assumed.

Evolutionary psychology is now grappling with ways to incorporate individual differences and species-typical psychological mechanisms within a unified conceptual framework (e.g., Bailey, 1998; Buss & Greiling, 1999; Gangestad & Simpson, 1990; MacDonald, 1995; Wilson, 1994). Several avenues look promising.

Individual differences can emerge from a variety of heritable and nonheritable sources. Evidence from behavioral genetic studies of personality strongly suggests that both are important. Personality characteristics commonly show evidence of moderate heritability, typically ranging from 30 to 50 percent (Plomin, DeFries, & McClearn, 1990). Simultaneously, these studies provide the strongest evidence of environmental sources of variance, ranging from 50 to 70 percent. Below are several suggestions for exploring adaptively patterned individual differences based on environmental and heritable sources, as well as interactions between these sources (Bailey, 1998; Buss & Greiling, 1999).

Alternative Niche Picking or Strategic Specialization

From an evolutionary perspective, competition is keenest among those pursuing the same strategy. As one niche becomes more and more crowded with competitors, success of those in the niche can suffer compared with those seeking alternative niches (Maynard Smith, 1982; Wilson, 1994). Selection favors mechanisms that cause some individuals to seek niches in which the competition is less intense, and hence in which the average payoff may be higher.

Mating provides some clear examples. If most women pursue the man with the highest status or greatest resources, then some women would achieve more success by courting males outside the arenas in which competition is keenest. In a mating system in which both polygyny and monogamy are possible, for example, a woman might be better off securing all of the resources of a lower-status monogamous man rather than having to settle for a fraction of the resources of a high-status polygynous man.

The ability to exploit a niche will depend on the resources and personal characteristics an individual brings to the situation. Consider a person's birth order. It is possible that first borns and later borns have faced, on average, recurrently different adaptive problems over human evolutionary history. The historian of science Frank Sulloway (1996), for example, argues that first borns occupy a niche characterized by strong identification with parents and other existing authority figures. Later borns, in contrast, have less to gain from authority identification, and more to gain by overthrowing the existing order. According to Sulloway, birth order influences niche specialization. Later borns develop a different personality marked by greater rebelliousness, lower levels of conscientiousness, and higher levels of openness to new experiences (Sulloway, 1996). Birth order differences show up strongly among scientists, where later borns tend to be strong advocates of scientific revolutions; first borns tend to strenuously resist such revolutions (Sulloway, 1996).

Whether the details of Sulloway's arguments turn out to be correct, the example illustrates strategic niche specialization. Individual differences are adaptively patterned, but they are *not* based on heritable individual differences. Rather, birth order, a nonheritable individual difference, provides input (presumably through interactions with family members) into a species-typical mechanism that shapes strategic niche specialization.

Heritable individual differences also can provide input into species-typical evolved psychological mechanisms and, in addition, can evolve as a consequence of strategic niche specialization—possibilities to which we now turn.

Adaptive Assessment of Heritable Qualities

Suppose all men have an evolved decision rule of this form: Pursue an aggressive strategy when aggression can be successfully implemented to achieve goals, but pursue a cooperative strategy when aggression cannot be successfully implemented (modified from Tooby & Cosmides, 1990, p. 58). Evolved decision rules are undoubtedly more complex than this. Given this simplified rule, however, those who happen to be mesomorphic (muscular) in body build can carry out an aggressive strategy more successfully than those who are ectomorphic (skinny) or endomorphic (rotund). Heritable individual differences in body build provide input into the decision rule, thereby producing stable individual differences in aggression and cooperativeness. In this example the proclivity toward aggression is not directly heritable, but rather would be "reactively heritable" in the sense that it is a secondary consequence of heritable body build that provides input into species-typical mechanisms of self-assessment and decision making.

Tooby and Cosmides (1990) coined the term "reactive heritability" to describe evolved psychological mechanisms designed to take as input heritable qualities as a guide to strategic solutions. According to this view, selection will favor the evolution of assessment mechanisms if such appraisals help a person choose wise strategies. Evolved mechanisms, in this view, are not only attuned to recurrent features of the external world, such as the reliability of parental provisioning, but can also be attuned to the evaluation of the self.

Assessment of heritable qualities may also aid in the choice of mating strategies. Recall from Chapter 12 the study that examined the physical appearances of teenage boys on two dimensions—the degree to which their faces looked dominant or submissive and how physically attractive others found them to be (Mazur, Halpern, & Udry, 1994). Photographs were used for the judgments of these features, with a dominant person being defined as someone who "tells other people what to do, is respected, influential, and often a leader" (p. 90). The teenagers who were judged to be more facially dominant and physically attractive were discovered to have had more heterosexual experience with "heavy petting" and sexual intercourse. Furthermore, dominant facial appearance predicted cumulative coital experience, even after statistically controlling for facial attractiveness and pubertal development.

On the assumption that facial features involved in appearing dominant and attractive are partially heritable, one can speculate that males have an evolved psychological mechanism designed to appraise the degree to which one appears dominant and attractive: "If high on these dimensions, pursue a short-term sexual strategy; if low, pursue a long-term sexual strategy." In this example, of course, one cannot rule out other variables, such as testosterone, which may simultaneously produce a more dominant-looking face and a higher sex drive.

According to the conception of evolved assessment mechanisms designed to appraise one's heritable qualities, stable individual differences in the pursuit of short-term and long-term sexual strategies are not directly heritable. Instead, they represent adaptive individual differences based on assessment of heritable information. Future research in evolutionary personality psychology can be expected to uncover the nature of evolved assessment mechanisms.

Frequency-Dependent Adaptive Strategies

In general, the process of directional selection tends to use up heritable variation. Heritable variants that are more successful tend to replace those that are less successful, resulting in species-typical adaptations that show little or no heritable variation in the presence or absence of basic functional components (Williams, 1966; 1975).

There is a major exception to this trend—frequency-dependent selection. In some contexts, two or more heritable variants can be sustained in equilibrium. The most obvious example is biological sex. In sexually reproducing species, the two sexes represent frequency-dependent suites of covarying adaptive complexes. If one sex becomes rare relative to the other, success increases for the rare sex, and hence selection favors parents who produce offspring of the less common sex. Typically the sexes are maintained in an approximately equal ratio through the process of frequency-dependent selection. Frequency-dependent selection requires that the payoff of each strategy decreases as its frequency increases, relative to other strategies in the population (see Maynard Smith, 1982, and D. S. Wilson, 1998, for extensive treatments in the context of game theory).

Alternative adaptive strategies can also be maintained *within the sexes* by frequency-dependent selection. Among bluegill sunfish, for example, three different male mating strategies are observed—a "parental" strategy that defends the nest, a "sneak" strategy that matures to only a small body size, and a "mimic" strategy that resembles the female form (Gross, 1982). The sneakers gain sexual access to the female eggs by avoiding detection because of their small size and the mimics gain access by resembling females and thus avoiding aggression from the parental males. As the mimic strategists increase in frequency, however, their success decreases—their existence depends on the parentals who guard the nest from predation. Parentals become rarer as the mimics and sneakers become more common, rendering these parasitic strategies more difficult to pursue. Thus, heritable alternative strategies within the sexes are maintained by the process of frequency-dependent selection. Theoretically these heritable individual differences can persist in the population indefinitely through frequency-dependent selection, unlike the process of directional selection, which tends to drive out heritable variation.

Mealey's Theory of Psychopathy. The evolutionary psychologist Linda Mealey (1995) proposed a theory of psychopathy based on frequency-dependent selection. Psychopathy (sometimes called sociopathy or antisocial personality disorder) represents a cluster of traits marked by irresponsible and unreliable behavior, egocentrism, impulsivity, an inability to form lasting relationships, superficial social charm, and a deficit of social emotions such as love, shame, guilt, and empathy (Cleckley, 1982). Psychopaths pursue a deceptive or "cheating" strategy in their social interactions. Psychopathy is more common among men than women, making up roughly 3 to 4 percent of the former and less than 1 percent of the latter (Mealey, 1995).

Psychopaths pursue a social strategy characterized by exploiting the reciprocity mechanisms of others. After feigning cooperation, psychopaths typically defect. This cheating strategy might be pursued by men who are unlikely to outcompete other men in a more traditional or mainstream status hierarchy (Mealey, 1995).

According to the theory, a psychopathic strategy can be maintained by frequency-dependent selection. As the number of cheaters increases, and hence the average cost to the cooperative hosts increases, mechanisms would presumably evolve to detect cheating and inflict costs on those pursuing a cheating strategy. As the prevalence of psychopaths increases, therefore, the average payoff of the psychopath strategy decreases. As long as the frequency of psychopaths is not too large, it can be maintained amidst a population composed primarily of cooperators (Mealey, 1995).

There is some evidence—albeit indirect—that is at least consistent with Mealey's theory of psychopathy. First, behavioral genetic studies suggest that psychopathy may be moderately heritable (Willerman, Loehlin, & Horn, 1992). Second, some psychopaths appear to pursue an exploitative short-term sexual strategy, which could be the primary route through which genes for psychopathy increase or are maintained (Rowe, 1995). Psychopathic men tend to be more sexually precocious, have sex with a larger number of people, have more illegitimate children, and are more likely to separate from their wives than nonpsychopathic men (Rowe, 1995). This short-term, opportunistic, exploitative sexual strategy would be expected to increase in populations marked by high mobility, where the reputational costs associated with such a strategy would be low (Wilson, 1995).

There are several challenges to this theory, such as whether it represents a type or a continuum (Baldwin, 1995), whether its frequency is sufficiently large to be maintained by frequency-dependent selection, and whether it represents a recently evolved cluster in modern populations or an ancient evolved strategy (Wilson, 1995).

Despite these complications, Mealey's theory of psychopathy nicely illustrates the possibility that heritable alternative strategies can be maintained by frequency-dependent selection. Frequency-dependent selection offers a potential explanation for integrating the cumulative results from behavioral genetic studies (e.g., Willerman, Loehlin, & Horn, 1992) and the findings on the sexual strategies apparently pursued by psychopaths (Rowe, 1995) with an evolutionary analysis of adaptive individual differences.

In summary, evolutionary psychology offers a framework for considering a variety of individual differences. Differences can arise from early environmental experiences, such as father presence or absence, which can channel an individual's development toward different adaptive strategies. Differences can arise from the occupancy of different environments in adulthood, which recurrently activate a particular mechanism. Differences can arise from alternative niche picking. And differences can arise through frequency-dependent selection. These sources of individual difference hold the promise of providing a truly integrative personality theory that includes both core premises about human nature and the major ways in which individuals differ.

Evolutionary Clinical Psychology

The concept of mental disorder occupies a central place in the field of clinical psychology. Clearly articulated conceptual criteria for identifying mental disorder are important for the advancement of psychological science and its applications. Such criteria provide a framework for determining when individuals are functioning well or poorly, and what can be done to successfully treat them as needed.

Psychologists often invoke terms such as *adjusted* and *maladjusted, adaptive* and *maladaptive, normal* and *abnormal* to identify mental disorder. However, these terms lack clear definitional criteria and thus beg the question why they imply disorder. Many authors implicitly appeal to intuitions, presumably shared by readers, about what is good or bad, desirable or undesirable. Indeed, the Diagnostic and Statistical Manual of Mental Disorders (American Psychiatric Association, 1994) offers such a model of mental disorder in its discussion of terms used to define disorder, including dyscontrol, disadvantage, inflexibility, and irrationality. When explicit criteria for mental disorder are specified they are often simple heuristic rules, such as notions of subjective distress, bizarreness, social harmfulness, and inefficiency (e.g., American Psychiatric Association, 1994).

Evolutionary psychology offers the potential for escaping intuitive appeals by providing a more rigorous set of explicit principles for identifying the presence of disorder (see Buss et al., 1997; Wakefield, 1992). Once an evolved psychological mechanism has been described and its proper function identified, a clear criterion exists for determining dysfunction: *Dysfunction occurs when the mechanism is not performing as it was designed to perform in the contexts in which it was designed to function.* A dysfunction of evolved mechanisms would be indicated, for example, if one's blood failed to clot after one's skin was cut, if one failed to sweat in response to external heat, or if one's larynx failed to rise to close off the passage to the lungs upon swallowing food.

According to the present definition of dysfunction, evolved mechanisms can fail in three distinct ways: (1) the mechanism fails to become activated when the relevant adaptive problem is confronted (e.g., one confronts a dangerous snake threatening to strike, but fails to get afraid or take evasive action); (2) the mechanism becomes activated in contexts in which it was not designed to become activated (e.g., becomes sexually attracted to inappropriate persons, such as close genetic relatives); and (3) the mechanism fails to coordinate as it was designed to coordinate with other mechanisms (e.g., self-assessments of mate value fail to guide the sorts of people to whom one devotes mating effort).

Causes of Mechanism Failure

Each of the three types of mechanism failure—activation failure, context failure, and coordination failure—can arise as a result of genetic factors (e.g., chance genetic variation or genetic defects) or developmental insults (e.g., brain injury), or a combination of these causes. Brain-injured aphasics, for example, experience failures of the evolved mechanisms underlying speech production and comprehension. They appear to understand language, but are unable to speak fluently. This suggests that language input is received and processed appropriately, but that the mechanisms underlying speech production are not properly coordinated with the speech comprehension mechanisms. Alternatively, there might exist activation or processing failures within the speech-production mechanisms themselves (Pinker, 1994).

Chance genetic variation might underlie some mechanism failures. Although natural selection tends to produce species-typical evolved mechanisms, heritable variation may remain in the surface features of a mechanism. Nearly all humans possess functionally similar eyes, hearts, and lungs, but there are heritable individual differences in the structural forms assumed by these mechanisms (e.g., there may be slight individual differences in lung shape). This variation is largely selectively neutral. There may be rare cases, however, in which genetic variants co-occur to produce mechanism failures. These variants are not harmful when they exist singularly, but in rare combinations they are dysfunctional. Some researchers have speculated that rare gene couplings may underlie certain types of schizophrenia (Gottesman, 1991).

Another source of variation is mutations. Although mutations provide the variation necessary for natural selection to occur, isolated mutations rarely enhance functioning and can be deleterious, leading to mechanism failures (Tooby & Cosmides, 1990; 1992). Yet mechanism failures may not be recognized by clinicians and researchers as dysfunctions. They may not be manifested as bizarre behavior, personal distress, an inability to care for oneself, or social harm. In some cases dysfunctions might lead to a more enjoyable life, as when the evolved mechanisms regulating anxiety and depression fail to operate as they were designed to do. In other cases mechanism failures do cause significant personal distress and social harm and are thus recognized by researchers and clinicians as worthy of treatment and further study. The implication of this analysis is not that only the three categories of dysfunction noted above should be treated by psychologists, however. Instead, this framework should serve to better inform clinical research and help to clarify the longstanding confusion about what is properly considered a dysfunction and what the treatment implications might be, given its causes.

Evolutionary Insights into Problems Erroneously Thought to Be Dysfunctions

Although a variety of human behaviors and experiences appear disordered, maladaptive, maladjusted, costly, or subjectively distressful, they are not dysfunctions. They are not caused by the failure of evolved mechanisms to function as they were designed by selection to do. These apparently disordered behaviors and experiences fall into several major classes.

First, there can be a *discrepancy between ancestral and modern environments* (Glantz & Pearce, 1989). Our modern environment differs in many ways, sometimes radically, from the environments present over most of human evolutionary history. An evolved mechanism could be functioning precisely as it was designed to function, but because the environment has changed the outcome may appear maladaptive. A discrepancy between ancestral and modern environments might change the nature of the adaptive problem, or it might render the adaptive problem irrelevant in current environments.

At a psychological level humans might have evolved mechanisms designed to assess their mate value relative to the individuals in their environment. Ancestral environments were probably populated with relatively small groups of people containing around fifty to one hundred individuals (Tooby & DeVore, 1987). Assessments of relative mate value were probably fairly accurate. One result of these accurate assessments might have been to focus individuals' attraction tactics on potential mates within their own mate value range. In our current environment, however, the population is substantially larger, and the images individuals are exposed to through various forms of media (especially television and print media) may present an unprecedented comparison standard. Fashion models and actresses, for example, are often highly physically attractive. Extremely attractive women are a tiny fraction of the population; yet images of these women are presented at a misleadingly high frequency. This might have the effect of artificially lowering women's judgments of their value as a potential mate, relative to competitors in the *local* pool of potential mates. This, in turn, might escalate intrasexual competition between women or cause them to take drastic measures to try to increase their attractiveness (Buss, 1996a). In extreme cases women might develop body image disorders, eating disorders such as anorexia and bulimia, or depression.

Evolutionarily novel contexts may also produce apparently disordered outcomes. A man's sexual jealousy mechanism, for example, may operate as it was designed to do—the mechanism detects cues to infidelity, weighs them, and generates the outputs of jealousy and anger. This man's anger and jealousy may no longer serve their intended-function, however. Ready access to evolutionarily novel weaponry such as guns might make killing his mate a more probable consequence of the man's anger and jealousy than frightening or intimidating her as a means of preventing further infidelity.

In sum, discrepancies between modern and ancestral contexts can produce psychological problems. These should not be construed as dysfunctions, however, because the evolved mechanisms are still operating in the manner in which they were designed to operate.

A second source of problems can arise from *normal mistakes accompanying the "on average" functioning of a mechanism*. All mechanisms work because, on average, the benefits outweighed the costs across a sample space of instances in ancestral environments, not because they work in all instances. Because evolved mechanisms are selected based on their "average" effects, a properly functioning mechanism can produce many mistakes, but these mistakes do not necessarily signify dysfunction (Schlager, 1995). Perceiving a dangerous animal behind a tree when one is not there and inferring sexual intent when none is there are mistakes but may not be dysfunctional because, on average, the threshold for perceiving these phenomena led to greater inclusive fitness than did alternative thresholds. These normal mistakes must be distinguished from instances of true dysfunction. This can be accomplished by specifying adaptive problems and modeling the costs and benefits associated with solving each adaptive problem. In inferring female sexual interest, for example, the costs ancestral men incurred when making a false-positive inference (assuming sexual interest when it did not exist) may have been outweighed by the costs of a false-negative inference (assuming no sexual interest when it did exist), leading to a lower sexual inference threshold than would yield maximal accuracy (Haselton & Buss, 1997). In sum, what might at first appear to be a disorder may simply be the proper functioning of an evolved mechanism that produces mistakes because it is designed to solve adaptive problems "on average" rather than successfully all of the time.

A third source of problems sometimes erroneously believed to represent disorders is *subjective distress produced by the normal operation of functional mechanisms*. Many of our evolved psychological mechanisms lead to outcomes that are subjectively distressful. Depression, for example, is experienced by an estimated 10 percent of young adults in the United States. Because of its prevalence and close relation to sadness, depressed mood has been proposed a reliable effect of the experience of loss (of money, mate, reputation, etc.; Nesse & Williams, 1994; Price & Sloman, 1987). Although the experience of depression can be incredibly frustrating for those so inflicted, this emotional pain may have adaptive functions. First, a depressed mood helps us to disengage from a hopeless enterprise that may be causing losses and consider other directions. Second, it deflates our "blind" human optimism, thus allowing us to more objectively reassess our goals (Nesse & Williams, 1994; Stevens & Price, 1996).

Anxiety, too, involves subjective distress, but is produced by the normal operation of a functional mechanism that, in the face of a threat, alters our thinking, behavior, and physiology in advantageous ways (Nesse & Williams, 1994). It keeps us cautious and attentive to the possibility of physical or social harm. Although useful, the stress response is costly (excessive calorie use, tissue damage); thus, there must be a reason why anxious responses occur so frequently. From an evolutionary perspective the answer is clear: Of one hundred potentially dangerous situations, one death is more costly than responding to ninety-nine false alarms (Nesse & Williams, 1994).

Panic attacks may represent a functional component of the anxiety system that protects against the specific threat of attack. The cues that elicit panic are well suited to its evolved function to protect in the face of potential attack: being in wide-open spaces, being unaccompanied and far from home, and being in places where intense fear has occurred before. Panic is a defense against a particular type of threat; *faulty regulation* of panic results in panic disorder (Nesse, 1990).

In sum, evolutionary psychology helps us understand why we experience negative mood states. Subjective distress may not always represent a clinical disorder, but may signal the proper functioning of an evolved psychological mechanism.

A fourth source of problems stems from *socially undesirable behavior produced by the normal operation of functional mechanisms*. Some of our evolved mechanisms lead to outcomes that are socially undesirable. Psychopathy is one example. Void of medical incapacitations, psychopaths are identified as diseased because of their disregard for societal norms regulating cooperative reciprocity. However, psychopaths may, in fact, display behavior that is produced by the normal function of a mechanism designed to promote cheating behavior in specific ancestral contexts. For example, when sustained social interactions were not expected to occur, successful cheaters would have been able to reap the benefits of a few skewed interactions within a certain group before having to pay a cost (e.g., moving on to a new group) once their cheating behaviors were detected (Harpending & Sobus, 1987). Psychopaths do appear to display several behaviors and traits that may be the effects of an evolved cheater mechanism. These traits and behaviors include sudden changes in plan, charm, high mobility, promiscuity, and use of aliases (Harpending & Sobus, 1987; Lykken, 1995). It is not surprising that evolutionary psychology helps us understand why psychopathic behaviors are judged undesirable—they jeopardize our own reproductive interests. Evolutionary psychology also helps us understand why we are so wary of potential cheaters: We have evolved mechanisms that function to protect our own interests.

Child abuse and neglect, including infanticide, may be undesirable behaviors produced by the normal operation of mechanisms that function to reduce the investment of resources in nonrelatives (Daly & Wilson, 1988). To illustrate, stepparenthood is the single best predictor of child abuse. In England, Scott (1973) reported that more than half of twenty battered baby cases involved a stepfather, although only 1 percent of babies in the general population were living with a stepfather at that time. In other words, infants and children living with a stepparent are more than forty times more likely to experience child abuse than those living with two genetic parents. According to Daly and Wilson (1988), the ambiguity of the stepparent's situation resides not in a lack of knowledge about the stepparent role, but rather in genuine conflicts of interest within the stepfamily that may, unfortunately, result in the abuse or neglect of an unrelated child.

The implications of evolutionizing clinical psychology are profound (Glantz & Pearce, 1989). Properly understanding the design of something greatly improves the chances you can fix the system when it breaks down. This is why you take your car to a mechanic—you only know how to drive it, but the mechanic knows more about precisely how it was designed and how its mechanisms are meant to function. An evolutionary perspective also gives guidance about when to intervene. In some cases we might only be treating the symptom, such as anxiety or depression, rather than the source (Nesse, 1990; 1991; Nesse & Williams, 1994). If we mask these symptoms we may thwart an otherwise natural healing process. This is analogous to treating a fever or a cough—these are mechanisms designed to help fix an infection or extrude foreign matter from the respiratory system, for example. If you medicate the fever or cough it is possible to damage the whole system. Similarly, treating depression or anxiety (e.g., through drugs such as Prozac) may fail to get at the underlying causes of depression and anxiety (Nesse & Williams, 1994). In sum, evolutionary psychology offers much promise of new and profound insights into clinical psychology.

Evolutionary Cultural Psychology

Some psychologists perpetuate the false dichotomy between "culture" and "biology" as though the two were somehow in causal competition. Statements to the effect that "culture overrides biology" and "animals have instincts, humans have culture" reflect this false dualism. Evolutionary psychology provides a true interactionist position that shows why these dichotomies are false. As we will see in this section, "culture" cannot be viewed as a separate cause because it rests on a foundation of evolved psychological mechanisms.

Social scientists who grapple with culture typically start with the observation that groups of people in one place differ in some ways from groups of people in other places. The Yanomamö Indians of Venezuela proudly reveal on the tops of their heads the scars they get in club fights. In other cultures men and women put bones through their noses, tattoo their lips, pierce their ears, or put safety pins though their cheeks. Psychologists note these differences and attribute them to "culture." They presume that "biology" refers to what is invariant across humans and "culture" refers to what is variable, so it seems self-evident that "culture" accounts for the variability (Tooby & Cosmides, 1992).

Evolutionary psychology provides a different perspective. To begin with, patterns of local within-group similarity and between-group differences are best regarded as phenomena that require explanation. Transforming these differences into an autonomous causal entity called "culture" confuses the phenomena that require explanation with a proper explanation of the phenomena. Attributing such phenomena to culture provides no more explanatory power than attributing them to God, consciousness, learning, socialization, or even evolution, unless the causal processes subsumed by these labels are properly described. Labels for phenomena are not proper causal explanations for them.

Once we have identified in a general way the phenomena we are interested in explaining—ideas, practices, rituals, artifacts, beliefs, representations, music, and art that are shared within some groups but not others—the next step is to outline the potential causal explanations for them. A start along these lines makes a distinction between evoked and transmitted culture (Tooby & Cosmides, 1992).

Evoked Culture

All evolved mechanisms are responsive to environmental conditions—the pupils of eyes, sweat glands, sexual arousal, and jealousy are a few obvious examples of such mechanisms. *Evoked culture* refers to phenomena that are triggered differentially in some groups more than others by differing environmental conditions. The deeper tans among Californians than among Oregonians, for example, appear to reflect the differing levels of exposure to sunlight in the two states. Such "cultural differences" are explained simply by invoking a universal shared evolved mechanism combined with local between-group differences in input into that mechanism.

A concrete potential example of evoked culture is found in the patterns of cooperative food sharing among different bands of hunter-gatherers (Cosmides & Tooby, 1992). Different classes of food have different variances in their distribution. Among the Ache tribe of Paraguay, for example, meat from hunting is a high-variance resource. On any given day, the odds that a hunter will come back with meat are only 60 percent. On any particular day, one hunter will be successful while another will come back empty handed. Gathering food, on the other hand, is a lower variance food resource, with yield depending more on the effort a person expends.

One variable triggering communal food sharing appears to be high variance in the food resource (Cosmides & Tooby, 1992). Under high-variance conditions there are tremendous benefits to sharing. You share your meat today with an unlucky friend who failed, but next week you might be the beneficiary of reciprocity, when you come back empty handed. The benefits of engaging in cooperative food sharing under conditions of high variance are compounded by the fact that a person can consume only so much meat, and further gorging after being full does not bring much benefit. Under low-variance conditions, on the other hand, the benefits of food sharing are far less. Because gathered food depends on individual effort, sharing merely entails giving by those who work hard to those who are lazy.

Within the Ache, meat is shared communally. Hunters deposit their kill with a "distributor," who then allocates portions to different families, based largely on family size. In the same tribe, however, gathered food is not shared outside the kin group. Halfway around the world, in the Kalahari desert, the evolutionist Elizabeth Cashden (1989) found that some San groups are more egalitarian than others, and that these cultural differences are closely linked with the variance in the food supply. The !Kung San's food supply is highly variable, and they show much food sharing. To be called a *stinge* (stingy) is one of the worst insults, and costly reputational damage is incurred for failing to share food. Among the Gana San, in contrast, food variance is low, and they tend to hoard their food more and rarely share it outside their extended families. These examples show that environmental conditions that differ from place to place can trigger the activation of different psychological mechanisms across groups. Cultural differences of this sort are examples of evoked culture. They are explained by understanding how universal evolved mechanisms are differentially activated across groups—in this case by differences in the variability of food sources.

Another example of evoked culture comes from an analysis of cultural differences in the importance attached to physical attractiveness. Evolutionary psychologist Steve Gangestad reasoned that because parasites are known to degrade physical appearance, people living in ecologies with a high prevalence of parasites should place a greater value on physical attractiveness in a mate than people living in ecologies with a low prevalence of parasites (Gangestad & Buss, 1993). To test this hypothesis the prevalence of parasites in twenty-nine cultures was correlated with the importance that the people in those cultures attached to physical attractiveness in a marriage partner. The results confirmed the hypothesis: The greater the parasite prevalence, the more important was physical attractiveness (see Figure 13.4). Although these findings can be interpreted in a variety of ways, they are at least consistent with the idea of evoked culture—cultural differences

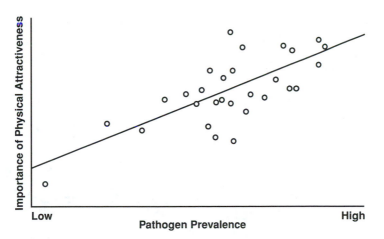

FIGURE 13.4 Parasite Prevalence and Importance of Attractiveness. The prevalance of parasites in the local ecology strongly predicts the importance people in the culture place on physical attractiveness in a long-term mate. Each circle in the graph represents one culture. This study illustrates that evolutionary psychology, in principle, can account for variability across cultures, in addition to human universals. Data from Gangestad & Buss (1993).

that are explained by a universal psychological mechanism that is differentially activated across groups.

Many other examples currently attributed to "culture" may eventually be explained as examples of evoked culture, such as cultural differences in reactions to insults (Nisbett, 1993), cultural differences in rates of infidelity (Buss, 1994), and cultural differences in preferences for thin versus plump body types (Symons, 1979).

Transmitted Culture

Transmitted culture represents another class of phenomena that requires a different sort of explanation. Transmitted culture refers to representations or ideas that originally exist in at least one mind and are transferred to other minds through observation or interaction (Tooby & Cosmides, 1992). The hula hoop craze, changes in clothing style or fashion, beliefs about alien beings, and jokes that are passed from one person to another are examples of transmitted culture. These phenomena require the existence of specialized inference mechanisms in the "recipients" that recreate the representation in their minds.

The existence of specialized inference mechanisms in accounting for transmitted culture is essential from the perspective of evolutionary psychology. Because "information" emanating from other individuals in one's social group is limitless, a potentially infinite array of ideas compete for the limited attention spans of humans. Evolved psychological mechanisms in the receivers must sift through this barrage of ideas, selecting only a small subset for psychological reconstruction. The subset that is selectively adopted and internally reconstructed in individuals depends on a foundation of evolved psychological mechanisms. Thus transmitted culture, like evoked culture, rests on a foundation of evolved psychological mechanisms.

At present, we do not know what these mechanisms are, but we do know what some of their properties must be. They must include procedures for *selectively attending* to some ideas and ignoring others; *selectively encoding* some in memory and forgetting others; and *selectively transmitting* some to other people while failing to transmit others. Presumably these mechanisms are highly saturated with content that determines relevance to the person—relevance on dimensions that would have affected fitness in ancestral environments.

Consider the tendency of humans to imitate the clothing styles of high-status members of their local social groups or the groups to which they aspire to belong. These cultural phenomena are examples of transmitted culture. But these phenomena rest on a foundation of evolved psychological mechanisms that cause people to attend to high-status people more than low-status people, encode in memory their clothing styles, access such memories when shopping for clothes, and so on.

A full account of transmitted culture ultimately will rest not just on the psychological mechanisms of those who "receive" the cultural representations of others. It will also rest on understanding mechanisms of those who *actively transmit* cultural representations. As Allport and Postman pointed out long ago, "Rumor is set in motion and continues to travel by its appeal to the strong personal interests of individuals involved in the transmission" (1947, p. 314). The intentional spread of rumors is a perfect example of transmitted culture, and understanding a rumor will require knowing the motivations and interests of those responsible for doing the spreading (e.g., derogating a rival to lower his or her perceived mate value).

Not all rumors are equally well remembered or transmitted. Nor is the same rumor equally encoded and transmitted by all individuals who are exposed to it. Consider the rumor "John is out to use women and would sleep with nearly anyone." In evaluating this rumor our psychological mechanisms undoubtedly cause us to selectively attend to certain features. Is the source of the rumor one of John's competitors or enemies? If so, perhaps the information will be discounted and fail to spread. Is the source the father or brother of a woman John is courting, whose goals are to protect her from exploitative men? Is the source a woman who is really interested in John herself and who spreads the rumor to dissuade other women from getting involved with him? The interests of the individuals who start rumors can determine which rumors get transmitted and by whom. The interests and intentions of the sources of rumors are critical in determining the degree to which each rumor is attended to, encoded, retrieved, and transmitted, perhaps with predictable distortions, to others.

This account of cultural phenomena is, of course, incomplete and simplified. But it is sufficient to draw the following conclusions: (1) "Culture" is not an autonomous causal agent in competition with "biology" for explanatory power; (2) cultural diversities—local within-group similarities and between-group differences—are phenomena to be explained, but do not, by themselves, provide an explanation for cultural phenomena; (3) cultural phenomena can be usefully divided into types, such as evoked culture and transmitted culture; (4) explanations for evoked culture require a foundation of evolved psychological mechanisms, without which the differently activated cultural diversity could not occur; and (5) transmitted culture also rests on a foundation of evolved psychological mechanisms that influence which ideas are attended to, encoded, retrieved from memory, and transmitted to other individuals.

The Evolution of Art, Fiction, Movies, and Music

Why do people engage in so many activities that seem to have nothing whatsoever to do with survival and reproduction? Why do people spend hours, days, months, and years creating and consuming art, literature, music, and sporting events? These seemingly "trivial pursuits" dominate some people's entire lives. These patterns require explanation. Bear in mind, however, that the proposed evolutionary explanations are highly speculative, albeit with some supporting empirical data.

Evolutionary psychologists have taken two basic approaches to answering these puzzles. The first approach may be called the *display hypothesis*. According to this hypothesis, culture is "an emergent phenomenon arising from sexual competition among vast numbers of individuals pursuing different mating strategies in different mating arenas" (Miller, 1998, p. 118). Men in particular tend to create and display art and music as a strategy for broadcasting courtship displays to a wide variety of women. The study's author, Geoffrey Miller, cites the rock musician Jimi Hendrix, who had affairs with hundreds of groupies and fathered children in four different countries before dying at age twenty-seven from a drug overdose. He also cites the numerous sexual liaisons of Pablo

Picasso, Charlie Chaplin, and Honoré de Balzac. Miller concludes: "As every teenager knows and most psychologists forget, cultural displays by males increase sexual access" (Miller, 1998, p. 119).

The display hypothesis can account for several known facts about the patterning of cultural displays. First, it can account for the sex differences in the production of cultural products. Men historically have produced more art, music, and literature than women across a wide variety of cultures. Women had less to gain by cultural displays, according to this argument, simply because increased short-term sexual access was rarely a goal for them (see Chapter 6). Women are more likely to engage in what Miller calls "narrowcasting," or displaying to one or a few men for long-term goals rather than to the masses for short-term sexual access. He cites the Scheherazade strategy, named after a woman who succeeded in avoiding getting killed and commanded the king's attention and investment for years by inventing dazzling stories for 1,001 nights. The display hypothesis thus accounts for sex differences in the nature and magnitude of effort devoted to cultural displays.

The display hypothesis can also account for the age distribution of cultural displays. Many major works of art and music are created by men in young adulthood—precisely the time when men are most intensely engaged in intrasexual mate competition (see Figure 13.5 on page 409). As men age and their efforts shift more to parental and grandparental effort, their production of dazzling cultural products declines.

The display hypothesis also accounts for why some products of art, music, and literature are linked with social status and resources. As the evolutionary psychologist Steve Pinker observes, "What better proof that you have money to spare than your being able to spend it on doodads and stunts that don't fill the belly or keep the rain out but that require precious resources, years of practice, a command of obscure texts, or intimacy with the elite . . . people find dignity in the signs of an honorably futile existence removed from all menial necessities" (Pinker, 1997, pp. 522–523). In short, the display hypothesis appears to account for the age and sex distribution of culture production.

The display hypothesis cannot explain several other facts about art, music, and literature, however. First, it cannot explain the *content* of these cultural products. Why do people find some songs moving, but show indifference to others? Why are Shakespeare's plays mesmerizing to some, while those of many other playwrights seem boring? Why do some movies draw millions of viewers, whereas others fade into obscurity? A complete theory of culture must explain the contents of cultural products, not just their age and sex distribution. Second, the display hypothesis cannot account for the fact that some people spend inordinate amounts of time in the *solitary* enjoyment of art, music, and literature, in contexts where no display is evident.

In a second approach to explaining culture, Pinker suggests a general answer to these puzzles, albeit a speculative one. He argues that the answer lies *not* in specific adaptations for art, music, and literature, but rather in the evolved mechanisms of the mind for other purposes that "let people take pleasure in shapes and colors and sounds and jokes and stories and myths" (1997, p. 523). A mechanism of color vision designed for locating ripe fruits, for example, can be pleasurably activated by creating paintings that mimic these patterns. Psychological preferences for cues to fertile females can be exploited by paintings, photographs, movies, and skin magazines to pleasurably mimic the

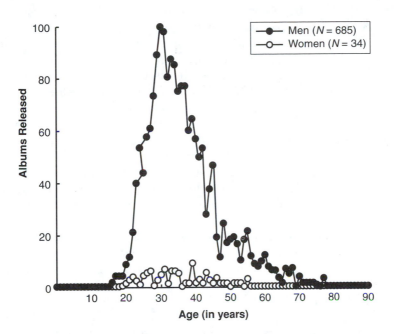

FIGURE 13.5   Jazz Music: 1,892 Albums by 719 Musicians. These findings support Geoffrey Miller's display hypothesis, which suggests that music, art, and literature are produced more by men than by women as a display tactic in attracting mates. In addition to the large sex difference, the age distribution roughly corresponds to the ages in which men engage in the heaviest mating effort. *N* refers to the sample size. Data from Carr, I., Fairweather, D., & Priestly, B., *The Essential Jazz Companion* (1988).

Source: From "Sexual Selection for Cultural Displays" by G. F. Miller, in R. Dunbar, C. Knight, & C. Power (Eds.), *The Evolution of Culture* (in press), Edinburgh: University of Edinburgh Press. Reprinted with permission.

patterns the mechanisms were originally designed to attend to and seek out. Just as artificial drugs can be created to "juice" our pleasure centers, art, music, and literature can be created to "juice" a variety of evolved psychological mechanisms. According to this hypothesis, humans have not evolved any specific adaptations to produce art, music, literature, and other cultural products. Rather, humans have learned how to artificially activate existing mechanisms by inventing cultural products that mimic in various ways the stimuli for which the mechanisms were originally designed. These cultural activities, in short, are not adaptations, but rather are nonadaptive byproducts.

Aspects of abstract art, for example, involve dots, parallels, circles, squares, spirals, and splashes of color that happen to mimic precisely the kinds of stimuli posited by vision researchers as essential to making sense of the objects and surfaces humans must navigate, and thus are pleasurable to us (Pinker, 1997). The paintings and landscapes we find drab, in contrast, come from mechanisms that perceive an environment to be devoid of resources. Dazzling objects of art, in short, mimic environments bursting with resources and hence worth attending to.

Pinker makes a similar argument for music: "I suspect that music is auditory cheesecake, an exquisite confection crafted to tickle the sensitive spots of at least six of our mental faculties" (1997, p. 534). These mental faculties include *language* (e.g., lyrics from songs), *auditory scene analysis* (e.g., we must segregate sounds coming from different sources, such as an animal call in a noisy forest), *emotional calls* (e.g., whining, crying, moaning, baying, and cheering are used as metaphors to describe musical passages), *habitat selection* (e.g., thunder, rushing water, growls, and other sounds might signal safe or unsafe environments), and *motor control* (e.g., rhythm, a universal component of music, mimics the motor control needed for a variety of tasks, including running and chopping, and signals qualities such as urgency, laziness, and confidence). The patterns of music we find pleasurable, according to this hypothesis, are those that artificially mimic natural stimuli that our evolved mechanisms were designed to process.

A similar argument can be made for fiction and movies. Words, plot lines, and stories depicting comedies and tragedies can activate pleasurable sensations by triggering a host of evolved mechanisms. It is probably no coincidence that the most successful novels and movies such as *Titanic* and *Gone With the Wind* contain patterns of intrasexual competition, mate choice, romance, and life-threatening hostile forces of nature. As Pinker noted, "When we are absorbed in a book or movie, we get to see breathtaking landscapes, hobnob with important people, fall in love with ravishing men and women, protect loved ones, attain impossible goals, and defeat wicked enemies. Not a bad deal for seven dollars and fifty cents!" (Pinker, 1997, p. 539).

One analysis of thirty-six common plot lines showed most were defined by one of four themes: love, sex, personal threat, or threat to the protagonist's kin (Carroll, 1995). Examples include "mistaken jealousy" (e.g., Shakespeare's *Othello*) and "discovery of the dishonor (infidelity) of a loved one" (one of the most common themes in novels and movies). Sex and violence lie at the heart of literature throughout written human history.

People invent and consume cultural products such as paintings, sculptures, novels, and movies, according to this hypothesis, not because these cultural activities are themselves adaptations, but rather because their form and content artificially activate adaptations that have evolved for different reasons. In this sense humans live with an ancient brain in a modern world filled with evolutionarily unprecedented cultural stimuli. The patterns of culture we create and consume, although not adaptations in themselves, may reveal about human evolutionary psychology as much as or more than the most carefully planned psychological experiments.

Toward a Unified Psychology

In this chapter we have considered how evolutionary psychology approaches the major branches of psychology including cognitive, social, developmental, personality, clinical, and cultural psychology. Evolutionary psychology has also proved informative for other subbranches of psychology, such as organizational and industrial psychology (Colarelli, 1998; Nicholson, 1997) and environmental psychology (Kaplan, 1992). Ultimately, however, evolutionary psychology can be expected to dissolve these traditional disciplinary boundaries. Human beings cannot be neatly partitioned into discrete elements such as personality, social, developmental, and cognitive. Stable individual differences traditionally have been relegated to the personality branch, but they often involve social orientations, have particular developmental antecedents, and are anchored in particular cognitive mechanisms. Social exchange and reciprocity have traditionally been regarded as belonging to social psychology. The mechanisms that underlie them, however, are information-processing devices that have developmental trajectories. The rapid changes occurring at puberty have been the traditional province of developmental psychologists. Individuals differ in the onset of puberty, however, and many of the most important changes at puberty are social. From the perspective of evolutionary psychology, many traditional disciplinary boundaries are not merely arbitrary, but are misleading and detrimental to scientific progress. They imply boundaries that cleave mechanisms in arbitrary and unnatural ways. Studying human psychology via adaptive problems and their solutions—the organizing principle of this book—provides a more natural means of "cleaving nature at its joints" and hence crossing current disciplinary boundaries.

A critical task in this new psychological science will be the identification of the key adaptive problems that humans have confronted repeatedly over human evolutionary history. Evolutionary psychologists have barely scratched the surface by identifying some of the problems most obviously and plausibly linked with survival and reproduction. Most adaptive problems remain unexplored, most psychological solutions undiscovered. It is not unreasonable to expect that the first scientists to explore these uncharted territories will come away with a great bounty.

Evolutionary psychology provides the conceptual tools for emerging from the fragmented state of current psychological science and linking psychology with the rest of the life sciences in a move toward larger scientific integration. Evolutionary psychology provides some of the most important tools for unlocking the mysteries of where humans came from and how they arrived at their current state, as well as the mechanisms of the mind that define what it means to be human.

BIBLIOGRAPHY

Abbey, A. (1982). Sex differences in attributions for friendly behavior: Do males misperceive females' friendliness? *Journal of Personality and Social Psychology, 32*, 830–838.

Abbey, A., & Melby, C. (1986). The effects of nonverbal cues on gender differences in perceptions of sexual intent. *Sex Roles, 15*, 283–298.

Ahmad, Y., & Smith, P. K. (1994). Bullying in schools and the issue of sex differences. In J. Archer (Ed.), *Male violence* (pp. 70–83). London: Routledge.

Alcock, J. (1989). *Animal behavior: An evolutionary approach* (4th ed.). Sunderland, MA: Sinauer.

Alcock, J. (1993). *Animal behavior: An evolutionary approach* (5th ed.). Sunderland, MA: Sinauer.

Alexander, R. D. (1961). Aggressiveness, territoriality, and sexual behavior in field crickets. *Behaviour, 17*, 130–223.

Alexander, R. D. (1979). *Darwinism and human affairs*. Seattle: University of Washington Press.

Alexander, R. D. (1987). *The biology of moral systems*. Hawthorne, NY: Aldine DeGruyter.

Alexander, R. D., Hoodland, J. L., Howard, R. D., Noonan, K. M., & Sherman, P. W. (1979). Sexual dimorphisms and breeding systems in pinnepeds, ungulates, primates, and humans. In N. A. Chagnon & W. Irons (Eds.), *Evolutionary biology and human social behavior*. North Scituate, MA: Duxbury Press.

Alexander, R. D., & Noonan, K. M. (1979). Concealment of ovulation, parental care, and human social evolution. In N. A. Chagnon & W. Irons (Eds.), *Evolutionary biology and human social behavior* (pp. 402–435). North Scituate, MA: Duxbury Press.

Allee, W. N., Collias, N., & Lutherman, C. (1939). Modification of the social order in flocks of hens by the injection of testosterone propionate. *Physiological Zoology, 12*, 412–440.

Allman, W. F. (1994). *The stone age present*. New York: Simon & Schuster.

Allport, G. W., & Postman, L. (1947). *The psychology of rumor*. New York: Holt.

American Psychiatric Association (1994). *Diagnostic and statistical manual of mental disorders* (4th ed.). Washington, DC: Author.

Anderson, J. G., Kaplan, H. S., & Lancaster, J. B. (1997, June). *Paying for children's college: The paternal investment strategies of Albuquerque men*. Paper presented at the Ninth Annual Conference of the Human Behavior and Evolution Society, University of Arizona, Tucson, AZ.

Appleton, J. (1975). *The experience of landscape*. New York: Wiley.

Archer, J. (1988). *The behavioural biology of aggression*. Cambridge, UK: Cambridge University Press.

Archer, J. (1998). *The nature of grief*. London: Routledge.

Ardener, E. W., Ardener, S. G., & Warmington, W. A. (1960). *Plantation and village in the Cameroons*. London: Oxford University Press.

Ardry, R. (1966). *The territorial imperative*. New York: Atheneum.

Argyle, M. (1994). *The psychology of social class*. New York: Routledge.

Athanasiou, R., Shaver, P., & Tavris, C. (1970, July). Sex. *Psychology Today*, pp. 37–52.

413

Atran, S. (1990). *The cognitive foundations of natural history.* New York: Cambridge University Press.

Atzwanger, K. (1995, June). *Biological aspects of driving behavior.* Paper presented to the Annual Conference of the Human Behavior and Evolution Society, Santa Barbara, CA.

Avis, J., & Harris, P. L. (1991). Belief-desire reasoning among Baka children: Evidence for a universal conception of mind. *Child Development, 62,* 460–467.

Axelrod, R. (1984). *The evolution of cooperation.* New York: Basic Books.

Axelrod, R., & Hamilton, W. D. (1981). The evolution of cooperation. *Science, 211,* 1390–1396.

Bahrick, H. P., Bahrick, P. O., & Wittlinger, R. P. (1975). Fifty years of memory for names and faces: A cross-sectional approach. *Journal of Experimental Psychology, 104,* 54–75.

Bailey, J. M. (1998). Can behavior genetics contribute to evolutionary behavioral science? In C. Crawford & D. L. Krebs (Eds.), *Handbook of evolutionary psychology* (pp. 221–234). Mahwah, NJ: Erlbaum.

Baize, H. R., & Schroeder, J. E. (1995). Personality and mate selection in personal ads: Evolutionary preferences in a public mate selection process. *Journal of Social Behavior and Personality, 10,* 517–536.

Baker, R. R., & Bellis, M. A. (1995). *Human sperm competition.* London: Chapman & Hall.

Baldwin, J. D. (1995). Continua outperform dichotomies. *Behavioral and Brain Sciences, 18,* 543–544.

Bandura, A. (1977). *Social learning theory.* Englewood Cliffs, NJ: Prentice Hall.

Barash, D. P., & Lipton, J. E. (1997). *Making sense of sex.* Washington, DC: Island Press/Shearwater Brooks.

Barber, N. (1995). The evolutionary psychology of physical attractiveness: Sexual selection and human morphology. *Ethology and Sociobiology, 16,* 395–424.

Barinaga, M. (1996). Social status sculpts activity of crayfish neurons. *Science, 271,* 290–291.

Barclay, A. M. (1973). Sexual fantasies in men and women. *Medical Aspects of Human Sexuality, 7,* 205–216.

Barkow, J. (1989). *Darwin, sex, and status: Biological approaches to mind and culture.* Toronto: University of Toronto Press.

Baron-Cohen, S., Leslie, A., & Frith, U. (1985). Does the autistic child have a "theory of mind"? *Cognition, 21,* 37–46.

Baumeister, R. F., & Leary, M. R. (1995). The need to belong: Desire for interpersonal attachments as a fundamental human motivation. *Psychological Bulletin, 117,* 497–529.

Belluck, P. (1997). A woman's killer is likely to be her partner, a study finds. *New York Times.*

Belsky, J. (1997). Attachment, mating, and parenting: An evolutionary interpretation. *Human Nature, 8,* 361–381.

Belsky, J., Steinberg, L., & Draper, P. (1991). Childhood experience, interpersonal development, and reproductive strategy: An evolutionary theory of socialization. *Child Development, 62,* 647–670.

Berkowitz, L. (1993). *Aggression: Its causes, consequences, and control.* New York: McGraw-Hill.

Berlin, B., Breedlove, D., & Raven, P. (1973). General principles of classification and nomenclature in field biology. *American Anthropologist, 75,* 214–242.

Bernhardt, P. C. (1997). Influences of serotonin and testosterone in aggression and dominance: Convergence with social psychology. *Current Directions in Psychological Science, 6,* 44–53.

Berscheid, E., & Walster, E. (1974). Physical attractiveness. In L. Berkowitz (Ed.), *Advances in experimental social psychology* (pp. 157–215). New York: Academic Press.

Bertenthal, B. I., Campos, J. J., & Caplovitz, K. S. (1983). Self-produced locomotion: An organizer of emotional, cognitive, and social development in infancy. In R. N. Emde &

R. Harmon (Eds.), *Continuities and discontinuities in development.* New York: Plenum.

Betzig, L. L. (1986). *Despotism and differential reproduction: A Darwinian view of history.* Hawthorne, NY: Aldine.

Betzig, L. (1989). Causes of conjugal dissolution. *Current Anthropology, 30,* 654–676.

Betzig, L. (1992). Roman polygyny. *Ethology and Sociobiology, 13,* 309–349.

Betzig, L. (1993). Sex, succession, and stratification in the first six civilizations. In L. Ellis (Ed.), *Social stratification and socioeconomic inequality* (pp. 37–74). Westport, CT: Praeger.

Bjorklund, D. F. (1997). The role of immaturity in human development. *Psychological Bulletin, 122,* 153–169.

Bjorklund, D. F., & Kipp, K. (1996). Parental investment theory and gender differences in the evolution of inhibition mechanisms. *Psychological Bulletin, 120,* 163–188.

Bjorkqvist, K., Lagerspetz, K. M. J., & Kaukiainen, A. (1992). Do girls manipulate and boys fight? Developmental trends in regard to direct and indirect aggression. *Aggressive Behavior, 18,* 117–127.

Bleske, A., & Buss, D. M. (under review). *Functions of friendship.* Department of Psychology, University of Texas, Austin.

Boone, J. (1986). Parental investment and elite family structure in preindustrial states: A case study of late medieval-early modern Portuguese genealogies. *American Anthropologist, 88,* 859–878.

Borgerhoff Mulder, M. (1988). Kipsigis bridewealth payments. In L. L. Betzig, M. Borgerhoff Mulder, & P. Turke (Eds.), *Human reproductive behavior* (pp. 65–82). New York: Cambridge University Press.

Botwin, M., Buss, D. M., & Shackelford, T. K. (1997). Personality and mate preferences: Five factors in mate selection and marital satisfaction. *Journal of Personality, 65,* 107–136.

Bouissou, M. F. (1978). Effects of injections of testosterone propionate on dominance relationships in a group of cows. *Hormones and Behavior, 11,* 388–400.

Bowlby, J. (1969). *Attachment and loss: Vol. 1.* New York: Basic Books.

Boyle, J. (1977). *A sense of freedom.* London: Pan Books.

Brandes, J. (1967). First trimester nausea and vomiting as related to outcome of pregnancy. *Obstetrics and Gynecology, 30,* 427–431.

Brewin, C. R. (1988). *Cognitive foundations of clinical psychology.* London: Erlbaum.

Brown, D. E. (1991). *Human universals.* New York: McGraw-Hill.

Brown, D. E., & Chia-yun, Y. (n.d.). *"Big man" as a statistical universal.* Department of Anthropology, University of California, Santa Barbara.

Brown, R. M., Dahlen, E., Mills, C., Rick, J., & Biblarz, A. (in press). Evaluation of an evolutionary model of self-preservation and self-destruction. *Suicide and Life Threatening Behavior.*

Bugos, P. E., & McCarthy, L. M. (1984). Ayoreo infanticide: A case study. In G. Hausfater & S. B. Hrdy (Eds.), *Infanticide: Comparative and evolutionary perspectives* (pp. 503–520). NY: Aldine de Gruyter.

Burbank, V. K. (1992). Sex, gender, and difference: Dimensions of aggression in an Australian aboriginal community. *Human Nature, 3,* 251–278.

Burley, N., & Symanski, R. (1981). Women without: An evolutionary and cross-cultural perspective on prostitution. In R. Symanski (Ed.), *The immoral landscape: Female prostitution in western societies* (pp. 239–274). Toronto: Butterworth.

Burnstein, E., Crandall, C., & Kitayama, S. (1994). Some neo-Darwinian decision rules for altruism: Weighing cues for inclusive fitness as a function of the biological importance of the decision. *Journal of Personality and Social Psychology, 67,* 773–789.

Buss, A. H. (1961). *The psychology of aggression.* New York: Wiley.

Buss, D. M. (1981). Sex differences in the evaluation and performance of dominant acts. *Journal of Personality and Social Psychology, 40,* 147–154.

Buss, D. M. (1985). Human mate selection. *American Scientist, 73,* 47–51.

Buss, D. M. (1987). Sex differences in human mate selection criteria: An evolutionary perspective. In C. Crawford, D. Krebs, & M. Smith (Eds.), *Sociobiology and psychology: Ideas, issues, and applications* (pp. 335–352). Hillsdale, NJ: Erlbaum.

Buss, D. M. (1988a). Love acts: The evolutionary biology of love. In R. J. Sternberg & M. L. Barnes (Eds.), *The psychology of love* (pp. 100–118). New Haven, CT: Yale University Press.

Buss, D. M. (1988b). The evolution of human intrasexual competition: Tactics of mate attraction. *Journal of Personality and Social Psychology, 54,* 616–628.

Buss, D. M. (1988c). From vigilance to violence: Tactics of mate retention. *Ethology and Sociobiology, 9,* 291–317.

Buss, D. M. (1989a). Sex differences in human mate preferences: Evolutionary hypotheses testing in 37 cultures. *Behavioral and Brain Sciences, 12,* 1–49.

Buss, D. M. (1989b). Conflict between the sexes: Strategic interference and the evocation of anger and upset. *Journal of Personality and Social Psychology, 56,* 735–747.

Buss, D. M. (1991). Conflict in married couples: Personality predictors of anger and upset. *Journal of Personality, 59,* 663–688.

Buss, D. M. (1994a). The strategies of human mating. *American Scientist, 82,* 238–249.

Buss, D. M. (1994b). *The evolution of desire: Strategies of human mating.* New York: Basic Books.

Buss, D. M. (1995a). Evolutionary psychology: A new paradigm for psychological science. *Psychological Inquiry, 6,* 1–49.

Buss, D. M. (1995b, June). *Human prestige criteria.* Paper presented to the Human Behavior and Evolution Society Annual Meeting, University of California, Santa Barbara, CA.

Buss, D. M. (1996a). Sexual conflict: Evolutionary insights into feminist and the "battle of the sexes." In D. M. Buss & N. M. Malamuth (Eds.), *Sex, power, conflict: Evolutionary and feminist perspectives* (pp. 296–318). New York: Oxford University Press.

Buss, D. M. (1996b). The evolutionary psychology of human social strategies. In E. T. Higgins & A. W. Kruglanski (Eds.), *Social psychology: Handbook of basic principles* (pp. 3–38). New York: Guilford.

Buss, D. M., Abbott, M., Angleitner, A., Asherian, A., Biaggio, A., and 45 other co-authors (1990). International preferences in selecting mates: A study of 37 cultures. *Journal of Cross-Cultural Psychology, 21,* 5–47.

Buss, D. M., & Barnes, M. F. (1986). Preferences in human mate selection. *Journal of Personality and Social Psychology, 50,* 559–570.

Buss, D. M., & Dedden, L. A. (1990). Derogation of competitors. *Journal of Social and Personal Relationships, 7,* 395–422.

Buss, D. M., & Duntley, J. (1998). *Evolved homicide modules.* Paper presented to the Annual Meeting of the Human Behavior and Evolution Society, Davis, California, July 10.

Buss, D. M., & Greiling, H. (1999). Adaptive individual differences. *Journal of Personality.*

Buss, D. M., Larsen, R. J., & Westen, D. (1996). Sex differences in jealousy: Not gone, not forgotten, and not explained by alternative hypotheses. *Psychological Science, 7,* 373–375.

Buss, D. M., Larsen, R., Westen, D., & Semmelroth, J. (1992). Sex differences in jealousy: Evolution, physiology, and psychology. *Psychological Science, 3,* 251–255.

Buss, D. M., & Schmitt, D. P. (1993). Sexual strategies theory: An evolutionary perspective on human mating. *Psychological Review, 100,* 204–232.

Buss, D. M., & Shackelford, T. K. (1997a). Susceptibility to infidelity in the first year of marriage. *Journal of Research in Personality, 31*, 1–29.

Buss, D. M., & Shackelford, T. K. (1997b). Human aggression in evolutionary psychological perspective. *Clinical Psychology Review, 17*, 605–619.

Buss, D. M., & Shackelford, T. K. (1997c). From vigilance to violence: Mate retention tactics in married couples. *Journal of Personality and Social Psychology, 72*, 346–361.

Buss, D. M., & Shackelford, T. K. (1997d). Susceptibility to infidelity in the first year of marriage. *Journal of Research in Personality, 31*, 193–221.

Buss, D. M., Shackelford, T. K., Haselton, M. G., & Bleske, A. (1997). *The Evolutionary psychology of mental disorder.* Unpublished manuscript, Department of Psychology, University of Texas, Austin.

Buss, D. M., Shackelford, T. K., Kirkpatrick, L. A., Choe, J., Hasegawa, M., Hasegawa, T., & Bennett, K. (1999). Jealousy and the nature of beliefs about infidelity: Tests of competing hypotheses about sex differences in the United States, Korea, and Japan. *Personal Relationships.*

Buss, D. M., Shackelford, T. K., Kirkpatrick, L. A., & Larsen, R. J. (under review). *A half century of American mate preferences.*

Buttery, R. G., Guadagni, D. G., Ling, L. C., Siefert, R. M., & Lipton, W. (1976). Additional volatile components of cabbage, broccoli, and cauliflower. *Journal of Agricultural and Food Chemistry, 24*, 829–832.

Buunk, A. P., Angleitner, A., Oubaid, V., & Buss, D. M. (1996). Sex differences in jealousy in evolutionary and cultural perspective: Tests from the Netherlands, Germany, and the United States. *Psychological Science, 7*, 359–363.

Buunk, A. P., & Hupka, R. B. (1987). Cross-cultural differences in the elicitation of sexual jealousy. *Journal of Sex Research, 23*, 12–22.

Byers, E. S., & Lewis, K. (1988). Dating couples' disagreements over desired level of sexual intimacy. *Journal of Sex Research, 24*, 15–29.

Campbell, A. (1993). *Men, women, and aggression.* New York: Basic Books.

Campbell, A. (1995). A few good men: Evolutionary psychology and female adolescent aggression. *Ethology and Sociobiology, 16*, 99–123.

Cameron, C., Oskamp, S., & Sparks, W. (1978). Courtship American style: Newspaper advertisements. *Family Coordinator, 26*, 27–30.

Carbonell, J. L. (1984). Sex roles and leadership revisited. *Journal of Applied Psychology, 69*, 44–49.

Carlson, C. A. (1984). *Intrafamilial homicide: A sociobiological perspective.* Unpublished bachelor's thesis, McMaster University, Hamilton, Ontario, Canada.

Carroll, J. (1995). *Evolution and literary theory.* Columbia: University of Missouri Press.

Cashden, E. (1989). Hunters and gatherers: Economic behavior in bands. In S. Plattner (Ed.), *Economic Anthropology* (pp. 21–48). Stanford, CA: Stanford University Press.

Cashden, E. (1995). Hormones, sex, and status in women. *Hormones and Behavior, 29*, 354–366.

Chagnon, N. A. (1981). Terminological kinship, genealogical relatedness and village fissioning among the Yanomamö Indians. In R. D. Alexander & D. W. Tinkle (Eds.), *Natural selection and social behavior* (pp. 490–508). New York: Chiron Press.

Chagnon, N. A. (1983). *Yanomamö: The fierce people* (3rd ed.). New York: Holt, Rinehart, & Winston.

Chagnon, N. A. (1988). Life histories, blood revenge, and warfare in a tribal population. *Science, 239*, 985–992.

Chagnon, N. A. (1992). *Yanomamö: The last days of Eden.* San Diego, CA: Harcourt Brace Jovanovich.

Chagnon, N. A., & Bugos, P. E. (1979). Kin selection and conflict: An analysis of a Yanomamö ax fight. In N. A. Chagnon & W. Irons (Eds.), *Evolutionary biology and human social behavior: An anthropological perspective* (pp. 213–249). North Scituate, MA: Duxbury Press.

Charnov, E. (1993). *Life history invariants.* Oxford: Oxford University Press.

Chisholm, J. S. (1996). The evolutionary ecology of attachment organization. *Human Nature, 7,* 1–38.

Christenfeld, N. J. S., & Hill, E. A. (1995). Whose baby are you? *Nature, 378,* 669.

Chomsky, N. (1957). *Syntactic structures.* The Hague: Mouton & Co.

Cieza de Leon, P. (1959). *The Incas.* Norman: University of Oklahoma Press.

Clarke, R. D., & Hatfield, E. (1989). Gender differences in receptivity to sexual offers. *Journal of Psychology and Human Sexuality, 2,* 39–55.

Cleckley, H. (1982). *The mask of sanity.* New York: New American Library.

Clutton-Brock, T. H. (1991). *The evolution of parental care.* Princeton, NJ: Princeton University Press.

Colarelli, S. M. (1998). Psychological interventions in organizations: An evolutionary perspective. *American Psychologist, 53,* 1044–1056.

Collias, N. W., & Collias, E. C. (1970). The behavior of the West African village weaverbird. *Ibis, 112,* 457–480.

Cosmides, L. L., & Tooby, J. (1989). Evolutionary psychology and the generation of culture. Part II. Case study: A computational theory of social exchange. *Ethology and Sociobiology, 10,* 51–97.

Cosmides, L., & Tooby, J. (1992). Cognitive adaptations for social exchange. In J. Barkow, L. Cosmides, & J. Tooby (Eds.), *The adapted mind* (pp. 163–228). New York: Oxford University Press.

Cosmides, L., & Tooby, J. (1994a). Beyond intuition and instinct blindness: Toward an evolutionarily rigorous cognitive science. *Cognition, 50,* 41–77.

Cosmides, L., & Tooby, J. (1994b). Origins of domain specificity: The evolution of functional organization. In S. Gelman & L. Hirshfeld (Eds.), *Mapping the mind: Domain specificity in cognition and culture* (pp. 85–116). New York: Cambridge University Press.

Cosmides, L., & Tooby, J. (1996). Are humans good intuitive statisticians after all? Rethinking some conclusions from the literature on judgment under uncertainty. *Cognition, 58,* 1–73.

Cowley, G., & Underwood, A. (1997, December 29). A little help from serotonin. *Newsweek,* pp. 78–81.

Cronin, H. (1991). *The ant and the peacock.* Cambridge, UK: Cambridge University Press.

Cronk, L. (1994). Group selection's new clothes. *Behavioral and Brain Sciences, 17,* 615–617.

Cross, J. F., & Cross, J. (1971). Age, sex, race, and the perception of facial beauty. *Developmental Psychology, 5,* 433–439.

Cummins, D. D. (1998). Social norms and other minds: The evolutionary roots of higher cognition. In D. D. Cummins & C. Allen (Eds.), *The evolution of mind* (pp. 30–50). New York: Oxford University Press.

Cummins, D. D., & Allen, C. (Eds.) (1998). *The evolution of mind.* New York: Oxford University Press.

Cunningham, M. R.., Roberts, A. R., Wu, C-H, Barbee, A. P., & Druen, P. B. (1995). "Their ideas of beauty are, on the whole, the same as ours": Consistency and variability in the cross-cultural perception of female attractiveness. *Journal of Personality and Social Psychology, 68,* 261–279.

Cutting, J. E., Profitt, D. R., & Kozlowski, L. T. (1978). A biomechanical invariant for gait perception. *Journal of Experimental Psychology, 4,* 357–372.

Dabbs, J. M. & Ruback, R. B. (1988). Saliva testosterone and personality of male college students. *Bulletin of the Psychonomic Society, 26,* 244–247.

Daly, M., Salmon, C., & Wilson, M. (1997). Kinship: The conceptual hole in psychological studies of social cognition and close relationships. In J. A. Simpson & D. T. Kenrick (Eds.), *Evolutionary social psychology* (pp. 265–296). Mahwah, NJ: Erlbaum.

Daly, M., & Wilson, M. (1981). Abuse and neglect of children in evolutionary perspective. In R. D. Alexander & D. W. Tinkle (Eds.), *Natural selection and social behavior* (pp. 405–416). New York: Chiron.

Daly, M., & Wilson, M. (1982). Whom are newborn babies said to resemble? *Ethology and Sociobiology, 3,* 69–78.

Daly, M., & Wilson, M. (1983). *Sex, evolution, and behavior* (2nd ed.). Boston: Willard Grant.

Daly, M., & Wilson, M. (1985). Child abuse and other risks of not living with both parents. *Ethology and Sociobiology, 6,* 197–210.

Daly, M., & Wilson, M. (1988). *Homicide.* Hawthorne, NY: Aldine.

Daly, M., & Wilson, M. (1990). Is parent–offspring conflict sex-linked? Freudian and Darwinian models. *Journal of Personality, 58,* 163–189.

Daly, M., & Wilson, M. (1994). Evolutionary psychology of male violence. In J. Archer (Ed.), *Male violence* (pp. 253–288). London: Routledge.

Daly, M., & Wilson, M. (1995). Discriminative parental solicitude and the relevance of evolutionary models to the analysis of motivational systems. In M. S. Gazzaniga (Ed.), *The cognitive neurosciences* (pp. 1269–1286). Cambridge, MA: MIT Press.

Daly, M., & Wilson, M. (1996a). Violence against stepchildren. *Current Directions in Psychological Science, 5,* 77–81.

Daly, M., & Wilson, M. (1996b). Evolutionary psychology and marital conflict: The relevance of stepchildren. In D. M. Buss & N. Malamuth (Eds.), *Sex, power, conflict: Evolutionary and feminist perspectives* (pp. 9–28). New York: Oxford University Press.

Daly, M., & Wilson, M. (1997). Kinship: The conceptual hole in psychological studies of social cognition and close relationships. In J. A. Simpson & D. T. Kenrick (Eds.), *Evolutionary social psychology* (pp. 265–296). Mahwah, NJ: Erlbaum.

Daly, M., Wilson, M., & Weghorst, S. J. (1982). Male sexual jealousy. *Ethology and Sociobiology, 3,* 11–27.

Dannenmaier, W. D., & Thumin, F. J. (1964). Authority status as a factor in perceptual distortion of size. *Journal of Social Psychology, 63,* 361–365.

Darwin, C. (1859). *On the origin of species.* London: Murray.

Darwin, C. (1871). *The descent of man and selection in relation to sex.* London: Murray.

Darwin, C. (1877). A biographical sketch of an infant. *Mind, 2,* 285–294.

Dass, J. (1970). *Maharaja.* Delhi: Hind.

Davis, B. M., & Gilbert, L. A. (1989). Effects of dispositional and situational influences on women's dominance expression in mixed-sex dyads. *Journal of Personality and Social Psychology, 57,* 294–300.

Davis, J. N., & Daly, M. (1997). Evolutionary theory and the human family. The *Quarterly Review of Biology, 72,* 407–435.

Dawkins, R. (1979). Twelve misunderstandings of kin selection. *Zeitschrift fur Tierpsychologie, 51,* 184–200.

Dawkins, R. (1982). *The extended phenotype.* Oxford: W. H. Freeman & Co.

Dawkins, R. (1986). *The blind watchmaker.* New York: Norton.

Dawkins, R. (1989). *The selfish gene* (new ed.). New York: Oxford University Press.

Dawkins, R. (1994). Burying the vehicle. *Behavioral and Brain Sciences, 17,* 617.

Dawkins, R. (1996). *Climbing mount improbable.* New York: Norton.

De Becker, G. (1997). *The gift of fear: Survival signals that protect us from violence.* Boston, MA: Little, Brown.

de Catanzaro, D. (1991). Evolutionary limits to self-preservation. *Ethology and Sociobiology, 12,* 13–28.

de Catanzaro, D. (1995). Reproductive status, family interactions, and suicidal ideation: Surveys of the general public and high-risk group. *Ethology and Sociobiology, 16,* 385–394.

DeGroat, B. (1997, April 1). Dating violence differs for teen-age girls, boys. *The University Record,* p. 15.

DeKay, W. T. (1995, July). *Grandparental investment and the uncertainty of kinship.* Paper presented to the Seventh Annual Meeting of the Human Behavior and Evolution Society, Santa Barbara, CA.

DeKay, W. T., & Buss, D. M. (1992). Human nature, individual differences, and the importance of context: Perspectives from evolutionary psychology. *Current Directions in Psychological Science, 1,* 184–189.

DeKay, W. T., Buss, D. M., & Stone, V. (under review). *Coalitions, mates, and friends: Toward an evolutionary psychology of relationship preferences.* Department of Psychology, University of Michigan, Ann Arbor.

Dennett, D. C. (1994). E pluribus unum? *Behavioral and Brain Sciences, 17,* 617–618.

Dennett, D. C. (1995). *Darwin's dangerous idea.* New York: Simon & Schuster.

DeSouza, E. R., Pierce, T., Zanelli, J. C., & Hutz, C. (1992). Perceived sexual intent in the U.S. and Brazil as a function of nature of encounter, subjects' nationality, and gender. *Journal of Sex Research, 29,* 251–260.

DeSteno, D. A., & Salovey, P. (1996). Evolutionary origins of sex differences in jealousy: Questioning the "fitness" of the model. *Psychological Science, 7,* 367–372.

DeVore, I., & Hall, K. R. L. (1965). Baboon ecology. In I. DeVore (Ed.), *Primate behavior: Field studies of monkeys and apes* (pp. 20–52). New York: Holt, Rinehart, & Winston.

de Waal, F. (1982). *Chimpanzee politics: Sex and power among apes.* Baltimore, MD: Johns Hopkins University Press.

de Waal, F. (1988). Chimpanzee politics. In R. W. Byrne & A. Whiten (Eds.), *Machiavellian intelligence* (pp. 122–131). Oxford: Oxford University Press.

Dickemann, M. (1979). Female infanticide, reproductive strategies and social stratification: A preliminary model. In N. A. Chagnon & W. Irons (Eds.), *Evolutionary biology and human social behavior* (pp. 312–367). North Scituate, MA: Duxbury Press.

Dickemann, M. (1981). Paternal confidence and dowry competition: A biocultural analysis of purdah. In R. D. Alexander & D. W. Tinkle (Eds.), *Natural selection and social behavior: Recent research and new theory* (pp. 417–438). New York: Chiron Press.

Dickens, G., & Trethowan, W. H. (1971). Cravings and aversions during pregnancy. *Journal of Psychosomatic Research, 15,* 259–268.

Dobash, R. E., & Dobash, R. P. (1984). The nature and antecedents of violent events. *British Journal of Criminology, 24,* 269–288.

Dobash, R. P., Dobash, R. E., Wilson, M., & Daly, M. (1992). The myth of sexual symmetry in marital violence. *Social Problems, 39,* 71–91.

Dobzhansky, T. (1937). *Genetics and the origins of species.* New York: Columbia University Press.

Dobzhansky, T. (1951). *Genetics and the origin of species* (3rd ed.). New York: Columbia University Press.

Domjan, M. (1997). Behavioral systems and the demise of equipotentiality: Historical antecedents and evidence from sexual conditioning. In M. E. Bouton & M. S. Fanselow (Eds.), *Learning, motivation, and cognition: The functional behaviorism of Robert C. Bolles* (pp. 31–51). Washington, DC: American Psychological Association.

Doran, T. F. et al. (1989). *Journal of Pediatrics, 114*, 1045–1048.

Duberman, L. (1975). *The reconstituted family: A study of remarried couples and their children.* Chicago, IL: Nelson-Hall.

Dunbar, R. I. M. (1993). Coevolution of neocortical size, group size, and language in humans. *Behavioral and Brain Sciences, 16*, 681–735.

Duntley, J., & Buss, D. M. (1998). *Evolved anti-homicide modules.* Paper presented to the Annual Meeting of the Human Behavior and Evolution Society, Davis, CA. July 10.

Dworkin, A. (1987). *Intercourse.* New York: Free Press.

Eibl-Eibesfeldt, I. (1989). *Human ethology.* New York: Aldine de Gruyter.

Eisenberg, N. (1986). *Altruistic emotion, cognition, and behavior.* Hillsdale, NJ: Erlbaum.

Ekman, P. (1973). Cross-cultural studies of facial expression. In P. Ekman (Ed.), *Darwin and facial expression: A century of research in review* (pp. 169–222). New York: Academic Press.

Elder, G. H., Jr. (1969). Appearance and education in marriage mobility. *American Sociological Review, 34*, 519–533.

Ellis, B. J. (1992). The evolution of sexual attraction: Evaluative mechanisms in women. In J. Barkow, L. Cosmides, & J. Tooby (Eds.), *The adapted mind* (pp. 267–288). New York: Oxford.

Ellis, B. J., & Symons, D. (1990). Sex differences in fantasy: An evolutionary psychological approach. *Journal of Sex Research, 27*, 527–556.

Ellis, L. (1995). Dominance and reproductive success among nonhuman animals: A cross-species comparison. *Ethology and Sociobiology, 16*, 257–333.

Emlen, S. T. (1995). An evolutionary theory of the family. *Proceedings of the National Academy of Science, 92*, 8092–8099.

Eron, L. D. (1982). Parent-child interaction, television violence, and aggression of children. *American Psychologist, 37*, 197–211.

Essock-Vitale, S. M., & McGuire, M. T. (1985). Women's lives viewed from an evolutionary perspective. II. Patterns of helping. *Ethology and Sociobiology, 6*, 155–173.

Euler, H. A., & Weitzel, B. (1996). Discriminative grandparental solicitude as reproductive strategy. *Human Nature, 7*, 39–59.

Evans, R., & Summers, R. J. (1986). Clinical aspects of Hymernoptera hypersensitivity (pp. 23–38). In M. I. Levine & R. F. Lockey (Eds.), *Monograph on insect allergy.* Pittsburgh, PA: Dave Lambert Associates.

Eysenck, H. J. (1976). *Sex and personality.* Austin, TX: University of Texas Press.

Faludi, S. (1991). *Backlash: The undeclared war against American women.* New York: Crown.

Farkas, L. G. (1981). *Anthropometry of the head and face in medicine.* New York: Elsevier.

Farrell, W. (1986). *Why men are the way they are.* New York: Berkeley Books.

Feather, N. T. (1994). Attitudes toward achievers and reactions to their fall: Theory and research concerning tall poppies. *Advances in Experimental Social Psychology, 26*, 1–73.

Feinsilber, M. (1997, December 6). Inflating personal histories irresistible to some. *Austin American Statesman,* p. A1.

Fielden, J., Lutter, C., & Dabbs, J. (1994). *Basking in glory: Testosterone changes in World Cup soccer fans.* Unpublished manuscript, Psychology Department, Georgia State University.

Figueredo, A. J. (1995). *Preliminary report: Family deterrence of domestic violence in Spain.* Department of Psychology, University of Arizona.

Fisek, M. H., & Ofshe, R. (1970). The process of status evolution. *Sociometry, 33*, 327–346.

Fisher, H. E. (1992). *Anatomy of Love.* New York: Norton.

Fisher, J. D., Nadler, A., & Whitcher-Alagna, S. (1982). Recipient reactions to aid. *Psychological Bulletin, 91*, 27–54.

Fisher, R. A. (1958). *The genetical theory of natural selection* (2nd ed.). New York: Dover.

Fisher, R. R. (1983). Transition to grandmotherhood. *International Journal of Aging and Human Development, 16*, 67–78.

Flinn, M. (1988a). Mate guarding in a Caribbean village. *Ethology and Sociobiology, 9*, 1–28.

Flinn, M. (1988b). Parent-offspring interactions in a Caribbean village: Daughter guarding. In L. Betzig, M. Borgerhoff Mulder, & P. Turke (Eds.), *Human reproductive behavior: A Darwinian perspective* (pp. 189–200). Cambridge, UK: Cambridge University Press.

Flinn, M. V. (1992). Parental care in a Caribbean village. In B. Hewlett (Ed.), *Father-child relations: Cultural and biosocial contexts* (pp. 57–84). Chicago: Aldine.

Ford, C. S., & Beach, F. A. (1951). *Patterns of sexual behavior.* New York: Harper & Row.

Forrest, M. S., & Hokanson, J. E. (1975). Depression and autonomic arousal reduction accompanying self-punitive behavior. *Journal of Abnormal Psychology, 84*, 346–357.

Fox, A. (1997, June). *The assessment of fighting ability in humans.* Paper presented to the Ninth Annual Meeting of the Human Behavior and Evolution Society, University of Arizona, Tucson, AZ.

Frank, R. H. (1985). *Choosing the right pond: Human behavior and the quest for status.* New York: Oxford University Press.

Frank, R. (1988). *Passions within reason.* New York: Norton.

Frayser, S. (1985). *Varieties of sexual experience: An anthropological perspective.* New Haven, CT: HRAF Press.

Freeman, D. (1983). *Margaret Mead and Samoa: The making and unmaking of an anthropological myth.* Cambridge, MA: Harvard University Press.

Freud, S. (1953). *The interpretation of dreams.* In J. Strachey (Ed. and Trans.), standard edition (Vol. 4, pp. 1–338; Vol. 5, pp. 339–721). New York: Basic Books. (Original work published 1900)

Friedman, B., & Duntley, J. D. (1998, July 12). *Parent-guarding: Offspring reactions to parental infidelity.* Paper presented to the Tenth Annual Meeting of the Human Behavior and Evolution Society, Davis, CA.

Friedman, H. S., Tucker, J. S., Schwartz, J. E., Tomlinson-Keasey, C., Martin, L. R., Wingard, D. L., & Criqui, M. H. (1995). Psychosocial and behavioral predictors of longevity: The aging and death of the "Termites." *American Psychologist, 50*, 69–78.

Gangestad, S. W., & Buss, D. M. (1993). Pathogen prevalence and human mate preferences. *Ethology and Sociobiology, 14*, 89–96.

Gangestad, S. W., & Simpson, J. A. (1990). Toward an evolutionary history of female sociosexual variation. *Journal of Personality, 58*, 69–96.

Gangestad, S. W., & Thornhill, R. (1997). Human sexual selection and developmental stability. In J. A. Simpson & D. T. Kenrick (Eds.), *Evolutionary social psychology* (pp. 169–195). Mahwah, NJ: Erlbaum.

Gangestad, S. W., Thornhill, R., & Yeo, R. A. (1994). Facial attractiveness, developmental stability, and fluctuating asymmetry. *Ethology and Sociobiology, 15*, 73–85.

Garcia, J., Ervin, F. R., & Koelling, R. A. (1966). Learning with prolonged delay of reinforcement. *Psychonomic Science, 5*, 121–122.

Garcia, J., & Koelling, R. A. (1966). Relation of cue to consequence in avoidance learning. *Psychonomic Science, 4*, 123–124.

Gardner, H. (1974). *The shattered mind.* New York: Random House.

Gaulin, S. J. C., McBurney, D. H., & Brakeman-Wartell, S. L. (1997). Matrilateral biases in the investment of aunts and uncles. *Human Nature, 8*, 139–151.

Gayford, J. J. (1975). *Wife battering: A preliminary survey of 100 cases.* London: British Medical Journal.

Geary, D. C. (1996). Sexual selection and sex differences in mathematical abilities. *Behavioral and Brain Sciences, 1996,* 229–284.

Geertz, C. (1973). The *interpretation of cultures.* New York: Basic Books.

Gigerenzer, G. (1991). How to make cognitive illusions disappear: Beyond "heuristics and biases." In W. Stoebe & M. Hewstone (Eds.), *European Review of Social Psychology,* Vol. 2 (pp. 83–115). Chichester, England: Wiley.

Gigerenzer, G. (1998). Ecological intelligence: An adaptation for frequencies. In D. D. Cummins & C. Allen (Eds.), *The evolution of mind* (pp. 9–29). New York: Oxford University Press.

Gigerenzer, G., & Hug, K. (1992). Domain specific reasoning: Social contracts, cheating and perspective change. *Cognition, 43,* 127–171.

Gilbert, D. T., & Malone, P. S. (1995). The correspondence bias. *Psychological Bulletin, 117,* 21–49.

Gilbert, P. (1989). *Human nature and suffering.* Hillsdale, NJ: Erlbaum.

Gilbert, P. (1990). Changes: Rank, status and mood. In S. Fischer & C. L. Cooper (Eds.), *On the move: The psychology of change and transition* (pp. 33–52). New York: Wiley.

Gillis, J. S. (1982). *Too tall, too small.* Champaign, IL: Institute for Personality and Ability Testing.

Gladue, B. A. (1991). Aggressive behavioral characteristics, hormones, and sexual orientation in men and women. *Aggressive Behavior, 17,* 313–326.

Gladue, B. A., Boechler, M., & McCaul, K. (1989). Hormonal response to competition in human males. *Aggressive Behavior, 15,* 409–422.

Gladue, B. A., & Delaney, J. J. (1990). Gender differences in perception of attractiveness of men and women in bars. *Personality and Social Psychology Bulletin, 16,* 378–391.

Glantz, K., & Pearce, J. (1989). *Exiles from Eden: Psychotherapy from an evolutionary perspective.* New York: Norton.

Glass, B., Temekin, O., Straus, W., Jr., (Eds.). (1959). *Forerunners of Darwin.* Baltimore, MD: Johns Hopkins University Press.

Glass, S. P., & Wright, T. L. (1985). Sex differences in type of extramarital involvement and marital dissatisfaction. *Sex Roles, 12,* 1101–1120.

Glass, S. P., & Wright, T. L. (1992). Justifications for extramarital relationships: The association between attitudes, behaviors, and gender. *Journal of Sex Research, 29,* 361–387.

Goldsmith, H. H., & Harman, C. (1994). Temperament and attachment: Individuals and relationships. *Current Directions in Psychological Science, 3,* 53–57.

Goldstein, J. H. (1986). *Aggression and crimes of violence* (2nd ed.). New York: Oxford University Press.

Gottesman, I. L. (1991). *Schizophrenia genesis.* New York: W. H. Freeman.

Gough, H. G. (1964). *Manual for the California Psychological Inventory* (Rev. ed.). Palo Alto, CA: Consulting Psychologists Press.

Gould, S. J. (1991). Exaptation: A crucial tool for evolutionary psychology. *Journal of Social Issues, 47,* 43–58.

Gould, S. J. (1997, October 9). Evolutionary psychology: An exchange. *New York Review of Books, XLIV,* 53–58.

Gould, S. J., & Eldredge, N. (1977). Punctuated equilibria: The tempo and mode of evolution reconsidered. *Paleobiology, 3,* 115–151.

Gove, P. B. (Ed.). (1986). *Webster's third new international dictionary of the English language unabridged.* Springfield, MA: Merriam-Webster.

Graham, N. M., et al. (1990). *Journal of Infectious Diseases, 162,* 1277–1282.

Grammer, K. (1992). Variations on a theme: Age dependent mate selection in humans. *Behavioral and Brain Sciences, 15,* 100–102.

Grammer, K. (1996, June). *The human mating game: The battle of the sexes and the war of signals.* Paper presented to the Human

Behavior and Evolution Society Annual Meeting, Northwestern University, Evanston, IL.

Grammer, K., & Thornhill, R. (1994). Human facial attractiveness and sexual selection: The roles of averageness and symmetry. *Journal of Comparative Psychology, 108,* 233–242.

Grant, P. R. (1991, October). Natural selection and Darwin's finches. *Scientific American, 265,* 82–87.

Gregor, T. (1985). *Anxious pleasures: The sexual lives of an Amazonian people.* Chicago: University of Chicago Press.

Greiling, H. (1995, July) *Women's mate preferences across contexts.* Paper presented to the Annual Meeting of the Human Behavior and Evolution Society, University of California, Santa Barbara, CA.

Greiling, H., & Buss, D. M. (under review). *Women's sexual strategies: The hidden dimension of short-term extra-pair mating.* Department of Psychology, University of Texas, Austin.

Gross, M. R. (1982). Sneakers, satellites and parentals: Polymorphic mating strategies in North American sunfishes. *Zeitschrift fur Tierpsychologie, 60,* 1–26.

Gross, M. R., & Sargent, R. C. (1985). The evolution of male and female parental care in fishes. *American Zoologist, 25,* 807–822.

Gross, M. R., & Shine, R. (1981). Parental care and mode of fertilization in ectothermic vertebrates. *Evolution, 35,* 775–793.

Gutek, B. A. (1985). *Sex and the workplace: The impact of sexual behavior and harassment on women, men, and the organization.* San Francisco: Jossey-Bass.

Gutierres, S. E., Kenrick, D. T., & Partch, J. (1994). *Effects of others' dominance and attractiveness on self-ratings.* Unpublished manuscript, Department of Psychology, Arizona State University, Tempe.

Guttentag, M., & Secord, P. (1983). *Too many women?* Beverly Hills, CA: Sage.

Guttmacher, M. S. (1955). Criminal responsibility in certain homicide cases involving family members. In P. H. Hoch & J. Zubin (Eds.), *Psychiatry and the law.* New York: Grune and Stratton.

Haig, D. (1993). Genetic conflicts in human pregnancy. *The Quarterly Review of Biology, 68,* 495–532.

Hames, R. B. (1988). The allocation of parental care among the Ye'kwana. In L. Betzig, M. Borgerhoff Mulder, & P. Turke (Eds.), *Human reproductive behavior: A Darwinian perspective* (pp. 237–252). Cambridge, UK: Cambridge University Press.

Hamilton, W. D. (1964). The genetical evolution of social behavior. I and II. *Journal of Theoretical Biology, 7,* 1–52.

Hamilton, W. D. (1980). Sex versus non-sex versus parasite. *Oikos, 35,* 282–290.

Hamilton, W. D. (1987). Discriminating nepotism: Expectable, common, overlooked. In D. J. C. Fletcher & C. D. Michener (Eds.), *Kin recognition in animals* (pp. 417–437). New York: Wiley.

Hamilton, W. D. (1996). *Narrow roads of gene land.* New York: W. H. Freeman.

Hamilton, W. D., & Zuk, M. (1982). Heritable true fitness and bright birds: A role for parasites? *Science, 218,* 384–387.

Harlow, H. F. (1971). *Learning to love.* San Francisco: Albion.

Harris, C. L. (1992). *Concepts in zoology.* New York: HarperCollins.

Hansen, R. D. (1980). Commonsense attribution. *Journal of Personality and Social Psychology, 39,* 996–1009.

Harpending, H. C., & Sobus, J. (1987). Sociopathy as an adaptation. *Ethology and Sociobiology, 8,* 63S–72S.

Hart, C. W., & Pilling, A. R. (1960). *The Tiwi of North Australia.* New York: Hart, Rinehart, & Winston.

Hartung, J. (1987). Deceiving down: Conjectures on the management of subordinate status. In J. Lockart & D. L. Paulhus (Eds.),

Self-deception: An adaptive mechanism? (pp. 170–185). Englewood Cliffs, NJ: Prentice-Hall.

Haselton, M. B., & Buss, D. M. (1997, June). *Errors in mind reading: Design flaws or design features?* Paper presented to the Ninth Annual Meeting of the Human Behavior and Evolution Society, University of Arizona, Tucson, AZ.

Hatfield, E., & Rapson, R. L. (1993). *Love, sex, and intimacy.* New York: HarperCollins.

Hatfield, E., & Rapson, R. L. (1996). *Love and sex: Cross-cultural perspectives.* Boston: Allyn & Bacon.

Hawkes, K. (1991). Showing off: Tests of another hypothesis about men's foraging goals. *Ethology and Sociobiology, 11,* 29–54.

Held, B. L., Nader, S., Rodriguez-Rigau, L. J., Smith, K. D., & Steinberger, E. (1984). Acne and hyperandroenism. *Journal of American Academy of Dermatology, 10,* 223–226.

Hendersen, R. W. (1985). Fearful memories: The motivational significance of forgetting. In F. R. Brush & J. B. Overmier (Eds.), *Affect, conditioning, and cognition: Essays on the determinants of behavior* (pp. 43–53). Hillsdale, NJ: Erlbaum.

Hendrick, S., & Hendrick, C. (1992). *Romantic love.* Newbury Park: Sage.

Henss, R. (1992). *Perceiving age and attractiveness in facial photographs.* Unpublished manuscript, Psychologisches Institut, University of Saarland, Germany.

Herrnstein, R. J. (1977). The evolution of behaviorism. *American Psychologist, 32,* 593–603.

Hess, E. H. (1975). *The tell-tale eye.* New York: Van Nostrand Reinhold.

Hewlett, B. S. (1991). *Intimate fathers: The nature and context of Aka pygmy paternal infant care.* Ann Arbor: University of Michigan Press.

Hilberman, E., & Munson, K. (1978). Sixty battered women. *Victimology, 2,* 460–470.

Hill, C. T., Rubin, Z., & Peplau, L. A. (1976). Breakups before marriage: The end of 103 affairs. *Journal of Social Issue, 32,* 147–168.

Hill, K. (1993). Life history theory and evolutionary anthropology. *Evolutionary Anthropology, 2,* 78–88.

Hill, K., & Hurtado, A. M. (1989). Ecological studies among some South American foragers. *American Scientist, 77,* 436–443.

Hill, K., & Hurtado, A. M. (1991). The evolution of premature reproductive senescence and menopause in human females. *Human Nature, 2,* 313–350.

Hill, K., & Hurtado, A. M. (1996). *Ache life history.* New York: Aldine De Gruyter.

Hill, K., & Kaplan, H. (1988). Tradeoffs in male and female reproductive strategies among the Ache. In L. Betzig, M. Borgerhoff Mulder, & P. Turke (Eds.), *Human reproductive behavior* (pp. 277–306). New York: Cambridge University Press.

Hill, R. (1945). Campus values in mate selection. *Journal of Home Economics, 37,* 554–558.

Hirsh, L. R. (1996, June). *"Quantity" and "quality" fathering strategies: Not all men follow in their fathers' footsteps.* Paper presented to the Eighth Annual Meeting of the Human Behavior and Evolution Society, Evanston, IL.

Hirshfeld, L. A., & Gelman, S. (1994). *Mapping the mind: Domain specificity in cognition and culture.* New York: Cambridge University Press.

Hite, S. (1987). *Women and love: A cultural revolution in progress.* New York: Knopf.

Hokanson, J. E. (1961). The effect of frustration and anxiety on overt aggression. *Journal of Abnormal and Social Psychology, 62,* 346–351.

Holmberg, A. R. (1950). *Nomads of the long bow: The Siriono of Eastern Bolivia.* Washington, DC: U.S. Government Printing Office.

Holmes, W. G., & Sherman, P. W. (1982). The ontogeny of kin recognition in two species of ground squirrels. *American Zoologist, 22,* 491–517.

hooks, b. (1984). *Feminist theory: From margin to center.* Boston: South End Press.

Horung, C. A., McCullough, C. B., & Sugimoto, T. (1981). Status relationships in marriage:

Risk factors in spouse abuse. *Journal of Marriage and the Family*, 675–692.

Hrdy, S. B. (1977). Infanticide as a primate reproductive strategy. *American Scientist, 65,* 40–49.

Hrdy, S. B. (1981). *The woman that never evolved.* Cambridge, MA: Harvard University Press.

Hudson, J. W., & Henze, L. F. (1969). Campus values in mate selection: A replication. *Journal of Marriage and the Family, 31,* 772–775.

Huesmann, L. R., & Eron, L. D. (1986). *Television and the aggressive child: A cross-national comparison.* Hillsdale, NJ: Erlbaum.

Hunt, M. (1974). *Sexual behavior in the 70's.* Chicago: Playboy Press.

Hurtado, A. M., Hill, K., Kaplan, H., & Hurtado, I. (1992). Trade-offs between female food acquisition and child care among Hiwi and Ache foragers. *Human Nature, 3,* 185–216.

Huxley, J. S. (1942). *Evolution: The modern synthesis.* London: Allen & Unwin.

Hyde, J. S. (1986). Gender differences in aggression. In J. S. Hyde & M. C. Linn (Eds.), *The psychology of gender: Advances through meta-analysis.* Baltimore, MD: Johns Hopkins University Press.

Isaac, G. (1978). The food-sharing behavior of protohuman hominids. *Scientific American, 238,* 90–108.

Jackson, D. N. (1967). *Personality Research Form manual.* Goshen, NY: Research Psychologists Press.

Jackson, L. A. (1992). *Physical appearance and gender: Sociobiological and sociocultural perspectives.* Albany: State University of New York Press.

Jagger, A. (1994). *Living with contradictions: Controversies in feminist social ethics.* Boulder, CO: Westview Press.

James, W. (1962). *Principles of psychology.* New York: Dover. (Original work published 1890)

Jankowiak, W. (Ed.). (1995). *Romantic passion: A universal experience?* New York: Columbia University Press.

Jankowiak, W., & Fischer, R. (1992). A cross-cultural perspective on romantic love. *Ethnology, 31,* 149–155.

Jankowiak, W. R., Hill, E. M., & Donovan, J. M. (1992). The effects of sex and sexual orientation on attractiveness judgments. *Ethology and Sociobiology, 13,* 73–85.

Jencks, C. (1979). *Who gets ahead? The determinants of economic success in America.* New York: Basic Books.

Johnston, V. S., & Franklin, M. (1993). Is beauty in the eyes of the beholder? *Ethology and Sociobiology, 14,* 183–199.

Jones, D. (1996). *Physical attractiveness and the theory of sexual selection.* Ann Arbor: University of Michigan Press.

Judge, D. S. (1995). American legacies and the variable life histories of women and men. *Human Nature, 6,* 291–323.

Kalma, A. (1991). Hierarchisation and dominance assessment at first glance. *European Journal of Social Psychology, 21,* 165–181.

Kaplan, S. (1992). Environmental preference in a knowledge-seeking, knowledge-using organism. In J. Barkow, L. Cosmides, & J. Tooby (Eds.), *The adapted mind* (pp. 581–598). New York: Oxford University Press.

Kaplan, S., & Kaplan, R. (1982). *Cognition and environment: Functioning in an uncertain world.* New York: Praeger.

Keller, M. C., Thiessen, D., & Young, R. K. (1996). Mate assortment in dating and married couples. *Personality and Individual Differences, 21,* 217–221.

Kenrick, D. T., Groth, G. E., Trost, M. R., & Sadalla, E. K. (1993). Integrating evolutionary and social exchange perspectives on relationships: Effects of gender, self-appraisal, and involvement level on mate selection. *Journal of Personality and Social Psychology, 64,* 951–969.

Kenrick, D. T., Gutierres, S. E., & Goldberg, L. (1989). Influence of erotica on ratings of strangers and mates. *Journal of Experimental Social Psychology, 25,* 159–167.

Kenrick, D. T., & Keefe, R. C. (1992). Age preferences in mates reflect sex differences in reproductive strategies. *Behavioral and Brain Sciences, 15,* 75–133.

Kenrick, D. T., Keefe, R. C., Gabrielidis, C., & Cornelius, J. S. (1996). Adolescents' age preferences for dating partners: Support for an evolutionary model of life-history strategies. *Child Development, 67,* 1499–1511.

Kenrick, D. T., Neuberg, S. L., Zierk, K. L., & Krones, J. M. (1994). Evolution and social cognition: Contrast effects as a function of sex, dominance, and physical attractiveness. *Personality and Social Psychology Bulletin, 20,* 210–217.

Kenrick, D. T., Sadalla, E. K., Groth, G., & Trost, M. R. (1990). Evolution, traits, and the stages of human courtship: Qualifying the parental investment model. *Journal of Personality, 58,* 97–116.

Kenrick, D. T., & Sheets, V. (1993). Homicidal fantasies. *Ethology and Sociobiology, 14,* 231–246.

Kim, K., Smith, P. K., & Palermiti, A. (1997). Conflict in childhood and reproductive development. *Evolution and Human Behavior, 18,* 109–142.

Kinsey, A. C., Pomeroy, W. B., & Martin, C. E. (1948). *Sexual behavior in the human male.* Philadelphia: Saunders.

Kinsey, A. C., Pomeroy, W. B., & Martin, C. E. (1953). *Sexual behavior in the human female.* Philadelphia: Saunders.

Kirkpatrick, L. A. (1998). Evolution, pair-bonding, and reproductive strategies: A reconceptualization of adult attachment. In J. A. Simpson & W. S. Rholes (Eds.), *Attachment theory and close relationships.* New York: Guilford.

Kluger, M. J. (1990). In P. A. MacKowiac (Ed.), *Fever: Basic measurement and management.* New York: Raven Press.

Kluger, M. J. (1991). The adaptive value of fever. In P. A. MacKowiac (Ed.), *Fever: Basic*

measurement and management (105–124). New York: Raven Press.

Konner, M. (1990). *Why the reckless survive.* New York, NY: Viking.

Kyl-Heku, L. M., & Buss, D. M. (1996). Tactics as units of analysis in personality psychology: An illustration using tactics of hierarchy negotiation. *Personality and Individual Differences, 21,* 497–517.

La Cerra, M. M. (1994). *Evolved mate preferences in women: Psychological adaptations for assessing a man's willingness to invest in offspring.* Unpublished doctoral dissertation, Department of Psychology, University of California, Santa Barbara.

Lakoff, G., & Johnson, M. (1980). *Metaphors we live by.* Chicago: University of Chicago Press.

Lalumiere, M. L., Chalmers, L. J., Quinsey, V. L., & Seto, M. C. (1996). A test of the mate deprivation hypothesis of sexual coercion. *Ethology and Sociobiology, 17,* 299–318.

Lalumiere, M. L, & Quinsey, V. L. (1996). Sexual deviance, antisociality, mating effort, and the use of sexually coercive behaviors. *Personality and Individual Differences, 21,* 33–48.

Lalumiere, M. L., Seto, M. C., & Quinsey, V. L. (1995). *Self-perceived mating success and the mating choices of human males and females.* Unpublished manuscript.

Lamarck, J. B. (1809). *Zoological Philosophy.* New York: McMillan & Co. [English Translation in 1914].

Lancaster, J. B., & King, B. J. (1985). An evolutionary perspective on menopause. In J. K. Brown & V. Kern (Eds.), *In her prime: A new view of middle-aged women* (pp. 13–20). Boston, MA: Bergin & Carvey.

Langhorne, M. C., & Secord, P. F. (1955). Variations in marital needs with age, sex, marital status, and regional composition. *Journal of Social Psychology, 41,* 19–37.

Langlois, J. H., & Roggman, L. A. (1990). Attractive faces are only average. *Psychological Science, 1,* 115–121.

Langlois, J. H., Roggman, L. A., Casey, R. J., Ritter, J. M., Rieser-Danner, L. A., & Jenkins, V. Y. (1987). Infant preferences for attractive faces: Rudiments of a stereotype. *Developmental Psychology, 23,* 363–369.

Langlois, J. H., Roggman, L. A., & Musselman, L. (1994). What is average and what is not average about attractive faces? *Psychological Science, 5,* 214–219.

Langlois, J. H., Roggman, L. A., & Reiser-Danner, L. A. (1990). Infants' differential social responses to attractive and unattractive faces. *Developmental Psychology, 26,* 153–159.

Latané, B. (1981). The psychology of social impact. *American Psychologist, 36,* 343–356.

Lauman, E. O., Gagnon, J. H., Michael, R. T., & Michaels, S. (1994). *The social organization of sexuality: Sexual practices in the United States.* Chicago: University of Chicago Press.

Leach, E. (1966). Virgin birth. *Proceedings of the Royal Anthropological Institute of Great Britain and Ireland,* 39–49.

Leakey, R., & Lewin, R. (1992). *Origins reconsidered: In search of what makes us human.* New York: Doubleday.

Leary, M. R., & Downs, D. L. (1995). Interpersonal functions of the self-esteem motive: The self-esteem system as a sociometer. In M. H. Kernis (Ed.), *Efficacy, agency, and self-esteem* (pp. 123–144). New York: Plenum.

Leary, M. R., Haupt, A. L., Strausser, K. S., & Chokel, J. T. (in press). Calibrating the sociometer: The relationship between interpersonal appraisals and state self-esteem. *Journal of Personality and Social Psychology.*

Leary, M. R., & Shepperd, J. A. (1986). Behavioral self-handicaps versus self-reported handicaps: A conceptual note. *Journal of Personality and Social Psychology, 51,* 1265–1268.

Le Boeuf, B. J., & Reiter, J. (1988). Lifetime reproductive success in northern elephant seals. In T. H. Clutton-Brock (Ed.), *Reproductive success* (pp. 344–362). Chicago: University of Chicago Press.

Lee, R. B. (1979). *The !Kung San: Men, women, and working in a foraging society.* New York: Cambridge University Press.

Lee, R., & DeVore, I. (Eds.). (1968). *Man the hunter.* Chicago: Aldine.

Leslie, A. M. (1991). The theory of mind impairment in autism: Evidence for modular mechanisms of development? In A. Whiten (Ed.), *The emergence of mind reading.* Oxford: Blackwell.

Levins, R. (1968). *Evolution in changing environments.* Princeton: University Press.

Little, B. R. (1989). Personal projects analysis: Trivial pursuits, magnificent obsessions, and the search for coherence. In D. M. Buss & N. Cantor (Eds.), *Personality psychology: Recent trends, emerging directions* (pp. 15–31). New York: Springer-Verlag.

Lorenz, K. (1941). Vergleichende Bewegungsstudien an Anatiden. *Journal of Ornithology, 89,* 194–294.

Lorenz, K. Z. (1965). *Evolution and the modification of behavior.* Chicago: University of Chicago Press.

Low, B. S. (1989). Cross-cultural patterns in the training of children: An evolutionary perspective. *Journal of Comparative Psychology, 103,* 313–319.

Low, B. S. (1991). Reproductive life in nineteenth century Sweden: An evolutionary perspective. *Ethology and Sociobiology, 12,* 411–448.

Lykken, D. (1995). *The antisocial personalities.* Hillsdale, NJ: Erlbaum.

Lynn, M., & Shurgot, B. A. (1984). Responses to lonely hearts advertisements: Effects of reported physical attractiveness, physique, and coloration. *Personality and Social Psychology Bulletin, 10,* 349–357.

Maccoby, E. E. (1990). Gender and relationships: A developmental account. *American Psychologist, 45,* 513–520.

Maccoby, E. E., & Jacklin, C. N. (1974). *The psychology of sex differences.* Stanford, CA: Stanford University Press.

MacDonald, K. B. (Ed.). (1988). *Sociobiological perspectives on human development.* New York: Springer-Verlag.

MacDonald, K. (1995). Evolution, the Five-Factor Model, and Levels of Personality. *Journal of Personality, 63,* 525–568.

MacDonald, K. (1996). What do children want? A conceptualization of evolutionary influences on children's motivation in the peer group. *International Journal of Behavioral Development, 19,* 53–73.

Mackey, W. C. Relationships between the human sex ratio and the woman's microenvironment: Four tests. *Human Nature, 4,* 175–198.

Mackey, W. C., & Daly, R. D. (1995). A test of the man-child bond: The predictive potency of the teeter-totter effect. *Genetic, Social, and General Psychology Monographs, 121,* 424–444.

MacKinnon, C. (1987). *Feminism unmodified.* Cambridge, MA: Harvard University Press.

Malamuth, N. M. (1996). The confluence model of sexual aggression: Feminist and evolutionary perspectives. In D. M. Buss & N. M. Malamuth (Eds.), *Sex, power, conflict: Evolutionary and feminist perspectives* (pp. 269–295). New York: Oxford University Press.

Malamuth, N. M., Sockloskie, R., Koss, M., & Tanaka, J. (1991). The characteristics of aggressors against women: Testing a model using a national sample of college women. *Journal of Consulting and Clinical Psychology, 59,* 670–681.

Malinowski, B. (1929). *The sexual life of savages in North-Western Melanesia.* London: Routledge.

Mann, J. (1992). Nurturance or negligence: Maternal psychology and behavioral preference among preterm twins. In J. Barkow, L. Cosmides, & J. Tooby (Eds.), *The adapted mind* (pp. 367–390). New York: Oxford University Press.

Manson, J. H. (1992). Measuring female mate choice in Cayo Santiago rhesus macaques. *Animal Behavior, 44,* 405–416.

Marks, I. (1987). *Fears, phobias, and rituals: Panic, anxiety, and their disorders.* New York: Oxford University Press.

Marks, I. M., & Nesse, R. M. (1994). Fear and fitness: An evolutionary analysis of anxiety disorders. *Ethology and Sociobiology, 15,* 247–261.

Marr, D. (1982). *Vision: A computational investigation into the human representation and processing of visual information.* San Francisco: Freeman.

Maslow, A. H. (1937). Dominance-feeling, behavior, and status. *Psychological Review, 44,* 404–429.

Mathews, A. M. (1978). Fear-reduction research and clinical phobias. *Psychological Bulletin, 85,* 390–404.

Maynard Smith, J. (1982). *Evolution and the theory of games.* Cambridge, UK: Cambridge University Press.

Mayr, E. (1942). *Systematics and the origin of species.* New York: Columbia University Press.

Mayr, E. (1982). *The growth of biological thought.* Cambridge, MA: Harvard University Press.

Mazur, A., & Booth, A. (in press). Testosterone and dominance in men. *Behavioral and Brain Science.*

Mazur, A., Booth, A., & Dabbs, J. (1992). Testosterone and chess competition. *Social Psychology Quarterly, 55,* 70–77.

Mazur, A., Halpern, C., & Udry, J. R. (1994). Dominant looking male teenagers copulate earlier. *Ethology and Sociobiology, 15,* 87–94.

McCracken, G. F. (1984). Communal nursing in Mexican free-tailed bat maternity colonies. *Science, 223,* 1090–1091.

McGinnis, R. (1958). Campus values in mate selection. *Social Forces, 35,* 368–373.

McGuire, A. M. (1994). Helping behaviors in the natural environment: Dimensions and correlates of helping. *Personality and Social Psychology Bulletin, 20,* 45–56.

McGuire, M. T., & Troisi, A. (1998). *Darwinian psychiatry*. New York: Oxford University Press.

McNally, R. J. (1987). Preparedness and phobias: A review. *Psychological Bulletin, 101*, 283–303.

Mealey, L. (1995). The sociobiology of sociopathy: An integrated evolutionary model. *Behavioral and Brain Sciences, 18*, 523–599.

Mealey, L., Daood, C., & Krage, M. (1996). Enhanced memory for faces of cheaters. *Ethology and Sociobiology, 17*, 119–128.

Megargee, E. I. (1969). Influence of sex roles on the manifestation of leadership. *Journal of Applied Psychology, 53*, 377–382.

Mesquida, C. G., & Wiener, N. I. (1996). Human collective aggression: A behavioral ecology perspective. *Ethology and Sociobiology, 17*, 247–262.

Milgram, S. (1974). *Obedience to authority*. New York: Harper & Row.

Miller, G. (1991). Personal communication.

Miller, G. F. (1998). How mate choice shaped human nature: A review of sexual selection and human evolution. In C. Crawford & D. Krebs (Eds.), *Handbook of Evolutionary Psychology* (pp. 87–129). Mahwah, NJ: Erlbaum.

Miller, G. F. (in press). Sexual selection for cultural displays. In R. Dunbar, C. Knight, & C. Power (Eds.), *Evolution of culture*. Edinburgh: Edinburgh University Press.

Miller, W. B. (1980). Gangs, groups and serious youth crime. In D. Shichor & D. H. Kelly (Eds.), *Critical issues in juvenile delinquency* (pp. 115–138). Lexington, MA: Lexington Books.

Mineka, S. (1992). Evolutionary memories, emotional processing, and the emotional disorders. *The Psychology of Learning and Motivation, 28*, 161–206.

Morse, S. T., Gruzen, J., & Reis, H. (1976). The "eye of the beholder": A neglected variable in the study of physical attractiveness. *Journal of Personality, 44*, 209–225.

Muehlenhard, C. L., & Linton, M. A. (1987). Date rape and sexual aggression in dating situations: Incidence and risk factors. *Journal of Counseling Psychology, 2*, 186–196.

Mueller, U., & Mazur, A. (1996). Facial dominance of West Point cadets as a predictor of later military rank. *Social Forces, 74*, 823–850.

Mulvihill, D. J., Tumin, M. M., & Curtis, L. A. (1969). *Crimes of violence* (Vol 11). Washington, DC: U.S. Government Printing Office.

Murdock, G. P. (1932). The science of culture. *American Anthropologist, 34*, 200–215.

Myers, D. G. (1995). *Social psychology* (5th ed.). New York: McGraw-Hill.

Nesse, R. M. (1990). Evolutionary explanations of emotions. *Human Nature, 1*, 261–289.

Nesse, R. M. (1991, November/December). What good is feeling bad?: The evolutionary benefits of psychic pain. *The Sciences*, 30–37.

Nesse, R. M., & Williams, G. C. (1994). *Why we get sick*. New York: Times Books Random House.

Nicholson, N. (1997). Evolutionary psychology: Toward a new view of human nature and organizational society. *Human Relations, 50*, 1053–1078.

Nida, S. A., & Koon, J. (1983). They get better looking at closing time around here, too. *Psychological Reports, 52*, 657–658.

Nisbett, R. E. (1993). Violence and U.S. regional culture. *American Psychologist, 48*, 441–449.

Nisbett, R. E., & Ross, L. (1980). *Human inference: Strategies and shortcomings of social judgment*. Englewood Cliffs, NJ: Prentice-Hall.

Nyquist, L. V., & Spence, J. T. (1986). Effects of dispositional dominance and sex role expectations on leadership behaviors. *Journal of Personality and Social Psychology, 50*, 97–98.

Olweus, D. (1978). *Aggression in schools*. New York: Wiley.

Orians, G. (1980). Habitat selection: General theory and applications to human behavior. In J. S. Lockard (Ed.), *The evolution of human social behavior* (pp. 49–66). Chicago: Elsevier.

Orians, G. (1986). An ecological and evolutionary approach to landscape aesthetics. In E. C. Penning-Rowsell & D. Lowenthal (Eds.), *Landscape meaning and values* (pp. 3–25). London: Allen & Unwin.

Orians, G. H., & Heerwagen, J. H. (1992). Evolved responses to landscapes. In J. Barkow, L. Cosmides, & J. Tooby (Eds.), *The adapted mind* (pp. 555–579). New York: Oxford University Press.

Ortner, S. B. (1974). Is female to male as nature is to nurture? In M. Z. Rosaldo & L. Lamphere (Eds.), *Women, culture, and society* (pp. 67–88). Stanford, CA: Stanford University Press.

Orwell, G. (1946). *Animal farm*. New York: Harcourt, Brace & Company.

Otterbein, K. (1979). *The evolution of war*. New Haven, CT: HRAF Press.

Packer, C. (1977). Reciprocal altruism in *Papio anubis*. *Nature, 265,* 441–443.

Padilla, F. M. (1992). *The gang as an American enterprise*. New Brunswick, NJ: Rutgers University Press.

Palmer, C. T., & Tilley, C. F. (1995). Sexual access to females as a motivation for joining gangs: An evolutionary approach. *The Journal of Sex Research, 32,* 213–217.

Parker, G. A. (1974). Assessment strategy and the evolution of fighting behaviour. *Journal of Theoretical Biology, 47,* 223–243.

Paton, W., & Mannison, M. (1995). Sexual coercion in high school dating. *Sex Roles, 33,* 447–457.

Patton, J. Q. (1997, June). *Are warriors altruistic? Reciprocal altruism and war in the Ecuadorian Amazon.* Paper presented at the Human Behavior and Evolution Society Meetings, University of Arizona, Tucson, AZ.

Pavlov, I. P. (1927). *Conditioned reflexes,* trans. G. V. Anrep. London: Oxford University Press.

Pedersen, F. A. (1991). Secular trends in human sex ratios: Their influence on individual and family behavior. *Human Nature, 2,* 271–291.

Pennebaker, J. W., Dyer, M. A., Caulkins, R. S., Litowixz, D. L., Ackerman, P. L., & Anderson, D. B. (1979). Don't the girls get prettier at closing time: A country and western application to psychology. *Personality and Social Psychology Bulletin, 5,* 122–125.

Perrett, D. I., May, K. A., & Yoshikawa, S. (1994). Facial shape and judgments of female attractiveness. *Nature, 368,* 239–242.

Perusse, D. (1993). Cultural and reproductive success in industrial societies: Testing the relationship at proximate and ultimate levels. *Behavioral and Brain Sciences, 16,* 267–322.

Piddocke, S. (1965). The potlatch system of the southern Kwakiutl: A new perspective. *Southwestern Journal of Anthropology, 21,* 244–264.

Pinker, S. (1994). *The language instinct.* New York: Morrow.

Pinker, S. (1997). *How the mind works.* New York: Norton.

Platts, J. T. (1960). *A dictionary of Urdu, Classical Hindi, and English.* Oxford: Oxford University Press.

Plomin, R., DeFries, J. C., & McClearn, G. E. (1990). *Behavioral genetics: A primer* (2nd ed.). New York: Freeman.

Plomin, R., DeFries, J. C., & McClearn, G. E. (1997). *Behavioral genetics: A primer* (3rd ed.). New York: Freeman.

Posner, R. A. (1992). *Sex and reason.* Cambridge, MA: Harvard University Press.

Pratto, F. (1996). Sexual politics: The gender gap in the bedroom, the cupboard, and the cabinet. In D. M. Buss & N. M. Malamuth (Eds.), *Sex, power, conflict: Evolutionary and feminist perspectives* (pp. 179–230). New York: Oxford University Press.

Pratto, F., Sidanius, J., & Stallworth, L. M. (1993). Sexual selection and the sexual and ethnic basis of social hierarchy. In L. Ellis (Ed.), *Social stratification and socioeconomic inequality* (pp. 111–137). Westport, CT: Praeger.

Price, J. S., & Sloman, L. (1987). Depression as yielding behavior: An animal model based on Schjelderup-Ebb's pecking order. *Ethology and Sociobiology, 8,* 85–98.

Profet, M. (1991). The function of allergy: Immunological defense against toxins. *Quarterly Review of Biology, 66,* 23–62.

Profet, M. (1992). Pregnancy sickness as adaptation: A deterrent to maternal ingestion of teratogens. In J. Barkow, L. Cosmides, & J. Tooby (Eds.), *The adapted mind* (pp. 327–366). New York: Oxford University Press.

Quinn, R. E. (1977). Coping with cupid: The formation, impact, and management of romantic relationships in organizations. *Administrative Science Quarterly, 22,* 30–45.

Quinsey, V. L., & Lalumiere, M. L. (1995). Evolutionary perspectives on sexual offending. *Sexual Abuse: A Journal of Research and Treatment, 7,* 301–315.

Ramson, W. S. (1988). *Australian national dictionary.* Melbourne: Oxford University Press.

Redford, D. (1984). *Akhenaten: The heretic king.* Princeton, NJ: Princeton University Press.

Regalski, J. M., & Gualin, S. J. C. (1993). Whom are Mexican infants said to resemble? Monitoring and fostering paternal confidence in the Yucatan. *Ethology and Sociobiology, 14,* 97–113.

Regan, P. C. (1998). Minimum mate selection standards as a function of perceived mate value, relationship context, and gender. *Journal of Psychology and Human Sexuality, 10,* 53–73.

Ridley, M. (1996). *Evolution* (2nd ed.). Cambridge, MA: Blackwell Science.

Rosenblatt, P. C. (1974). Cross-cultural perspectives on attractiveness. In T. L. Huston (Ed.), *Foundations of interpersonal attraction* (pp. 79–95). New York: Academic Press.

Røskaft, E., Wara, A., & Viken, A. (1992). Reproductive success in relation to resource-access

and parental age in a small Norwegian farming parish during the period 1700–1900. *Ethology and Sociobiology, 13,* 443–461.

Ross, L. (1981). The "intuitive scientist" formulation and its developmental implications. In J. H. Flavell & L. Ross (Eds.), *Social cognitive development* (pp. 1–41). Cambridge, UK: Cambridge University Press.

Rowe, D. C. (1995). Evolution, mating effort, and crime. *Behavioral and Brain Sciences, 18,* 573–574.

Rozin, P. (1976). The selection of food by rats, humans and other animals. In J. Rosenblatt, R. A. Hinde, & E. Shaw (Eds.), *Advances in the study of behavior: Vol 6* (pp. 21–76). New York: Academic Press.

Rozin, P. (1996). Towards a psychology of food and eating: From motivation to module to model to marker, morality, meaning and metaphor. *Current Directions in Psychological Science, 5,* 18–24.

Rozin, P., & Fallon, A. (1988). Body image, attitudes to weight, and misperceptions of figure preferences of the opposite sex: A comparison of men and women in two generations. *Journal of Abnormal Psychology, 97,* 342–345.

Rozin, P., & Schull, J. (1988). The adaptive-evolutionary point of view in experimental psychology. In R. C. Atkinson, R. J. Herrnstein, G. Lindzey, & R. D. Luce (Eds.), *Stevens' handbook of experimental psychology: Vol. 1. Perception and motivation* (2nd ed., pp. 503–546). New York: Wiley.

Saal, F. E., Johnson, C. B., & Weber, N. (1989). Friendly or sexy? It may depend on whom you ask. *Psychology of Women Quarterly, 13,* 263–276.

Sabini, J. (1995). *Social psychology* (2nd ed.). New York: Norton.

Safilios-Rothschild, C. (1969). Attitudes of Greek spouses toward marital infidelity. In G. Neubeck (Ed.), *Extramarital relations* (pp. 78–79). Englewood Cliffs, NJ: Prentice-Hall.

Sahlins, M. (1977). *The use and abuse of biology.* Ann Arbor: University of Michigan Press.

Salmon, C. (1997). *Birth order and the salience of the family.* Manuscript submitted for publication.

Salmon, C., & Daly, M. (1996). On the importance of kin relations to Canadian women and men. *Ethology and Sociobiology, 17,* 289–297.

Salovey, P., & Rodin, J. (1984). Some antecedents and consequences of social-comparison jealousy. *Journal of Personality and Social Psychology, 47,* 780–792.

Scarr, S., & Salapatek, P. (1970). Patterns of fear development during infancy. *Merrill-Palmer Quarterly, 16,* 53–90.

Schapera, I. (1940). *Married life in an African tribe.* London: Faber & Faber.

Scheib, J. E. (1997, June). *Context-specific mate choice criteria: Women's trade-offs in the contexts of long-term and extra-pair mateships.* Paper presented to the Annual Meeting of the Human Behavior and Evolution Society, University of Arizona, Tucson, AZ.

Schlager, D. (1995). Evolutionary perspectives on paranoid disorder. *The Psychiatric Clinics of North America, 18,* 263–279.

Schmitt, A., & Atzwanger, K. (1995). Walking fast—ranking high: A sociobiological perspective on pace. *Evolution and Human Behavior, 16,* 451–462.

Schmitt, D. P., & Buss, D. M. (1996). Strategic self-promotion and competitor derogation: Sex and context effects on perceived effectiveness of mate attraction tactics. *Journal of Personality and Social Psychology, 70,* 1185–1204.

Scott, P. D. (1973). Fatal battered baby cases. *Medicine, Science, and the Law, 13,* 120–126.

Segal, N. L., Wilson, S. M., Bouchard, T. J., & Gitlin, D. G. (1995). Comparative grief experiences of bereaved twins and other bereaved relatives. *Personality and Individual Differences, 18,* 511–524.

Segal, N. L., Weisfeld, G. E., & Weisfeld, C. C. (1997). *Uniting psychology and biology: Integrative perspectives on human development.* Washington, DC: American Psychological Association.

Seligman, M., & Hager, J. (1972). *Biological boundaries of learning.* New York: Appleton-Century-Crofts.

Seyfarth, R. M., & Cheney, D. L. (1984). Grooming, alliances and reciprocal altruism in vervet monkeys. *Nature, 308,* 541–543.

Shackelford, T. K., & Buss, D. M. (1996). Betrayal in mateships, friendships, and coalitions. *Personality and Social Psychology Bulletin, 22,* 1151–1164.

Shackelford, T. K., & Larsen, R. J. (1997). Facial asymmetry as indicator of psychological, emotional, and physiological distress. *Journal of Personality and Social Psychology, 72,* 456–466.

Shepard, R. N. (1992). The perceptual organization of colors: An adaptation to regularities of the terrestrial world? In J. Barkow, L. Cosmides, & J. Tooby (Eds.), *The adapted mind* (pp. 495–532). New York: Oxford University Press.

Sherman, P. W. (1977). Nepotism and the evolution of alarm calls. *Science, 197,* 1246–1253.

Sherman, P. W. (1981). Kinship, demography and Belding's ground squirrel nepotism. *Behavioral Ecology and Sociobiology, 8,* 251–259.

Shipman, P. (1985). The ancestor that wasn't. *The Sciences, 25,* 43–48.

Short, R. V. (1979). Sexual selection and its component parts, somatic and genital selection, as illustrated by man and great apes. *Advances in the Study of Behavior, 9,* 131–158.

Shostak, M. (1981). *Nisa: The life and words of a !Kung woman.* Cambridge, MA: Harvard University Press.

Sigall, H., & Landy, D. (1973). Radiating beauty: The effects of having a physically attractive partner on person perception. *Journal of Personality and Social Psychology, 28,* 218–224.

Silverman, I., & Eals, M. (1992). Sex differences in spatial abilities: Evolutionary theory and data. In J. H. Barkow, L. Cosmides, & J. Tooby (Eds.), *The adapted mind* (pp. 533–549). New York: Oxford University Press.

Silverman, I., & Phillips, K. (1998). The evolutionary psychology of spatial sex differences. In C. Crawford & D. L. Krebs (Eds.), *Handbook of evolutionary psychology* (pp. 595–612). Mahwah, NJ: Erlbaum.

Simpson, G. G. (1944). *Tempo and mode in evolution.* New York: Columbia University Press.

Simpson, J. A. (in press). Attachment theory in a modern evolutionary perspective. In J. Cassidy & P. R. Shaver (Eds.), *Handbook of attachment theory and research.* New York: Guilford.

Simpson, J. A., & Kenrick, D. T. (1997). *Evolutionary social psychology.* Mahwah, NJ: Erlbaum.

Simpson, J. A., & Weiner, W. S. C. (1989). *The Oxford English Dictionary* (Second ed.). Oxford: Clarendon Press.

Singh, D. (1993). Adaptive significance of waist-to-hip ratio and female physical attractiveness. *Journal of Personality and Social Psychology, 65,* 293–307.

Singh, D., & Luis, S. (1995). Ethnic and gender consensus for the effect of waist-to-hip ratio on judgments of women's attractiveness. *Human Nature, 6,* 51–65.

Singh, D., & Young, R. K. (1995). Body weight, waist-to-hip ratio, breasts, and hips: Role in judgments of female attractiveness and desirability for relationships. *Ethology and Sociobiology, 16,* 483–507.

Skinner, B. F. (1981). Selection by consequences. *Science, 213,* 501–504.

Small, M. (1992). The evolution of female sexuality and mate selection in humans. *Human Nature, 3,* 133–156.

Smith, M. S., Kish, B. J., & Crawford, C. B. (1987). Inheritance of wealth as human kin investment. *Ethology and Sociobiology, 8,* 171–182.

Smith, P. K. (1979). The ontogeny of fear in children. In W. Sluckin (Ed.), *Fear in animals and man* (pp. 164–168). London: Van Nostrand.

Smith, R. L. (1984). Human sperm competition. In R. L. Smith (Ed.), *Sperm competition and the evolution of mating systems* (pp. 601–659). New York: Academic Press.

Smuts, B. B. (1985). *Sex and friendship in baboons.* New York: Aldine de Gruyter.

Smuts, B. B. (1992). Men's aggression against women. *Human Nature, 6,* 1–32.

Smuts, B. B. (1995). The evolutionary origins of patriarchy. *Human Nature, 6,* 1–32.

Smuts, B. B., & Gubernick, D. J. (1992). Male-infant relationships in nonhuman primates: Paternal investment or mating effort? In B. S. Hewlett (Ed.), *Father-child relations: Cultural and bio-social contexts* (pp. 1–30). Hawthorne, NY: Aldine de Gruyter.

Sober, E., & Wilson, D. S. (1998). *Unto others: The evolution and psychology of unselfish behavior.* Cambridge, MA: Harvard University Press.

Sprecher, S., Aron, A., Hatfield, E., Cortese, A., Potapova, E., & Levitskaya, A. (1994). Love: American style, Russian style, and Japanese style. *Personal Relationships, 1,* 349–369.

Stanislaw, H., & Rice, F. J. (1988). Correlation between sexual desire and menstrual cycle characteristics. *Archives of Sexual Behavior, 17,* 499–508.

Stearns, S. (1992). *The evolution of life histories.* New York: Oxford University Press.

Steinberger, E., Rodriguez-Rigau, L. J., Smith, K. D., & Held, B. (1981). The menstrual cycle and plasma testosterone levels in women with acne. *Journal of the American Academy of Dermatology, 4,* 54–58.

Sternberg, R. (1986). A triangular theory of love. *Psychological Review, 93,* 119–135.

Stevens, A., & Price, J. (1996). *Evolutionary Psychiatry.* London: Routledge.

Strassman, B. I. (1981). Sexual selection, parental care, and concealed ovulation in humans. *Ethology and Sociobiology, 2,* 31–40.

Strum, S. C. (1981). Processes and products of change: Baboon predatory behavior at Gilgil, Kenya. In R. Harding & G. Teleki (Eds.), *Omnivorous primates* (pp. 255–302). New York: Columbia University Press.

Studd, M. V. (1996). Sexual harassment. In D. M. Buss & N. M. Malamuth (Eds.), *Sex, power, conflict: Evolutionary and feminist perspectives* (pp. 54–89). New York: Oxford University Press.

Studd, M. V., & Gattiker, U. E. (1991). The evolutionary psychology of sexual harassment in organizations. *Ethology and Sociobiology, 12,* 249–290.

Sugiyama, M. S. (1996). On the origins of narrative: Storyteller bias as a fitness-enhancing strategy. *Human Nature, 7,* 403–425.

Sulloway, F. (1979). *Freud: Biologist of the mind.* New York: Basic Books.

Sulloway, F. (1996). *Born to rebel.* New York: Pantheon.

Surbey, M. K. (1998). Developmental psychology and modern Darwinism. In C. Crawford & D. Krebs (Eds.), *Handbook of evolutionary psychology* (pp. 369–403). Mahwah, NJ: Erlbaum.

Surbey, M. K. (1998). Parent and offspring strategies in the transition at adolescence. *Human Nature, 9,* 67–94.

Symons, D. (1979). *The evolution of human sexuality.* New York: Oxford.

Symons, D. (1987). If we're all Darwinians, what's the fuss about. In C. Crawford, D. Krebs, & M. Smith (Eds.), *Sociobiology and psychology* (pp. 121–145). Hillsdale, NJ: Erlbaum.

Symons, D. (1989). The psychology of human mate preferences. *Behavioral and Brain Sciences, 12,* 34–45.

Symons, D. (1992). On the use and misuse of Darwinism in the study of human behavior. In J. Barkow, L. Cosmides, & J. Tooby (Eds.), *The adapted mind* (pp. 137–159). New York: Oxford University Press.

Symons, D. (1993). How risky is sex? *The Journal of Sex Research, 30,* 344–346.

Symons, D. (1995). Beauty is in the adaptations of the beholder: The evolutionary psychology of human female sexual attractiveness. In P. R. Abramson & S. D. Pinkerton (Eds.), *Sexual nature, sexual culture* (pp. 80–118). Chicago: University of Chicago Press.

Tanner, N. M. (1983). Hunters, gatherers, and sex roles in space and time. *American Anthropologist, 85,* 335–341.

Tanner, N. M., & Zihlman, A. (1976). Women in evolution part 1: Innovation and selection in human origins. *Signs: Women, Culture, and Society, 1,* 585–608.

Taylor, P. A., & Glenn, N. D. (1976). The utility of education and attractiveness for females' status attainment through marriage. *American Sociological Review, 41,* 484–498.

Teisman, M. W., & Moser, D. L. (1978). Jealous conflict in dating couples. *Psychological Reports, 42,* 1211–1216.

Terpstra, D. E., & Cook, S. E. (1985). Complainant characteristics and reported behaviors and consequences associated with formal sexual harassment charges. *Personnel Psychology, 38,* 559–574.

Thakerar, J. N., & Iwawaki, S. (1979). Cross-cultural comparisons in interpersonal attraction of females toward males. *Journal of Social Psychology, 108,* 121–122.

Than-Than, R. A., Hutton, Myint-Lwin, Khin-EiHan, Soe-Soe, Tin-Nu-Swe, Phillips, R. E., & Warrell, D. A. (1988). Haemostatic disturbances in patients bitten by Russell's Viber (*Vipera russelli siamensis*) in Burma. *British Journal of Haematology, 69,* 513–520.

Thiessen, D. D. (1972). A move toward species-specific analysis in behavior genetics. *Behavior Genetics, 2,* 115–126.

Thiessen, D. D., & Gregg, B. (1980). Human assortative mating and genetic equilibrium: An evolutionary perspective. *Ethology and Sociobiology, 1,* 111–140.

Thiessen, D. D., Young, R. K., & Burroughs, R. (1993). Lonely hearts advertisements reflect sexually dimorphic mating strategies. *Ethology and Sociobiology, 14,* 209–229.

Thompson, A. P. (1983). Extramarital sex: A review of the research literature. *Journal of Sex Research, 19,* 1–22.

Thompson, S. (1955). *Motif-index of folk-literature.* Vols. 1–6. Bloomington, IN: Indiana University Press.

Thornhill, N. (1992). *Human inbreeding* (Research Report No. 10/92). Bielefeld, Germany: Research Group on Biological Foundations of Human Culture, Center for Interdisciplinary Research, University of Bielefeld.

Thornhill, N. (1996). Psychological adaptation to sexual coercion in victims and offenders. In D. M. Buss & N. M. Malamuth (Eds.), *Sex, power, conflict: Evolutionary and feminist perspectives* (pp. 90—104). New York: Oxford University Press.

Thornhill, R. (1997). The concept of an evolved adaptation. In G. R. Bock & G. Cardew (Eds.), *Characterizing human psychological adaptations* (pp. 4–22). Chichester, England: Wiley.

Thornhill, R., & Møeller, A. P. (1997). Developmental stability, disease, and medicine. *Biological Review, 72,* 497–548.

Thornhill, R., & Thornhill, N. (1983). Human rape: An evolutionary perspective. *Ethology and Sociobiology, 4,* 137–173.

Thornhill, R., & Thornhill, N. (1992). The evolutionary psychology of men's coercive sexuality. *Behavioral and Brain Sciences, 15,* 363–421.

Thornhill, R., Thornhill, N., & Dizinno, G. (1986). The biology of rape. In S. Tomaselli & R. Porter (Eds.), *Rape.* London: Basic Blackwell.

Tierson, F. D., Olsen, C. L., & Hook, E. B. (1985). Influence of cravings and aversions on diet in pregnancy. *Ecology of Food and Nutrition, 17,* 117–129.

Tierson, F. D., Olsen, C. L., & Hook, E. B. (1986). Nausea and vomiting of pregnancy and association with pregnancy outcome. *American Journal of Obstetrics and Gynecology, 155,* 1017–1022.

Tiger, L. (1996). My life in the human nature wars. *The Wilson Quarterly, 20,* 14–25.

Tiger, L., & Fox, R. (1971). *The imperial animal.* New York: Holt, Rinehart, & Winston.

Tinbergen, N. (1951). *The study of instinct.* New York: Oxford University Press.

Tinbergen, N. (1963). The shell menace. *Natural History, 72,* 28–35.

Tomarken, A. J., Mineka, S., & Cook, M. (1989). Fear-relevant selective associations and covariation bias. *Journal of Abnormal Psychology, 98,* 381–394.

Tooby, J. (1982). Pathogens, polymorphism, and the evolution of sex. *Journal of Theoretical Biology, 97,* 557–576.

Tooby, J., & Cosmides, L. (1988). *The evolution of war and its cognitive foundations.* Institute for Evolutionary Studies, Technical Report #88-1.

Tooby, J., & Cosmides, L. (1989). The innate and the manifest: How universal does universal have to be? *Behavioral and Brain Sciences, 12,* 36–37.

Tooby, J., & Cosmides, L. (1990). On the universality of human nature and the uniqueness of the individual: The role of genetics and adaptation. *Journal of Personality, 58,* 17–68.

Tooby, J., & Cosmides, L. (1992). Psychological foundations of culture. In J. Barkow, L. Cosmides, & J. Tooby (Eds.), *The adapted mind* (pp. 19–136). New York: Oxford University Press.

Tooby, J., & Cosmides, L. (1996). Friendship and the banker's paradox: Other pathways to the evolution of adaptations for altruism. *Proceedings of the British Academy, 88,* 119–143.

Tooby, J., & Cosmides, L. (under review). Ecological rationality and the multimodular mind: Grounding normative theories in adaptive problems. *Psychological Review.*

Tooby, J., & DeVore, I. (1987). The reconstruction of hominid behavioral evolution through strategic modeling. In W. G. Kinzey (Ed.), *The evolution of human behavior* (pp. 183–237). New York: State University of New York Press.

Tooke, W., & Camire, L. (1991). Patterns of deception in intersexual and intrasexual mating strategies. *Ethology and Sociobiology, 12,* 345–364.

Townsend, J. M. (1989). Mate selection criteria: A pilot study. *Ethology and Sociobiology, 10,* 241–253.

Townsend, J. M. (1995). Sex without emotional involvement: An evolutionary interpretation of sex differences. *Archives of Sexual Behavior, 24,* 173–206.

Townsend, J. M., & Levy, G. D. (1990). Effects of potential partners' physical attractiveness and socioeconomic status on sexuality and partner selection. *Archives of Sexual Behavior, 19,* 149–164.

Trinkaus, E., & Zimmerman, M. R. (1982). Trauma among the Shanidar Neandertals. *American Journal of Physical Anthropology, 57,* 61–76.

Trivers, R. L. (1971). The evolution of reciprocal altruism. *Quarterly Review of Biology, 46,* 35–57.

Trivers, R. L. (1972). Parental investment and sexual selection. In B. Campbell (Ed.), *Sexual selection and the descent of man: 1871–1971* (pp. 136–179). Chicago: Aldine.

Trivers, R. (1974). Parent–offspring conflict. *American Zoologist, 14,* 249–264.

Trivers, R. (1985). *Social evolution.* Menlo Park, CA: Benjamin/Cummings.

Trivers, R. L., & Willard, D. E. (1973). Natural selection of parental ability to vary the sex ratio of offspring. *Science, 179,* 90–92.

Tversky, A., & Kahneman, D. (1974). Judgment under uncertainty: Heuristics and biases. *Science, 185,* 1124–1131.

Udry, J. R., & Eckland, B. K. (1984). Benefits of being attractive: Differential payoffs for men and women. *Psychological Reports, 54,* 47–56.

Ulrich, R. (1983). Aesthetic and affective response to natural environment. In I. Altman & J. F. Wohlwill (Eds.), *Behavior and the natural environment* (pp. 85–125). New York: Plenum.

Ulrich, R. (1984). View through a window may influence recovery from surgery. *Science, 224,* 420–421.

Ulrich, R. (1986). Human response to vegetation and landscapes. *Landscape and Urban Planning, 13,* 29–44.

U.S. Bureau of the Census (1978). 1976 survey of institutionalized persons: A study of persons receiving long-term care. *Current population reports.* (Special Studies Series P-23, No. 69.) Washington, DC: U.S. Government Printing Office.

van den Berghe, P. L., & Frost, P. (1986). Skin color preference, sexual dimorphism and sexual selection: A case of gene culture coevolution. *Ethnic and Racial Studies, 9,* 87–113.

van der Dennen, J. M. G. (1995). *The origin of war* (Vols. 1 & 2). Groningen, The Netherlands: Origin Press.

van Gulik, R. H. (1974). *Sexual life in ancient China.* London: E. J. Brill.

Vayda, A. P. (1961). A re-examination of Northwest Coast economic systems. *Transactions of the New York Academy of Sciences, (Series 2), 23,* 618–624.

Voland, E. (1984). Human sex ratio manipulation: Historical data from a German parish. *Journal of Human Evolution, 13,* 99–77.

Voland, E., & Engel, C. (1990). Female choice in humans: A conditional mate selection strategy of the Krummerhörn women (Germany 1720–1874). *Ethology, 84*, 144–154.

Wade, N. (1997, June 24). Dainty worm tells secrets on the human genetic code. *New York Times,* p. B9.

Wakefield, J. C. (1992). The concept of mental disorder: On the boundary between biological facts and social values. *American Psychologist, 47*, 373–388.

Walker, P. (1995). *Documenting patterns of violence in earlier societies: The problems and promise of using bioarchaeological data for testing evolutionary theories.* Paper presented at the Annual Conference of the Human Behavior and Evolution Society, Santa Barbara, CA: July 2.

Wallace, A. R. (1858). On the tendency of varieties to depart indefinitely from the original type. *Journal of the Proceedings of the Linnean Society (Zoology), 3*, 53–62.

Waller, A. L. (1993). The Hatfield-McCoy feud. In W. Graebner (Ed.), *True stories from the American past* (pp. 35–54). New York: McGraw-Hill.

Walster, E., Traupmann, J., & Berscheid, E. (1978). Equity and Extramarital sexuality. *Archives of Sexual Behavior, 7*, 127–141.

Wang, X. T. (1996). Evolutionary hypotheses of risk-sensitive choice: Age differences and perspective change. *Ethology and Sociobiology, 17*, 1–15.

Wason, P. (1966). Reasoning. In B. M. Foss (Ed.), *New horizons in psychology.* London: Penguin.

Watson, D., & Burlingame, A. W. (1960). *Therapy through horticulture.* New York: Macmillan.

Watson, J. B. (1924). *Behaviorism.* New York: Norton.

Weinberg, E. D. (1984). Iron withholding: A defense against infection and neoplasia. *Physiological Review, 64*, 65–102.

Weisfeld, G. (1997). Puberty rites as clues to the nature of human adolescence. *Cross-Cultural Research, 31*, 27–54.

Weisfeld, G. E., & Billings, R. (1988). Observations on adolescence. In K. B. MacDonald (Ed.), *Sociobiological perspectives on human development* (pp. 207–233). New York: Springer-Verlag.

Weiss, D. L., & Slosnerick, M. (1981). Attitudes toward sexual and nonsexual extramarital involvements among a sample of college students. *Journal of Marriage and the Family, 43*, 349–358.

Weissner, P. (1982). Risk, reciprocity and social influences on !Kung San economics. In E. Leacock & R. B. Lee (Eds.), *Politics and history in band societies.* Cambridge, UK: Cambridge University Press.

Wellman, H. (1990). *The child's theory of mind.* Cambridge, MA: MIT Press.

White, G. L. (1980). Inducing jealousy: A power perspective. *Personality and Social Psychology Bulletin, 6*, 222–227.

White, G. L. (1981). Some correlates of romantic jealousy. *Journal of Personality, 49*, 129–147.

Whitehurst, R. N. (1971). Violence potential in extramarital sexual responses. *Journal of Marriage and the Family, 33*, 683–691.

Whiting, B., & Edwards, C. P. (1988). *Children of different worlds.* Cambridge, MA: Harvard University Press.

Whyte, M. K. (1990). Changes in mate choice in Chengdu. In D. Davis & E. Vogel (Eds.), *China on the eve of Tiananmen.* Cambridge, MA: Harvard University Press.

Wicker, F. W., Payne, G. C., & Morgan, R. D. (1983). Participant descriptions of guilt and shame. *Motivation and Emotion, 7*, 25–39.

Wiederman, M. W. (1993). Evolved gender differences in mate preferences: Evidence from personal advertisements. *Ethology and Sociobiology, 14*, 331–352.

Wiederman, M. W., & Allgeier, E. R. (1992). Gender differences in mate selection criteria: Sociobiological or socioeconomic explanation? *Ethology and Sociobiology, 13,* 115–124.

Wilkinson, G. W. (1984). Reciprocal food sharing in the vampire bat. *Nature, 308,* 181–184.

Willerman, L. (1979). *The psychology of individual and group differences.* San Francisco: Freeman.

Willerman, L., Loehlin, J. C., & Horn, J. M. (1992). An adoption and a cross-fostering study of the Minnesota Multiphasic Personality Inventory (MMPI) Psychopathic Deviate scale. *Behavior Genetics, 22,* 515–529.

Williams, G. C. (1957). Pleiotropy, natural selection, and the evolution of senescence. *Evolution, 11,* 398–411.

Williams, G. C. (1966). *Adaptation and natural selection.* Princeton, NJ: Princeton University Press.

Williams, G. C. (1975). *Sex and evolution.* Princeton, NJ: Princeton University Press.

Williams, G. C. (1992). *Natural selection.* New York: Oxford University Press.

Williams, G. C., & Nesse, R. M. (1991). The dawn of Darwinian medicine. *Quarterly Review of Biology, 66,* 1–22.

Wilson, D. S. (1994). Adaptive genetic variation and human evolutionary psychology. *Ethology and Sociobiology, 15,* 219–235.

Wilson, D. S. (1995). Sociopathy within and between small groups. *Behavioral and Brain Sciences, 18,* 577.

Wilson, D. S. (1998). Game theory and human behavior. In L. A. Dugatkin & H. K. Reeve (Eds.), *Game theory and animal behavior* (pp. 261–282). New York: Oxford University Press.

Wilson, D. S., Near, D., & Miller, R. R. (1996). Machiavellianism: A synthesis of the evolutionary and psychological literatures. *Psychological Bulletin, 119,* 285–299.

Wilson, D. S., & Sober, E. (1994). Reintroducing group selection to the human behavioral sciences. *Behavioral and Brain Sciences, 17,* 585–654.

Wilson, E. O. (1975). *Sociobiology: The new synthesis.* Cambridge, MA: Harvard University Press.

Wilson, E. O. (1998). *Consilience: The unity of knowledge.* New York: Knopf.

Wilson, G. D. (1987). Male-female differences in sexual activity, enjoyment, and fantasies. *Personality and Individual Differences, 8,* 125–126.

Wilson, M., & Daly, M. (1985). Competitiveness, risk-taking, and violence: The young male syndrome. *Ethology and Sociobiology, 6,* 59–73.

Wilson, M., & Daly, M. (1992). The man who mistook his wife for a chattel. In J. Barkow, L. Cosmides, & J. Tooby (Eds.), *The adapted mind: Evolutionary psychology and the generation of culture* (pp. 289–322). New York: Oxford University Press.

Wilson, M., & Daly, M. (1993). An evolutionary psychological perspective on male sexual proprietariness and violence against wives. *Violence and Victims, 8,* 271–294.

Wilson, M., & Daly, M. (1996). Male sexual proprietariness and violence against wives. *Current Directions in Psychological Science, 5,* 2–7.

Wilson, M., Johnson, H., & Daly, M. (1995). Lethal and nonlethal violence against wives. *Canadian Journal of Criminology, 37,* 331–361.

Wilson, P. R. (1968). Perceptual distortion of height as a function of ascribed academic status. *Journal of Social Psychology, 74,* 97.

Wolf, N. (1991). *The beauty myth.* New York: Anchor Books.

Wolfe, L. (1975). *Playing around: Women and extramarital sex.* New York: William Morrow.

Wrangham, R. W. (1993). The evolution of sexuality in chimpanzees and bonobos. *Human Nature, 4,* 47–79.

Wrangham, R., & Peterson, D. (1996). *Demonic males*. Boston: Houghton Mifflin.

Wright, R. (1995). The biology of violence. *The New Yorker*, pp. 68–77, March 13.

Wynne-Edwards, V. C. (1962). *Animal dispersion in relation to social behavior*. Edinburgh: Oliver & Boyd.

Yerushalmy, J., & Milkovich, L. (1965). Evaluation of the teratogenic effects of meclizine in man. *American Journal of Obstetrics and Gynecology, 93*, 553–562.

Yosef, R. (1991, June). Female seek males with ready cache. *Natural History*, 37.

Zahavi, A., & Zahavi, A. (1996). *The handicap principle*. New York: Oxford University Press.

Zihlman, A. L. (1981). Women as shapers of the human adaptation. In F. Dahlberg (Ed.), *Woman the gatherer* (pp. 77–120). New Haven, CT: Yale University Press.

PHOTO CREDITS

INDEX

Note: Italicized letters *f* and *t* following page numbers indicate figures and tables, respectively.